FABIO BOURBO

PETRA REVEALED

HISTORY, CIVILIZATION AND MONUMENTS OF THE CITY CARVED INTO THE ROCK

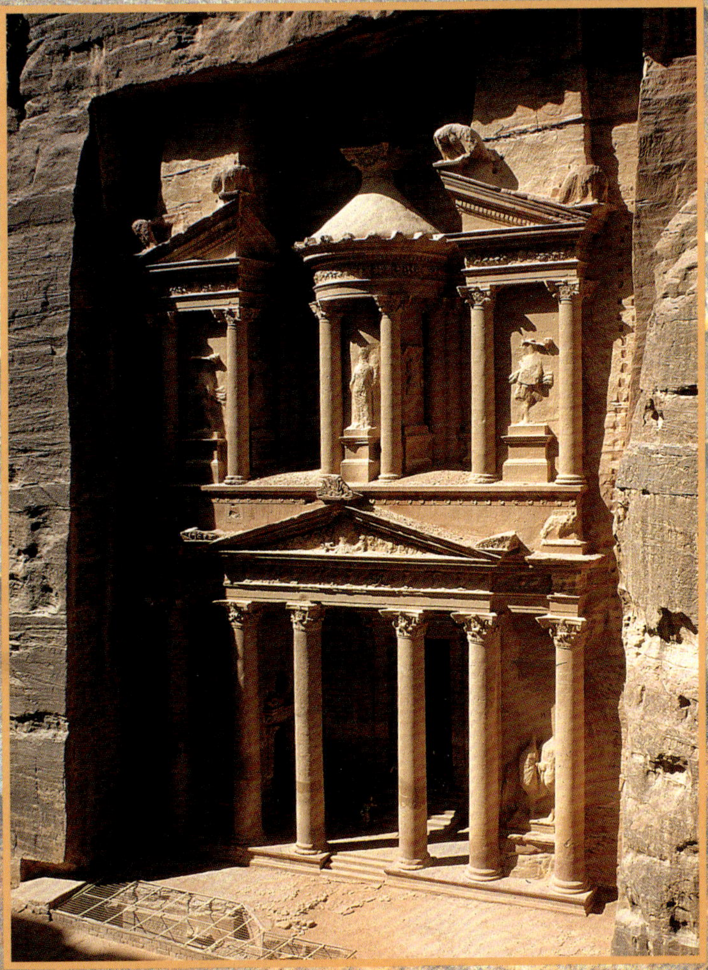

"You will never know what Petra is really like, unless you come in person"

Lawrence of Arabia

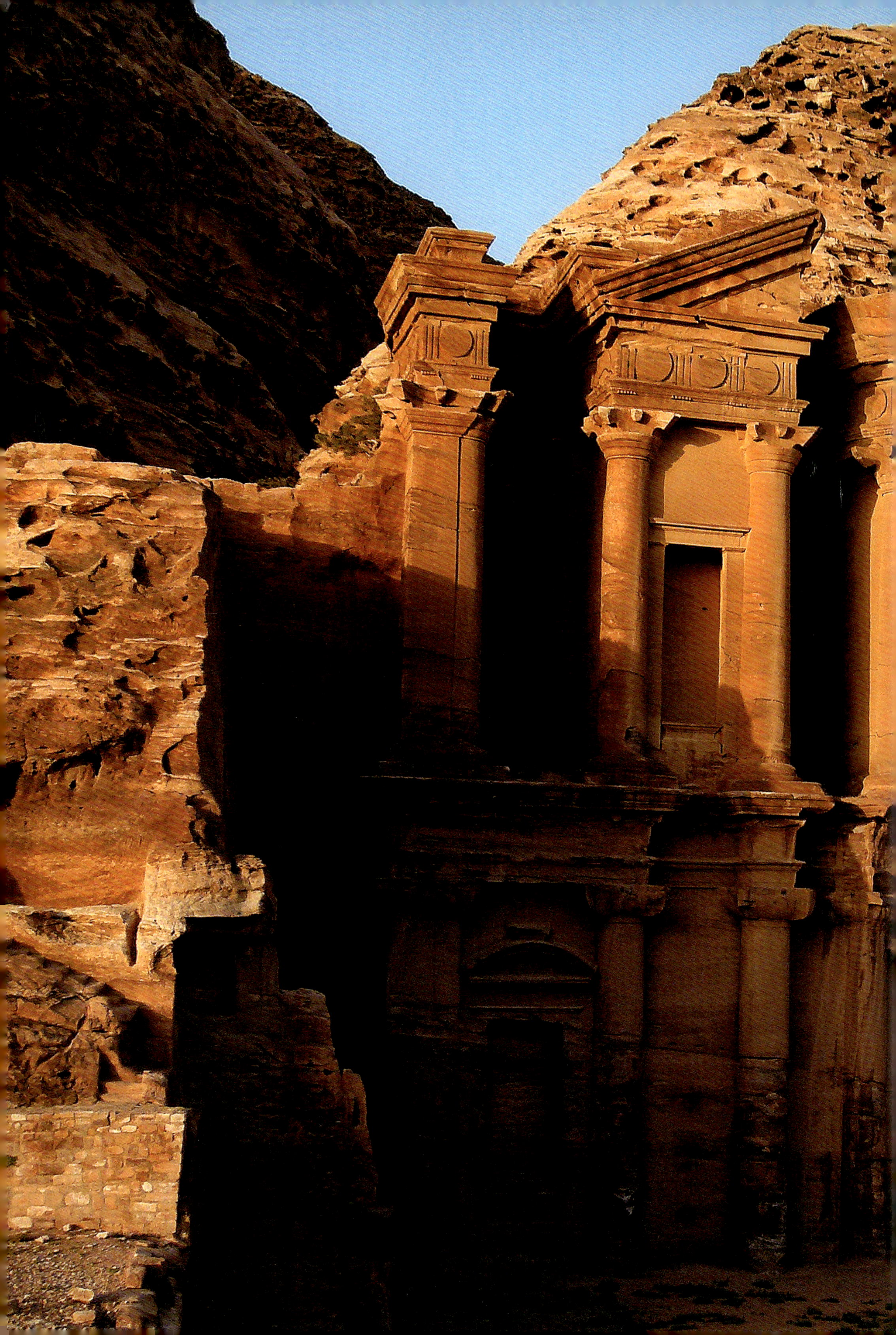

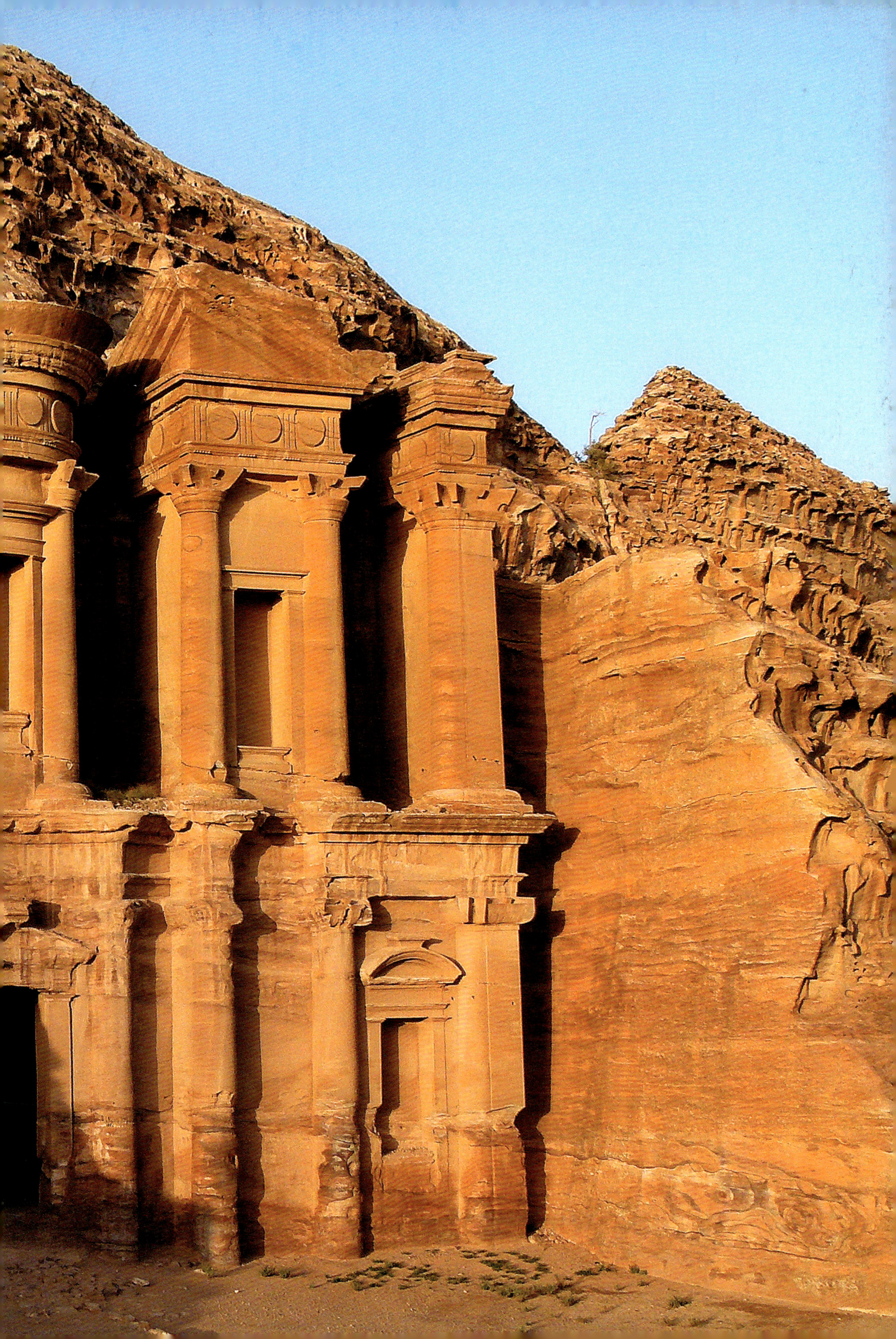

PETRA REVEALED

HISTORY, CIVILIZATION AND MONUMENTS OF THE CITY CARVED INTO THE ROCK

Texts, photographs and layout
FABIO BOURBON

Maps and drawings
MONICA FALCONE BOURBON

Digital anastylosis
MARCO BAVAGNOLI, IDA CIRILLO, FABIO BOURBON

Translation
Julius F. Woodman

ISBN 978-88-95847-69-6

Page 1 - *The Khazneh, the very symbol of Petra.*

Pages 2-3 - *The superb Deir (or Monastery), one of the absolute pinnacles of Nabataean architecture and an unconscious forerunner to Baroque art.*

Below - *Asphodelus flowers in front of the Armour Tomb, in the Mughar an Nasara area*

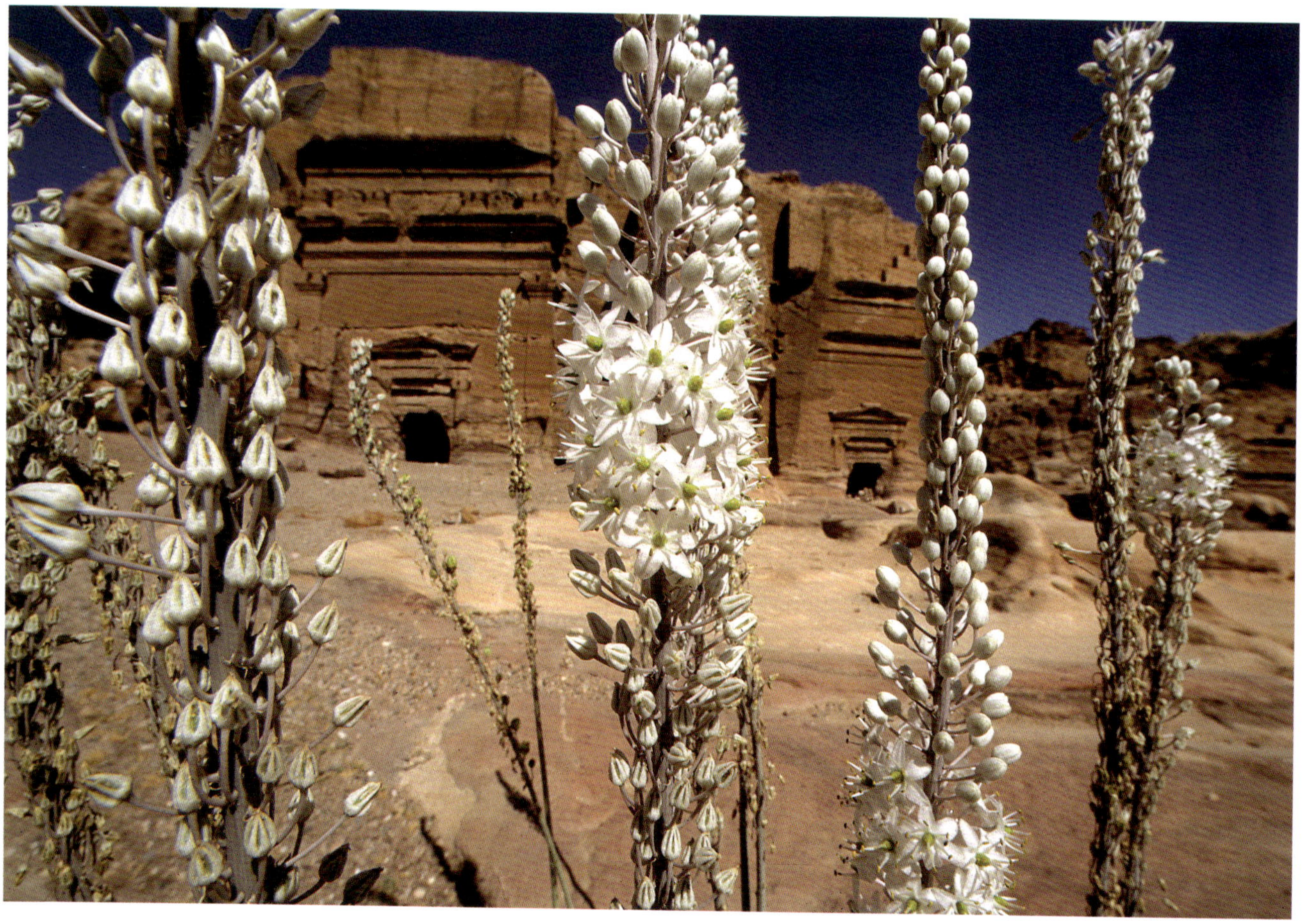

CONTENTS

PREFACE

Fundamentally, this book is a sincere act of love. I fell in love with Petra the first time I saw it, and even now, years later, I still have a feeling of trepidation when I go back to visit it, like a teenager on a first date.
I have produced several publications about the "Rose City", which were favourably received by the public and "professionals in the field", but for years I harboured the dream of putting all the information I had gathered over time into one book. In effect, this guide is the sum of all the previous ones. However, on this occasion I wanted to go further, and make the results of the most recent archaeological investigations, carried out in the area of Petra by teams from many different parts of the world, available to the public. At the same time, I wanted to present the intuitions and hypotheses I had arrived at over the course of numerous explorations of the sites, followed by laborious research, comparisons with other architectural works and texts, and even practical tests. During many explorations of the Petra area, I wore out the soles of my boots, climbing all over the place, observing minute details, taking thousands of photographs, and (with permission from the local authorities) reaching places that are usually off limits.
I listened to the most disparate opinions of researchers from the area and abroad, and compared them, but I also paid just as much attention to what the locals told me, and their ideas often seemed equally valid, as they

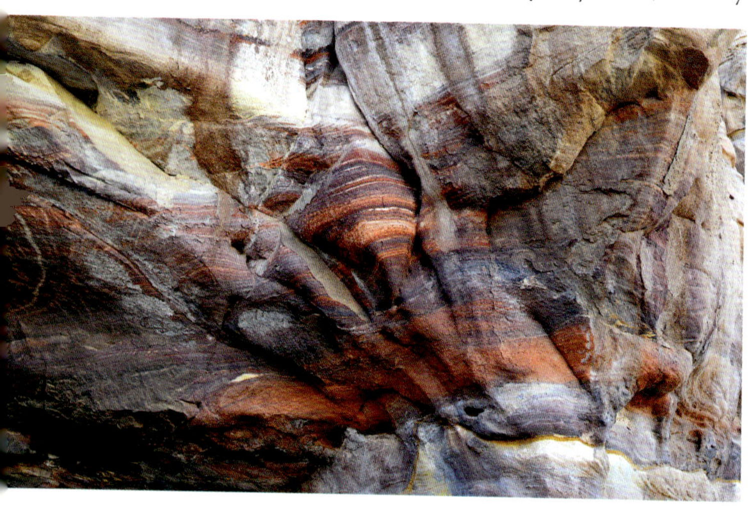

were based on an atavistic knowledge of the places as well as personal experience. Being careful not to break my neck, I climbed vertical ladders carved into the rock by the Nabataeans two thousand years ago, and dangled from ropes threaded through rings and toeholds put in place by ancient builders, all to establish how realistic some ideas I had come up with during laborious studies and sleepless nights might be (isn't this what happens to people when they are in love?).
I also visited places thousands of kilometres away, where I was able to study ancient techniques of rupestrian architecture, and evaluate their technical similarities. I even learned how to use some simple tools, which are still skilfully handled by old stonemasons. This opened my eyes to working practices and allowed me to read the traces left on the stone as invaluable clues. I will never forget the excitement I felt in a quarry of volcanic tuff (whose grain is very similar to the sandstone of Petra) on the island of Santa Maria in the Azores, when I noticed the peculiar marks left on the rock face by pickaxe blows, identical to those seen at Petra. Seeing an old labourer, who showed me some of the tricks of the trade, left me in no doubt. Some may say that almost two millennia have passed between the creation of the monuments at Petra and this experience, but it should not be forgotten that when human beings' needs and living conditions are the same, they develop almost identical techniques, regardless of time and space. Do today's craftsmen not model clay on their wheels, just as innumerable generations of their predecessors did before them? Do glass makers not blow and shape hot glass just as the artisans of old did? In fact, at the root of my curiosity is a real craving to understand how things are made. As I believe that this curiosity is common to many people, I hope to be able to provide answers to many of their questions in the pages that follow.
I do not claim to have a solution for everything, but I do consider myself an honest reporter. Over the years, I have studied everything it is possible to study about Petra and Nabataean civilization (and I owe a debt to numerous authors for this), and then, from time to time, I have taken stock and corroborated what I have learned in the field. In this way, I have continued examining and comparing different theories, and also formulated new ones, all the while seeking to do so in a logical and methodical way. This has been a great source of satisfaction for me. When I proposed the first anastyloses of the Palace Tomb, the Deir and the nearby Room 468, I could not have hoped that those reconstructions would be so favourably received in such a short space of time. Today, I feel a sense of pride when I see the drawings, done by myself and my wife Monica over twenty years ago, reproduced in various formats (and sometimes in other people's publications).
I clearly owe a debt of gratitude to many people. I am grateful to the Jordanian archaeologist Sami Mohammed Al Nawafleh for the time he dedicated to me, keeping me up to date with what was discovered during the excavations being carried out in front of the Khazneh, the most famous of Petra's monuments. I can say the same thing about the conversations I had with the archaeologist Andrea Polcaro. I have fond memories of a meeting with Professor Dan Bahat, who particularly appreciated the reconstruction of the Palace Tomb, and some exchanges of ideas with the then director of the Archaeological Area of Petra, Dr. Suleyman Farajat, and also with the current director Dr. Emad Hijazeen, to whom I showed the other anastyloses while they were being completed. Their positive judgements encouraged me to continue using my perhaps somewhat unorthodox method. I am convinced that you need to know how to take risks, and in the end, I decided to continue following this path. The book you are now reading is the result of that decision. Thanks to the invaluable help I received from some extraordinary people - our dear departed friend Gianni

Gè, Marco Bavagnoli, Ida Cirillo and my wife Monica, a real guardian angel - I have, among other things, been able to see some of my intuitions take shape in the form of graphic and digital reconstructions.
In this book I have emphasised the practical aspect, but I have also given a complete account of the history of Petra, and other aspects of Nabataean civilization. Ultimately, I consider this to be a guide that is suitable for both researchers and non-professionals, and indeed any visitor, including "armchair" sightseers, as well as a useful tool for fully exploring the extensive archaeological area of Petra.
The Rose City is an absolutely unique place, which should be completely understood and respected. If you are able to grasp its magic, by listening to the poetry of silence, observing the never ending kaleidoscopic changing of its colours and admiring the superb balance of its rupestrian architecture, you will be rewarded with a profound and intimate perception of one of the most beautiful sights on earth. Above all, you will return home with a treasure in your heart. This is the reason why I would invite anyone who wishes to visit the site, to do so with awareness and respect. To preserve it for as long as possible and pass it on to future generations.
Lastly, one final point: I believe it is important to keep interest in Petra and the whole of Jordan alive. A peaceful and productive land, among the most welcoming and hospitable, which has been at the centre of events for thousands of years. Neolithic hunters left their mark here, as did the Edomites, the Greeks, the Romans, the caravans of the rich Nabataean spice merchants, the Byzantines, the Crusaders, the Ottomans, the armies of Prince Feisal Bin Ali and Lawrence of Arabia. It was here that the language currently written by millions of Arabs took shape from the elegant calligraphy of the Nabataeans. Today, the Hashemite Kingdom, wisely ruled over by King Abdallah Ibn Al Hussein, is a small rich prestigious nation that wants to build itself a future that lives up to its past. Jordan is a land where many different peoples have left an important legacy, making it an immense museum, telling that complex tale which is history. Today that history reminds us of our duty to live together in a civilized way, respect the traditions and beliefs of others, and also to participate and show solidarity. In this country, which an austere environment has endowed with few natural resources, the greatest and most splendid treasure are the people who live here, the Jordanians. Visitors are greeted with the words "ahlan wa sahlan" - welcome - wherever they go, said with a smile, even by the children. Personally, I have always felt welcome, both in the big cities and in the remotest villages, and even in the ancient hypogea of Petra, where a few Bedouin families still live today. With this book, I also want to show my sincere gratitude. One day, time and fate permitting, I will go further. *F.B.*

Opposite page and below - *Sandstone is a sedimentary rock composed of tiny grains of sand, heavily compressed during geological eras. For this reason it is a material that is not very resistant to erosion.*

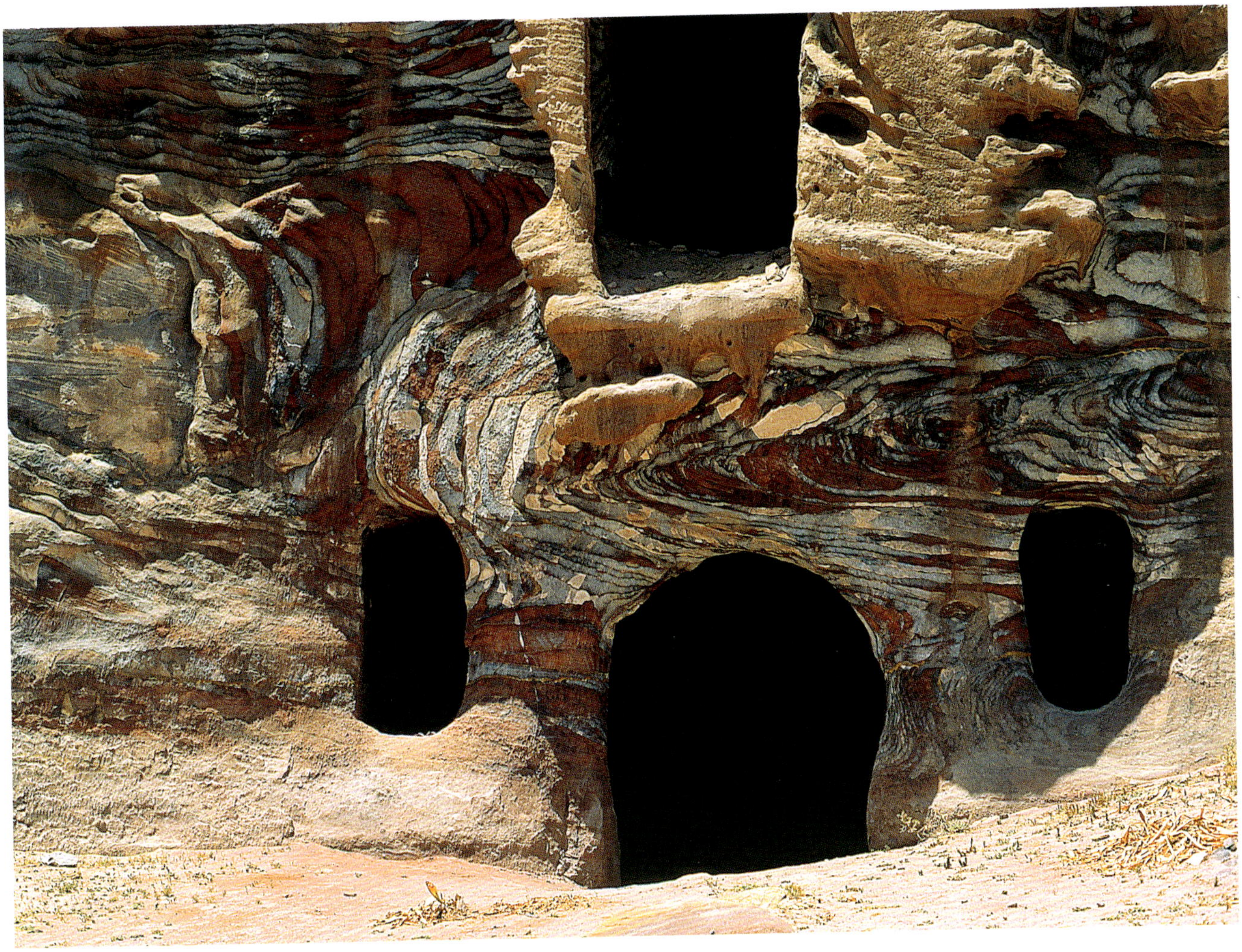

HISTORICAL INTRODUCTION

Situated in southern Jordan, about 300 kilometres south of Amman, Petra is mentioned in the Bible with the name Sela' - which means "Rock" in Hebrew. Petra is the Greek translation, but not all historians agree that this name refers to the rupestrian city, as there is another place with the same name located about forty kilometres to the north of Petra. Two other historical sources also provide some useful information - the *Library* of Diodorus Siculus (about 90-20 BC) and the *Geographica* by Strabo (64 BC - about 23 AD) - which both describe the city as the sumptuous capital of the Nabataeans, a

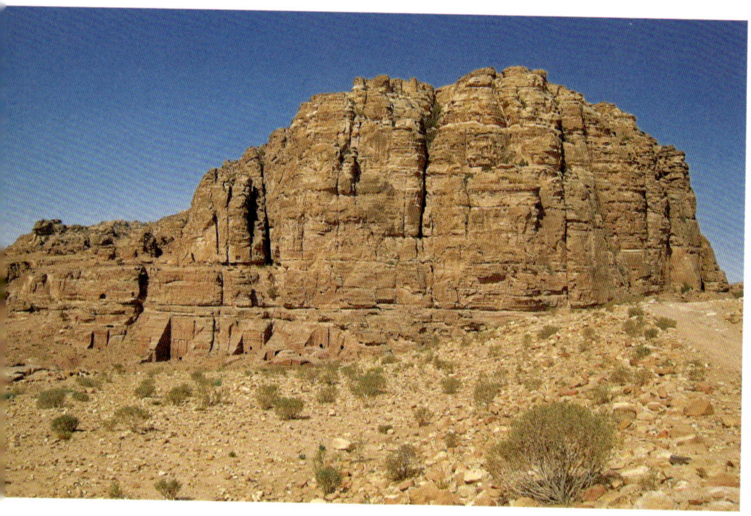

nomadic people who became rich through caravan trading. Diodorus specifies that they arrived in this land shortly after the death of Alexander the Great (in 323 BC). It is now known that the entire area was already inhabited in the Palaeolithic era, well before the arrival of this population, by groups of hunter-gatherers, who were continually on the move in search of food. In a site a few kilometres north of Petra, known as Beidha, the remains of a human settlement dating back to 7000 BC were discovered. This is believed to have been the first permanent settlement in the region. Ba'aja and Shkarat Mess'aed are other Neolithic villages identified and excavated in the area around Petra. In the Chalcolithic period and during the Bronze Age (between 4000 and 2500 BC), the encampments of nomadic groups and the villages of farmers that had already settled in one place coexisted. Over the course of the next two millennia the region was probably affected by climate change and many villages were suddenly abandoned, and only a few sporadic groups of nomads continued to roam the area. It was not until the Iron Age (8th-7th century BC) that a group of humans settled permanently in the valley of Petra again. They built fortifications on top of a rocky prominence known as Al Habis, and the area was soon densely populated once more.
In the same period, which we know about thanks to the Old Testament, the whole region that corresponds to modern Jordan was occupied by the kingdoms of the Ammonites (in the north), the Moabites (in the central area) and the Edomites (in the south). This particular group, who were a Semitic people, came to occupy the lands between the Dead Sea and the Gulf of Aqaba. One of their permanent settlements was situated on top of Jebel Umm al Biyara, the mountain that looks out over the valley of Petra from the west. Relations between the Edomites and the nearby Israelites were problematic, if not abysmal, for a long period of time. In fact, after the fall of Jerusalem to the Babylonians (587 BC), the Edomites repeatedly attacked and looted the Kingdom of Judah. However, for some time they had been under pressure themselves from a determined nomadic population, who almost certainly came from the Arabian Peninsula: the Nabataeans, then known as the Nabatu (*Nbtw*). They in turn were being pushed further and further to the north-west by the expansionism of the Babylonians. Although their exact place of origin is still unknown today, they were certainly a resolute and industrious people, who were able to progress from the limited possibilities of a nomadic society and become part of a much wider system of political and economic relations. Towards the end of the 4th century BC, the caravans of the Nabataean merchants extended from Arabia to the Mediterranean on a north-south axis, and Syria to Egypt from east to west. Today, it is believed that the Nabatu "inherited" control of the caravan routes and the defensive system in the region from the Edomites. The two populations probably fused together peacefully, leading to the creation of what is now commonly known as Nabataean civilization.

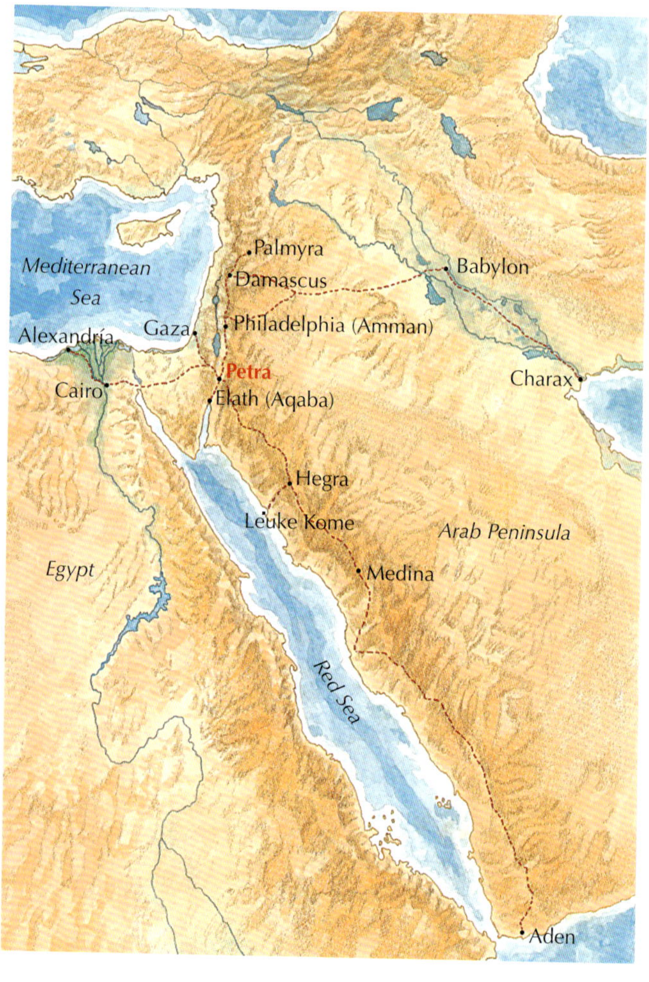

Monica Falcone

To conduct their trade, the Nabataeans used Aramaic, the language of commerce of the time, which was spoken all over the Near East. Although they were described in the earliest reliable historical documents (those already mentioned by Diodorus and Strabo) as inhabitants of the desert, dedicated to pastoralism and unaware of agriculture, incapable of building houses and scornful of wine, they drastically changed their way of life in a short space of time. However, the various phases of this epochal transformation remain a mystery. The land occupied by the Nabataeans certainly had few resources, apart from the bitumen of the Dead Sea, which was exported to Egypt as a raw material for the mummification of the deceased, and the rich copper mines at Al Sabrah and in the Wadi Faynan (a valley situated on the eastern side of the Wadi Arabah, the enormous depression in the Earth's crust that connects the Dead Sea and the Gulf of Aqaba, on the southern side of which lies the valley of Petra). The Nabataean caravans were so immense that they actually seemed like armies on the move to the historian Strabo. The commercial abilities of the Nabataeans lay in their skill at identifying what were the most valuable and sought after goods in the most distant countries on their routes of communication. In southern Arabia, modern Yemen, they bought myrrh, incense and spices, which they then sold for a high price in Gaza, Alexandria and other ports on the Mediterranean coast. These products reached as far as Greece and Italy, where they were used during religious rites, and also for the production of cosmetics or medicine. It should be remembered that in those days incense was as valuable as gold, because it was used in all civil and religious ceremonies, as well as for medicines and personal hygiene. Other precious goods included gold, silver, glass, orpiment, damasks and also silk, which was imported from as far away as China! The enormous profits earned from this trade made the Nabataean merchants richer and richer, and as a consequence they were continually able to expand their sphere of influence over the trade routes from the Gulf of Persia to far-off Abyssinia. Another important source of income were the taxes that the Nabataeans imposed on foreign traders for passing through their lands. In short, the Nabataeans ended up with a trade monopoly over the whole region, and to consolidate this they built a network of staging posts, caravanserais and watchtowers to guarantee the safety of their caravans. Today, the remains of one of these well-equipped staging posts can be seen in the desert, a few kilometres from the modern village of Wadi Musa, not far from the tarmac road.

In the meantime, the Nabataeans had developed their own form of language, derived from Aramaic but also with characteristics of its own. In particular, the writing took on an elegant calligraphic appearance, and it was widely used both for official inscriptions, which have been found mainly at Hegra, and in the many examples of graffiti left by merchants on the move, in Petra and all over the Nabataean territories. Unfortunately, no Nabataean literature has survived. However, it has now been confirmed that modern Arabic originates from this written language.

In this historic period, the Nabataeans effectively con-

THE LANGUAGE OF THE NABATAEANS

Nabataean was a Semitic language that originated from Aramaic, which was the lingua franca throughout the Near East used for political and commercial relations until the end of the 4th century BC. After that Greek was also used.

Starting from the 2nd century BC, the Nabataeans, who must have originally spoken a northern Arabic dialect, began to develop their own written language taking their alphabet from Aramaic and developing it into a distinctive cursive form of rather rounded letters. Nabataean was read from right to left.

The Arabic alphabet was derived from Nabataean in the 5th century AD.

The most popular written languages in the Near East during the Nabataean reign are compared in the adjacent table.

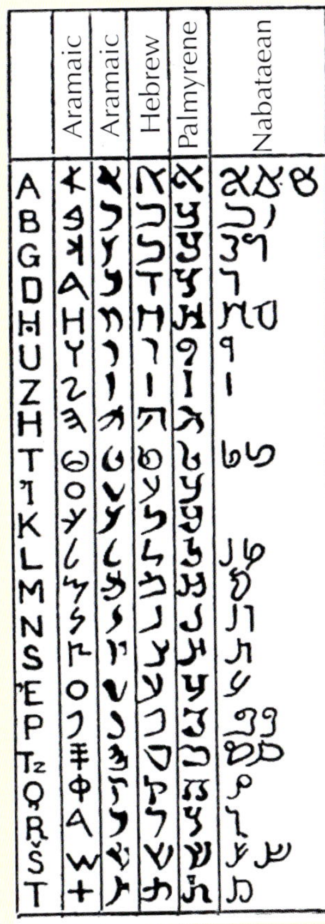

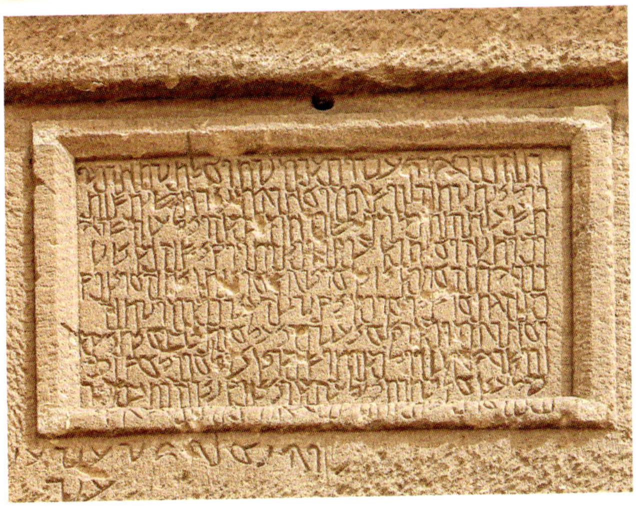

Opposite page, left - *The characteristic shape of Jebel Umm al Biyara, on whose flat top first the Edomites settled and then the Nabataeans, entrenching themselves to repel the siege of Antigonus I Monophthalmus.*
The Edomite settlement was excavated in the 1960s by the English archaeologist Crystal Bennett and dates back to the Iron Age (7th-6th century BC). It had no walls and consisted of long stone houses.

Opposite page, right - *Map of the main Nabataean caravan routes.*

Above - *One of the many Nabataean inscriptions on the facades of the rupestrian tombs in Hegra, a place in Saudi Arabia known today as Mada'in Saleh.*
131 rock tombs have been identified here, dating back to a period between the 1st century BC and the 2nd century AD.

tinued with their nomadic way of life, although they did control safe places where they could stay, sometimes for long periods of time, when the weather was bad. Hegra, in modern Saudi Arabia, which lay on the route from Sheba to the Mediterranean, was one of these outposts. During that period, even Petra, which the Nabataeans called Raqmu (Multicoloured), was little more than a huge caravanserai on the route known as the Road of the Kings, a protected place to pitch tents and quench your thirst, thanks to the perennial springs in the area. It was in this period that the village of Gaia must have appeared. Its site is now occupied by the modern town of Wadi Musa, where tourists stay when they visit Petra. The presence of the perennial spring of Ain Musa, and the fact that the valley bottom is suitable for agriculture, made it the main settlement in the area for some time, and it was only much later that Gaia became a suburb of Petra.

In the meantime, the Nabataeans had to confront the expansionist aims of two Hellenistic kingdoms formed after the break-up of the empire of Alexander the Great: the Selucids in Syria and the Lagids in Egypt. In the summer of 311 BC, the citizens of Petra managed to resist an attempt to conquer them by Antigonus I Monophthalmus (one of Alexander's former generals, who was fighting against his old comrades in arms in order to take control of the region). They barricaded themselves on top of the mountain range of Umm Al Biyara, where several enormous cisterns for gathering rainwater can still be seen today, as well as the remains of a grand building, which may have been a royal palace or perhaps a sanctuary erected in memory of this event. Antigonus' son Demetrius also tried to invade the region several times, but without success.

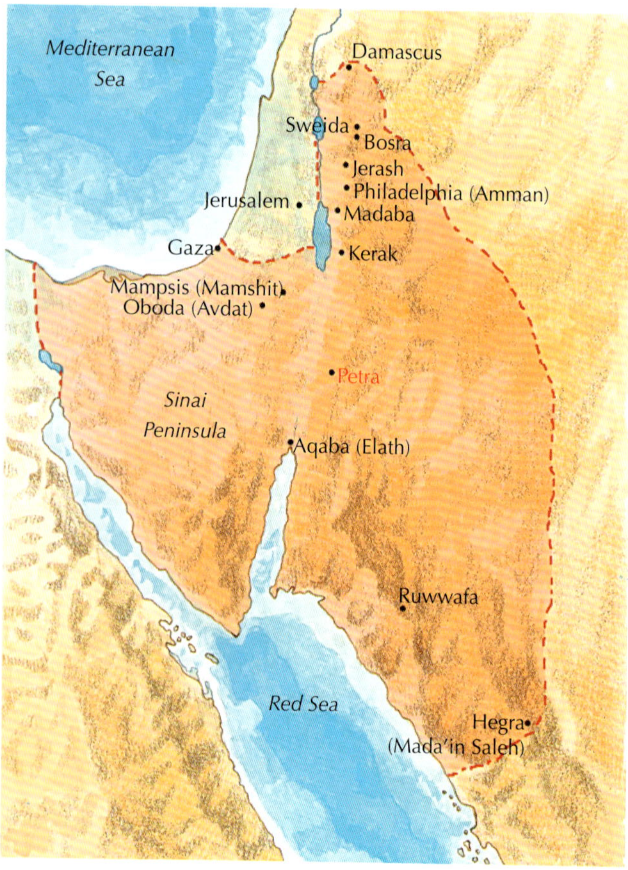

Monica Falcone

The "cultural revolution" that led to the birth of the Nabataean Kingdom, in the true sense of the word, took place between the 3rd and 1st centuries BC. Politically, this was made possible by the progressive weakening of the Seleucid Kingdom, which by then was coming into conflict with Roman expansionism. The Nabataeans progressively consolidated their control over the area that stretches from modern Palestine to the Arabian Desert and from the Gulf of Aqaba to the border of Syria, while at the same time becoming sedentary more and more rapidly. During the same period, their social

SELA': AN ALTERNATIVE HISTORICAL THEORY

According to some historians, Petra does not correspond to the biblical Sela'. This would instead be to be found in a settlement (Khirbat as Sela) located just south of Tafilah, along the King's Highway that connects Petra to Amman. The settlement was situated on the flat top of a rocky mountain, surrounded by steep walls. Access was by a steep staircase cut into the rock, overlooked by guard posts. A long inscription in neo-Babylonian cuneiform, many rupestrian structures, several cisterns and channels, an unusual bas-relief in the form of a bull, plus two spectacular "high places of sacrifice" similar to those in Petra, have all been found here. The high places are formed of terraces hewn into the living rock, overlooking the chasm and accessible by staircases, where priests made ritual offerings to the gods above. If this is the Sela' mentioned by Greek historians, it must be assumed that the siege carried out by Antigonus I Monophthalmus happened here and not on the slopes of Umm al Biyara as is currently believed. Yet Strabo's description (XVI.4.26) leaves many doubts, "the metropolis of the Nabataeans is Petra, as it is called; for it lies on a site which is otherwise smooth and level, but it is fortified all round by a rock, the outside parts of the site being precipitous and sheer, while the inside parts having springs in abundance, both for domestic purposes and for watering the gardens". However, there are no springs in the locality identified as Sela' today and it is clear the settlement never experienced any great development. Additionally, although the site has never been excavated or systematically studied, it seems likely that it was actually an Edomite stronghold dating from the Iron Age. In fact, the already mentioned inscription appears to celebrate the conquest of the Kingdom of Edom during the military campaign carried out in the middle of the 6th century BC by the Babylonian king Nabonidus (556-539 BC).

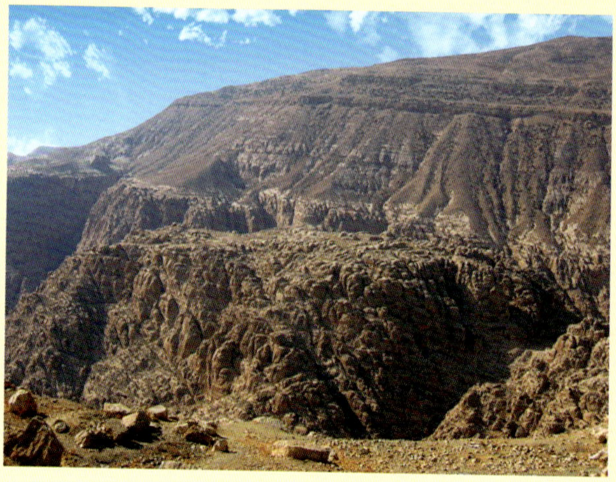

system evolved from a tribal type of organization (in which the chief had to have his power recognized by an assembly of his peers) to a monarchy based on and inspired by Hellenistic models of the time. A quotation from the *Book of Maccabees*, which dates back to about 168 BC, unfortunately the only of its kind, mentions a king named Aretas (Al Harith), who is today believed to be the first sovereign of the newly formed Nabataean Kingdom. His successors took to using an epithet after their names, as the Hellenistic sovereigns did (for example, Aretas III was known as the Philhellen, or friend of the Greeks). Nabataean society evolved very quickly. Permanent cities were founded (not only Petra and Hegra, but also Haluza, Avdat, Mamshit and Shivta, in the Negev), an army was established and under Aretas II (110-96 BC) they even began minting coins. In the 1st century BC, the extensive Nabataean trading system already included a series of permanent caravan stations, complete with temples, barracks and even banking services, so that money did not have to be transported over long distances. However, these permanent settlements still looked like great tent cities, at least up until the Roman conquest, as only official religious and public buildings were made of stone (the ruins of Avdat in Israel are a classic example of this). It was probably during this period that Petra was made the capital, thanks to its strategic position. At the same time, the influence of the Hellenistic world, especially Alexandria, which was favoured by close commercial ties, became more and more obvious in society.

Around 90 BC King Obodas I ('Ubayda) destroyed the Israelite army near Gadara, putting a stop to the expansionist aims of the Hasmonean sovereign Alexander Jannaeus. In 86 BC, the Seleucid monarch Antiochus XII Dionysus invaded the Nabataean Kingdom. Obodas personally led his army into battle and in the violent clash Antiochus was killed. The Nabataean Kingdom was saved. Obodas was buried a little later in the Negev Desert in a place on the "Incense Route" now known as Avdat, which was given his name. Thereafter, the heroic monarch was honoured as a deity, and he became the quintessential symbol of the indomitable Nabataean spirit.

During the reign of his brother, Aretas III (84-62 BC), the kingdom reached its maximum territorial expansion, with control over the modern territories of Jordan, Negev, Sinai, and part of Arabia, as far as Hegra. His greatest achievement, however, was the capture of Damascus (84 BC), which at the time was in the hands of the Seleucid Empire. Shortly afterwards he invaded the Hasmonean Kingdom and convincingly defeated Alexander Jannaeus. Aretas III was also the first Nabataean sovereign to order the minting of silver coins, which had Greek writing on them instead of Nabataean, a testimony to his admiration for Hellenistic culture. This admiration led him to introduce architectural styles that originated from Alexandria and the Roman world to Petra, probably by encouraging foreign craftsmen to come to the city. These artisans changed its face. At the same time, communities of Nabataean merchants established themselves in the major port cities in the Near East (including Sidon) and the western Mediterranean (Pozzuoli), and also in Rome, consolidating the exchange of goods as well as ideas.

Opposite page - *The map shows the boundaries of the Nabataean kingdom at the time of its greatest splendour, in the first century AD.*

Top - *Avdat, today in Israeli territory, once famous for breeding horses; the city, located along the Incense Route, owed its wealth to caravan business and mining.*

Centre - *Some of the Nabataean tombs of Hegra (in present day Saudi Arabia), which is considered second only to Petra, by virtue of its rock cut monuments.*

Bottom - *The Greek legend on this rare copper coin, minted under Aretas III, confirms the powerful monarch's love for Hellenistic culture.*

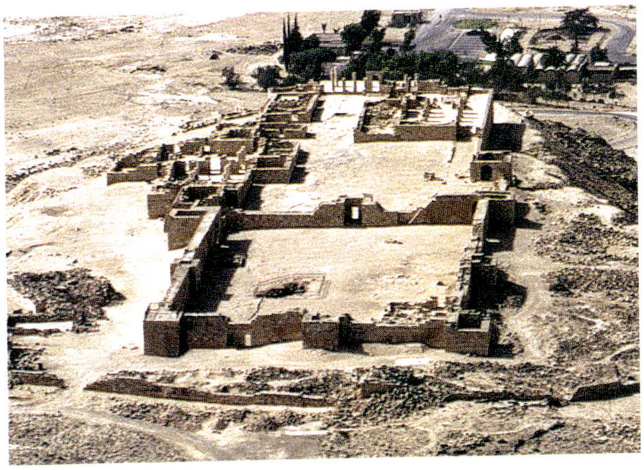

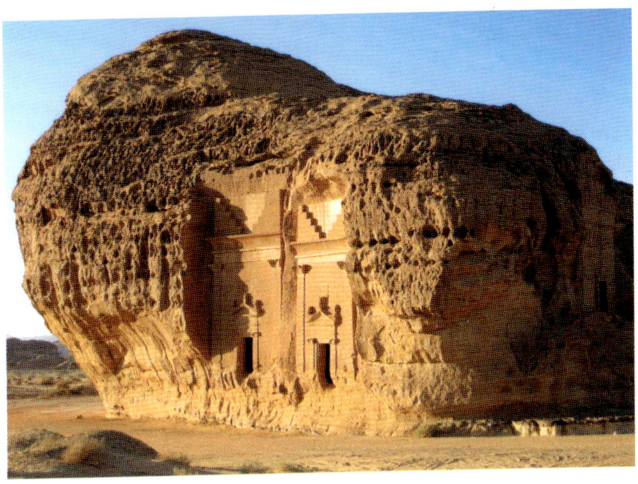

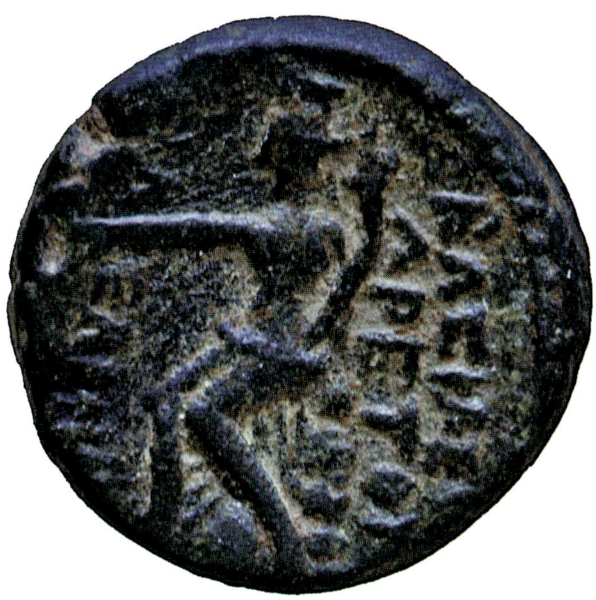

The special relationship with Egypt also continued, and an important Nabataean settlement sprung up in the north of the Nile Delta at Wadi Tumilat. Meanwhile, the Nabataean merchant ships continued to ply the Gulf of Aqaba and the Red Sea, heading for the ports of Egypt.
Although at the beginning of the 1st century BC the main enemy of the Nabataeans was the Hasmonean Kingdom in Palestine, paradoxically, it was soon the Romans who would become the biggest threat, when the legions of Pompey arrived and permanently took control of Syria and Palestine between 64 BC and the following year. In 67 BC, the Hasmonean prince Hyrcanus II (who had been supported by Alexander Jannaeus' wife, Queen Shlomtzion, for some time after the death of her husband) succeeded to the throne of Judah, but was soon deposed by his brother Aristobulus II. Hyrcanus then took refuge in Petra, asking Aretas III for help and promising in return to give back the Nabataean cities that had been occupied by the Hasmoneans. The Nabataean king marched on Jerusalem (65 BC) and laid siege to it, but at this point, Aristobulus II requested the intervention of the Roman tribune Marcus Aemilius Scaurus, Pompey's right-hand man. He forced Aretas to retreat and the Nabataean king suffered a serious defeat while returning to Petra. Scaurus was nominated governor of Syria, and in 62 BC he laid siege to the Nabataean capital. However, the siege was soon lifted as the Nabataeans agreed to pay a tribute of 300 talents (about 10 tons of silver!) and recognize

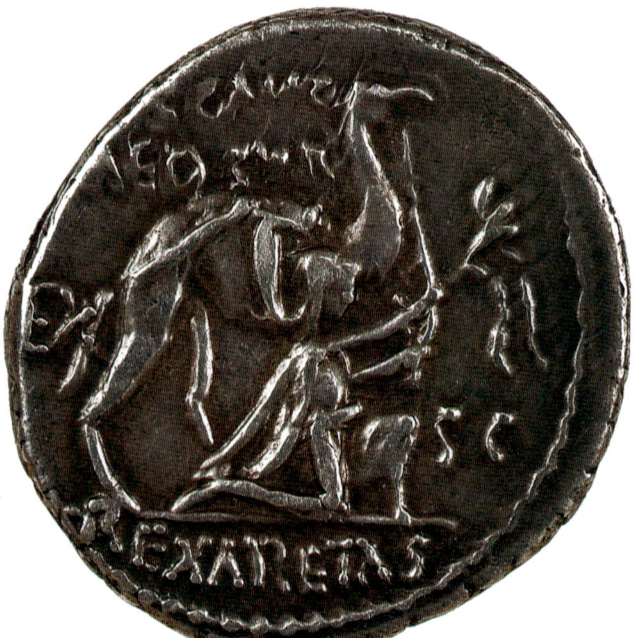

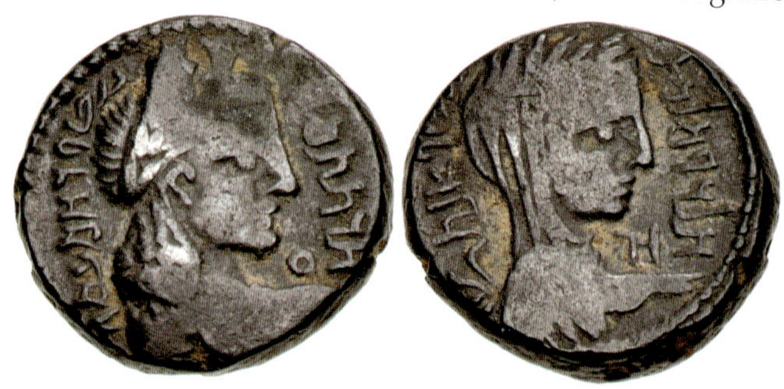

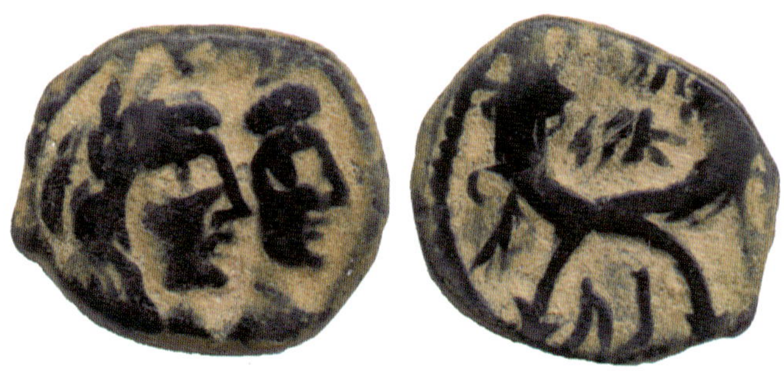

Roman supremacy over the region. In the end, the Nabataean Kingdom became a vassal of Rome.
It was the beginning of a delicate period, but the successors of Aretas III, King Obodas II (62-60 BC) and King Malichos I (Malik, 60-30 BC) managed to remain reasonably independent, thanks to their diplomatic skills and the payment of large sums in taxes. On one occasion in 40 BC, Malichos had the bad idea of supporting the Parthians in one of their offensives against the Roman forces in Syria and Palestine. After the legions had driven off the Parthians in 34 BC, the Romans forced Malichos to pay a heavy tribute. The king also had to confront the expansionist aims of Herod the Great, king of Judah and close ally of Rome. During this period, the Nabataean army suffered the humiliation of being defeated near Philadelphia (modern Amman).
In the meantime, however, continuing involvement in the major flows of trade and culture, as well as significant economic prosperity, had made Petra a cosmopolitan and vibrant city of the arts, where influences from Syria, Hellenized Egypt and the Romanized world came together. During the reigns of Obodas III (30-80 BC) and Aretas IV (8 BC-40 AD), the appearance of the city drastically changed, with urban development based on the Hellenistic model, and a colonnade and grand public monuments were built. The traditional tents had now

CHRONOLOGICAL LIST OF NABATAEAN KINGS

Due to the lack of written sources and a lot of disagreement on the subject, the sequence of Nabataean kings is still uncertain. The following is currently believed to be the most reliable:

Aretas I	ca. 168 - ? BC
Aretas II	120 o 110 - 96 BC
Obodas I	96 - 85 BC
Rabbel I	85 - 84 BC
Aretas III	84 - 62 BC
Obodas II	62 - 60 BC
Malichos I	60 - 30 BC
Obodas III	30 - 9 BC
Aretas IV	9 BC - 40 AD (Queens Huldu and Shaqilath)
Malichos II	40 - 70 AD (Queen Shaqilath II)*
Rabbel II	70 - 106 AD (Queens Gamilath and Hagiru)

** Shaqilath, daughter of Aretas IV and namesake of his second wife, reigned together with her husband Malichos II. Upon their deaths, their very young son Rabbel II ruled for six years.*

Based on fragmentary inscriptions, several historians believe that between Aretas I and Rabbel I a Malichos and an Erotimus ruled, although this is not certain.

been substituted by houses with walls, which were in no way inferior to the most luxurious homes in the Mediterranean basin, as the recent excavations on the Ez-Zantur hill demonstrate. The rooms were sumptuously decorated with floors in mosaic or precious stones, and walls covered with colourful frescoes and plasterwork. Many rupestrian houses, which are particularly suitable for the climate in the region, also had extensive wall decorations, as can be seen in some of the rooms in the Wadi Siyyagh. During the same period, the city's water supply system was hugely improved, with absolutely superb engineering, and the most picturesque access route to the city, the Siq gorge, was most probably paved.

Although the Romans were weakening the Nabataean caravan trade, having opened up their own sea trade route along the coast of the Red Sea, the Nabataeans handled the situation by massively increasing their own agricultural and mineral resources. In fact, copper from their mines was exported all over the Near East. Their heyday came under the reign of Aretas IV, who has already been mentioned. Probably the most spectacular monument in Petra, the Khazneh, was dedicated to him, and it was during his reign that Petra blossomed architecturally more than at any other time. This king, also known as Philopatris, or friend of the people, was extremely skilful at dealing with the Romans, and he offered military support for Publius Quinctilius Varus' expedition against Jerusalem in 4 BC. According to the historian Flavius Josephus, in 26 AD, Aretas defeated the army of Herod Antipas, tetrarch of Galilee, and conquered some territories on the west bank of the Jordan and the lands around Qumran, on the Dead Sea. In around 37 AD, he was given responsibility for the administration of Damascus by the emperor Caligula, and thus control over the affairs of Syria. His successors, Malichos II (40-70 AD) and Rabbel II (70-106 AD), continued resisting Roman expansionism with mixed success. Malichos II lost control of Damascus (even though he had helped the Romans to suppress the Jewish revolt in 67) and Rabbel II even went as far as making Bosra (in the south of modern Syria) the second capital of the kingdom, perhaps fearing that Petra might fall. In spite of everything, this happened after the death of Rabbel II, when on 22 March 106 AD, the legions of the emperor Trajan, led by Aulus Cornelius Palma, took possession of the capital of the kingdom without bloodshed. In the end continuing to resist Rome would have been suicide, and the Nabataeans preferred to be absorbed into the Roman Empire whilst still maintaining a series of privileges.

Opposite page, left - *Back of a silver denarius issued in 58 BC by Marcus Aemilius Scaurus: King Aretas III is depicted pleading and offering an olive branch as a sign of surrender. Behind him is the unmistakable silhouette of a dromedary.*

Opposite page, right - *Front and back of two coins minted under Aretas IV. The one above is a very rare silver drachma dating back to the seventeenth year of his reign (8 AD). It depicts the bust of the sovereign on the obverse and Queen Huldu, his consort, on the reverse. The one below is a copper coin, portraying the king on the obverse with Queen Shaqilath. Thanks to this coinage we know that Aretas had two wives: Huldu (who had given three sons and three daughters to Aretas) and presumably died in 16 AD, and Shaqilath whom the king married two years later.*

Below - *Long excavation campaigns have brought to light the remains of sumptuous houses in the Ez Zantur sector. Not far from the one illustrated here, a large housing unit dating back to the 1st century AD was discovered, the interiors of which retain part of the refined polychrome wall decora-*

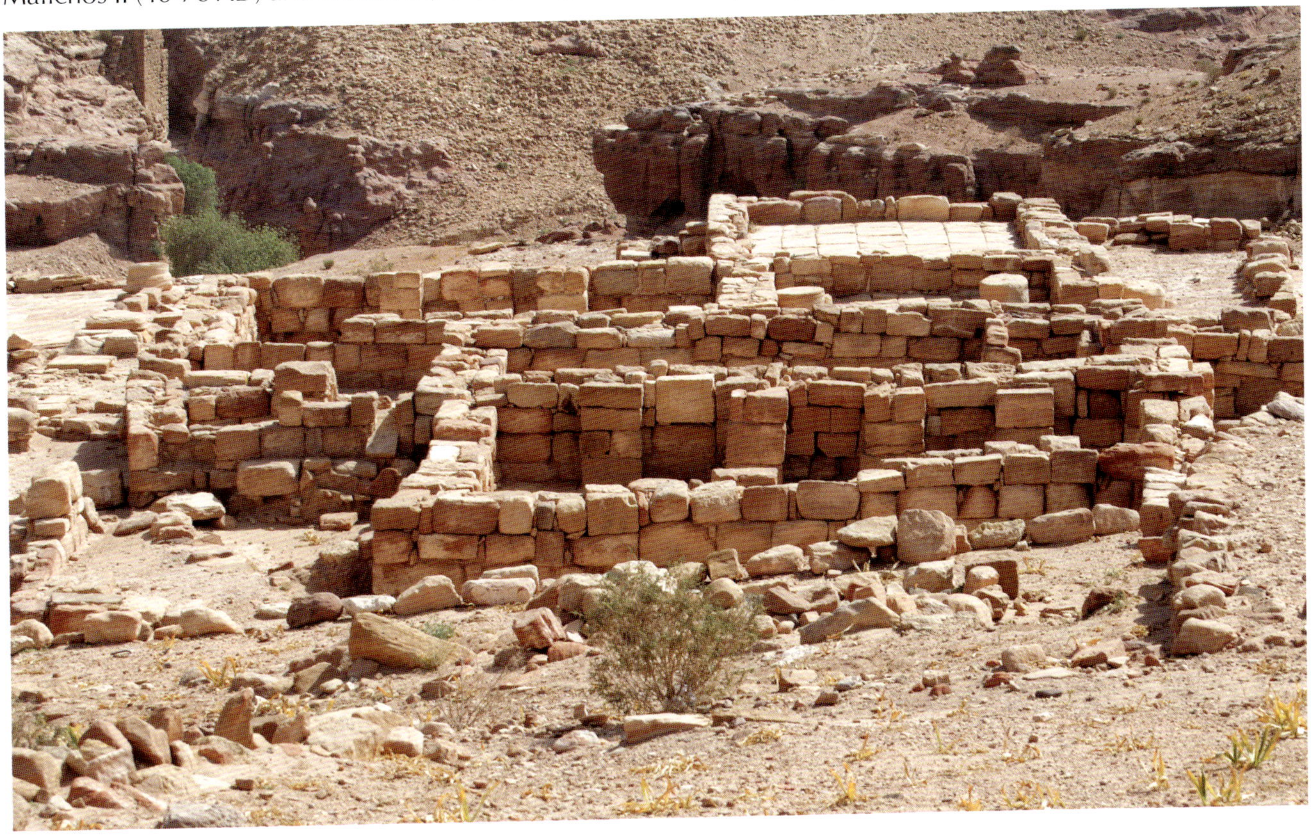

An imperial envoy and a detachment of the Cyrenaica 3rd Legion from Egypt were installed in Petra, which was annexed to the Roman province of Arabia Petraea, and made its capital (together with Bosra). It continued to be a flourishing commercial city for several decades. The most important street in the city was enlarged during this period, and grandiose civil and religious buildings were erected, including a great altar dedicated to the emperors Marcus Aurelius and Lucius Verus. However, the development of maritime trading routes and other centres for the caravan trade in the north, like Gerasa and Palmyra, as well as the transfer of administrative powers to Bosra, signalled the slow but inevitable decline of the city. Between 111 and 114 Trajan also opened a new road from Bosra to the Gulf of Aqaba (*Via Nova Traiana*), which passed a long way to the east of Petra, and the city was only connected to it with a side road. This fatally weakened it, relegating it to the role of a city of secondary importance, even though Trajan had honoured it with the title of metropolis. Hadrian, his successor, also gave the city the title of *Adrianea* (Hadrianic) during his visit in 131, implicitly recognizing its status as a cultural and economic centre.
In this period, the Greek language, which had already been introduced in the time of Aretas IV, spread to all social classes and was used both for official purposes and colloquially, until it had practically replaced Aramaic and its Nabataean variety. This is attested to by the large num-

Above - *This sestertius in orichalcus, coined under Trajan, celebrates the Roman annexation of the Nabataean kingdom, which took place without true military glory. This is demonstrated by the fact that Trajan was not adorned with the title of Arabicus (instead he was given the appellation of Dacicus after the victory over the bellicose Dacia). Furthermore, on the reverse,* Arabia adquisita *(namely Arabia annexed) is written, and not* Arabia capta *(i.e. Arabia conquered). Indeed, the annexation of the Nabataean kingdom was not officially celebrated until the completion of Trajan's* Via Nova.

Below - *A detail of the magnificent mosaic floor of the Byzantine church, in which Christian figurative themes merge with others in the Greco-Roman pagan tradition. The girl is the personification of Spring (Εαρινη).*

Opposite page - *View of the crusader castle of Al Wu'eira, strategically located on the edge of a deep chasm.*

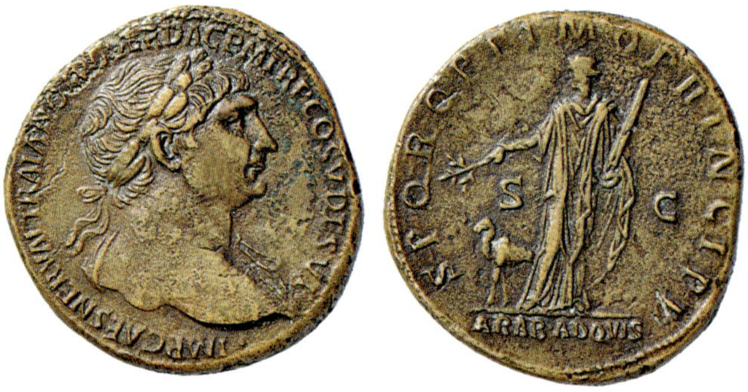

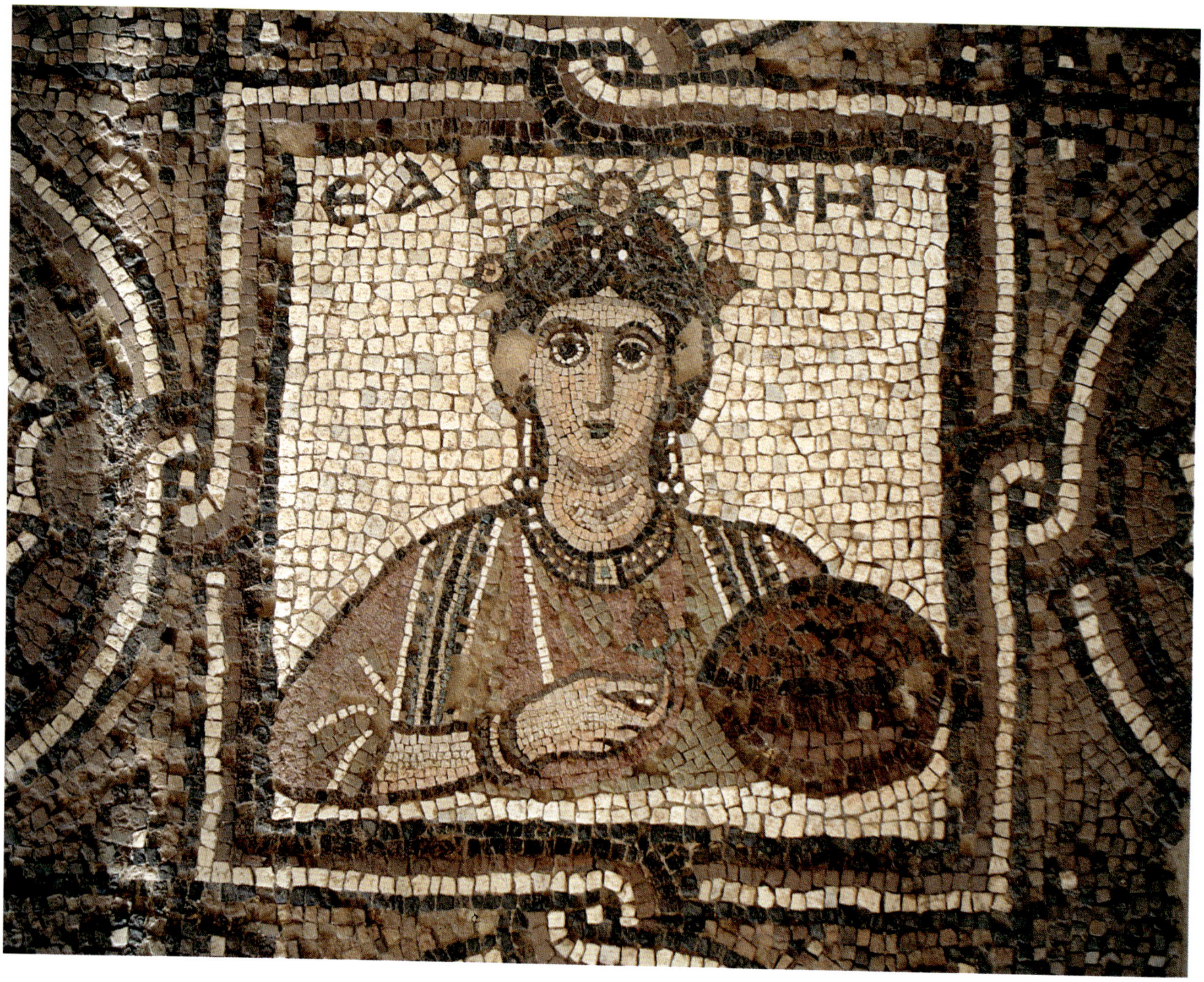

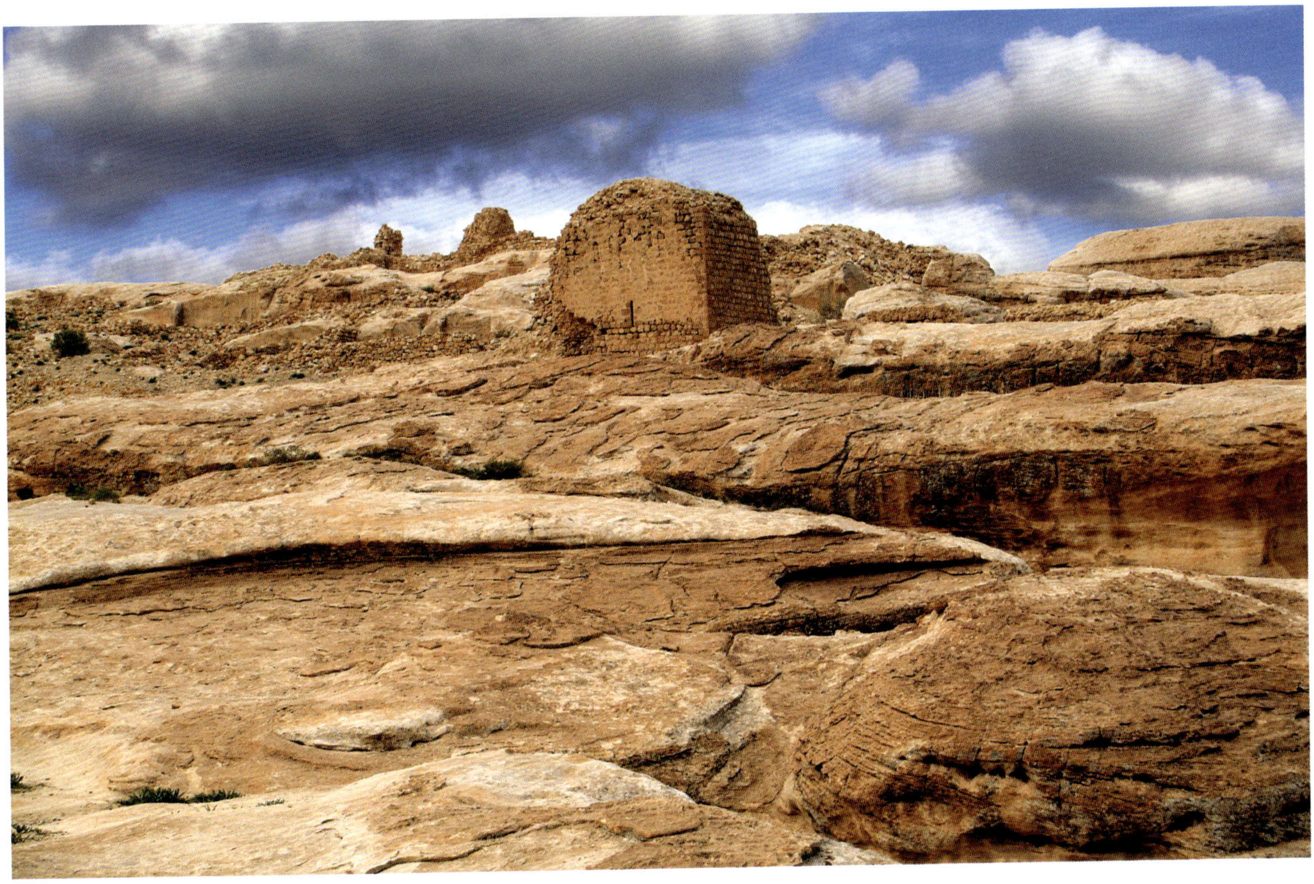

ber of inscriptions in this language that can be found in Petra and the surrounding area. Latin, on the other hand, was very rarely used. (In Petra, only the inscription on the tomb of the propraetor Sextius Florentinus is notable).

For a couple of centuries Petra stubbornly struggled on as an active commercial centre, and towards the end of the 3rd century, during the political reorganization of the eastern part of the empire carried out by Diocletian, it was designated capital of the province known as *Palaestina Tertia*. Petra's official title of "metropolis" was re-established, its Christian community rapidly increased in size and it soon became a bishopric. A wall was built around the city and basilicas sprung up, with wonderful mosaic floors in the Byzantine style. Many of the rupestrian buildings were converted into churches, including the so-called Urn Tomb (converted in 447).

In spite of being struck by two violent earthquakes in 363 (perhaps followed by a catastrophic flood caused by the collapse of the dams) and 419, life in the city continued much as before, although the original Nabataean population was starting to thin out as a result of an increase in migration, mainly from the Arabian peninsula. However, it became almost completely depopulated following the terrifying earthquake of 551, which brusquely interrupted its slow but continuous evolution. After the region was conquered by the Arabs of the Umayyad dynasty in 663, and yet another devastating earthquake in 747, Petra was virtually abandoned, and the slow decline of what was left of its magnificent monuments began.

Probably only the suburb of Gaia was still permanently inhabited, as the excavations of some of the residential and trade buildings (including oil presses, water mills and water tanks) have revealed. In the first years of the 12th century, the crusaders of Baldwin I arrived and named the place Li Vaux Moise, or the "Valley of Moses", in the belief that the biblical patriarch had passed through while leading the people of Israel on their long journey from Sinai to the Promised Land. They built the great castle of Al Wu'eira a few kilometres from where Wadi Musa stands today, and a smaller fortress on the Al Habis rock, right in the heart of Petra, using building materials taken from the ruins of the Nabataean capital. The crusaders were also responsible for the construction of three other small fortresses in the area, which are ruins today.

After 1189, the year in which Li Vaux Moise was taken by Saladin, Petra was finally abandoned and its name was forgotten. Only a few learned people knew of its existence (including the Sultan Baibars, who visited it in the 13th century), and it remained in obscurity right up until 1812 when the young Swiss explorer and Orientalist Johann Ludwig Burckhardt managed to pass himself off as a Muslim pilgrim visiting the nearby tomb of Aaron, thanks to his perfect knowledge of the Arabic language and culture. Thanks to this ploy, Burckhardt was able to see the astonishing rupestrian monuments, but he did not stay long in order not to arouse the suspicions of the locals. In fact, at the time, Petra was inhabited by some rather belligerent Bedouin tribes, who were always fighting amongst themselves. Although Burckhardt was not able to stay for more than a few hours, the fabulous city carved into the rock had finally been rediscovered. The news spread rapidly throughout the western world and soon attracted the attention of adventurous new visitors travelling under the protection of various local sheiks, who gave them safe passage in exchange for large sums of money. It should be pointed out that the hostility towards foreigners of the Bedouin tribes that had settled in Petra was the result of centuries of isolation, and the

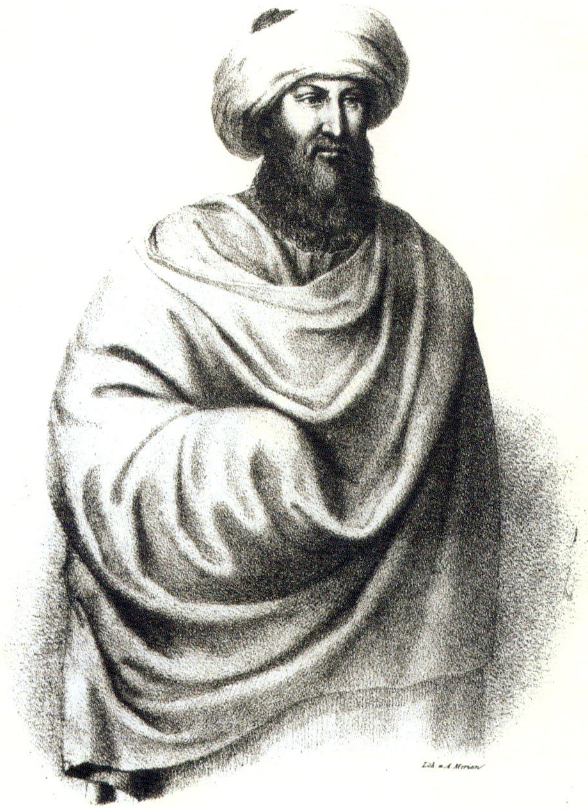

and to this day they are some of the best known representations of Petra. This wave of romantic explorers, adventurers and artists in the mid nineteenth century was followed by the first recognized researchers, who began a systematic exploration of the archaeological area. These included respected figures like the Englishmen Austen Henry Layard and Edward Beer (who identified the Nabataean language as a form of Aramaic), and the Frenchmen Honoré d'Albert and Melchior de Vogüé, but it was the Germans Rudolf Ernst Brünnow and Alfred von Domaszewski who completed the first systematic study of the Nabataean monuments in Petra, cataloguing them on the basis of their position, with a numbering system that is still being used and added to today. Not by chance is their work, *Die Provincia Arabia*, published between 1904 and 1909, still considered a milestone. Gustav Dalman, who was especially interested in the Nabataen religious sites, later added to the text. In 1914, Thomas Edward Lawrence, the famous Lawrence of Arabia, came to Petra and was quite literally enchanted by it.
Unfortunately, during the course of the twentieth century the region was affected by military conflicts including the First World War, the Arab Israeli War in 1948 and the Yom Kippur War, which interrupted the archaeological investigations. However, following the signing of the peace treaty between Jordan and Israel, they began again with renewed impetus. Recent discoveries that have taken place in various areas of the city, thanks to excavations carried out by international teams in cooperation with the local authorities, are a testament to this. In particular, the excavations that identified some tombs under

false belief that treasures of immeasurable value were hidden in the ruins, left by a phantom "Pharaoh". In fact, the biblical stories had been distorted by popular imagination and the figure of Moses was transformed into a sort of good magician, while his historic rival became a miserly evil sorcerer. Among the first visitors were the Englishmen Charles Irby and James Mangles in 1818. They were both officers in the Royal Navy and were accompanied by the painter William Bankes, who wrote a vivid account of their visit. Like many others after them, there were amazed especially when they saw the Khazneh, which they described as "a work unlike any other in the world". They were followed, ten years later, by two Frenchmen, Count Léon de Laborde and Adolphe Linant de Bellefonds, who produced the first reliable reproductions of the monuments of Petra. The lithographs made from their reliefs and sketches, which were published in Paris in 1830 in a wide-ranging work entitled *Voyage de l'Arabie Pétrée*, soon became famous all over Europe. These images had a profound effect on a young American named John Lloyd Stephens (who later became famous for "discovering" the Maya civilization). In February 1836, after countless adventures, he finally reached Petra. He later described it with great passion in *Incidents of Travel in Egypt, Arabia Petraea, and the Holy Land*, which soon became a best seller. It was the increasing fame of Petra, immortalized by the English poet John William Burgon, who described it as "a rose-red city half as old as time", which attracted the Scottish draughtsman and painter David Roberts, today considered one of the most talented and influential landscape artists of the 19th century. The lithographs made from drawings done on location, originally published in the huge collection entitled *Holy Land* and published between 1842 and 1849, brought him fame in perpetuity,

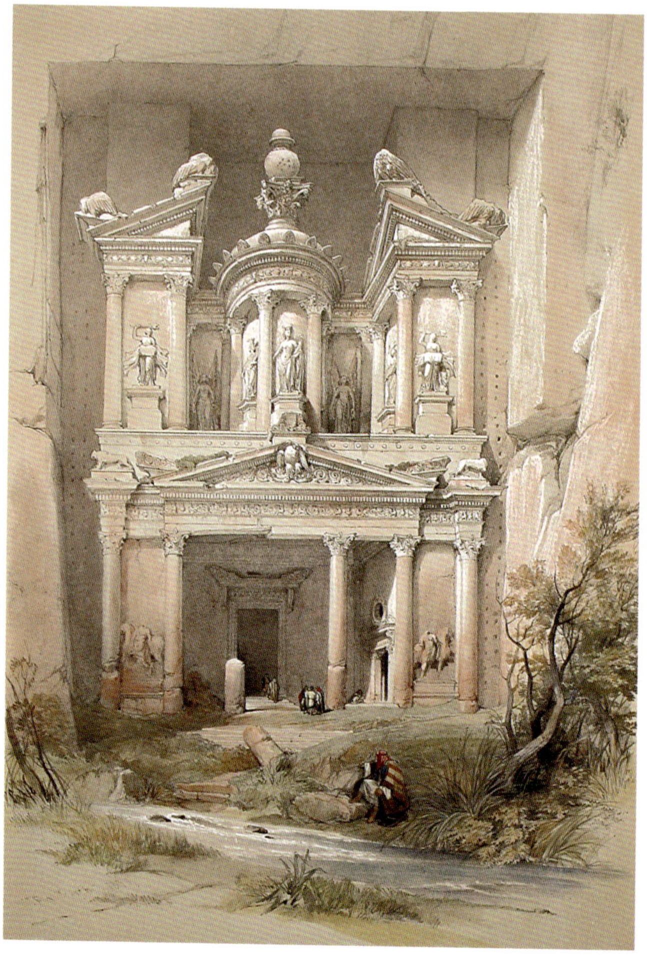

the Khazneh, carried out by the Jordanian Antiquities Department, should be mentioned. The investigations of the Swiss mission, organized by the University of Basel, concentrated on the central area of Petra, where residential buildings dating back to the 1st century AD were found. In the late nineties, archaeologists from the University of Pennsylvania discovered that the so-called "Lower Market" was in fact a garden, which had a large pool of water with a pavilion at its centre. It was a real *paradeisos*, or ornamental garden, designed according to the principles of Hellenistic town planning. The results of an extensive excavation carried out by the prestigious Brown University from Providence, in the area of the so-called "Great Temple", were even more spectacular. They revealed a building that is one of a kind and in many ways still enigmatic. Between 1992 and 2002. The American Center of Oriental Research unearthed three Byzantine churches to the north of the Colonnade. In particular, the papyrus scrolls discovered near the Petra Church shed light on life in Petra in the 6th century. The work carried out by the Petra Survey Project, which identified and catalogued more than three thousand rupestrian buildings and artefacts in the Petra area, and promoted an invaluable series of restorations, has also been of fundamental importance. Finally, it should not be forgotten that in 2007 Petra was included in the list of the "new" Seven Wonders of the World, which considerably increased the number of visitors. This tourist boom has highlighted how important it is to protect this unique and exceptional archaeological site, which absolutely must be safeguarded for future generations.

Opposite page, left - *Portrait of Johann Ludwig Burckhardt, the Swiss explorer and orientalist who "discovered" Petra in 1812. As he converted to the Islamic religion, when he died in 1817 he was buried in Cairo with the Arabic name of Ibrahim Ibn Abdallah.*

Opposite page, right - *Between 1842 and 1849 David Roberts published a colossal work, entitled* Holy Land, *made up of six volumes and comprising 247 lithographs, 14 of which have Petra as a subject. This, which has become famous, portrays the facade of the Khazneh.*

In this page - *Another two lithographs from Roberts' work: the so-called "Royal Tombs" (above) and the Deir, or Monastery (below) are reproduced.*

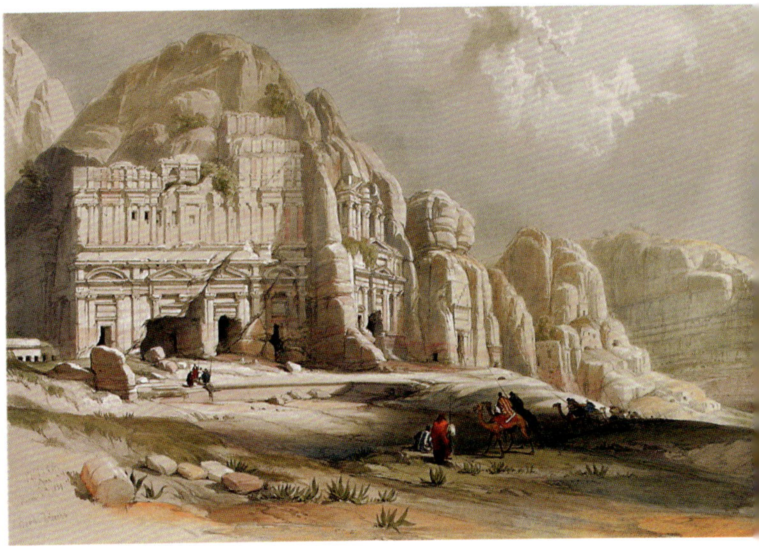

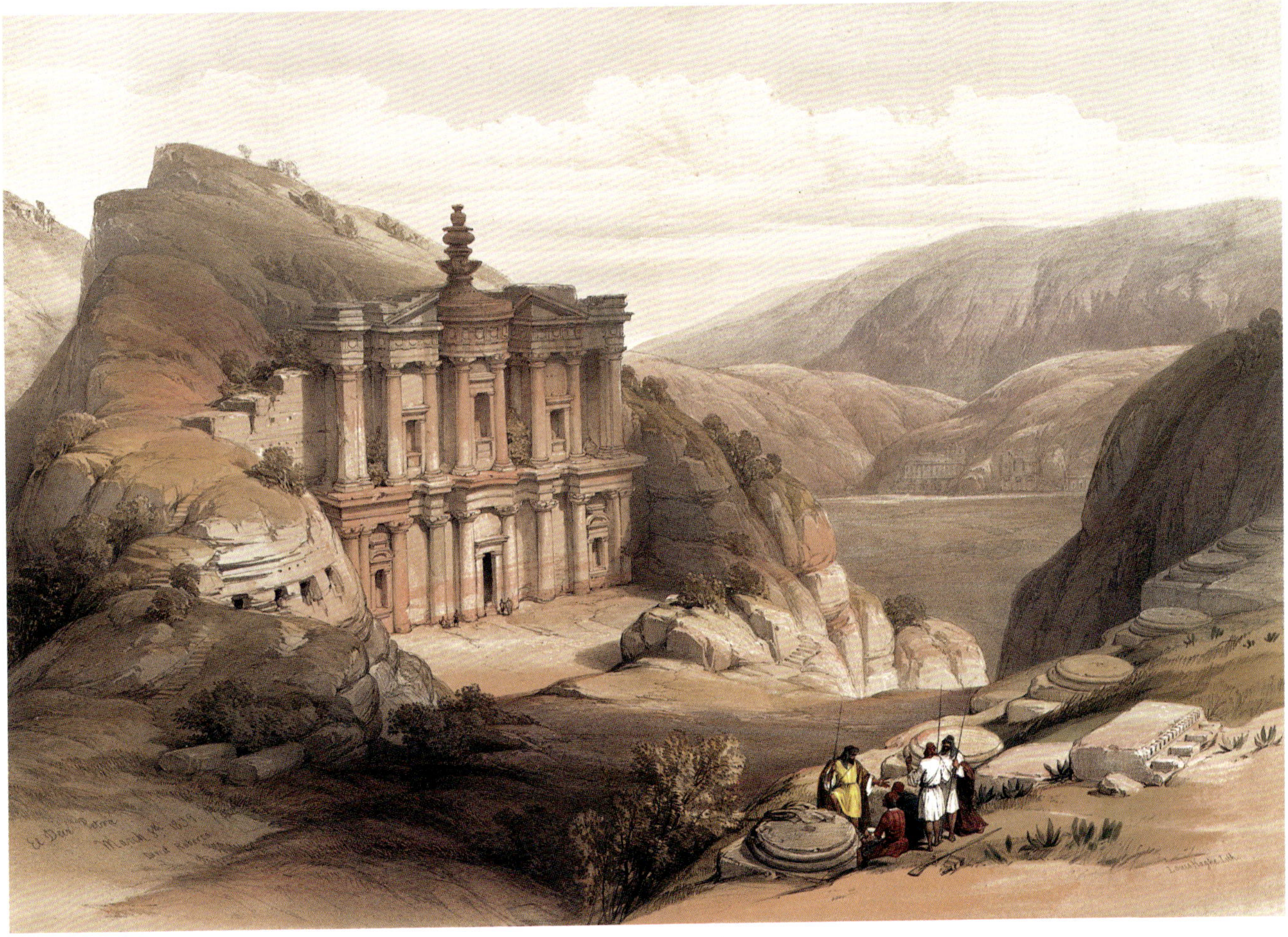

Illustrations – paintings, watercolours, lithographs – produced by the first western travellers who reached Petra, not only constitute an important artistic patrimony, but are often a precious source of information. De Laborde, Mangles and Roberts were indeed privileged to visit the dead city when several of its monuments appeared differently to how they do today; in fact, one and a half centuries have passed since those pioneers explored Petra.
For example, in a map drawn by De Laborde, the position of the so-called Room 468 is shown directly in front of the Deir, fronted by a large pronaos completely missing today, but the French explorer could still see the column bases in situ. David Roberts also noticed the building's ruins, which he immortalised in his famous lithograph, reproduced on the preceding page. Another view by the talented Scottish artist portrays the so-called Palace Tomb; the monument, semi-destroyed by earthquakes, is not very dissimilar to how it appears today, but it is interesting to note that the large courtyard in front of the facade is not that cluttered with debris. This confirms that all the building material (with which the top part was built), raised to the ground by a violent earthquake, had already been cleared in antiquity. This fact supports the commonly held belief that the adjacent, northern city wall – today hardly noticeable – does not date back to the beginning of the settlement, but was erected in the Byzantine era due to a strong phase of depopulation and the urban area shrinking. The wall was probably made out of the large amount of building material resulting from the earthquake in 419. It is easy to imagine that the ruins of the Palace Tomb were also used for this purpose.
Photographs prior to the First World War have the same historical value. Thanks to them, we can see how various monuments looked before the excavation and restauration campaigns (ceaselessly ongoing today), which have led to their current appearance. These photographs allow us to fully evaluate the enormous scale of the manual work and research that have been necessary to preserve Petra's monuments, so that thousands of tourists can still admire them today.
It is surprising to see the Urn Tomb before a painstaking anastylosis reconstructed at least in part the large, vaulted rooms facing it. More disheartening is seeing the magnificent facade of the Khazneh with of one of its columns missing, surrounded by a messy heap of rubble and bushes. This detail, also evident in Robert's lithographs and in a famous painting by Frederic Edwin Church, reminds us that until the middle of the last century, the Siq was not the privileged entrance to Petra, but rather, a wild gorge with an almost perennial stream. Today that has dried up due to the modern town of Wadi Musa's voracity for water. Back then, travellers usually arrived from the opposite side of Petra, from Aqaba along the Wadi Thughra, and the Khazneh was one of the last monuments they saw, which is very different to what tourists experience today.
Regarding visitors, it is touching to see how the legendary Nazzal's Camp, a basic campsite until the '20s, offered such a Spartan welcome. No doubt there were hardships and discomforts, but how can those heroic times not be viewed without nostalgia and even envy?

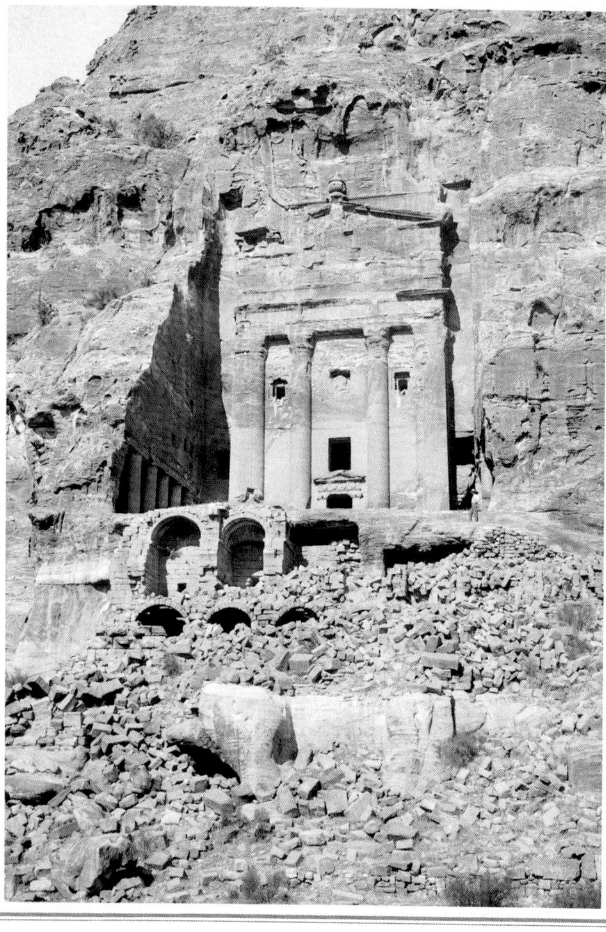

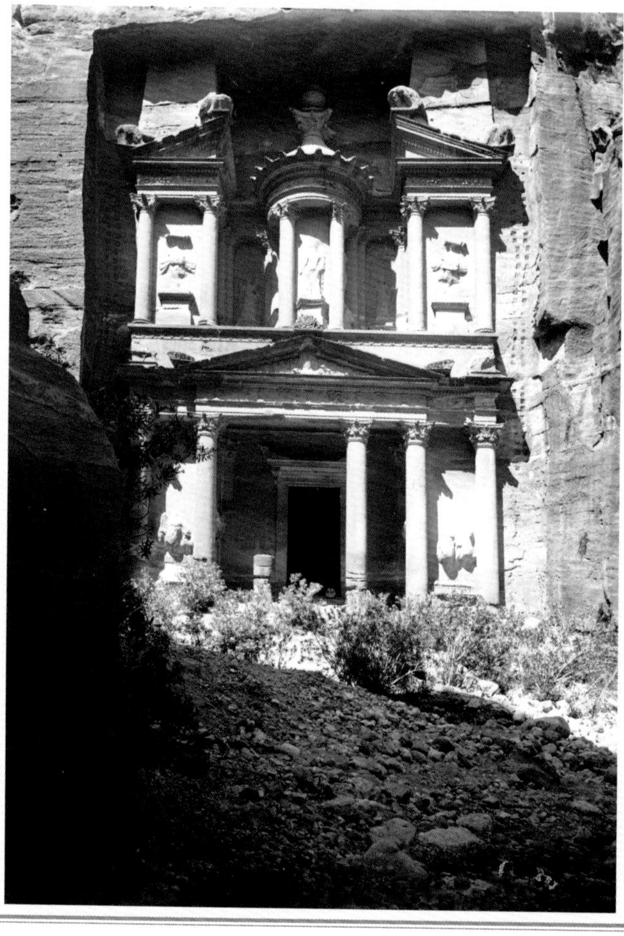

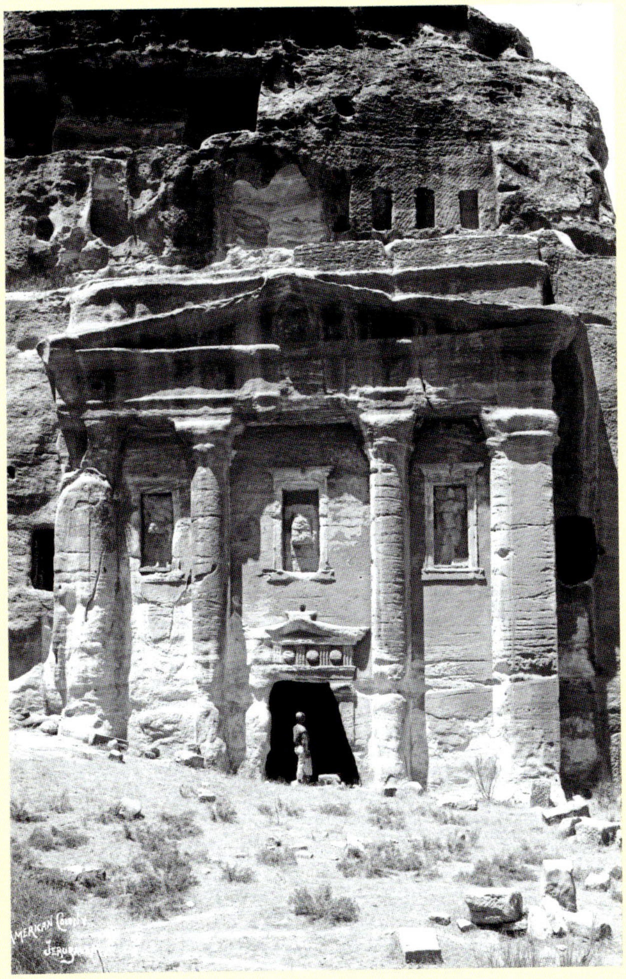

Opposite page, left - *In this photo, prior to 1914 (along with the others), the Urn Tomb is portrayed with its large substructures still in ruins.*

Opposite page, right - *The facade of the Khazneh with its southern column missing.*

Top left - *The Tomb of the Roman Soldier.*

Top right - *The Palace-Tomb; as can be seen, the mass of rubble in front of the facade was small.*

Below - *The white tents of Nazzal's Camp.*

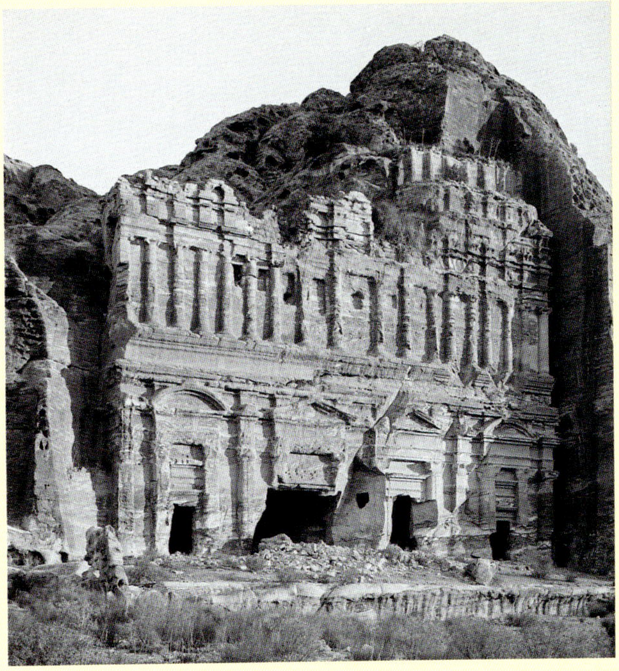

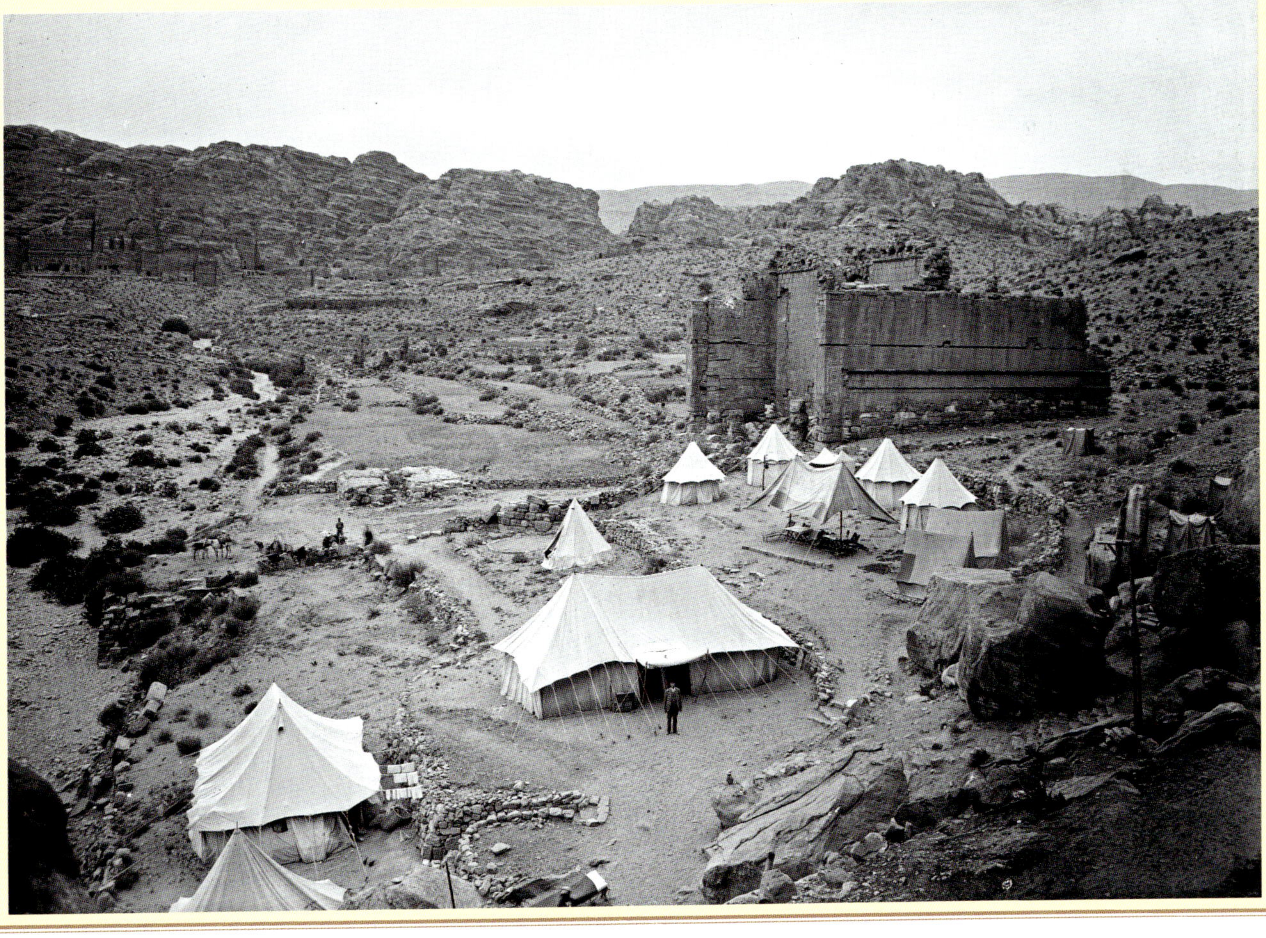

LEGEND

1 Visitors centre, museum and entrance gate
2 Djinn Blocks
3 Obelisk Tomb and Bab el Siq Triclinium
4 Tunnel
5 Eagle Niche
6 Entrance arch
7 Khazneh (the Treasury)
8 Uneishu Tomb
9 Theatre
10 Urn Tomb
11 Silk Tomb
12 Corinthian Tomb
13 Palace Tomb
14 Sextius Florentinus Tomb
15 Carmine Facade
16 Dorotheos House
17 Tomb with the Armour
18 TurkmaniyyaTomb
19 Colonnaded Street (Decumanus maximus)
20 Great Temple
21 Temenos Gate
22 Qasr el Bint
23 Unfinished Tomb
24 Old museum and restaurant
25 Winged Lions Temple
26 Blue Chapel
27 Byzantine Church
28 Pharaoh's Column
29 Lion Triclinium
30 Ed Deir (the Monastery)
31 Room 468
32 Serpent Monument
33 Broken Pediment Tomb
34 Renaissance Tomb
35 Wadi al Najir Tomb
36 Roman Soldier Tomb
37 Roman Soldier Triclinium
38 Garden Triclinium (or Temple)
39 Lion Monument
40 Great Obelisks
41 High Place of Sacrifice
42 Al Wu'eira Crusader Castle
43 Khubtha North aqueduct bridge
44 Large reservoir (Zurrabah, or al Birka)

Main Nabataean dams
●● Course of the main Nabataean aqueducts

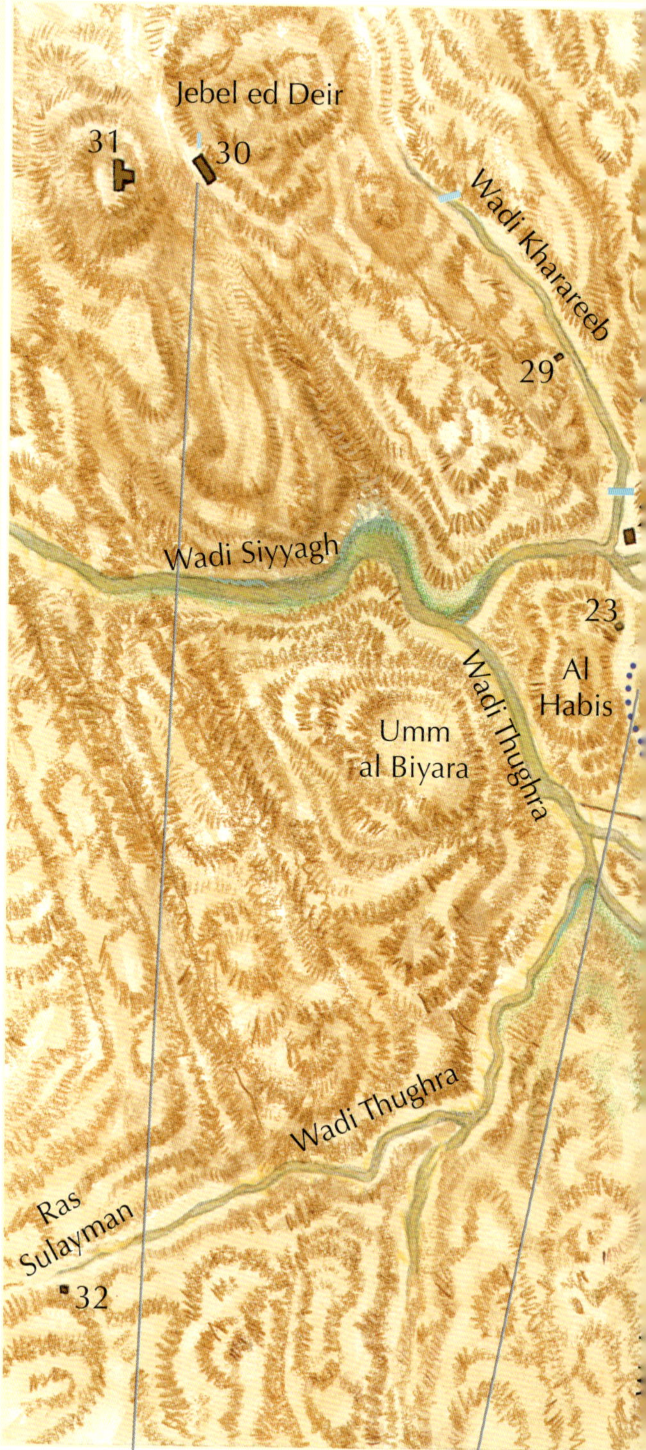

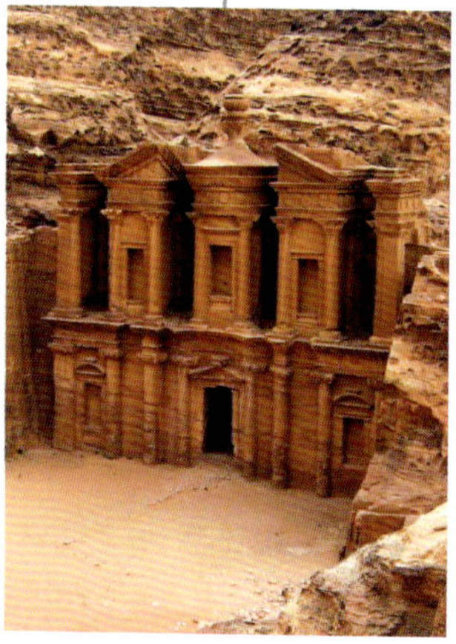

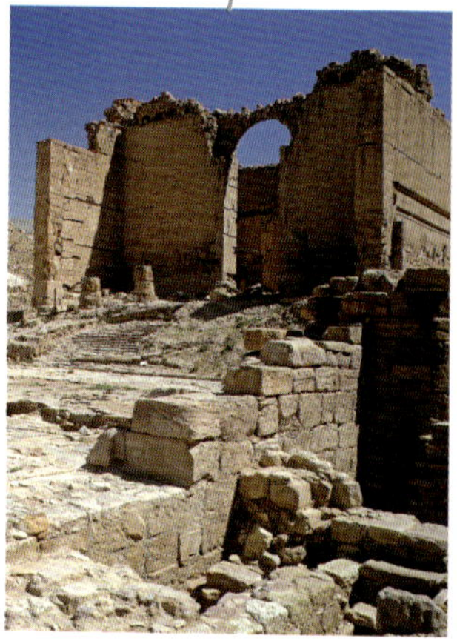

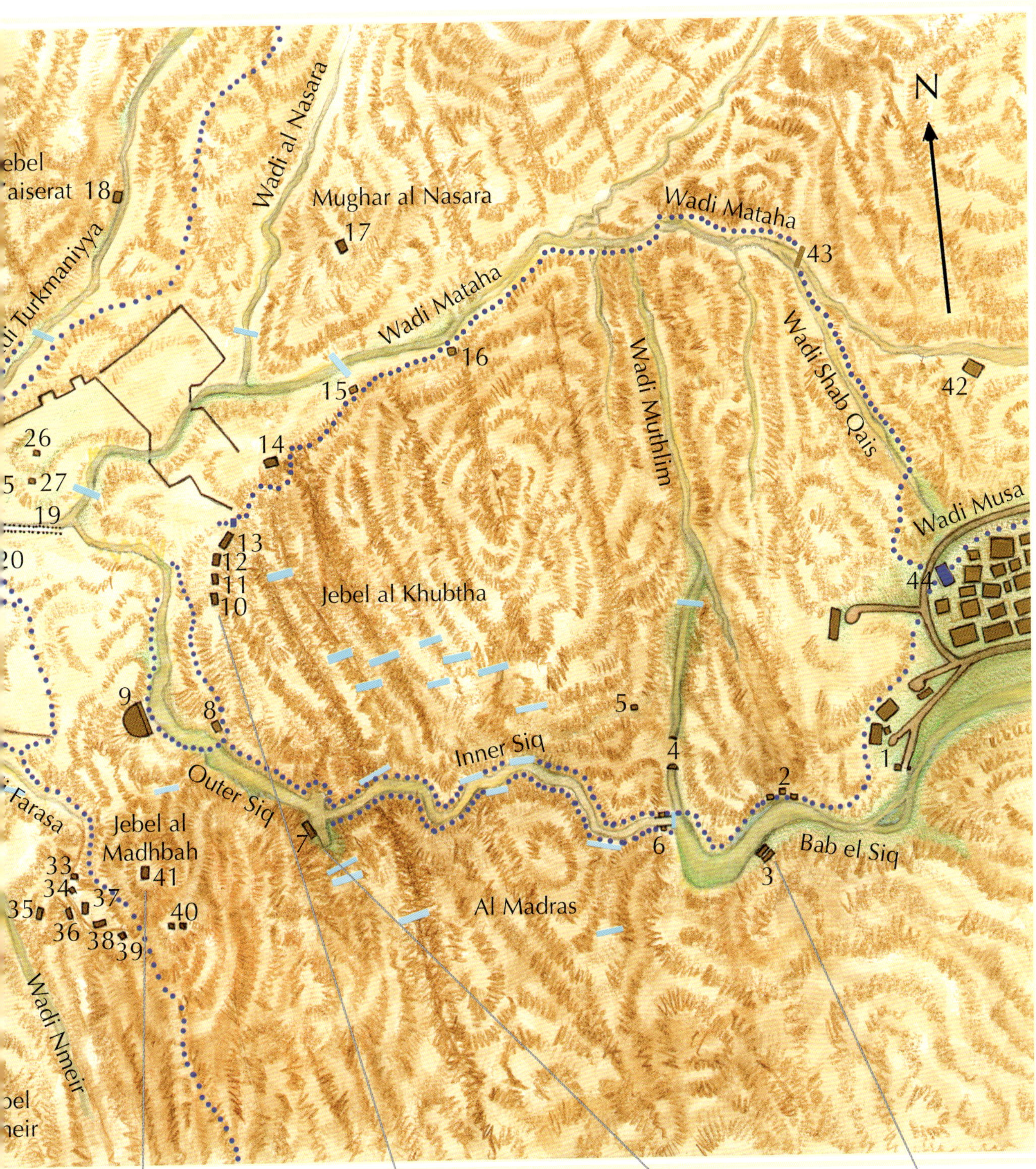

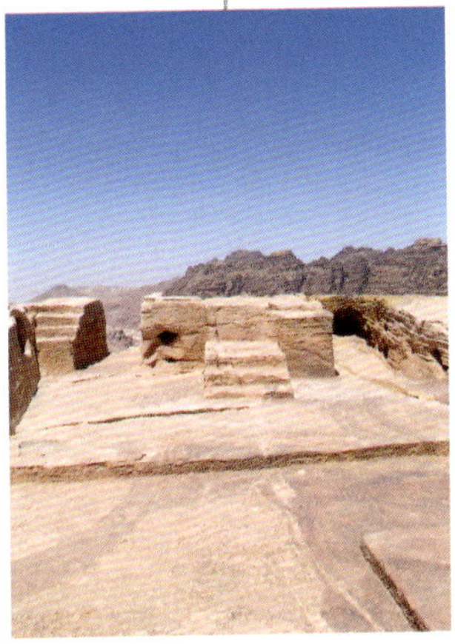

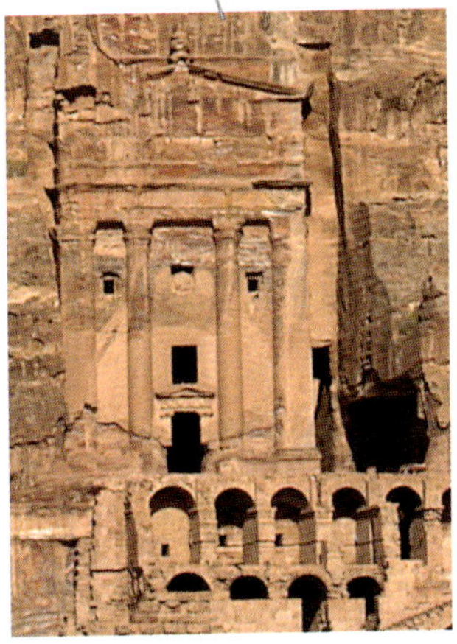

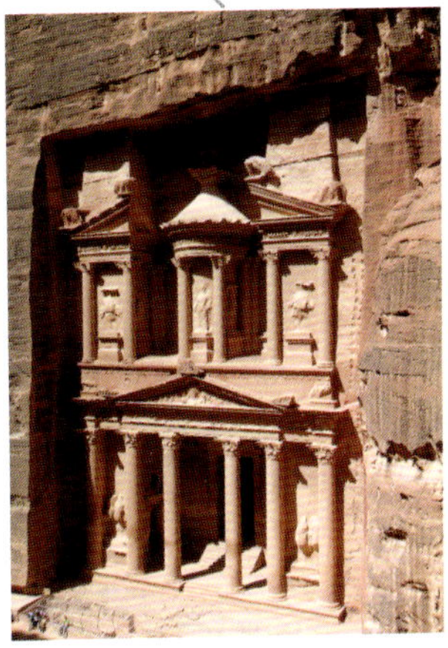

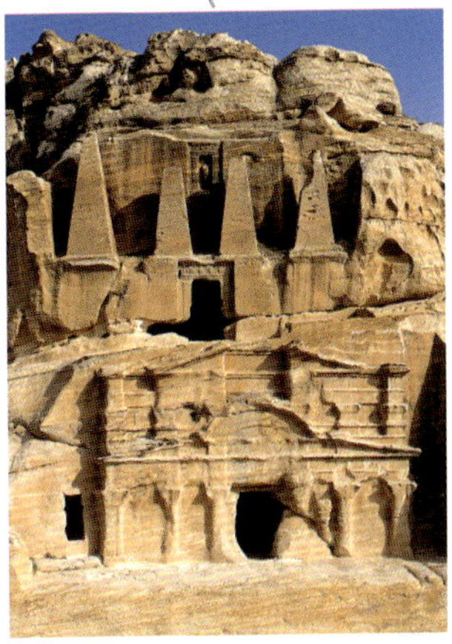

Monica Falcone

PETRA AND THE NABATAEANS

Today, Petra is one of the most famous places in the world, but paradoxically, there are more unanswered questions about this archaeological site than certainties. As far as the historical events that affected the metropolis and the surrounding region are concerned, Nabataean civilization has never been the subject of thorough analysis, largely because of the lack of written sources. Unfortunately, there is little information that can be confirmed, and it tends to be fragmented. At the moment, only archaeological investigation seems capable of penetrating the darkness, albeit slow-ly. A fairly reliable chronological sequence of Nabataean kings has been worked out thanks to inscriptions and especially coins, but numerous other aspects of this unique civilization, like the people's daily life, their religion, customs, farming methods and architectural techniques, are only partially understood.
It is not known exactly which part of the Arabian Peninsula the Nabataeans (or Nabatu as they were known as in ancient times) originated from either. There is so much uncertainty that some people maintain that they came from Mesopotamia or the Persian Gulf, although that theory now seems very unlikely. This uncertainty is a result of the fact that all Nabataean documents written on perishable materials like papyrus and parchment have been destroyed. Today, there are only a few rupestrian inscriptions, which are mainly declarations of faith and unfortunately contain little historical information.
However, archaeological investigations have established that the Nabataeans started settling in the Petra Valley towards the end of the 4th century B.C. This choice was undoubtedly justified by its strategic location along two of the main caravan routes in the region. One went south from Gaza, on the Mediterranean, to Hegra and the port of Leuke Kome on the Arabian Peninsula, and the other pushed north from Alexandria, through Sinai, towards Bosra and Damascus. The area was also naturally well protected and above all had several permanent springs, which were vital in such an arid region. The place where the Rose City is located is shaped like an amphitheatre, enclosed by high mountain ranges approximately 2 kilometres apart from north-east to south-west and one kilometre apart from east to west. The bed of a creek called the Wadi Musa, which is almost always dry, crosses the valley and borders two low rocky plateaus, where the main part of the city, later razed to the ground by earthquakes, used to stand. The peaks of some of the surrounding mountains were easy to reach if it was necessary to take refuge on higher ground to escape from enemies. The main access routes to the city ran along the bottom of gorges and valleys. They could therefore be guarded without difficulty by garrisons of a few

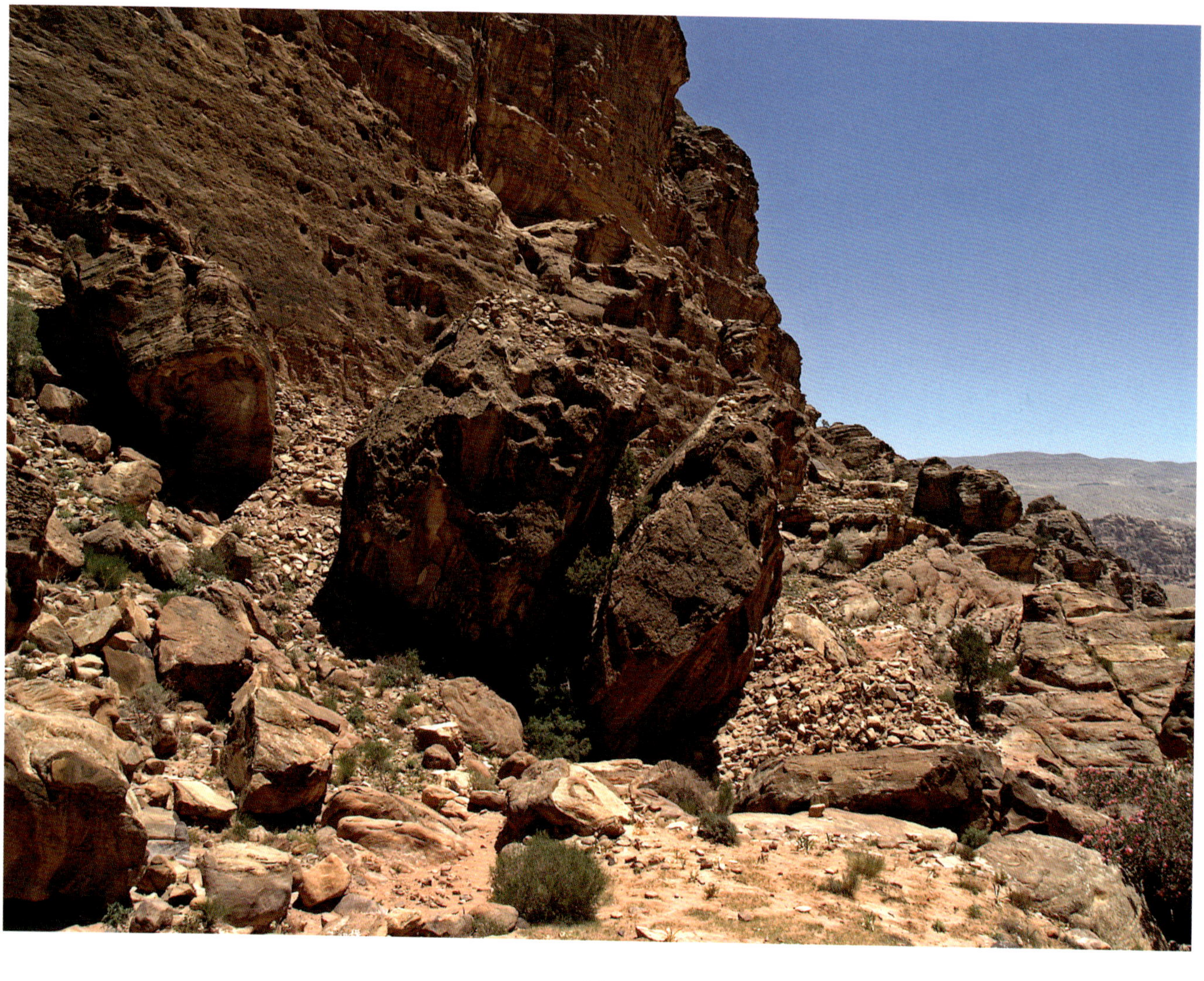

men and defended fairly easily if necessary. The remains of one of these forts are visible in the Wadi Kharareeb, along the track that joined the city with the caravan suburb of Siq al Barid (today known as Little Petra).
In the first centuries of its existence, Petra must have looked like a big disorganized encampment of tents. Little by little, its inhabitants abandoned their nomadic lifestyles and learned all the techniques necessary to erect buildings and create the infrastructure needed to survive in a community with an ever growing population. At the beginning it must have been rather difficult, because the Nabataeans did not have their own traditions in these areas. They were not farmers, or skilled builders or town-planners. In fact, they had to learn everything they needed to know by observing the peoples they traded with and experimenting as they went along. Their major influences came from the Hellenized world, but for a lot of things, the Nabataeans came up with solutions that were entirely original. The field in which they were most inventive and certainly excelled was hydraulic engineering.

THE WATER SYSTEM OF PETRA

The most compelling problem for a community that was constantly growing was supplying it with water. In fact, the springs in the region were only able to provide for part of their requirement. Petra was not actually situated exactly on the caravan routes mentioned, but a few kilometres away. The settlement of Gaia, today's Wadi Musa, was closer to this thoroughfare, and also had the most abundant spring, called Ain Musa. However, Petra was situated on the floor of a large valley and the Nabataeans realized that this could solve their problem. In fact, they devised an extremely complicated system of channels carved into the living rock. Some of them were used to carry water to the city from the springs of Ain Musa, Ain Braq and Ain Debdebeh, but most were for gathering rainwater from a wide area and carrying it to ever larger waterways, which in turn filled enormous cisterns, carved into the rock and lined with thick layers of watertight plaster. These cisterns were mostly covered over. Keeping the water in total darkness prevented the growth of algae and killed bacteria, which made it drinkable, even after a long period of time.
Although the annual rainfall was very low, with these sophisticated techniques the inhabitants of Petra managed to gather a large proportion of the rain that fell on an area of over 250 square kilometres! Obviously, this involved a careful study of the geography of the local area, which the Nabataeans were able to exploit with extraordinary skill. In fact, the courses of all the seasonal streams that converge in the valley of Petra (the Wadi Musa, the Wadi Muthlim, the Wadi An Nasara, the Wadi Farasa and many others of a smaller size) were carefully directed by constructing massive barriers, which had a threefold purpose. Firstly, these dams (often built in a sequence along the same wadi) drastically slowed down the extreme speed of bodies of water produced by the most violent storms, which otherwise would have moved enormous quantities of rock, devastating everything in their path (as recently

Opposite page - *In Wadi Kharareeb, there are some remains of a probable Nabataean fortification, partly built on a huge boulder in order to monitor the valley better. It is possible that the structure was remodelled in the Byzantine or Crusader period.*

Above - *One of the Nabataean dams rebuilt along the Siq to prevent sudden floodings.*

Below - *A section of the rock-cut aqueduct that runs along the northern side of the Jebel al Khubtha.*

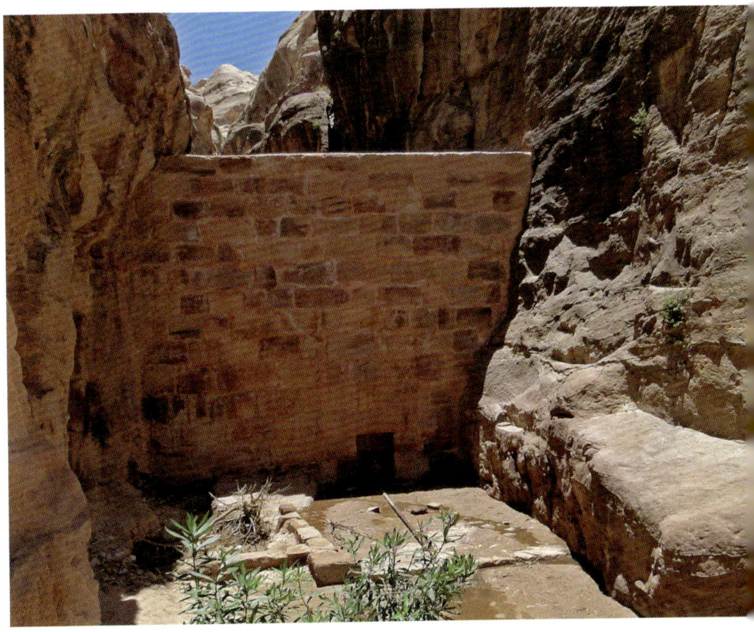

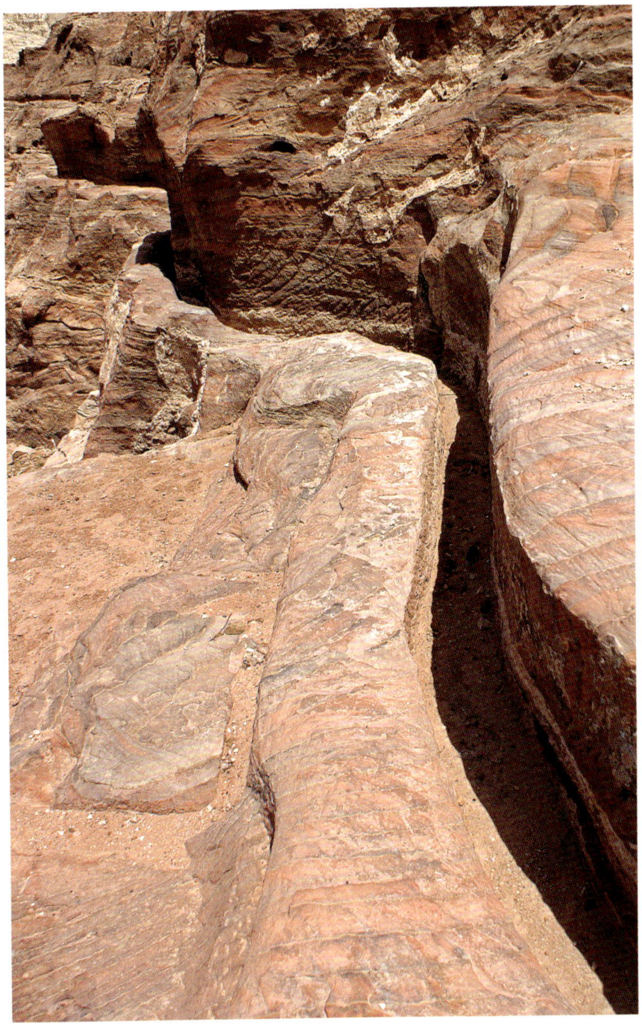

as 1963, a group of tourists was wiped out in the Siq by one of these sudden waves). Secondly, the dams created little pools of water that were actually quite deep, which then supplied the channels that had been made both to supply drinking water to the city, and for irrigation. Finally, the barriers were also a good defensive system, especially if a guard post was set up nearby.

From the nineteen-nineties onwards, the Petra National Trust have restored (or rather rebuilt) the Nabataean dams that blocked the side gorges along the Siq. This allows visitors to get a clear idea of what these structures originally looked like. They are massive walls built with well-squared blocks of stone held together with mortar, which are easily robust enough to resist the pressure of the water.

In general it can be said that practically all the gorges and valleys surrounding the urban area of Petra were closed by one or more dams, sometimes built in sequence to collect as much water as possible. In many valleys, these barriers have been fairly well preserved up to the present time. For example, in the Little Siq the remains of one of them can be seen, and it is immediately apparent that the wall was firmly fixed to the rock face, thanks to deep mortices carved into the rock. Another extraordinarily well preserved dam (12 and a half metres high) is located in the valley to the right of the Khazneh (the Wadi al Jarra), to the left of the Danqur el Khazneh staircase. The purpose of this barrier, and the other four situated nearby, was clearly to protect the mouth of the Siq and the great paved courtyard in front of the Khazneh from possible flood waves. A small rupestrian aqueduct starts from the dam downstream and leads towards the forecourt, so it is possible that this pipeline fed a monumental fountain, which was among

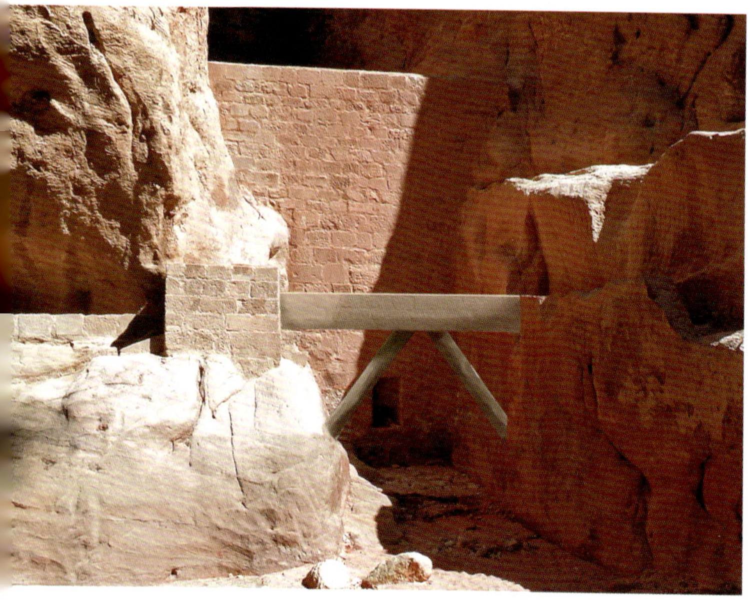

F. Bourbon

Above - *The dam of the Shaqq al Ajuss, tributary of the internal Siq, has been rebuilt. In front of it, the northern aqueduct would have crossed the narrow gorge on a small viaduct, with a span supported by struts (possibly wooden) fitted into deep square holes, still visible in the sandstone bank today. The graphic reconstruction suggests how this interesting system would have looked, including a distribution tank (on the left).*

PETRA'S AQUEDUCTS

The origin of a water system as complex as it is sophisticated has long been debated. Until a few years ago, many dated it to the period of Roman rule or even to the Byzantine era, but it is now certain that it was an original Nabataean concept, although influenced by contact with other civilizations including the Persians and Romans. The fact remains, however, that no civilization up until then had succeeded in ensuring its people with a constant water supply in such an arid region, where less than 10 centimetres of rain fall per year (Morris, 1961) from October to March. This resource not only allowed man and beast to quench their thirst but also allowed for effective personal hygiene. In addition to the fact that every Nabataean household had at least one cistern, the cities, not only Petra, even had public bath complexes to welcome the tired men and their large caravans.

Such hydraulic technology and its associated operating systems indicate that there was real urban planning and

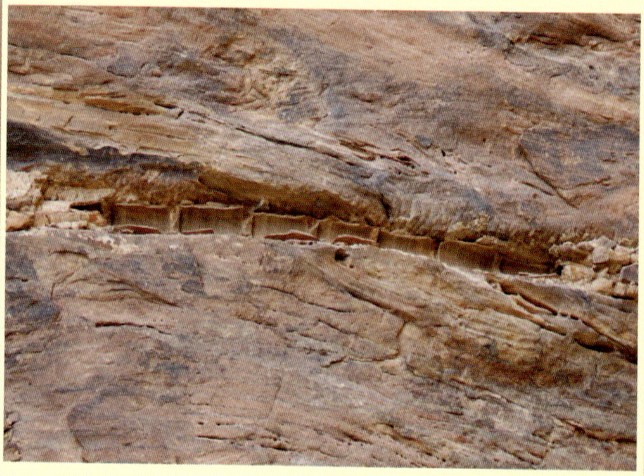

management, with specialised personnel and supervisors. Maintenance must have been continual; one need only think of the large cisterns that had to be periodically replastered and how the inside of pipes needed to be cleaned of silt deposits. The mountains around Petra are covered by approximately 200 kilometres of channels cut into the rock and dotted with innumerable cisterns. Sometimes the ducts had to go over extreme drops thus forming small waterfalls; overflow basins were positioned at their feet so as to let the water settle and slow it down before it continued down the next section of pipeline. Seen elsewhere are interconnected basins arranged in sequence, so that the water could gradually deposit its sediments, and become purified.

Recent studies have shown that Nabataean engineers knew how to calculate the flow of various springs so as to create pipelines that could absorb the maximum internal load, avoiding even the slightest loss. Additionally, they demonstrated abilities in designing and creating terracotta pipelines able to withstand hydrostatically pressurised water flows without caving in or leaking. The various components were made to perfectly fit each other (with a remarkably modern design) and the joints were sealed with mortar with excellent resistance (photo above).

Archaeological evidence proves that the first aqueduct built in Petra must have supplied the city with water from the Ain Musa spring (at the entrance of the modern town of Wadi Musa), combined with water from the smaller spring of Ain Umm Sar'ab, running along the Wadi Musa valley and inside the Siq. Although the first part of the track has been erased by the town's urban development, it becomes visible close to the entrance gate of the archaeological site. The channel, cut into the sandstone, coated with waterproof mortar and covered with stone slabs, mostly ran underground, even inside the Siq, and followed the path on the bottom of the gorge well before this was cleaned up and paved during the first century AD. A section of this ancient aqueduct has been located near the the arch of the temenos *((page 110), so it is certain that it reached the centre of Petra. The aqueduct was badly damaged or destroyed by a flash flood in the middle of the 1st century BC. It was exactly in this period that Petra saw an important development, taking on all the characteristics of a Hellenistic city complete with grand public monuments. Urban expansion required the creation of a more effective water supply system to support the needs of a rapidly growing population.*

The first major (and more technologically advanced) aqueduct built to support the expansion of the Nabataean capital was the one known today as Khubtha North. It was the first to be built in sight and pass over the natural depressions found along its path, thanks to stone bridges. The first section must have used the pre-existing track, it then curved northwards, reaching the area of Ramla where the Movenpick Hotel stands today, just above the entrance gate of the archaeological site. Here the double artificial basin known as the Zurrabah (or al Birka) supplied water and provided the driving force for several mills and facilities producing earthenware, whose ruins are partially visible at the parking lot near the hotel. From here it passed through the deep valley of Wadi Shab Qais, running along its western slope, then over the deep chasm of Wadi Mataha through an arch spanning seven metres, the only one preserved in all of Petra and still visible today. Then it crossed the gorge again a little further down, on a bridge nearly equal in size, now destroyed. It continued along the wall of Jebel al Khubtha, following every twist and turn, winding along the prominence (perhaps on yet another bridge) where the Sextius Florentinus Tomb is carved, and terminated in a great rectangular reservoir positioned to the left of the Palace Tomb. Three smaller cisterns, dug out opposite the reservoir and connected to it, gave Petra's population a daily supply of drinking water. Along the entire course of over seven and a half kilometres, the aqueduct was covered with stone slabs and fitted

Opposite page – *Along the outer Siq the track of the ancient aqueduct clearly stands out; in several points collapses have made the terracotta water pipes visible.*

Above - *The only remaining arch of the Khubtha North aqueduct; here the gorge is about 22 metres deep.*

Below – *Along the walls of the Jebel al Khubtha, the track of the aqueduct can be clearly seen.*

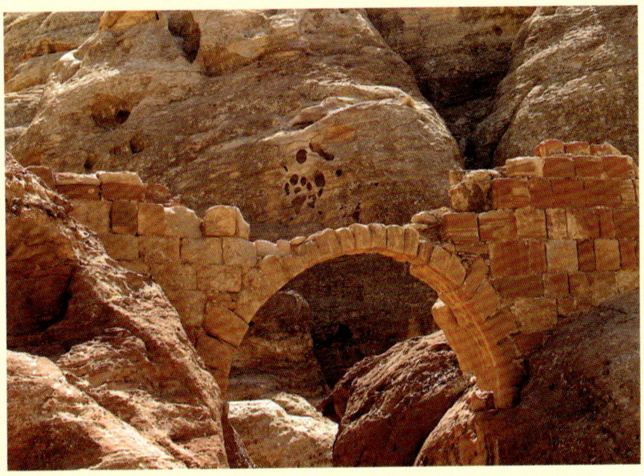

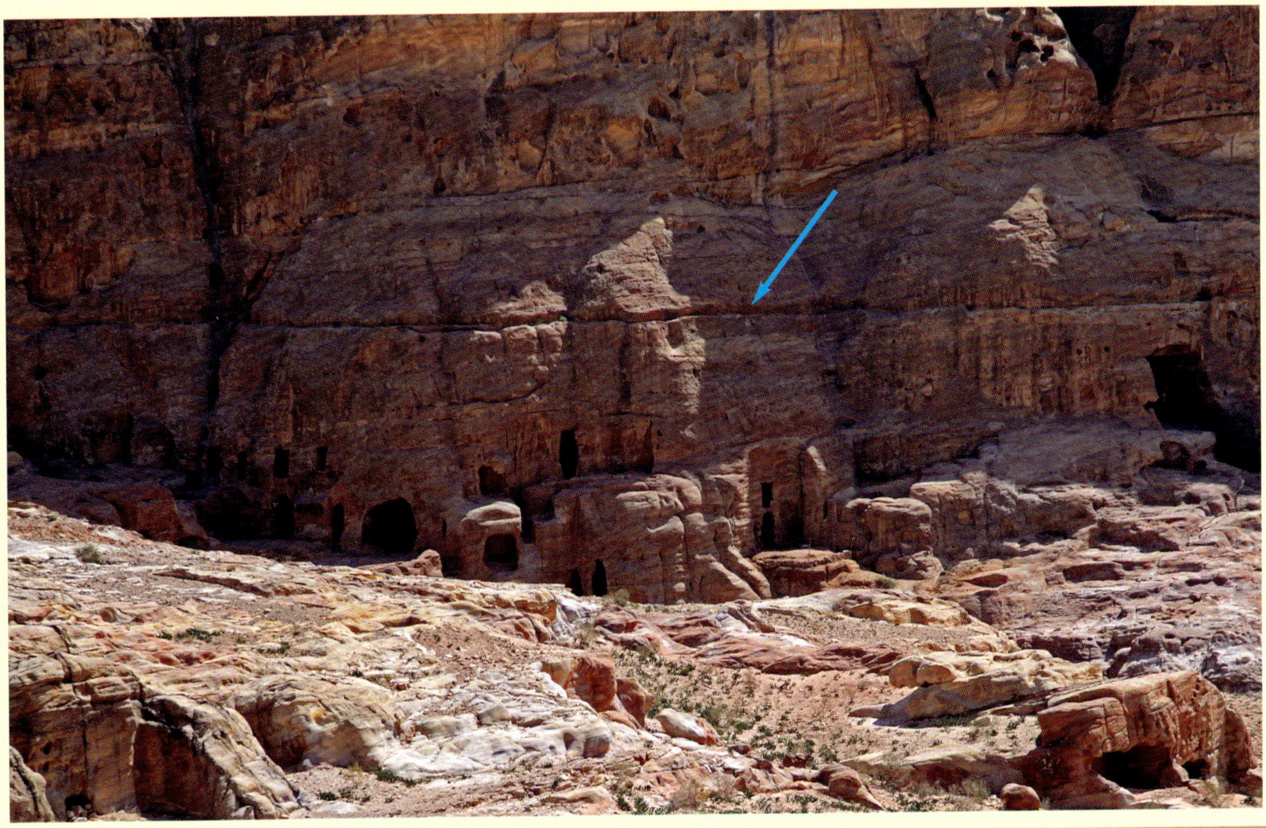

with settling tanks. The great earthquake of 363 most probably put the aqueduct out of use, never to be restored again.
The existence of the above-mentioned bridges and others that have been destroyed in the Petra area have raised several questions such as when and from whom Nabataean engineers learnt the art of bridge building. Contact with the Roman world most likely granted this technological evolution. Roman engineers were indeed the best bridge builders of ancient times; take for example the town of Pont Saint Martin in northern Italy where a bridge built around 25 BC, boasting a span of 36 metres and in perfect condition, can still be found today! In any case, the Nabataeans took full advantage of this resource. Petra's most well-known aqueduct, probably created in the third quarter of the 1st century BC, runs inside the Siq and ends in the city at the eastern end of the Colonnade, where a monumental nymphaeum served as a public fountain. This route was doubled in the first century AD and later enlarged with a side-channel that was used to supply the inhabited area opposite the great theatre. It has been ascertained that the southern track of the aqueduct was restored in the Byzantine era.
The third major aqueduct collected water from the springs of Ain Braq and Ain Ammon, located on the hills south-east of the town. This was a double track, one formed by a channel covered with stone slabs, the other equipped with terracotta pipes and decompression chambers. It supplied the south-west neighbourhoods of Petra, overcoming a significant difference in height on the way up thanks to internal pressure. One channel brought water to the residential neighbourhood of Ez Zantur (where several wealthy residences had running water), the other one supplied the paradeisos (page 104) discovered next to the Great Temple.
A similar aqueduct, composed of two different conduits, carried water from the source at Ain Debdebeh, located several kilometres north-east, and passed close to the current Bedouin village of Umm Sayhoum, suppling the north-west area of Petra.
Lastly, the Ain Abu Olleqa spring, which flows from the bottom of the Wadi Turkmaniyya was collected by a double aqueduct, formed by a gravity duct and a pressurized pipeline, and served the urban area around the Qasr el Bint.
An interesting point briefly examined here is the appearance of the cisterns and their dating. According to several authors, the most ancient among these distinctive structures are the ones that are entirely carved into the rock, characterised by their rounded form that tapers towards the top like a "demijohn", so to speak, with the opening consisting of a round hole presumably sealed by a stone manhole. It is thought that these cisterns were used to store drinking water and that they were not used for irrigation purposes. At a later stage, the cisterns were more elaborately constructed with a rectangular or square form (although there are also examples of round ones), fitted with a cover formed by a series of parallel arches, which in turn supported large stone slabs connected by mortar. A stone staircase ensured access for maintenance and periodic removal of silt deposited at the bottom; the inside was carefully plastered with waterproof cement so as to avoid water seeping into the sandstone walls, and the manhole covers could have been made of metal.
The inlets of the pipelines were always positioned a little above the bottom of the cistern, so that if there were any sediments left at the bottom, they would not be picked up and introduced into the water system. These large cisterns were used for both farming and storing drinking water, and over time the way they worked became more refined and complex. In several areas of Petra there are indeed examples of these interesting complexes, consist-ing of a conduit dug into the stone, which funnelled rain water into an initial, large settling basin from where, through a series of bulkheads, the water purified by gravity ran into a second

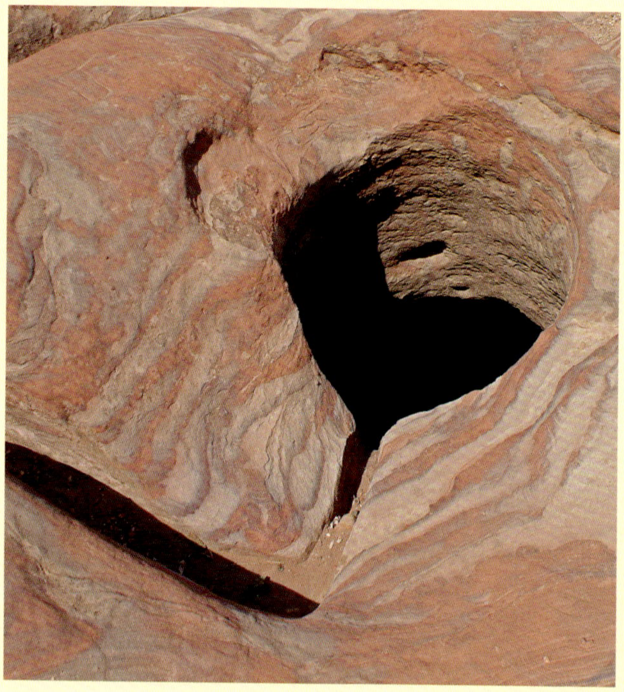

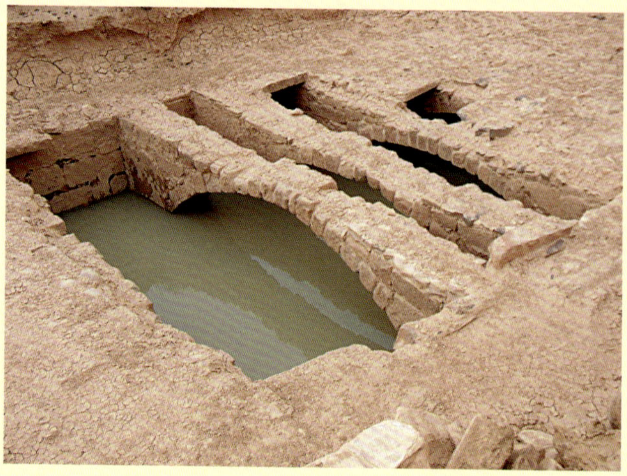

basin and sometimes even into a third one, which constituted the actual cistern, where drinking water could be conserved for months in total darkness. From these cisterns, water was transported to settlements or fields through channels carved into the sandstone. Needless to say, drinking water flowed inside the carefully covered conduits or in clay pipelines. One of the most interesting systems of this type is found on the slopes of Jebel Ma'aiserat (or Jebel Mu'aysarat), more or less in the area of the Turkmaniyya Tomb. The internal staircase, which was used for the maintenance of the large cistern, is also well preserved.

Opposite page, above – *An ancient type of cistern in the area of the Royal Tombs.*

Opposite page, below – *A well-preserved Nabataean cistern with its arched covering system, at the Hawara (Humayma) site.*

Above – *The triple basin and cisterns complex of Jebel Ma'aiserat.*

Below, left – *The small room at the base of the shallow dam in the Wadi al Jarra.*

Below, right – *A bronze, "male" type, Roman valve.*

A THEORY ABOUT THE REGULATIONS OF THE FLOWS

Several dams (for example in the Wadi al Jarra, to the left of the Khazneh) and the huge retaining walls of the large reservoirs (like the one to the right of the so-called Garden Tomb), have an interesting feature at their base. It consists of a rectangular small room within the masonry structure, generally plastered with hydraulic mortar, which can only be accessed by one person. In the back wall there is a round hole, which was evidently for collecting the water of the cistern, in fact, in some cases a little humidity still seeps out of it. On careful analysis, it is clear that a pipe came out of this opening.
Although nothing remains, it is logical to assume that these rooms contained a valve that allowed the flow of water out of the cistern to be regulated. Since devices of this kind are known to have existed in the Roman world (described by Sextus Julius Frontinus in the treatise De Aquaeductu urbis Romae *and frequently found in the territory of the empire), it is possible that they were male taps in bronze. These valves were constructed in such a way as to allow for the flow to be turned on and off, and also for the flow rate to be regulated at will. The presence of highly oxidised metal remains in some of the above mentioned rooms, would appear to support this theory.*
In any case, it is clear that a system to regulate the flow would have been necessary. The Nabataeans came into contact with Roman civilization well before the annexation to the empire in 106. It is therefore impossible to say whether this technological innovation - like that of the terracotta pipes, which was already found in the Roman world in the 2nd century BC - is form a period before or after that date. Regardless of probable external influences, the fact remains that the Nabataean hydraulic system was one of the most refined and complex in the ancient world.

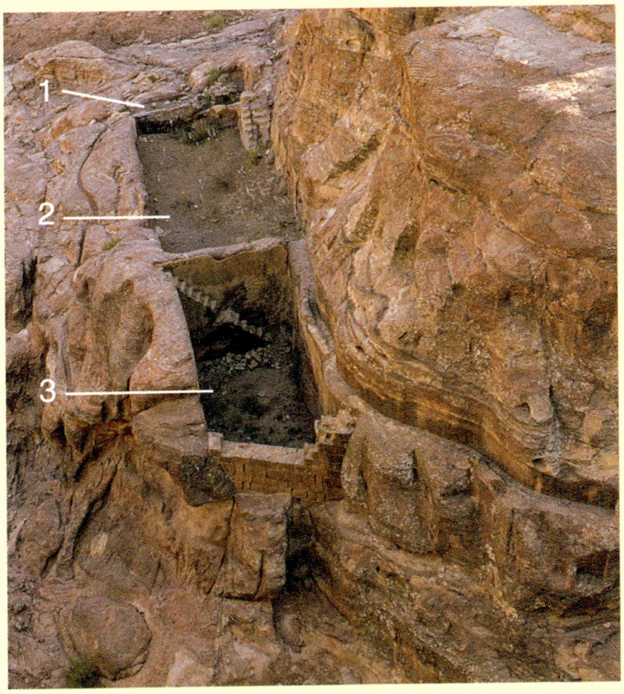

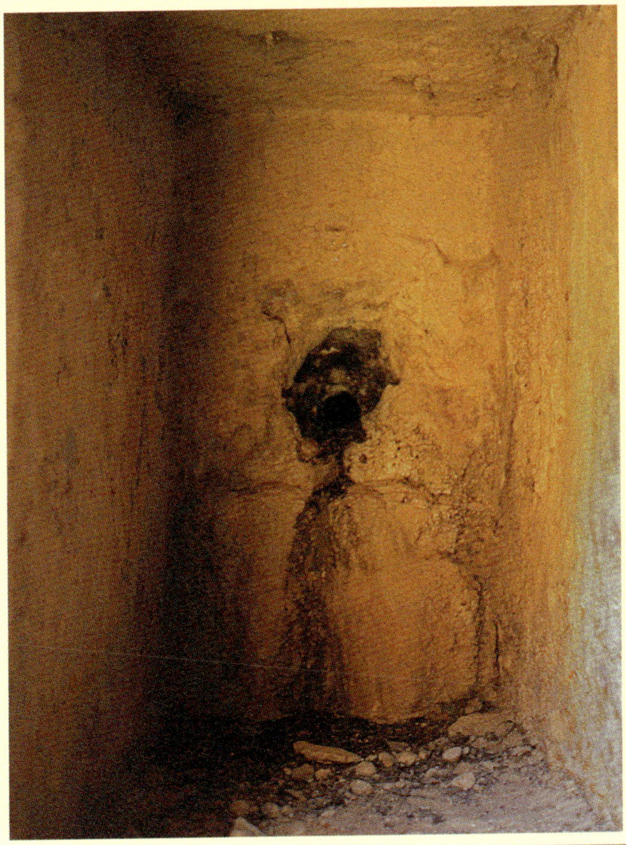

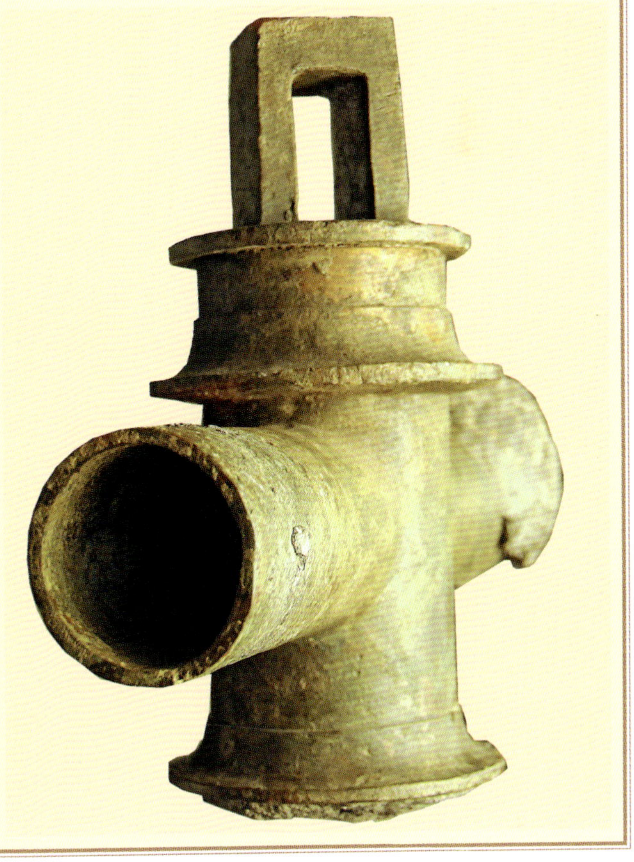

the architectural features surrounding one of the most important monuments of Petra. The recent excavations have allowed the functioning of this extraordinary series of barriers and pools to be researched, as well as restoring the path, and the flights of stairs cut into the rock, to their original function. These were used as service routes and were indispensable for the maintenance of the water systems. There are similar walkways next to many other dams in the Petra area.
Archaeological investigations have shown that many Nabataean water systems were so sophisticated that they made use of diversion dams and drainage channels, which were essential when the most violent flood waves occurred.
Over time, the Nabataeans set up ever more sophisticated systems of collection and distribution, making use of terracotta pipelines (perhaps derived from similar Babylonian techniques), watercourses built above ground in order to cross valleys and other natural depressions, bridges, sluice gates, and settling basins for purifying drinking water. In this way they managed to satisfy their water needs so effectively that they were able to place fountains and nymphaeums in the city.
To get an idea of the engineering feat achieved by the Nabataeans, it is sufficient to consider that the investigations carried out by the Petra National Trust identified 143 barriers, 136 terraces, 30 dams and 7 cisterns, just in the area of the Siq (the gorge that acts as the main access route to Petra).
At the same time, the Nabataeans also learned farming techniques and built large terraces (some of which can still be seen among the houses in Wadi Musa). In some cases, the fields were situated along the wadis, and they were irrigated by making water overflow from the nearest dam. Many areas were also used for grazing herds of sheep and goats, as well as dromedaries.
To sum up, the Nabataeans' hydraulic engineering was every bit as good as the Romans' and it allowed them to create agricultural wealth that was unprecedented in the region.

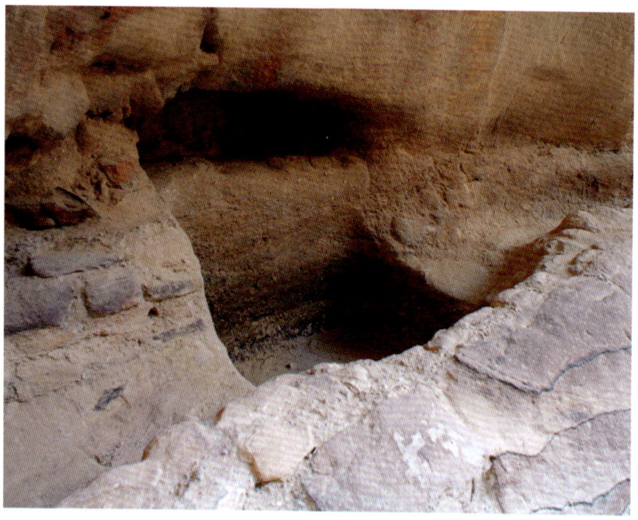

URBAN STRUCTURE AND SOCIAL FABRIC

Petra developed enormously between the 1st century BC and the 2nd century AD, when its population reached at least 20,000 inhabitants (though many believe it was as high as 30,000). Today it is hard to imagine that at the time of its greatest splendour, between the reigns of Aretas III and Aretas IV, the city's buildings spread out over an area of about 4 square kilometres, within a radius of 2 km from the Colonnade at its centre. In fact, Petra was not like a classic Roman or Hellenistic city, whose streets were built up along perpendicular axes. The residential areas were mixed up with the public and religious buildings and satellite towns, including the settlements of Al Barid and Al Sabrah, which even had its own rupestrian theatre,

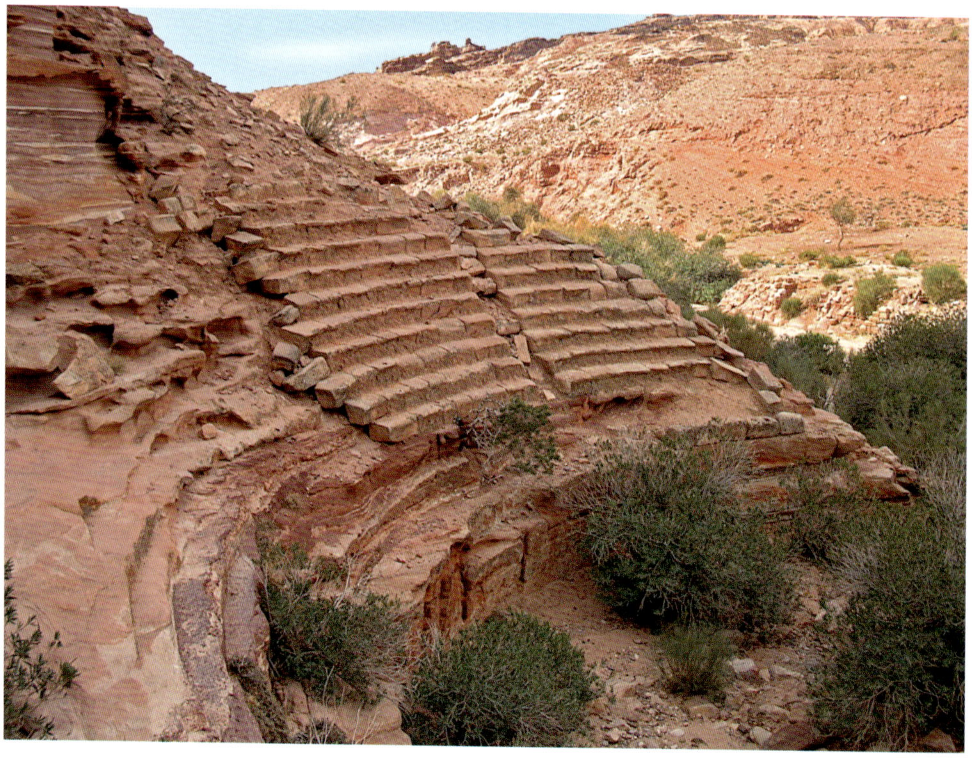

Above - *One of the settling basins positioned along one of the two aqueducts excavated from inside the Siq: its function was to slow down the speed of the water flow, decreasing the pressure inside the pipeline and making any water impurities fall to the bottom.*

Below - *The small rupestrian theatre of Al Sabrah, a suburb of Petra still not very well known. This satellite settlement of Petra arose near the perennial spring of Ain Sabrah and had agricultural and industrial functions. In fact, nearby there were outcrops of copper and iron, metals that were processed on site.*

were spread out around the city itself, sometimes even at considerably different altitudes. One of the reasons for this was the necessity to protect the few flat areas fit for growing crops from urbanisation. As a result, the city seen from above would have looked like a curious patchwork of built-up areas, gardens and farmland. These fertile areas were chiefly made up of large fields of sesame (the oil of which was used for food and also burnt in lamps for lighting), cereals and vines, as well as orchards and vegetable gardens.

Although it was naturally protected, defending a metropolis of this kind must have been difficult. A perimeter wall would have required an enormous effort, and in fact, Strabo reported that Petra did not have city walls. The remains of the barricades partially visible to the south-west and north-east of the city probably date back to the Byzantine period, by which time the urban area was much smaller. The Nabataeans preferred to place a system of interconnected forts and watchtowers along the edge of the city, whose garrisons could warn the population of imminent danger using visual signals (fires and mirrors). The roads cut into the rock could also easily be blocked, and the lines of communication along the gorges were defended by guard posts in strategic positions, which would have allowed a small garrison to keep any attackers at bay.

Such complex hydraulic engineering and defences were clearly very expensive, which means a system of government capable of providing for them must have existed, as well as a stable and well organized power structure. These were all confirmed by Strabo, who mentions the existence of a royal family, and describes Petra as a city in all respects, where people traded, and legal and tax issues were dealt with. It should not be overlooked that forming immense caravans, like the ones described by the Greek historian, would have required very rich investors in control of actual companies with many different "branches" spread out along the various commercial routes. The resulting necessity to centralize their power and capital was what led the Nabataeans to settle down in fixed locations. As a logical consequence, this resulted in the creation of a proper form of government and an organized society. In effect, the Nabataeans had now moved on to a sedentary way of life, with a hereditary monarchy modelled on those in nearby Hellenistic kingdoms, which had military and political authority, and perhaps also religious power, without being too conditioned by it. In fact, there never seems to have been great rivalries between the clergy and the royal house, which was actually very stable. The fact that most of the Nabataean kings reigned for a considerable length of time suggests that there were not many internal tensions in society.

The Nabataean state was of a democratic type, which was unusual for that period, and women played an active and very important role in society. This has been

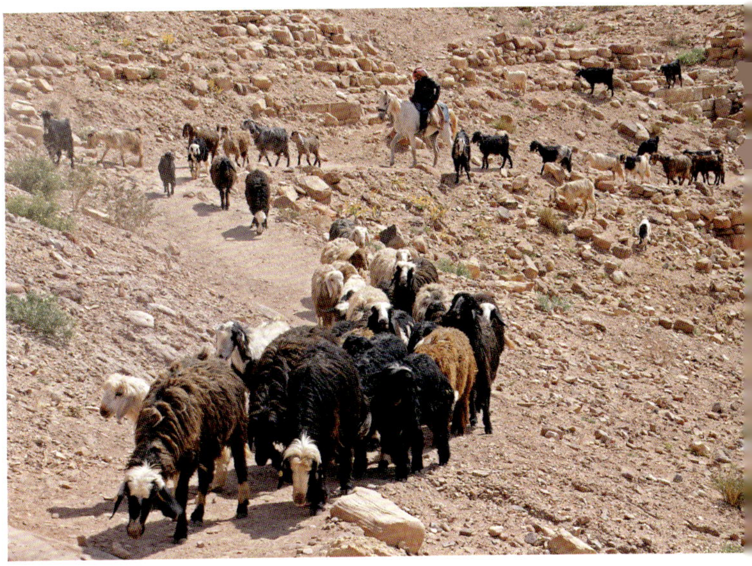

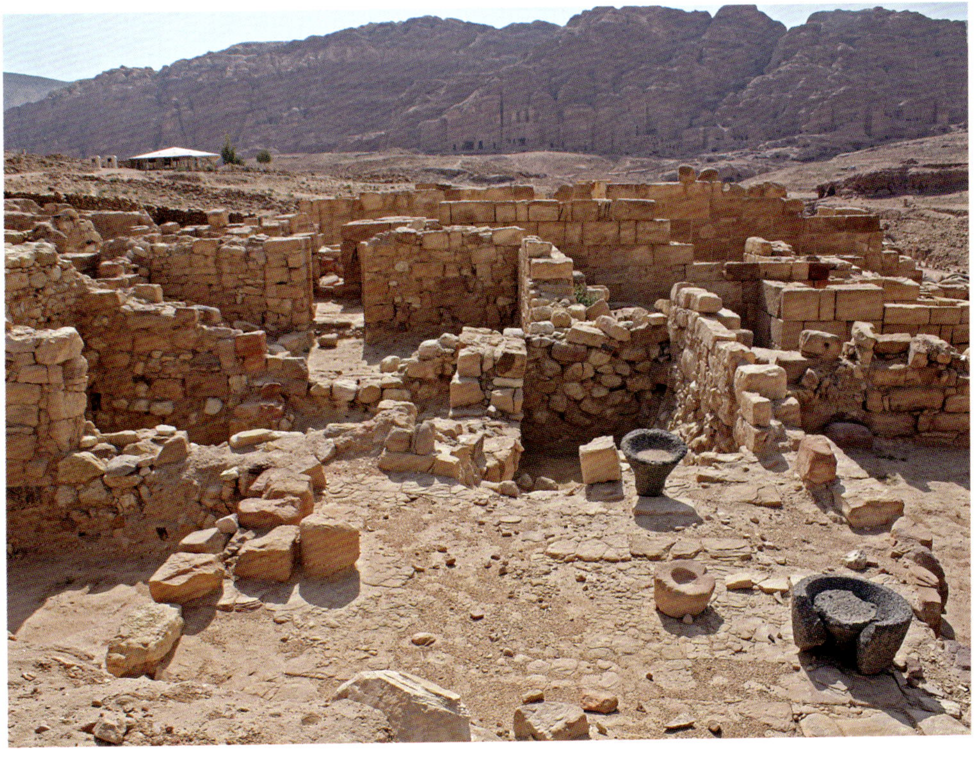

Above - *A Bedouin from the Bdoul tribe grazes his flock of sheep in the ruins of Petra. Today, like two millennia ago, sheep farming is still an important source of livelihood in this region.*

Below - *Near the Winged Lions Temple, the excavation campaigns have uncovered the remains of laboratories and workshops that demonstrate that Petra was an active production centre. The remarkable proximity between the various buildings suggests a fairly dense urban network and, consequently, a population well above to what was once imagined.*

confirmed by several funeral inscriptions that indicate they had their own land, goods and employees. It has also been established that women could accede to the throne, as the names of several queens were passed on, including the particularly important figure of Shaquilat, who was the mother of Rabbel II and ruled over the kingdom for many years. In any case, the wives of the kings took on the title of queen and their influence in political life must have been considerable, given that the effigies of some of them appear on coins, next to those of their husbands.
The few historical documents that exist confirm that public life was governed by legislators and judges, whose importance was only subordinate to that of the monarchs and the priests. Merchants were obviously at the top of the social pyramid, followed by artisans and the military. Sculptors and artists also had a certain amount of prestige, and it has been demonstrated that many of them passed on their profession from father to son. This is confirmed by some inscriptions at Hegra from the first half of the 1st century BC, in which three sculptors who were brothers are mentioned. The son of one of them appears to have followed in his father's footsteps. Similar inscriptions indicate the existence of close family ties between other sculptors. Then came the farmers, shepherds, stonemasons and labourers. There were not very many slaves (as Strabo reports) and their lives were not too hard. In many cases they were considered part of the family.
The numerous votive inscriptions found in Petra, in Aramaic, Nabataean and Greek, appear to demonstrate that literacy was fairly widespread, at least among the higher social classes.
Although the prosperity of the Nabataean Kingdom centred around the lucrative caravan trade, the manufacturing sector boasted at least one speciality, which was the production of ceramics. Nabataean ceramics, which was a continuation of the Edomite craft, was unique for its highly evolved workmanship. The crockery, for example, was extraordinarily subtle, with a very fine texture and elegant patterns in dark red on a lighter background. Near the Zurrabah cistern in Wadi Musah, the remains of some large ovens have been uncovered, which are evidence that Petra was a regional centre for the production of ceramics up until the end of the 3rd century AD.

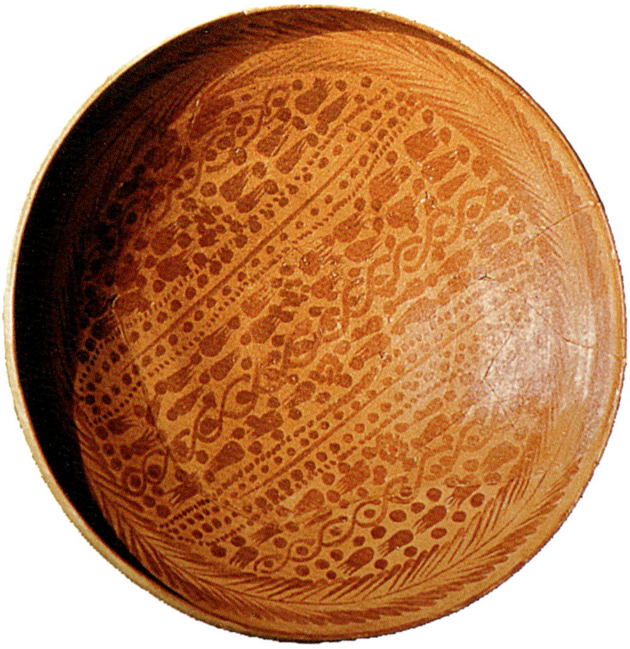

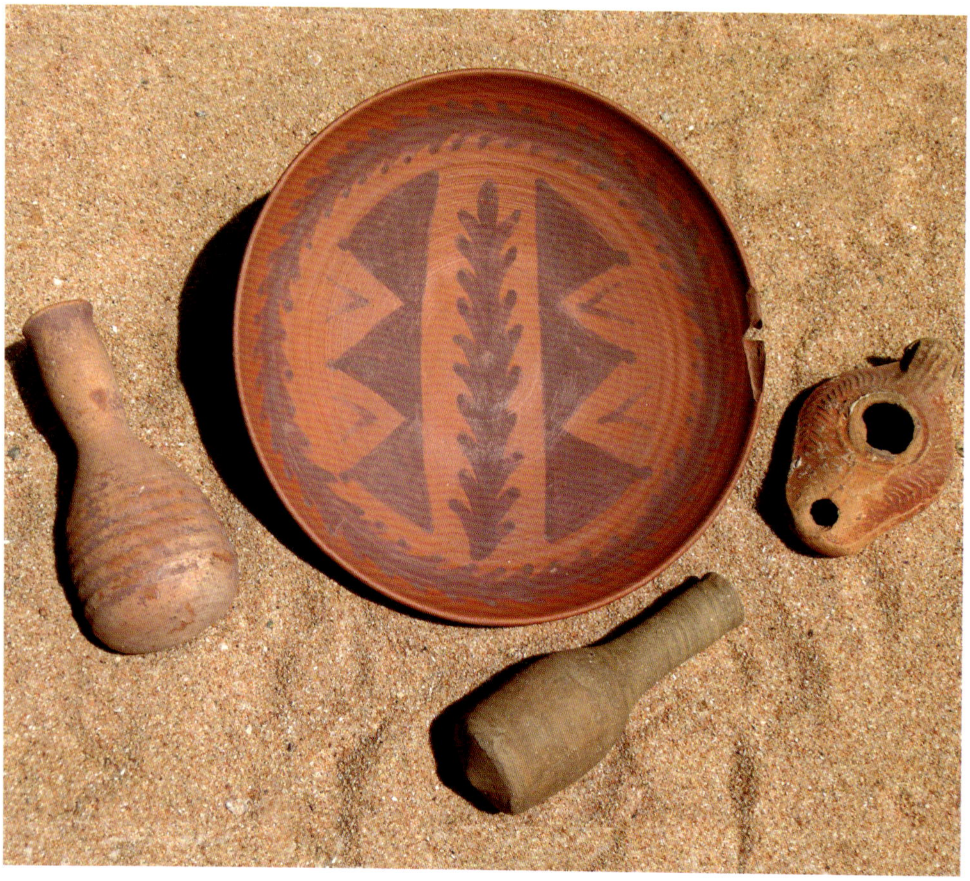

Above - *This magnificent ceramic plate is elegantly decorated with small brush strokes. For its subtlety, almost unique in the ancient world, this type of ceramic is called "eggshell".*

Below - *Other examples of Nabataean pottery. The small flasks with a characteristic shape were used to store incense and other perfumed essences, which formed the fulcrum of Nabataean commercial activities. Thousands of similar objects have been found, not only in Petra, but throughout the Nabataean kingdom.*
The oil lamp was fuelled with sesame oil.
Nabataean ceramic production began in the first century BC and ended in the Byzantine era. The typical red clay of these artefacts (which owed its colour to iron oxide) was extracted in some places near Petra.

Having settled in a region that had not shown any signs of a substantial figurative culture, and with no real artistic tradition of their own, the Nabataeans were initially influenced by the already partially Hellenised Syrian art world. However, Nabataean art is essentially Hellenistic in origin. While in some places this is expressed in rather rough forms, in Petra it is much more refined, clearly borrowed from the Alexandrian tradition.
While at first the representations of gods were strictly aniconic, or at the most made up of simple rectangular stelae with basic facial features, from the 1st century BC onwards, Hellenism became more and more pervasive. It is quite probable that at least court art was produced by Greek artists of Alexandrian origin, but it is clear that a local school was soon formed, the same one that has given us the bas-relief decorations on the temenos *arch or in the temple area known as Qasr el Bint. These sculptures reveal a clear Alexandrian style, although the unusual custom of vertically aligning carved panels onto the pillars of buildings is clearly a local stylistic element. Friezes with lively spirals, Erotes and lions facing each other, also seem like distinct replicas of Hellenistic models. The same can be said for the extremely rare murals, such as those in a rupestrian chamber of al Barid, otherwise known as Little Petra. Here a pergola of vines with birds of different species and Erotes covers the ceiling, while the walls are covered with an illusionary architectural composition recalling the First Pompeian Style. The surviving murals in the so-called Painted House, in Wadi Thughra, echo the Second Style and allow us to imagine what the decorations in private buildings must have been like.*
Despite the extreme scarcity of sculptural fragments, Petra's art ultimately appears to be one of the rare testimonies to Alexandrian art. However, in its less courtly expressions, it reveals a recomposition of elements typical of the bare nomadic tradition: minimal form, frontal composition, fixed expressions and subjective proportions, mainly with enormous, wide open eyes.

Left - *This stone head, perhaps a portrait of a priest and dated to the 1st century AD, displays a clear Syrian influence in its treatment of the headdress and beard with ringlets.*

Right, above - *Architectural high-relief with the Nabataean god Dushara, represented as Dionysius (1st century AD).*

Right, below - *The girl gripping a mask of Pan displayed in this high-relief, which clearly shows a Hellenistic influence, is generally identified with Melpomene, the Muse of Tragedy (1st century AD).*

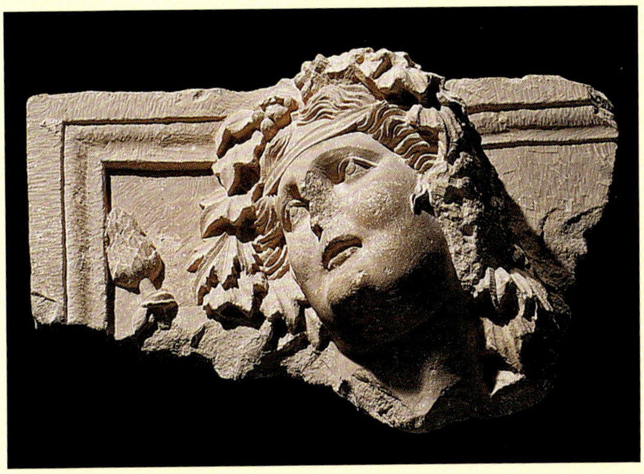

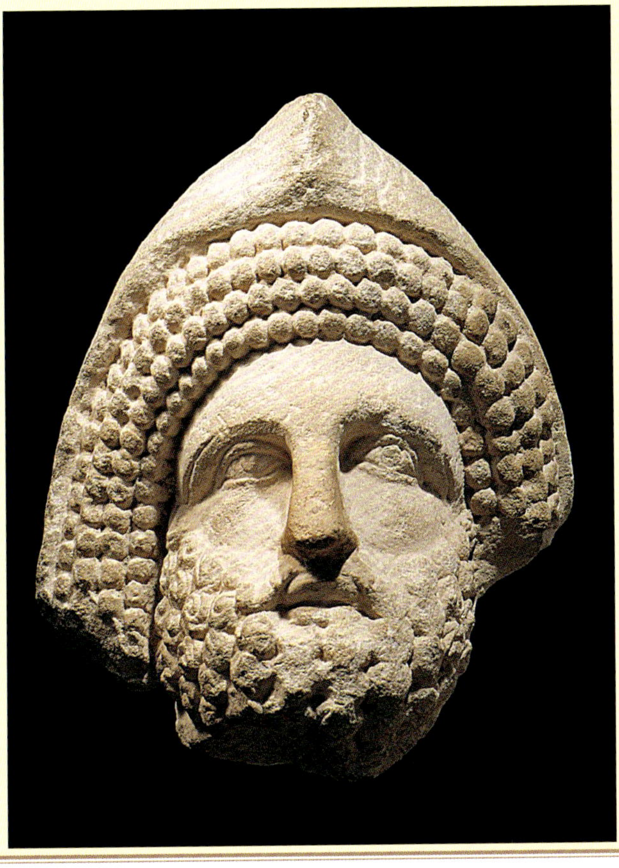

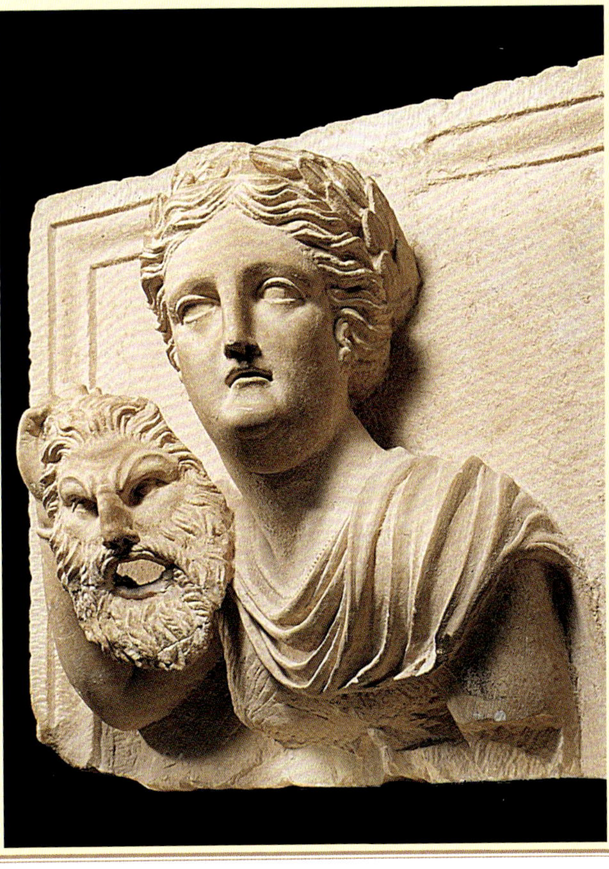

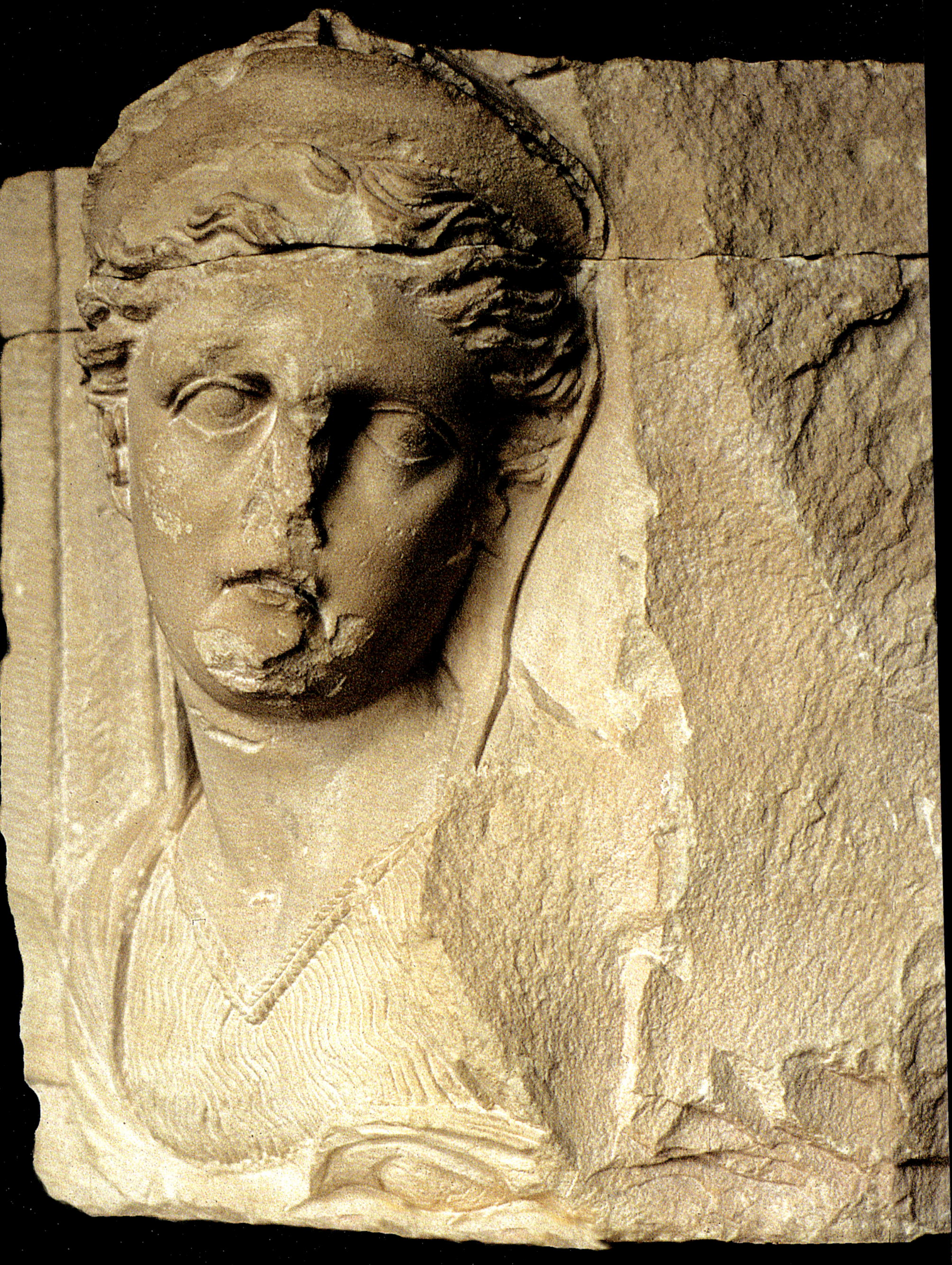

RELIGIOUS BELIEFS

The Nabataeans were polytheists and they worshipped pre-Islamic Arabian gods. Because of their frequent and wide-ranging contacts with different peoples and cultures, they were also at the forefront of an extensive process of religious syncretism, that is, the tendency to reconcile a variety of elements belonging to different faiths. They first absorbed elements of religions from Syria, Egypt and Babylonia. Later on, the increasing infiltration into the Nabatean civilization of cultural components from the Hellenized Mediterranean became evident with the assimilation of the local gods to divinities belonging to the Greek religion, which in turn had been already influenced by the religions of the Middle East.

Broadly speaking, we can say that the main god was Dushara, who lived on the mountains and ruled over natural phenomena and the changing seasons, guaranteed the fertility of the land and living beings, and watched over the royal house as guarantor of the common law. Archaeological evidence also shows that he was connected with the cult of the dead. It is generally believed that his name means "the god of Shara", which is the mountain that overlooks the valley of Petra to the east, where the city of Gaia was situated, but not all researchers agree about this.

Al Kutba, the patron of writing and divination, was also worshipped, as well as a female trio made up of Al Uzza ("the powerful"), Allat ("the Goddess") and Manawat (or Manat), the goddess of destiny. In other Nabataean settlements, like Bosra, it seems that Allat was the most powerful goddess (assimilated with Athena and Atargatis, as well as the cult of sun worshipping), but in Petra it was certainly Al Uzza, ruler of love and life, assimilated with the Greek Aphrodite, the Canaanite Astarte and the Egyptian Isis, as well as the personification of Venus, the Morning Star. According to some inscriptions she had close relations with Dushara and Al Kutba. In any case, it is clear that in the pantheon of Petra, Dushara and Al Uzza had the dominant roles. Since there are many shrines with two baetyli side by side, and it is generally believed that the larger one depicts Al Uzza, and the smaller one the god Dushara, it is thought that this implies a mother-son relationship, like the one between Isis and Horus in the Egyptian pantheon.

These deities were not anthropomorphic and as a result the Nabataean religion was aniconic, especially in the early centuries. The gods were not therefore depicted in human form, but represented with baetyli, which had simple geometrical shapes (cubes or parallelepipeds) and

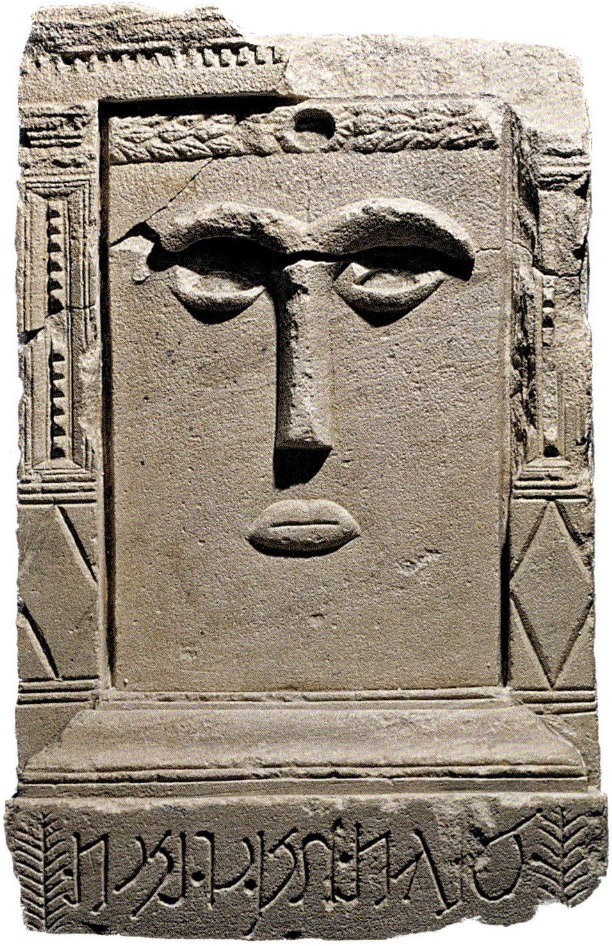

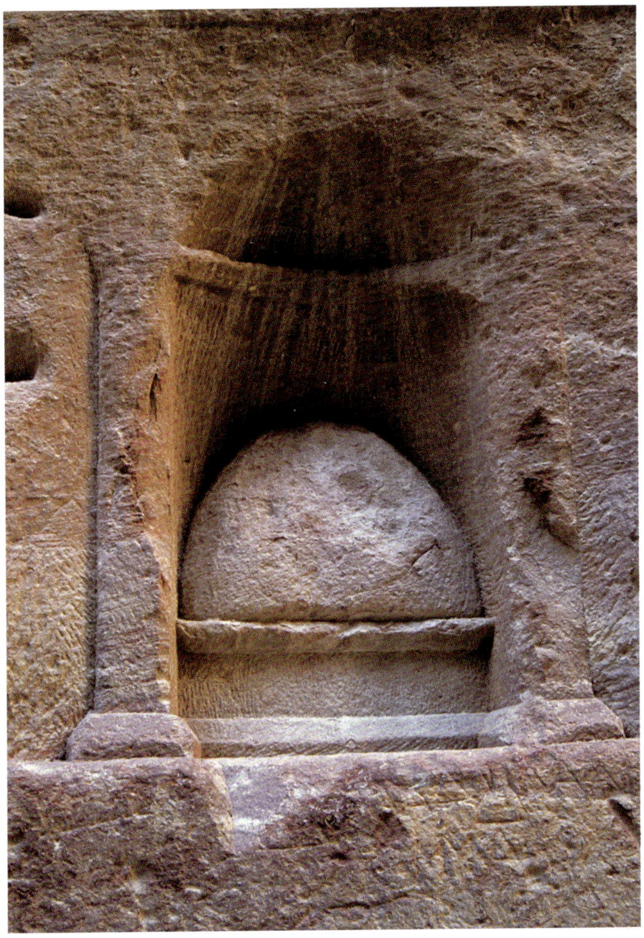

Opposite page - *This elegant high-relief depicting the goddess Al Uzza, assimilated to Venus, dates back to the second half of the 1st century AD. Clearly it is of Hellenistic influence, if not actually the work of Alexandrian craftsmen who had moved to Petra.*

Left - *The baetylus within this votive niche is carved into the southern wall of the Siq, and is an aniconic depiction of the god Dushara.*

Right - *This stele, found in the Winged Lions Temple, is a representation of the goddess Al Uzza. Dated to the beginning of the 1st century AD, with its rudimentary physiognomic features it marks the transition from the ancestral aniconic tradition to the figurative phase.*

were not symbols of the gods but rather of their presence. The thrones (*motab*) of the deities were themselves objects of worship. These were seats or simply plinths on which the baetylus rested. Similarly, the bas-reliefs in the shape of obelisks (*nefesh*) found on many tombs represent the soul of the deceased in an aniconic way.

Over time, the Nabataeans absorbed deities from the neighbouring Syrians and Edomites, like the god Ba'alshamin and the god of storms and rainbows Qaws (or Qaush) with his consort Atargatis (goddess of harvests and fertility), who in turn became assimilated with the Greek goddess Tyche, and also with Allat. Contact with Greco-Roman civilization led to a progressive assimilation of the local gods with foreign ones. Dushara was sometimes identified with Dionysus-Bacchus and sometimes with Zeus-Jupiter, Al Uzza with Aphrodite-Venus, Allat with Athena-Minerva, Manawat with Nemesis, and Al Kutba with Hermes-Mercury.

In addition to all these deities, it should be remembered that the Nabataean king Obodas (96-85 B.C.) was deified after his death in battle.

Contact with the western world also led to an iconographic revolution, and in the 1st century AD, figurative representations of the various deities appeared alongside the baetyli. Unfortunately, these images were largely destroyed by the iconoclastic Muslims who demolished all representations of the human form in Muslim lands following the edict by the Caliph Yazid II (720-724).

Through the various deities in their pantheon, the Nabataeans worshipped the primordial forces of nature, and in particular, water and light in their various manifestations (the Sun, the Moon, Venus). This explains the existence of numerous "high places of sacrifice" around Petra, arranged like a sort of mystic crown on the highest mountains (Jebel al Madhbah to the south, Jebel Umm al Biyara to the west, Jebel ed Deir to the north-west, Jebel al Khubtha to the east), clearly to protect the city and its inhabitants. There are also several rupestrian sanctuaries near springs or water courses (like in the Wadi Siyyagh or in the Wadi Muthlim).

The "high places of sacrifice" are open-air sanctuaries that can be reached via rugged processional paths cut into the living rock, along which priests and worshippers periodically climbed, in order to offer the blood of sacrificial victims to the gods (usually lambs and young goats). However, there were also bloodless offerings like cereals and other agricultural products. In general they seemed to focus on astronomical elements (in particular, the "movement" of the sun from east to west), but this specific aspect has still not been studied in great detail. In any case, it is clear that the god Dushara was associated with the sun, the goddess Allat with the moon and the goddess Al Uzza with Venus, forming a radiant trinity. It is the recent excavations carried out at the sites of the mountain sanctuaries of Khirbet et Tannur and Khirbet ed Dharih, both to the north-west of Petra, that have

Below - *In the absence of epigraphic evidence, it is usually impossible to tell which deity is represented by a baetylus. While it seems certain that the pairs of side-by-side baetyli refer to Al Uzza and Dushara, the not infrequent cases of the triple juxtaposition (as in this votive niche, carved in the internal Siq) are more debatable. It is generally believed to be a feminine triad, composed of Al Uzza, Allat and Manawat.*

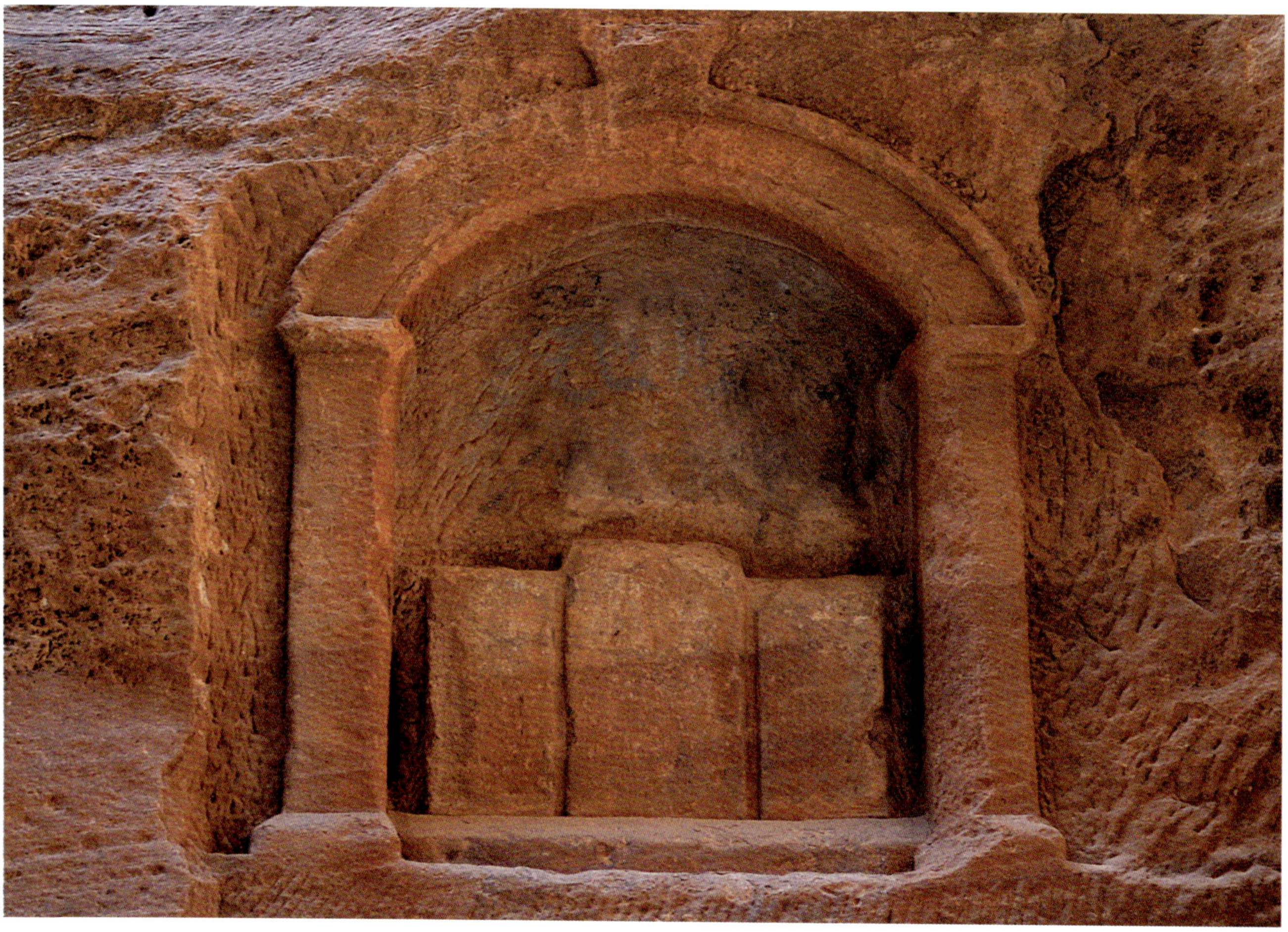

A FEW NOTES ON ARCHAEOASTRONOMY

Although a lack of written sources prevent us from establishing what the relationship was between Nabataean religious beliefs and astronomical knowledge, some of Petra's monuments appear to be positioned in accordance with very precise astronomical alignments and clearly a connection between the two did influence the local architecture to a certain degree. The historian Strabo describes how the Nabataeans usually worshiped the sun disc from the rooftops of their houses. Therefore, if the sun was one of the fundamental aspects of their religion, they must have given a lot of attention to the solstices and equinoxes. In this respect, it is significant that the two enormous obelisks at the top of Jebel al Madhbah are aligned along the east-west axis. They most likely acted as gnomons, whose shadows were used to mark the passing of time and pinpoint the exact moments of the equinoxes. This information must have been of fundamental importance for monitoring the lunisolar calendar.

Recently, the scholars Juan Antonio Belmonte, César González-Garcia and Andrea Polcaro have shown clear connections between the position of several rupestrian structures and the apparent movement of the sun. One of the most striking results of their research is finding that during the winter solstice (21 December), the light of the setting sun, which filters through the entrance of the Deir, strikes the motab *carved into the recess of the arcosolium where the baetylus (object of worship), was placed. Seen from inside, the effect is even more spectacular because the sun lights up a rocky prominence opposite the Deir, recreating the profile of a lion's head. The lion was the sacred animal of Al Uzza, and this does not seem to be accidental. The presence on the same mountain pass of an enormous circular basin carved into the rock, an altar and the temple known as Room 468 confirm that this place was one of the most sacred in the Petra area, where processions coming from the town centre must have gone on special occasions, perhaps connected to the movement of celestial bodies. In fact, the 4th century writer Epiphanius of Salamis, mentions in his work* Panarion adversus omnes haereses *how the winter solstice and the movements of Venus and Mercury were so important to the Nabataean religion.*

The same team of scholars discovered an interesting astronomical phenomenon connected to the position of the Urn Tomb. This structure, whose facade is preceded by a deep colonnaded courtyard carved into the living rock, rises on the western slopes of Jabal al Khubta and faces the towering mountain of Umm al Biyara. During the two equinoxes, the last rays of sun that set behind Umm al Biyara, cross the monument's doorstep and touch the back wall of the great underground chamber. On the winter solstice, the sun rays that enter, light-up the north-east corner of the room, while on the summer solstice they light up the opposite corner. The potential presence of a third porticoed wing at the end of the courtyard opposite the facade would not have hindered these events due to the incline of the sun's rays.

For his part, the author of this book has noticed other features which could be related to astronomical events. Firstly, the rupestrian altars carved on the summit of the so-called "high places of sacrifice", particularly at the top of Jabal al Madhbah, Jabal al Khubtha and Jebel al Madras are aligned with the two axes north-south and east-west. Other analogous structures, which some authors describe as "open-air triclinia", found in several places very far apart from each other, have very similar characteristics. Possibly related to the events discovered at the Urn Tomb, is the great stone mound at the top of al Umm al Biyara. Clearly it must have been a tall structure, reduced to ruins by earthquakes and thus difficult to decipher. It is however interesting to note that this prominence is still very visible from the Urn Tomb, constituting a kind of gnomon perhaps, linked to the solar alignments just described.

The Khazneh could also be hiding a connection to the stars. Indeed, very little sky can be seen from the monument because of its unusual position, and the sun never shows any particular alignment to it, although things change during the full moon. The superb facade is totally illuminated by the cold lunar light and completely transforms, bathed by a poignant, pale blue glow. In some periods of the year the bright rays go as far as to briefly skim the doorstep of the great underground chamber. Although this phenomenon has not been sufficiently studied during the course of an entire year, it is possible that at specific moments, the moon was able to light up several features of the facade or within the monument. In this regard, the curious and as yet unexplained window positioned above the large doorway in the main chamber could reveal a specific function. It should be noted that in actual fact, it is possible to glimpse a narrow sliver of sky through the above-mentioned window only from the most inner recess of the Khazneh (probably the naos in which a sacred figure was kept). This close relationship with the moon would reinforce the hypothesis of a consecration of the monument to a female divinity.

In short, all these elements highlight how the Nabataean religion, like so many ancient cults, was inextricably linked to astronomical events.

Below - *A diagram of astronomical phenomena seen from inside the Urn Tomb.*

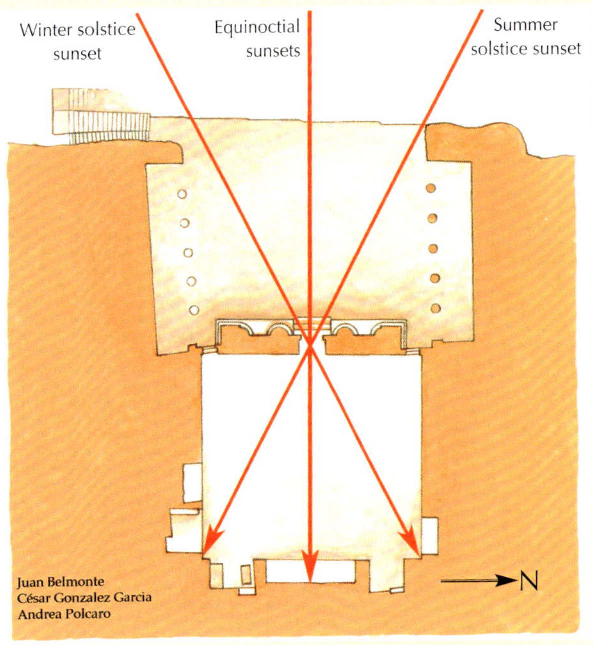

brought to light the existence of Nabataean cults based on the celestial sphere.
Among other things, the historian Strabo mentioned that on certain occasions the Nabataeans used to go up onto the flat roofs of their houses to send prayers up to the heavens, while burning incense. Although the great temples of Petra have been destroyed, with the exception of Qasr el Bint, it is possible that they too had flat roofs, like great terraces, similar to that found in the unfortunately destroyed temple of Bel, in Palmyra, whose architecture may have influenced the Nabataean one. In fact, the ruins of Qasr el Bint have two flights of stairs that undoubtedly led to the roof.
Apart from the sacrifices and the burning of incense, one constant element of the cult was the banquet, during which the diners entered into communion with their gods. Tricliniums cut into the living rock are common in every part of Petra. In this regard, Strabo wrote that the Nabataeans often held banquets for groups of thirteen people, and that two girls were responsible for accompanying each of these events with songs. The monarch (or the highest ranking person) would propose a number of toasts, but none of the guests ever drank more than eleven cups, and they changed them after each toast. In his descriptions, Strabo mentions the fact that the sovereign was so democratic that not only did he often serve himself, but even used to serve the other diners.
The Greek historian also highlighted the existence of a large number of fraternities (*thiasoi*), which played an important role in the social and religious fabric of Petra. Each of them would meet periodically in particular locations with religious significance, on mountain tops or at the bottom of wadis, to hold communal ceremonies in honour of specific deities.
The Nabataeans certainly believed in life after death, and also that the souls of the deceased became supernatural entities, who in some way continued to watch over the world of the living. This explains their resolve to dig huge burial sites all around their city. Archaeological finds have shown that the dead were covered with a shroud made of cloth, or sometimes animal hide, before being placed in the loculus. There is also evidence of the practice of cremation, after which the ashes were placed in an urn and then buried. It seem that there was a very close relationship between the dead and the living. In fact, rooms for families to meet, and hold banquets in honour of their ancestors, or *marzeah* in Nabataean, were often made alongside the tombs. In these chambers, there was typically a triclinium couch carved from the living rock along three sides of the room (or occasionally along two, in which case the term biclinium is used) and the diners would lie down on their sides. These tricliniums were sometimes in the open air, rather than in a hypogeum.

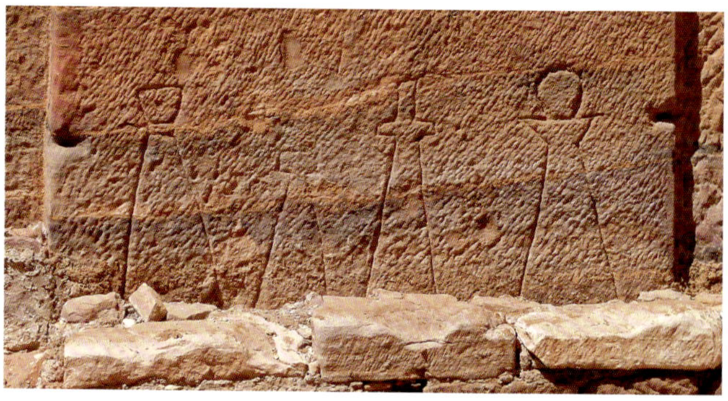

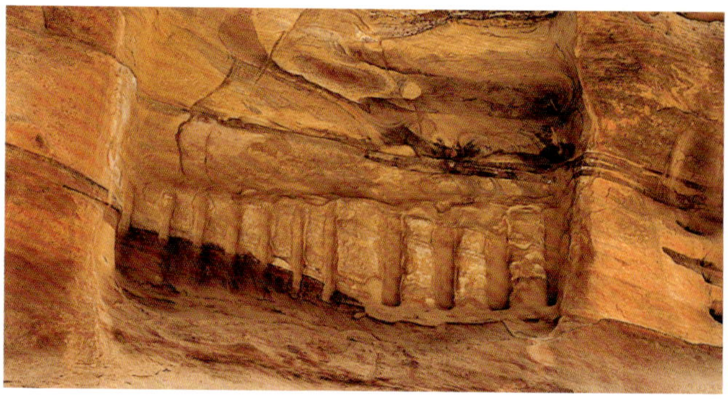

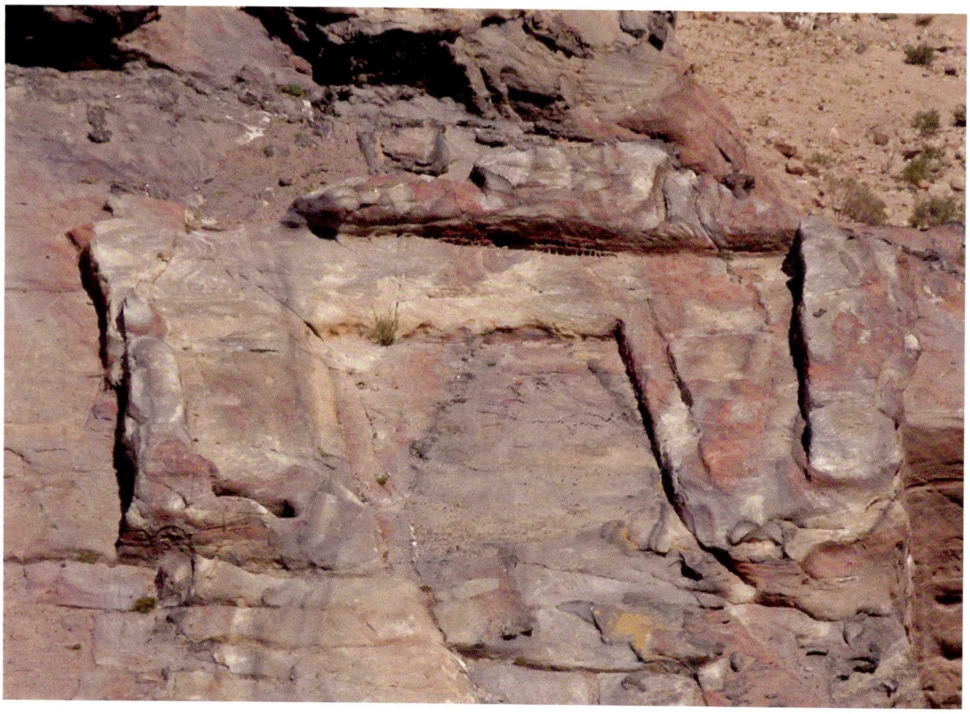

Top - *The* nefesh *were aniconic representations of the deceased's soul: these ones are engraved on the facade of Tomb 69, in the Outer Siq.*

Centre - *In the northern wall of the Siq this distinctive series of ten baetyli has been carved, a case unique in Petra. It should be remembered that, in addition to the main gods of their pantheon, the Nabataeans worshipped a certain number of gods, or minor deities (so to speak), comparable to the penates of the Roman religious tradition, that is, the spirit protectors of single individuals or families.*

Bottom - *An open-air triclinium, excavated in the northern slopes of Jebel al Madhbah.*

THE ARCHITECTURE

Razed to the ground by several earthquakes and abandoned for many centuries, today Petra is an expanse of rubble covered with sand and sparse seasonal vegetation, so it is very difficult to work out what the inhabited city would have looked like after the end of the semi-nomadic phase.
The valley of Petra was occupied by a monumental centre, whose pole consisted of the colonnaded road that ran along the well-regimented course of the wadi Musa, surrounded by residential neighbourhoods and the more distant suburbs The densely populated area was surrounded by the sumptuous facades of the great tombs as well as the more modest ones carved into the

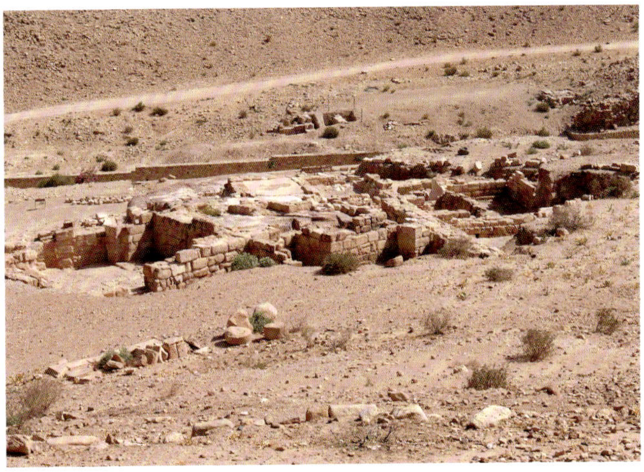

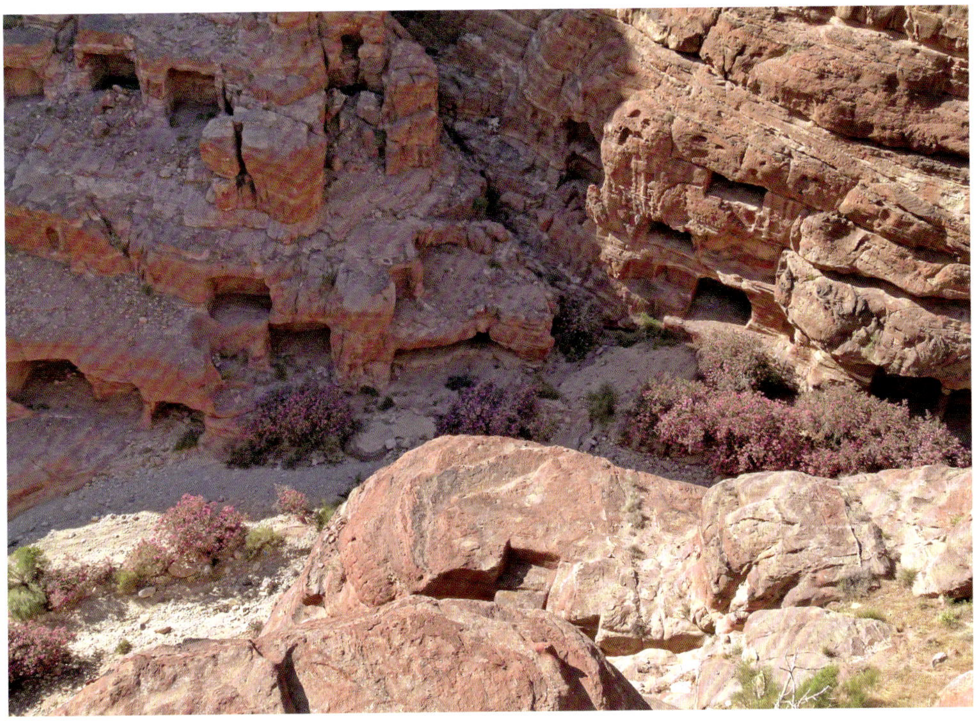

Above - *On the low ridge that borders the south of the Wadi Musa, called el Katuteh, there was a residential area known as Ez Zantur. Over the years, the remains of four large houses built in masonry have been brought to light. The one shown here stands behind the Great Temple.*

Below - *The almost vertical walls of the Siyyagh Wadi are perforated by dozens of cavities, placed on different levels and connected to each other by bold flights of stairs. These rock cut complexes would have housed a large part of the population in Petra.*

rock faces, which are now all that remains of the glorious past. The houses of ordinary people must have been simple buildings with one or two floors, made of stone, with flat roofs, plastered in white and with the windows that usually looked out onto the internal courtyards, which were as full of vegetation as possible. Clustered together in a disorganized way, these houses gave rise to a maze of little streets, which followed the lie of the land, and were quite narrow in order to create as much shade as possible. In fact, Petra did not have a perpendicular layout like Roman and Hellenistic cities. It was more like a "encampment made of stone", almost as if the inhabitants had one day decided to substitute the poles and fabric of their great tents with stone and bricks.
Because wood was very scarce in the region, structural elements like beams, doors and windows had to be reused many times. The rooms were also not very spacious, because of the limited size of the beams used for roofing. It is also possible that in the hottest months, people slept in tents put up on the flat roofs.
All in all, Petra must have been a bit like an old Jordanian village, but rather more disorganized. This expanse of little houses was interspersed with agricultural areas and orchards (the American archaeologist Nelson Gluek appropriately talks about a "garden city"), and the imposing structures of the public and religious buildings were spread about here and there. Thanks to its abundant supply of water, the metropolis was adorned with fountains and nymphaea, as well as public gardens and even an artificial lake, situated on the main street, next to what is today known as the Great Temple.
Other houses, made up of several rooms connected by staircases and terraces, were cut into the rock of the wadis surrounding the centre of the city. These were cool and comfortable, and their walls were decorated with moulding, plasterwork and multi-coloured paintings, which evoked the style of the Hellenistic and Roman world: architectural facades, false doors, or more imaginative creations including pergolas or floral motifs. In the Wadi Siyyagh, a room with some well preserved multi-coloured wall panels sports a ceiling decorated with an unbelievable black and white pattern radiating out from the centre point.
As the excavations in various areas of the "district" known as Ez Zantur (behind the Great Temple) demon-

strate, towards the end of the 1st century BC, the wealthy were already living in sumptuous houses, the beauty of which was even mentioned by Strabo. They contained large numbers of spacious rooms for socializing, which were arranged around peristyles and vestibules, in the Hellenistic-Roman style. These rooms, which had stone floors, were plastered and profusely decorated with rich multi-coloured paintings. The residential sector of the house, less cared for, was instead set out in a more random way, according to Eastern custom.
Temples and public buildings, like the Qasr el Bint, the Great Temple and the Winged Lions Temple, were built with the stone that was tirelessly extracted from the

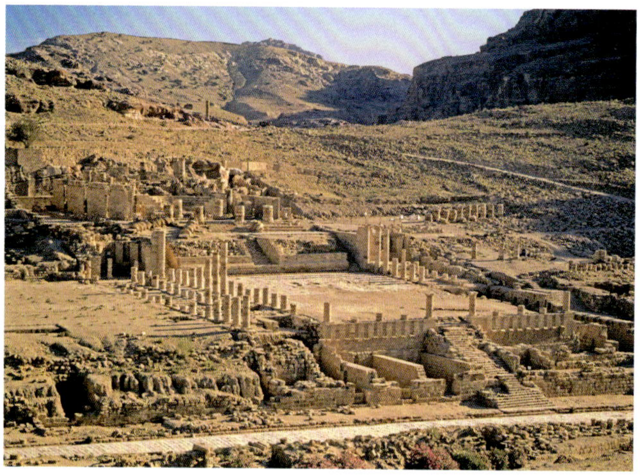

quarries surrounding the city. Although they were influenced by the Hellenistic and later the Roman styles, these monuments have structural and decorative characteristics that are entirely original.
Even the Qasr el Bint, which resembles a tetrastyle *in antis* temple of Roman origin on the outside, in reality shows the considerable independence from the classical traditions that the local builders demonstrated.
The Nabataeans were like sponges, ready to absorb ideas from all the peoples they came into contact with, and Syrian, Egyptian, Greek and Roman elements freely converged in the great buildings of Petra, combing to create previously unheard of solutions, including the so-called Nabataean or "horned" capital, which was a local invention. It is also clear, for example in the facade of the Palace Tomb, that the "golden ratio", a common factor in Greek and Roman building, was scarcely taken into account.
This situation was also evident in the sculptural decorations. The Nabataeans did not have their own figurative tradition, as has already been mentioned, and from the end of the 1st century BC, there must have been sculptors, plasterers and artists in the city, who had either trained abroad, or were actually foreigners themselves.
Along its perimeter, the inhabited city gradually merged with the city of the dead. This unusual combination, which is hard for us to comprehend, must have seemed natural for the Nabataeans because of their religious beliefs about the afterlife. Anyone who could afford it would prepare themselves a prestigious tomb, sculpted from the rock, to keep the memory of the deceased alive and perhaps confirm their social status in the afterlife. Recent finds have also shown that in Petra, like in the rest of the ancient world, the dead were put in their last resting place together with a wealth of grave goods.
As almost nothing now remains of the metropolis itself, the attention of visitors is mainly directed towards the burial sites, where there are many hundreds of tombs of varying shapes and sizes. (In Petra, at least 3,000 structures have been catalogued, from tombs to simple baetyli cut into the rock). Some of these are extraordinary works, even when compared with Greek and Roman masterpieces of the same era. Many are rather more modest, but still fascinating. There is quite a wide

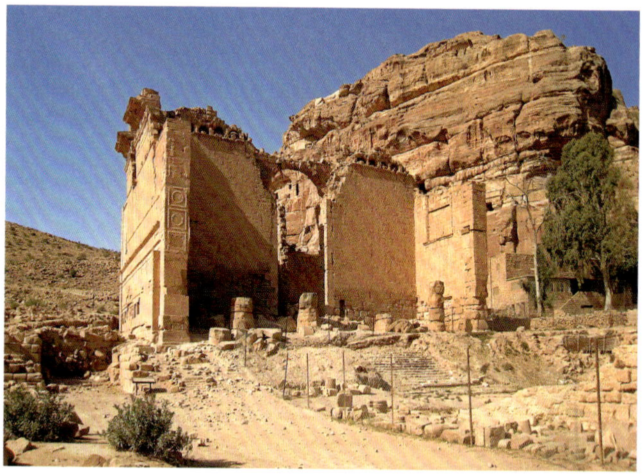

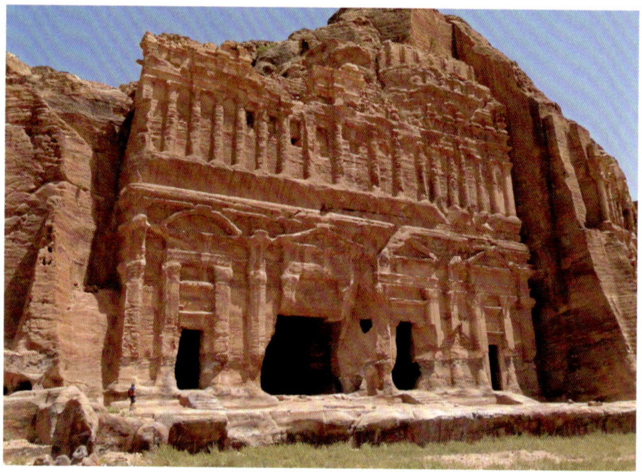

variety of different styles and in the past, many researchers believed that each of them was evidence of a different cultural influx and a different historical period. Today, on the other hand, it is thought that the various different architectural models do not correspond to a chronological sequence, but that they were used simultaneously over a period of at least three and a half centuries, which seems logical given the scarcity of tombs in the more "recent" styles. This theory is also supported by the fact that in Hegra there is a large number of rupestrian tombs that are similar to those in Petra, but with perfectly legible inscriptions, and the dating of these has confirmed that the various architectural styles were being used at the same time and and that they do not reflect a chronological order.
It is certainly a strange thought that a people of nomadic

origin, and therefore without an architectural tradition, settled down, and within the space of a few decades had developed sophisticated techniques for working stone, which were then applied on a scale that is still astonishing today. The Nabataeans were certainly helped by the natural characteristic of the local rock, which is sandstone. It is a compact, resistant and yet easily workable sedimentary rock, made up of grains the size of sand. On the other hand, the idea of excavating rock cut buildings already had ancient origins at the time. The rock cut sanctuaries of the Hitites, like that of Yazilikaya (near the capital Hattusha), date back to about 1250 BC, and during the same period the famous Egyptian temple of Abu Simbel was built by order of Ramesses II. In central Italy, the Etruscans excavated immense underground necropolises, giving rise to spectacular architectural creations like the Ildebranda Tomb in Sovana, which dates back to the 3rd century BC, and has similar characteristics to some of the tombs of Petra. The magnificent Lycian tombs on the south coast of Turkey were carved in the 4th century BC, while much further to the east, the Persian emperor Darius I had his own tomb (dated 486 B.C.) carved into the rock face of Naqsh-e Rostam, near the capital Persepolis. This began a tradition that was followed by his successors up until Darius III (336-330 BC), the last king of the Achaemenid dynasty. Great rock cut buildings are also common in the Far East, from China to India, where the underground Buddhist sanctuaries of Ajanta, Ellora and Elephanta (to name but a few) are situated.

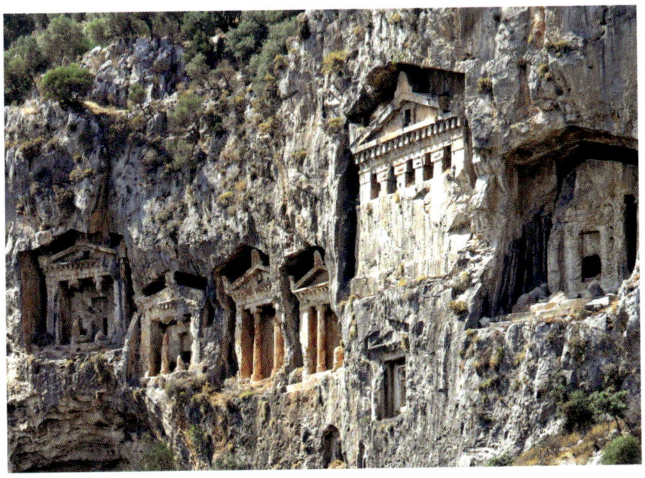

So the Nabataeans had illustrious predecessors, and undoubtedly learned the basics of rock cut architecture thanks to their wide ranging trading contacts with different peoples, both in the east and the west.
As in all the cases above, the secret of this form of architecture lies in the approach. In fact, the labourers must work in reverse compared with traditional methods, or rather from top to bottom. This is fundamental for two reasons. Firstly, if they had worked from the bottom upwards, the stonemasons would have been hit by the chippings and dust produced during their work. Secondly, working from the top down allowed them not to damage the structure when they jettisoned the materials resulting from the excavation of the mass of rock.
Obviously, this required a different way of planning and considering the work. If we think about this way of working, we realize that it must have involved a considerable number of technical problems, and required an extraordinary capacity for abstract thought, because it would have been necessary to "see" the architectural shape while it was still hidden in the raw material, as the work proceeded. This is particularly true in the case of the more complex monuments, like the Khazneh, the Deir and the Corinthian Tomb. It also must have entailed excellent technique and astonishing precision, as no errors, except very minor ones, can be permitted. Nabataean rock cut architecture, which is in fact more like sculpture, was therefore an authentic masterpiece of artistic sensitivity and ingenuity.

Opposite page, left - *The so-called Great Temple was one of the most extensive monuments in Petra to be built in masonry.*

Opposite page, top right - *The temple known as Qasr el Bint is the only structure built in masonry left in Petra, despite the earthquakes.*

Opposite page, bottom right *The so-called Palace Tomb has very peculiar proportions.*

Left - *The rupestrian tombs in Dalyan, on the southwestern coast of Turkey, were carved by the Lycians around 390 BC; they have constructive characteristics similar to those of the monuments in Petra.*

Right - *The pit graves, covered with stone slabs, were the first type of tomb used in the Petra area and continued to be carved for centuries, for the lower social classes.*
This one is located in the Outer Siq.

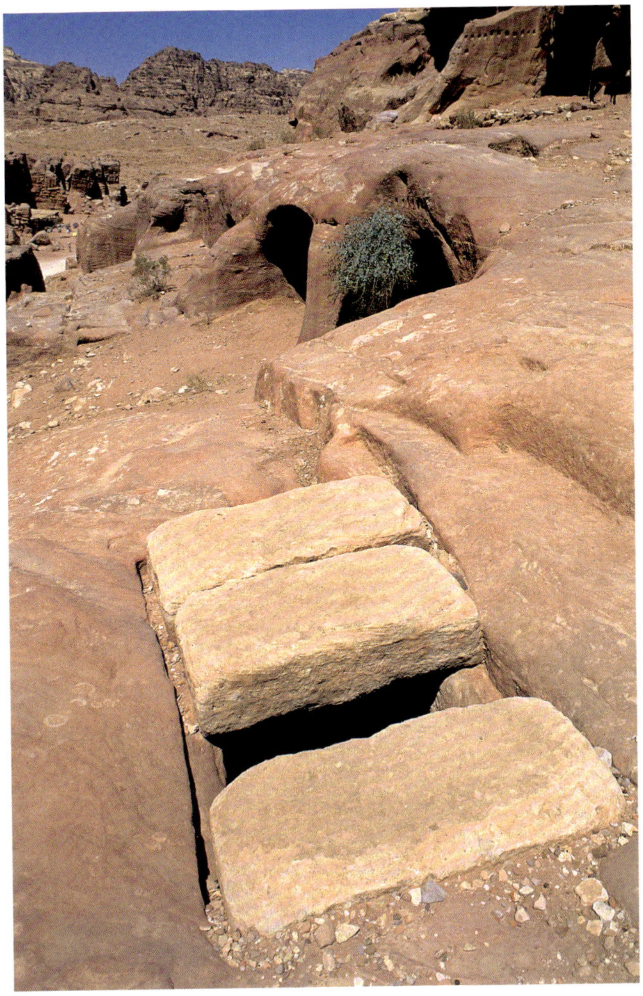

THE ARCHITECTURAL MODELS

For convenience, the various archaeological styles have been classified by type.

The first burial places, which date back to the 4th -3rd century BC, are **pit graves**, or simple rectangular spaces cut into the rock and closed off with stone slabs. As they were simple to construct, these tombs continued to be used by the less well off until the Byzantine period. The **shaft tombs** are a bit more recent. They consist of bare underground chambers that can be reached through a kind of chimney (or well). The **dromos tombs** are very similar, but instead of a well, they have a corridor that gives access to the burial chamber with the loculi in its floor. From the 3rd century B.C. onwards, **Assyrian style tombs** (or pylon tombs) became common, with a simple smooth facade crowned with one or two rows of crowsteps, which were imported from Syria. The door can be framed between pilasters (or half-columns or half-pillars) and crowned with a simple cornice. The tombs with two lines of crowsteps (double pylon tombs) can have a more elaborate doorway, crowned with a triangular tympanum with a Hellenistic look. A particular form of the previous type are the **block tombs** (or tower tombs), which are carved into the rock on three or four sides, taking on the appearance of a parallelepiped. Of the 22 recorded examples in the Petra area, only six have all for sides free, and the rest are partly attached to the mass of rock behind. The crowsteps can be carved from the living sandstone (as in the case of Tomb 70 (page 78), or built in masonry. The **cavetto tombs** (or step tombs) are from the same period or a little later. The facades of these tombs are surmounted with a concave cornice similar to Egyptian (or Phoenician) moulding, which is in fact called cavetto, on which two enormous half merlons rest, usually consisting of five steps.

In the meantime a type of capital evolved based on the classical Corinthian style, but much simpler, which is known as "horned" or Nabataean. This was widely used in the tombs called **proto Hegra**, which are the same as the previous ones, but the front is enclosed between pilasters, and the doors have added trabeations with varying degrees of complexity. The **Hegra tombs**, also known as double cornice tombs, are an elaboration of this model in which a trabeation with a classical cornice is added underneath the cavetto cornice. The lower attic, between the two entablatures, may have short pilasters with Nabataean capitals placed at regular intervals, while the facade is sometimes divided up by four pilasters. In some cases, the pilasters further out have an elegant development: they are supplemented by quarter columns on the inner sides (a good example of this is the Turkmaniyya Tomb). The door is usually surmounted by a pediment with a tympanum and acroterions.

Now that it has been established that the types of tomb described so far were in use at the same time over centuries, it is believed that the differences in style are related to the social status of the patron: the higher their status, the grander and more elaborate the tomb.

From the second half of the 1st century BC, Nabataean architecture had acquired architectural and decorative designs from the Hellenized world, in particular from Alexandria, which gave rise to a small number of monuments known as **classical Nabataean** tombs. The Khazneh is the most spectacular example of this. In their search for an ever more exaggerated grandeur, the tombs reached colossal dimensions. Innovative solutions, like overlapping orders of columns and the use of the *tholos*, were applied, alongside elements that were already obsolete, like rosettes or animals facing each other. This highlights the provincial, but very original, character of Nabataean architecture. As well as the Khazneh, there are also other examples of this, including the Corinthian Tomb (which is clearly a continuation of the style), the Bab Al Siq Triclinium (influenced in turn by the Corithian Tomb), the Tomb of the Broken Pediment, and the extraordinary and little known Tomb 154. Another distinctive example is the so-called Palace

Monica Falcone

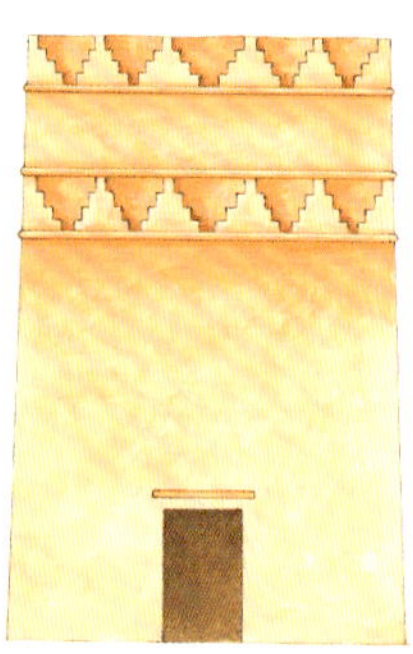

Assyrian style tomb (or pylon tomb) with double crowsteps

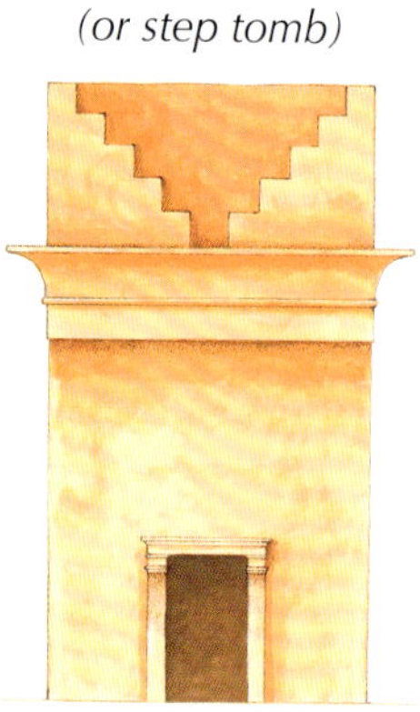

Cavetto tomb (or step tomb)

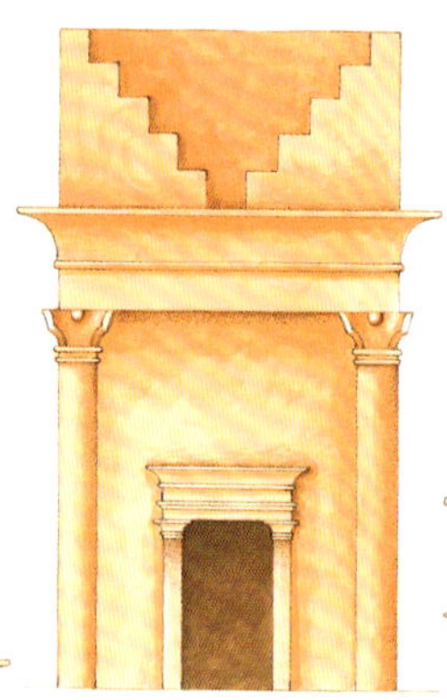

Proto Hegra tomb

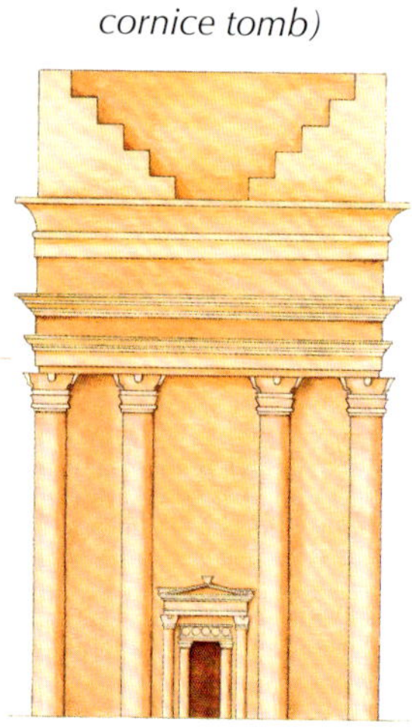

Hegra tomb (or double cornice tomb)

Although catalogued according to their most obvious typological characteristics, the architectural models of Petra show an extraordinary number of variants, which are especially evident in the tombs with half merlons.
There are graves with two overlapping burial chambers and even a double cornice tomb topped by crowsteps.

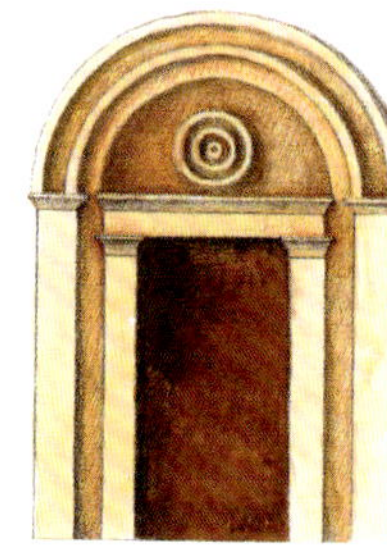

Arch tomb

Tomb, with its recurring use of horizontal lines and a disconcerting asymmetrical composition, which are both absolutely unique architectural solutions.
The magnificent Deir can be considered the swan song of this particular phase of Nabataean architecture. Although it is similar to the Khazneh in appearance, the imported Hellenistic decorative designs are noticeably simpler (the floral capitals are substituted with Nabataean ones), as if to confirm a return to indigenous stylistic features. In this building, the lightness and slightly affected appearance of the Khazneh are replaced with a stark severity, which is a testimony to a reformation that took place in Nabataean art from the 2nd century A.D. onwards and led to the rejection of the more elaborate models brought to Petra from the Hellenistic-Roman world.
One particular category of hypogeum that belongs to the classical Nabataean style is that of the **simple classical tombs** (or pediment tombs), in which the facade is enclosed between two pilasters surmounted by a classical pediment with a triangular tympanum. The Carmine Facade, the Lion Triclinium, the Monument (or Temple) 846 in Little Petra, the Renaissance Tomb, the Tomb of Sextius Florentinus and several other smaller tombs (Tombs 269, 455) are perfect examples of this.
The rare examples of tombs in the **Roman style**, which are very similar to tertrastyle temples, are also part of this category. These include the Urn Tomb, the Roman Soldier Tomb and the almost identical Tomb 258 in the Wadi al Najir. The few other examples are so badly preserved that they cannot be identified with any certainty.
Three unique monuments of their kind, which are temples *in antis* with two free-standing columns, are also categorized as classical Nabataean style. These include the so-called Garden Triclinium (or Temple), the temple of Little Petra and the great Unfinished Tomb.
The **arch tombs**, the doors of which are surmounted with a simple curved tympanum, have proved difficult to date. According to some, they are from the same period as the Assyrian and cavetto tombs, but others believe they date back to the Roman occupation.
Regardless of the architectural style, every now and again, the craftsmen had to deal with problems caused by the consistency of the sandstone in which they were sculpting the tomb. As a result, it was not uncommon for them to carve the elements with more complex details in a harder stone, and then embed them into the facade in special slots, fixing them in place with mortar (*photo below*). This explains the noticeable fissures in the facades of many of the tombs, where these elements have become detached over the course of time.

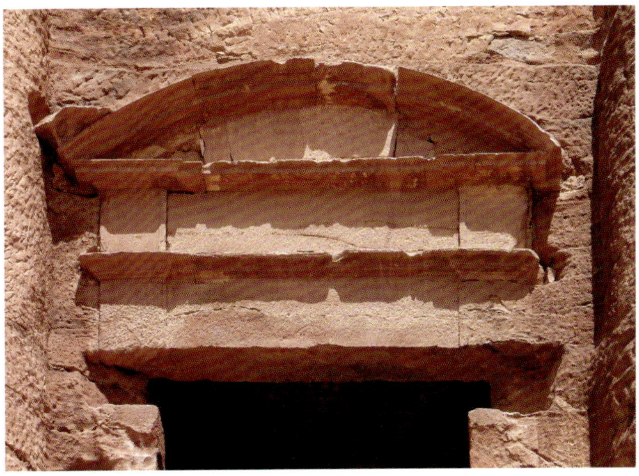

Monica Falcone

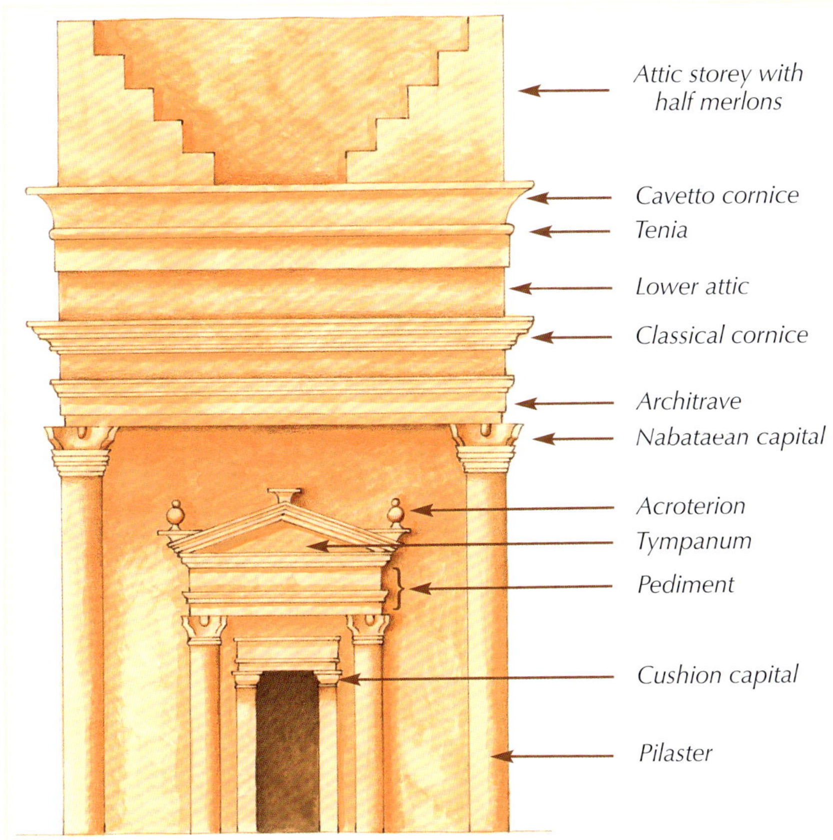

Hegra tomb, (or double cornice tomb)

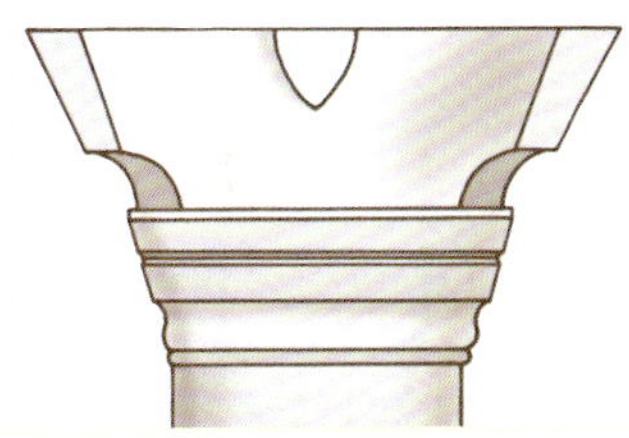

Nabataean capital

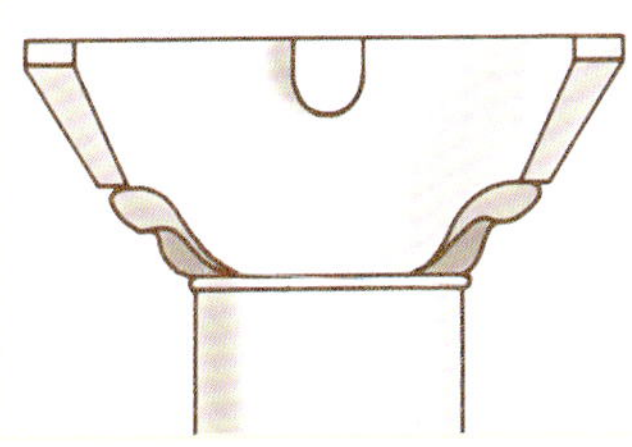

Nabataean capital, variant

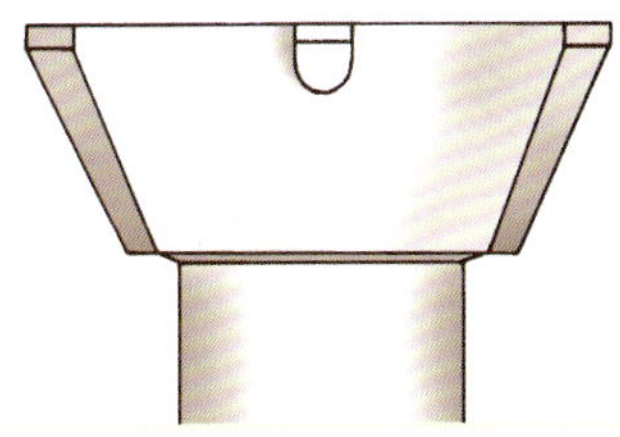

Nabataean capital, variant

To get a clearer idea of what the funerary monuments of Petra must have looked like, we need to consider that all the tombs had wooden doors with hinges, which turned in special holes made in the rock, or in wooden frames tightly fitted into the doorways. In the case of the more opulent burial chambers, the doors were probably decorated in relief or overlaid with metal plates.

One issue about which there has been much debate is whether the facades of the tombs were plastered or not. There is actually a lot of evidence to suggest that they were, at least partially. In fact, fragments of plaster have survived on several tombs, like Tomb 67. However, it was a close observation of a pillar tomb in the outer Siq, and the remains of the Assyrian crowsteps of the Block Tomb 303, that convinced the author that the crowsteps had a white strip beneath them. The battlements themselves must have been painted dark red, with the spaces between them coloured white. This colour contrast would have made the monuments more visible, creating a clear juxtaposition with the surrounding surface of the rock. It is also unlikely that the facades were completely plastered and painted. It is evident that the rich array of colours of the sandstone fades over time, partly because of the effects of oxidization. In fact, the marbling is more pronounced where the rock is more eroded. This would have made the appearance of the facades much more uniform than it is today.

In the area of Petra, 619 tombs with facades have been discovered as well as 100 *triclinia*, *biclinia* and *stibadia*, or tricliniums with a circular shape. At least thirty *triclinia* in Petra are clearly connected with a nearby tomb. The others may not have been used for events related to funeral rites, but rather for community prayers and banquets in honour of the gods. However, the possibility that the so-called "open-air *triclinia*" were connected with the celebration of the previously mentioned *marzeah* cannot be ruled out. Surprisingly, some triclinium halls have loculi inside them. In the absence of other explanations, we can only imagine that these were made at a later date in history.

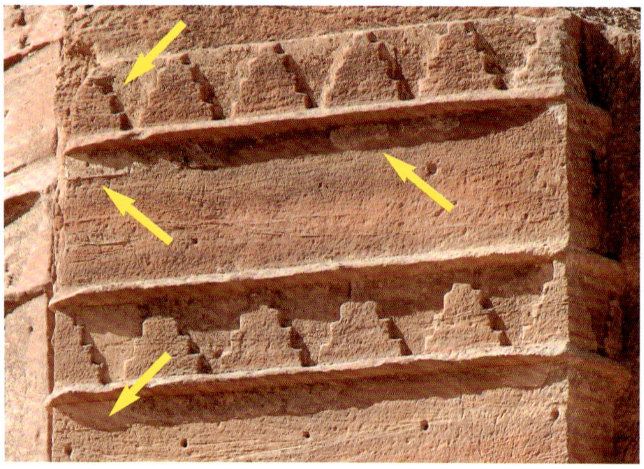

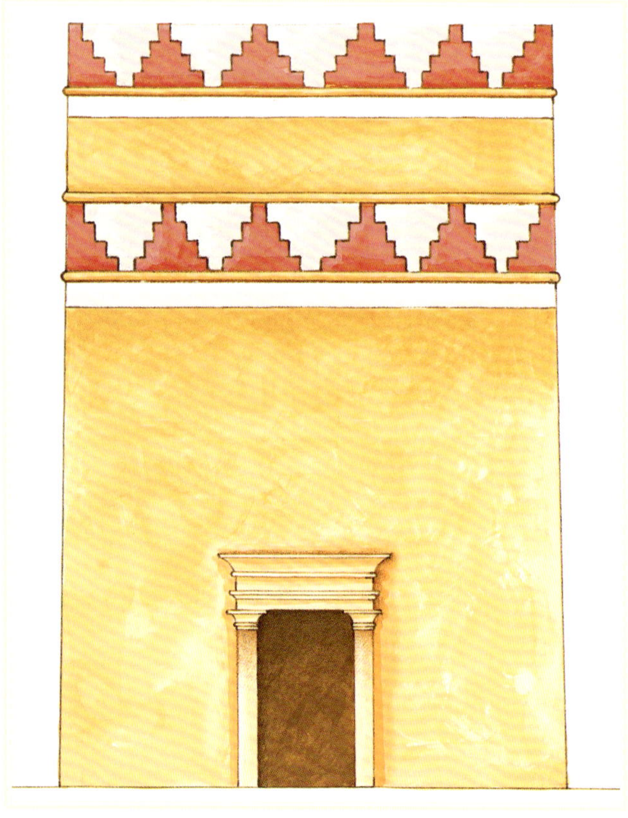

Monica Falcone

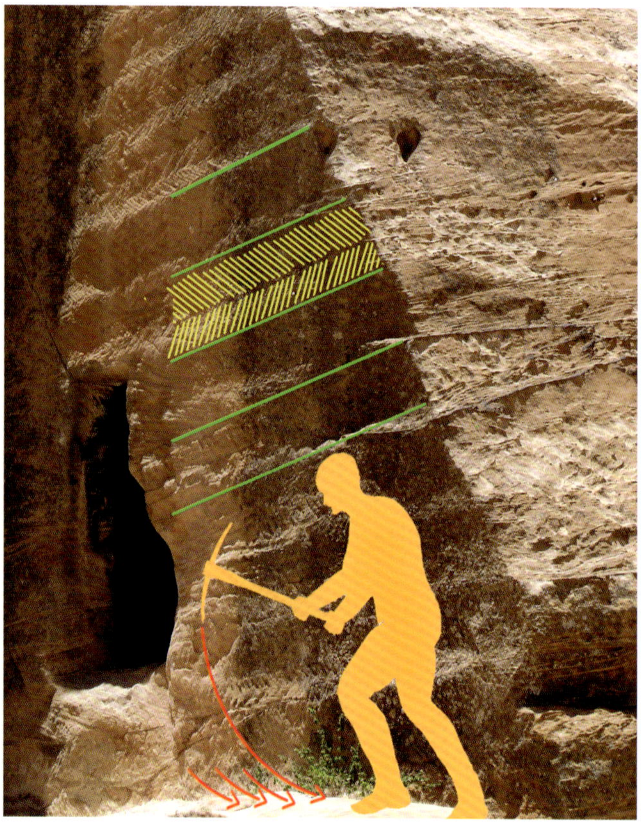

Left top - *The arrows indicate the clearly visible remains of painted plaster on an Assyrian-style tomb (No. 114) located in the Outer Siq, along the Streets of the Facades. Fragments of plaster are also preserved in the spaces between the crowsteps.*

Left bottom - *This was probably the appearance of the rupestrian tombs; it is possible that the colour scheme had variations, but red and white (obtainable from the widespread iron oxide in the Petra area) would seem to have been the most common colours.*

Right - *The prominent rocky buttress on the right of the Bab el Siq Triclinium (see also the image on the opposite page) clearly shows the herringbone signs left by pickaxes (highlighted in yellow). The subsequent horizontal excavation planes (highlighted in green) are also perfectly distinguishable.*

BUILDING TECHNIQUES

Petra's rock-cut tombs may look like a lot of time and effort went into them, but carving an environment and a facade out of the soft sandstone is in many respects less tiring (and costly) than building in masonry, also because the ceilings are self-supporting. The study of the Unfinished Tomb (small photo above) and other unfinished tombs (small photo below) confirm that carving was carried out from top to bottom.

Tools essentially consisted of pickaxes, clubs and chisels, along with files and smaller chisels for the finer details. They regularly needed to be sharpened being made of iron rather than steel. The worksites should therefore be imagined as a perfectly run organisation consisting of stonemasons, blacksmiths, ropemakers, carpenters and a drove of helpers to carry, amongst other things, water and provisions.

If the tomb was to be hewn along a slope, builders started with its peak, then began digging a kind of horizontal platform, slightly wider than the facade, whose surface gradually increased as it went down. The builders worked on the flat surface along long parallel tracks, based on a checkerboard pattern. Standing and slowly moving forward, they gave the pickaxes the same repetitive curvilinear movements. Once they reached the end of the track, they turned back and restarted from the beginning until they reached the desired depth (large image). By doing this, they created a distinctive fishbone pattern on the vertical surface of the sandstone, still visible almost everywhere today. The last groove was cut under the block as outlined, and iron (or wooden) wedges were stuck into it, then by beating violently against them, they caused the block to split right to the back of the groove and become detached. These ashlars were then used for other building purposes.

While the construction work continued towards the bottom, various architectural elements were traced onto the now obtained flat, vertical surface using plumb-lines and ropes, which were then sculpted in relief form into the solid rock. Then came the smoothing and finishing of every component, making the rocky surface as uniform as possible. As already mentioned, since the soft sandstone was generally not good for sculpting the finer, decorative details, in some cases (mainly above portals) the mouldings were made of harder stone, which was better for sculpting finer details, and wedged into special grooves. In other cases, dark pigments were used to simulate decorative features like dentils under the cornices; this is clearly seen in the so-called Palace Tomb. Obviously, the burial chamber and any other internal, underground rooms were dug last. In most cases, burial chambers were devoid of any sort of decoration and deep burial niches were dug into the ground or along the walls, sometimes inside the cavity of an arcosolium.

Working along a vertical wall was more complex, as in the case of the Khazneh. It was necessary to reach the top of the cliff first and carve through-holes into the rock (dozens of them can be seen in the Petra area), in which ropes were passed that secured the pulleys. In these ran the ropes that allowed the scaffolding to move (a bit like the external maintenance of skyscrapers today). Having reached the predetermined height, the builders made a deep horizontal cut into the mountain, slightly larger than the planned facade. Once the gap had been sufficiently enlarged, it was possible to work standing up, cutting the rock and unloading the resulting debris as they continued carving towards the bottom. In other cases, to create a kind of hanging platform, aligned holes were drilled along the façade, into which metal rods were inserted to hold shafts on which workers could easily move and work. This platform was easy to set up and progressively move downwards.

Obviously, all of these techniques required a huge amount of professionalism and supervision by expert workers.

As Judith McKenzie revealed by analysing the epigraphs carved on the Hegra tombs, the average period of activity for a stonemason was about twenty-five years and they could all probably sculpt facades in different styles.

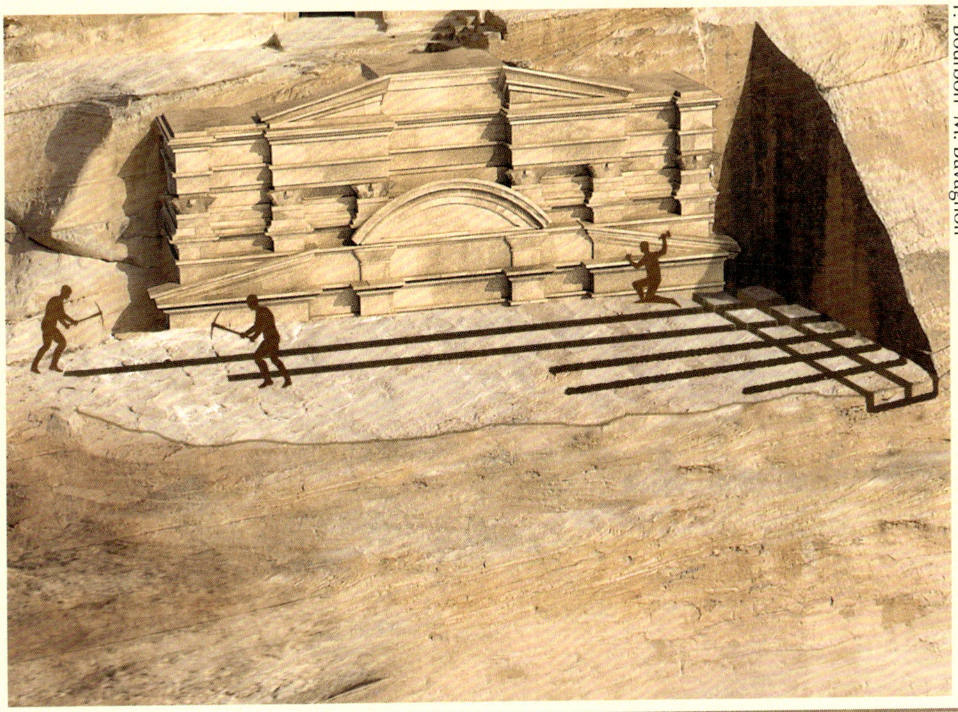

F. Bourbon M. Bavagnoli

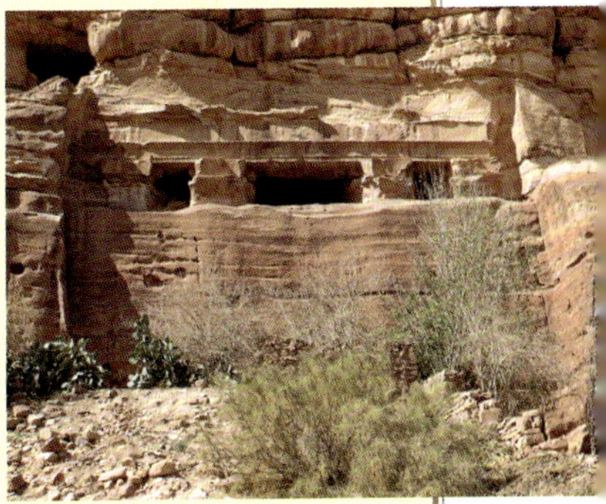

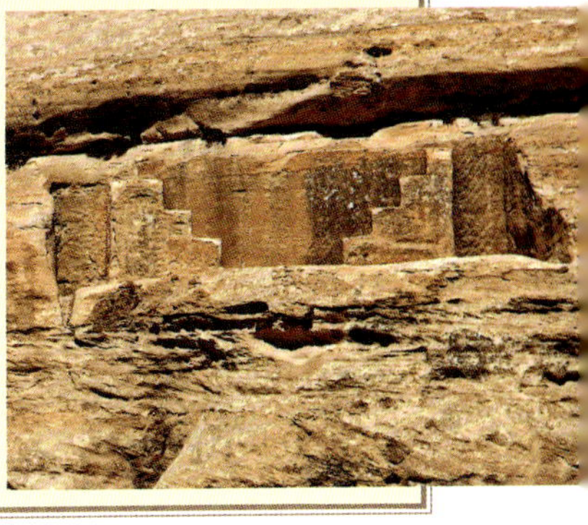

PRACTICAL INFORMATION AND ADVICE

Petra is the legacy left by the Nabataeans for future generations and has been declared a World Heritage Site by UNESCO. It is an incomparable place and it must be carefully preserved. It should be visited with awareness, which means respecting it, so that others who follow will be able to experience the same beauty and the same exhilaration. Only a responsible attitude adopted by everyone will enable the wonderful heritage of the builders of antiquity, and a place where one of nature's most original creations can be seen, to remain intact over time.

It takes at least three days to visit the site. However, considering the distance between the most important monuments, the large number of rock cut buildings and the natural beauty of the place, the ideal length of time to stay is four or five days, in order to be able to explore the archaeological area properly. As a general rule, bear in mind that from the entrance gates to the Khazneh it takes about thirty minutes to go down the Siq, and from the Khazneh it takes another half hour to reach the refreshment area known as Nazzal's Camp. From here to the Deir - an absolute must - is another three quarters of an hour on foot. The time spent getting from one place of interest to the next is therefore an important consideration, and you should plan your excursions carefully.

Petra can be visited all year round (although July and August are very hot), but it is useful to know that in the hottest months the difference in temperature between day and night is about 12-15 degrees, and therefore quite noticeable. For example, while the temperature on a fine day in June can reach 35°C, in the evening it can easily go down to 21, or even lower. A jumper with long sleeves is useful to have with you in a situation like this.

To avoid the crowds and the hottest time of day, it is a good idea to start your visit early in the morning, take a long break to unwind, and then continue in the late afternoon.

Near the entrance gate to the archaeological area, it is possible to hire a horse to get to the entrance to the Siq (about a kilometre away). Horse drawn carriages are available to go all the way along the Siq as far as the Khazneh (always escorted by someone). However, it is worth finding out how far they will actually take you before paying for the service. You can also hire a ride on a donkey or a mule in the area around Nazzal's Camp, to go up to the Deir or the Jebel al Madhbah. (The prices are generally reasonable and the guides are competent).

For visitors who are used to managing on their own, Petra is a wonderful place, where it is possible to experience an air of adventure in complete safety, just by following a few basic rules. The archaeological park is really huge and it is not unusual to spend time in pleasant solitude, sometimes for hours, especially in the area of the Armour Tomb and in the Wadi Thughra, on the way to the enigmatic Serpent Monument. Also, the whole area is patrolled by an efficient tourist police force (whose officers can be recognised by their striking

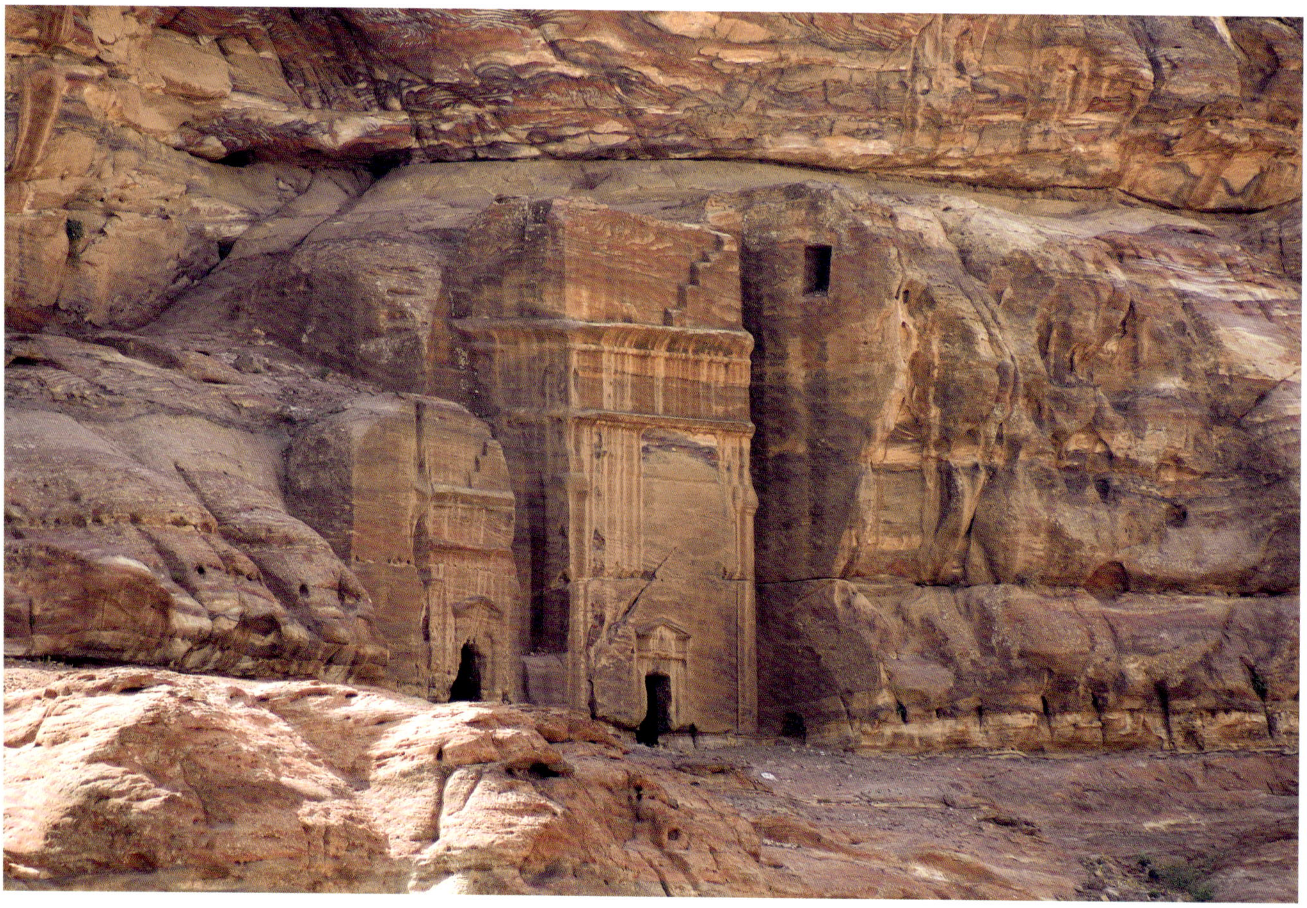

uniforms). For those who prefer to be accompanied, it is easy to find contact details for specialist guides in the village of Wadi Musa, near the entrance gates or in the reception areas of the hotels. In general, they know what they are doing and the prices are reasonable.
It is important to remember that Petra is a mountain location. The urban area itself lies at an altitude of about 800 metres, but many of the monuments and places of interest (like the Deir) are higher than 1000 metres. You will be walking quite a lot, so it is a good idea to wear suitable shoes. Forget sandals, flip-flops and any kind of shoes that are too light or have a smooth sole. Walking for hours on gravel or climbing steep paths cut into the living rock without proper footwear can easily turn into torture, made even worse by the sand that gets everywhere, and the bushes, many of which are pretty thorny. If you want to be comfortable, it is best to wear light boots. So-called "commando boots" in canvas are ideal. Clothes are also important. Do not be deceived by the magnificent sunshine and the breeze that often blows. Avoid going out with too much skin exposed, because it is easy to get burnt, or end up with sun stroke while walking amongst the rocks, so don't forget to bring a hat, sunglasses and sunscreen. At the beginning of spring it will be useful to bring a light sweatshirt with you, or in any case something with long sleeves, as unexpected changes in the weather are not uncommon, and after a downpour, the temperature in the shade can suddenly fall by several degrees. Rain is rare in Petra, and normally falls between November and March. Waterproof clothes are not essential, as it is usually easy to find somewhere to shelter, and after a shower the wind and sun dry your clothes off in a few

Opposite page - *These tombs are located at the foot of the Jebel al Madhbah, facing the Wadi Farasa, in one of the less visited areas of the archaeological park.*

Left - *This stairway carved into the rock, is located in the Wadi Siyyagh, on the slopes of jebel al Habis. It is one of many similar rupestrian structures scattered throughout Petra.*

Right top - *Aloe vera* (Aloe barbadensis) *is a perennial fleshy plant, which is widespread in Petra. It is similar in appearance to an agave plant and is recognizable by its flamboyant reddish inflorescence.*

Right bottom - *Petra is extraordinary not only for its monuments, but also for the rock formations, which show fabulous color ranges.*

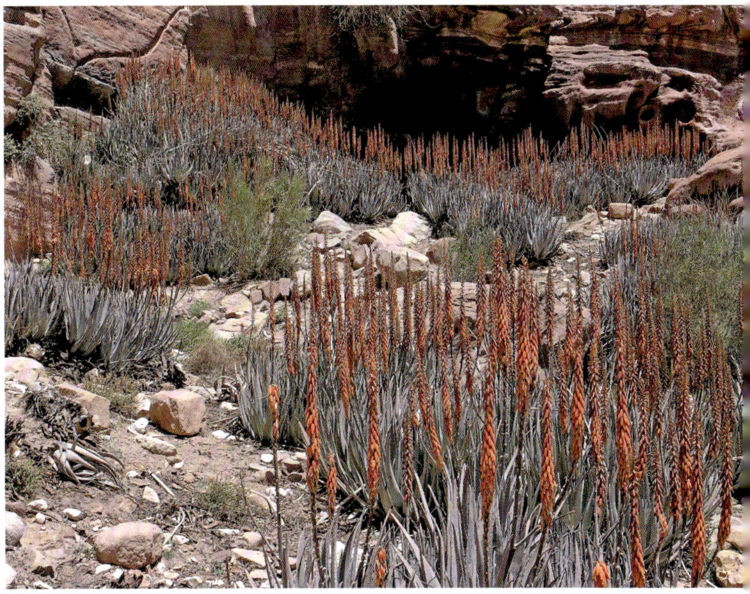

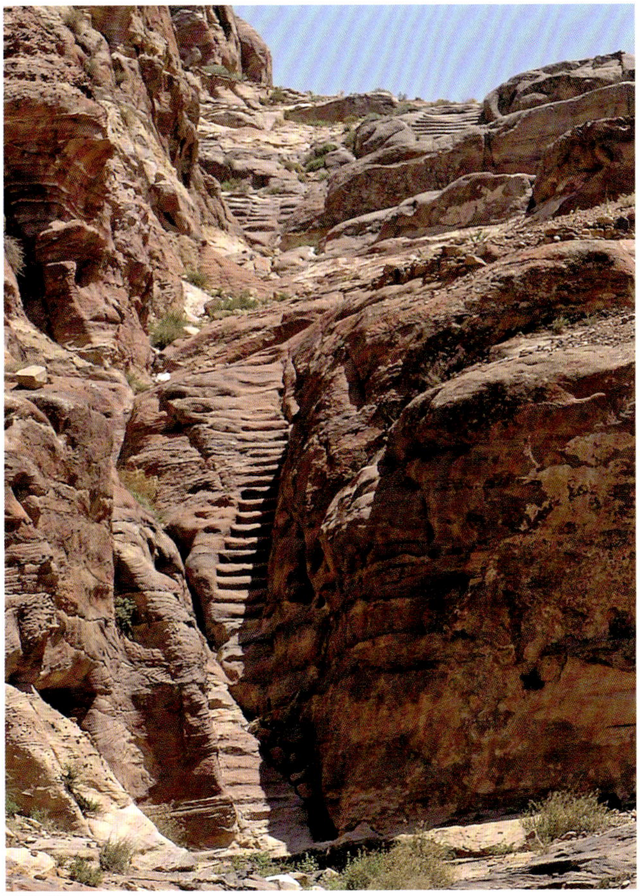

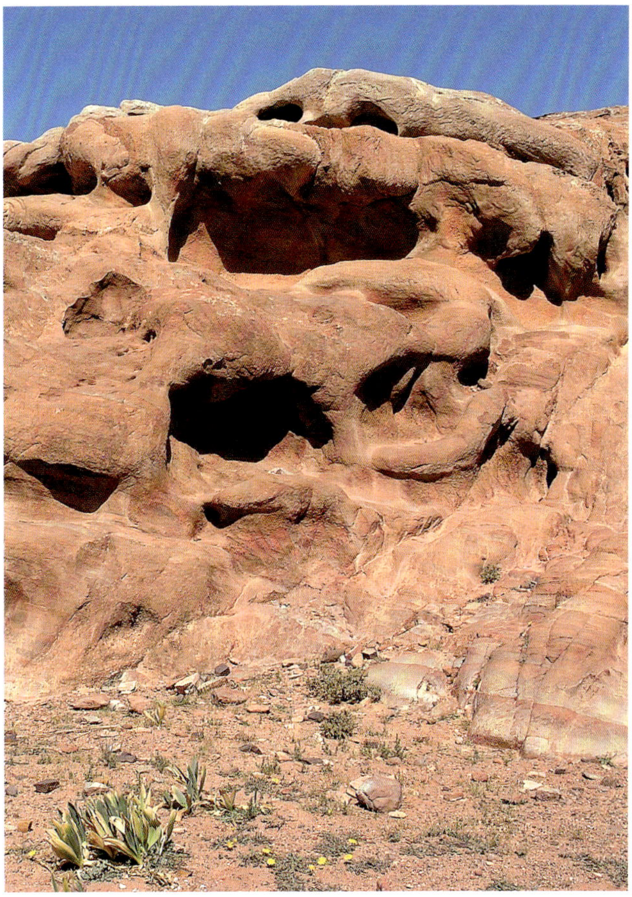

minutes. However, it should be remembered that when the sky is overcast, you need to be careful of storms, especially if you are in one of the steep narrow valleys. Even if it takes place several kilometres away, a downpour can cause sudden flash floods, which hurtle downhill violently. The ancient processional paths cut into the rock, which lead up to the summits of the highest mountains (Jebel al Madhbah, Jebel al Khubtha, Jebel Umm al Biyara), can also become torrents during storms. When the sky is clear, on the other hand, which is most of the time, do not expose yourself to direct sunlight for longer than necessary, and avoid moving around too much at the hottest times of day. Eat something light but nutritious (fruit is ideal) and have a rest while you wait for an exciting afternoon. It is better not to drink alcohol, including beer, because in a hot dry climate it is harmful, increases perspiration and can cause shortness of breath.
Once you have seen the main monuments, if you have a few more days, it can be very rewarding to venture into the Wadi Siyyagh and the Wadi Mataha, or climb up to the summit of the Umm al Biyara, all places which are particularly interesting for their extraordinary landscapes. These excursions, especially the climb up Umm al Biyara, are suitable for expert walkers, on days that are not too hot. The suburb known as "Little Petra" (al Barid) is also worth a visit, especially now that the frescoes in the Painted House have been restored. A visit to the silent al Sabrah is much more demanding. It is a sort of miniature Petra, several hours walk from the centre, and if you want to venture this far, it is a good idea to go with an expert guide.

REFRESHMENT KIOSKS

Water is the basic necessity for a comfortable visit to Petra. Dehydration is not to be under estimated here. Your skin can feel dry due to the almost continual breeze, but this does not mean you are not perspiring a lot. Refreshment kiosks look like traditional Bedouin tents where souvenir counters and benches for serving fresh drinks and traditional mint tea take refuge in the welcoming shade. Quality varies, but generally it is more than sufficient. Prices between the kiosks are the same on average.
The first is situated at the opening of the Siq. The ones in front of the Khazneh and just before the theatre are always crowded (this is where you'll find the restrooms, by the way). Located at the end of the Colonnaded Street is the area known as Nazzal's Camp where the only hotel in Petra once stood; it is known for hosting the famous detective writer Agatha Christie in 1933. Here you'll find the old Archaeological Museum (replaced in 2019 by a modern building erected beside the Visitor Centre) and a number of restaurants offering a wide range of menus to suit everybody's budget. Other tents can be found near the Deir and close to the panoramic view point (also known as "The view at the end of the world"), where the view extends over the immense Wadi Arabah chasm. There is a tent at the entrance of the Wadi Farasa just before the Roman Soldier Tomb; another awaits tired tourists at the top of the Jebel al Madhbah, a short distance from the famous "High Place of Sacrifice".

Petra is a real paradise for lovers of walking because of the kilometres and kilometres of paths and flights of stairs cut into the living rock. The ever changing scenery is extraordinary and provides unique subject matter for photographers. Some routes lead to breath taking views, from which all the main monuments can be seen from strategic angles. You can choose the most suitable path for your own abilities, but I would recommend proceeding with extreme caution. It is best not to stray off the beaten track if you are not used to the mountains or long challenging walks, because not taking things seriously could have dangerous consequences.
In some areas right on the edge of Petra, there are still a few families of Bedouins, most of whom are members of the Bdoul tribe. They are the current inhabitants of the Rose City. In reality, the government has built modern houses for them in Umm Sayhoun, near Wadi Musa, but in spite of this, some of them prefer their traditional way of life. In general, they live in groups of rupestrian tombs that are suitable for their needs. You may come across them in the Wadi Mataha and in the Wadi Thughra, but also elsewhere. They live off animal herding and agriculture (it may seem unbelievable, but there are still irrigated, cultivated spaces in the Petra area), or work in the archaeological digs that are taking place in various parts of the dead city. They are proud, reserved and well mannered. The women are often busy doing traditional activities like preparing and baking bread the old-fashioned way. Their presence is announced by fences, the occasional tent, a barrel for water or a rudimentary door attached to an old hypogeum, or sometimes by clotheslines outside the

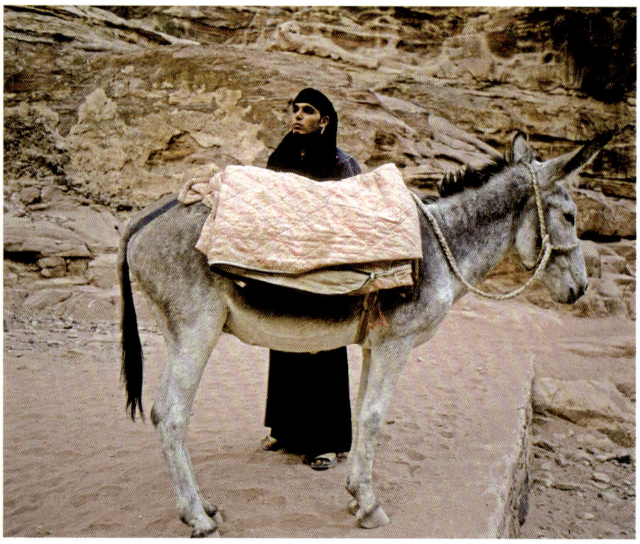

openings of the tombs. It is a good idea to respect their privacy and their culture. Visitors who are able to establish a good human contact with them, as with the ever present donkey and dromedary drivers, will undoubtedly learn something interesting: an anecdote, a suggestion for a particular itinerary, or some practical advice. It will certainly be a good experience, in any case.
It is much less common, though not impossible, to have a meeting with a bizarre reptile that is a kind of large lizard. The strange thing about these is the unlikely colour of the males of the species. In fact, the Sinai

agama (*Pseudotrapelus sinaitus*) is bright blue in the mating season, to attract a mate. The females, on the other hand, have a less gaudy livery of beige with rust coloured spots. About thirty centimetres long, including its very slim tail, this elegant reptile is completely harmless and very shy. Another typical inhabitant of Petra, which is equally elusive, is the stellagama (*Laudakia stellio*). A large lizard, which can be more than 35 centimetres in length, with a vaguely prehistoric appearance because of the short spines on its tail. This species is also completely inoffensive, although it can be quite a surprise when it suddenly appears. However, off the beaten track you should be careful where you put your hands. Although rare, there are snakes, scorpions and spiders in the area. In particular, those who decide to leave the centre of the archaeological area to walk along the more remote paths should be careful of the Palestine viper (*Daboia palaestinae*). It can be up to 120 cm long and its lethal bite occasionally causes deaths among the locals. One of the reasons why the Bedouins that still live in the ancient tombs always have cats is because they are very good at spotting snakes, and they immediately warn of the danger by hissing.
Petra is now one of the most famous tourist destinations in the world, and as a result, there are souvenir sellers everywhere, and even characters dressed in unlikely "Nabataean" or "Roman" clothes, who have photographs taken in exchange for money. Sellers and hawkers, like the dromedary and donkey drivers, are not usually too insistent, but the solitary romantic atmosphere that pervaded Petra a few decades ago has certainly been lost, at least in the most popular areas. Unfortunately, this is one of the prices of progress.
The most common items of local craftsmanship are glass bottles expertly filled with multi-coloured sand, generally gathered on site, jewellery in silver alloy, and reproductions of ancient Nabataean artefacts. It should be stressed that even the best quality souvenirs, like the terracotta oil lamps and the coins, are still modern replicas. In amongst all the junk, you might find that a Bedouin woman or boy offers you an authentic relic, for a high price. These are generally Nabataean and Roman ointment bottles or coins, but it is worth remembering that exporting archaeological artefacts is quite rightly prohibited (and punishable) by the Jordanian government.
Around many of the tombs, the ground is literally covered with fragments of earthenware. Taking away a few fragments as a souvenir is tolerated, but considering that once you get back home they will almost certainly end up at the bottom of a draw, all in all, it is better to leave them where they are.
Finally, I would strongly encourage you to respect both Petra and the entire natural environment that the Rose City is an integral part of. It is essential not to drop litter, and causing as little damage as possible to the rock cut monuments is also of fundamental importance. Millions of tramping feet are slowly but surely wearing away the rock they are made of. We should not forget this, as we are enthusiastically walking around the hypogea and other monuments, so that we can leave something more than just colourful sand for future generations.

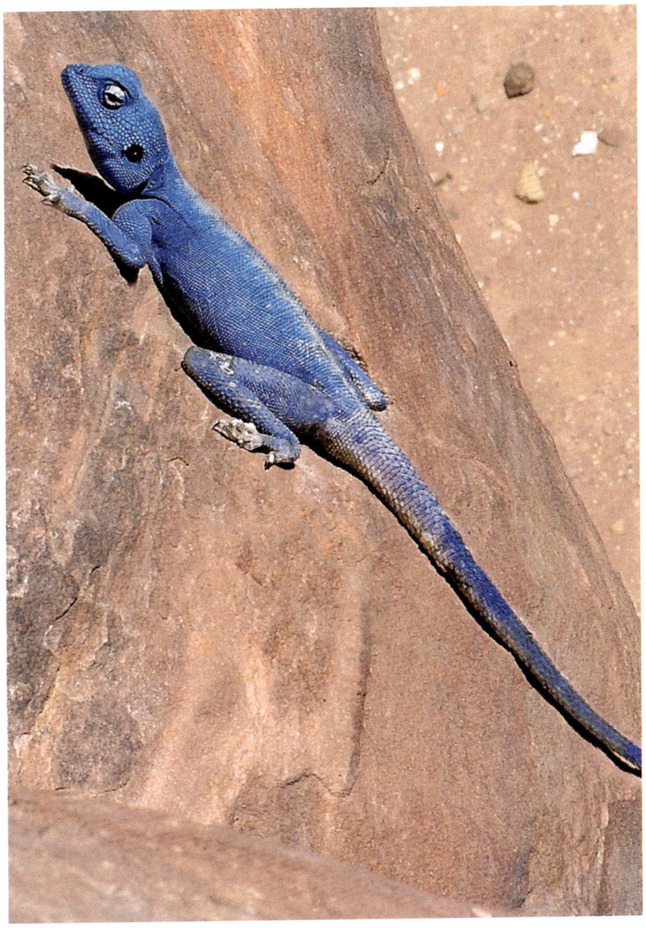

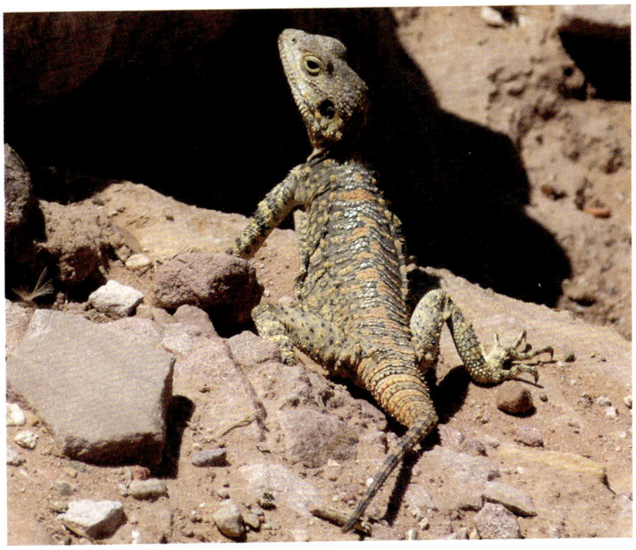

Opposite page - *Most of Petra's inhabitants today belong to the ancient Bedouin tribe of the Bdoul; their help as guides can be invaluable.*

Left - *The Sinai agama, a reptile belonging to the Agamid family, is well known for the spectacular livery of the males in the breeding season. During the day it is active and feeds on insects and fruits. It is very shy and shuns humans.*

Right - *A typical inhabitant of Petra is the stellagama, a saurian who also belongs to the Agamid family. This large lizard is diurnal and willingly exposes itself to the sun to regulate its body temperature; as a result, its livery tends to darken. It feeds on insects and fruits and is harmless to humans.*

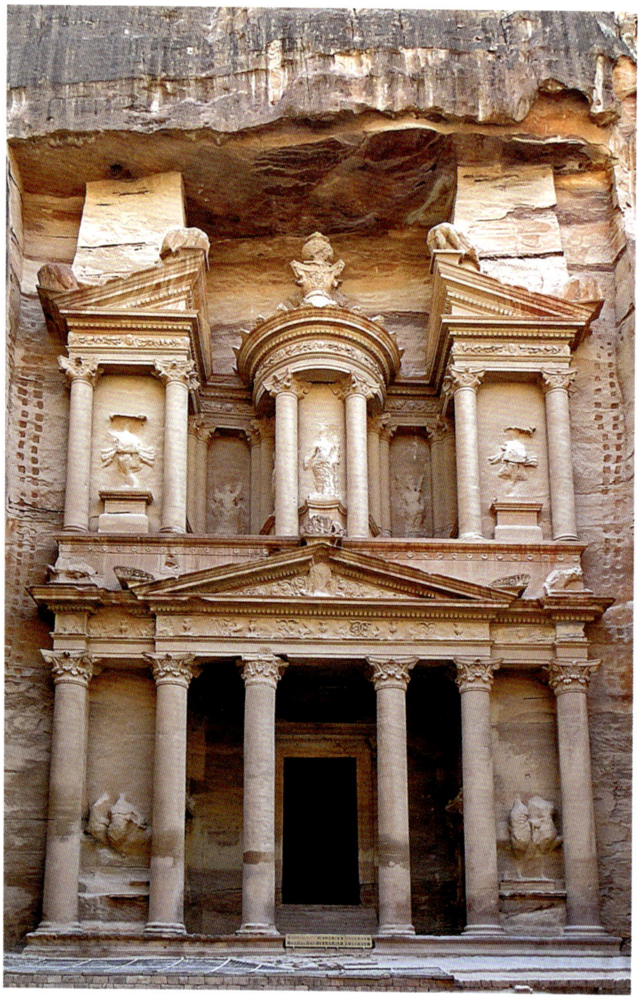

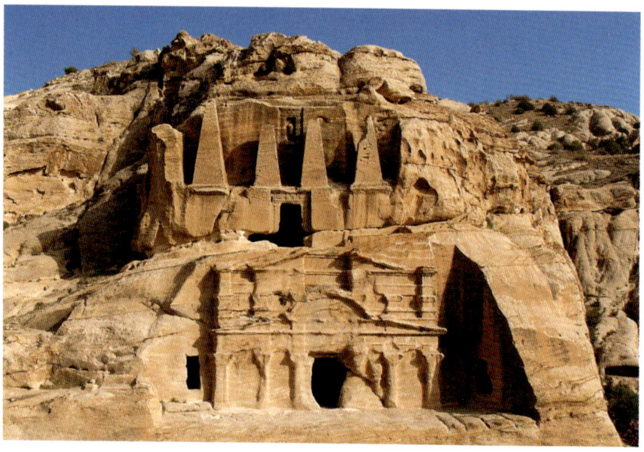

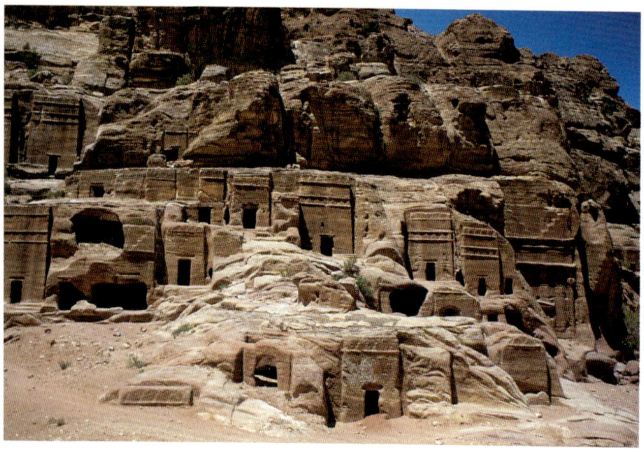

Top left - *The spectacular facade of the Khazneh, or "The Pharaoh's Treasury", has become the symbol of Petra. Its sudden appearance, at the end of the shady Siq gorge, is an indescribable emotion.*

Centre left - *The unique Obelisk Tomb and the underlying Triclinium, located on the southern slope of Wadi Musa, are the first large rupestrian monuments to be encountered by the visitor.*

Bottom left - *A glimpse of the so-called "Streets of the Facades", in the Outer Siq. These alignments of rock-cut tombs are a compendium of the different architectural styles that can be seen in Petra and confirm that the various models were in use simultaneously for several centuries.*

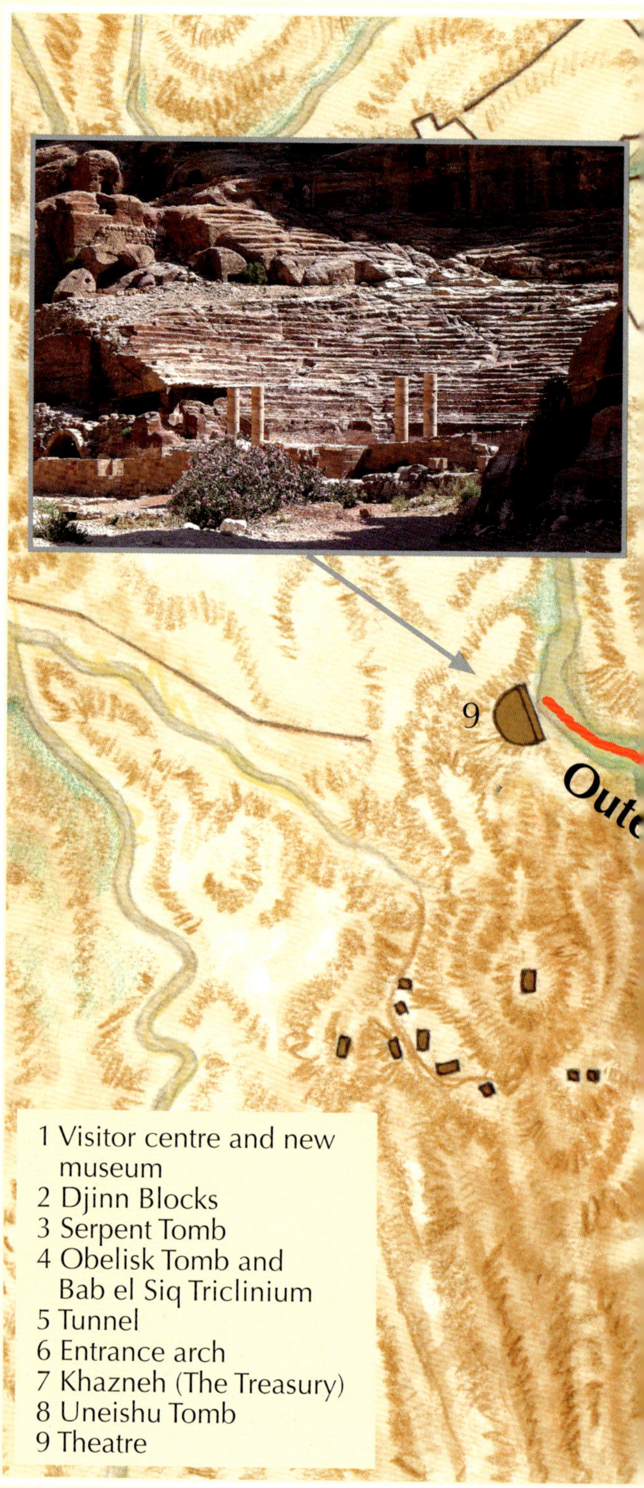

FROM BAB EL SIQ TO THE THEATRE

The first approach to Petra can only take place by going along its most famous and spectacular access route, which winds along the remarkable gorge known as the Siq. Along the way you will see some of the most important monuments of Petra, from the architectural point of view, like the Djinn Blocks, the Obelisk Tomb and the Bab el Siq Triclinium, the Uneishu Tomb, and the grand rock cut theatre. However, none of these can compare with the fame, beauty and majesty of the Khazneh, the symbol of the Rose City, which awaits the visitor at the end of the ravine. Although its image is well known to so many, the excitement that you feel when its sublime shapes suddenly appear is a unique and unforgettable experience.

The path is suitable for everyone, and it takes at least an hour each way. However, the magic of the Treasure and the other rock cut structures, as well as the amazing colours of the sands and the natural landscape, deserves a much longer visit to fully appreciate the allure of these mysterious places.

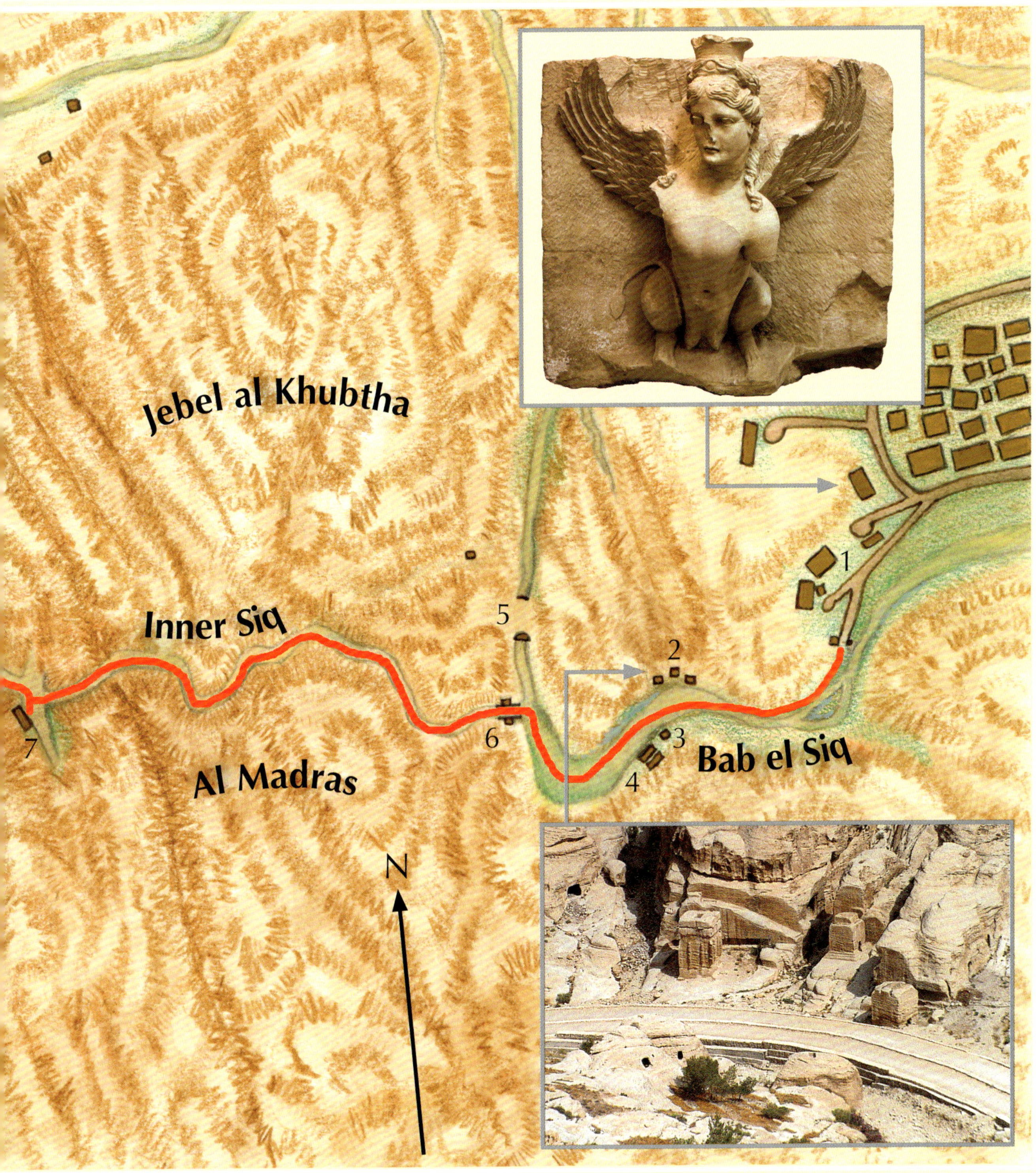

Monica Falcone

Before starting your visit to Petra and going through the entrance gates of the archaeological area, you should take a quick look at the modern town of Wadi Musa (also known as al Ji). This chaotic but picturesque expanse of buildings probably lies on the site of an ancient Edomite settlement, the ancient Gaia, which became a Nabataean centre of considerable importance, and perhaps also the seat of the local sovereigns before the court moved to Petra. Its inhabitants worshipped Dushara, the supreme god in the Nabataean pantheon, and it is no coincidence that he was also known as the "God of Gaia".
In the upper part of the village, at the entrance to the urban area, there is a small white building similar to a mosque, which houses the perennial spring known as **Ain Musa** (Musa is the Arabic translation of Moses). According to the Bible (*Exodus 17: 1-7*), the patriarch made the water spring forth by touching it with his staff, in order to quench the thirst of the people of Israel, as they walked towards the Promised Land. The presence of this spring was the main reason for the existence of the settlement. When Petra developed as an autonomous town, the water was diverted into a channel and led into the city along the walls of the deep gorge that is today known as Siq. In and around the modern Wadi Musa, you can still see a number of rock cut tombs (which were once part of the local necropolis), some cisterns, and above all the remains of terracing built by the Nabataeans for agricultural purposes. Near Wadi Musa, you can also visit the archaeological excavations of the Edomite site of Tawilan.
Next to the entrance gate of the archaeological area, incorporated into the luxurious Petra Forum Hotel, there is a beautiful tomb of considerable size, known

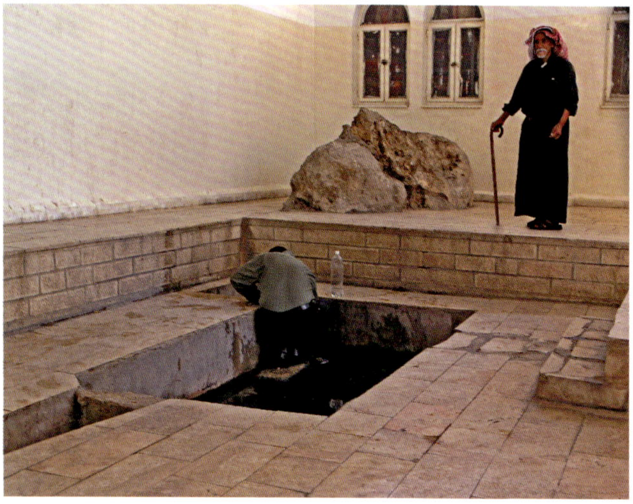

as **al Khan** (No. 4), which is now used as a bar. It is a double cornice tomb, and although the two large half merlons are now missing, it is particularly interesting because of the colonnade that precedes to it on two sides, carved into the living rock. It surrounded a consecrated space facing the burial site, and was typical of many of the monumental tombs of Petra. These enclosures (including ones that were smaller in size) were usually built in masonry, which explains why almost none of them remain intact today. In fact, over the centuries the region has been hit by powerful earthquakes, which destroyed almost all the buildings that were not rupestrian. The half merlons (which have now disappeared) on top of the facade were probably freestanding and not cut from the living rock. As we can see, the combination of rupestrian and traditional architecture in Petra was not as unusual as one might think.
Near al Khan, there are the remains of a kiln for firing Nabataean pottery (discovered in 1980), and an enormous reservoir (known as Zurrabah or al Birka), in which the water from the Moses spring was collected, before continuing on its way towards Petra.
At this point it is a good idea to stop for a moment and contemplate the surrounding valley. It is clear that the rare rainwater that falls over this vast area, all ends up flowing along the seasonal stream known as Wadi Musa, alongside the convenient dirt track that the tourists walk along. It seems impossible that such an insignificant trickle of water, when it is not completely dried up, could be transformed into a threatening mass of water, often several metres high, during violent storms. However, it was exactly this type of problem that the Nabataeans had to overcome in order to guarantee safe access to their capital.
We now find ourselves in the **Bab el Siq**, or rather the "Gateway to the Siq", a section of the valley hollowed

GAMEBOARDS

On the right side of the dirt track that goes down towards Petra, just before the Djinn Blocks, some curious patterns, formed of parallel rows of shallow holes, can be seen dug into the flat, sandstone surface. These are gameboards for the game of tab*, perhaps already used in the Nabataean period. Players had to arrange their "pawns" (stones or seeds in two different colours) in various holes – or boxes – then move them following complex rules with the aim of "eating" their rival's pieces. The movement of the pawns were linked to throwing four contoured sticks (used like a kind of dice).*
Many of these "chessboards" have been located in the Petra area thanks to archaeologist Bilal Khrisat's research; some can be seen near the shops at the gate of the archaeological park, others along the ancient rock-cut streets, one is close to the Urn Tomb, another is opposite the Deir.
Although many of the gameboards identified to date vary in their number of rows and holes, the most common board has four rows, each with twelve holes. These chessboards (several with truly incomprehensible game plans) are not easy to identify but give us an open window onto the daily life of Petra's ancient inhabitants.

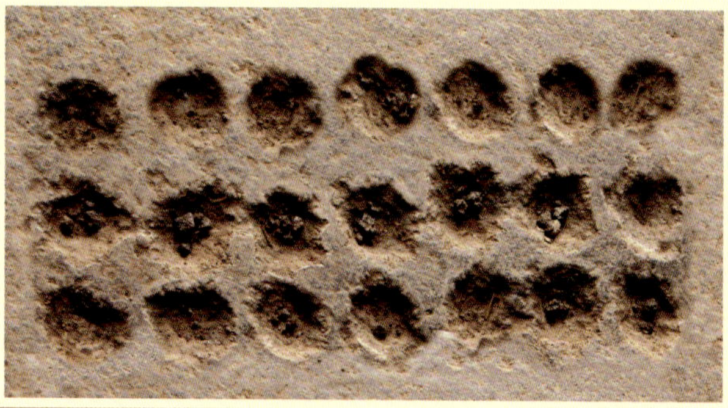

out by the Wadi Musa in a thick bed of sandstone, the whiteness of which is a contrast with the reddish colour of the surrounding peaks. It is a lunar landscape, with rounded rocks pockmarked with holes and cavities produced by wind erosion.
A few hundred metres from the entrance, where the first rock cut tombs start to appear, there are three curious monuments on the right hand side, with a distinctive shape. They are the so-called **Djinn Blocks** (Nos. 7, 8, 9), cut from the mass of rock of a large sandstone outcrop. In all probability, this enormous effort was necessary to widen the bed of the stream, and above all to make space for the road that went down towards Petra; at the same time, this huge excavation allowed the monolithic blocks to be created. The three enigmatic monuments, which the Bedouins once believed were inhabited by evil spirits (the *Djinn*) capable of scaring whoever they met to death, probably date back to a period between 50 BC and 50 AD, and they were used as tombs. The little rooms cut into the two smaller blocks, and the loculus carved out on top of the largest block, would appear to confirm this theory. The imposing ramp carved into the rock face behind it must have been used to raise the body, which would then have been placed in the rectangular cavity using a gangway. The loculus was originally covered with limestone slabs and sealed with mortar, but it was looted centuries ago.
According to the French archaeologist Michel Mouton, on the other hand, the Djinn Blocks in reality date back to the 2nd century BC or the first decades of the following century. He believes they were part of a funeral tradition from the Arabian Peninsula, and that they were not used as tombs, but rather as commemorative monuments close to the actual underground burial sites, excavated nearby. The loculus on the top of the main block and the rooms inside them would have been added later when the use was changed, according to this theory.
The first of the three blocks, which are between 5 and 8 metres tall, has Assyrian crowsteps carved around it in bas-relief, which are very eroded (they can only be seen when the light is at a particular angle). The second does not have decorations of any kind. The faces of the third one are each adorned with four pilasters. The plinths, capitals and cornices were made of another type of rock, which was harder, embedded into wide grooves and later wrenched off by raiders or just shaken off during one of the many earthquakes that struck the region in the past. Some fragments of them are still in place.

Opposite page - *The Ain Musa spring, from which a flow of perennial water gushes out.*

Above and below - *The Djinn Blocks were obtained thanks to an huge excavation work. Behind them we can see the groove in which the aqueduct ran that led to Petra the water of the Ain Musa spring.*

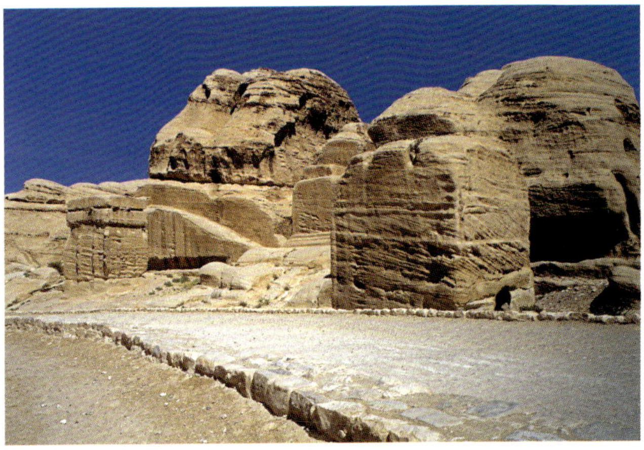

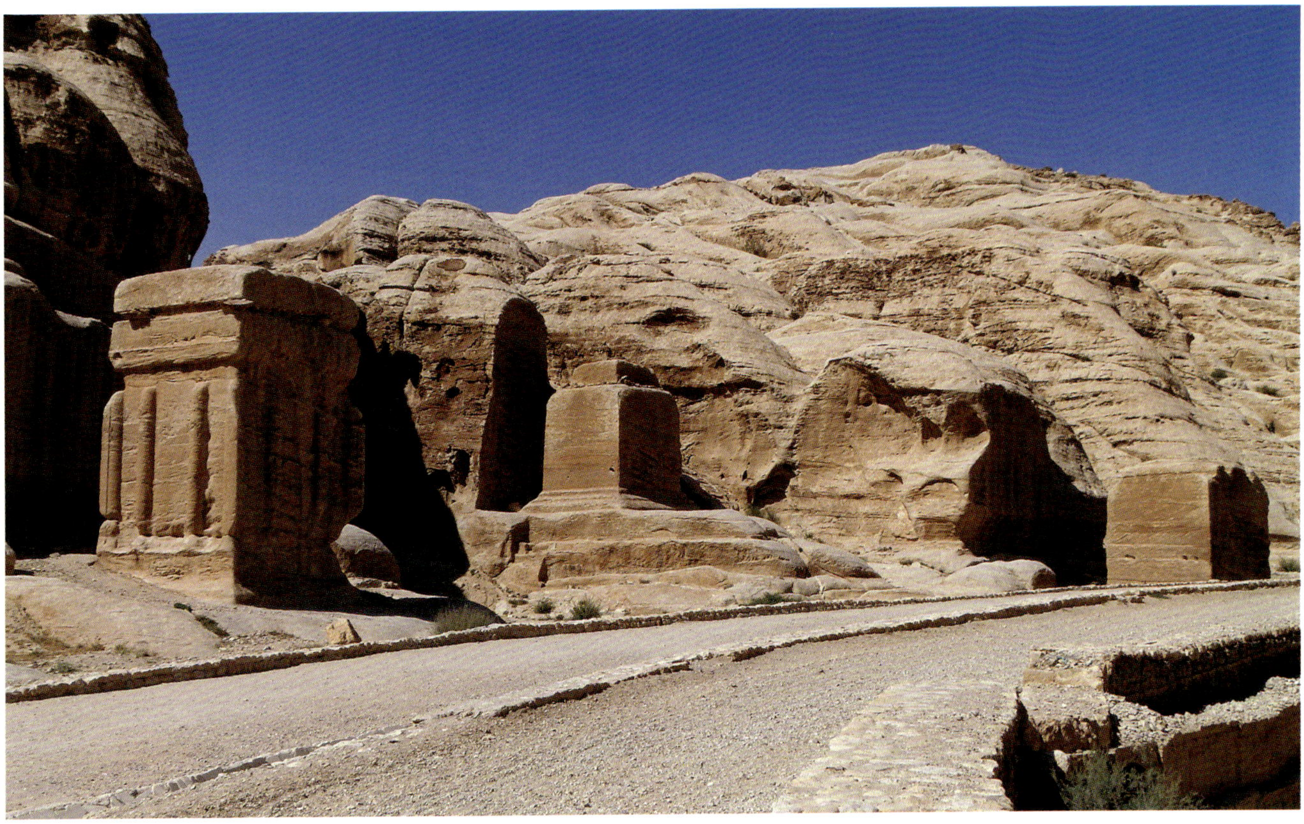

As has already been highlighted in the chapter dedicated to architecture, it should be remembered that the three Djinn Blocks originally looked different, as they had freestanding Assyrian crowsteps on top of them. In the case of the largest monument, these battlements were placed directly onto the top of the block, but in the case of the one situated higher up, they were set into the distinctive recesses on the top of the rock cut structure (together with the cornices).
It should be pointed out that, according to some researchers, the Djinn Blocks were actually divine resemblances dedicated to Dushara (often depicted in the shape of a cube), and put there to protect the path, as well as the entrance to Petra. According to others, the name Djinn (or "spirit") is a reminder of their function as receptacles for the guardian spirits of the Nabataean city. Finally, it should be remembered that the other Arabic name that they are known by - as Sahrij - means "water tank". This interpretation seems entirely misplaced. However, the recent discovery made by Mouton of an underground cistern next to monolith No. 7 (the one crowned with Assyrian crowsteps), which was fed by a channel that perhaps captured the water of the wadi Musa during the seasonal floods, would explain the strange name given to these monuments by the Bedouins.
Behind the Djinn Blocks, there is a deep crevice cut into the sandstone, which follows the line of the rocky reliefs. It is a section of the aqueduct that carried water from the Moses spring to Petra. It then proceeds with an almost constant gradient (4%) and continues all the way to the city. Observing its course, it seems clear that where it crossed deep valleys or other natural depressions, it must have flowed over little bridges that were specially built.
In the area where the three monoliths are situated, there are also some monumental tombs, mainly of the cavetto or Hegra type. One of these, which was partially completed (only two half merlons can be seen; photo on page 43), is very helpful for our understanding of the excavation techniques used by the Nabataeans. There are also several pit graves, probably for the lower social classes, which are believed to be some of the oldest in Petra, dating back to the end of the 2nd century BC and the middle of the 1st.
Right opposite the Djinn Blocks, on the other side of the wadi, a curious outcrop of sandstone can be seen, which is rounded off by erosion and has a short flight of stairs. This is the **Serpent Tomb**, a dromos tomb with a narrow entrance leading into a funerary chamber, which has 12 loculi dug into the floor. There is a bizarre bas-relief on one of the walls, which appears to depict two snakes attacking a quadruped, and another image showing a horse carrying a rectangular object on its back, probably a rider that was never completed. However, it should be said that Dalman thought it was a baetylus. The meaning of this representation remains a mystery, although the symbol of the snake was connected with the world of the afterlife, of which it was a guardian. The rather rough style suggests that the bas-relief was from a relatively late period.

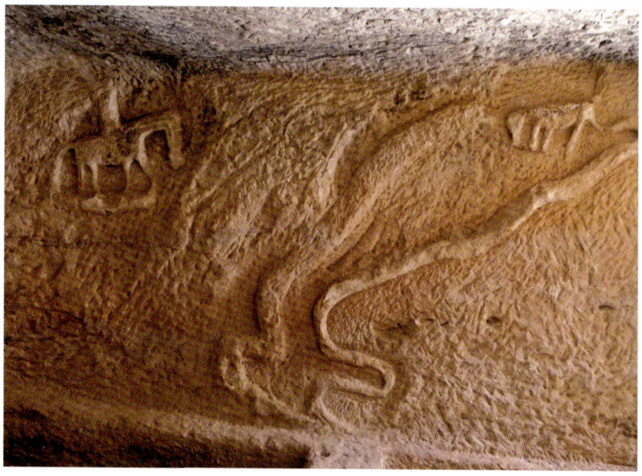

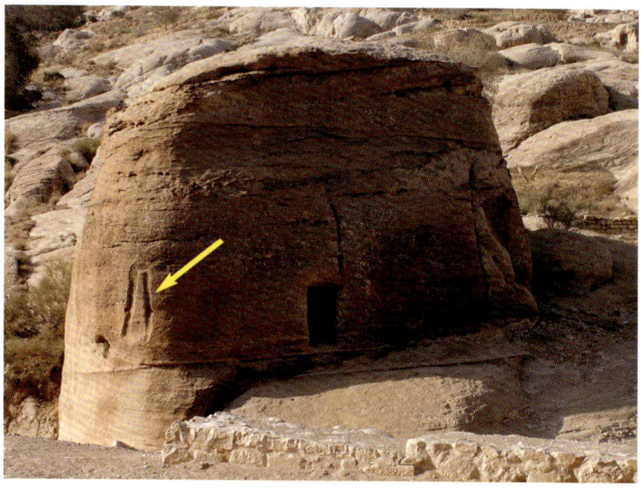

THE DJINN BLOCKS: A RECONSTRUCTIVE SUGGESTION

The so-called "Djinn Blocks" belong to a specific funerary monument typology called block (or tower) tomb and are a kind of three-dimensional version of the more widespread Assyrian style tombs.
Tomb 70 (page 78) and Tomb 824 close by, confirm that these tombs were adorned with a band of crowsteps. These could be carved from the solid rock or built in masonry just like the underlying protruding cornice.
The colouration suggested here is inferred from pigment traces still present on several tombs including Tomb 303, an enormous block tomb, situated close to the Snake Monument in Wadi Thughra.

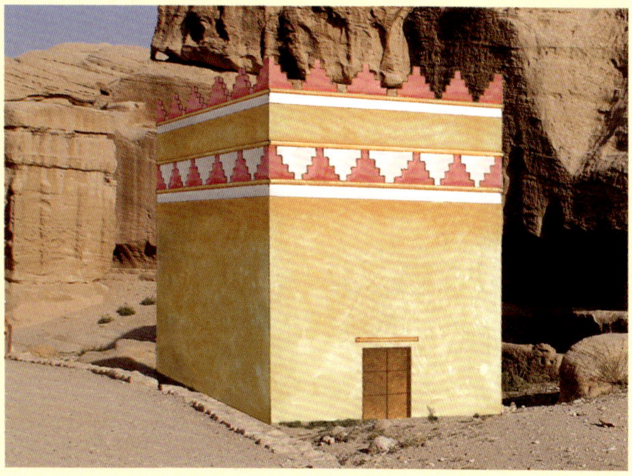

F. Bourbon M. Falcone

Next to the Serpent Tomb, another mass of sandstone is also noticeable because of its rounded shape. It has an unadorned door, to the left of which a bas-relief of a shape resembling an obelisk can be seen. It is a *nefesh*, or an aniconic representation of the soul of the deceased, used as a symbol to denote a grave. In the area of Petra, there are dozens of them, all more or less identical in shape. Some *nefesh* are adorned with a stylized crown, a flower or a pinecone, and the name of the deceased is sometimes engraved on the rectangular base. The fact remains that some of these bas-reliefs are to be found along the rupestrian paths, and are not connected with any of the tombs. In this case, it is thought they should be considered similar to the baetyli, which were aniconic representations of the Nabataean deities.

A few metres beyond the Djinn Blocks, on the left hand side of the wadi, the first two great monumental buildings of Petra immediately catch the eye. They are situated one on top of the other, so at first sight they seem to be a single architectural whole. The one above is known as the **Obelisk Tomb** (No. 34), which obviously takes its name from the four obelisks on top of it, originally about 7 metres tall and sculpted directly from the rock. Probably of Egyptian origin, and absolutely unique in Petra, in reality they would be as many *nefesh*, exceptionally made in three dimensions. Each one is thought to represent the soul of a deceased person. The relief carved into the wall behind the obelisks, which is inside a niche surmounted by a doric Nabataean frieze (one in which the triglyphs alternate with simple pateras, or discs), depicts a male figure, dressed in a Hellenistic or Roman style. The head, unfortunately, is missing. Some believe that he may be a fifth deceased person, whose body was placed in the tomb at a later date. The time difference between the different burials would explain the drastic change in the style of the monument. In fact, according to one plausible theory, the four obelisks were carved in the first phase, together with the funerary chamber, and later on, the monument was altered by adding the niche with the bas relief, and the Doric frieze over the door. This would explain the striking similarity between the ornamental motifs on the two architraves, clearly from the same period.

Dating the tomb is still a problem, however, in spite of the double inscription in Nabataean and Greek on the opposite side of the wadi (now very worn away, but already transcribed and translated in the nineteenth century), which mentions the burial of "'Abdmank, son of 'Akayus, son of Shullay, son of 'Utaih", who lived at

Opposite page, top - *The enigmatic bas-relief inside the Serpent Tomb. Although the equestrian image is unfinished, the crownpiece, the mouthpiece and the bridle of the animal are rendered with remarkable precision.*

Opposite page, bottom - *The arrow indicates the position of the* nefesh *visible next to the entrance of this tomb, dug into an isolated monolith.*

Below - *Although they look like a single entity, the Obelisk Tomb and the underlying Triclinium are indeed two very distinct monuments that were probably made in different eras.*

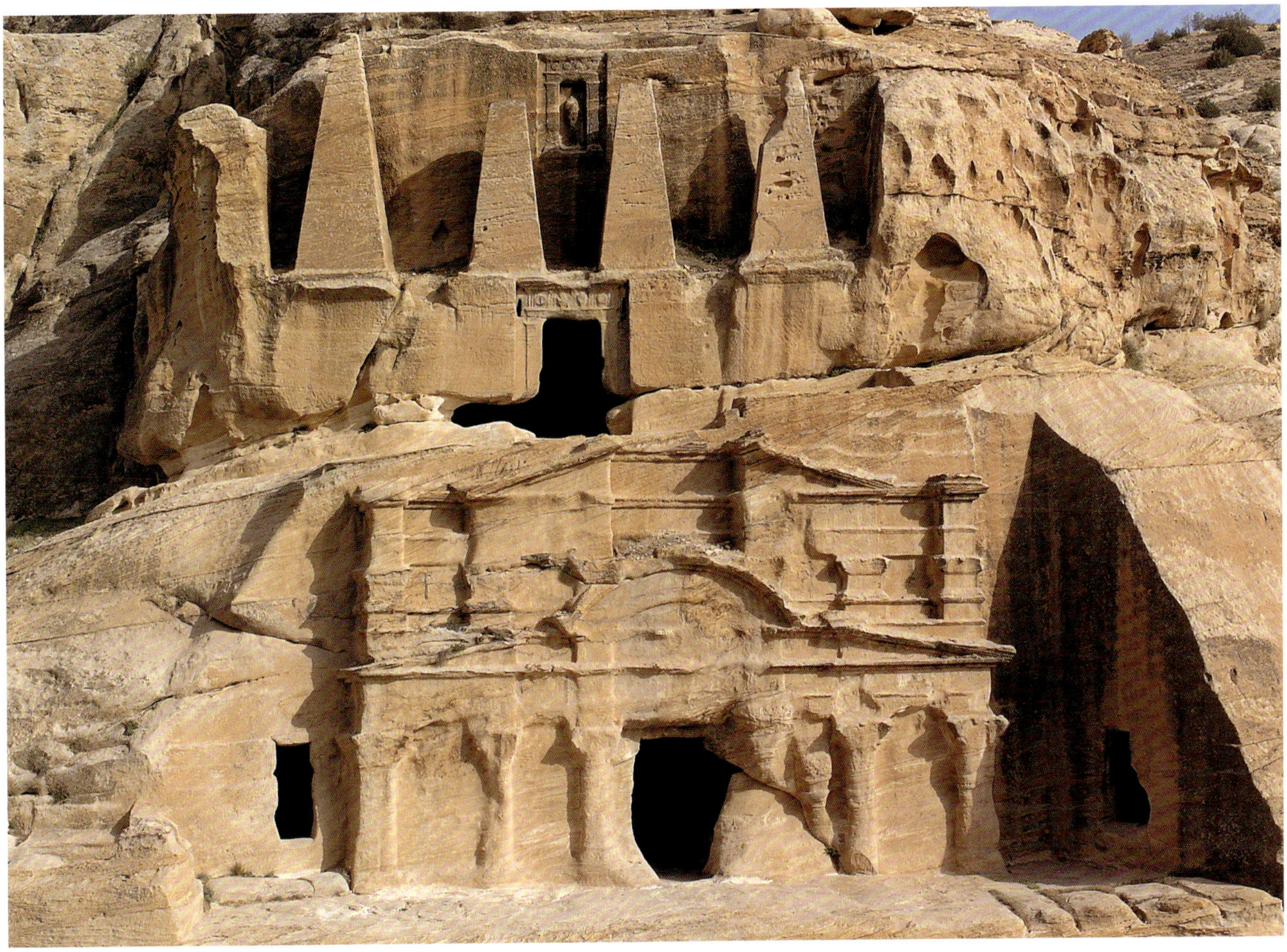

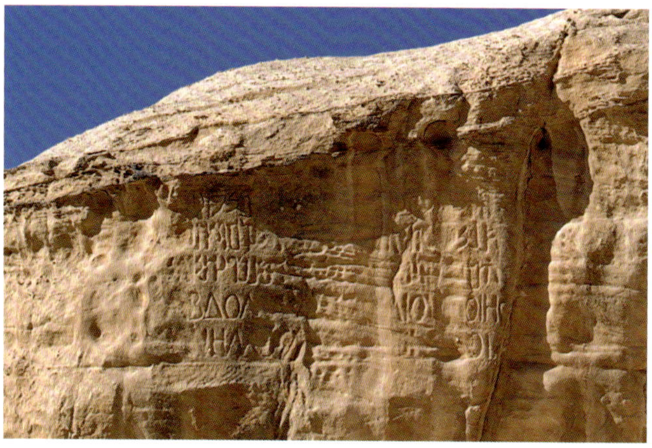

the time of King Malichos. Even if the inscription refers to the Obelisk Tomb, as it seems to, the fact remains that two kings called Malichos reigned in Petra, one from 60 to 30 BC, and the other from 40 to 70 AD. The use of Greek also shows that Petra was already a cosmopolitan city between the 1st century BC and the 1st century AD. In any case, inside the hypogeum, which is accessed through a door surmounted with a Doric Nabataean frieze, there are four loculi carved into the side walls and a fifth carved into the end wall, in the shape of an arcosolium. Another loculus is carved into the floor of the funerary chamber, to the left of the door. What seems to be a shaft tomb is accessible from the terrace in front of the facade, but the real function of this excavation is uncertain (some believe it was a cistern).
Only visible from above (or by climbing up to it, which is obviously not recommended), a deep duct has been dug out, about a metre above the site of the four obelisks, parallel to the line of the rock, and as long as the entire facade. In addition to gathering rainwater, this channel had the fundamental role of preventing the monument below from being worn away by erosion caused by the rainwater. This precaution was common to almost all the major rock cut works of Petra, and it is a testimony to the sophistication of the hydraulic engineering of the Nabataeans.
Under the Obelisk Tomb, but not perfectly in line with it, is the so-called **Bab el Siq Triclinium** (No. 35), a great triclinium hall for hosting banquets and symposiums, which took place periodically in honour of the dead. In fact, on the inside, which is completely unadorned, the benches running along three sides of the rectangular hall are well preserved. Unfortunately, this monument seems much more eroded than the tomb above. The elaborate design of the facade, with its series of pilasters, the curvilinear pediment over the door and the two half-pediments above, resembles the Corinthian Tomb (page 91), which suggests it is more recent that Obelisk Tomb. This is now believed to date back to the first half of the 1st century AD, and the triclinium is thought to have been built in the second half (during the reign of Rabbel II, the last Nabataean king), or even the 2nd century AD, during the Roman period. However, it should also be said that the British researcher Judith McKenzie believes the structures are from the same period.
Another question is what the real function of the monument was. In fact, some people think that the triclinium hall was built as part of the tomb above, while others believe that the tombs connected to the triclinium are

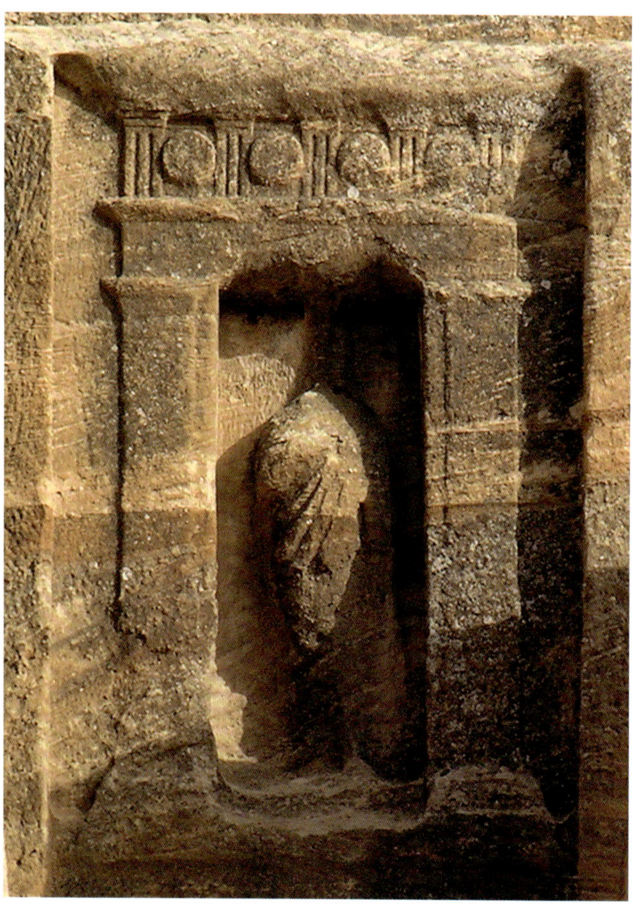

Plan of the Obelisk Tomb

A Burial chamber
B Arcosolium
(arched recess)
C Niches
D Shaft tomb (?)
E Stibadium (?)

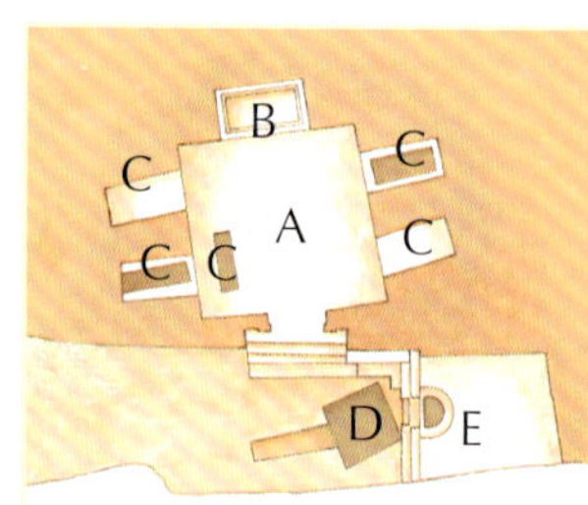

Map of Bab Al Siq Triclinium

A Great hall
B Triclinium benches
C Burial chambers
(or service rooms)

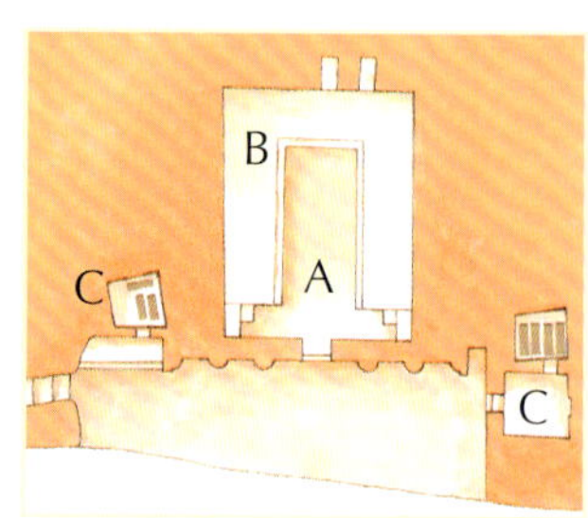

Left top - *The large bilingual inscription, carved on a rock facing the Obelisk Tomb. The Nabataean text reads: "This is the burial place chosen by 'Abdmank, son of 'Akayus, son of Shullay, son of 'Utaih, for the construction of a tomb for himself, for his heirs and for the heirs of his heirs, for eternity and beyond. He had made it in his lifetime, in the... year of the reign of Malichos".*

Left bottom - *The high-relief in the niche of the same tomb depicts a draped male figure.*

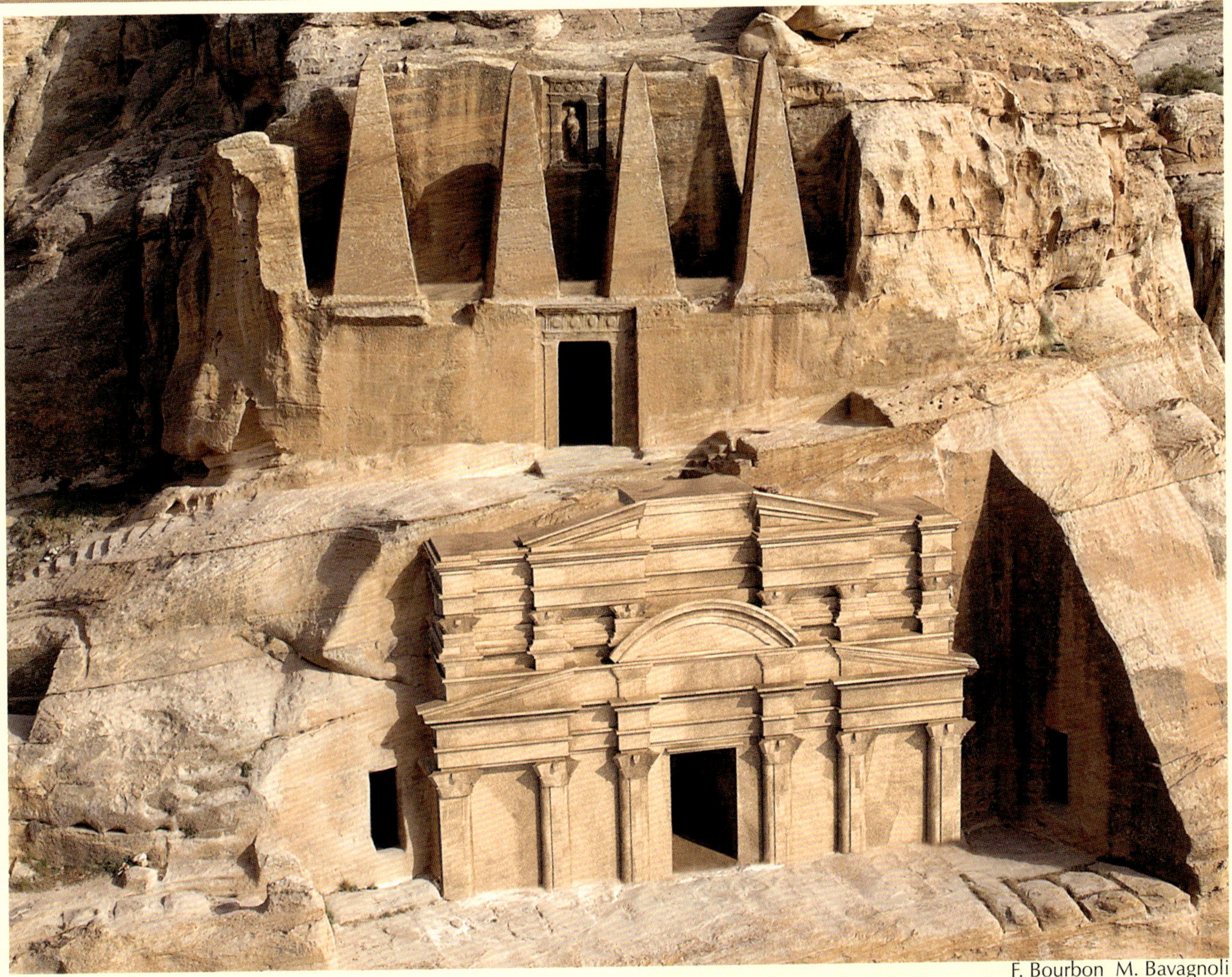

F. Bourbon M. Bavagnoli

THE BAB EL SIQ TRICLINIUM: A RECONSTRUCTIVE SUGGESTION

This is what the monumental complex consisting of the Obelisk Tomb and the Bab el Siq Triclinium, whose facade is now very damaged from erosion, must originally have looked like. This rock-cut structure is a good example of what has been defined as "Classical Nabataean Style" and displays many similarities with other monuments in Petra with a broken pediment, especially the Corinthian Tomb. Regarding the origin of the Obelisk Tomb, one piece of evidence supporting the theory of two distinct construction phases derives from the prominent cornices seen at the base of the outermost obelisks, instead missing in correspondence with the internal ones, plus the rearward position of the door in relation to the surface of the façade, which is most unusual in Petra's architecture. Probably, in the first instance (small image), the builders designed a kind of enormous altar on which the four impressive nefesh soar, with one simple door leading to the burial chamber. Later, the monument, which judging by several features may not have been finished, was reworked to contain a deceased person of high social ranking from the same family, and it was decided that a portrait in bass-relief should be sculpted in the niche and the doorway decorated more ornately with a similar frieze. This led to the two central cornices being removed and the door jambs being set back, so as to be able to sculpt the Nabataean frieze on the architrave. At the same time, in the funerary chamber, where there were already four funeral niches, two on each side, the arcosolium was carved into the back wall to contain the additional deceased person. This feature seems to have appeared rather late on the local architectural scene, hence it would be another confirmation supporting the theory. The loculus carved into the floor is probably the last burial to have taken place inside the great tomb.

Lastly, but worth mentioning, is the mostly unsubstantiated theory that the four obelisks were originally like mazeboth, or representations of aniconic divinities, which in virtue of their position at the entrance of the Siq would have offered powerful protection to the city. It is a compelling theory although it is highly improbable that a sacred monument was then transformed into a private tomb.

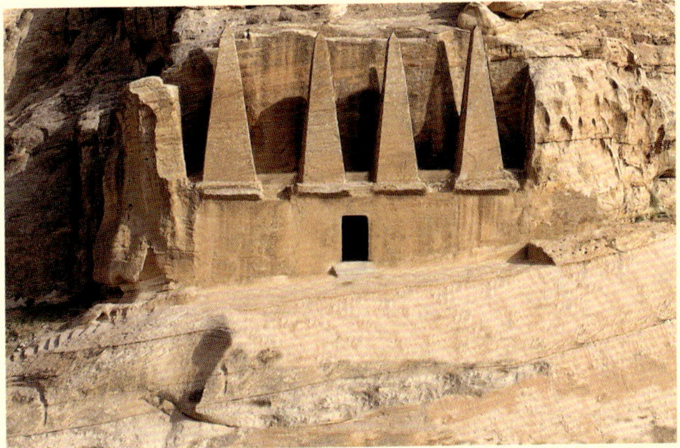

F. Bourbon

the bare chambers with loculi in the floor, which can be seen to the sides of the facade. However, they may have been service rooms, as can be seen near many other triclinia all over Petra, and the tombs excavated in the floors of the chambers could be the result of a later change of use, like the two loculi with graves in the back wall of the same triclinium hall. On the other hand, the presence of burials inside the triclinia, a notable feature in Petra, may suggest fluid boundaries between the living and the dead (as pointed out by the scholar Lucy Wadeson).

In the platform in front of the facade there are some deep fissures cut into the rock, which are evidence that the work was never completed by the stonemasons, as the general irregularity of the court would also suggest.

Leaving the Obelisk Tomb and the triclinium behind us, we continue along the Bab el Siq. We soon realize that the valley where Wadi Musa is situated is an immense funnel that gets progressively narrower, directing all the rainwater towards a huge bed of sandstone, against which the kinetic energy of the seasonal surges has been unleashed over the course of the millennia. This has opened up a fissure, possibly caused by an earthquake, giving rise to the actual Siq, or rather the Inner Siq. Before heading into this spectacular ravine, however, it is worth noticing a few other details. At this point, the course of the Wadi Musa, which is crossed by a reinforced concrete bridge, is blocked by a dam (dating back to 1964, and rebuilt in 1991), which redirects flash floods towards an impressive ditch cut in the solid rock, about a hundred metres long, which suddenly changes into an actual **tunnel**, 86 metres in length. Both the bridge and the dam have replaced similar structures already built in the 1st century AD by the Nabataeans, who were also responsible for the new course of the river and the tunnel. In fact, in order to prevent the flood waves from entering the Siq, which in the meantime had become one of the main access routes to the city, the Nabataeans diverted the course of the water into the nearby Wadi Muthlim, also known as the Little Siq. This meant that the waters of the Wadi Musa made a long deviation around the Jebel al Khubtha massif, and then returned to the ancient riverbed in the valley of Petra, right at the beginning of the Colonnade Street, now flowing much more slowly. Near the mouth of the tunnel, on higher ground, and completely isolated, a block tomb can clearly be seen (No. 30), decorated with Assyrian crowsteps in bas-relief. Not far from this is the interesting **Aslah Triclinium** (BD17), which according to an inscription dated 96-95 BC, was built by a certain Aslah in honour of the god Dushara and king Obodas I.

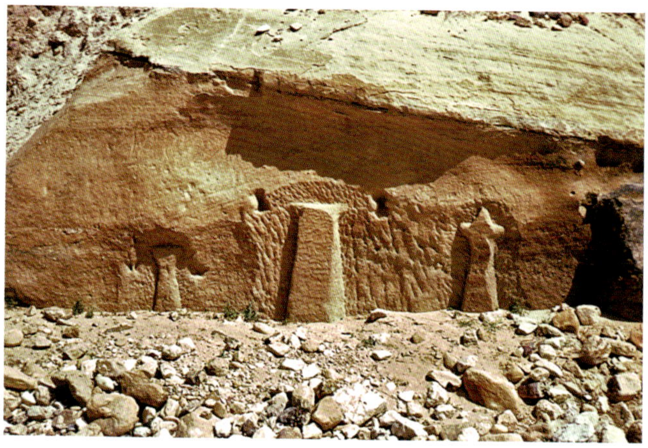

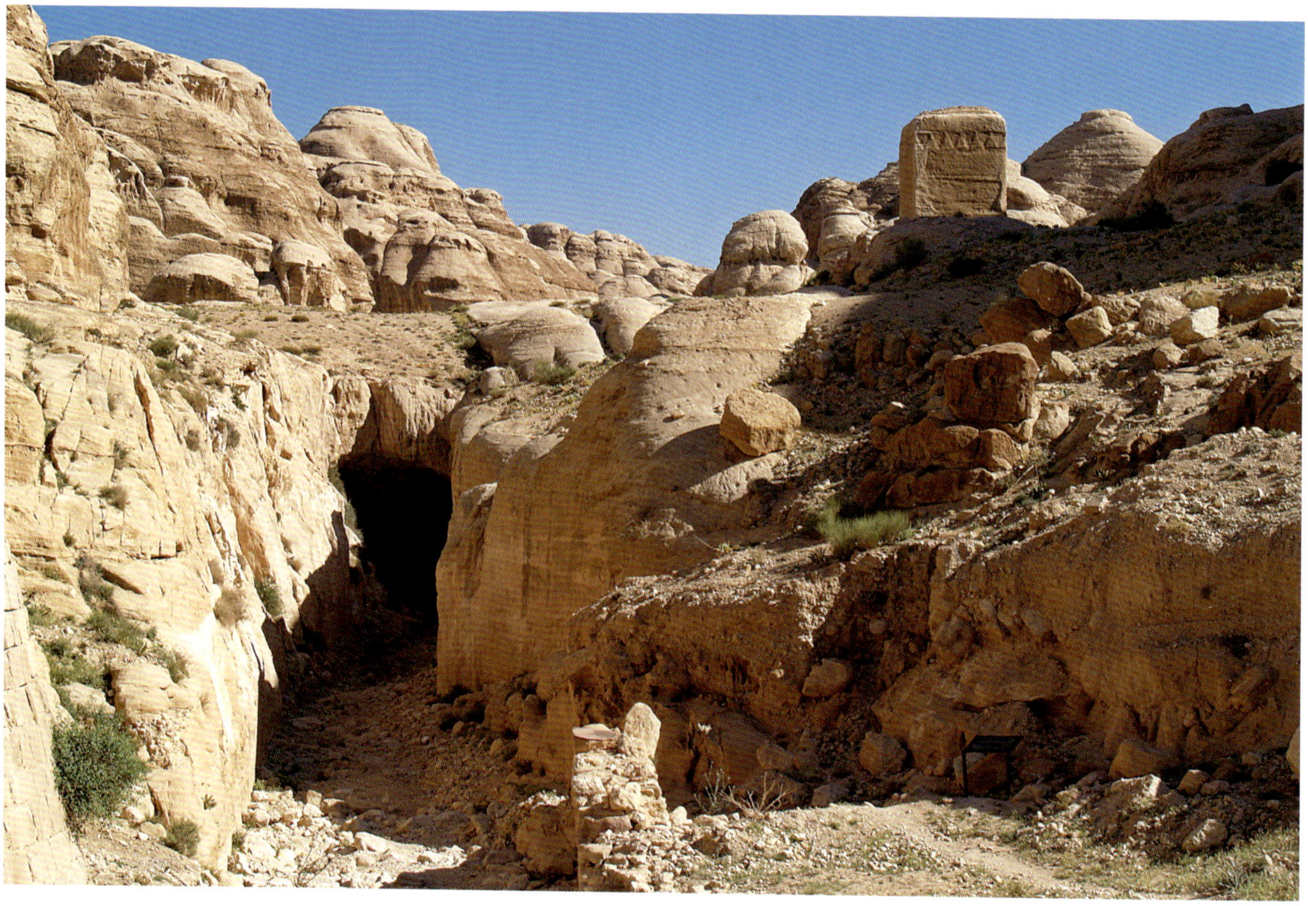

During the construction of the modern dam, some *nefesh* were discovered, one of which bore an inscription paying tribute to "Petraios, son of Threptos, born in Raqmu, who died and was buried in Garshu" (probably Jerash of the Decapolis, or perhaps Jurash in Saudi Arabia, on the border with Yemen). This Petraios probably died during a caravan expedition, but the most significant thing is that the ancient name of Petra was used here, that is *Raqmu*, which means "Multi-coloured". Never has a place name been more appropriate. Unfortunately, these *nefesh* are today hidden from view, covered by the modern dam.

Still on the right side of the wadi, looking towards the mouth of the Siq, on the rocky spur on the left, a deep groove, which appears to actually start at this point, can clearly be seen. In reality, it is necessary to visualize the water from the Ain Musa spring crossing the bed of the seasonal stream here, on an aqueduct made of masonry, which linked up with the one cut into the rock at this very point, and then continued on towards the city.

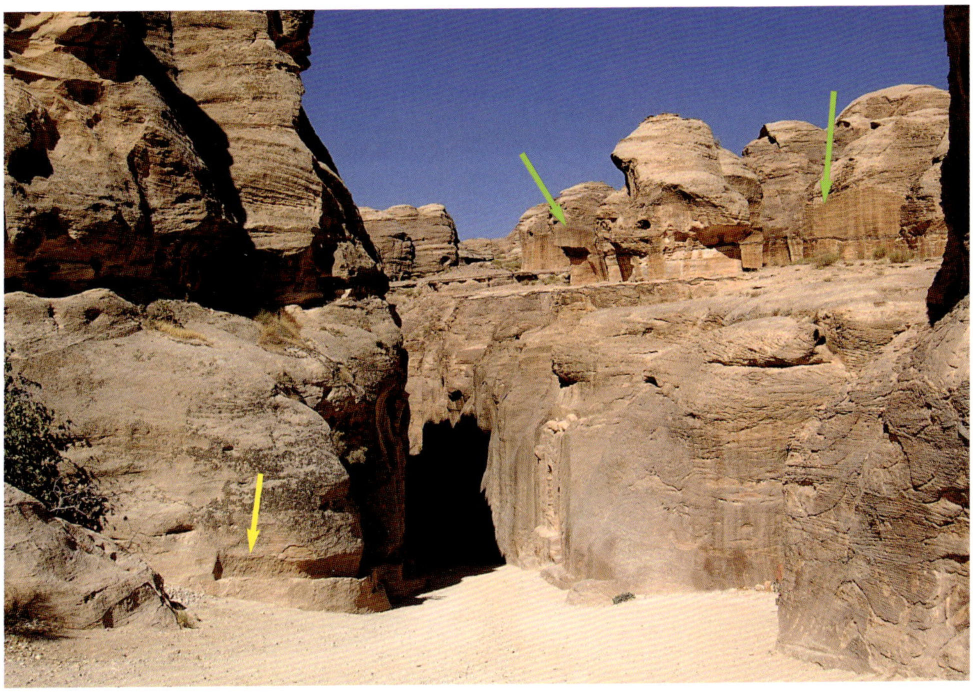

Opposite page, top - *A photo from 1976 showing the* nefesh *carvings next to which the ancient name of Petra was written.*

Opposite page, bottom - *The tunnel that diverts the waters of the Wadi Musa to the nearby Wadi Muthlim.*

Left - *The mouth of the Inner Siq. The yellow arrow indicates the point where the aqueduct, coming from the Ain Musa spring, which here crossed the wadi on a bridge, connected with the channel cut in the southern side of the gorge.*
The green arrows indicate the position of some Nabataean stone quarries.

AN ALTERNATIVE TRAIL: AL MADRAS

This hike is fairly demanding but very satisfying. It is recommended for those who have already done the classic Siq route but have more days to dedicate to their visit to Petra. However, it is only recommended for experienced hikers, otherwise it is advisable to use a local guide (and inquire if the path is viable). It takes a couple of hours.
A few metres after the Obelisk Tomb and on the same slope, a rather rugged and not very well signposted path leads westwards across an incredible landscape to al Madras, once one of Petra's suburbs. Once at the top of al Madras mountain (1107 m), where two large caves open up, you will be able to see a platform used for worship (or "high place of sacrifice"), carved as always into the living rock; opposite it is a long row of votive niches, some containing a baetylus. Nearby there are also several oil presses, cisterns and an underground chamber once used for religious symposiums.
A barely noticeable inscription dedicated to Dushara reveals that al Madras is the original toponym of the area, the only one in Petra to have kept its Nabataean name.
From here the view extends to Jabal Haroun, recognisable by the white chapel built on its summit. The path then continues across a barren plateau known as Jebel al Jilf. It is easy to lose your way here so a lot of attention is required. Passing a couple of modest Bedouin dwellings, the path continues towards a viewpoint at the end of the Siq where it opens up in front of the great Khazneh, Petra's most famous monument. The aerial view enjoyed from this vertiginous position is unparalleled.
To descend towards the Khazneh from here, you need to backtrack a few steps then veer left, going down an endless staircase carved into the rock, along what is known as Danqur el Khazneh. The way down is fairly worn in places, but it is really worth the effort. From the top, the ruins of several Nabataean dams and connected channels can be seen on the right. The route ends at the open space in front of the Treasury which is always crowded with tourists.

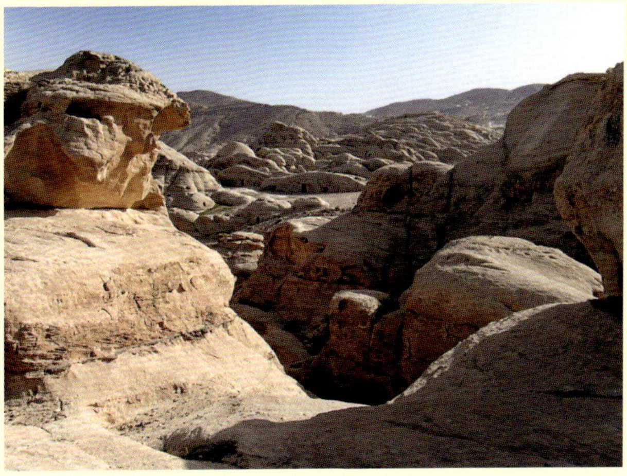

On the other side of the modern bridge, the dirt road suddenly becomes quite steep and abruptly enters the inner Siq, which is a fissure (*thaniya*) in the mountain formed after an earthquake in ages past, and then shaped by the tireless erosion of rain and wind. The spectacular gorge is just over 1,200 metres long, and its sides, which are 90 to 180 metre high, are no more than three metres apart in some places. The entrance to this natural wonder is marked by the remains of an imposing **arch**, whose abutments, which were carved into the rock, are eroded but still visible. The two niches between semi-columns probably had statues in them. The deep aedicula (or shrine) that can be seen next to the right abutment of the arch, however, must have contained a sacred image and therefore had a religious function. This likeness could be reached by climbing three high steps cut into the living rock. The date of construction of this monumental doorway is not known, but given the obvious Roman influence, it must date back to either the second half of the 1st century AD, or perhaps even the period after the conquest of Petra by Trajan. However, it is certain that the arch itself, which is depicted in a lithograph by the Scottish landscape painter David Roberts, collapsed in 1895 or the year after, although a few stones are miraculously still in place.

If you look at what is left of the arch from a few metres uphill and then look towards the rocky foothills above, on the right hand side, you will notice the face of an old stone quarry, recognizable by the straight lines cut into the rock, in stark contrast with the surrounding

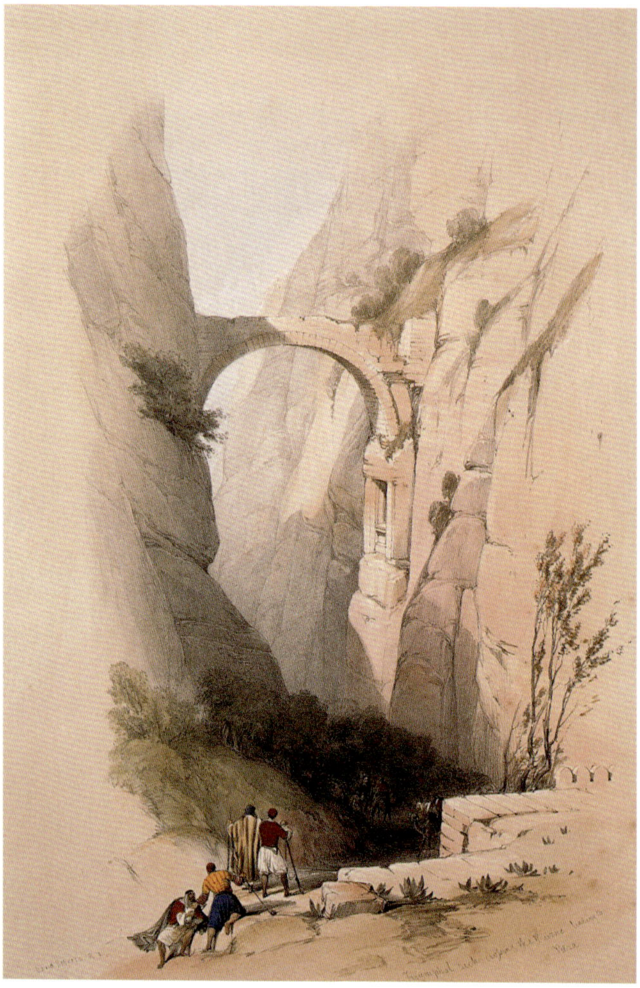

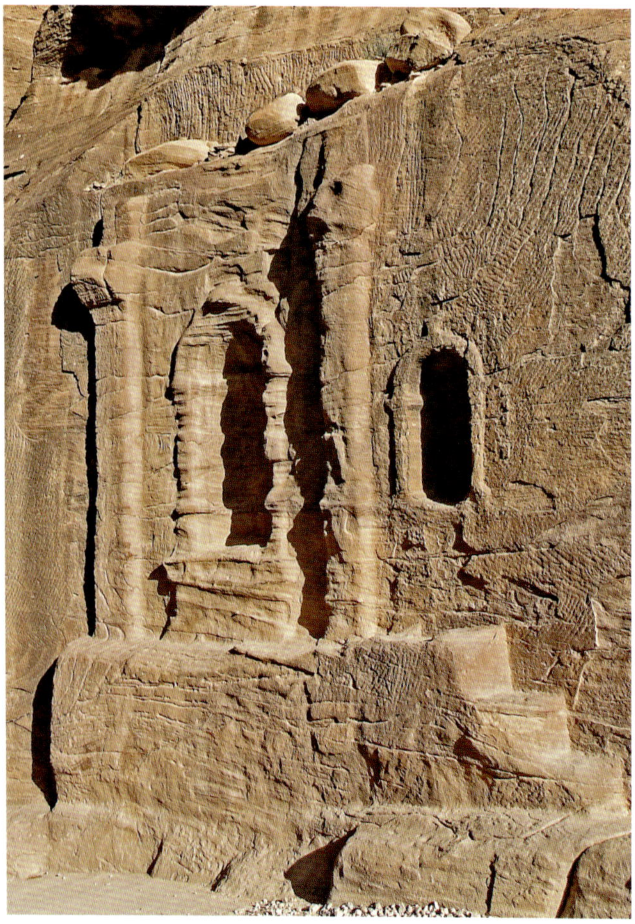

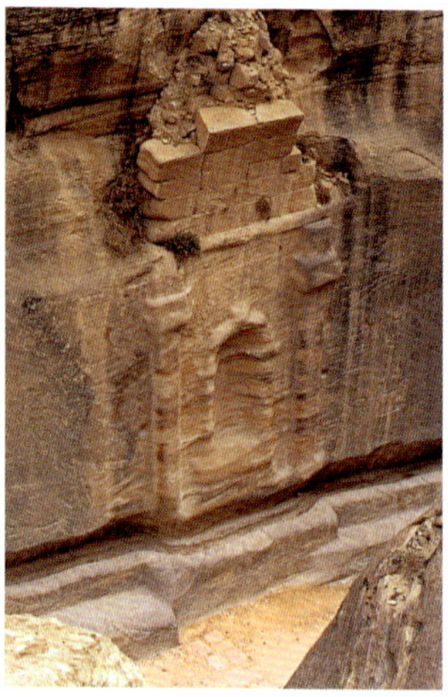

Left - *The northern abutment of the arch, with the votive niche next to it.*

Top right - *This lithograph by David Roberts depicts the arch that once stood at the mouth of the Siq.*

Below right -*The southern abutment of the arch, with the groove of the aqueduct.*

Opposite page - *Two views of the Inner Siq with the deep grooves of the aqueducts.*

landscape with its uneven shapes. The ashlars used to build the dam and the Nabataean bridge were probably extracted from it, as well as the slabs necessary to erect the arch, surmounted with an attic. If you climb up there on a very steep rock cut staircase (which is not recommended), you will notice some sloping surfaces cut into the sandstone, which were used for transporting the material extracted to the ancient building sites. What may have been a room, partially excavated into the rock, and the ruins of some walls adjoining it, are difficult to interpret. Perhaps there was a guard post here, situated on high ground, and therefore strategic for keeping watch over the entrance to the city.

Before moving on, it is important to remember that the

appearance of the Siq has changed a lot over the years. In fact, when the dam that protected the opening of the canyon fell into ruin, because of the abandonment of the city and the earthquakes that affected the region, the waters of the wadi had free rein once again. The erosion upstream and the depositing of detritus downstream (with the addition of sediment from the surrounding valleys) changed the face of the Siq, and caused the serious erosion of many of the artifacts along its course. It has been calculated that in the first section, the original surface of the road was about two and a half metres higher than it is today, while towards the bottom, the ancient paving is more than 4 metres below the current ground level. It is generally thought that the gorge was regulated with a constant gradient (5%), and was paved with stone in the second half of the 1st century AD. Remains of the original paving, uncovered between 1996 and 2002, are visible in several places.
All the way along the Siq, carved into both sides of the ravine, two deep grooves with a familiar appearance can be seen. These are the channels made in various different historical periods, which carried water to Petra from the Moses spring. The one on the northern side (or the right, if you are going down) is the oldest. Strangely, the groove in the rock is missing for several metres, downstream from the monumental arch, and it then starts suddenly. In reality, this can be explained by the fact that this aqueduct was built before the dam. When the Nabataeans erected the dam, they had to raise the level of the earth by at least two metres, and the old channel was buried under the paving in this section, and then returned to the surface in correspondence with the evident carving. If we look at the abutments of the arch, it is immediately obvious that the left hand one was carved away at the base, to allow the channel to pass. This suggests that the southern channel was made quite late on, after the arch was built in any case. As well as having to bring the water of the Ain Musa to the city, the Nabataeans also had to deal with a problem that seems unimaginable today, which was regulating the sudden surges of rainwater inside the Siq. During the spring and autumn, as already mentioned, a considerable amount of rain can fall in a short space of time. The water flows down the

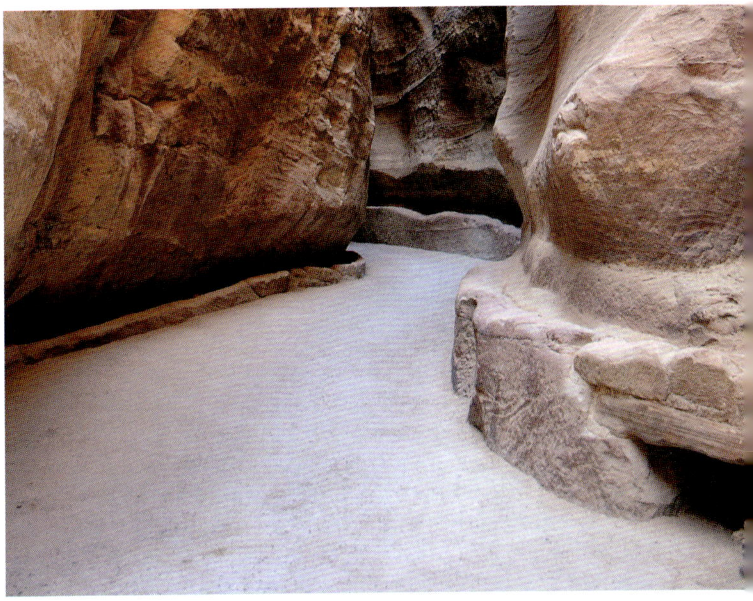

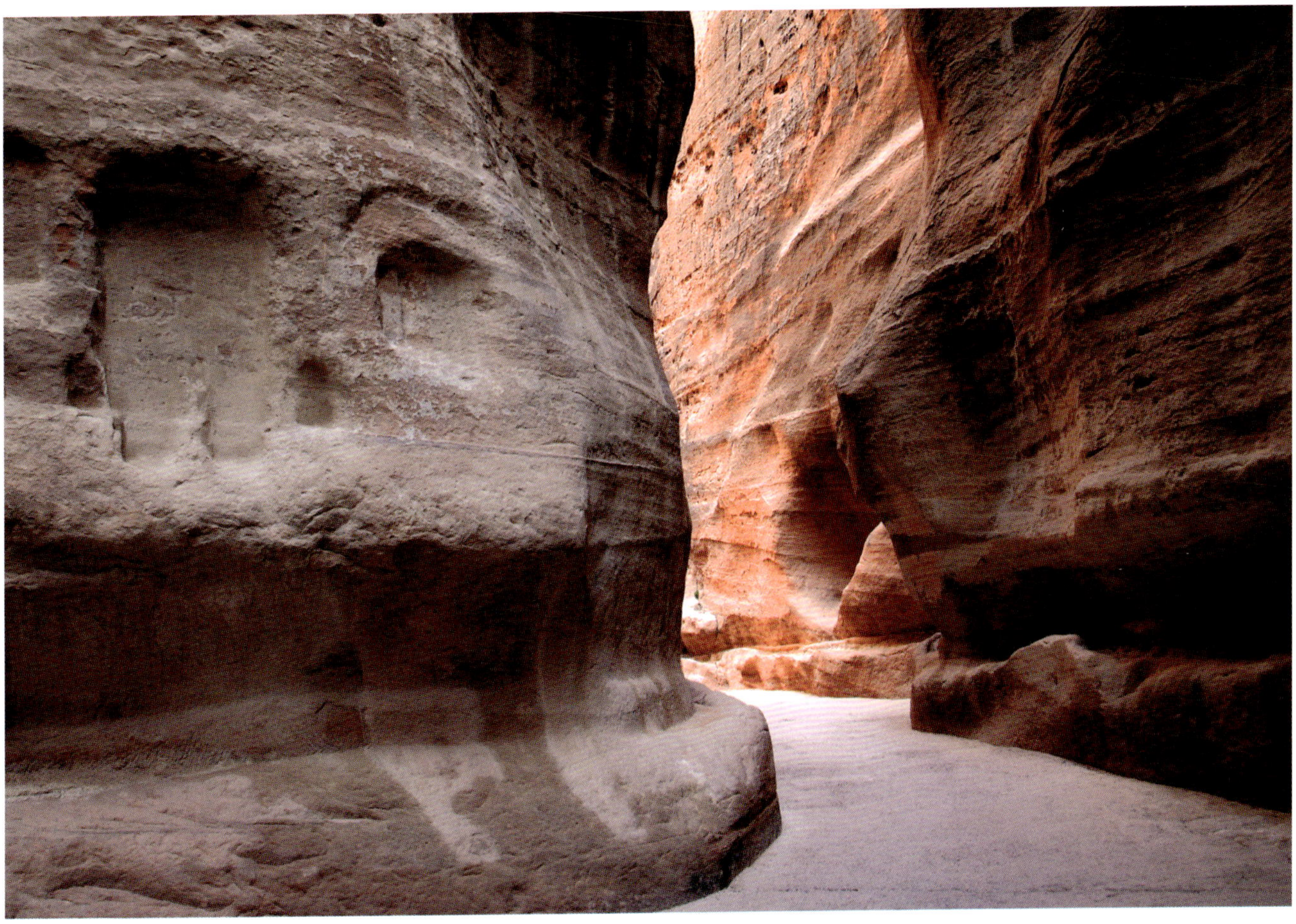

slopes of bare rock and speeds up, rapidly forming rivulets and little waterfalls, and then actual streams that hurtle along the side valleys and converge in the Siq, forming a flood wave that can be several metres high. The Nabataeans were well aware of this danger, and they designed an intricate and effective network of channels, dams and pools, which had the dual purpose of preventing the floods and feeding the system for supplying the city with water. In the last few decades, in order to make the most famous entrance to Petra safe, the local authorities have restored a large part of this system, by rebuilding the dams in the side valleys of the Siq (al Madrass, al Jilf, al Qantara to the south; al Khubtha and al Ajuss to the north) and restoring long stretches of channelling, so visitors can now go into the gorge in complete safety. In particular, the dams situated at the bottom of the Wadi Madrass and the Wadi Khubtha give us a realistic idea of what the ancient Nabataean dams must have been like.
Continuing along the Siq, you will notice that the channels are at different heights, so much so that in some places the right hand one is almost at the level of the paving (or below it), while the one opposite is always fairly high, and follows a more regular course. This suggests a more advanced design, and therefore that it is from a later period. In any case, the water in the two aqueducts did not flow in the open air. The older one, on the north side of the Siq, was made up of a fissure cut into the rock, with a earthenware pipe made of cylindrical sections (some of which are still in place), specially designed with male and female terminations to allow a tightfitting conduit and joined together with plenty of mortar. This limited leakage, and also regulated the pressure. Some of these terracotta pipes are on display in the museum. In the more recent aqueduct, on the south side, the water flowed in a channel lined with hydraulic mortar and covered with slabs of stone carefully connected with mortar.
These ancient builders clearly had a good knowledge of hydraulics, as the gradient of the aqueducts was as constant as possible and never assumed an inclination greater than 4 degrees. This was to avoid creating turbulence inside the pipes, which would have led to rapid internal deterioration.
Archaeological investigations have also established that the two aqueducts were restored on several occasions, in ancient times. In particular, the southern one was altered in the Byzantine era using cement (which in some cases partly obliterated pre-existing shrines).

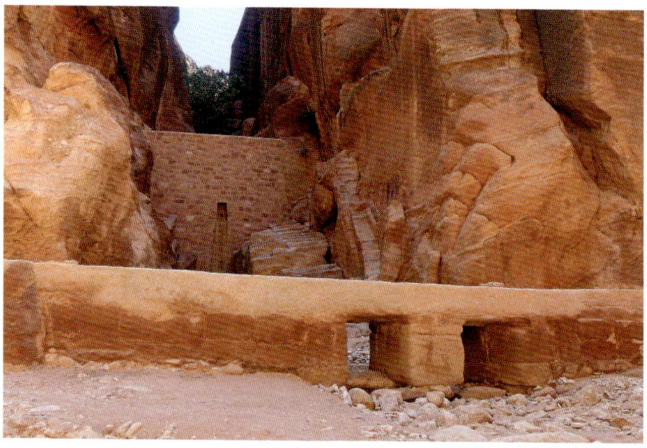

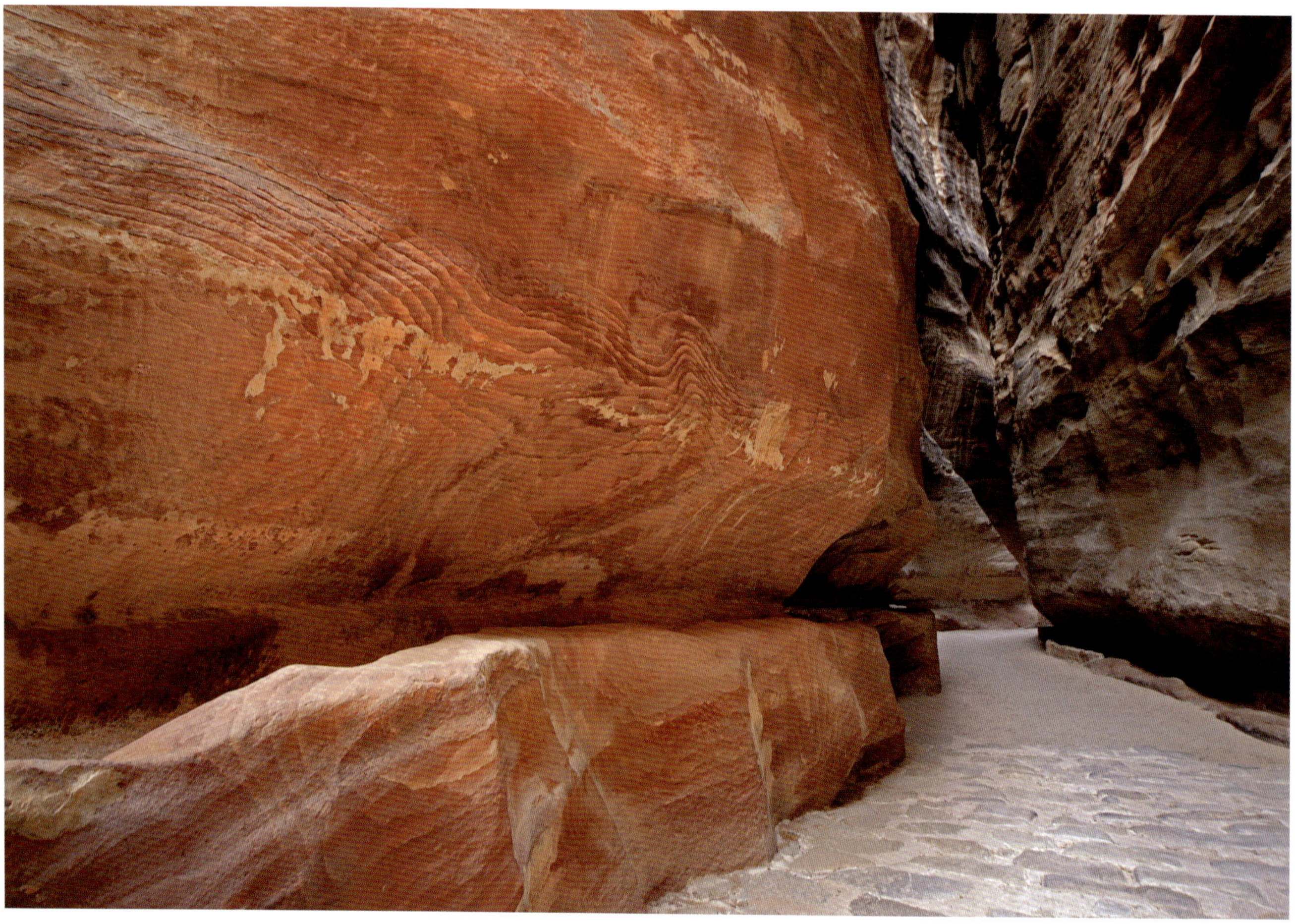

The excavation and restoration work has also brought other details to light, and as a result, sections can be seen where the pipe ran along the top of walls built in masonry, rather than carved into the rock. Where the Wadi al Ajuss opens into the Siq (*page 24*), recesses can be seen, in which were inserted the struts of the viaduct that allowed the watercourse to continue unbroken. Elsewhere, four small fountains used by wayfarers have been discovered, as well as some settling basins, which are rectangular pools, where the water from the aqueducts was discharged and purified, as the finer sediments were deposited on the bottom. These basins also probably helped release the pressure, or in any case reduce the speed of the flow in the channels and pipes.
Along the Siq there are about fifty baetyli and niches carved into the rock, as well as numerous inscriptions in Nabataean and Greek, which is evidence of the sacred atmosphere that permeated it. These were mainly testimonies of faith, or offerings left by the Nabataean merchants arriving in Petra and leaving it. Authentic historical testimony is an inscription that directly refers to the Cyrenaica 3rd Legion. This was the unit of the Roman army that – coming from Egypt – played the most important role in the occupation of Petra in 106 AD, and from then on, it was stationed in the city.
Many of the niches contain a single baetylus, and others have up to ten. About a third of the way down the Siq, where the gorge widens, stands a solitary boulder of sandstone with a wild fig tree growing next to it. The downhill side has a large niche flanked by two pillars with Nabataean capitals, surmounted by an architrave with a Doric frieze. Inside it, there are two baetyli, side by side. The one on the right, which is smaller, is

Opposite page, top - *The Wadi al Qantara dam; where the aqueducts intersected the mouth of the lateral valleys of the Siq, the pipeline passed over bridges built in masonry, which today have largely been rebuilt.*

Opposite page, bottom - *A glimpse of the Siq, with a well preserved section of the original paving. It should be noted that the two aqueducts run at different heights.*

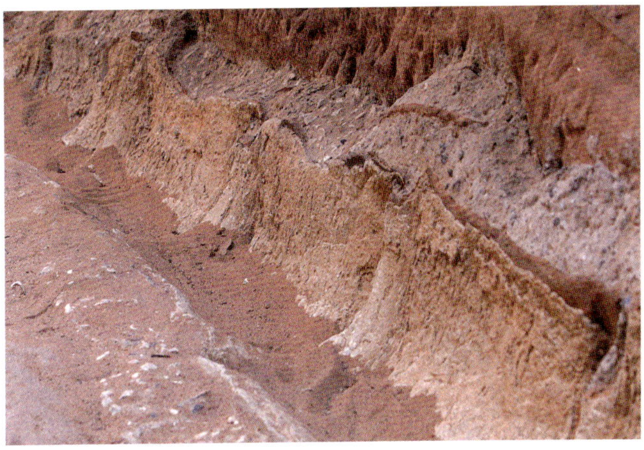

Above - *At various points along its route, the northern aqueduct has preserved traces of the terracotta pipes, which were housed in the groove cut in the rock with an abundant layer of mortar.*

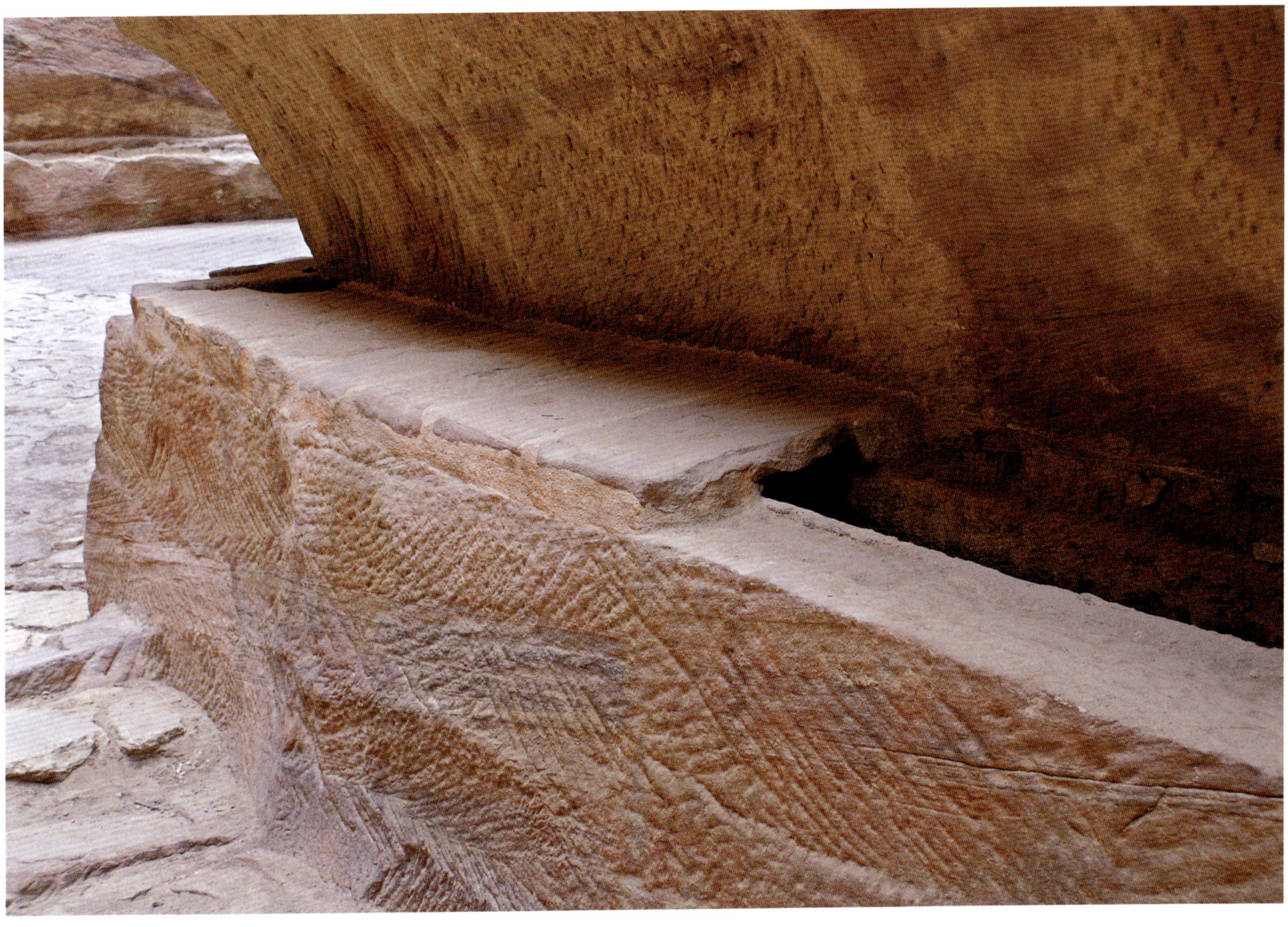

Below - *The southern aqueduct has been carefully restored in some sections. Here, the ancient conduit still retains the original covering in stone slabs connected with mortar.*

smooth, while the one on the left has a highly stylized face with rectangular eyes and a linear nose. It is believed to represent Al Uzza, one of the most important Nabataean deities. The shrine, which is the biggest in the Siq, is generally believed to date back to the reign of Malichos II (40-70 AD).

The natural widening of the canyon, like the smaller ones upstream and downstream, must have served as a caravanserai, or rather a stopping place for the caravans that passed through Petra, as they went back and forth between the Mediterranean and Arabia, or Syria and Egypt. At this point, some artificial rooms can be seen along the rock faces. They were certainly not tombs or houses, but probably served as guard posts or "offices" for tax collectors. In some places, if you look very carefully, you can see some through-holes for passing ropes through, cut into the rock a few metres from the ground. On close observation, a peculiar kind of erosion can be seen, like the wear produced by running a rope through it over a long period of time. You can imagine that during the hottest months, in some sections of the Siq, especially where there were caravanserais, great tarpaulins were stretched from one side of the gorge to the other using a system of ropes and pulleys, to provide shade. Similar systems are still used today in the streets of many cities in areas where there is a hot climate (for example in Seville). This also explains the presence of some stairs cut into the sandstone, which may have been used for manoeuvring the large tarpaulins, and would otherwise be difficult to account for.

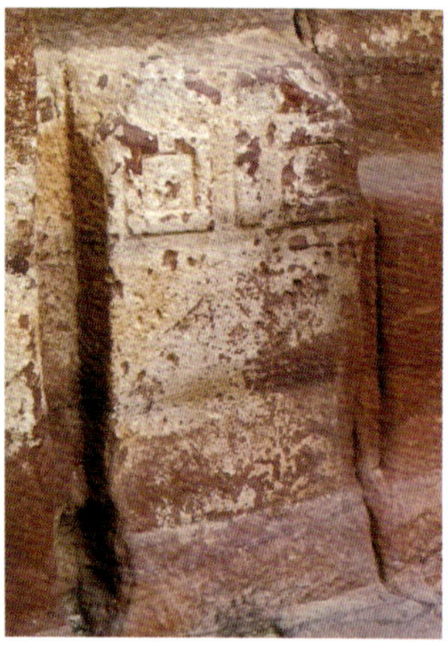

Below - *The large votive aedicula carved in a sandstone outcrop, in a place about one third of the way along Siq. The two pilasters with typical Nabataean capitals are surmounted by an elegant architrave with a Doric frieze; in the centre there are two baetyli side by side.*

Left - *The strongly stylized face of the larger baetylus is believed to represent the goddess Al Uzza.*

Further along from this natural widening of the Siq, there is another one, which is smaller in size. On the southern rock face there are three niches with inscriptions in Greek. One contains an oval shaped baetylus dedicated to the god Dushara, dating back to the 2nd century AD, which is unusual. Next to this, there is another shrine with a divine effigy, which although very eroded, is certainly of a figurative type. This confirms that during a particular period, both the aniconic and the figurative styles were used to represent the gods.

A little further on, still on the southern side of the Siq, there is a group of sculptures, which were discovered in 1998 during the work that led to the lowering of the level of the road by more than 2 metres. The enormous high relief dates back to the middle of the 1st century AD. Although the upper part is very eroded, the figures

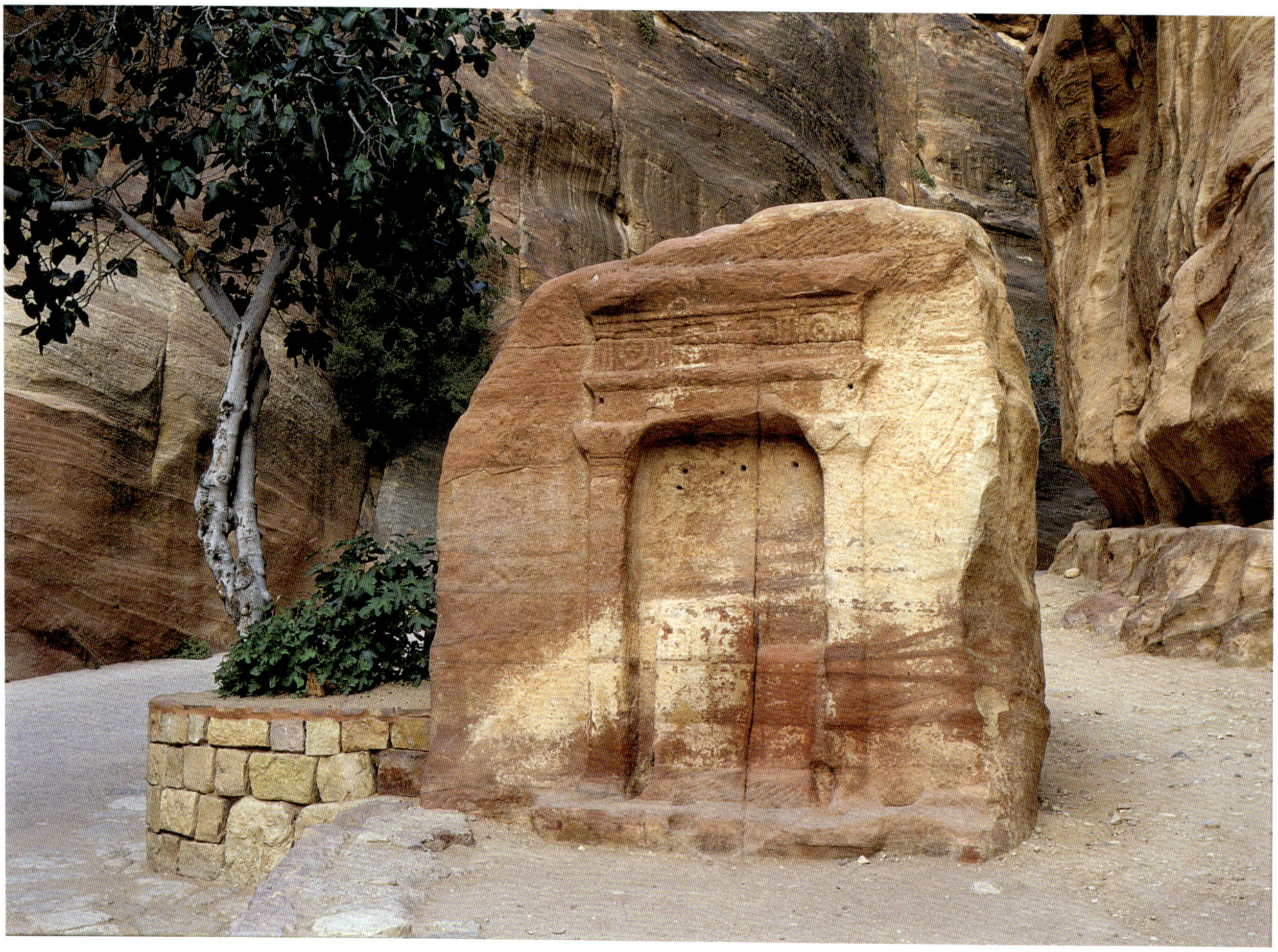

VOTIVE NICHES: TWO RECONSTRUCTIVE SUGGESTIONS

There are also some figurative representations in the Siq next to the aniconic representations of the Nabataean gods, although they are barely recognisable today due to iconoclasts of the Umayyad period. On the north side of the Siq, in a votive niche (D 144) with pilasters crowned with a tympanum with three acroteria, you can make out a seated human figure. Given its likeness to two similar and better-preserved reliefs (one in Wadi Siyyagh, the other in Wadi Dalaw), we can deduce that the divinity portrayed is Al Uzza-Isis. The three masks joined by two garlands seen on the architrave, are based on a pattern that is reproduced on a larger scale in the frieze that crowns the Khazneh's broken pediment (photo page 67 below). Although this niche is often mistakenly presented as a sort of representation of the Khazneh itself, it actually references a much simpler architectural model than the Treasury and well attested to Petra; indeed, its similarity to the Urn Tomb or to the Roman Soldier Tomb is clear. In any case, in the reconstructions presented here, the appearance of the acroteria are purely speculative, inspired by those of the Khazneh.

Another niche with a distinct human figure is carved next to a typical niche containing a baetylus in the shape of an egg (with an inscription in Greek dedicated to Dushara). Based on well-known iconography, the presence of two bulls at the god's feet suggests that this is Dushara assimilated with Zeus-Jupiter. The inscription below the niche reminds us that it was cared for by Sabinus Alexander, the "panegyrist" (master of religious ceremonies during the festivals), who came from the Syrian city of Adhri'at (Der'a today). Both niches can be dated back to the end of the 2nd century AD.

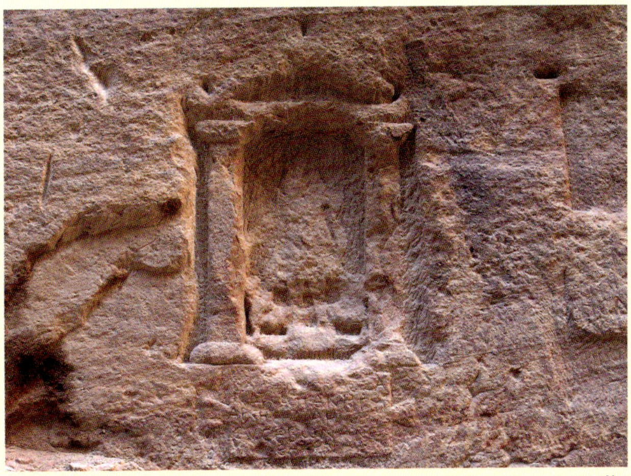

F. Bourbon I. Cirillo

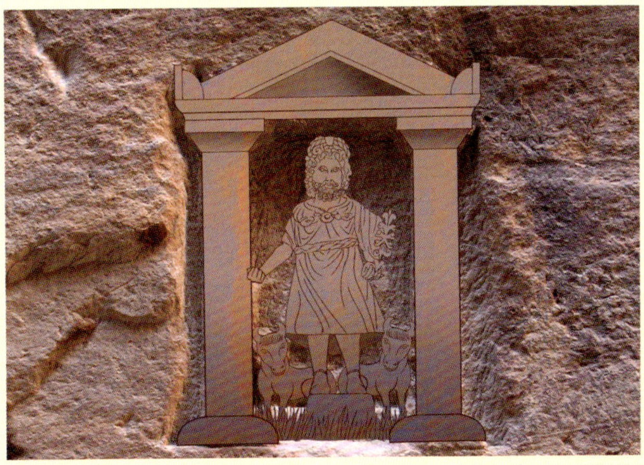

F. Bourbon I. Cirillo

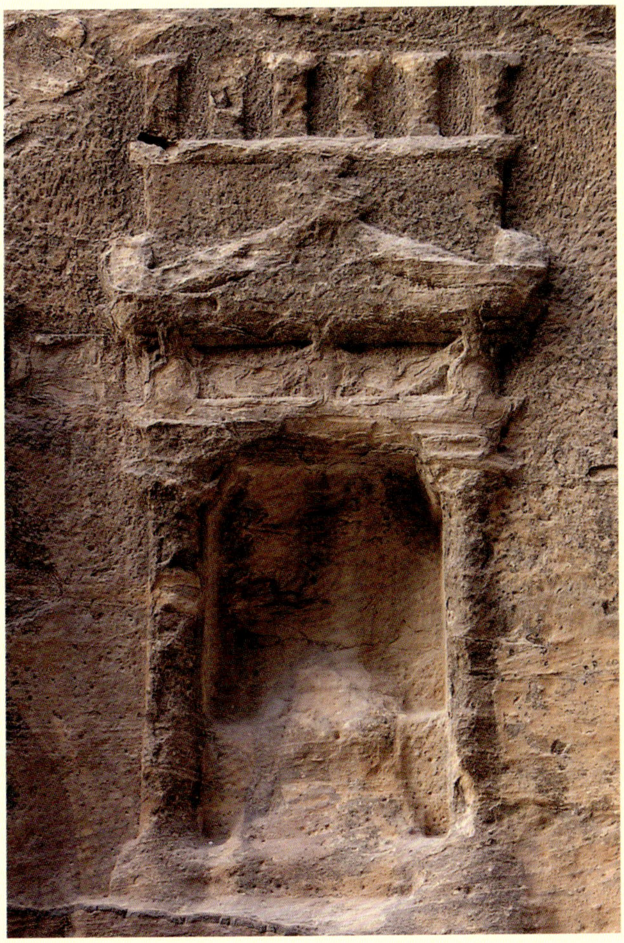

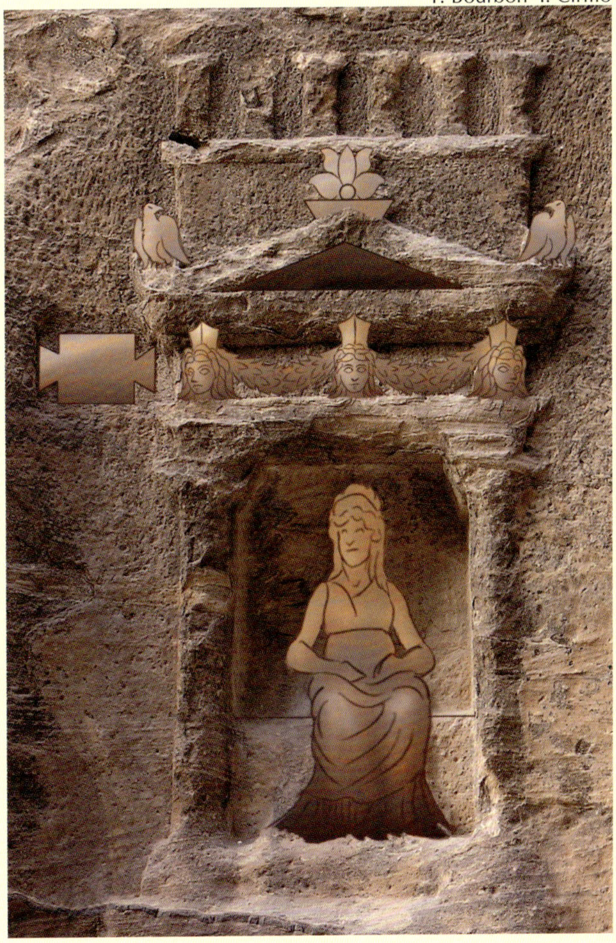

of two merchants, each leading a dromedary, can still be recognized. After centuries covered and protected by layers of sediment, the hooves of the animals and the feet of the two men, shod with caligae-like sandals, can still be seen. The legs of the human figure further down, wrapped in a long tunic, are also well preserved. The man was also leaning on a thin stick. The dimensions of the figures are larger than life, and it is easy to imagine what the emotional impact of this unexpected vision would have been on those who passed through the Siq for the first time. A few metres further along, there was another group of figures that was exactly the same (now almost invisible), moving in the opposite direction.
If you look closely at the high relief, it is clear that the deep cut of the aqueduct was made in a period after the group was carved. This is demonstrated by the fact that there are still small portions of the original rocky surface next to the legs of the merchant further down, which form an incongruous sort of frame around the figure. Likewise, if the carvings and the aqueduct had been made at the same time, the tunic would be wrapped around the figure with a more three dimensional effect. This also seems to support the theory that the aqueduct on the south side was built quite late on, perhaps after the earthquake of 363.
It is still not possible to see what the subsequent course of the pipeline was. Since the alluvial deposits in the last section of the Siq, and then in the outer Siq, are several metres higher than the old paving, it is clear that the last section of the aqueduct lies buried under debris. However, it is certain that it ran along the south-western side of the outer Siq, and this has been confirmed by an excavation carried out in front of Tomb 67.
A little further on from the striking group of statues, the unmistakable shape of the Khazneh, which is undoubtedly the symbol of Petra (No. 62), suddenly appears.

Above and below - *During the spring of 1998 in the Inner Siq a statuary group was discovered, larger than the natural size, depicting a caravan. Unfortunately the high-relief was seriously damaged by erosion and so the virtual reconstruction helps us to imagine its real proportions and aspect.*

Opposite page - *When you come to the end of the narrow gorge of the Siq, the sudden appearance of the Khazneh, bathed in sunlight, is a unique and unrepeatable experience. The best time to enjoy this incomparable spectacle is early in the morning, when the facade is fully exposed to the sun.*

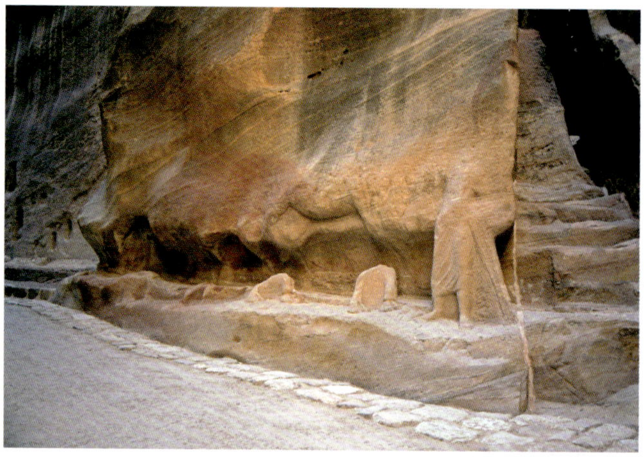

F. Bourbon I. Cirillo

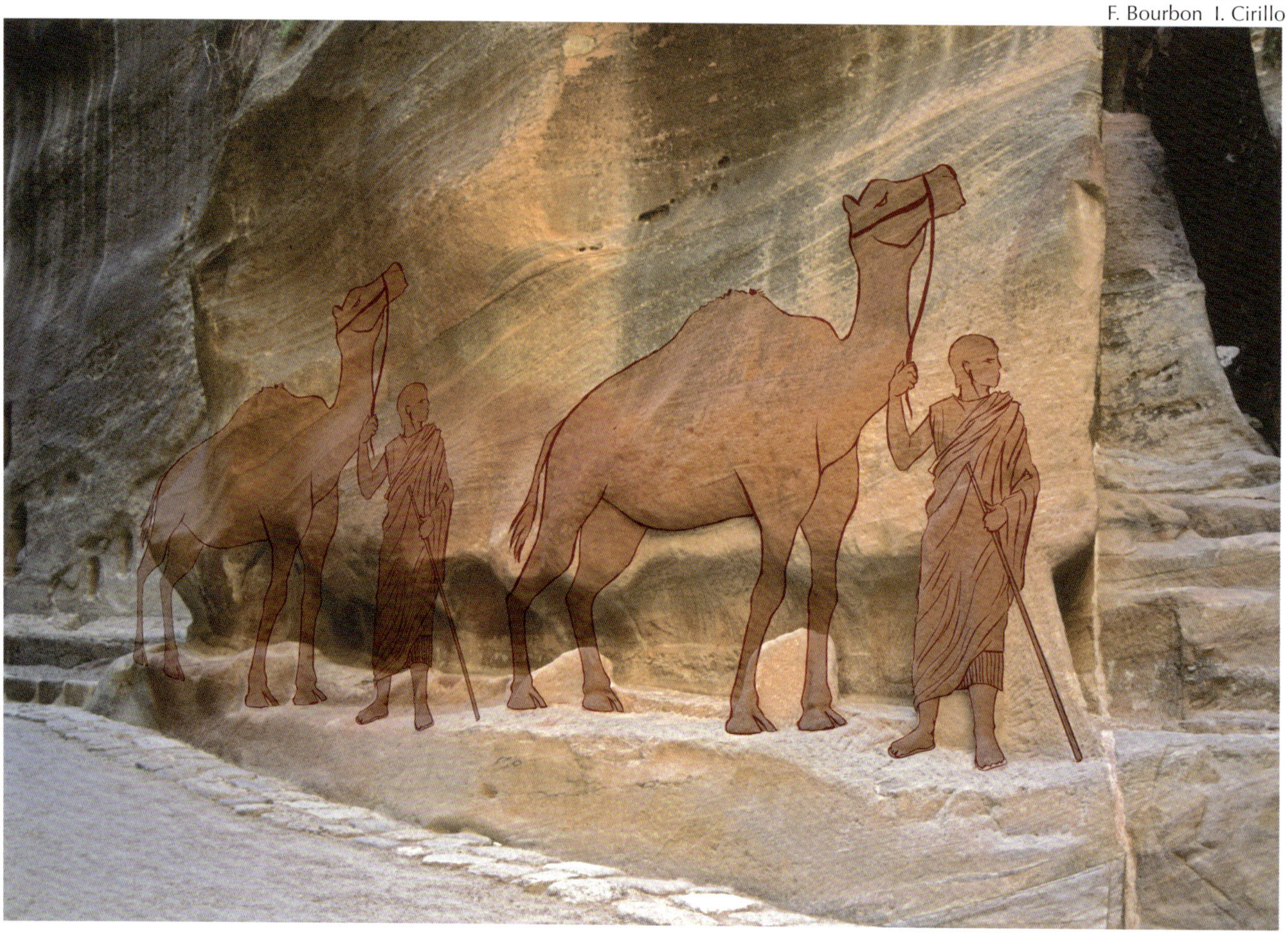

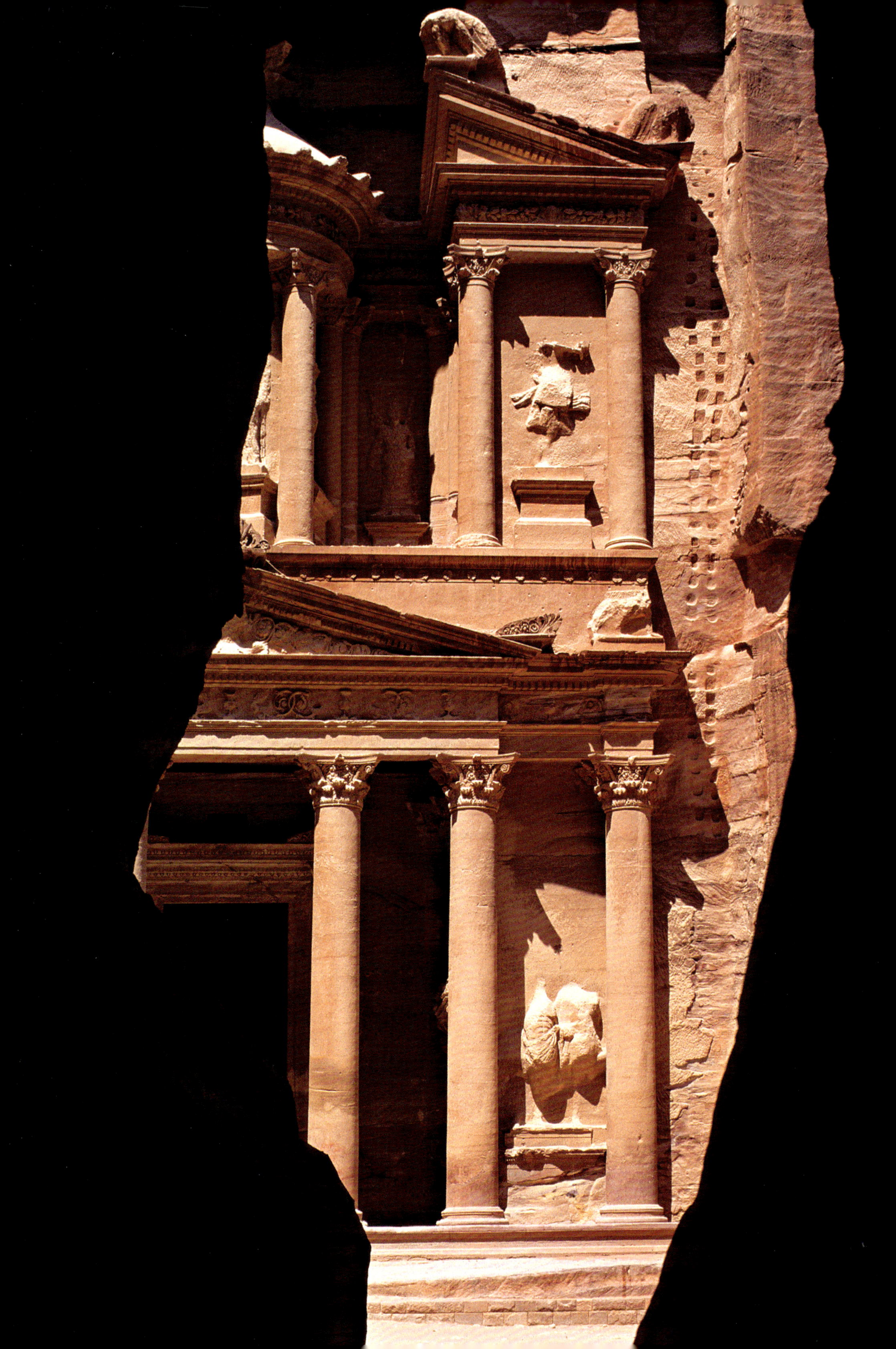

THE KHAZNEH (or THE PHARAOH'S TREASURY)

The enchanting beauty of the Khazneh and its scenic position are literally breathtaking. The colossal facade is carved into the rock face that looks out over the narrow mouth of the Siq, where the canyon widens naturally and makes a sharp turning to the right. The sense of wonder is intensified by the monument's almost perfect state of preservation, which also astonished the first European visitors, like Léon de Laborde, Charles Irby, James Mangles and David Roberts, all of whom were convinced that they were looking at an incomparable masterpiece. The sheer size of the monument is formidable in itself, 39.6 metres in height and 25.3 wide, and the position of the facade, behind the natural line of the vertical rock face, emphasises the sense of majesty (and has also protected it from the action of the weather over the centuries). The lower part of the monument is made up of a portico with a pediment, whose six columns with Corinthian capitals are twelve and a half metres high. In spite of appearances, only the two central columns are free-standing (the one on the left, which was damaged at the base in ancient times, was restored in the early sixties), while the others are connected to the mass of the rock behind. In the two external intercolumniations, there are two equestrian sculptures depicting the Dioscuri, Castor and Pollux, which are unfortunately very worn away, like the other nine human figures carved in relief, which decorated the upper section. This is the result of the destructive acts of iconoclasts, who were obeying the edict of the Umayyad Caliph, Yazid II (720-724) to destroy all human representations in the Muslim lands.

The long frieze that runs above the colonnade is made up of racemes and volutes alternated with cups supported by griffins facing each other. The tympanum, which may have had a Gorgon's head at its centre (although some researchers believe it was an eagle), has an elegant decoration consisting of volutes. At the ends of the attic above, the upper part of which has a continuous line of rosettes (all depicting different botanical species), two lions serve as acroterions. The second storey is subdivided into three elements. At the centre is the *tholos*, which is a small round temple with a conical roof, crowned with a great Corinthian capital with an urn on top of it, which is also damaged. It is this element that gave the monument its Arabic name, Khazneh el Faroun, or "Treasury of the Pharaoh", because of an ancient belief that the phantom Pharaoh (who became an evil magician with supernatural powers in the folk tales of the Bedouins), enemy of Moses, hid an immense fortune there. In an attempt to get hold of it, generations of Bedouins took aim at the urn with there rifles, and tried to split it to make the treasure fall to the ground. This explains the myriad of holes the surface is pitted with, caused by the bullets. The female figure carved in high relief in the central intercolumniation of the *tholos* is probably the goddess Tyche (Destiny, but also Fortune, the deity who protected cities and states). It is interesting to note, however, that the acroterion at the apex of the pediment, right at the feet of the goddess, is made up of

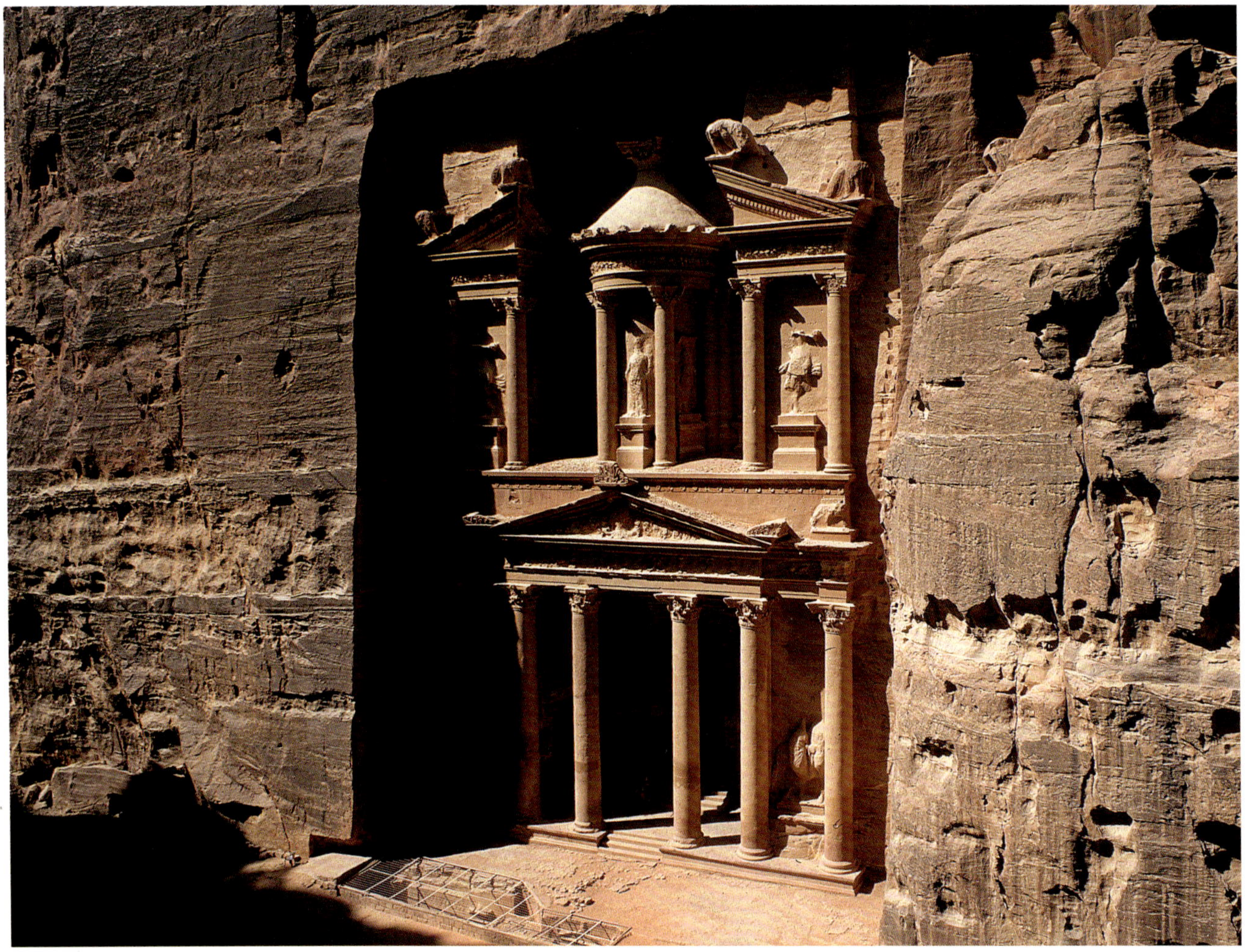

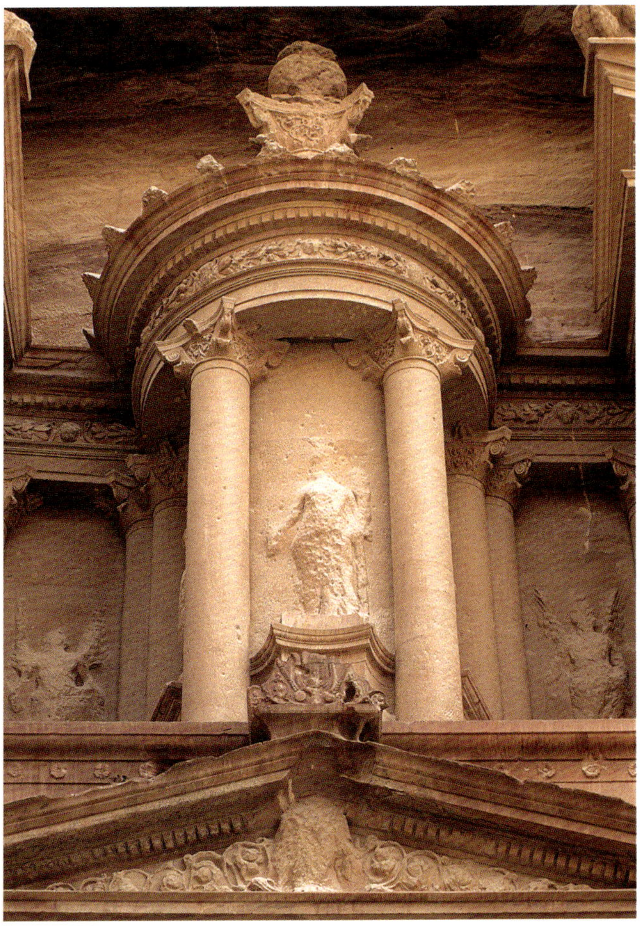

Opposite - *The image highlights the position of the Khazneh facade, carved deeply into the rock, and allows us to evaluate the enormous extent of the excavation work.*

Left - *The* tholos, *with the obliterated female figure.*

Top right - *The capitals are local reworkings of the Corinthian models imported from the Hellenistic Alexandrian world. The arrow indicates the vase (or cup) that still has traces of paint on it.*

Bottom right - *The right half pediment, with its frieze.*

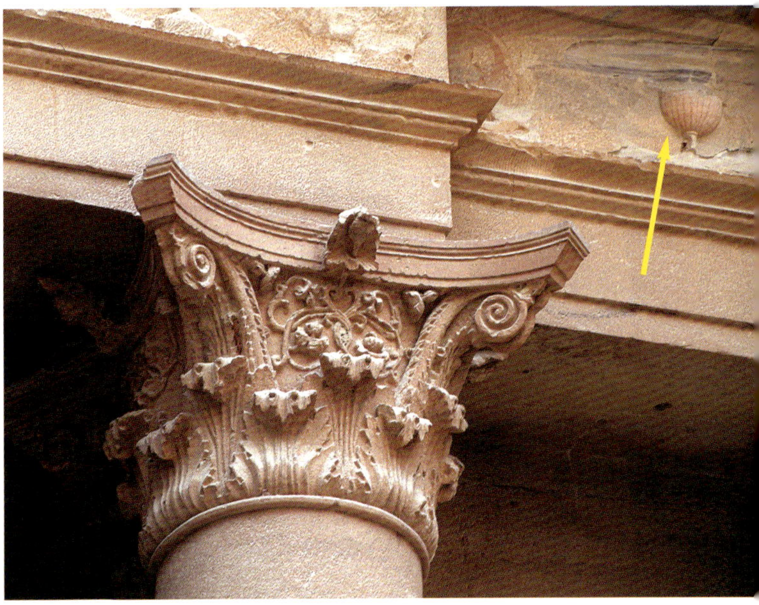

a solar disc between two ears of corn and two cow horns. This symbolism, which comes from Egyptian iconography, is connected with the goddess Isis, and it is therefore believed that the mysterious figure should in fact be interpreted as Isis, assimilated with Tyche and the Nabataean goddess Al Uzza, in accordance with a form of syncretism often seen in the Hellenistic era. This identification is supported by the posture of the goddess and a similar image of Tyche-Isis on several vases made in Alexandria and, in particular, on a Ptolemaic jug in relief kept in Stockholm.

The other two bas-reliefs on the sides of the *tholos* are still recognizable as Amazons brandishing an axe, like the ones in the intercolumniations of the two semi-pediments. Finally, the figures between the two semi-pediments and the *tholos*, attached to the back wall, are two winged Nikes. The two semi-pediments are held up by false corner columns, with capitals that are the same as the ones below. The two niches in the background are framed by two pairs of half columns. The continuous trabeation above the capitals of the upper floor is adorned with a frieze with garlands of leaves and acorns, and three giant eagles, which are very worn away and have no heads, act as acroterions.

It has been confirmed that there was a layer of plaster on some of the decorative elements (in particular the frieze with cups), which suggests that the facade was originally plastered and painted, at least partially. This is demonstrated by the fact that the fluting on one of the cups was painted, not sculpted. To a certain degree, this must have made the appearance of the monument more vivid, compared with our perception of it today.

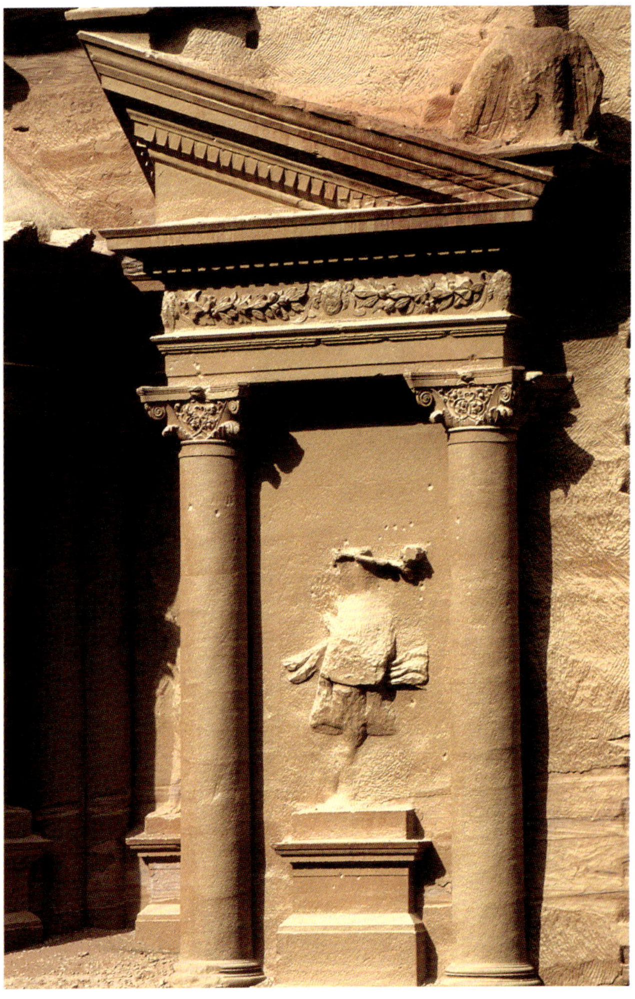

The inside of the Khazneh is made up of the great vestibule (or *pronaos*), that is 14 metres wide and 6 metres deep. From here, there are eight steps up to the main chamber, a cubic hall that is 12 metres wide and about 13 metres high, with three smaller rooms that open onto it. The only decorations are the elegant pediment frames of the doors. The great chamber may seem bare compared with the exterior, but the natural colouring of the walls is spectacular. Two smaller rooms, which also have steps leading up to them, look out onto the short sides of the vestibule. Here, too, the frames of the doors are decorated, and there are two great oculi above them. The acroterions above the door frames were decorated with eagles with outstretched wings. Unfortunately they were decapitated by the iconoclasts. On the thresholds of the doorways that lead into the main chamber and the two side rooms, the holes where the hinges of the great wooden doors were attached can be seen. These doors may have been covered with sheets of bronze, like the ones in the Pantheon in Rome, for example.

On the walls next to the main entrance, some rectangular holes can be seen, arranged in a seemingly random way. Wooden dowels were probably placed in these to support two stone slabs carved in bas-relief, or even two groups of high-reliefs made of bronze plates , which were destroyed or looted in ancient times. Unfortunately, this is a mystery that will probably never be solved.

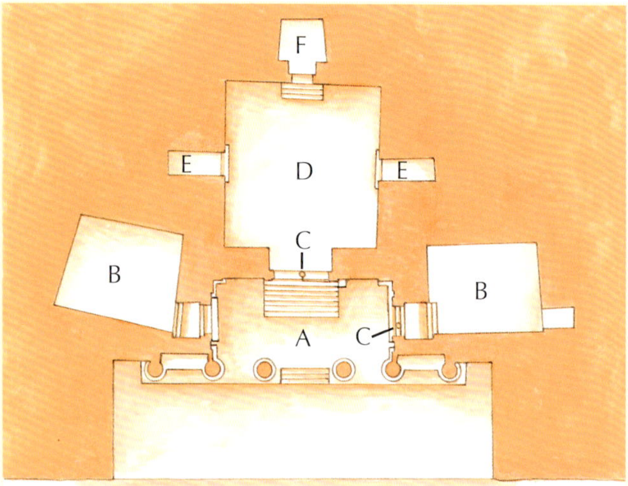

Plan of the Khazneh

A Vestibule (or pronaos)
B Side rooms
C Lustral basins
D Large chamber
E Side rooms
F Sanctuary (or naos)

Access to the interior of the Khazneh is today generally precluded to protect it from the wear and tear of the stone, caused over the years by the passage of thousands of visitors.

Below - *The large cubic chamber that constitutes the main space of the Khazneh.*

Opposite, left - *The doorway of one of the rooms that open onto the vestibule.*

Opposite, top right - *One of the royal tombs discovered at the foot of the Khazneh.*

Opposite, bottom right - *The lustral basin carved into the threshold of the main chamber; the rectangular hole housed the vertical door post.*

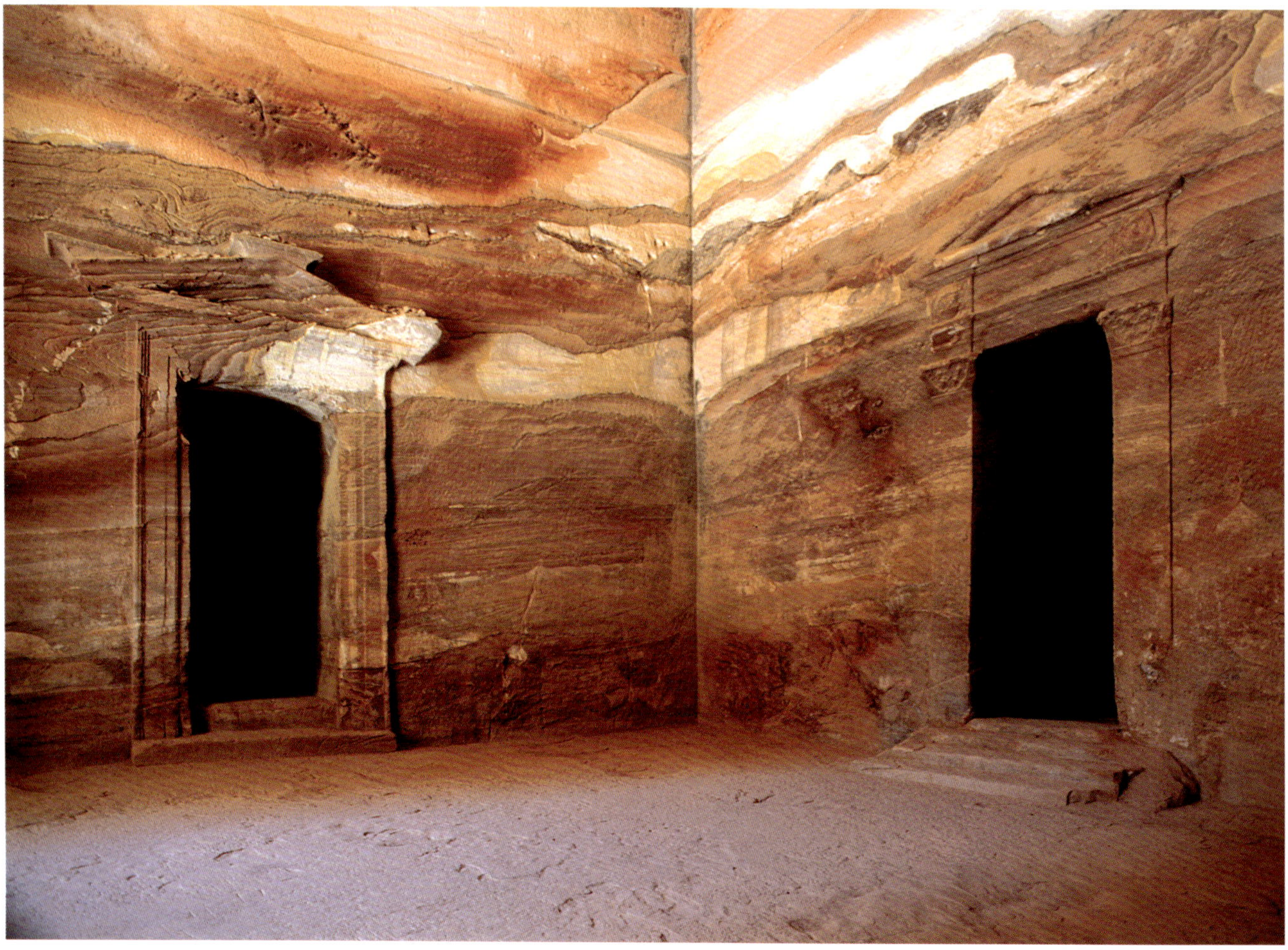

The date and the real function of the Khazneh have been the subject of speculation since the moment it was discovered. Some thought it was a temple, others a royal tomb, or a cenotaph. Some believed it dated back to the reign of Aretas III (84-62 BC), or even the emperor Hadrian (117-18 AD). The archaeological excavations carried out from 2003 onwards have, however, dispelled the doubts. First of all we need to bear in mind that the original level of the open space in front of the monument was about 7/8 metres lower than it is now. Sand and stones were piled up there over the centuries, after the collapse of the Nabataean dam placed at the mouth of the Siq. Initially, five tombs crowned with battlements were carved into the rock face opposite the gorge. Later,

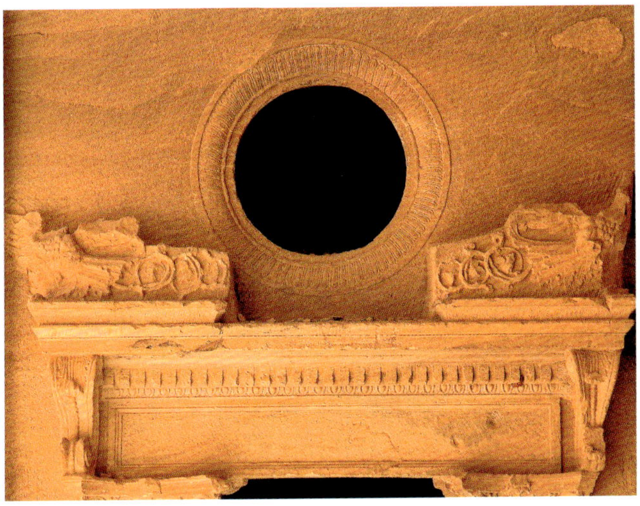

a large masonry staircase was built against their facades, designed in a way that it would not damage the tombs. An ingenious window was opened into it, in order to illuminate and ventilate one of the tombs (the 62D, called the Window Tomb). Access to this tomb - which must have been considered very important - was made possible by building a small staircase on the left hand side, the entrance to which opened up at the level of the terrace situated in front of the facade of the Khazneh. It is therefore clear that the rupestrian building accessible via the monumental staircase, which was the Khazneh, was constructed after the tombs below. The finds discovered inside them (including human bone fragments) revealed that people of a very high status were buried here, almost certainly a sovereign and his family, and they were dated to a period between the end of the first century BC and the beginning of the next one. It is therefore reasonable to suppose that it was the powerful Aretas IV (9 BC - 40 AD) who commissioned the Khazneh, as a funerary temple in honor of his father Oboda III or, more likely, of his first wife Huldu, who died around 16 AD. The queen would then have been deified and assimilated to Isis-Thyche, whose effigy adorned the *tholos* of the Khazneh. The Treasury must therefore have been built in the first decades of the 1st century AD. It is also probable that Aretas IV himself was buried in the royal tomb beneath it.
The small lustral basin carved into the threshold of the great chamber (used for ceremonial ablutions, and also to collect blood from sacrifices) suggests that the monument was used for religious purposes. In the light of this, the various bas-reliefs on the facade should be interpreted as funerary symbols. For example, in Greek mythology it was the Dioscuri who led the souls of the deceased to the Elysian Fields. As well as being the goddess of fertility and maternity, Isis, sister and bride of Osiris, reigned in the afterlife and also led the spirits of the dead with her to a new life.
It is still not known if the incomparable rock cut building was the work of craftsmen from the Hellenized world (probably Alexandria), or Nabataean artisans, trained in a Hellenistic setting. In fact, the exceptional nature of the architectural style, and the complexity and sophistication of the decorative design would suggest an external contribution, probably assisted by local workers. As Judith McKenzie rightly pointed out, the

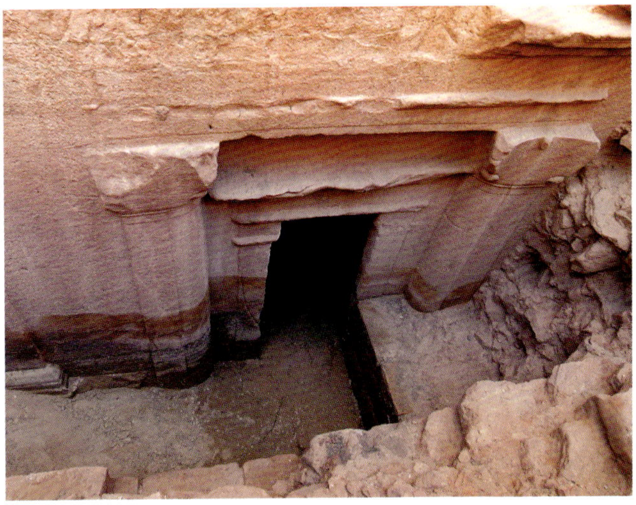

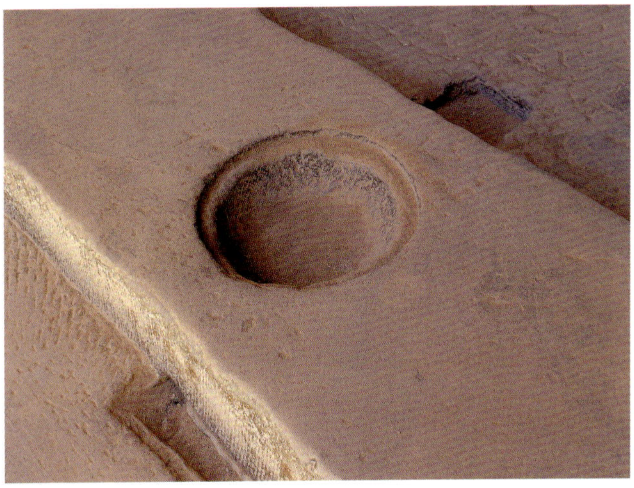

Alexandrian influence is certainly very clear.
Archaeological surveys have shown that the original level of the open space in front of the Khazneh (part of the Wadi al Jarra, or Wadi of the Urn) lies at a depth of several metres below ground. It is therefore possible to imagine how much more spectacular the sight of the facade was, rising up on top of a grand staircase about six or seven metres high, for those arriving from the shady Siq. In ancient times, the space where the tourists queue up today was paved with hexagonal slabs, and there were probably many other tombs in the surrounding rock faces, as well as votive niches or even highreliefs. It is also known that under the flagstones there was a system of channels, which may have fed a fountain. The upper part of a pair of monumental tombs is visible on the rock

face, too, opposite the Khazneh, to the left of the mouth of the Siq. As a whole, it must have been a magnificent sight, enough to astound the most experienced traveller. Not that the modern tourist should be any less amazed, especially considering the technical aspect of a rock cut structure of this size. Today it seems impossible that the Khazneh was carved without using machinery, but only pickaxes, hammers and chisels, and perhaps this is the most extraordinary aspect. In fact, it is even harder to imagine how they were able to do the work considering they carried it out starting from the top and moving downwards, as we know. There has been a lot of speculation on the subject, but none of the various different theories have been confirmed.

Another unsolved question concerns the two conspicuous sequences of holes bored out on both sides of the facade. Many have suggested that they were foot holes (like those that can be seen on many quarry walls all over Petra), used by the workers to climb up as far as the two acroterions in the shape of eagles, where they stop. According to the archaeologist Naif Haddad's recent theory, however, beams would have been fitted into these large slots to make up an ingenious self supporting scaffolding, which could easily have been assembled and disassembled. The fact that these slots start several metres from the ground can be explained bearing in mind that all the stone debris produced by the excavation work would have tumbled down, and gradually formed a pile at the foot of the facade being carved. When the work reached this cone of rubble, it would no longer have been necessary for the Nabataean workers to use scaffolding, as it was then possible to work standing on the mass of detritus, which would have been pushed downhill as the carving continued towards the bottom, and then removed from the building site.

On the other hand, it is certain that the Nabataean stonecutters were able to make their way along the prominent fissure that runs obliquely, many metres above the colossal facade. In fact, on the natural terrace situated vertically above the great rectangular space in which the Khazneh stands, there is a deep channel, used as a gutter. This prevents the rainwater from dripping down the rock face, and makes it flow down the valley along the natural fissure. This ingenious device, which is further

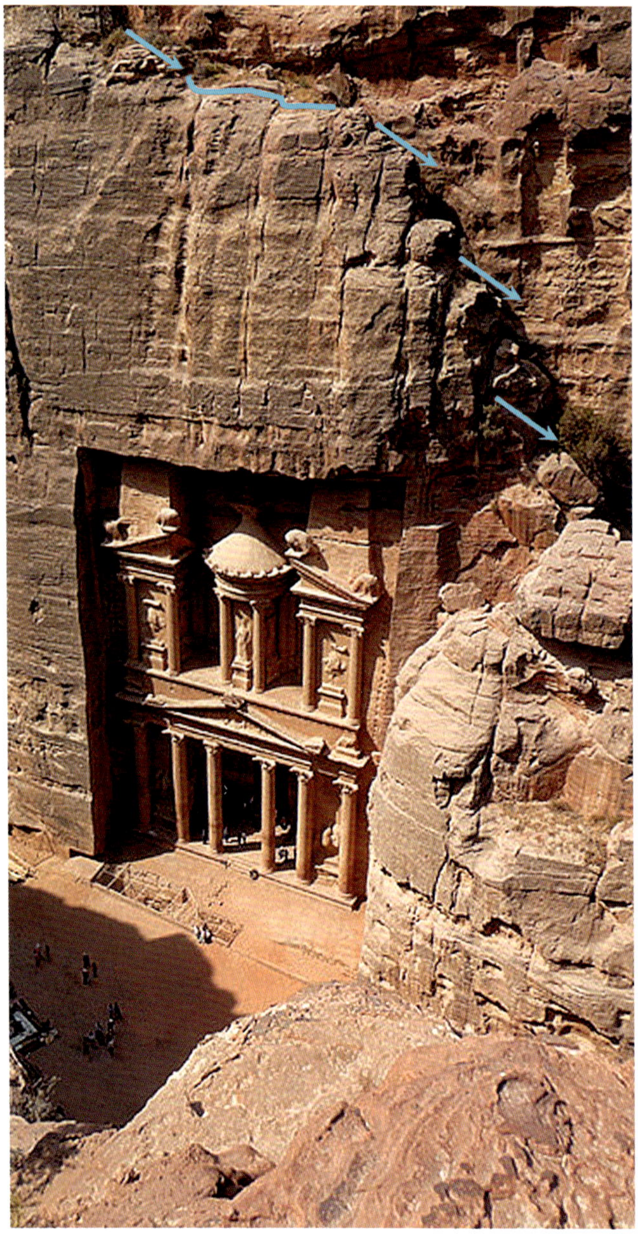

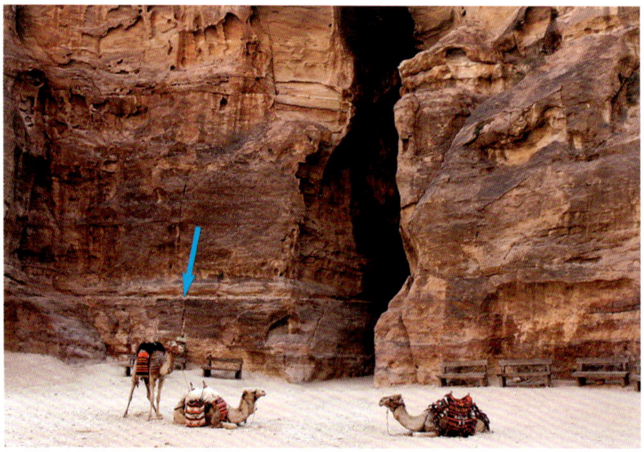

confirmation of the engineering expertise of the Nabataeans, prevents water from falling onto the terrace in front of the Khazneh, and once protected the great staircase, which is still buried under detritus today.

Before saying goodbye to the Pharaoh's Treasure, it is worth turning around and having a good look at the sombre fissure of the Siq. On the left hand side, a few metres from the ground, you will notice the cutting of the northern aqueduct, with some pieces of earthenware pipes still clearly visible. However, there is no trace of the southern aqueduct.

Left - *The blue line highlights the path of the groove carved into the rocky prominence situated above the facade of the Khazneh. It was used to drain rainwater downstream, which otherwise could have damaged the underlying monument.*

Right - *In this image of the outlet of the Inner Siq in the wadi al Jarra (which includes the esplanade in front of the Khazneh), the arrow highlights the layout of the aqueduct.*

Opposite page - *The red arrow indicates the steep staircase carved into the fissure (nowadays cluttered with debris) to the right of the Khazneh, while the yellow arrow highlights the curious ledge (or passage) that gave access to the attic floor of the monument.*

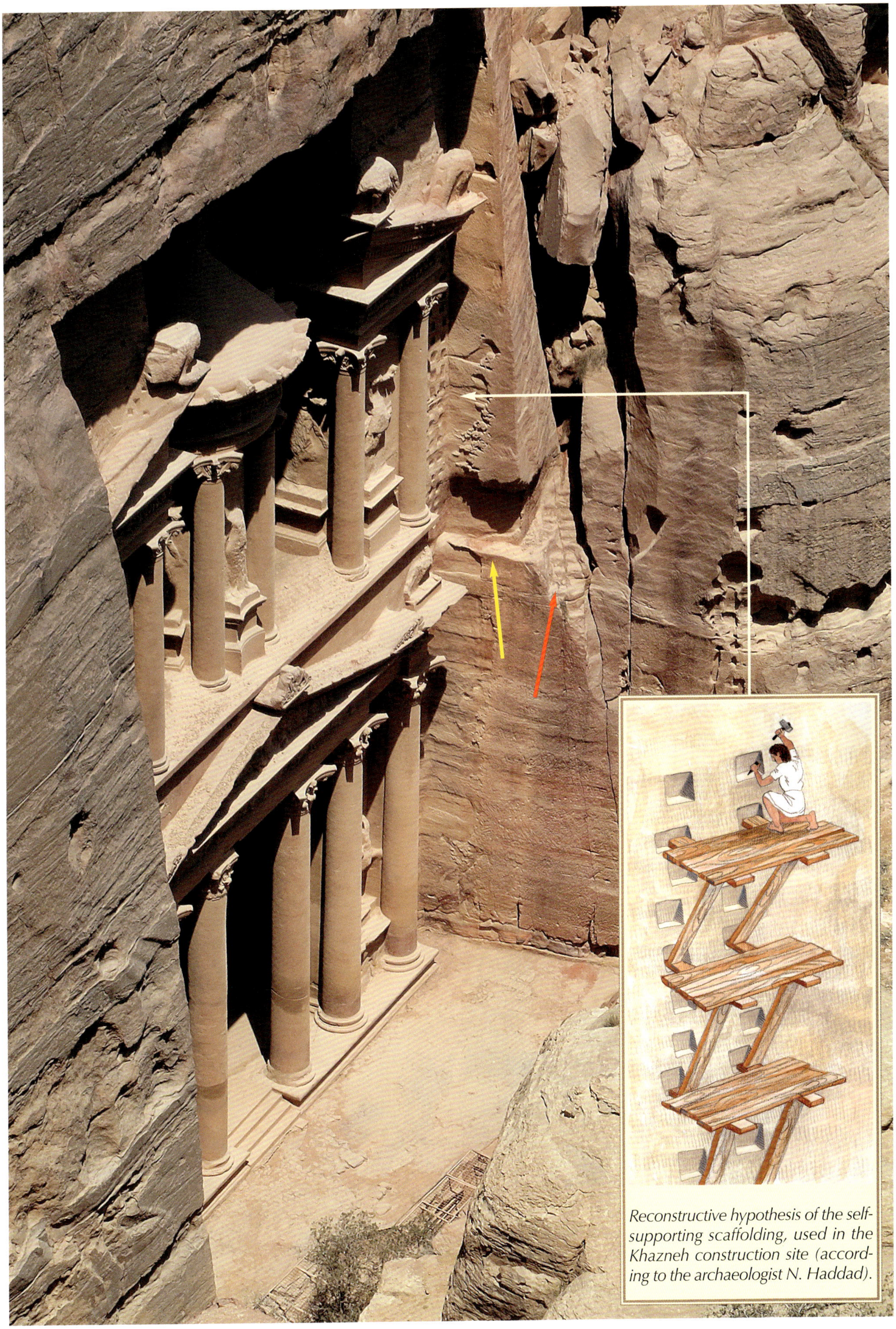

Reconstructive hypothesis of the self-supporting scaffolding, used in the Khazneh construction site (according to the archaeologist N. Haddad).

A HYPOTHESIS CONCERNING THE GENESIS OF THE KHAZNEH

After many years of in situ observations and studying and comparing other theories, the author here expresses his premise on how the Khazneh was created.

First of all, it is evident that the mountain wall on the sides of the facade, mostly in the upper right area, shows clear signs left by stonemasons: this means that the natural profile of the mountain was different and that it was modified. Even more evident from above is that the massive rock buttress located to the right of the facade, originally slanted onwards for several metres until converging with the vertical wall, more or less corresponding with the left side of the great rectangular recess (photo below). Therefore, it was necessary to eliminate this conspicuous mass of rock in order to create a free surface down to the ground, as becomes immediately apparent when viewing the facade obliquely from the far left side). On what remains of the rocky promontory, an ancient and vertiginous staircase leading to the top still exists; its starting point is located on the left side of the Outer Siq, before the great monumental tombs. Here you can see some excavation works and a sort of platform whose function is uncertain; however, it is clear that the stairway allowed one to climb quite easily here (it is definitely not advisable to take this very dangerous and worn route). From this position you can see that between the rock buttress and the vertical wall behind it, a narrow fissure meanders for several metres deep. In an indeterminable period this was obstructed by the falling of enormous boulders. If you look at the Khazneh from a favorable position – that is, obliquely from the far left – you can clearly see the existence of this chasm and a staircase carved on the bottom of it. This curiously ends in the void (see photo on the previous page), on the upper edge of the cut buttress to the right of the facade.

Summing up, originally a massive sandstone shoulder was leaning against the vertical wall; a fissure several metres deep and a couple of metres wide ran through the top part of it. A staircase was hewn into this crevice, which ran from the bottom of Wadi al Jarra to the top of the shoulder (where a sacred space may have been or a look out point to control the Siq); a second staircase went down into the Outer Siq from the opposite side.

The five royal tombs, brought to light by excavations, were first carved at the feet of the shoulder. At this stage, the staircase in the fissure was probably still accessible. When it was decided to sculpt the enormous facade of the Khazneh, the work initially consisted in carving the upper part of the enormous, rectangular dig, working from top to bottom as usual, and most certainly with the help of suspended scaffolding. At this point the flights of stairs became serviceable for the construction site, for the movement of the workers and the transport of the stone extracted from the mountain. The upper part of the monument, including the two half-pediments and the tholos, *were made in the first phase of the works. Initially, teams outlined the vertical front of the dig, then they carved the basic shape of the monument from the rock mass behind it. Specialists who had the task of carving the architectural details then took over. To move up and down in the building site, mobile scaffolding was used. It was put in place using the two lines of holes cut into the rock, which are clearly visible to the sides of the upper half of the facade. Access to this section of the worksite was ensured by a ledge carved next to the staircase, still clearly visible to the right of the facade (as seen in the preceding page).*

Once the upper part was finished, carving the lower part began, this time using a different procedure. A large part of the prominent mass of rock had to be demolished, down to the bottom of the wadi. Now the workers could move more easily and the excavation work proceeded by horizontal levels: as the buttress was gradually dismantled, they continued working towards the bottom, delineating the volumes of the lower part of the facade and specialists were able to sculpt friezes and other sculptural elements without having to climb any longer. This would explain the absence of the two rows of holes towards the bottom. In the meantime, the ancient staircase that descended from the top of the buttress was demolished together with the rest. Two free-standing columns were outlined under the pediment, the vestibule was dug out, and the terrace overlooking the facades of the four tombs below took took shape. The internal rooms were then created and finally the great staircase was built, rising from the bottom of the gorge to the grandiose, memorial temple. In order to be able to attach the staircase to the rock, it became necessary to carve the upper part of the tombs, which therefore lost their half merlons.

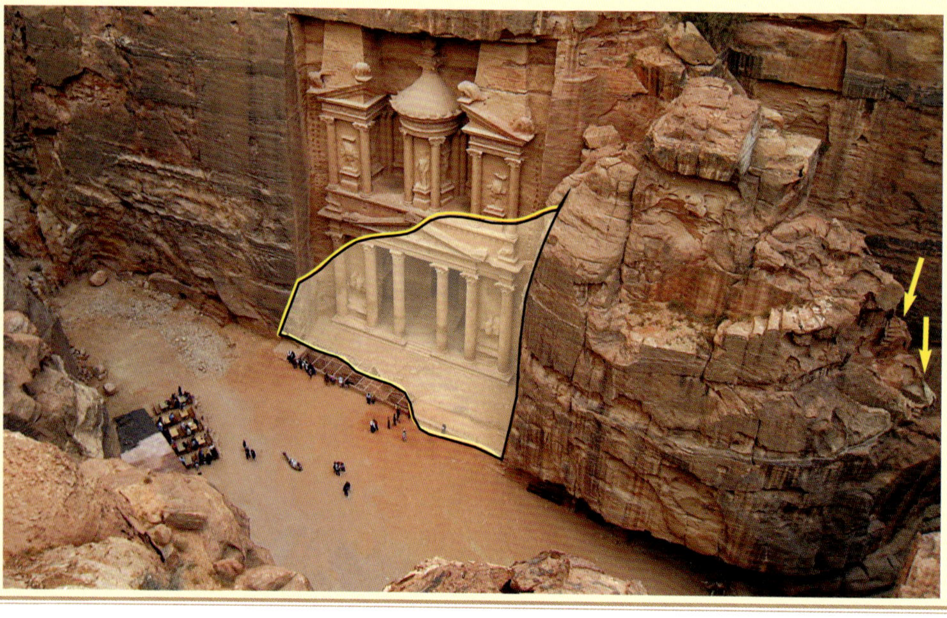

Left - *The two arrows indicate the route of the steep staircase that leads to the top of the rock buttress. The highlighted area suggests the volume of the mass of rock that must have been demolished to build the Khazneh.*

Opposite page - *The six pictures show hypotheses about the various phases of the construction of the Khazneh. In the second the pre-existing tombs are shown; in the fifth the monumental staircase that went up to the vestibule of the monument can be seen.*

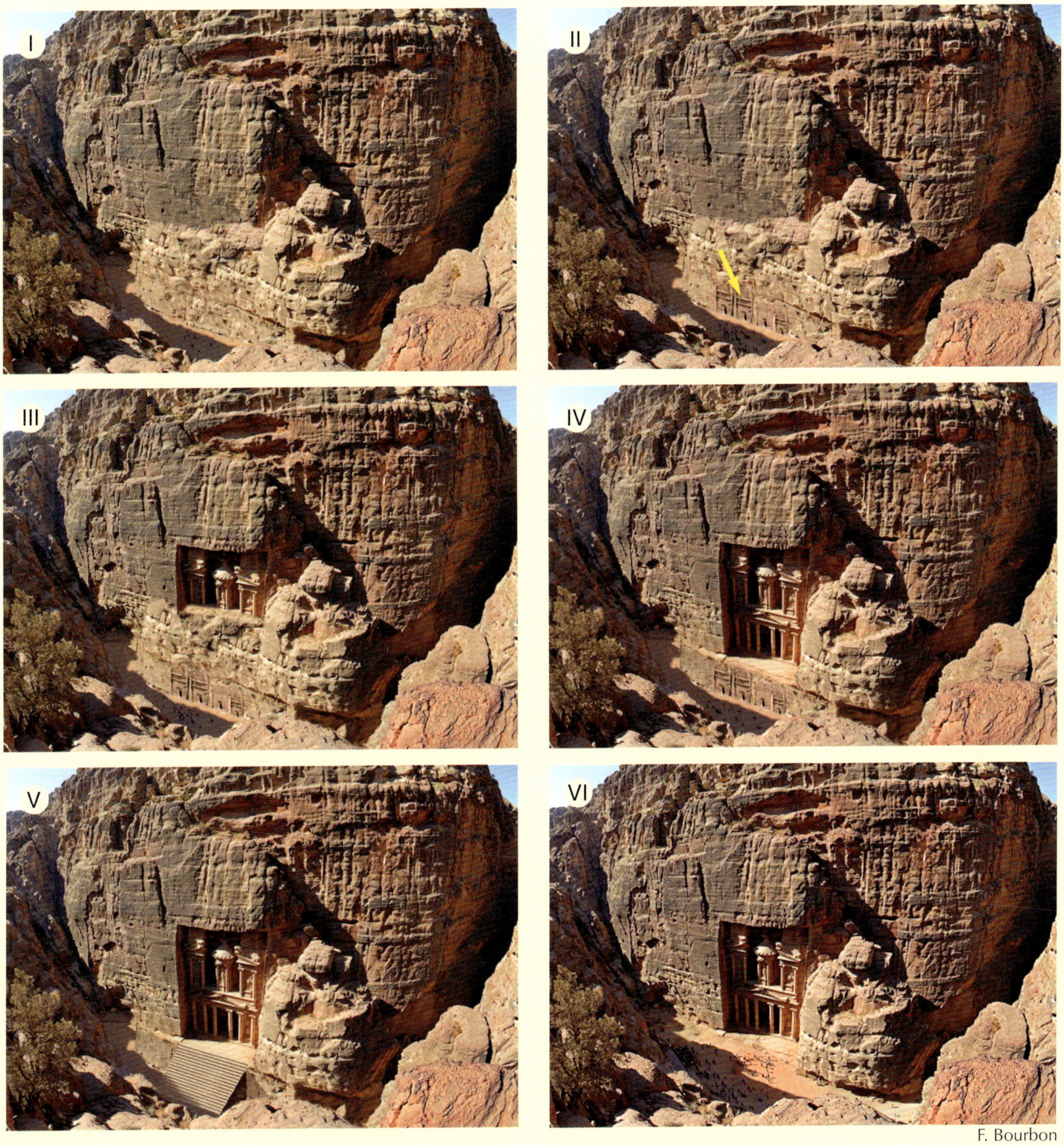

F. Bourbon

Another conjecture concerns the decorative reliefs of the Khazneh depicting humans, works that were obliterated by the iconoclasts who followed the dictates of Caliph Yazid II. While a couple of simple wooden ladders may have sufficed to allow them to reach and destroy the images of the Dioscuri, the procedure must have been completely different when it came to demolishing what was above the column capitals. However, if at the time (first half of the 8th century) the stairway that descended from the top of the rocky shoulder had not yet been obstructed by the boulders that had fallen from above, the iconoclasts needed merely go down the stairs and onto the ledge and, perhaps with the help of a couple of boards, reach the attic, where they could continue to vent their destructive fervor. Lastly, the two vertical flights of holes were all they needed to reach and decapitate the acroterion eagles. Since by adopting the same method they could also have gone onto the roof of the tholos *without any difficulty and verify the presence, in the urn, of the legendary 'Pharaoh's treasure', it can be assumed that the birth of this myth is to be dated to a period subsequent to that of Yazid II and the landslide that blocked the crevice.*

Lastly, a final thought on the Khazneh's real function, indebted to what Iain Browning has already expressed. The internal structure itself of the monument suggests that it was a temple, not a tomb. As is the case with masonry temples, there is in fact a vestibule that affords access to the cella, at the bottom of which the small chamber that can be reached via three steps would be the naos, where a sacred image was kept. The side rooms would be service rooms, where the sacred vestments and other items related to the sacred offices were stored. The total lack of loculi seems to substantiate this supposition: while it is true, as some authors claim, that the remains of the sovereign could have been placed in a sarcophagus, nonetheless it is strange that no trace of this latter has remained, not to mention the fact that in all Petra the use of stone sarcophagi has not been attested.

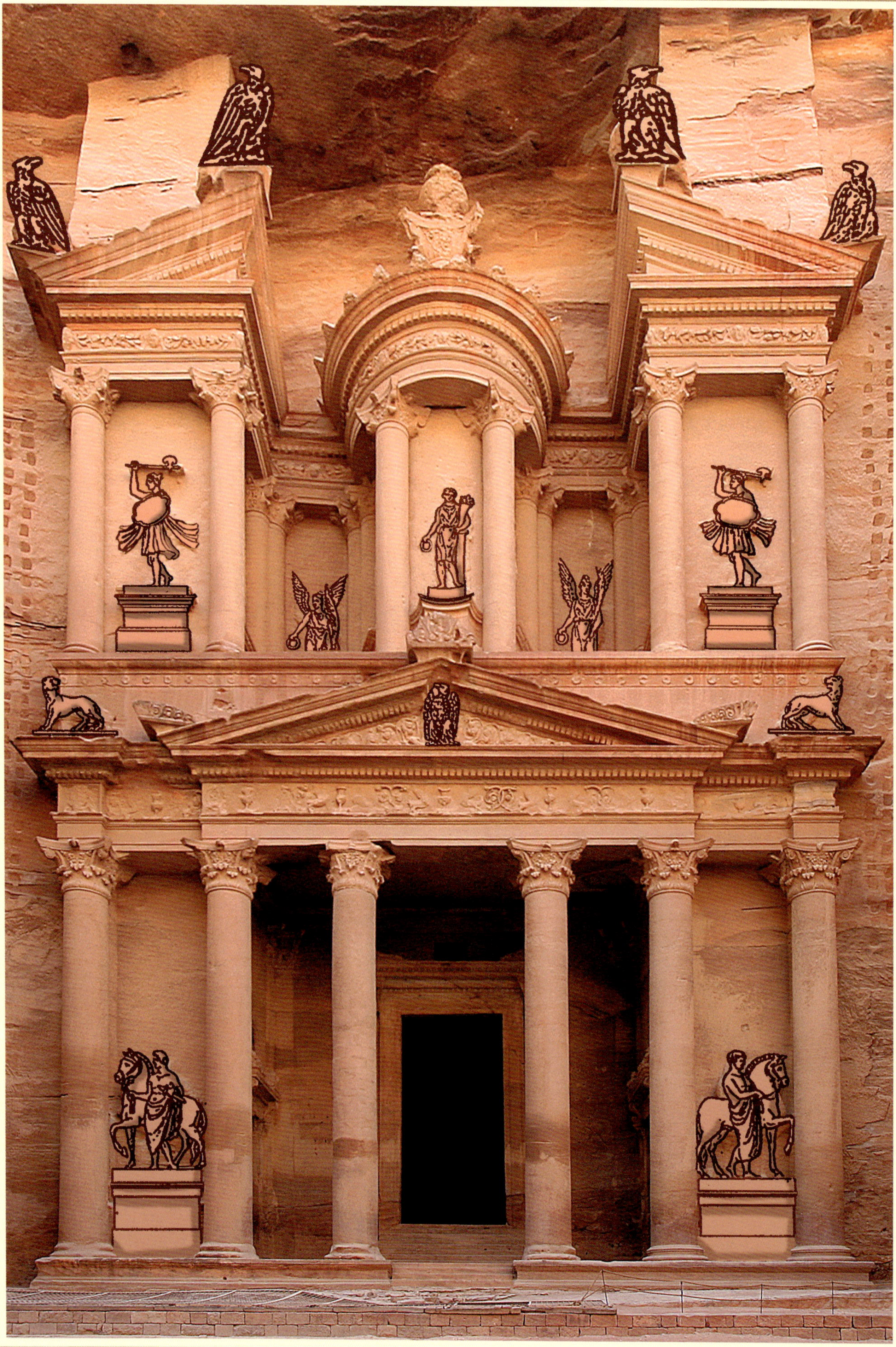

F. Bourbon I. Cirillo

THE KHAZNEH REVEALS ITSELF

Dating the Khazneh is one of the great dilemmas that has puzzled scholars of Petra since the dawn of Petra's archaeology. The historian Mikhail Rostovtzeff attributed it to the Hellenistic period on the basis of style elements. Donald S. Robertson thought otherwise: he dated it to the time of the Trajan emperor on the basis of similar comparisons. Other academics, including Herbert Wiegand and Konstantin Ronczewski, date it to no later than the reign of Augustus based on its decorative schemes, in particular the capitals and garlands of the frieze. Others opt for the reign of Aretas III Philhellen, while some even believe the monument dates back to the reign of the emperor Hadrian. Indeed, British scholar Judith McKenzie, dated it to the 1st century BC.
Excavations carried out in front of the Treasury from the beginning of 2003, suddenly threw new light on the monument, not only giving us a highly probable date, but also an explanation regarding its function. The five tombs (all built within the space of forty years) have been named as the Incense Tomb, the Window Tomb, the Staircase Tomb, the Obliterated Tomb and Tomb 62C. It is very likely that the Staircase Tomb (62E) and the Window Tomb (62D) were made just a few years before the Khazneh. The Incense Tomb (62A) owes its name to the fact that an hearth was located in front of it where a huge amount of frankincense was burnt in antiquity, remains of which have been recovered and studied. Conspicuous remains of incense were also found at the level of the original pavement of the square, where an altar must have stood; this attests that the Khazneh and the tombs were for a long time the object of a devoted veneration. Additionally, some surveys have shown that the flat area in front of the Treasury was paved with large, hexagonal, stone slabs. A sophisticated drainage system for rain water ran under the paving slabs, which was undoubtedly connected to a series of dams and channels set in the Wadi al Jarra, the gorge that opens to the left of the Treasury. Several clues suggest that all these were set in place, as well as the monumental staircase, at the same time or just after the creation of the Khazneh. This large-scale creation of monuments in the area was designed to suitably welcome the many pilgrims who gathered here to perform sacred rites in memory of an important deified person, which, among other things, required the use of incense.
Finally, a plausible theory is that this area began to be used as a necropolis towards the end of the 1st century BC when the tombs, half-buried in gravel today, were carved. This was possible as the Siq had finally been made secure by the construction of the large dam designed to stop devastating floodwaters, which until then had periodically destroyed the bottom of it, making the entire area a danger zone. The person behind this radical transformation was Aretas IV Philopatris (9 BC - 40 AD), in the context of a massive monumentalization of Petra. During his almost fifty-year reign, the sovereign had the grandiose rock temple sculpted, most likely dedicating it to the memory of his late wife Huldu, who had given him three sons and as many daughters. She was probably assimilated to the goddess Isis, highly revered in the Nabataean capital. The rupestrian building therefore became one of the major religious buildings in Petra and, probably, the sovereign himself was then buried in one of the tombs below (or in one of the rooms overlooking the pronaos).

It is believed that for the realization of the Treasury Aretas IV called Alexandrian architects to Petra, responsible for a completely innovative work in the local architectural panorama, but in line with the progressive westernization of the Nabataean society. Work that was carried out by the now expert local workers. This approach to the aesthetic canons of the Hellenized West and the influence of western iconography on the Nabataean religion – already active for several decades – explain the abandonment of the aniconic representations in favour of the figurative ones and therefore the extraordinary decorative program of the Treasury.
This last one was unfortunately destroyed centuries later by iconoclastic rage, but the first western visitors to Petra were fortunate enough to enjoy the rock-cut monument when the reliefs were not as ruined as they are today. Indeed, Laborde, Roberts and others all mentioned in their diaries how Bedouins continued to shoot at the reliefs, not only out of respect for the Islamic prohibition to depict the human form, but also to show off their shooting skills. It is only thanks to comparing Laborde's reliefs, Roberts' engravings and the current state of the structure, that we can formulate a highly possible reconstructive theory of how the Khazneh must have originally appeared (image on opposite page).
The creation of the Treasury coincided with the last phase of authentic splendor of the Nabataean reign and became its symbol, strategically positioned at the end of what had become the new and more scenic entrance to the city.
Several clues allow us to make an assumption as to when the Siq was transformed. Firstly, nearly all the inscriptions in Nabataean attested to Petra, date back to the period of the kingdom, that is, prior to the Roman conquest in 106 AD. Although it is unknown how widespread Greek was in Petra before the 2nd century AD, epigraphic data suggests that the use of Nabataean was replaced by Greek (or both were used) after being annexed by the Roman empire. The majority of the visible inscriptions in the Siq are written in Greek and therefore rather late, datable to between the 2nd and 4th centuries AD based on lexical and stylistic factors.
Additionally, there are several votive niches in the gorge that contain human representations of gods in accordance with a popular custom which only spread in the late period. The high relief groups of merchants with their dromedaries could be from the same period as the Khazneh and perhaps created by the same sculptors who had worked on the Khazneh. The monumental arch located at the entrance to the Siq, influenced by Roman architecture, is later than 50 AD. The nefesh *at the entrance to the Siq, along with the name of Petra in Nabataean,* Raqmu*, were well preserved since part of the Nabataean dam had been attached to them shortly after they had been engraved. The inscriptions' style dates them to the first years of the 1st century AD. As they were concealed by the dam, it is clear that it was built under the reign of Aretas IV.*
All these factors suggest that initially the Siq was simply a seasonal waterway that was barely functional, but on the bottom of which was first carved (on the north side) a covered aqueduct that carried water to the city from the Ain Musa spring. When Petra experienced its heyday, namely in the first years of the 1st century AD, it was decided to drastically change the situation and the now paved gorge took on its current appearance. Merchants and pilgrims then got into the habit of carving the votive offerings that we still see today.

THE OUTER SIQ

From the space the Khazneh looks out over, the gorge of the Wadi al Jarra turns right and heads northwards. From this point on it is called the Outer Siq, as it begins to descend towards the valley where Petra lies, skirting along the overhanging face of the Jebel al Khubtha. The first rupestrian structure that attracts our attention is a great cube shaped cavity, which opens out, high up on the right hand rock face, and can be reached by climbing a flight of stairs. It is a vast triclinium hall (No. 65, one of the largest in Petra), probably built to accompany the Khazneh or rather the royal tombs below it. In the rock just above the upper edge of the room, a strange and very rare stylized human figure has been carved between two baetyli. Its meaning is unknown, but it may have had the function of warding off evil spirits.

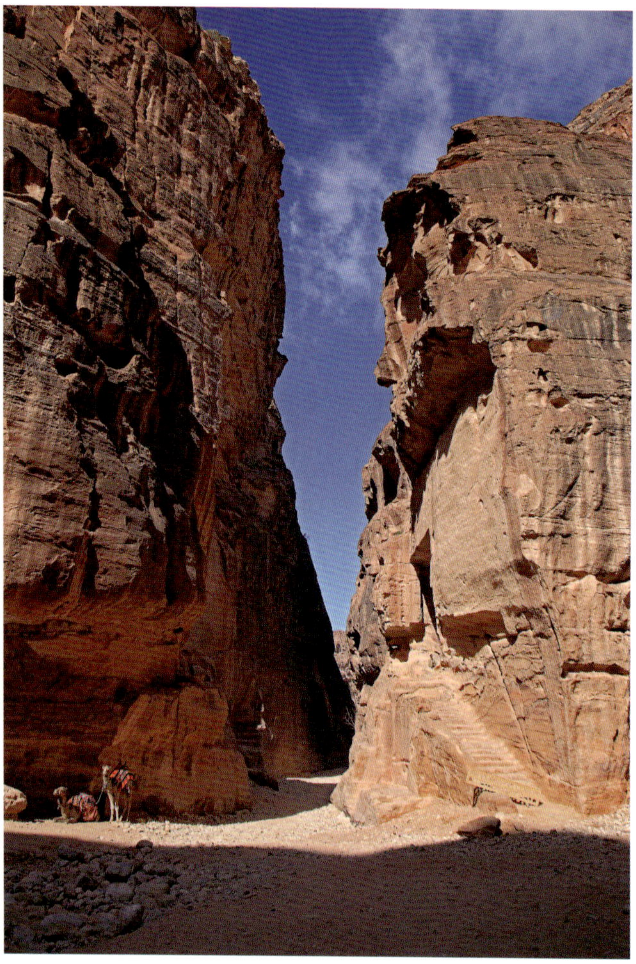

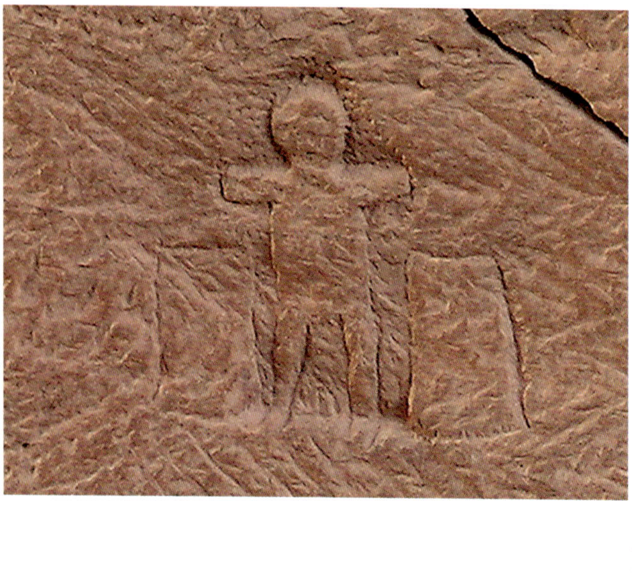

Almost opposite the triclinium, the remains of **Tomb 66** (in the Brünnow classification) can be seen. Only the base, carved in circles and lozenges, and the right pilaster are almost intact. The tomb had a long inscription in Greek on it, which was destroyed when it collapsed in 1847, perhaps after an earthquake. Fortunately, however, a transcription was made by the first westerners to visit Petra. The words commemorate the deceased, a twenty-seven-year-old named Arrian, who died of "a sickness that subdues all", and was mourned by his elderly mother.

For a while, the gorge is still quite narrow and deep, between the sheer rock faces. High up on the right hand side, you can clearly see the course of the aqueduct, with several pieces of terracotta pipes still in place. These were not left in the open, but covered by stonework, which in turn was covered with a thick layer of plaster. This hid the aqueduct from view, but above all it protected the tubing and prevented any possible leakage of the precious liquid. Considering the height of the aqueduct above the ground, it is difficult to imagine that the workers with the extremely difficult task of cutting the channel into the vertical rock face could have used wooden scaffolding, as it would have needed to be enormous in size. Instead, they likely worked using a hanging scaffold, whose wooden planks were supported by simple metal bars stuck in holes

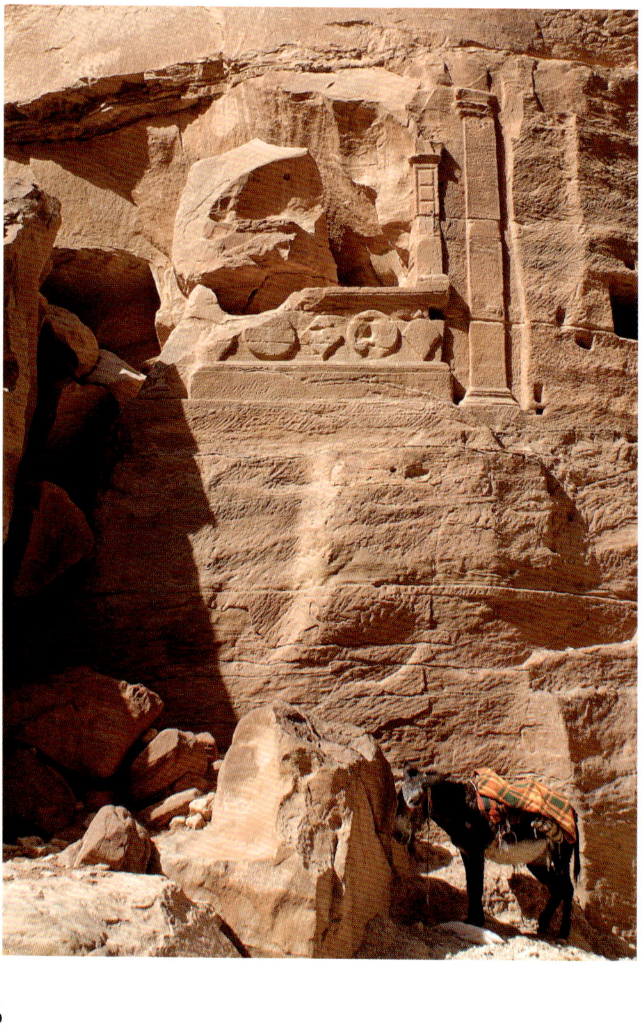

made in the rock wall as the building site progressed. Suddenly, a series of five magnificent tombs appears, carved into the left (western) side of the canyon (n.67, 68, 69, 70, 71). **Tomb 67** has a double cornice (Hegra type) and an unusual burial chamber placed on the attic between the two half merlons, framed between pilasters surmounted with a pediment, an element that is almost unique in the rock cut architecture of Petra. In the early sixties, the loculus was reached by a famous British rock climber, the legendary Joe Brown, who found it had already been robbed by ancient looters. However, this exploration revealed traces of a layer of plaster on the upper part of the facade, which may have originally been coloured. This detail, which has been confirmed in other rock cut monuments in Petra, suggests that in some cases a part of the facade was plastered and perhaps also multi-coloured. This would certainly have altered their appearance compared with how they look today. Some holes made symmetrically in the thickness of the half merlons and the upper cornice are believed by archaeologists to have been for anchoring some kind of lifting machinery, used to raise the body up to the funerary chamber. Other similar holes found elsewhere in the area suggest that this equipment was commonly used in Petra. This raises interesting questions about exactly what kind of construction technologies the Nabataean craftsmen possessed, and what their specific skills were.
The imposing **Tomb 69** is of the double cornice (Hegra) type, with a facade with four pilasters resting on a high

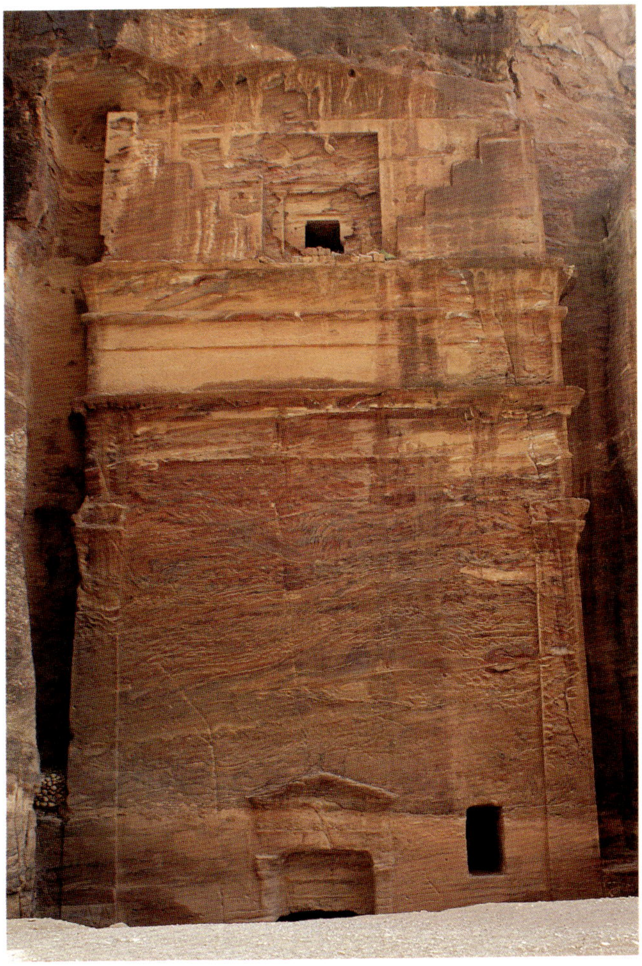

Opposite, top left - *The beginning of the Outer Siq, where on the right, a large triclinium hall can be accessed with a flight of stairs.*

Opposite, bottom left - *The mysterious stylized human figure, carved on the architrave in the triclinium hall.*

Opposite, right - *What remains of Tomb 66; the decoration of the innermost pilaster is curiously similar (and perhaps contemporary) to that of the splendid aedicule located inside Room 468, near the Deir (pag.132).*

Left - *Tomb 67, with the distinctive burial chamber on its attic.*

Right - *Possible method of construction of the rock aqueduct, with the use of a hanging scaffold.*

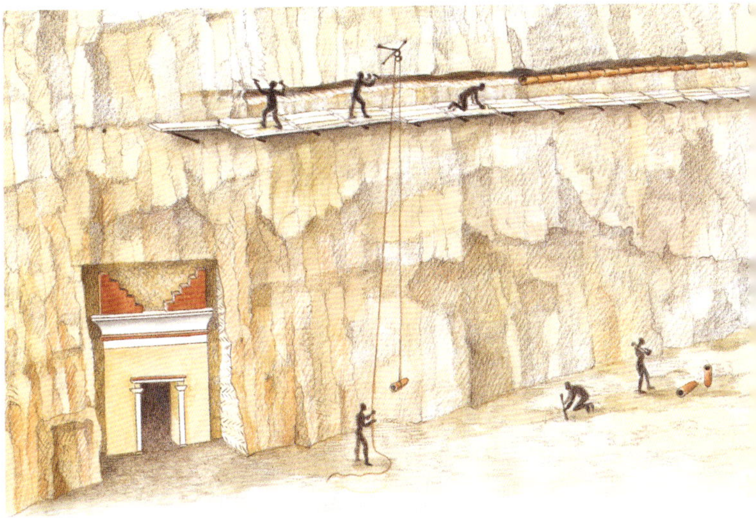

© F. Bourbon M. Falcone

THE NEFESH OF TOMB 67

The entrance to Tomb 67 has only recently become accessible again thanks to the massive excavation work of slowly clearing away the alluvial debris in the Outer Siq. The height of what was ground level until a few years ago can be calculated by the different colourations on the lower part of the facade. The excavations have also revealed a series of nefesh *engraved on both sides of the doorway – about twenty of them – one of the largest concentrations of them found in Petra to date.*
The strange masonry structure, which was evidently added onto the facade at a later date, is a part of the aqueduct built in the 4th century AD on the western side of the Outer Siq to provide the city with a water supply in the Byzantine era, after the earthquake of 363 that left the older aqueducts unusable.

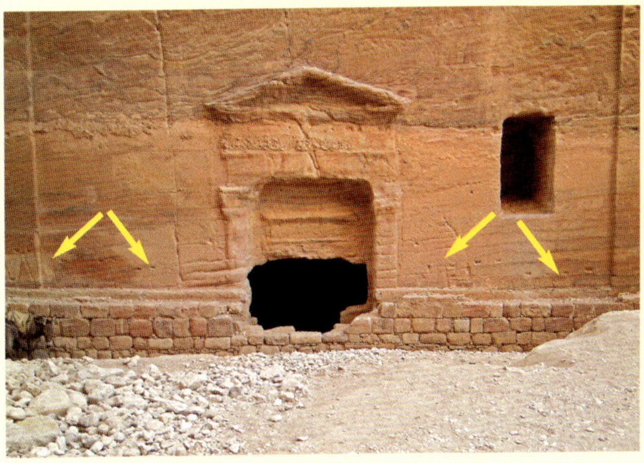

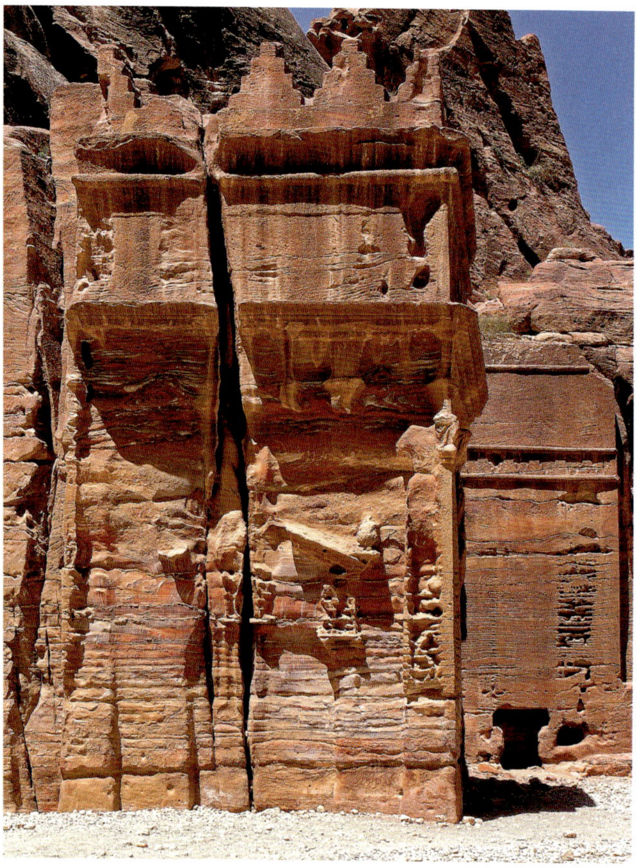

podium, crowned with typical Nabataean capitals. The doorway is decorated with pilasters with "horned" capitals surmounted by an elaborate tympanum.
The multi-coloured **Tomb 70** is even more interesting, and very prominent in relation to the mass of rock. It is crowned with Assyrian crowsteps on three sides, which are almost intact. It is a block tomb, similar to the Djinn Blocks, but in this case the crownsteps were carved from the mass of the sandstone, and for this reason they have been preserved. The three sides of the tomb are very eroded. The ones facing east and north have false doors between pilasters with floral capitals, surmounted by an architrave with no frieze and a tympanum with three acroterions (the top acroterion had a human form, perhaps of a winged genius). The west side, however, seems never to have been completed.
If you look closely at the tombs described above, and the others nearby, you get a sense of how the level of the ground has risen by several metres since the time when the monuments were carved. In fact, only the upper part of some of the tombs can now be seen, and you can imagine the power of the seasonal stream that dragged thousands of cubic metres of detritus downstream over the course of the centuries, once the dam in the Siq had collapsed.
Opposite the group of tombs mentioned, there are six others, side by side. The most interesting ones are **Tomb 825** and **Tomb 826** (the two most northerly), because

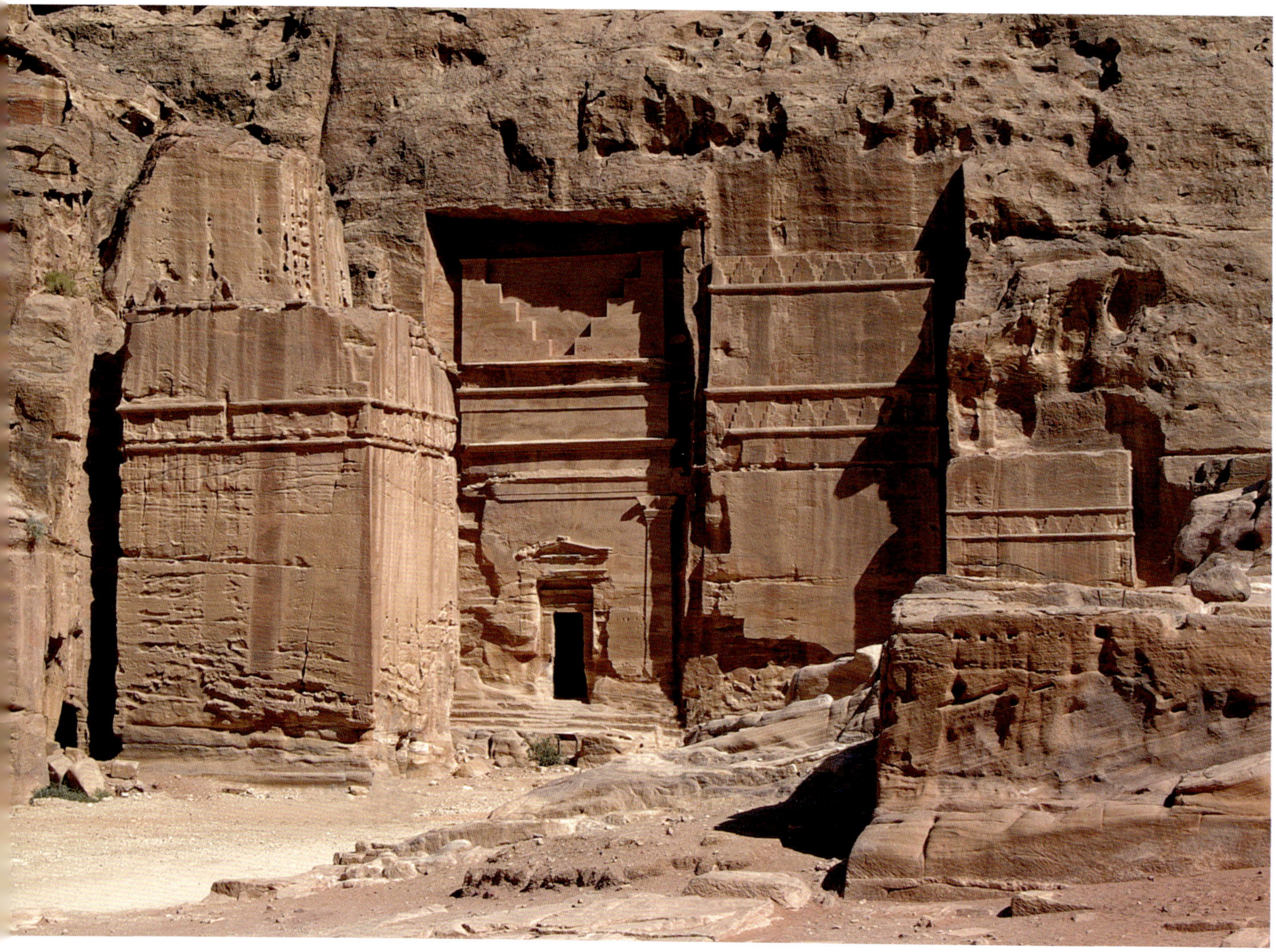

their facades are crossed by the channels of the aqueduct. Originally, the cut where the earthenware pipeline was placed was sealed with mortar and plaster to conceal it. This leaves us in no doubt that the aqueduct was made after the tombs, and therefore relatively recently, later than the so-called Khubtha north aqueduct. The connection between the two facades in masonry and plaster – that became necessary in order to house the earthenware pipes – is curious, in that it rests directly on top of the right capital of Tomb 825.

Tomb 825 is also interesting for a number of other reasons. Firstly, it is noticeable that on the facade, the pilaster on the left and its capital are missing, and in its place there is a groove that reveals its proportions. As sometimes happened, the Nabataean artisans came across a vein of sandstone that was too soft and decided to deal with the problem by embedding a piece carved from a more resistant stone in the gap, which can be seen so clearly today. Devices of this kind, which can also be found in other monuments in Petra, are further evidence that the facades were partly plastered. In fact, in this case a layer of plaster would have concealed the unappealing sight of the large insert. Finally, inside the tomb, which contains 17 loculi, there are five *nefesh*, which are not easy to identify in the dark. One of these has an inscription in Nabataean on it, which names the descendants of a certain Iakun. This detail is a confirmation of the connection between the *nefesh* and their funerary function.

The adjacent **Tomb 824**, at right angles to the other six, also deserves a mention. Its imposing bulk juts out forcefully from the mass of rock behind. It is another block tomb, similar to the Djinn Blocks. The crowning is badly damaged, but Assyrian crowsteps are still visible, carved in relief on the lower level, and made with stone slabs and plaster above, (three of them can still be seen on the western side). On the south side, we can see that part of the upper section of the monument was built in masonry, with big blocks of sandstone.

The more observant will notice some footholds carved into the rock face behind Tomb 829 (the fifth of the six in this line), which go up as far as the line of the aqueduct. It is difficult to say whether this stair was part of the building site or if it was used for maintenance. What is certain is that similar stairs are visible along the course of the various aqueducts in Petra.

The flight of steps that climbs up the rock face just to the left of Tomb 831 (of which only the two half merlons of the crowning are visible) is more noticeable. It led up to an ingenious system for gathering rainwater, carved into the mass of rock above, and connected by channels and walkways put in place for maintenance. The fact that the staircase ends suddenly in the middle of nowhere, several metres from the ground, and cannot therefore now be reached, might be explained by the fact that this water system was abandoned at some point (probably after the construction of the aqueduct).

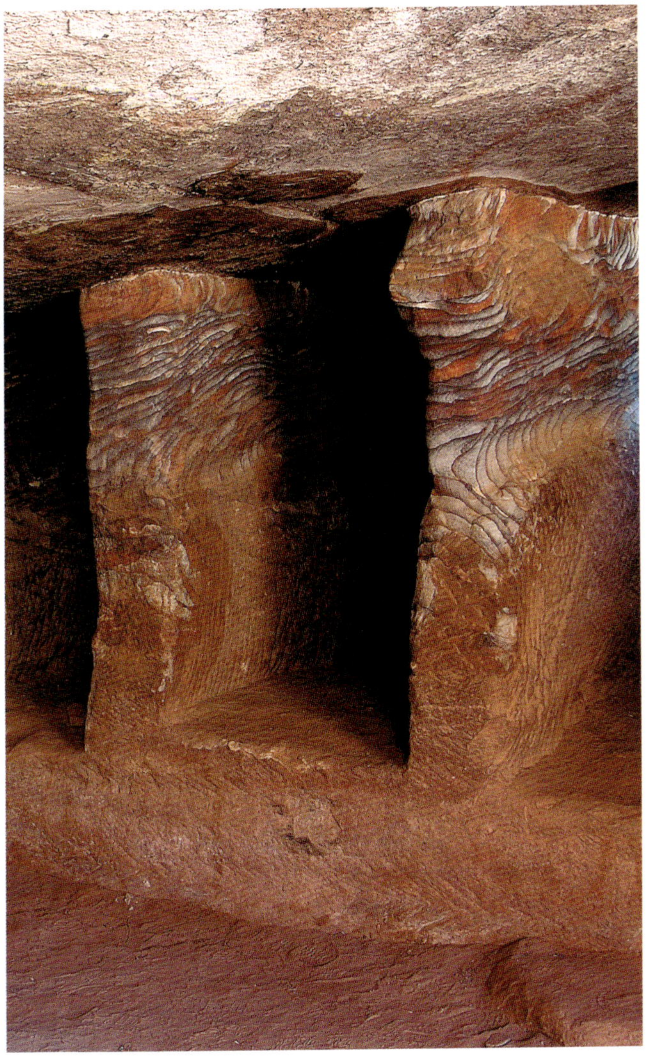

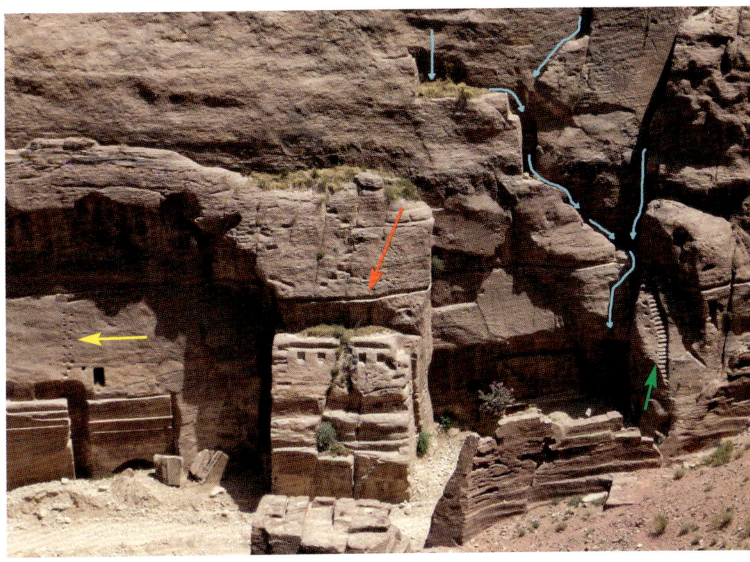

Opposite page, top - *The unmistakable shape of Tomb 70, crowned with Assyrian-type crowsteps.*

Opposite page, bottom - *Tomb 824, Tomb 825, Tomb 826 and the upper part of Tomb 825 can be seen from left to right. The groove where the aqueduct would have flowed is also clearly distinguishable, although its path from this point on is not as easy to identify.*

Left - *The interior of one of the many hypogea overlooking the Outer Siq. This area is famous for its fabulous range of sandstone colours.*

Right - *The rainwater collection system in the Outer Siq. The red arrow indicates the line of the aqueduct coming from the Inner Siq, the yellow one the footholds above Tomb 829 and the green one the staircase next to Tomb 831.*

The building of the tombs below probably necessitated the demolition of that section of rock and therefore of the lower part of the staircase.
A few metres further along the Siq, high up on the right hand side, slightly behind the line of the rock face, a majestic double cornice (Hegra) facade can be seen. This is Tomb 813, known as the **Tomb of 'Uneishu** from a fragment of an inscription that must have been part of the slab of stone that closed off one of the loculi inside, on which "'Uneishu, brother of Shaqilath, Queen of the Nabataeans" is written. The fact that there were two Queen Shaqilath complicates the dating of the monument considerably. One was the second consort of King Aretas IV (who married in 18 AD), and the other was the bride of Malichos II and mother of Rabbel II. She reigned for six years while her son was still a child. It is also known that the title of queen was given to all the princesses that belonged to the royal family, and not only to the wife of the reigning monarch, which complicates the situation even more. However, as a coin of Malichos II was found during the exploration of the tomb, it makes sense to date the tomb back to the period between 40 and 76 AD. Finally, it should be noted that the term "brother" should be understood as a synonym for prime minister here. The tomb had a courtyard with a portico in front of it (unfortunately the colonnade has been destroyed), onto which a triclinium hall also opened. Inside, along the walls of the funerary chamber there are thirteen loculi, which is a sign that the tomb was used by the relatives of an illustrious person for several decades, in line with an established tradition. Next to the Tomb of 'Uneishu, there are some very large sepulchres including Tomb 808, which is very similar but of even greater dimensions. This part of the Necropolis probably housed the tombs of the wealthiest and most important families in Petra in the 1st century AD. The courtyard in front of the Tomb of 'Uneishu looks out over the Outer Siq, the original level of which was two or three metres lower than it is today. In the golden age of Petra, from the reign of Aretas IV onwards, the road was paved, and must have run next to a channel that gathered the rainwater coming from the side valleys. Later on, the seasonal stream may even have been covered, in such a way that its water returned to the surface further downstream, near a nymphaeum.

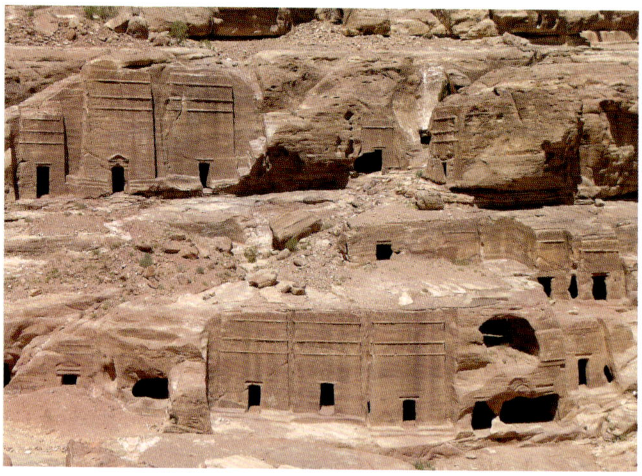

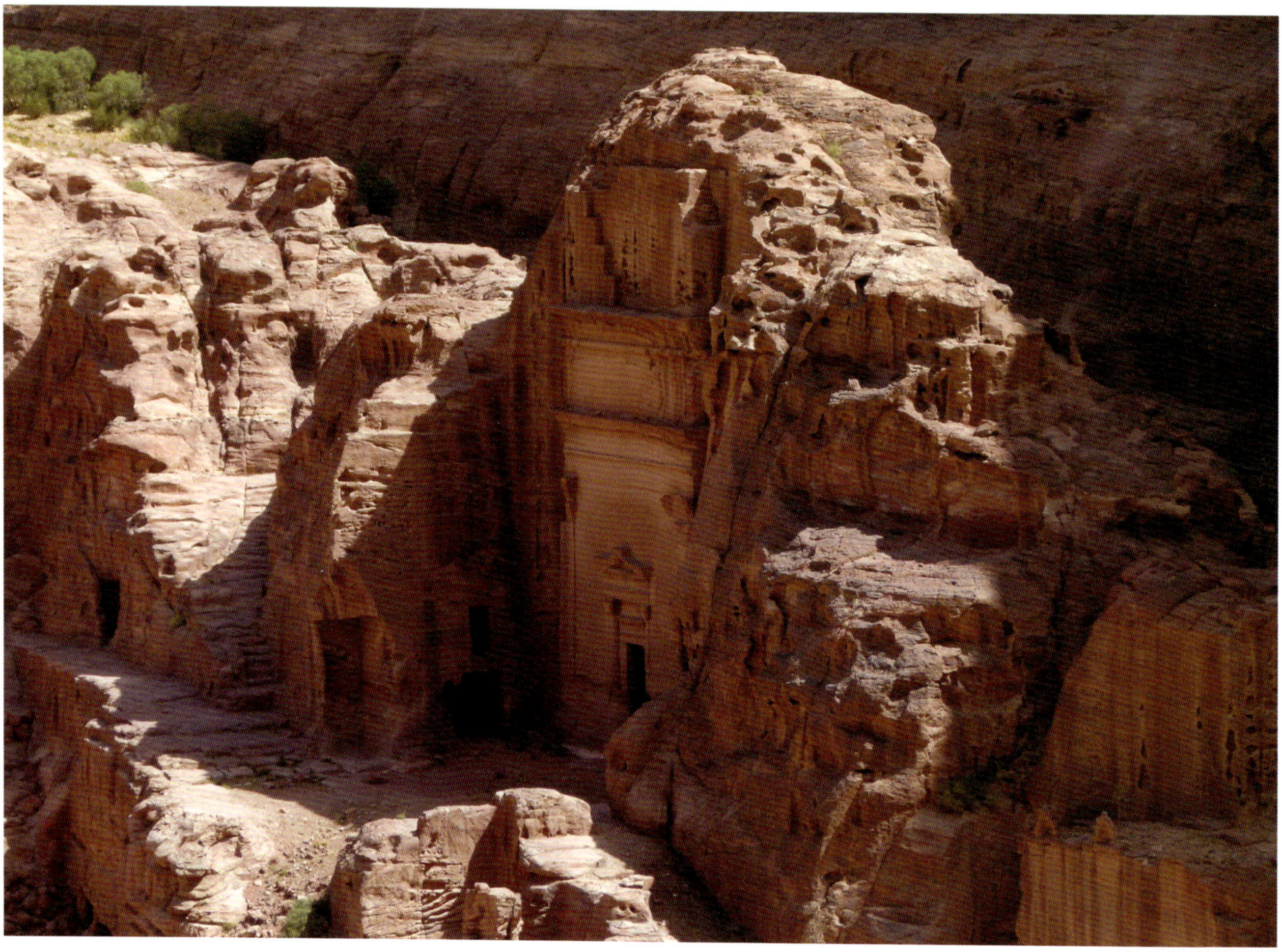

From this point on, the outer Siq opens up more and more and the west face of the valley seems literally covered with the dark holes of dozens and dozens of tombs, spread out on many different levels to make up what the first western visitors called the **Streets of the Facades**. This spectacular array of rock cut structures is a compendium of the most common architectural types in Petra, from the tombs in the Assyrian style to the arched ones. The sepulchres are connected with staircases and narrow passages, which gives the impression that they are actual streets with buildings along them. Several of the tombs on the lowers levels are also half buried by the alluvial detritus, so that not even the doors are visible.
The existence of such a huge necropolis along the main access route to a city may seem strange to a modern visitor, but it was completely normal in the ancient world, both in the Hellenistic and Roman spheres of influence. This remarkable connection between the city of the dead and the city of the living is highlighted by the presence of some rupestrian structures on the eastern side of the valley, which have been irrefutably identified as homes. One in particular, which was damaged by earthquakes, making its underground rooms visible as result of the collapse of the entire facade, has a layout that is surprisingly similar to a modern house, with a large central room, surrounded by six other smaller rooms. Unfortunately, it has not been possible to establish what these rooms were originally used for, and the same can be said for practically all the rock cut houses in the Petra area.

Opposite page, top - *The so-called Streets of the Facades are authentic compendiums of the different architectural types in Petra, from the Assyrian-style tombs to the arch tombs.*

Opposite page, bottom - *The Tomb of 'Uneishu is of the double-cornice type, with the elegant door framed by pilasters with Nabataean capitals and crowned by a triangular pediment of evident classical inspiration.*

Above - *The unmistakable shape of one of the arch tombs carved on the western side of the Outer Siq, along the Streets of the Facades.*

Below - *The large rupestrian house, still relatively well preserved, which is located opposite the theatre.*

Following pages - *View from above of the spectacular theatre cavea, cut into the rock. On the right there are some massive tower tombs.*

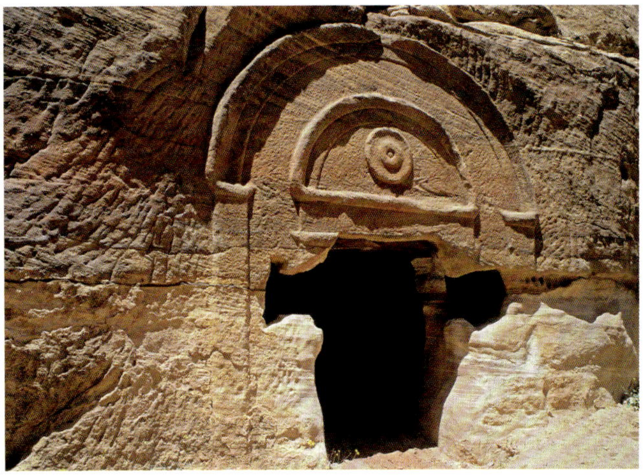

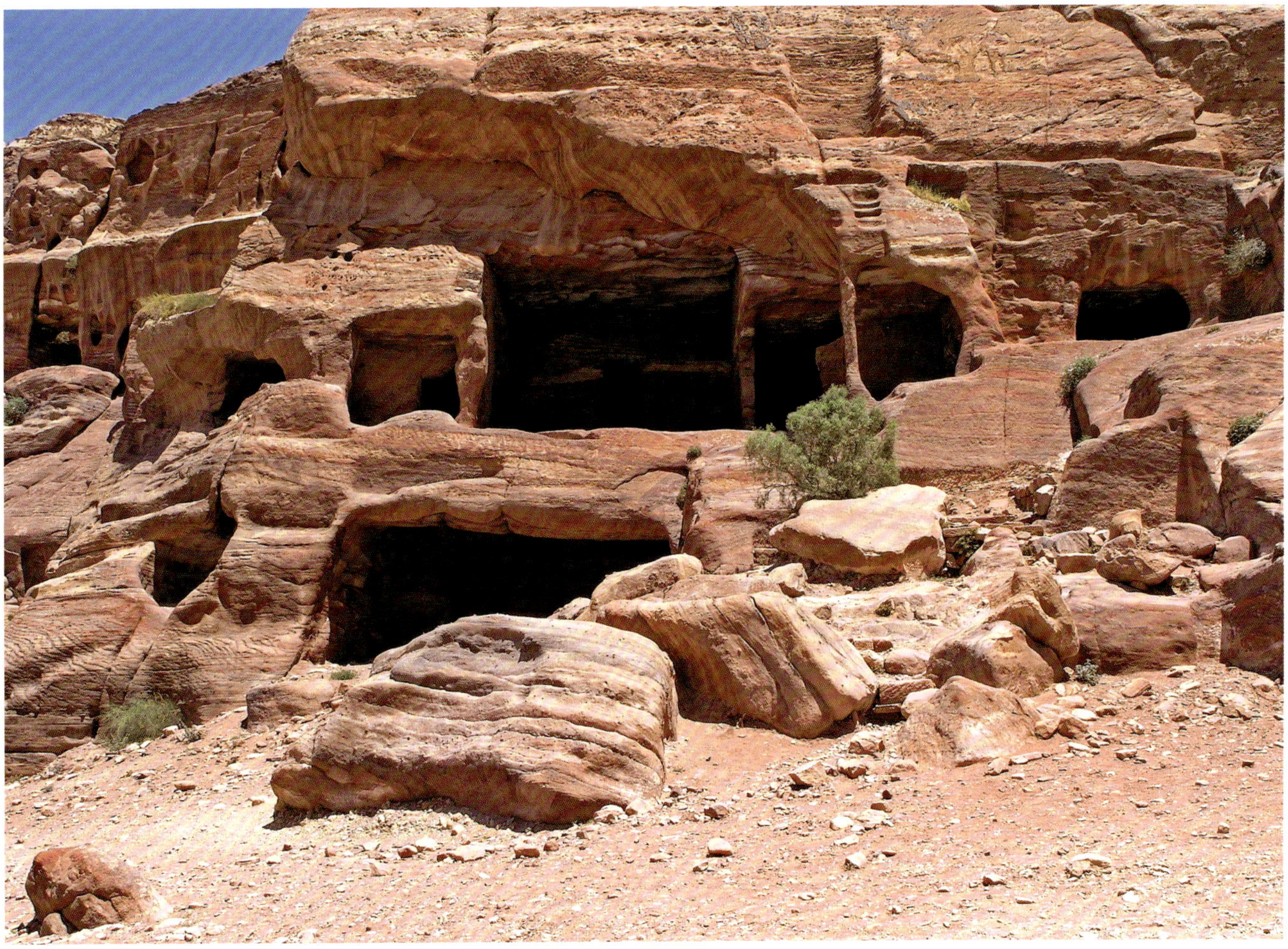

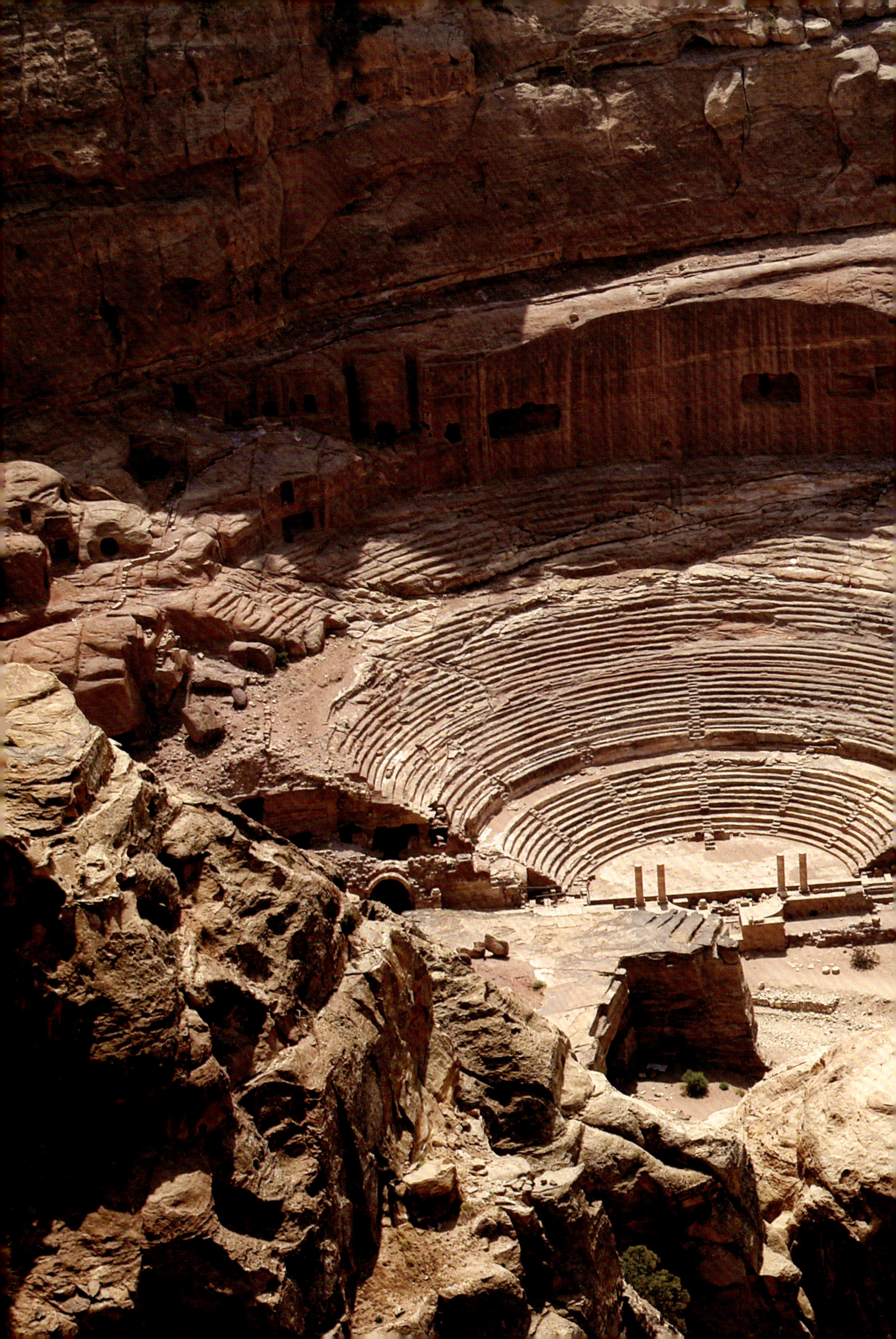

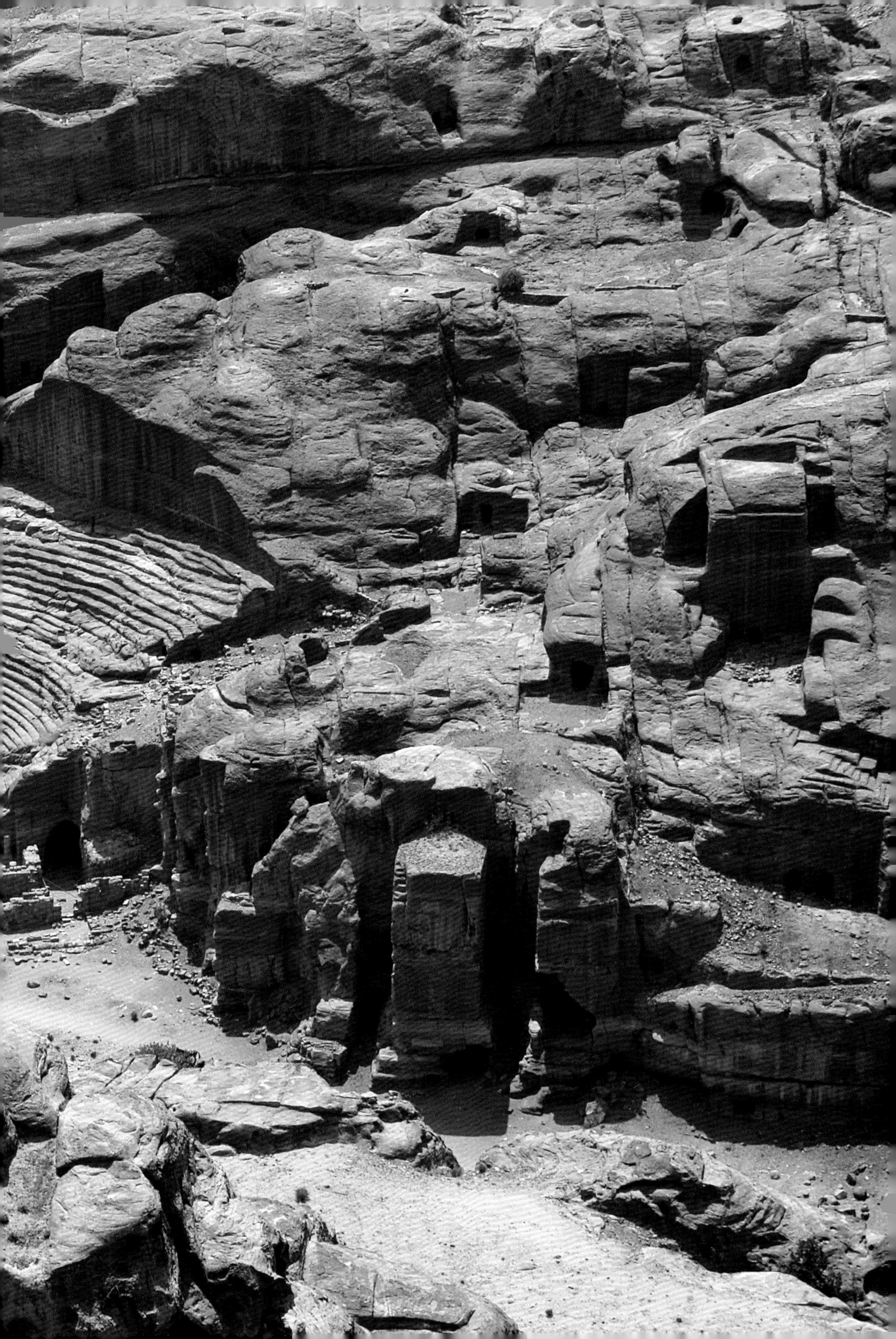

On the opposite side of the Siq, the enormous sweeping curve of the **Theatre** catches the eye, with its *cavea* entirely sculpted out of the living rock. Although this monument has a quintessentially Roman structure (with an orchestra that consists of a perfect semicircle), it is believed to have been built during the reign of Aretas IV (8 BC - 40 AD), a period in which Petra was still independent, but had nonetheless entered into the sphere of influence of Rome. It was then modified during the reign of his successor Malichos II, and finally enlarged after the Trajan's annexation of the city. In its first phase, the theatre must have reached the height of the second ring of seats, but the structure was considerably enlarged after Trajan annexed Petra to the empire in 106 AD. This involved the demolition of some of the tombs behind, along one of the "Streets of the Facades"which was completely dug up to become part of the *summa cavea* (or third horizontal section of the cavea). The alignment of the surviving facades allows us to imagine what the original route of street would have been. The funerary chambers, broken through, thus came to appear incongruously along the rock wall, although it is probable that originally these cavities had been concealed with masonry walls, which later collapsed following earthquakes. The *cavea* has a diameter of 95 metres and is made up of 45 rows of seats (sections made of masonry were only added at the ends), divided into three sections and six *cunei* (or vertical sections) by staircases that allowed the spectators to reach their seats. A complex drainage system, including earthenware tubes, allowed rainwater to be removed. The surface of the orchestra (which has a diameter of 25 metres) was also also cut from the living rock. The stage, which was fronted with a 38 metre long *pulpitum* (a low wall with niches), and the stage wall (*scaenae frons*) behind, were built in masonry, and therefore demolished by earthquakes and floods. Today only the partially reconstructed ruins remain, which allow us to imagine the customary three doorways, framed by colonnades on two floors. To the sides of the stage two barrel vaulted passages (*aditi maximi*) can be seen, originally plastered and painted, which allowed access to the orchestra and the *cavea* through a series of corridors and staircases.

The *cavea*, which still has an exceptional acoustic, could seat between 6,000 and 8,000 spectators. However, some researchers have raised this limit up to 10,000, which was one third of the entire population of Petra. On the outside, the building must have had a fairly sober appearance, with a wall about 18-20 metres high and 65 metres long. The entrances for the public would have been at the base of this wall, which had no windows at all on the upper floors. Finally, it was crowned with a row of corbels and rings in stone, in which the wooden poles would have been fixed to support the great awning that covered the stage. Given its position inside the necropolis, some researchers believe that religious ceremonies and sacred representations, about which little or nothing is known, were probably held in the theatre, in addition to tragedies and comedies. The building was probably destroyed during the great earthquake of 363, but it is believed that by then it had not been used as a venue for shows for quite some time.

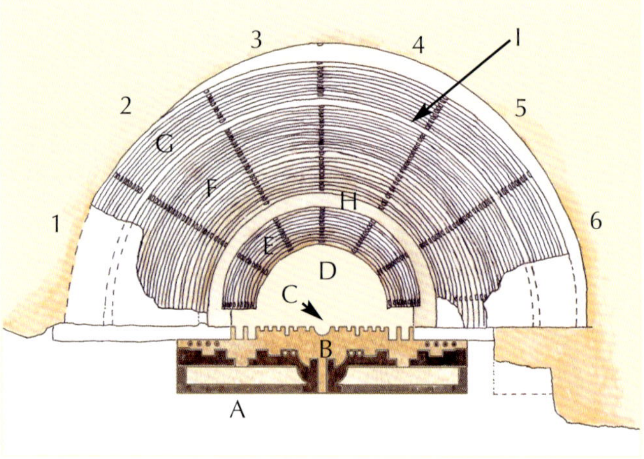

Plan of the theatre

A Scaenae frons
B Proscaenium (stage)
C Pulpitum
D Orchestra
E Ima cavea
F Media cavea
G Summa cavea
H Ima praecinctio (first curved walkway)
I Summa praecinctio (second curved walkway)
1-6 Cunei (vertical sections)

AN ALTERNATIVE TRAIL

Whoever goes up from the bottom of the Outer Siq to the 'Uneishu Tomb, which, incidentally, is one of the most complete burial complexes amongst those that have come down to us, will easily notice a staircase on the left that winds its way to the top. Used with caution, the staircase allows you to reach the top of the rocky hill where the tomb and adjoining sepulchres are carved. It is a long narrow ridge, cleanly separated from the imposing face of Jebel al Khubtha by a deep and narrow gorge. The area is intersected by other staircases and walkways carved into the rock, making it possible to explore the place quite easily.

Once you've reached the extreme north of the rocky relief (nearly opposite the theatre) you can see the continuation of the Siq's aqueduct and a water system as interesting as it is elaborate. It is a series of large collection and settling basins cut into the vertical wall of Jebel al Khubtha, arranged on several levels and interconnected. An ingenuous system of staircases and walkways ensured the maintenance of the system, which was obviously there to collect rainwater from this side of the mountain.

From this vantage point you can enjoy the spectacular view of the stone-cut theatre and the entire Outer Siq.

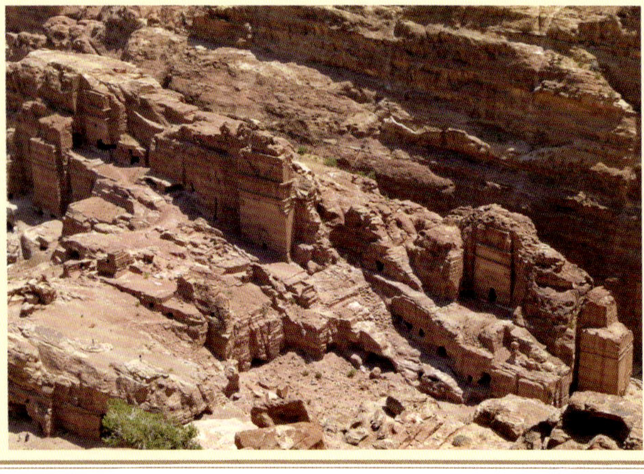

Curiously, the *pulpitum* has some niches filled in using massive blocks of stone. It is thought that this was done to simplify its appearance, making it more austere. This may be evidence of a particular phase in the architecture of Petra known as the Oriental Reaction, which took place in the 2nd century AD and coincided with a rejection of the more elaborate models that came from the Hellenic-Roman world.

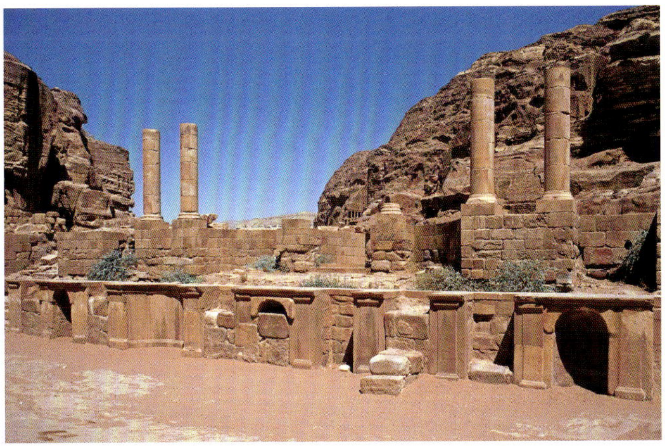

Above - *A detail of the theatre's* pulpitum*: you can see the niches that were filled in with blocks of stone. Archaeological investigations have shown that the whole* pulpitum, *made more sober in appearance, was then plastered.*

Below - *The drawing shows a hypothetical reconstruction of what the appearance of the* scaenae frons *would have been like after the annexation of Petra to the Roman Empire, and the great enlargement and restructuring works that the theatre underwent. The presence of elegant architectural decorations has been evidenced by the discovery in situ of numerous fragments of coatings in precious marble, as well as iron and copper brackets that were once used to fix the cladding slabs to the walls. The fact that statues were almost certainly inserted into the niches of the elaborate* scaenae frons *is certain, not only because this was the custom for this type of buildings, but also because in the excavations conducted in the 1960s a marble statue of Hercules and fragments of a second one were found, along with some Ionic and Corinthian capitals. The excavations also uncovered some of the roof tiles of the scene building. As usual, the stage was covered by a series of beams that jutted out, among which hemp awnings, forming the velarium, were stretched.*

F. Bourbon M. Falcone

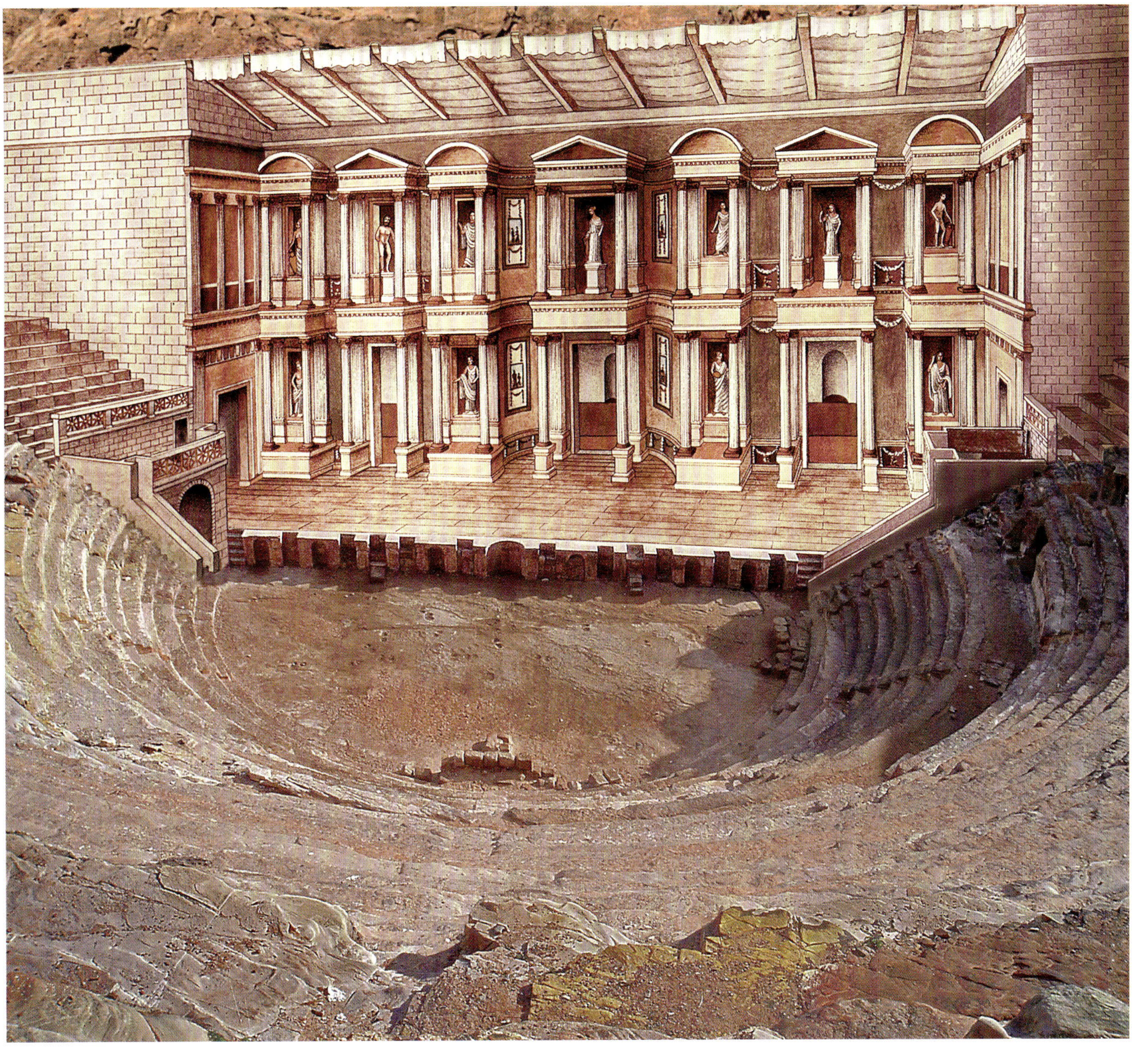

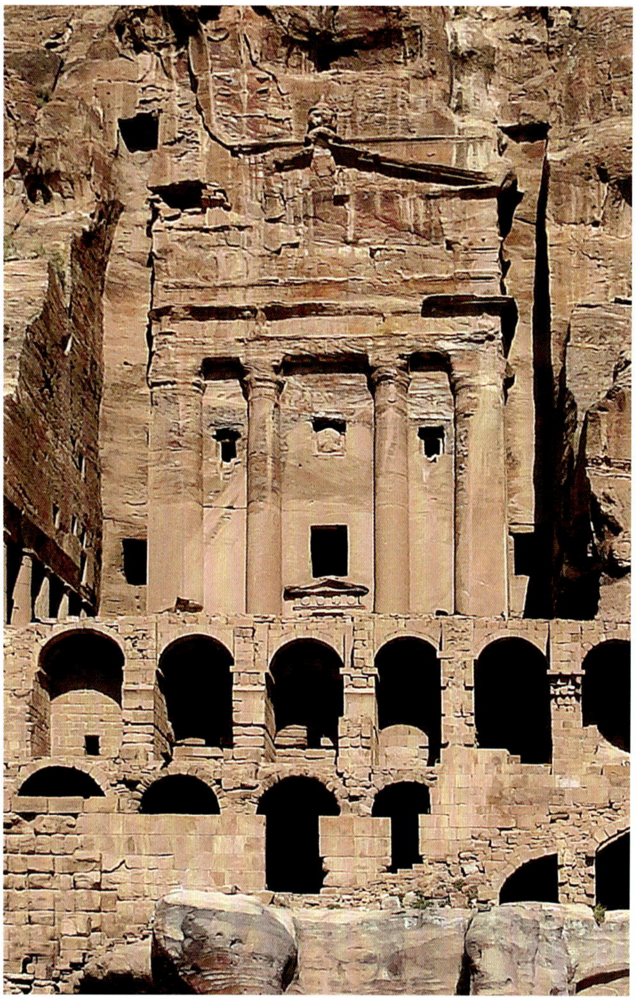

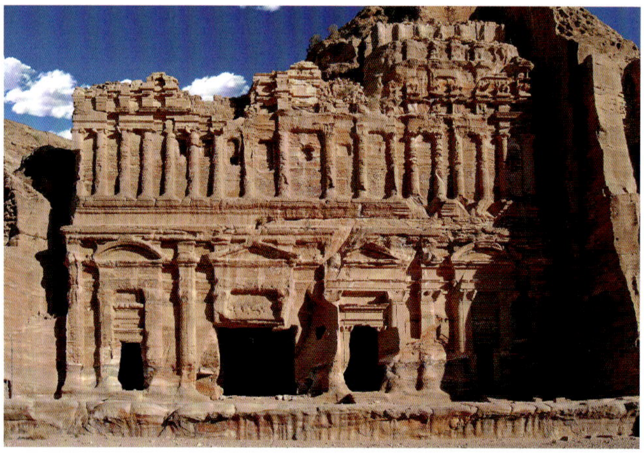

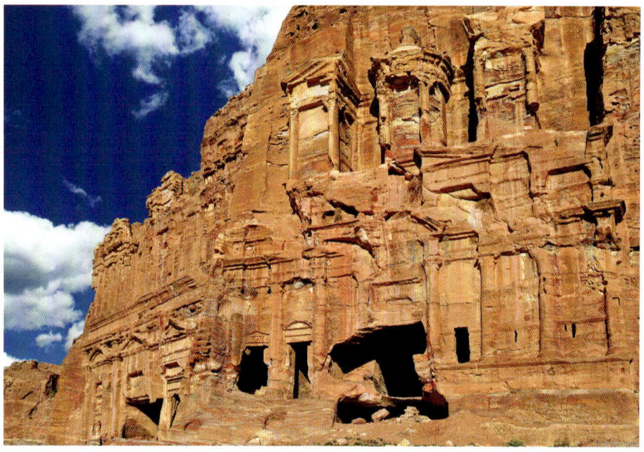

Top left - *View of the Urn Tomb, facing a colonnaded court and preceded by a complex system of two-storey substructures, the real function of which remains unknown.*

Centre left - *The so-called Palace Tomb is the largest rock cut structure in Petra. It was enormous in size and visible from every part of the city, and this suggests that the monument played a very important role: perhaps it was a public building, linked to the royal family or in any case to royal prerogatives.*

Bottom left - *Although it has been badly damaged by the erosive action of the weather, the Corinthian Tomb remains one of the most magnificent monuments in Petra.*

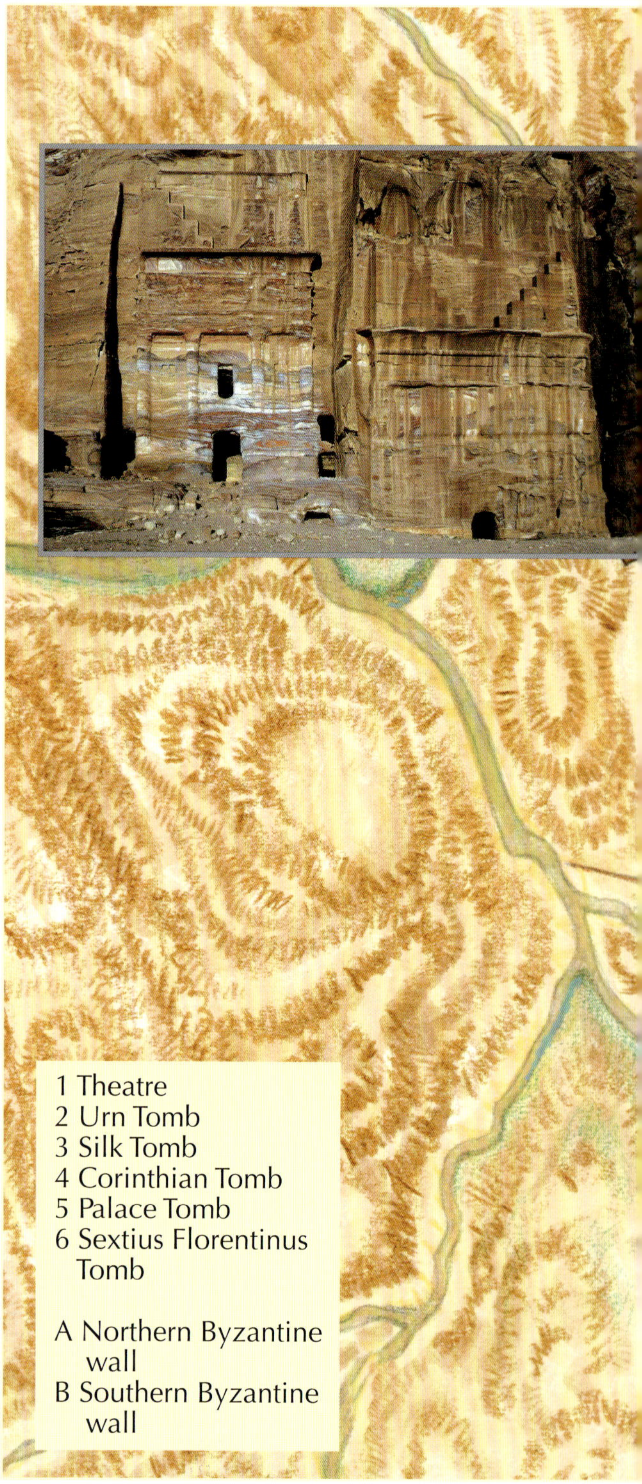

THE ROYAL TOMBS

Actually, there are no inscriptions or other historical documentary evidence to support their modern classification as Royal Tombs, but the unusual size of these structures and the amount it must have cost to build them suggest that it is probably an accurate description. Just over an hour is enough to complete this straightforward itinerary, which starts from the Outer Siq, just beyond the Theatre. On the right hand side of the dirt track that leads to the lower part of Petra, behind the refreshment kiosk, a modern staircase goes up towards the imposing rock face of the Jebel al Khubtha, which is dotted with caves carved into it. Visits usually start from the grand Urn Tomb, but if you have more time on your hands, you can take a detour to the right and explore numerous other rock cut structures in this vast necropolis. Some of the most photogenic hypogea in Petra are to be found here, because of the spectacular grain of the sandstone with its incredible colour contrasts.
The sun shines on the facades in the afternoon.

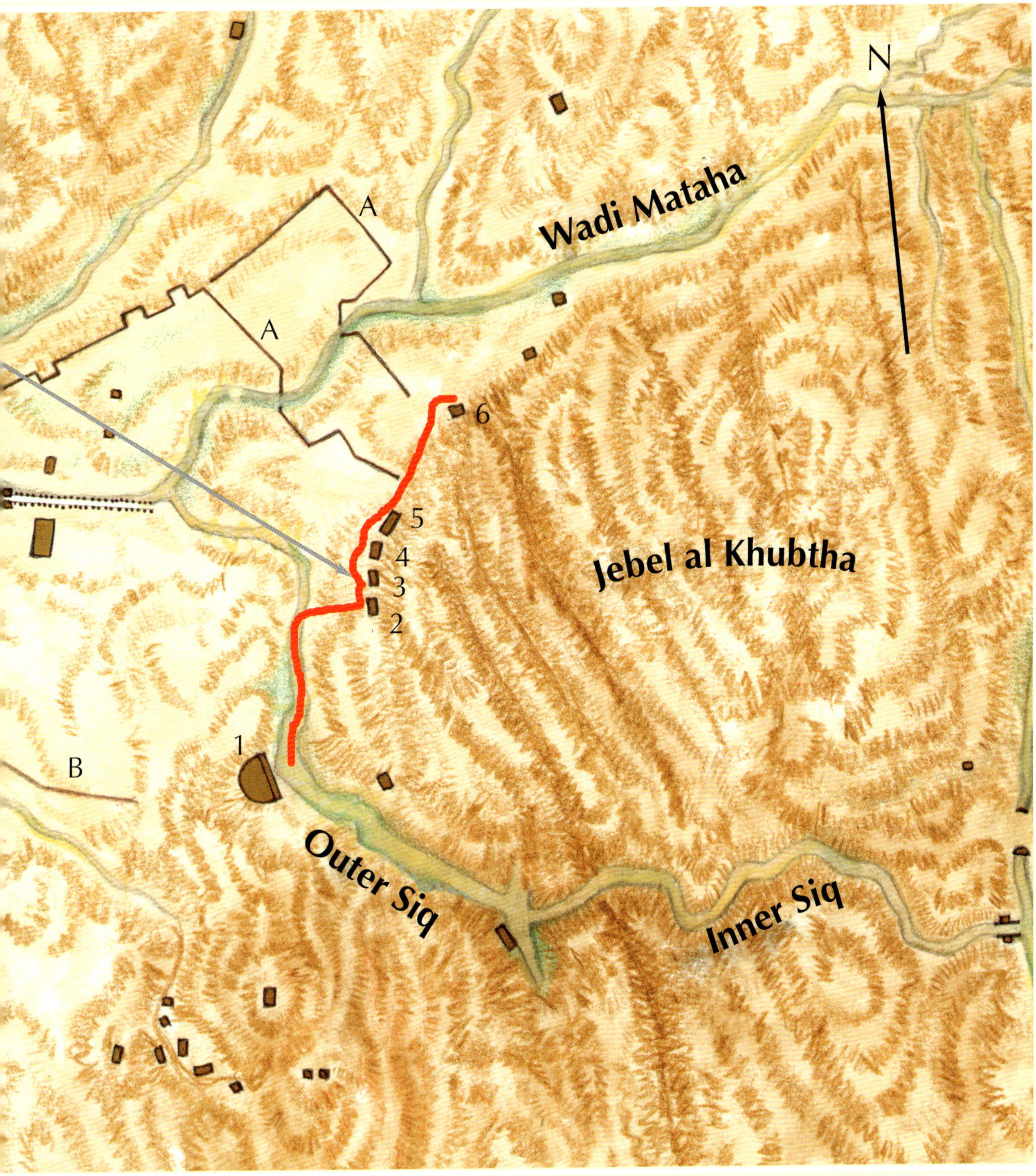

Monica Falcone

THE URN TOMB

The Urn Tomb (No. 772) is easily recognizable because of the eye-catching vaulted substructures on the front of the colonnaded courtyard, the only ones of their kind in Petra. For some strange reason, the tomb takes its name from a small insignificant urn that serves as an acroterion. Its facade is a long way back from the natural line of the mountain. The large courtyard (21.5 metres wide), which was cut out of the living rock, has two colonnades carved into the stone on its shorter sides. One of them still has its columns (three monolithic and two made from 5 cylindrical blocks), while the other has none. The rectangular loculi that can be seen above the northern colonnade are not relevant, as they were made after the tomb. The open space was enlarged by erecting a massive platform (wider than the courtyard) made up of vaulted rooms, set out on two floors. It has now partly collapsed, making it impossible to say whether or not these structures supported a third colonnade facing down the valley, although it is probable that they did. It is this complex structure, much of which has been restored, that gave the monument its local name, al Makhamah, or "Court of Justice", as the Bedouins believed that the tomb was a court, and the rooms in front of it a prison.

The facade, which resembles a tetrastyle Roman temple, although it does not have the classical proportions, is of the simple classical type. It stands out because of its height (it is 26 metres tall) and has a slim angular pillar on either side, onto which quarter columns with Nabataean capitals are adjoined. Two tall half columns on podiums frame the great doorway, which is crowned with the classic Nabataean Doric frieze, in which triglyphs alternate with simple discs in relief, and has a low pediment. The window above the entrance was added at a later date, in 447, when the tomb was converted into a Christian church. In the three intercolumnations, a long way off the ground, there are as many loculi. Only the central one still has a part of the stone slab used to close it off, which is decorated in relief with the bust of a man wearing a toga. It may have been a likeness of the owner of the tomb, but today it is badly damaged. According to the most common theory, it was King Malichos II (40-70 AD), and the two side tombs, which were also sealed with busts originally, might have been his closest family members, maybe his wives. Four busts in relief, perhaps effigies of deities, are just visible above each of the capitals on the main architrave of the high tripartite attic, which supports a pediment with triangular tympanum. This appears not to have any decoration, but originally it was decorated with floral garlands, which are now terribly eroded.

The great chamber (19 metres wide by 17 metres deep) is very austere, as usual, and has a wide arched recess (or apse) in the centre of the rear wall. Originally, there were two recesses, which were later joined together. In the Byzantine era, there must have been the bishop's seat (*cathedra*) here, and in the floor opposite, the holes

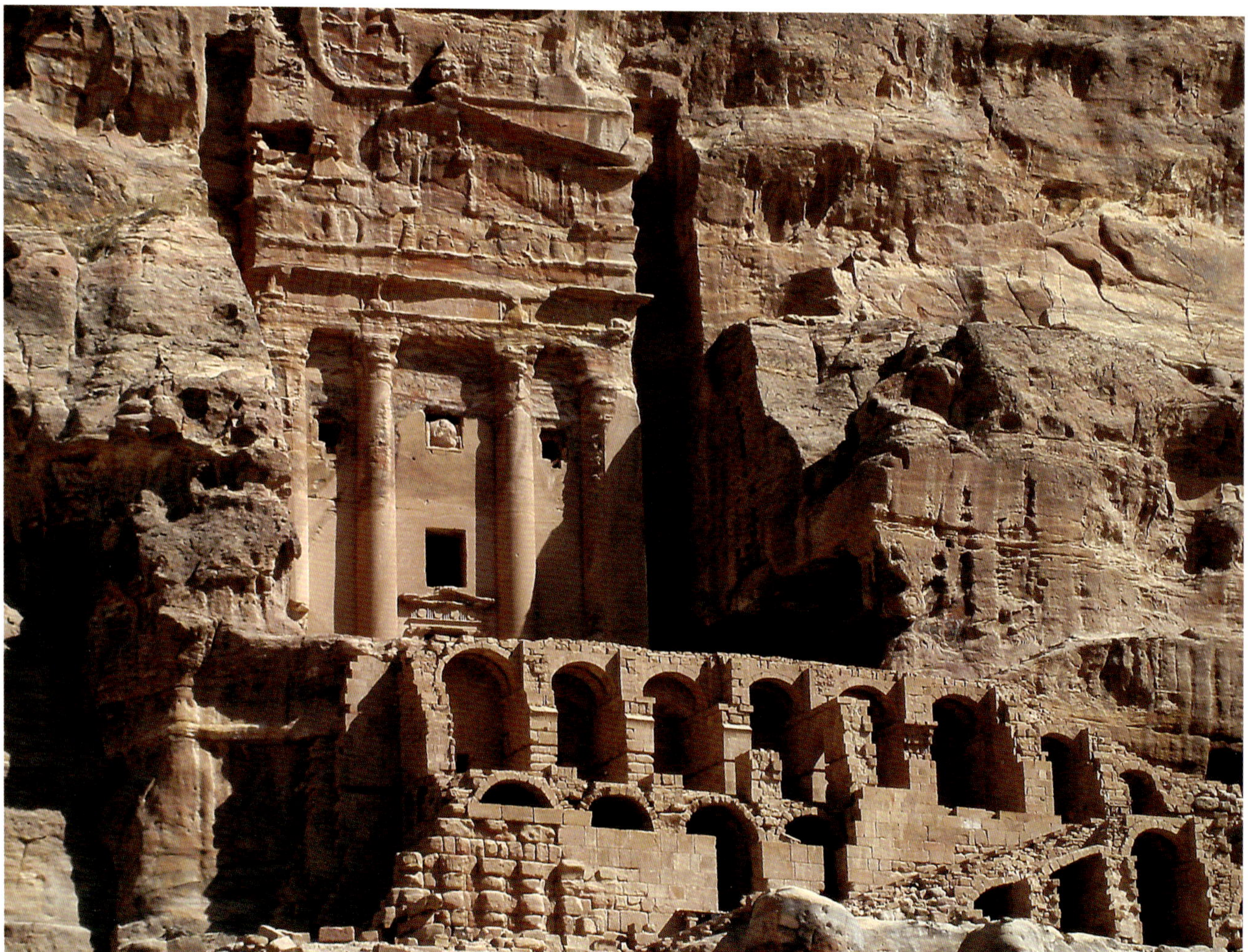

left by the posts that supported the balustrade around the altar can be seen, a customary feature in the Eastern Orthodox Church. There are two other smaller recesses to the right and left of the apse. The researcher John Wilkinson believes they were converted into *martyria*, or spaces where the relics of martyrs were displayed, in the Christian era. A long inscription in Greek, painted on the wall to the left of the most northerly niche celebrates the consecration of the building as a church by the bishop Jason. The three large niches in the side walls (one to the north and two to the south) may have been used as sacristies.
Since the tombs were situated in the facade, this space must originally have been a triclinium hall, where banquets in honour of the deceased were held. However, when it was transformed into a church, the benches were demolished, the floor was levelled and two side doors were added to the facade, surmounted by two more windows, outside the external angular pillars. The lines of little square holes that can be seen on the walls date back to the conversion phase, and blocks of wood must have been inserted into them, to anchor the sacred adornments, lamps and ornaments that are typical of a church.
Although there have been many theories on the subject, there is still no satisfactory explanation as to the function of the large interconnected vaulted spaces, which were laid out on two floors and formed the enormous substructure in front of the tomb. The flight of stairs that gave access to the colonnaded courtyard was built on top of it. The use of so many rounded arches is unique in the architecture of Petra. In spite of its massive size, this structure has a certain elegance and the arches show that the Nabataeans had acquired considerable technical knowledge and become expert at building. It also clearly indicates a Roman influence, as it is well known that the Romans were excellent builders of arches, but in the territory of the Nabataean kingdom, structures of this type are very rare. Some researchers have even suggested that the substructure was built in the Byzantine era, when the monument was converted into a church, but this seems unlikely, given that the structure was essential to access the rock cut tomb and therefore must be from the same period. This suggests that the work dates back to a time when the Roman influence on the architecture of Petra was already well established. In fact, if the Khazneh was constructed during the reign of Aretas IV Philopatris, then it is possible that the Urn Tomb is actually the resting place of Malichos II (or Rabbel II, the last king of Petra).
From the terrace, a flight of stairs facing south and a walkway lead to a picturesque part of the rupestrian necropolis, where some interesting hypogea dug into the magnificent multi-coloured sandstone can be found.

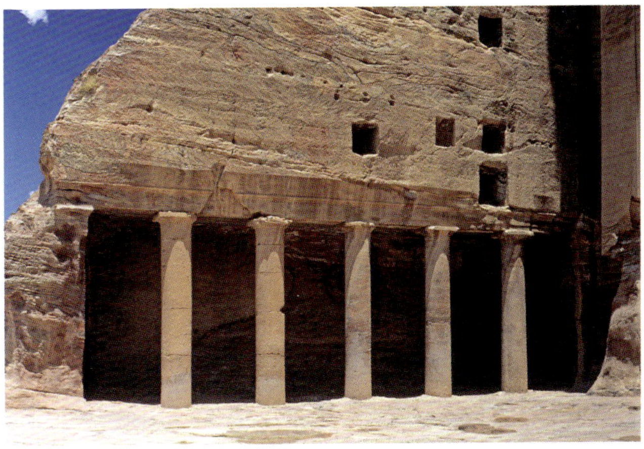

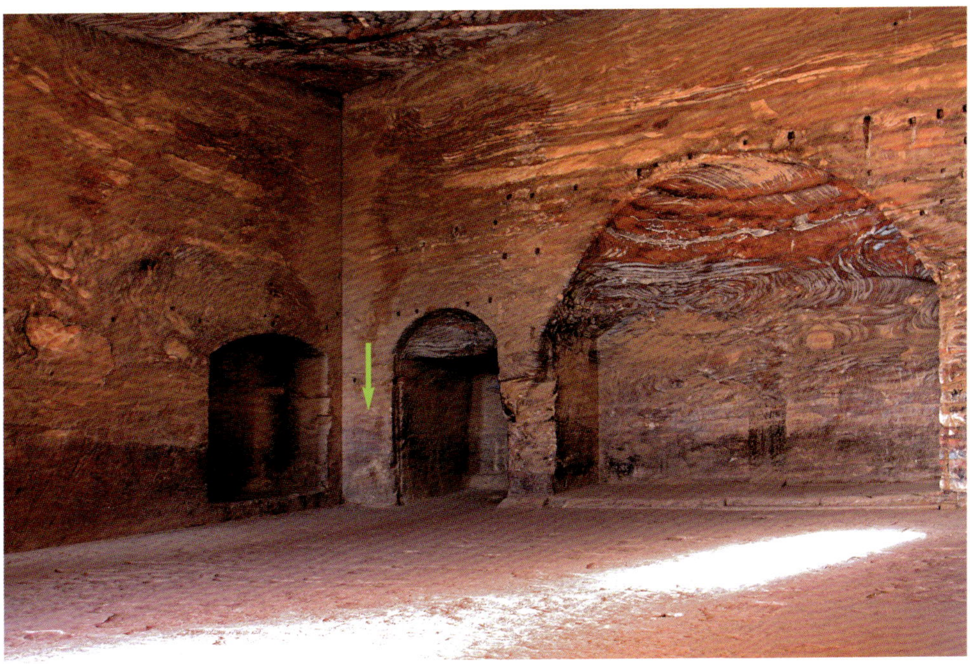

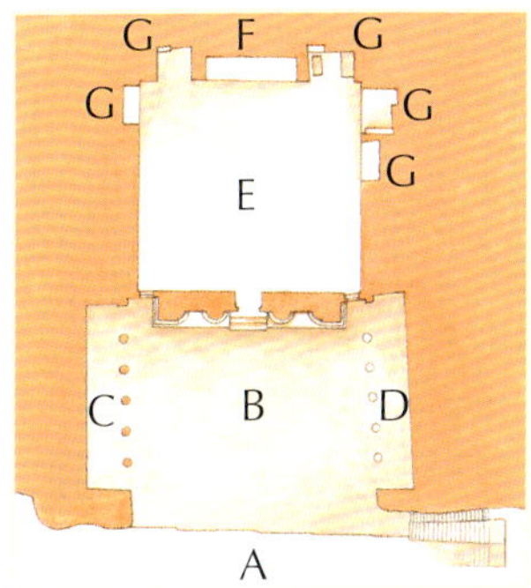

Plan of the Urn Tomb

A Substructures
B Courtyard
C Northern colonnade
D Southern colonnade
E Chamber or triclinium
F Arched recess (or apse)
G Recesses

Opposite - *The unmistakable silhouette of the Urn Tomb. Originally, perhaps the huge arched substructures supported a portico, a continuation of the two lateral ones carved into the stone. Archaeological evidence suggests that a courtyard closed on three sides was typical of funeral complexes in Petra.*

Above - *The northern colonnade still retains its five smooth columns, with simple capitals.*

Below - *A glimpse of the large room, with the wide apse excavated in the rear wall; the arrow indicates the position of the commemorative inscription in Greek.*

THE SILK TOMB

To the left of the Urn Tomb, there is a proto Hegra tomb, the facade of which is very eroded. The only interesting thing about it is that, unusually, the great half merlons are made up of six steps, instead of the usual five. This is a clear demonstration of the fact that the architectural canons were not always faithfully adhered to.
A little further along, the unmistakable facade of the so-called Silk Tomb can be seen. It owes its name to the spectacular colours and silky appearance of the grain of the stone, made even more vivid by erosion. The streaks in the sandstone display a superb range of hues, including ochre, saffron yellow, powder pink and sugar paper blue, in a palette of enchanting beauty. In addition to its striking colours, the tomb is also interesting for some of its architectural characteristics. The facade is of the Hegra type (or double cornice type), and the lower part has four pilasters crowned with Nabataean capitals. Two niches are carved in the intercolumniations, which unusually contain as many human figures in relief. Unfortunately, these are no longer recognizable. Above the door there is a large loculus, which is not a very common element. The lower attic is split up into sections by three cornices and divided by short pilasters in line with those below. As usual, the facade is crowned by two half merlons. The two rooms to the sides of the facade were probably service rooms.

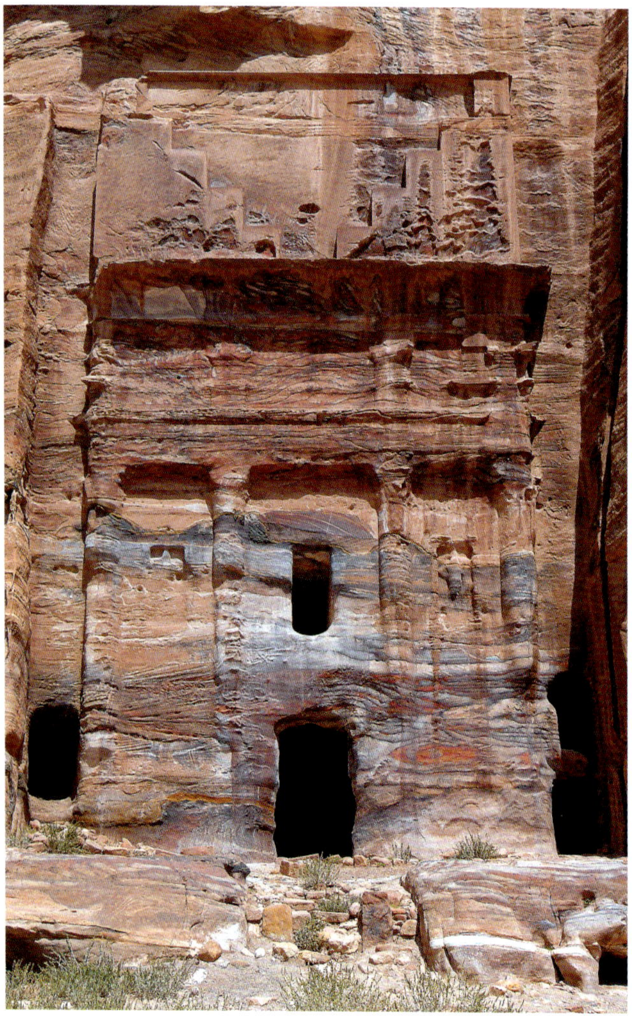

HYDRAULIC CONDUITS

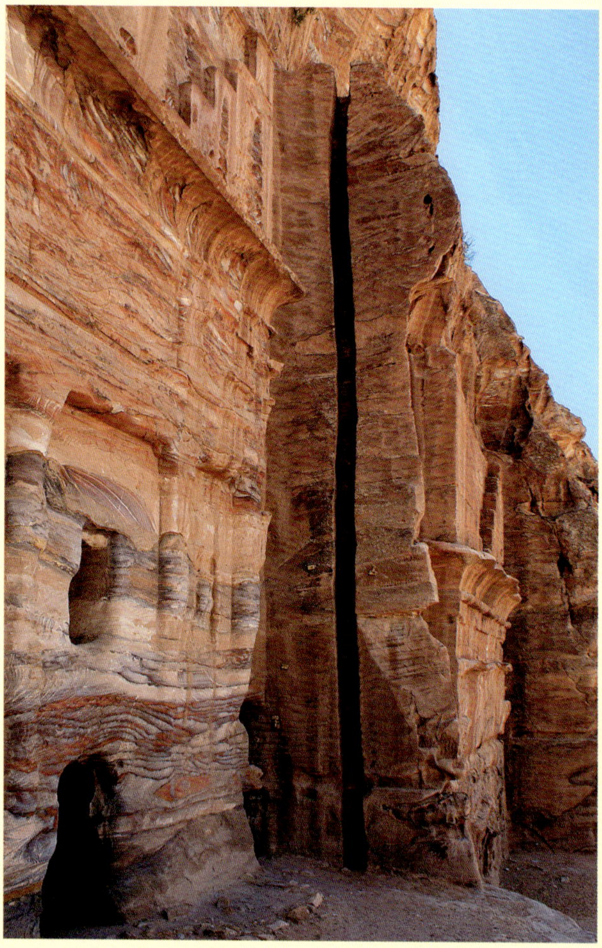

Once you have sufficiently admired the brilliant colours of the Silk Tomb, it is worth having a look at the vertical groove cut into the prominence to the right of the facade. A very similar groove is visible a little further on, next to the gigantic Palace Tomb. It is clearly a drainpipe that was part of a hydraulic system that collected rainwater from a natural fissure that runs above along the wall of the Jebel al Khubtha, behind the group of hypogea that includes the Urn Tomb. From this small ravine, rainwater was redirected downwards through a deep cut and flowed into a square basin carved right at the top of the rock buttress; from here, decanted, it went down the drainpipe and presumably finished its journey in a cistern that still lies underground at the foot of the Silk Tomb.
This effective water supply system, visible in several other tombs in Petra confirms what was learnt from the inscription of the Turkmaniyya Tomb, which describes the sepulchre as a complex heterogenous structure, including the actual tomb itself, a courtyard in front of it, service rooms, the triclinium and, of course, one or more cisterns.
Drinking water was essential during funeral ceremonies for washing and ablutions and during the symposiums and banquets that periodically took place in honour of the deceased. Among other things, in classical antiquity wine had a higher alcohol content than it does today and had to be diluted with water to be drunk.
From the gorge described above, another channel carved into the rock face brought water to the Corinthian Tomb.

THE CORINTHIAN TOMB

A few metres from the Silk Tomb, beyond the facade of a hypogeum that was never completed, stands the magnificent, though badly damaged, Corinthian Tomb (No. 776). In spite of having suffered the ravages of time more than the others, as a result of being carved in a position particularly exposed to the wind and rain, it remains a monument of great architectural interest, and impressive dimensions. It is 24.5 m wide by about 28 m high. It was given its name by the British travellers Irby and Mangles at the beginning of the nineteenth century (or according to some by the Frenchman Léon de Laborde in 1828), who classified the floral style of the capitals, which are similar to those of the Khazneh though less elaborate, as Corinthian. Underlining this similarity, the Corinthian Tomb has often been considered a sort of "rough copy" of the Pharaoh's Treasure. In fact, however, since the resemblance only applies to the upper floor, it would be more accurate to say that the monument represents an attempt to mediate between the imported Hellenistic style and the strictly Nabataean one. Indeed, the lower part of the facade appears to have been designed in line with local architectural canons. It has eight rather squat semi-columns standing on a high platform, with the main doorway surmounted by a curvilinear pediment and a broken pediment above. The repetition of the horizontal lines of the cornices and the vertical ones of the short pilasters closely resembles the Bab el Siq Triclinium. The upper part, on the other hand, with its central *tholos*, two half pediments, floral capitals and overall vertical momentum, is like the Khazneh.

Opposite - *The Silk Tomb is famous for the myriad of shades that give the facade the appearance of a multi-coloured fabric.*

Below - *The Corinthian Tomb, severely damaged by earthquakes and atmospheric events, displays unique architectural inconsistencies that compromise the symmetry of the facade.*

Plan of the Corinthian Tomb

A Burial chamber
B Recesses (or loculi)
1,2,3 Small chambers

Léon de Laborde, who in 1828 saw the tomb in a state of better conservation, designed its plan with the third small room communicating with the main chamber through a door.

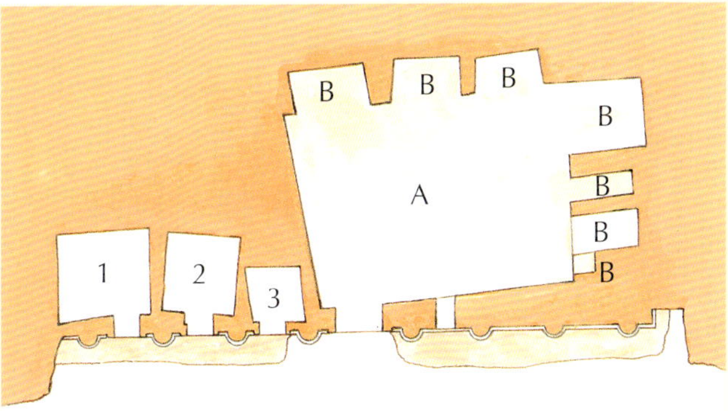

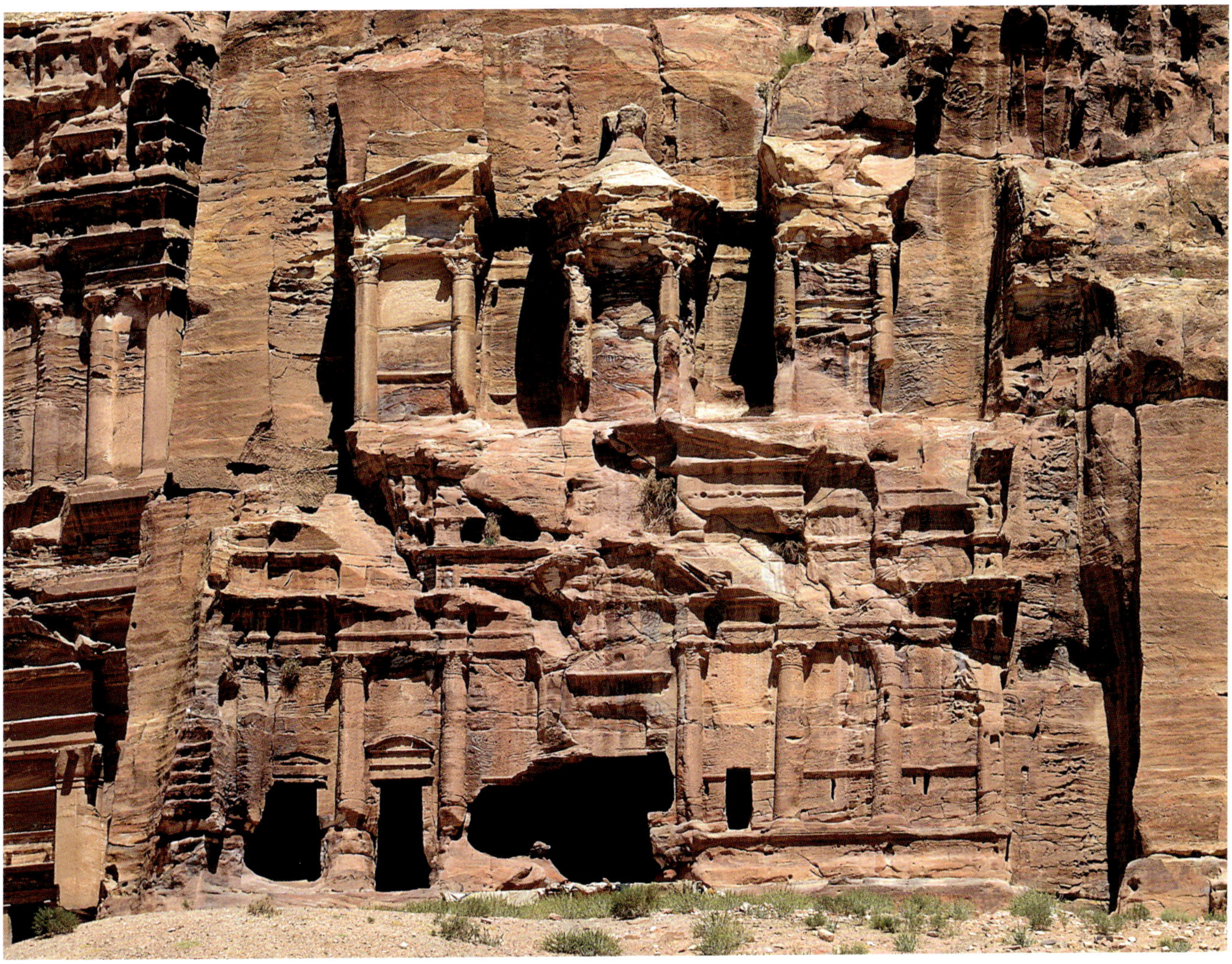

However, there are no relief decorations and the frieze is also made up of triglyphs alternating with typical Nabataean metopes, consisting of simple discs slightly in relief.
The clear asymmetry of the first floor is absolutely unique, and certainly discordant. It has three doors to the left of the main entrance, which access rooms with no communicating doors between them, and a window to the right. These are not the only discrepancies, however. While the floor of the two rooms furthest to the left is at a roughly similar height to that of the main hall (though not the same), the floor of the small room next to it, on the other hand, is considerably higher, which leaves a certain amount of perplexity as to how it could have been accessible from the outside. The large window that lights the main chamber seems unexplainable, and the two narrow embrasures carved out of the two neighbouring intercolumniations even more so. They appear to have been added at a later date, after the monument had been built. The three smaller doors and the window also have architectural designs that are very different from each other. The window to the right is completely bare, while the two doors furthest out are crowned, one with a carved triangular pediment, and the other with a inserted curvilinear pediment. The four rooms in the Corinthian Tomb are also strangely asymmetrical, and not perfectly in line with the facade. Finally, the cave that opens up in correspondence with the main doorway and continues under the floor of the large hall, making access to it almost impossible, is very strange. This vast underground space was originally made up of several interconnected rooms, and was probably a large cistern, the function of which was connected with funeral rites.
There are no traces of loculi in the smaller rooms, but in the large hall, which measures 12 m by 9 m, there are three recesses cut into the end wall, and four in the right hand wall, at different levels.
A deep gutter for the rainwater was carved into the bell-shaped roof of the *tholos*.
Ultimately, the appearance of the Corinthian Tomb may seem redundant and not very successful, but its poor state of preservation undoubtedly contributes to this bad impression. We should bear in mind that this building had a privileged position, perfectly in line with the great Colonnade, and at the time of its greatest splendour, it must have had an impressive visual impact. This suggests that it was the burial place of a very important person. At one time it was believed to be the tomb of King Aretas III the Philhellen (86-62 BC), but the current dating of the Khazneh contradicts this theory. If the Corinthian Tomb is in fact later than the Pharaoh's Treasure, as seems likely given the stylistic similarity, it should be dated to at least the second half of the 1st century AD. It is therefore reasonable to presume that the Corinthian Tomb may have contained the mortal remains of Malichos II (40-70 AD) or Rabbel II (70-106). However, there are no inscriptions or historical data to support this theory.

Below - *The upper order of the Corinthian Tomb reveals a clear Hellenistic architectural influence, with the* tholos *inserted between the two half pediments applied in Khazneh with decidedly more balanced outcomes.*

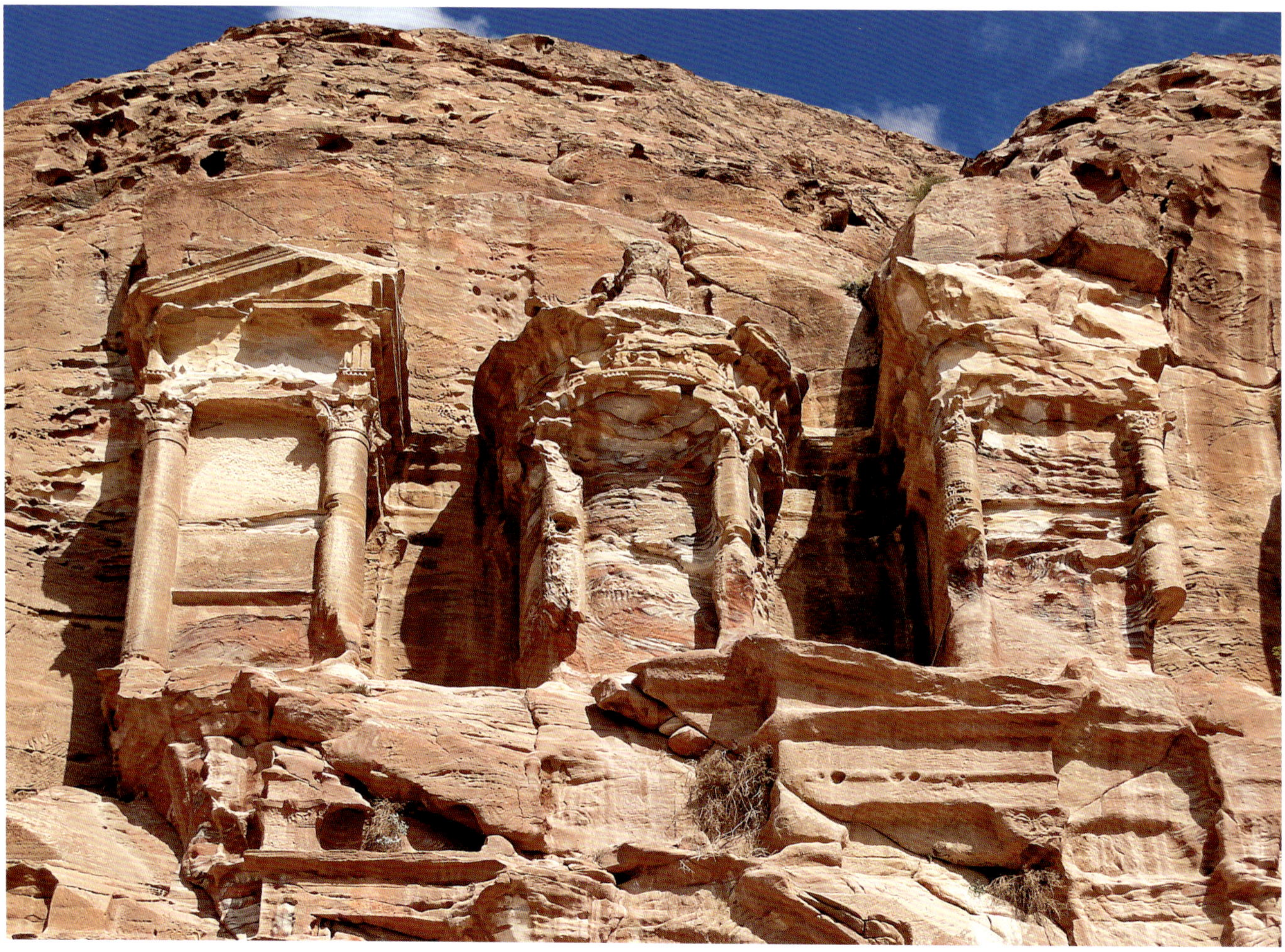

THE CORINTHIAN TOMB: A RECONSTRUCTIVE SUGGESTION

Explaining a monument as enigmatic as the Corinthian Tomb can seem ambitious but highlighting several features may help to understand the monument better.
Firstly, it is interesting how the internal rooms are so dissimilar in terms of size and floor height. The rooms are not orthogonal to each other, nor in line with the facade and appear to be the result of a not a perfectly executed job. Additionally, the most northern part of the facade (namely the left side) clearly appears unfinished, so much so as to lack depth, unlike the opposite side. However, this was intentional as the rock's thickness is greatly reduced at this point, so carving it would have broken through into the most northern room.
The two smaller doorways, besides the fact that they lead to rooms completely void of both loculi and triclinium-benches, appear rather incongruous. However, it can be admitted that in the architectural taste of the time, symmetry was not a fundamental requirement, and therefore they did not disturb the overall aesthetics of the tomb, being functional for some specific purposes. Now also considering that between the Corinthian Tomb and the Silk Tomb there is a wide section of rock face visibly excavated, in which two hypogea without facade open, it is possible that some rooms had already been carved into this section. Perhaps two of them were reworked, provided with two elegant portals and incorporated into the front of the Corinthian Tomb, during the monumentalization phase of this area.
The two openings to the side of the main doorway seem absurd considering that the monument was in fact a tomb, as already established. Perhaps these doors/windows were the result of a later reworking of the monument for another function, as in the case of the Urn Tomb, where two doors and three large windows were opened when it was transformed into a church. Even the two embrasures would have been coeval with the transformation.
All said and done, this tomb had its own regal splendour before being devastated by the ravages of time, and today remains a monument of imposing proportions.

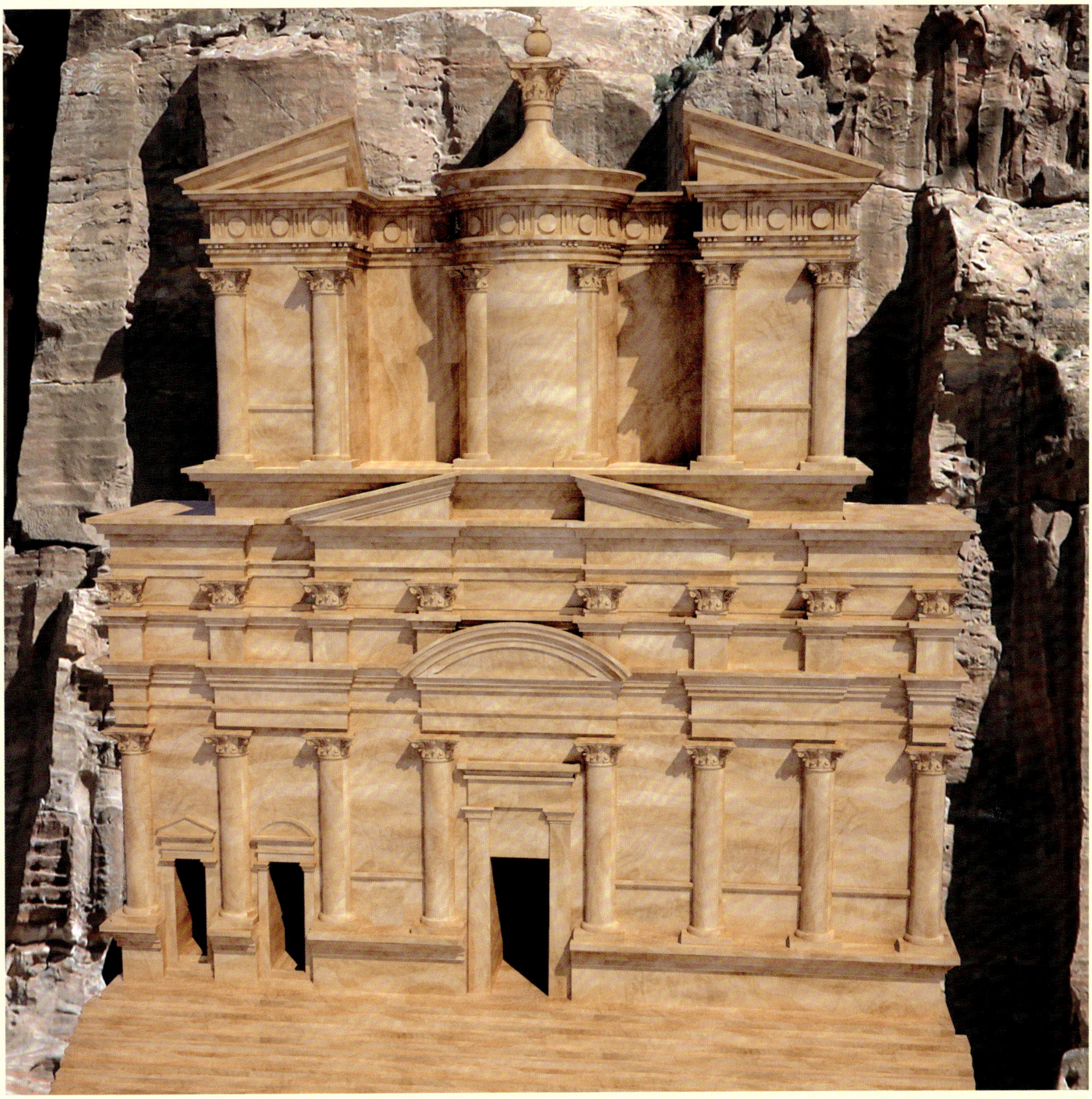

F. Bourbon - M. Bavagnoli

THE PALACE TOMB

Immediately to the left of the Corinthian Tomb stands the gigantic facade of the so-called Palace Tomb (Tomb 765). Although all of the upper part is badly damaged, it is still the largest tomb in Petra, 49 metres wide and more than 45 metres high. It has an extremely complex shape, and it is called the Palace Tomb because it was originally believed to be an imitation of the great Hellenistic or Roman palaces. Some people even suggested that it was influenced by the Domus Neroniana, the sumptuous royal palace that Nero had built in Rome. The only thing we can say for sure is that its appearance is as unlike that building as any other Nabataean rock cut structure, and it is therefore unique, both because of its unusual architectural features, and because of the obvious difference between the styles of the ground floor and the upper floors.

The facade is preceded by a large stage-like platform, entirely carved from the bed of sandstone, and higher than ground level. From here, four staircases, cut into the rock, lead to the great doorways, which are framed by pilasters. These in turn are set between half-pillars supplemented by quarter columns, crowned by great Nabataean capitals with magnificent pediments on top of them. The two outermost of these are curvilinear, and the other two are triangular.

The second floor rises up above an unusual continuous trabeation, which is completely smooth and creates an effect of disconcerting contrast. In fact, the eighteen semi-columns, divided into pairs, are not in any way aligned with the verticals of the floor below. This sort of blind arcade supports an alternately recessed and advanced double trabeation with no frieze, on which a third storey, or attic, stands. It is made up of short pilasters with Nabataean capitals, which are extensions of the semi-columns below, and divided into several horizontal sections by a number of cornices. Only the right hand section of the third floor carved out of the

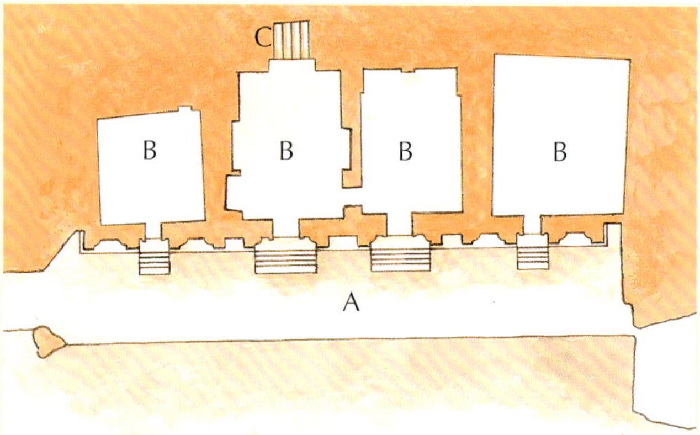

Plan of the Palace Tomb

A Terrace
B Chambers
C Large niche

Below - *The peculiar proportions of the so-called Palace Tomb are rather unique in the architectural panorama of Petra.*

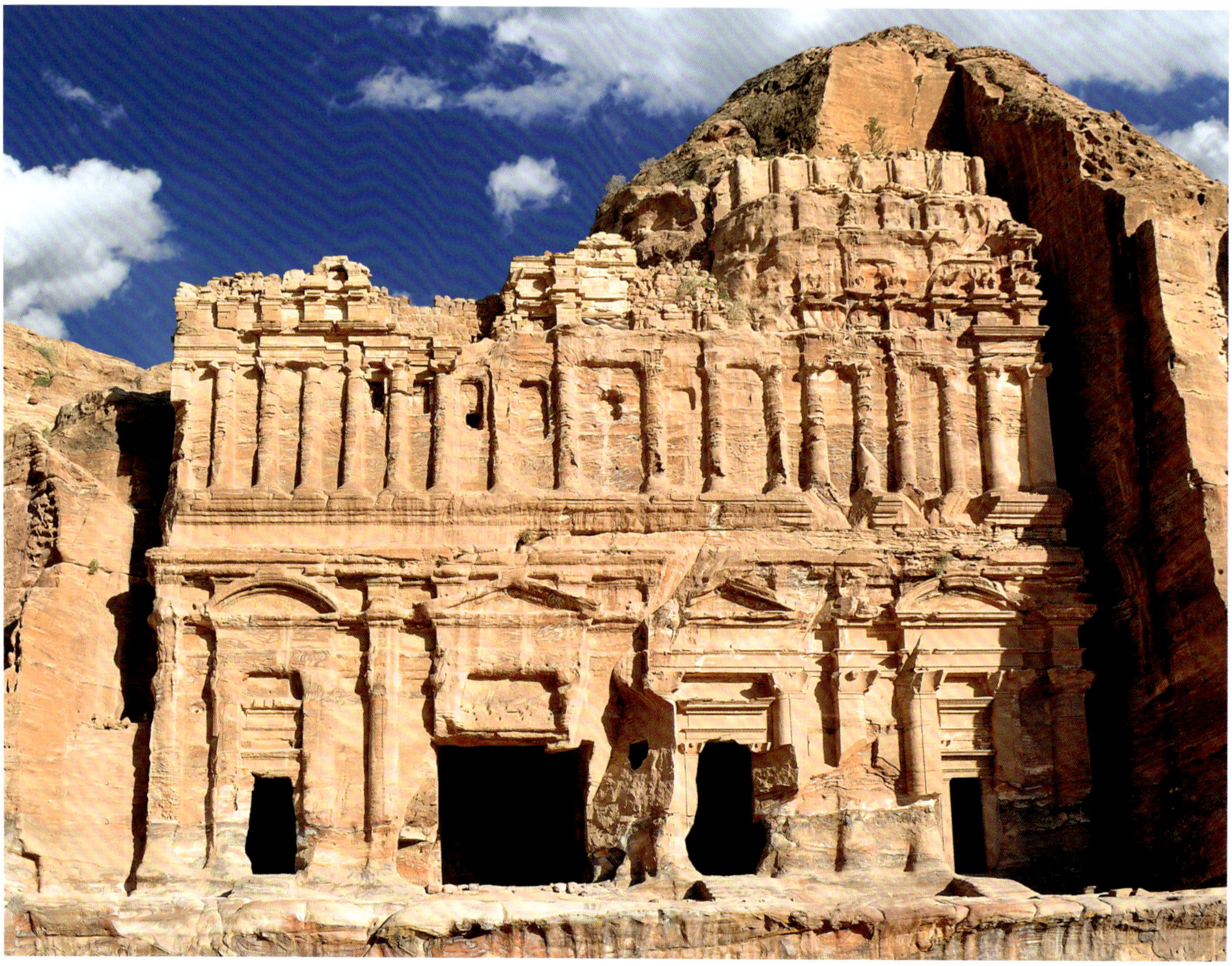

THE PALACE TOMB: A RECONSTRUTIVE SUGGESTION

This digital anastylosis suggests what the Palace Tomb would have been like. Its reconstruction is not difficult as far up as the cornice on the third floor, as the top right corner is relatively well preserved and it is therefore possible to deduce how the structure was before the top part collapsed. The appearance of the top floor (or attic floor) is harder to imagine, but the seven pilasters carved in a backward position and the enormous incision in the rock buttress to the right, suggest that the building rose few metres higher.
Perfectly visible on the left side, at the height of the middle of the second floor, is a large, natural fissure blocked by a masonry work that rests on a relieving arch which constitutes the mouth of a gallery. A staircase cut into the sandstone gave access to this "tunnel" running parallel to the edge of the facade, whose purpose is completely unknown. However, clearly this very impressive substructure (including several wooden beams) must have supported a considerable mass.
What remains of the facade denotes a reoccurring scheme of identical elements. This, plus the bases of several columns in front of the seven pilasters, justify the theory that there was actually an arcade; a three-dimensional replica of the blind arcade that forms the second floor. The arcade would have boosted the whole structure and balanced the overall appearance of the monument with its full and empty spaces. Thus, the facade would have taken on features similar to theatrical facades, particularly those erected between the Flavian and Severian periods, as is attested by Hierapolis of Phrygia (Turkey), Sabratha (Libya) and Merida (Spain) where the alternation of protruding and receding parts of the colonnade, distributed on many levels, also appear. This would date the monument to between the last decades of the 1st century AD and the first half of the 2nd century AD. Although it is reasonable to assume that even after annexation to the Roman empire, sumptuous celebratory monuments continued to be built in Petra, as the altar built in front of Qasr el Bint during the reign of Marcus Aurelius (161-189 AD) demonstrates, it is more likely that a monument of this scale was made at the behest of a Nabataean king. This can only be Rabbel II (70-106), the last king of Petra, in a period already strongly influenced by imperial Roman architecture.

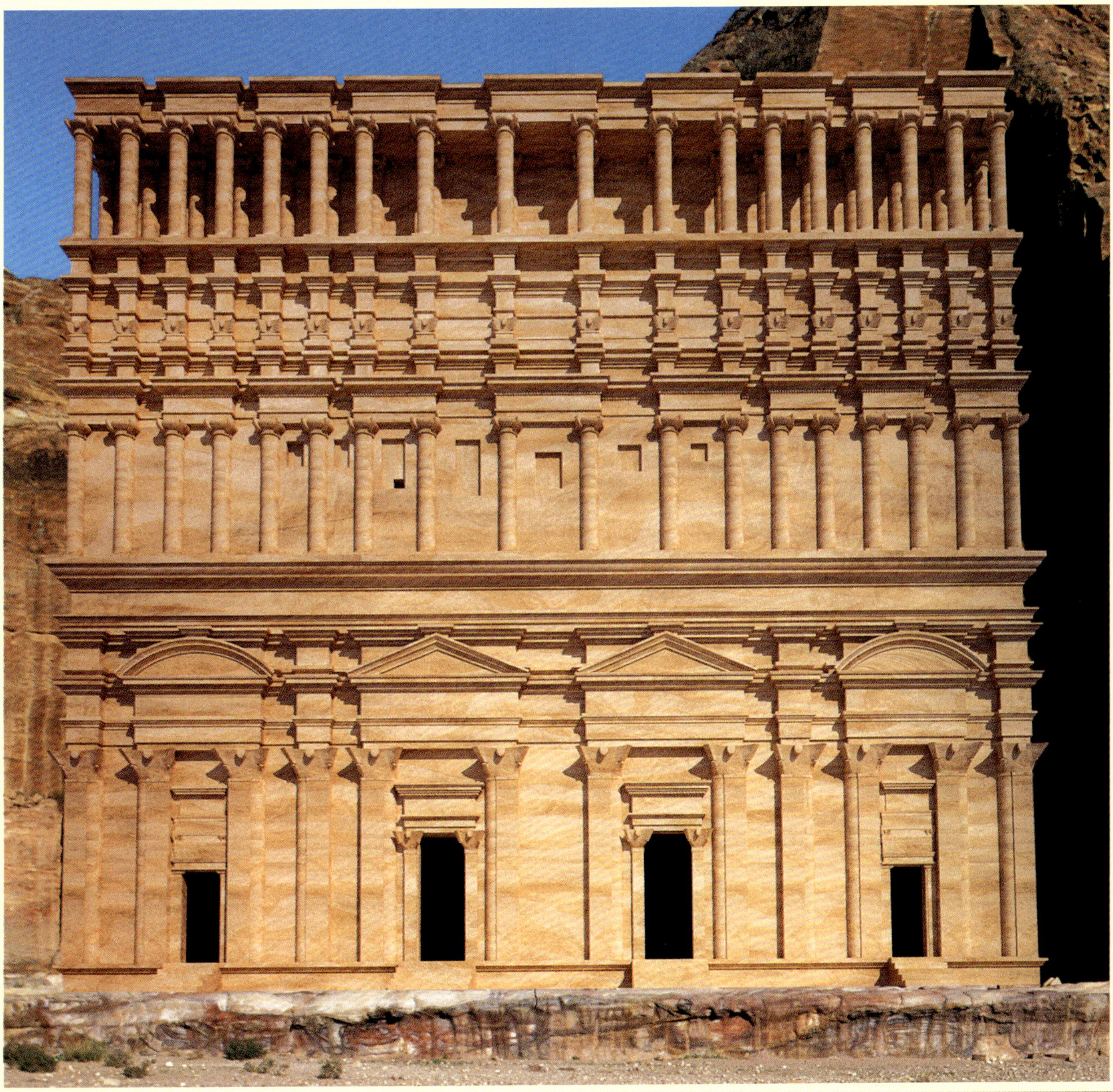

F. Bourbon - M. Bavagnoli

rock, while the rest was built in masonry. Unfortunately, earthquakes have destroyed most of it. Finally, at the top, on the right hand side, the fact that there was originally a fourth storey can be perceived from seven surviving pilasters, a little behind the line of the facade and partially cut into the living rock. In correspondence with each of these, and in front of them, there are the bases of as many columns (the presence of which was established by the author in 1998), aligned with the pilasters and semicolumns on the second and third floors. It is therefore possible to imagine that the facade was topped with an arcade that supported a crowning entablature.

While the appearance of the ground floor is majestic and elegant, the architectural decorations above seem to be a juxtaposition of identical elements that are repeated, which certainly creates a bizarre overall effect. However, we should bear in mind that in ancient

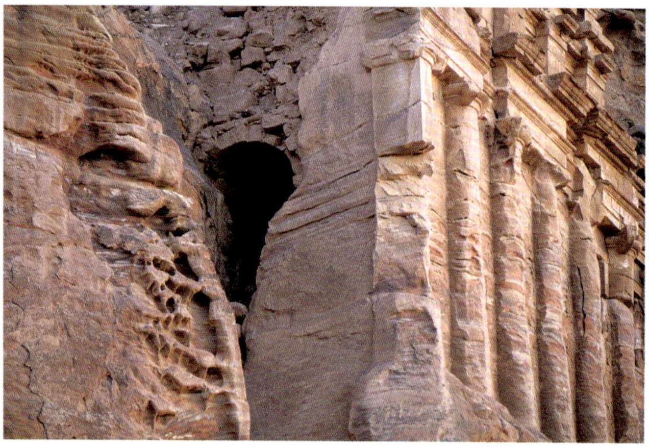

times, in contrast to how it looks today, the facade was characterized by a marked vertical momentum (exceeding 50 meters in height). As a result, its overall appearance must have been like that of the *scaenae frons* in a Roman theatre (the partially reconstructed ones in Merida in Spain, Sabratha in Libia, and Plovdiv in Bulgaria come to mind), and it would therefore have seemed much more balanced than it does today. Obviously, instead of the usual five great doors of the playhouses, there are four doors here, but as has already been mentioned, the architecture of Petra was in itself a combination of various elements, taken from different regional traditions and adapted to local needs.

These needs often led to unusual solutions that cannot be explained today. These include the seven niches, all of different sizes and depths, in the intercolumniations on the second floor. Their function is unknown, but some researchers (including P. J. Parr and Iain Browning) believe that they contained stone or bronze slabs, like those found in Hegra, with commemorative inscriptions on them. However, given its great height, they would have been illegible, and they would also have broken the alternating equilibrium of full and empty suggested by the false colonnade. The fact that the first two niches from the left were originally framed by pilasters with simple capitals, while the rest are bare recesses with no cornice or decoration, is strange. The presence of an obvious square hole in the lower part of the third niche from the left is even more puzzling. Following an investigation carried out in the early nineteen sixties, it was found to be connected to a vertical shaft, adjoining the upper part of the monument. The fact that there are two cisterns behind the facade built in masonry

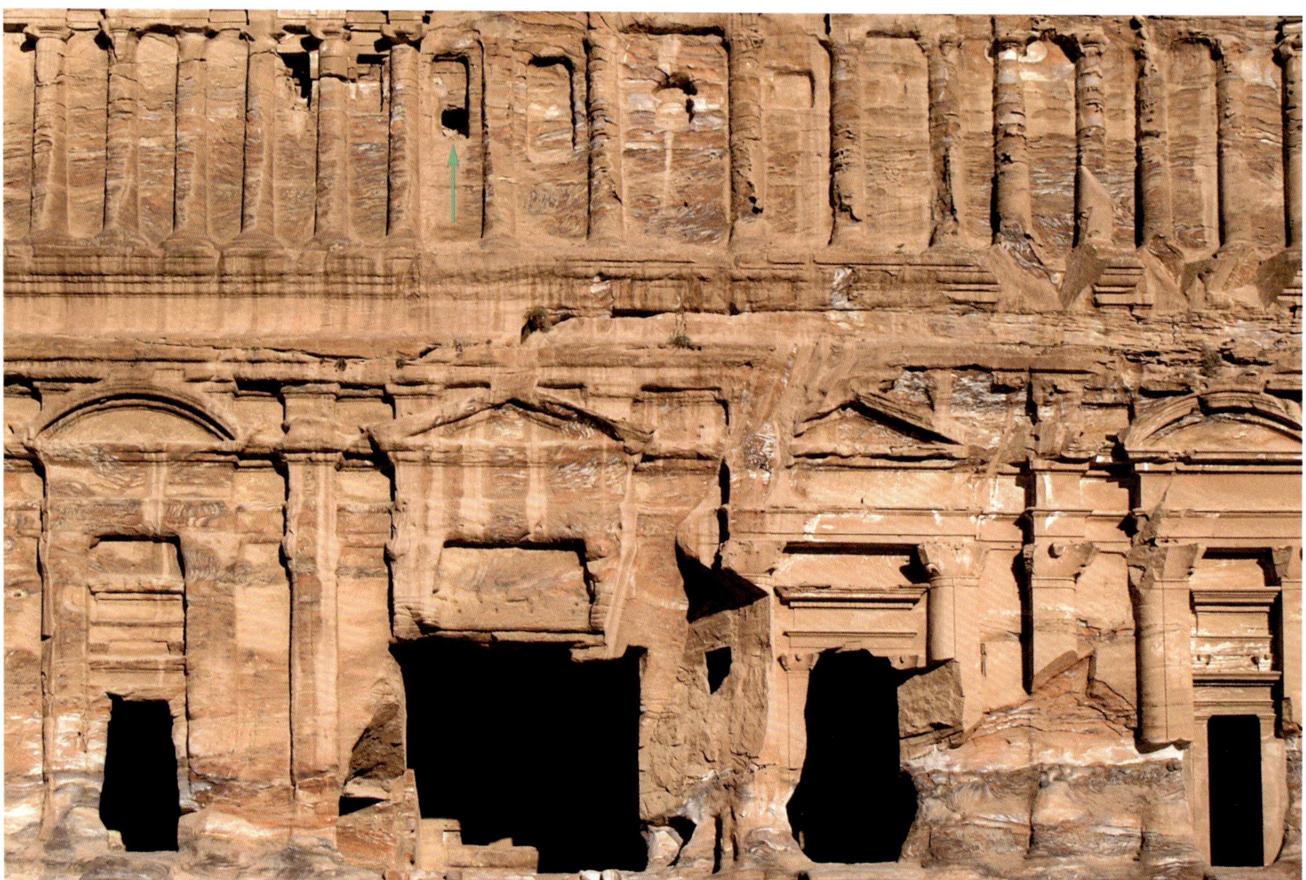

makes the situation even more mysterious. In fact, it could be assumed that water may have flowed into the well from these cisterns, and then gushed out from the facade, perhaps during special ceremonies, but this is just a theory.
The inside of the monument is rather bare, and was undoubtedly altered in ancient times. The four doors access other rooms with no decoration, which may originally have been plastered. Only the two central chambers are interconnected. In the left hand one, in the end wall, there is deep recess, which is rather unusual and was framed between pilasters with bases and capitals made of other materials, inserted into deep gaps. The inside of the niche has an unusual appearance, with four strange pedestals separated by shallow fissures. According to some researchers, including Judith McKenzie, the four plinths are simply the remains of extension work done to the recess, which was not completed for some reason. Although this theory seems likely, others think they may be *motabs* of as many baetyli, and the niche was therefore an altar dedicated to the most important deities of the pantheon of Petra. This would obviously invalidate the theory that the monument was used as a burial place. It should be remembered that although tradition has it that this was the tomb of the last Nabataean monarch, Rabbel II (70-106 AD), it is much more likely that in reality it was a representative building, or in any case a structure connected with royal prerogatives. It is possible that the platform in front of the facade was in fact a stage where religious performances may have been put on, or the king may have appeared in public during particular events, in line with lavish etiquette of oriental influence. The elevated position of the monument, which was visible from all over the city, and its impressive appearance would have made it the ideal place for public events of this kind. Iain Browning, on the other hand, maintains that it was a place used for royal funeral ceremonies. He does not, however, go as far as supporting the theory that it was a royal tomb, and there does in fact seem to be a lot of evidence against the hypothesis that the four underground rooms were used as burial chambers. There is no sign of loculi inside them, or of any pedestals for sarcophagi. Another architectural detail that almost goes unnoticed substantiates the hypothesis that it was not used for a funerary purpose, namely, a little rectangular window, carefully shaped and cut out, near the right semi-pillar of the second doorway from the right. It also seems to date back to the same period as the rest of the monument. There is a similar slit window on the opposite side of the doorway and the third doorway had the exact same arrangement. In spite of their small size, the purpose of these windows was clearly to illuminate and ventilate the inside of the two central halls, and a precaution of this kind would seem entirely out of place for a funeral chamber, which should presumably be shrouded in darkness.
As far as its date is concerned, the Palace Tomb seems considerably later than the Khazneh, and the Roman architectural influence is clear. This makes the monument date to a period not earlier than the last years of the first century AD.

Opposite, top - *The mysterious arch which is visible on the left side of the monument gave access to a tunnel, although its purpose is completely unknown.*

Opposite, bottom - *The arrow highlights the enigmatic square hole that opens on the facade, in an intercolumniation of the blind gallery.*

Above - *The deep niche that opens into the back wall of the large room on the left.*

Below - *The green arrow indicates the window opening next to the second portal from the right. Note that the dentils of the entablatures (yellow arrows) are not carved, but painted with a dark pigment.*

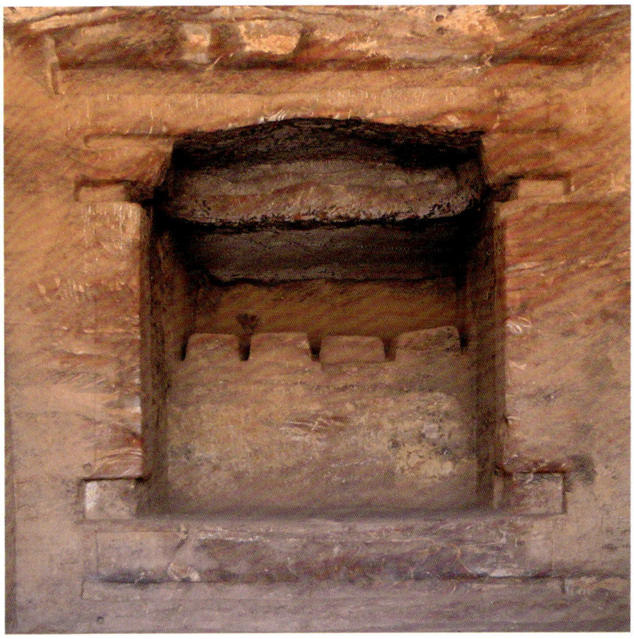

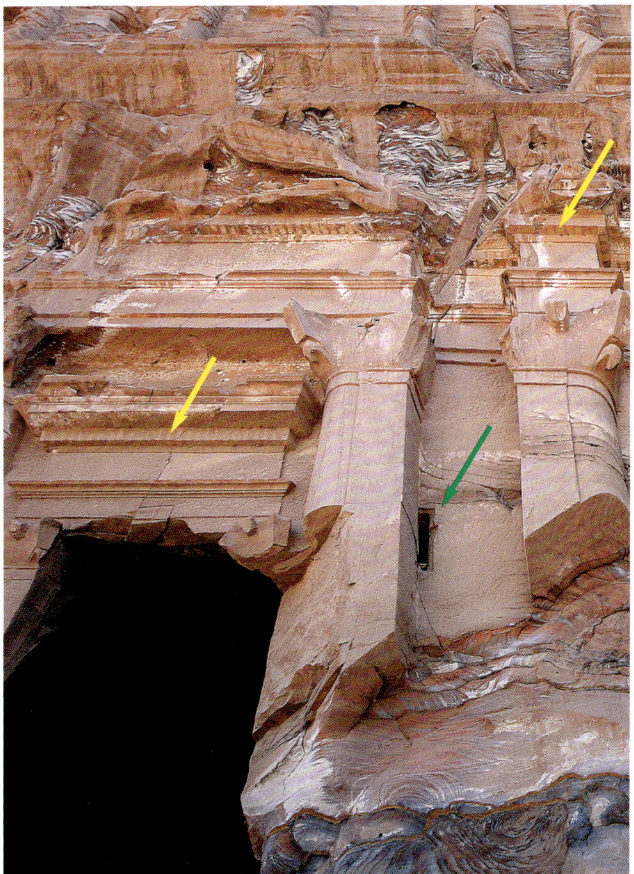

THE TOMB OF SEXTIUS FLORENTINUS

Immediately to the left of the so-called Palace Tomb you can see that the natural profile of the mountain has been altered by a massive excavation. At the foot of the rock face, still mostly buried, there is an enormous, roughly rectangular reservoir. This was the destination of the aqueduct from the Wadi Mataha, which runs along the northern face of the Jebel al Kubtha. This open-air reservoir must have been one of the most important water resources in Petra.

The Palace Tomb is the last of the Royal Tombs, but a short distance away, there is another very beautiful and interesting monument. To reach it you need to follow the path that leads north east, which is clearly visible and runs along the face of the Jebel al Kubtha. After a few metres, you go past what in the Byzantine era was a wall erected to defend the northern section of the city, which is now reduced to rubble. It is only just visible and looks like a low mass of stones, stretching out towards the west as far as the bed of the Wadi Mataha, and continuing on the opposite side. It was probably built using leftover materials. In fact, it is very likely that all the rubble from the upper section of the Palace Tomb was used here.

You soon come to a fork. To the right is the beginning of the steep processional road that climbs up to the top of the mountain (page 157), while the path to the left goes down to the Tomb of Sextius Florentinus (Tomb 763), whose facade, which is carved into the end of a low crag, faces north, and is therefore not visible until the last moment. Although it has been very worn away over time, it still has a harmonious elegance, and where the sandstone is more eroded, a spectacular array of colours has been revealed. The facade is very elaborate, and although it dates back to the Roman period, it is still regarded as a masterpiece of Nabataean architecture. The lower order has four pilasters that support a continuous trabeation, and a beautiful doorway surmounted by a pediment with a triangular tympanum. The upper order, above a continuous trabeation with no frieze, is dominated by a curvilinear pediment, the tympanum of which is adorned with a Gorgon's head, which is very eroded, surrounded by elegant floral spirals. The acroterion is an imperial Roman eagle, and the attic is divided into sections by two cornices and four short pilasters with Nabataean capitals. The whole thing is crowned with a low triangular pediment, with a small acroterion in the form of an urn on top of it. A very worn away inscription, carved into the lower trabeation, tells us that the tomb was commissioned by his son for Titus Aninius Sextius Florentinus, legatus of Hadrian and propraetor of the province of Arabia, who died in Petra in 129 or 130. Thanks to the inscription, this is the only tomb in Petra that can be dated with any certainty. Inside the funerary chamber there are five loculi in the end wall, which is decorated with pilasters, and three others in the right hand wall. The tomb has a rectangular courtyard carved into the rock in front of it. This was almost certainly surrounded by a portico originally, as is indicated by some cylindrical blocks from columns that can still be seen there.

From here, it is a good idea to go back towards the Palace Tomb. Those who wish to continue exploring this area, however, can continue along the Wadi Mataha (see the itinerary described on page 154).

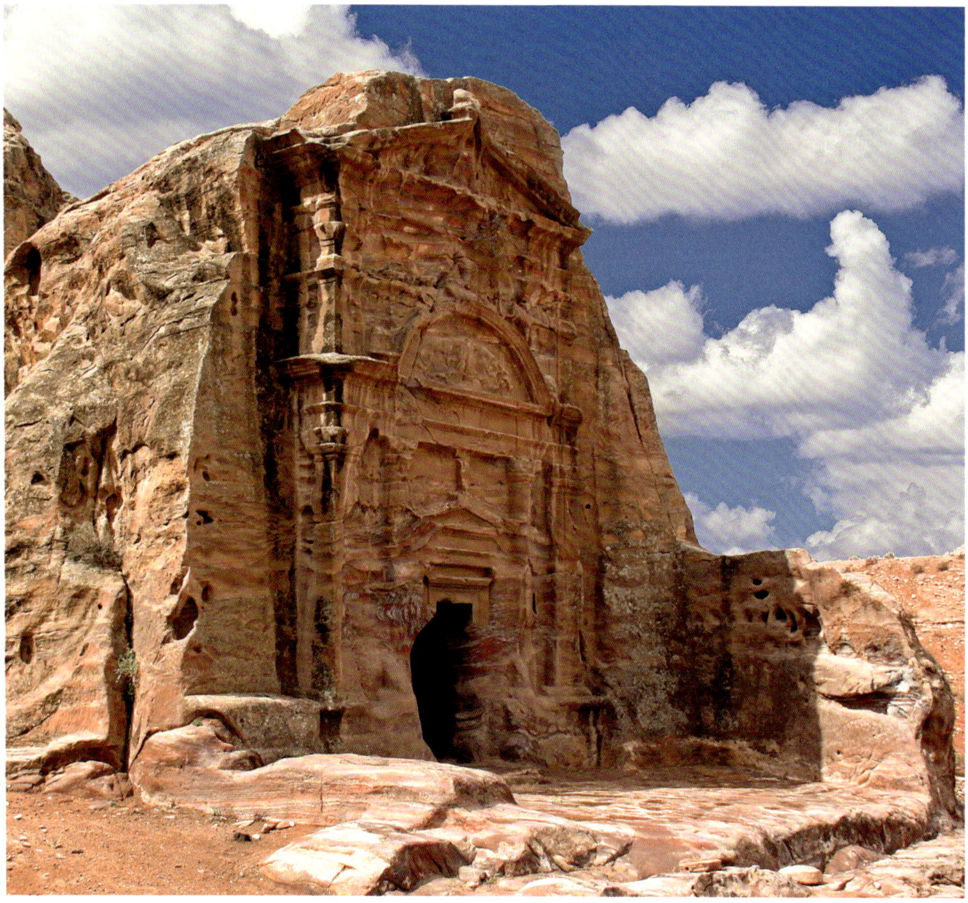

Left - *The Sextius Florentinus Tomb is the result of a composite style that combines Hellenistic architectural elements with the most fluent statements of Nabataean style.*

Opposite page, top - *A detail of the tomb,s doorway.*

Opposite page, bottom - *The inside of the sepulchre has a vibrant array of colours.*

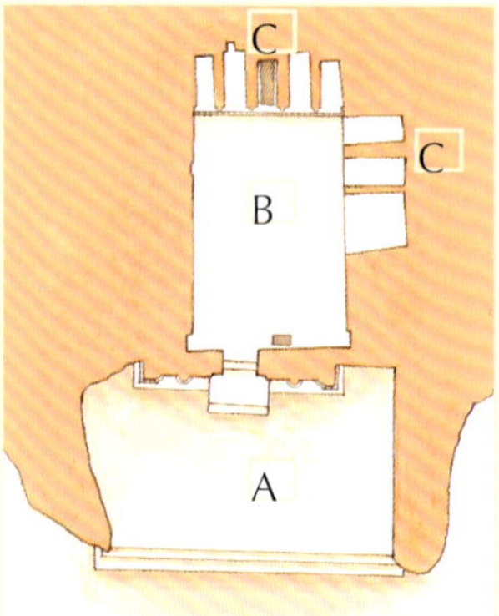

A Court
B Burial Chamber
C Loculi

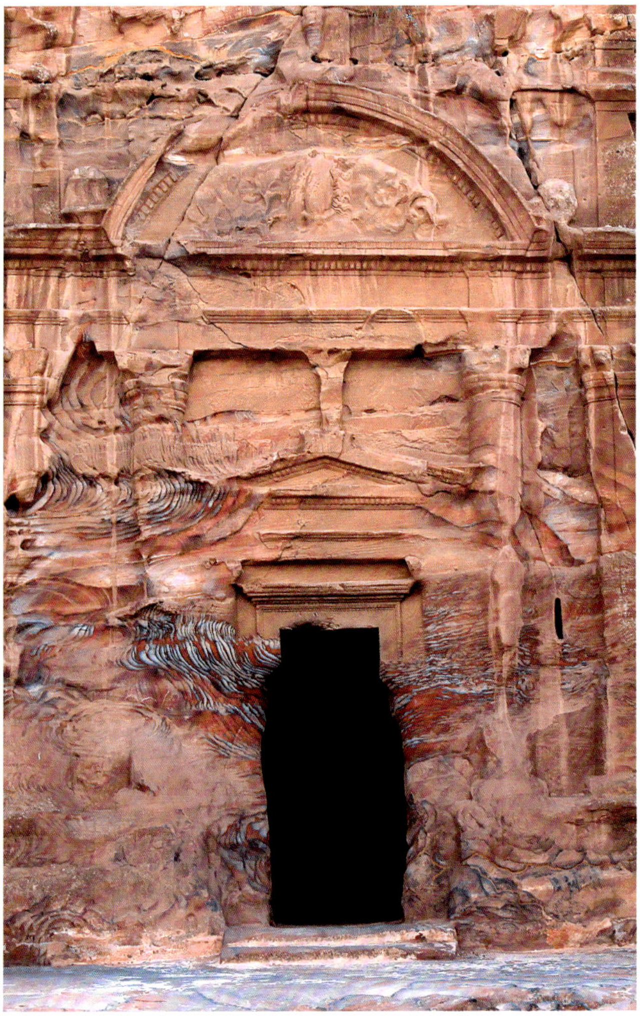

TWO CURIOUS HISTORICAL FACTS

The name Sextius Florentinus is linked to the well known Legio IX Hispana, *elite unit of the Imperial Roman army. This legion was sent by Emperor Claudius in 43 AD to crush the resistance of the British people, and forty years after supported the effort of two other legions to suppress the rebellion by Queen Boadicea. For a long time it was thought that the legion had been destroyed in an ambush on British soil. However, the epigraph of Sextius Florentinus' tomb has proven that the* Legio IX *did not end up in that province of the empire. Senator Titus Annius Sextius Florentinus was, in fact, initially a military tribune in the* Legio I Minervia *and then treasurer of the province of Achaia. In around 121 he became legate of the* Legio IX, *perhaps still stationed in Britain but most probably already deployed to a more southern region. Then Sextius was appointed proconsul of* Gallia Narbonensis, *and finally in 127 he had the governorship of the* Arabia Petrea *province. Today it is believed that in 161, under Marcus Aurelius, the* IX Hispana *was transferred to Cappadocia to face the Parthians. It was finally destroyed in Elegeia, in Armenia, during an ambush. Nevertheless, this legion, now known as "the lost legion" is still shrouded in mystery.*

The legion that occupied Petra was the III Cyrenaica, *coming from Egypt; the* VI Ferrata *(unit stationed in Syria) occupied Bosra instead. Proving the diversity in the origin of the legionaries, a votive stele was rediscovered in 1994 in Turin (the Roman* Augusta Taurinorum*) and preserved in the local Archaeological Museum. It is dedicated to Diana by the city magistrate Caius Valerius Clemens, head centurion of the same* III Cyrenaica *legion around 71 AD.*

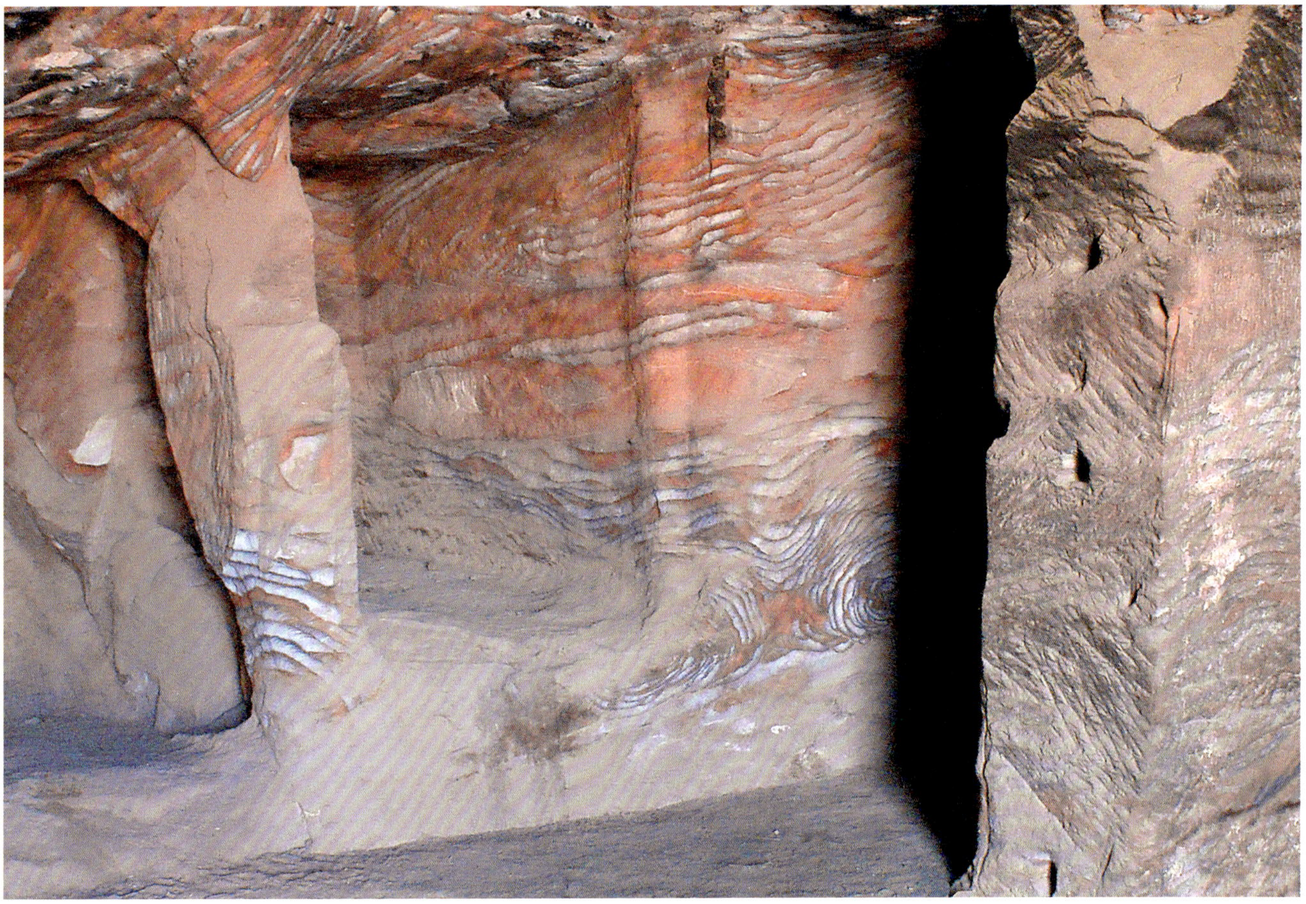

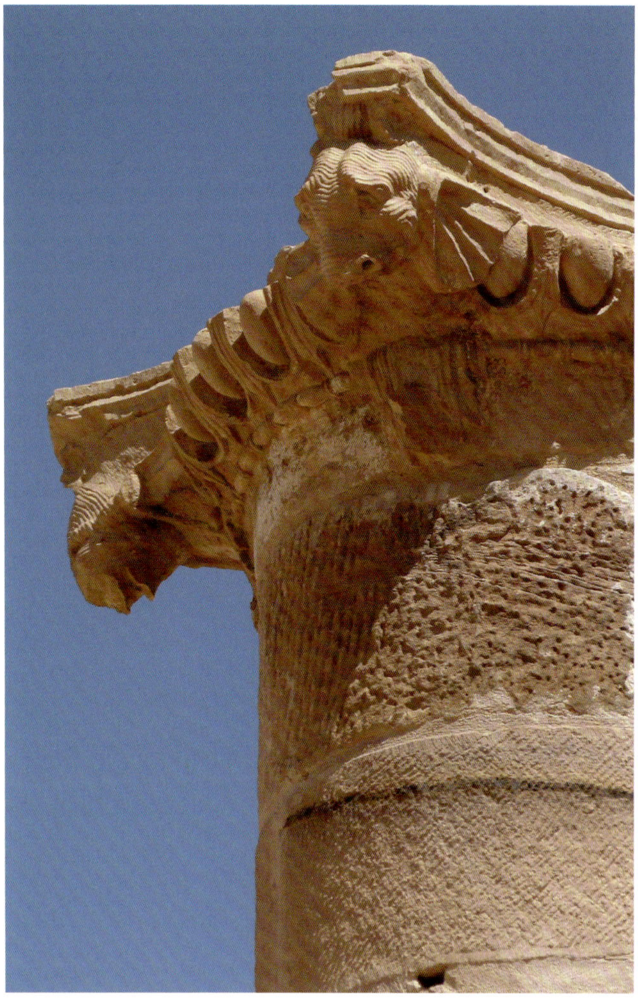

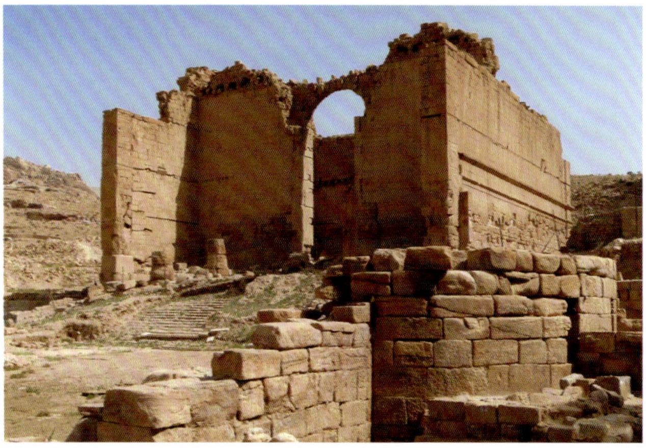

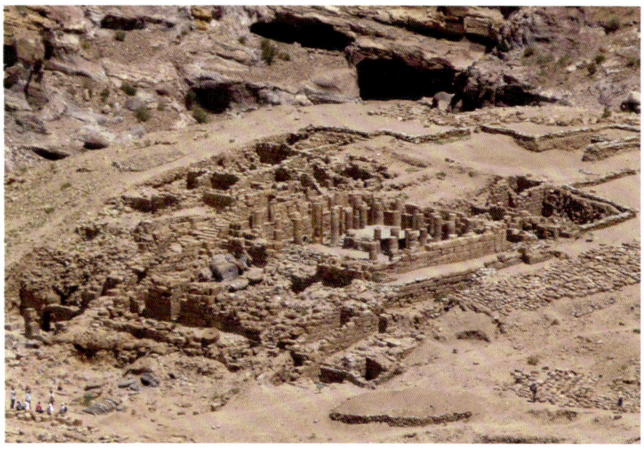

Top left - *The spectacular portico facing the so-called Great Temple was made up of 115 unfluted columns, originally surmounted by unique capitals, each formed by four realistic elephant protomes. Unfortunately one has been damaged by vandals.*

Centre left - *Of all the buildings built in masonry that made up the urban fabric of Petra, the Qasr el Bint is the best preserved one: the only one to have survived the earthquakes that repeatedly razed the rest of the splendid Nabataean capital.*

Bottom left - *Today reduced to a heap of ruins patiently restored during long excavation campaigns, the Temple of the Winged Lions (actually consecrated to the goddess Al Uzza) was one of the major sanctuaries of Petra.*

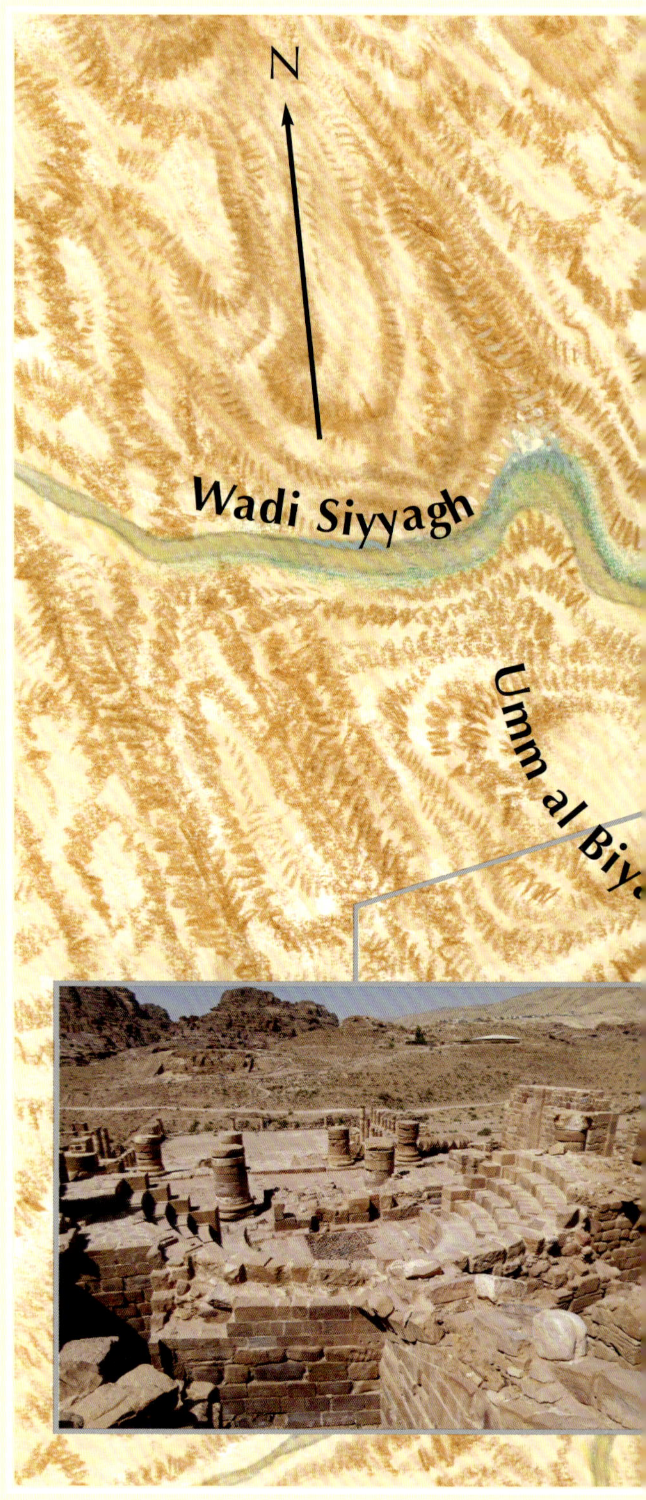

THE URBAN AREA

At first sight, the urban area may seem a little disappointing compared with the monumental splendour of the rock cut tombs seen so far. In fact, much of urban fabric still lies beneath a layer of sand and rubble. However, long archaeological excavations have gradually uncovered the remains of grandiose religious and public buildings, as well as three churches from the Byzantine era. The vast complex of the so-called Great Temple stands out because of the surprising originality of its architecture and decorative designs. Its unusual architectural characteristics raise a lot of questions about what its real function was. The majestic complex stands opposite what remains of the Winged Lions Temple, near to which there were some workshops for processing stone and metal. Also situated in this area is the only structure in Petra built in masonry that has survived: the monumental Qasr el Bint, a temple where the most important Nabataean gods were worshipped. Finally, a walk around the sheer-sided rock of the Jebel al Habis is not to be missed.

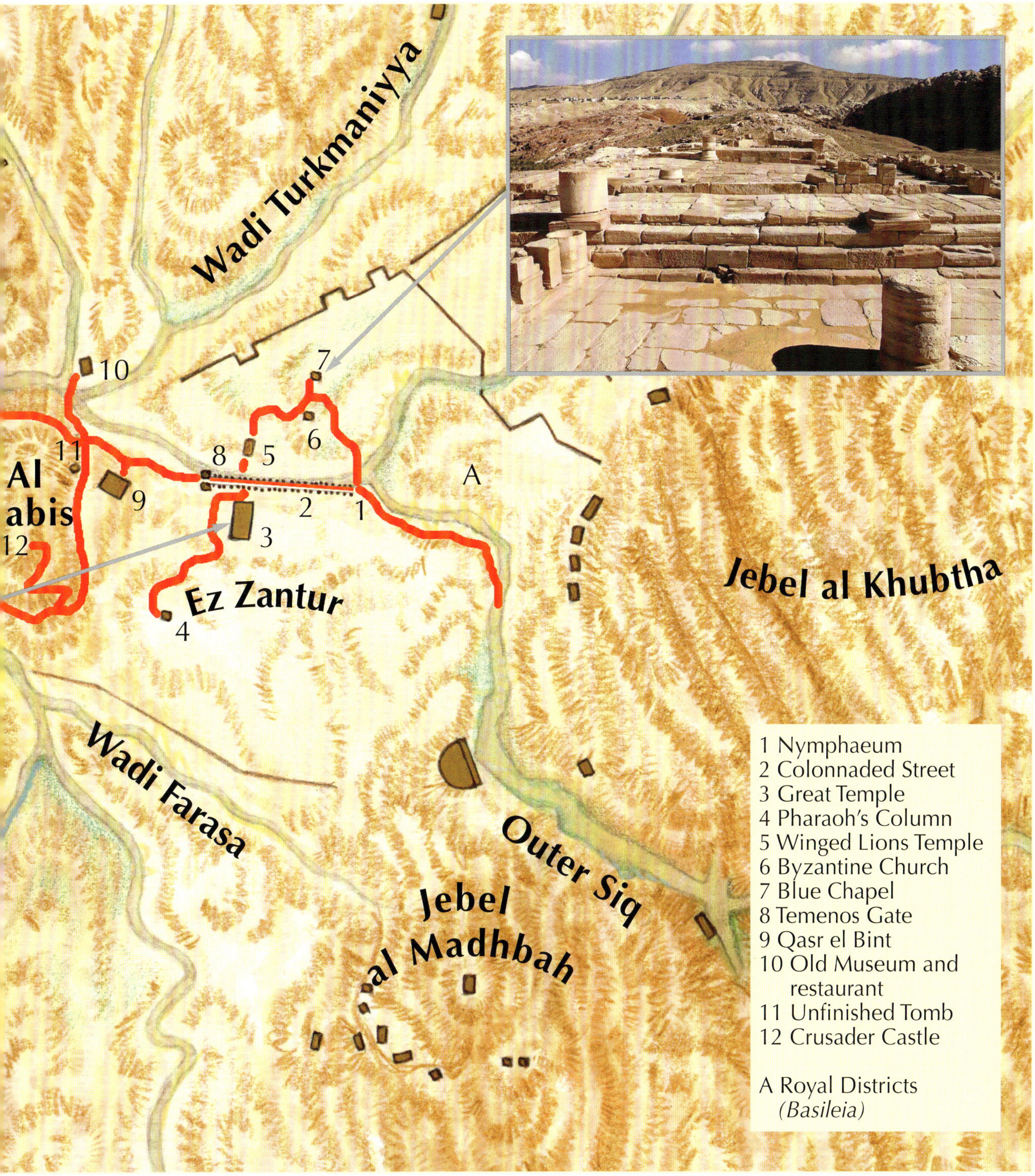

Monica Falcone

THE CENTRAL CITY AREA

A short distance beyond the theatre, the dirt track turns sharply to the left, while on the right stands the towering mass of the Jebel al Kubtha, at the foot of which the Royal Tombs were carved. Here, the Outer Siq opens up into the valley where the Nabataean capital lay. The ancient bed of the Wadi Musa joins with that of the Wadi Mataha, into which the Nabataeans directed the waters diverted through the tunnel that opened at the mouth of the Inner Siq. At this exact spot there was a monumental building, which was described as a "little theatre" in the nineteenth century, but which in reality must have served as scenic semi-circular architectural screen, or rather as a junction between the north-south main road coming from the Outer Siq, and the east-west one, which was the Colonnaded Street.

Looking around at the view gives you the impression of being in the middle of a vast deserted space. However, you need to imagine the valley covered with an expanse of flat roofed houses covered in white plaster. Here and there, the imposing masses of the temples and great public buildings looked out over this dense urban fabric, interspersed with gardens and orchards. The main part of the city extended as far as the al Habis rock, while the suburbs occupied the areas to the north and south, as well as the sides of the nearest valleys. Today it seems impossible that such a large number of buildings could have stood here, but it is enough to look around at the low hills to realize that you are quite literally walking on an expanse of rubble, which is still almost entirely unexplored. In particular, the entire area situated to the northeast of the point at which the two wadis meet (where the remains of a nymphaeum are) was densely built up. If you look carefully at the ground, the remains of walls are immediately noticeable, evidence of large buildings that have yet to be uncovered. A walk around this area, which is connected to the Byzantine basilica by a modern walkway that crosses the Wadi Mataha, allows you to imagine how big Petra originally was, and how splendid it must have been. Above all, it disproves beyond doubt the antiquated and erroneous theory that described Petra as a sort of "great encampment", or a kind of enormous sanctuary with a lot of temples but no houses or palaces. In fact, the excavations carried out from 2011 onwards by the North-Eastern Petra Project have identified a number of buildings, some of which were originally several storeys high. It seems that one of them was a sort of large tower used used for water features. Others are solid foundations that must have supported buildings of considerable size. In fact, the roughness of the terrain was tamed thanks to the terracing and the retaining walls, making the architectural context quite varied and amenable. It is also clear that some of the monumental buildings must have had an official function, and were in any case connected with the so-called "Palace Tomb", which in reality was probably not a tomb. Its position, looking out over the urban area, the fact that this part of the city had an abundant supply of drinking water thanks to the "Khuthba North" aqueduct, and the presence of a considerable amount of high quality ceramics (*terra sigillata*) in the rubble, suggests that there were royal residences in the north-eastern area of Petra. This residential area would seem to be a local adaptation of the so-called *basileia*, which was the noble part of the Hel-

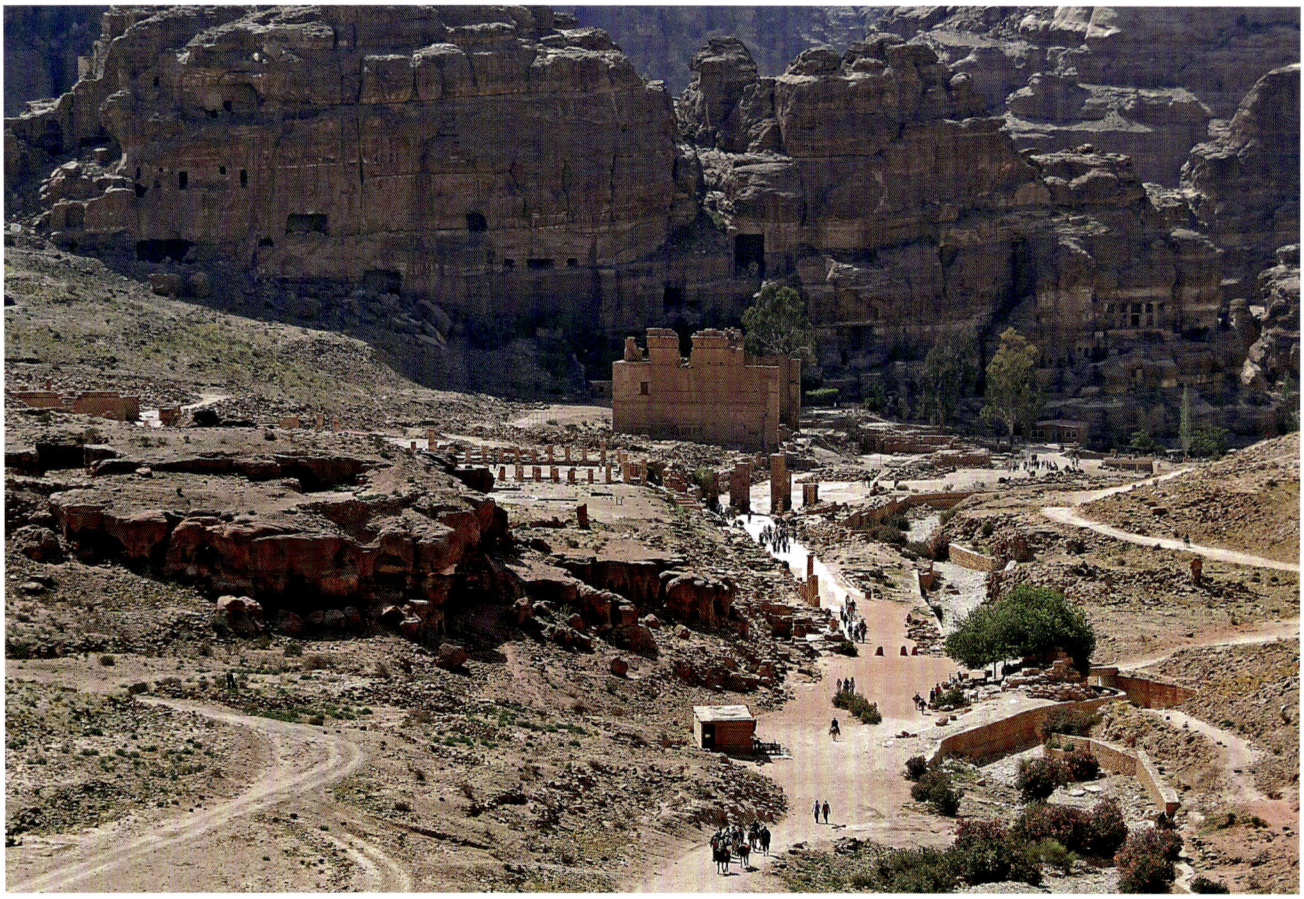

lenistic capitals, including Alexandria. This supports the theory that Nabataean society underwent a pervasive process of Hellenisation from the 1st century BC onwards.
Finally, it should be mentioned that the city was protected by two walls, which are at least partly visible, one to the north-west and one to the south. Although some researchers still believe that they date back to the 1st century BC, it now seems more likely that Petra did not have walls until the first decades of the 2nd century AD at the earliest, if not the years after the powerful earthquake of 363 AD.

THE COLONNADED STREET

The stony bed of the Wadi Musa, which descends in a westerly direction between what remains of the high masonry banks erected by the Nabataeans, ran along next to the main street of Petra, which was entirely paved and is 300 metres long today. Although originally it must also have continued towards the east, it now starts near a nymphaeum, the remains of which lie in the shade of a solitary tree, next to a modern bridge. This monumental fountain, originally adorned with marble columns and statues, was fed by the aqueduct from the Siq. Just opposite, at the time of the Roman emperor Septimius Severus (193-211), a second nymphaeum was erected, the remains of which are barely discernible. They certainly must have been an impressive sight for those arriving from the arid expanses of desert in the region, as must the existence of an efficient urban water supply. Unfortunately, as things stand it is not possible to investigate how large the distribution network of running water was, but at various different points, fragments of earthenware pipes amongst the rubble suggest that it was quite extensive, and served all the public buildings. There were probably fountains spread around the city, so that the inhabitants did not have to go too far from their houses to fetch water. In any case, it has been calculated that thanks to the aqueducts fed by the perennial springs and the large cisterns supplied with rainwater, which backed up the system during the period in the summer when the supply was less plentiful, each inhabitant had a daily availability of at least 40 to 50 litres of water, which was more than sufficient to provide a comfortable standard of living, even in a desert climate
Many of the main public buildings in Petra, and presumably a lot of shops and offices, were situated along the **Colonnaded Street**. Six metres wide and situated along the east-west axis (as the *decumanus maximus* in Roman cities), it was perfectly in line with the facade of the Corinthian Tomb, which with the adjoining Palace Tomb must have had a formidable visual impact. The eastern part of the street has been washed away by floods, while the western part still retains a lot of its paving stones, the sidewalk and the bases of numerous columns, partially raised.
In the shade of the arcades that ran along the street on both sides, deals were done, money was changed, refreshments were consumed, and the latest events were discussed. Although archaeological evidence shows that the street was significantly altered after the Trajan conquest in 106 AD, it has still not been established

F. Bourbon, M. Bavagnoli

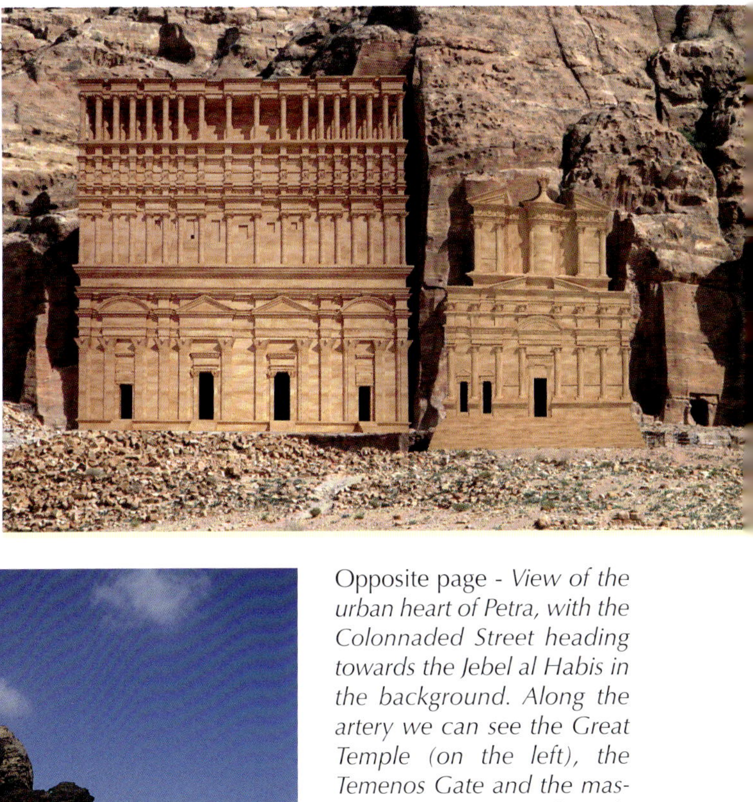

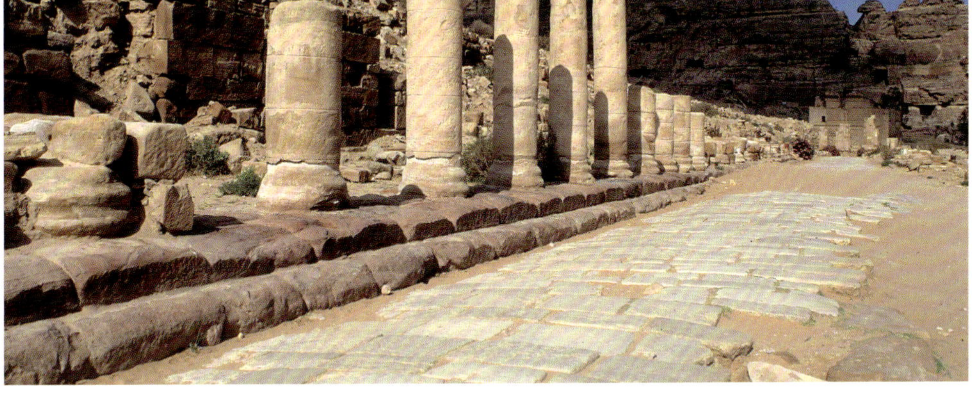

Opposite page - *View of the urban heart of Petra, with the Colonnaded Street heading towards the Jebel al Habis in the background. Along the artery we can see the Great Temple (on the left), the Temenos Gate and the massive Qasr el Bint. So far only 4 or 5% of the urban fabric has been excavated.*

Above - *A virtual reconstruction of the Corinthian Tomb and the nearby Palace Tomb, which were to form a formidable scenographic backdrop.*

Below - *The southern side of the Colonnaded Street, with partially raised columns (the capital is not pertinent).*

whether the paving and the two colonnades were added by Aretas IV as part of his grand design for the city, or if they date back to a later period.
Proceeding along this main road, several ruins, some of considerable size, can be seen along the northern bank of the wadi. It is difficult to say what the function of these buildings was, but it is certain that several stone bridges crossed the bed of the river in front of the most important buildings. It must therefore have been quite easy to pass from the southern to the northern part of the city. At a certain point, just west of the nymphaeum, there is a massive masonry structure with an arch. It was once believed to be a Byzantine palace (or tower), but recent excavations have identified it as part of a large bath complex, which was in use from the Roman era until the end of the 5th century.
On the left hand side of the Colonnaded Street, there are three vast areas, partly cut out of the rocky hillside, with a formidable excavation work. They are commonly known as the Upper Market, the Central Market and the Lower Market (from east to west), and today they are covered with sand and rubble. It is currently believed that the area furthest east, which can be reached from the Colonnaded Street via a monumental staircase, was in fact used as a square surrounded by porticoes, a sort of forum where business was done and the daily meetings of the metropolis took place. The monuments in this area probably were built after Petra was annexed to the Roman Empire.
Little is known about the "Central Market", although some believe that the area was occupied by a luxuriant garden, whose plants and flower beds were watered by the usual network of channels and earthenware pipes.
This should not be a surprise, because archaeological digs have revealed that there was a large pool (43 m x 23 m, and two and a half metres deep), with steps around the sides to allow people to enter the water, in the southern part of the third open space (or "Lower Market"). The investigations that began in 1998 identified the foundations of a rectangular pavilion in the centre, connected to the sides by two little bridges. An elaborate system of pipes was used to water the northern terrace, which was used as a garden. It was probably commissioned by Aretas IV towards the end of the 1st century BC, and it is believed that the pool was originally a royal *paradeisos*, or rather a place of delights, which was part of a larger complex. In fact, just on the opposite side of the wadi are the ruins of what is generally considered to be a royal palace. A scenic

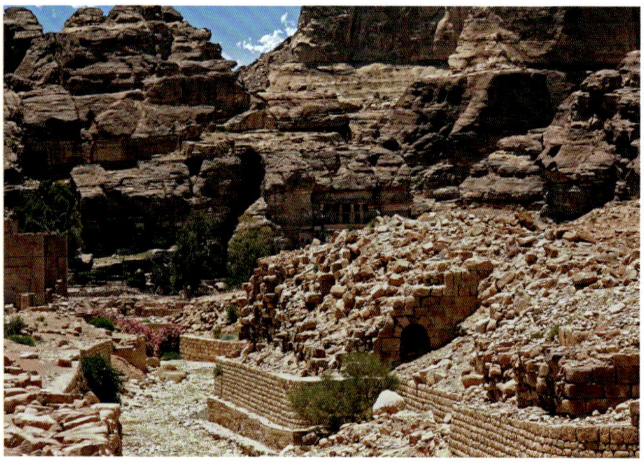

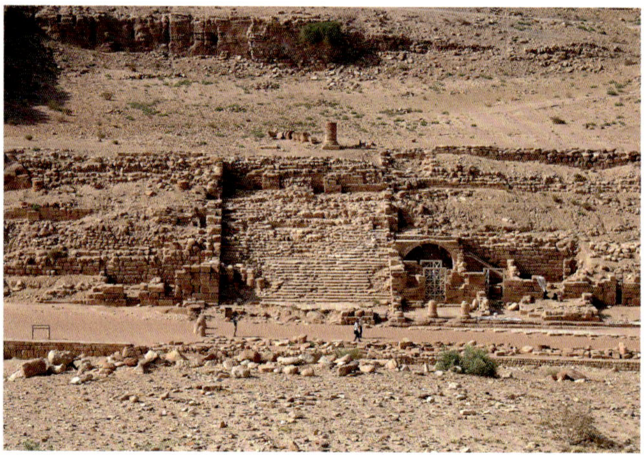

Plan of the central city area

A Colonnaded Street
B Nymphaeum
C "Upper Market"
D "Central Market"
E Paradeisos ("Lower Market")
F Great Temple
G Temenos Gate
H Temenos
I Little Temple
J Qasr El Bint Faroun
K Roman Baths
L Royal Palace
M Winged Lions Temple
N Byzantine Church
O Blue Chapel
P Northern Ridge Church

(from Fournet, Kanellopoulos, Bedal, Joukowski, Shiyyab)

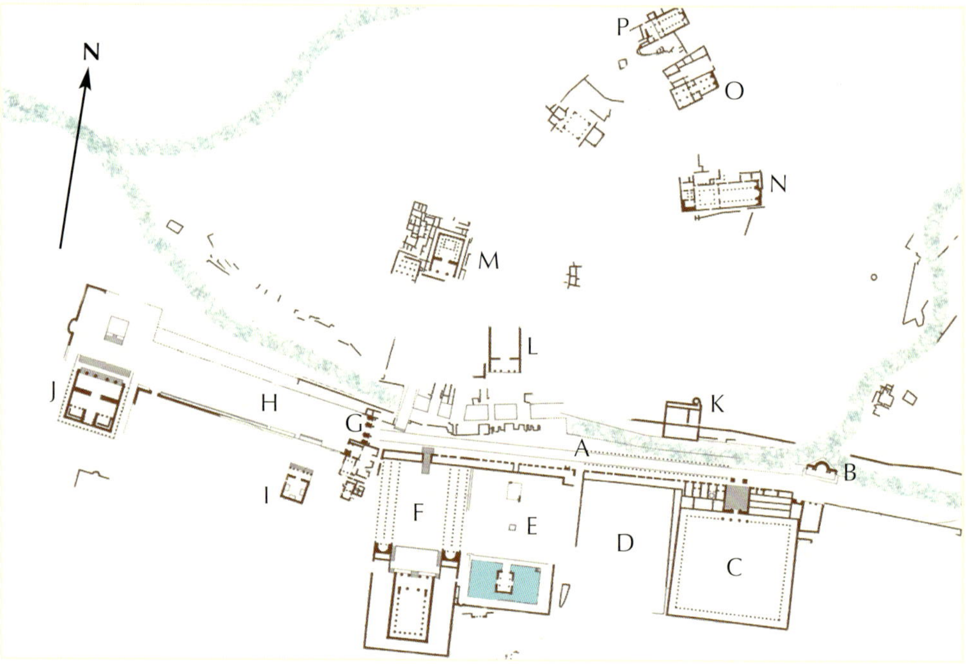

feature of this kind had the purpose of confirming the power of the monarch, and legitimising his role in a social context that was heavily influenced by the Hellenistic and Roman world. In fact, at the time, it was usual for those in power to use architecture as a political metaphor. Just think of Herod the Great, king of nearby Judah (from 37 to 4 BC), who had the majestic palace-fortress of Herodion built, with its gigantic pool, as well as the sumptuous royal palace on the rock of Masada. Considering how close it is to the Great Temple, the pool may have had a religious and ceremonial role, like the Egyptian "sacred lakes", although it is difficult to say for certain. Considering their popularity in this geographical area, it is also possible that the pool was used for the Maiuma celebrations, a religious festival involving collective bathing.

After being annexed to the Roman Empire, the *paradeisos* probably lost its royal status and was transformed into a sort of public park, until it was destroyed by the earthquake of 363. In any case it is clear that in their capital the Nabataeans wanted to show the world all their hydraulic engineering abilities, and their absolute control over that most precious of assets: water. It must have flowed into the pool through a connecting channel from the aqueduct that came from the south-east, supplied by the Ain Braq and Ain Ammon springs. This demonstrates that Petra had more water than the minimum necessary for daily life, and could use it for recreational and aesthetic purposes. The gardens, nymphaeums and water pools must have had a considerable psychological impact on visitors from abroad, as they were a powerful and effective symbol of how Petra was flourishing.

A little further on is the "**Great Temple**", one of the most enigmatic monuments in Petra. It can be accessed from the Colonnaded Street by climbing a staircase. This enormous structure covered an area of over 7,600 m^2. It was built in the last quarter of the 1st century BC, and at one time it was believed to have been a religious building. However, archaeological excavations carried out from 1993 onwards gave rise to different theories. It was preceded by a vast rectangular courtyard (known as lower *temenos*) oriented along the north-south axis, paved with hexagonal slabs and surrounded on three sides by great porticoes. The ones on the eastern and western sides, with an exedra at each end, were supported by three rows of columns. The capitals that surmounted this forest of columns were a very original Nabataean interpretation of the Ionic style, with four elephant heads on the corners, whose rolled up trunks took the place of the classic curls. The tusks (which are missing) must have been made of ivory or other perishable materials. The extraordinary accuracy of these protomes suggests that the sculptors were well aware of what Indian elephants looked like, and the Nabataean merchants certainly traded with far off India quite frequently.

Under the paving, there was an intricate system of tubing, which must have been used for collecting rainwater. A bronze manhole has even been preserved, which

Opposite page, left - *The remains of the large bath complex overlooking the banks of the Wadi Musa.*

Opposite page, right - *A large staircase leads to the so-called "Upper Market", an arcaded square that probably served as a forum.*

Below - *The Great Temple was the most impressive building in all of Petra.*

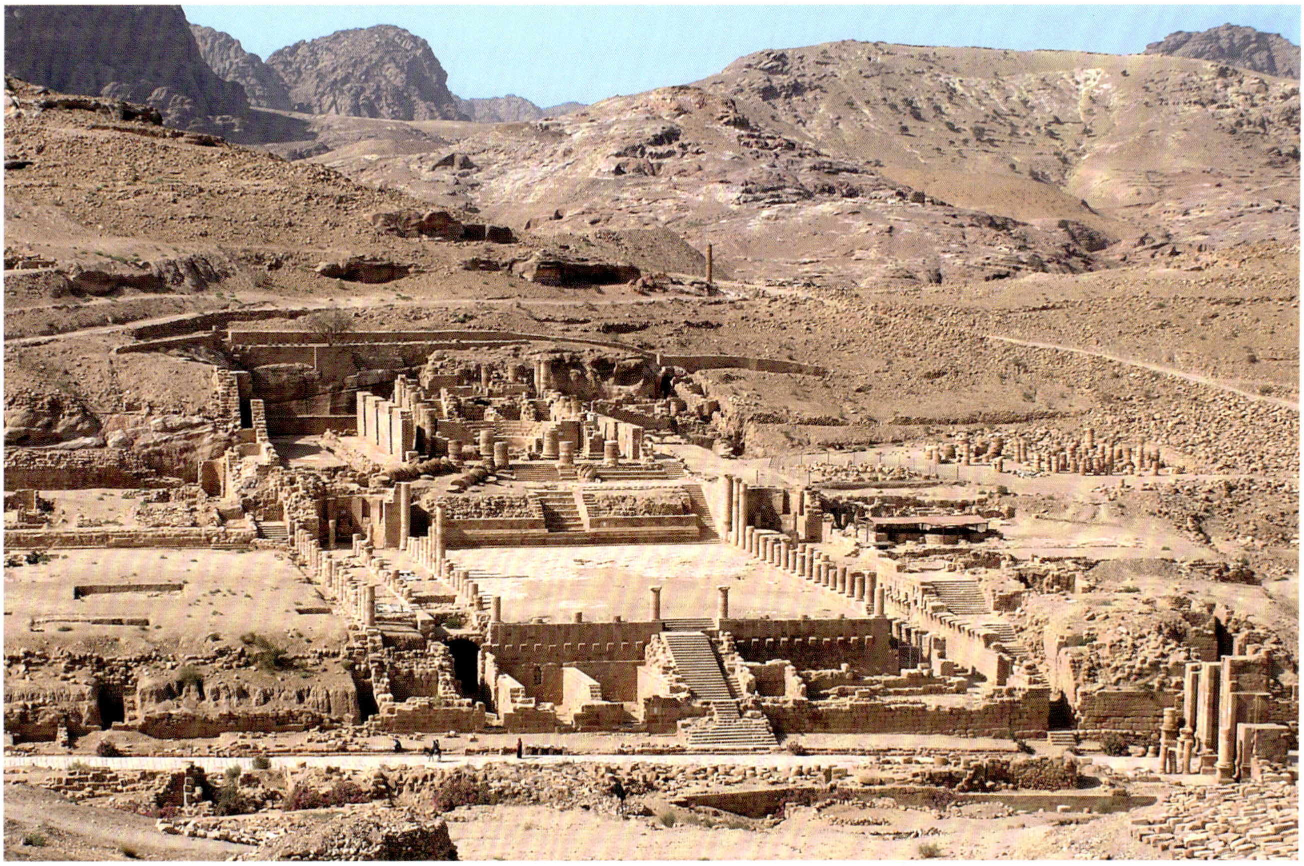

Above - *The wide lower temenos of the Great Temple, seen from the upper terrace (or upper* temenos*). The hexagonal slabs of the paving seem to be a recurring element in Nabataean architecture, used in the most varied sizes.*

Below - *It is evident that the Great Temple was heavily modified due the construction of the* theatron, *which completely occupied the internal space.*

Plan of the Great Temple

A Propylaea
B Lower Temenos
C East Portico
D West Portico
E Exedras
F Western entrance
G Upper temenos
H Cistern or storage room
I Pronaos
J Theatron
K Large cistern
L Residential quarter
M Cistern
N Roman-Byzantine baths

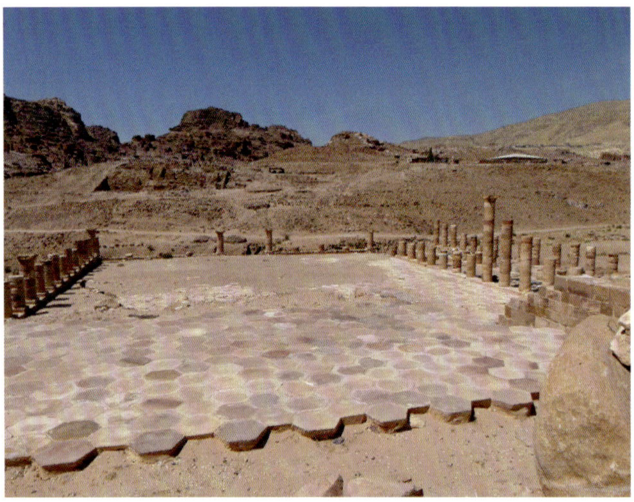

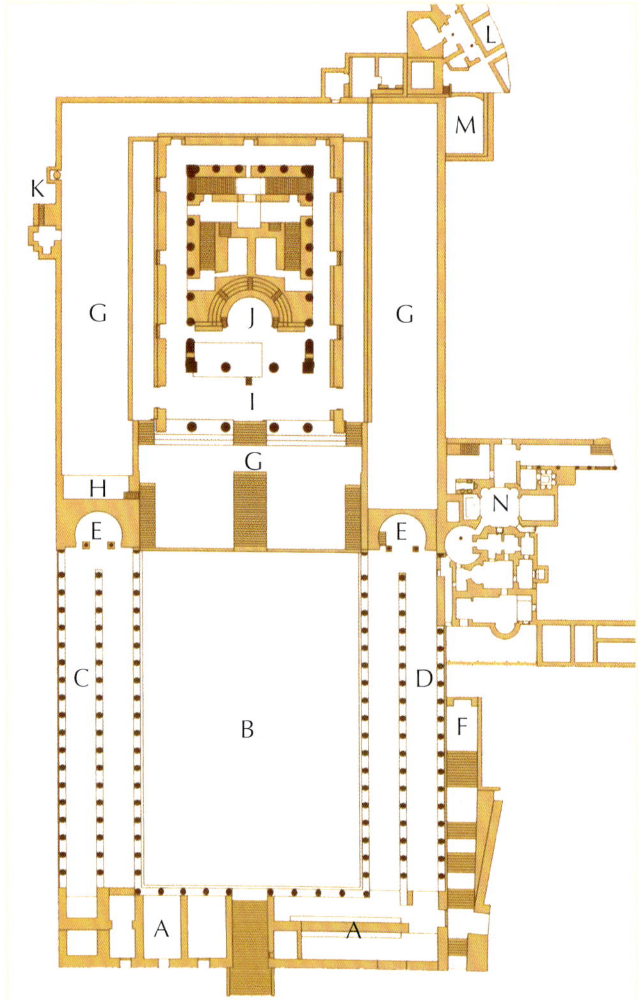

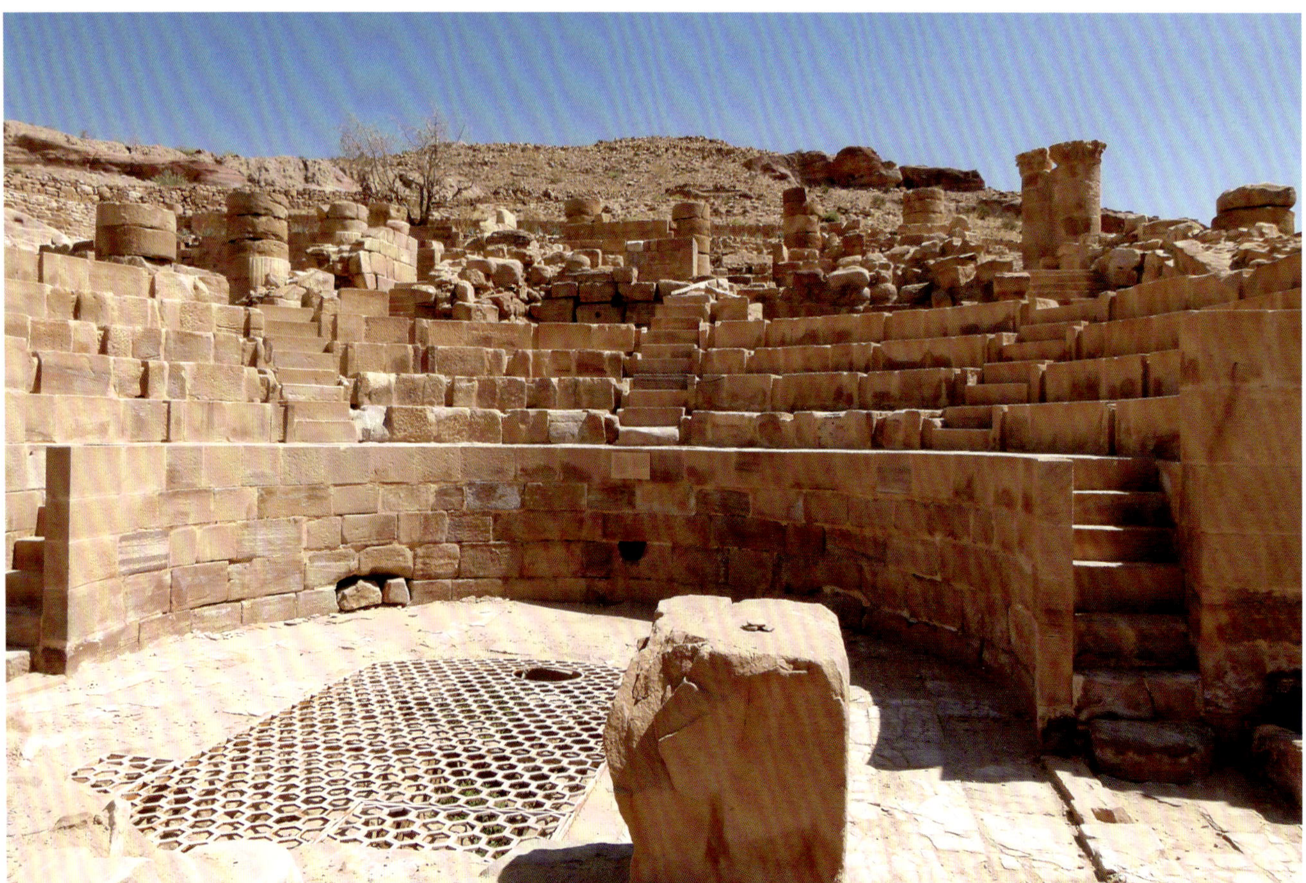

is also hexagonal. From the great courtyard, a central staircase, later replaced with two side staircases, went up to a second open space (known as the upper *temenos*), which was paved with hexagonal stones as well. From here, some more steps led to the main part of the building, the facade of which was made up of four columns of about 15 metres in height framed between two pillars, or *antae*, which must have supported a classically inspired pediment. These columns were plastered and painted red and white, as was the entire building. At about 35 metres wide, 42 long and about 20 high, this was the biggest monument in Petra.
In a first phase, the pronaos was followed by a spacious hall delimited by thick perimeter walls; the internal space was marked by plastered and painted columns. Later, that is in the first decades of the first century AD,

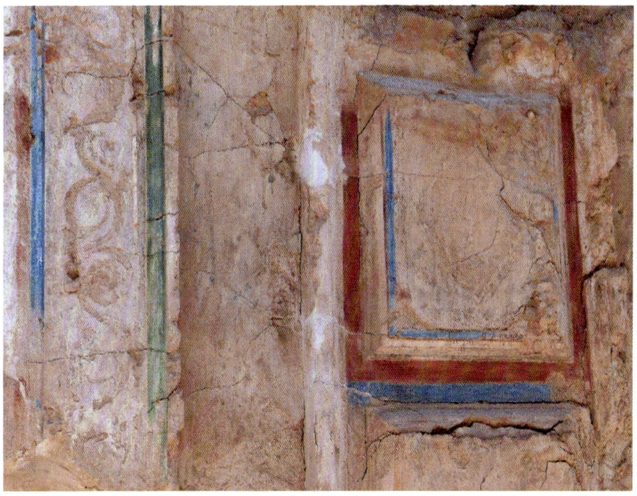

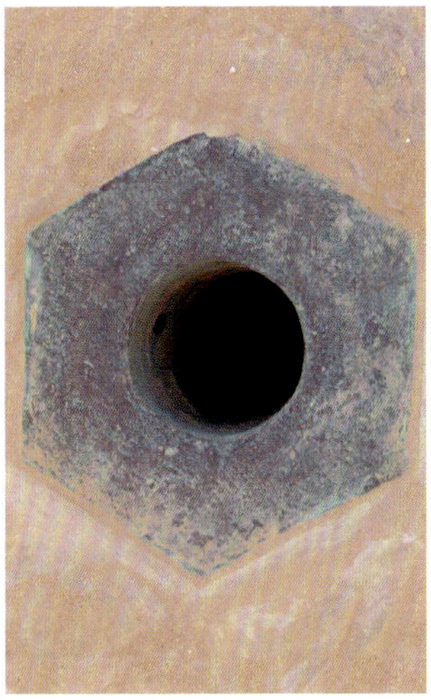

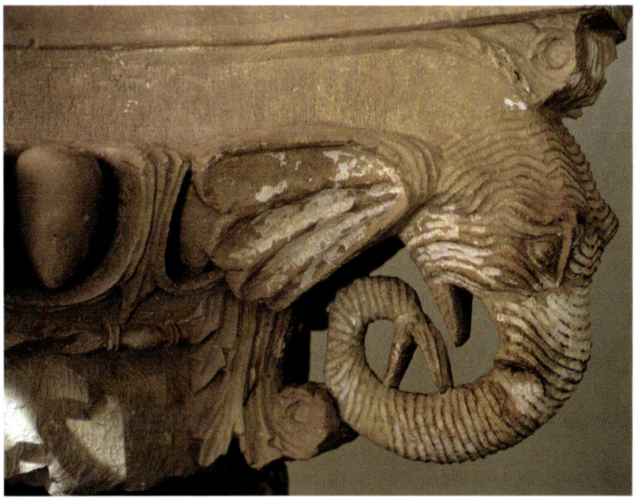

Right - *This bronze hexagonal manhole shows a remarkable metallurgical skill.*

Top left - *The Great Temple was decorated with panels of moulded and painted plaster depicting illusionist architectures, with an extensive use of primary colours.*

Bottom left - *The best preserved of the capitals with elephantine protomes, that adorned the porticoes of the lower temenos, is kept in the Archaeological Museum.*

the building underwent a drastic transformation, possibly at the behest of Aretas IV. The intercolumniations were filled in with walls that incorporated columns. The internal space, now surrounded by a continuous corridor, was occupied by a semi-circular structure known as a *theatron*, which could accommodate about 600 people on its steps. After some patient restoration work, the lower part of this surprising cavea is now clearly visible, as are the four flights of stairs that gave access to the upper part of the hemicycle, and two spacious halls situated to the east and west. This structure raises some important questions. While some people believe that it was an odeon, i.e. a little theatre used for music recitals, others point out that it seems unlikely that a sacred building could have been transformed into a secular one in such a flagrant way. Consequently, we can formulate the following hypothesis. The so-called "Great Temple" was in fact not a sanctuary originally, but rather a structure similar to the civil basilicas, that is buildings used as a place for public meetings and for the administration of justice, which originated in the Eastern Hellenistic world and then widespread in the Roman area. In fact, the floor plan of the original building tallies perfectly with that of a basilica: rectangular, divided up into naves by lines of columns, and able to hold huge numbers of people. If the building had had a civil function, such as the seat of the local government or city council, and probably a place where the economy and the business of the Nabataean Kingdom were discussed, this would also explain the strange capitals on the two huge terraces. They would have been completely out of place in a religious context, but perfect for drawing attention to the flourishing capital city, and its commercial links with far off places. In time, the space probably became insufficient and was therefore drastically altered by erecting a cavea that could accommodate a large number of people sitting down, based on the idea of the Greek *bouleuteria* (buildings where the council of representatives of the city, or *boulé*, would meet). From this point of view, a comparison between the monument in Petra and the various *bouleuteria* preserved in the Eastern Mediterranean area is convincing. In particular, the *bouleuterion* in Stratonikeia, a Hellenistic-Roman city in modern Turkey, has precise architectural similarities with the structure inside the Great Temple, including the lateral flights of stairs that provide access to the upper part of the cavea. The civil function of the building seems confirmed by the presence (ascertained in 2005) of a sumptuous Roman-Byzantine bath complex built close to the eastern exedra of the upper *temenos*.
Finally, it should be mentioned that precious fragments of modelled plaster and multi-coloured wall decorations have been found, which indicate just how colourful the public buildings in Petra must have been.
The Grand Temple was in use up until the 5th century AD, i.e. during the Byzantine period, and was renovated several times over time. It was later destroyed by an earthquake. The cylindrical blocks that made up the

columns of the pronaos, still lined up on the ground following their catastrophic collapse, bear witness to this terrible event. Behind the "Great Temple", a few dozen metres to the south-west, the **Pharaoh's Column** stands alone, the only clearly visible reminder of what must have been either a temple or a palace, but in any case a very large monumental structure. Next to it, the drums of an identical column are spread about on the ground, as if they had just been broken up by the fatal earthquake. In fact, it is not clear by what freak of nature the Pharaoh's Column has remained upright over the course of the centuries. It is also known as Zibb Faroun, because of its appearance (the word *zibb* being a crude term for a phallus). Obviously, any connection with an Egyptian Pharaoh comes from the many Bedouin legends relating to Petra.

Nearby, on the hill known as Ez Zantur, the excavations of a large two storey house (known as EZ IV) can be seen. It was built in the first half of the 1st century AD on the foundations of an older house (the excavations are still going on and it cannot be visited). Its floor plan shows a clear Hellenistic-Roman influence. The most luxurious rooms, where guests were received, as well as the service rooms, were arranged around a central peristyle (that is, a courtyard with a portico). The living quarters consisted of a central vestibule, with a hall on either side. The three rooms had beautiful stone paving, and the walls were decorated with stucco and painted panels with a lively variety of colours that resemble the First Pompeian Style. However, the centre of the house is a smaller room, with the remains of pictorial decorations on the lower section of the walls, that reproduce illusionary architectural perspectives. These murals have obvious similarities with the Second Pompeian Style, which was very much in vogue in the Roman Empire during the reign of Augustus (31 BC - 14 AD). The fact that some of the floors in the house are made with hexagonal paving stones is interesting. This shape was rather unusual in the ancient world, but in Petra it must have been quite fashionable, as it has also been found in many other places. Archaeological investigations have established that this sumptuous home had a large cistern, vaulted with arches, and supplied by a channel from the aqueduct that brought the waters of the springs of Ain Braq and Ain Ammon into the city. As there was a considerable difference in level between the distribution chamber of the aqueduct and the top of the hill where the cistern had been carved out, there must have been quite a lot of pressure inside the earthenware tubes to make the water flow.

In this area of the city, which enjoyed an exceptional view over the centre of the metropolis, several other houses that were supplied with drinking water from the same aqueduct, and had private cisterns, have been identified and explored. The house known as EZ I had two storeys and dates back to the IV century AD. It was covered by an interesting system of parallel arches, which supported flat roofs. Although these remains might seem rather modest to inexpert eyes, they have led to important discoveries about the civic life of Petra. At the same time, the excavations carried out in the Ez Zantur area have proved the reliability of the ancient texts that described Petra in its initial phase of settlement as a vast assembly of tents, where the Nabataeans continued to live like a nomadic people. In fact, rubbish dumps from this long period have been discovered, and even holes in which the poles that held up the tents

Top left- *The solitary Pharaoh's Column, which stands behind the Great Temple.*

Bottom left - *The large house, discovered on the Ez Zantur hill and known as EZ IV, has been partially reconstructed to protect the delicate interior decorations.*

Right - *An image of the goddess Al Uzza may have been worshipped on the* motab *of the Winged Lions Temple.*

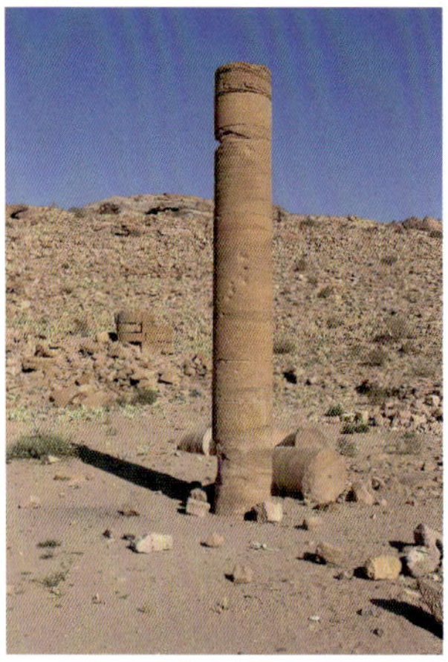

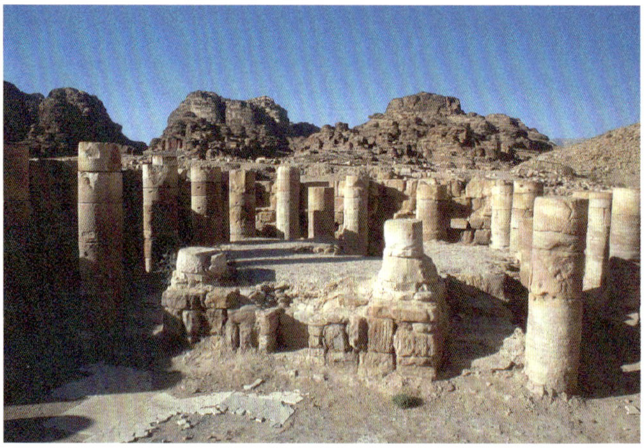

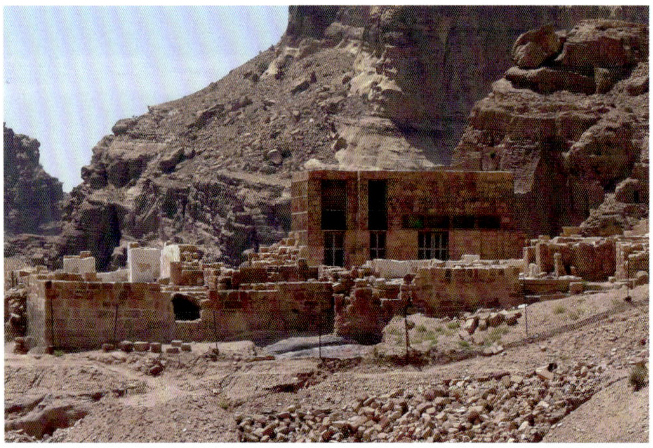

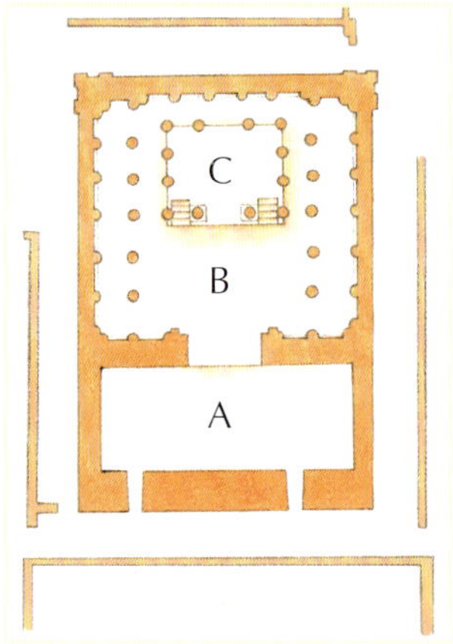

Plan of the Winged Lions Temple.

A Pronaos
B Cella
C Motab

Opposite page, above - *Part of the complex of workshops built around the temple.*

Opposite page, below - *The Winged Lions Temple is a typical early Nabataean monumental building.*

were fixed. The great fan that overlooks the valley of the Wadi Thughra, behind the domus EZ IV, is actually an enormous dump of inert materials, which was in use up until the end of the 1st century AD, by which time Petra was already a metropolis.

On the opposite side of the Colonnade, right opposite the "Great Temple", are the ruins of the **Winged Lions Temple**, so called because of the capitals decorated with these mythological animals that were found there. The building probably dates back to the first half of the 1st century BC, but it was renovated several times, and damaged by the earthquakes of 113 (or 114) and 363. The excavation of the complex, which began in 1974, revealed that there was a large bridge over the water course of the Wadi Musa in front of this religious building, giving access to the first terrace, which was surrounded by a portico with columns (the big drums of which are spread out on the ground). There was a second courtyard above, in front of the main temple building. This was made up of a large portico, supported by the massive substructures that are still visible. A doorway led to the square cella, which was paved in marble, with semi-columns framing deep niches in the walls. Five freestanding columns, in line with the pilasters, were aligned on the eastern and western sides. In the centre, but slightly towards the northern wall, there was a high square platform (the *motab*), surrounded by 12 columns and accessible via two ladders on the front, between the external intercolumniations. This platform was used as an altar, where a simulacrum of the goddess Al Uzza, to whom the temple was probably dedicated, was worshipped. There was a little room inside the *motab*, which was similar to a crypt and accessible from the rear. Religious artefacts may have been kept in it. The lower parts of the columns and walls were adorned with marble, and the upper parts with painted plaster. A famous stele was found in the temple, with highly stylized human features, which was identified with the goddess Al Uzza assimilated with Isis. It is now kept in the Archaeological Museum. Another interesting find was a female statuette in ivory, probably from India, which is an indication of the vast area covered by the Nabataeans' trade network.

Alongside the temple, to the west, the excavations of an inhabited neighbourhood, two workshops for processing metal and marble, and the studio of a painter or decorator can be seen. On the opposite side, towards the east, the ruins of an enormous building have yet to be investigated. It too once had a large bridge in front of it, and in the absence of reliable information, it has been given the evocative name of the Royal Palace.

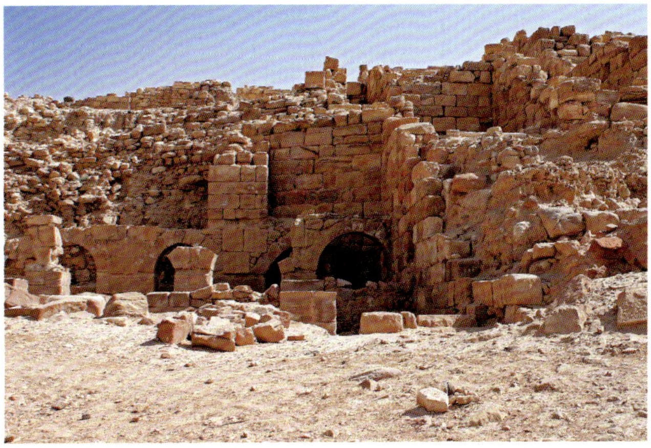

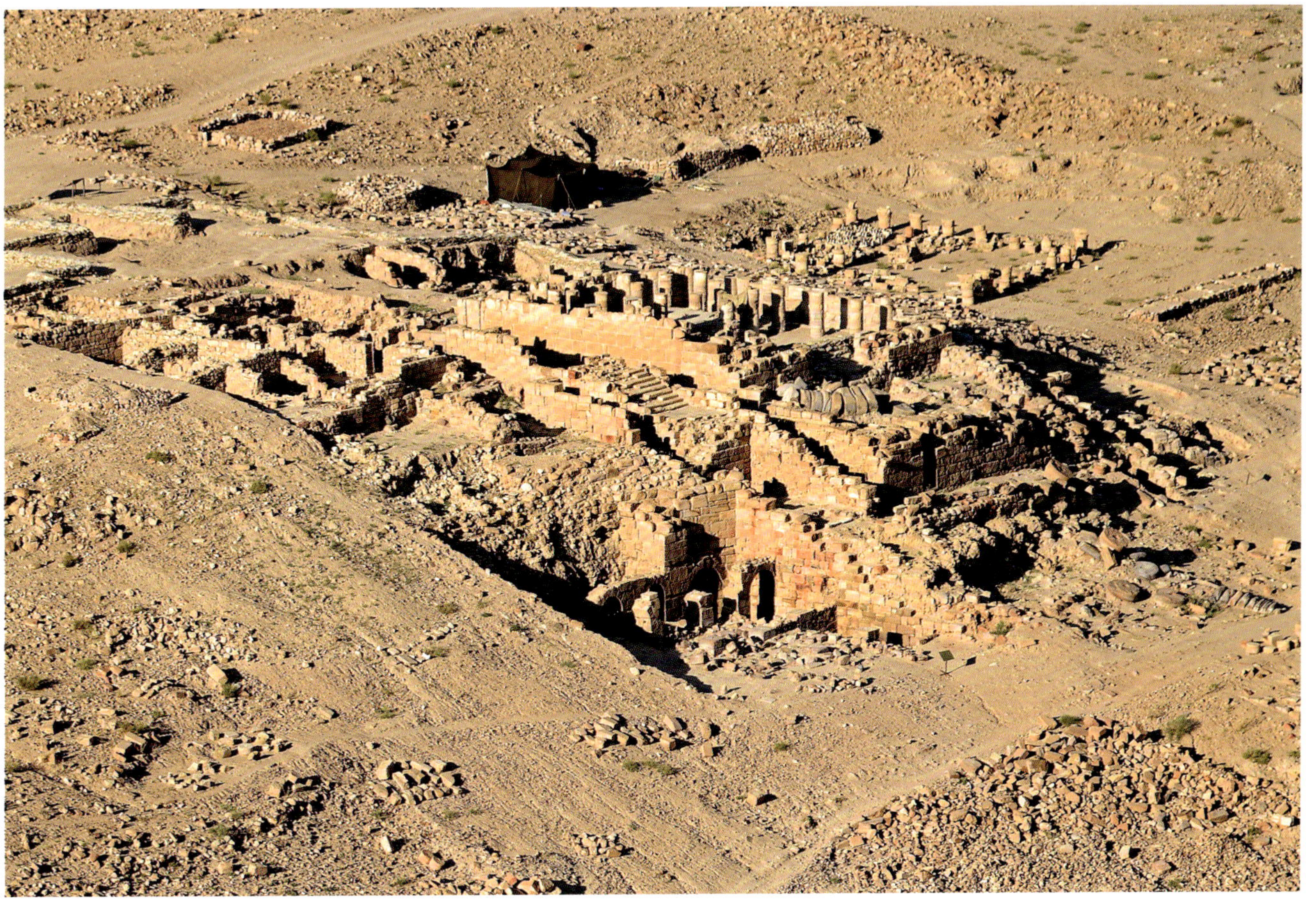

THE TEMENOS

The Colonnaded Street ends to the west with the remains of a monumental archway with three passageways, which is known as the **Temenos Gate**. The building has been partly reconstructed thanks to an accurate anastylosis. It had elaborate sculptural decorations in which the busts of deities alternated with elegant rosettes. For a long time it was believed to be a Roman triumphal arch erected in honour of Trajan, because of its appearance. However, in reality it was a gate that closed off the adjoining open air sacred precinct (the *temenos*). This is demonstrated by the fact that although the monument is slightly askew in relation to the Colonnaded Street, it is in line with the sacred enclosure. The existing structure is today thought to date back to the Severan period of the Roman domination (193-235), based on an analysis of its decorative design, and it was built on top of an older structure of a similar type. The bas-relief panels appear to be the work of several different artists, all influenced by Western taste, but more or less sensitive in the interpretation of the original models. It should be noted that the side of the arch facing the street was more architecturally complex, with four free standing columns that enlivened the facade (absent on the opposite side). Some of the sculptural decorations (a head of Hermes, busts of Dushara and Ares, and a winged Tyche) can be seen in the Museum. In the stone threshold of the central arch, two holes can be seen, for the hinges of the two heavy wooden doors that separated the chaos of everyday life from the silence of the sacred enclosure. To the sides of the Temenos Gate there were two tower-like structures, which have still not been fully understood. The one on the left served as the vestibule for a colonnaded hall, in turn communicating with three underground rooms covered with domes (wnot open to visitors). At one time they were believed to be pertinent to a bath complex, but now it is thought that it was part of a religious building, or in any case a much larger structure, perhaps connected with the "Great Temple". With regard to dilemmas that have not yet been resolved, it should be remembered that a set of fragments of sculptures and panels carved with effigies of the deities of the Graeco-Roman pantheon were found around the door in 1967. They were accurate copies of western models, undoubtedly made by local artists, and it seems evident that they were not part of the decoration of the gate, but rather of some nearby building. Among the best preserved pieces is a splendid bust of a veiled woman, identified as Venus Al-Uzza (page 32), a head of Dionysus (page 31), the bust of a Muse holding a tragic mask (page 31), and a sphinx (page 49). They are all on display in the Museum. On the southern side (to the left if you are coming from the Colonnaded Street), the **temenos** (about 140 m x 40 m) still seems to be bordered by a long wall, against which two continuous rows of benches were placed, perhaps for the priests and the worshippers during religious ceremonies. The northern side must have had a similar arrangement, but the floods from the Wadi Musa have cancelled all trace of the retaining wall. A number of buildings, which are today nothing more than a pile of rubble, looked out over the sacred precinct. One of these must have been a little prostyle temple. In 1964, an inscription dedicated to King Aretas IV was discovered on a block of sandstone that had been set into the southern wall of the *temenos* after the enclosure itself was built, and another similar one was found in 1990.

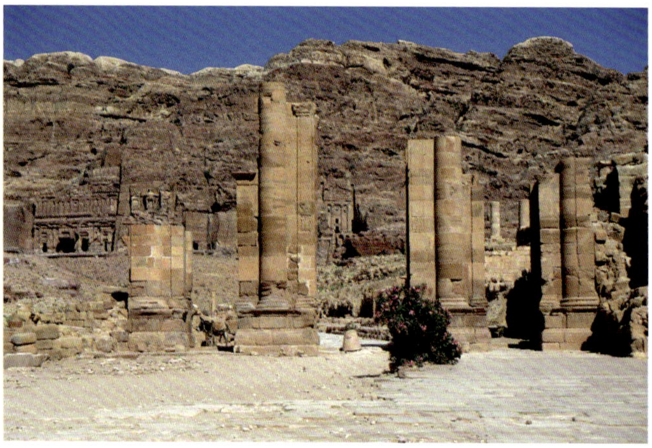

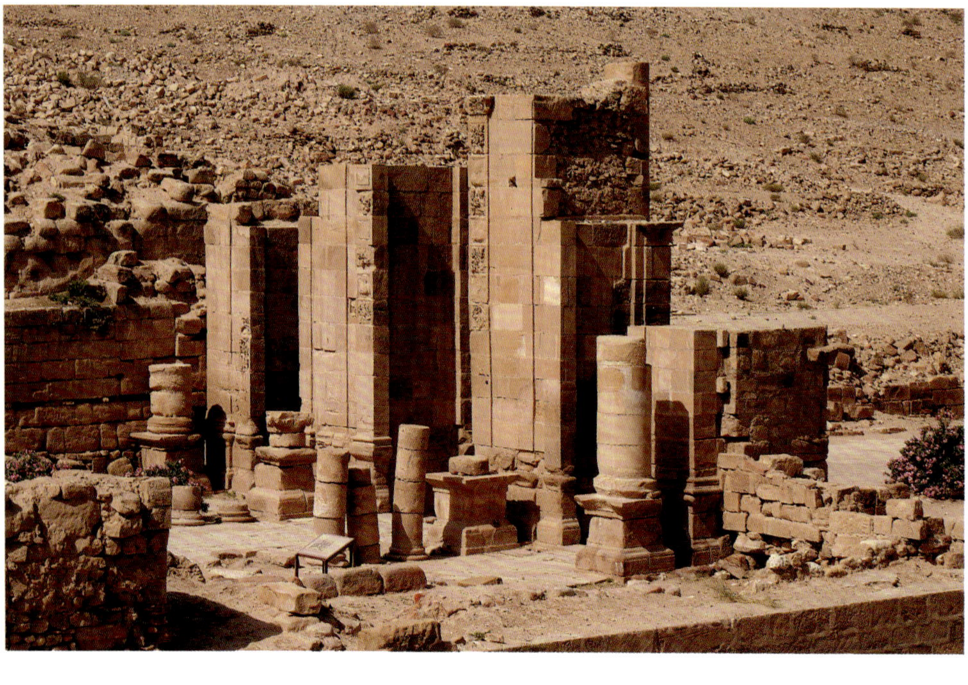

Above - *On the western side, facing the* temenos, *the gate was architecturally less articulated: here, in fact, the arches were framed between four simple pilasters, while to the east there were four free-standing columns on a high podium, which created a chiaroscuro effect especially suitable for scenically ending the Colonnaded Street.*

Below - *The monumental Temenos Gate is very similar to a Roman triumphal arch.*

Opposite page - *The Qasr El Bint stood at the point where the main roads of the city converged.*

Apart from the fact the two blocks may have had statues on them (which suggests the enclosure of the *temenos* was decorated with other statues), their presence has not only allowed the sacred area (situated in an area previously occupied by houses) to be dated to the second half of the 1st century BC, but also the colossal monument for which the *temenos* was created, that is, the **Qasr el Bint** (No. 403). This imposing building is the only one built in masonry in Petra that is still relatively well preserved, and today its towering ruins are about 23 metres high. At one time this temple was thought to have been built in the Roman era, but it has now been established that it was erected in the last quarter of the 1st century BC, probably during the reign of Obodas III (30-9 BC). Archaeological investigations carried out under the building have identified the remains of walls that were probably part of a house, dating back to the 4th and 3rd centuries BC. The excavations have confirmed a long building continuity here, and that there was already a Nabataean settlement in Petra in 312 BC, or even before.
The proportions and the layout of the building can be considered typically Nabataean. It has a square floor plan, it faces from north to south, it was built with ashlars of sandstone bound with mortar, it was 32 metres wide, and it stood on a high podium with a large staircase covered in marble in front of it. Its overall height must have been about 29 metres. The facade was of the *in antis* type, with four non-fluted columns, which were plastered and crowned with capitals, perhaps similar to those in the Khazneh. Curiously, the intercolumniations are all of different sizes. In fact, the two furthest out are 3 metres wide, the two in between 3.8, and the central one 6.3. The two side pillars have an unusual coloured plaster decoration, with circles alternating with octagons. The frieze that adorned the trabeation and also ran along the other three sides of the building was made up of triglyphs and unusual metopes in the shape of round medallions with the bust of a deity in the centre, alternated with pairs of rosettes. Unfortunately all the protomes were destroyed by the iconoclasts (except one, which is now kept in the Museum). The facade must have had a tympanum pediment with a high parapet, and the building probably had a flat, or a slightly gabled roof. As can be seen by observing the rear wall, the entire temple was plastered with a thick layer of stucco, which was modelled and painted with illusionistic architectural patterns. There is some evidence to suggest that a low portico was added to the east, south and west sides of the temple.
The cella is a spacious room with a rectangular floor plan, illuminated by two large windows high up on the short sides. It is accessed from the pronaos through a high doorway, which has lost its lintel, but miraculously still

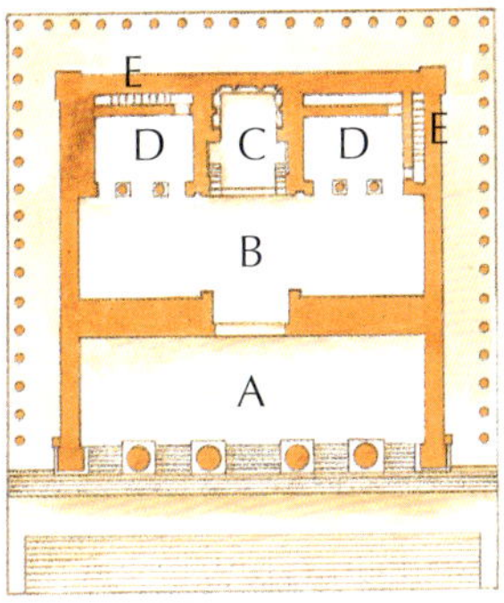

Plan of the Qasr el Bint

A Pronaos (or vestibule)
B Cella
C Adyton (or naos)
D Side adytons
E Stairs

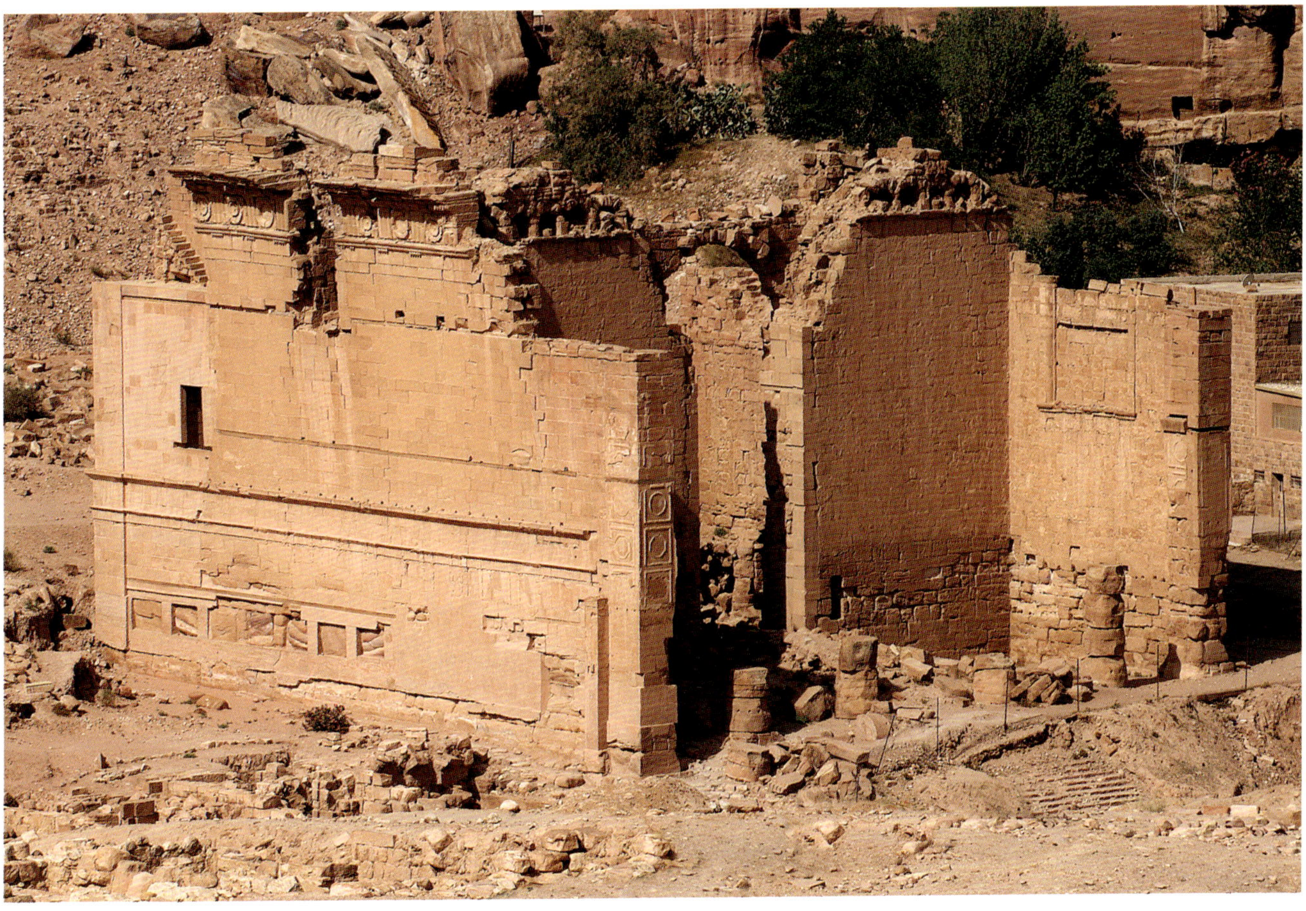

THE QASR EL BINT: A RECONSTRUCTIVE SUGGESTION

Scholars do not agree on what the Qasr el Bint aspect was; the main doubts concern the type of roof. According to some, including François Larché and Fawzi Zayadine, the temple was covered by a roof with two slightly inclined slopes; some holes in the upper internal part of the walls, which would have welcomed the beams of the trusses, and numerous terracotta fragments of what have been identified as roof tiles, found among the rubble of the internal rooms, would demonstrate this. Others, such as Iain Browning and G.R. Wright, believe that the roof was flat and that at least one of the two steep stairs built into the thickness of the walls served to reach this sort of large terrace, protected by a parapet and suitable for hosting religious functions. Certainly the presence of an attic above the large pediment, would have given the temple a remarkable resemblance to the Tomb of the Roman Soldier (page 140) and the other similar monuments in Petra, constituting the stylistic feature of a local architectural tradition.
A secondary question regards the appearance of the walls. Although it is an established fact that the interiors and the sections below the portico were covered in a thick layer of painted plaster, it is much harder to say the same for the rest of the monument. On the back of the temple (photo on the right) a large part of the stucco decoration, originally multi-coloured, is preserved, although very damaged. The architectural plasterwork, with a curved pediment framed between two broken pediments, denotes a clear influence of Alexandrian art and recalls the Second Pompeian Style (see p. 173). At the same time, it closely resembles the lower part of the Bab el Siq Triclinium (p. 53), and also the decorative elements of Trajan's Market in Rome. This leads to the idea that the portico and decorative elements are the result of a later intervention.
A technical device as interesting as it is astounding, is the structure of the monument's walls, in whose thickness were inserted wooden courses, running the length of the walls. Undoubtedly, this was to make the walls more flexible. Probably an anti-seismic device, which was ahead of its time, but proved effective.

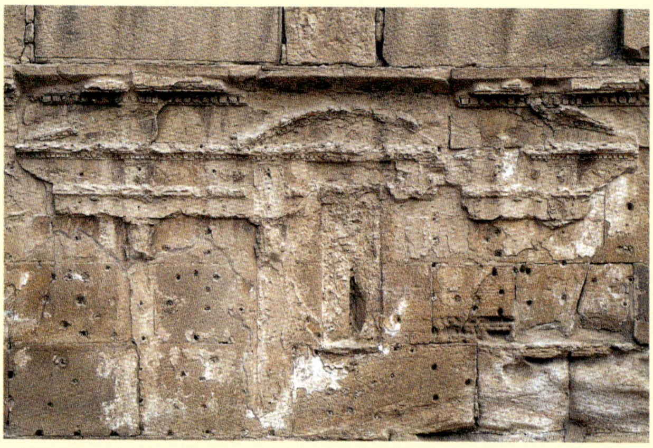

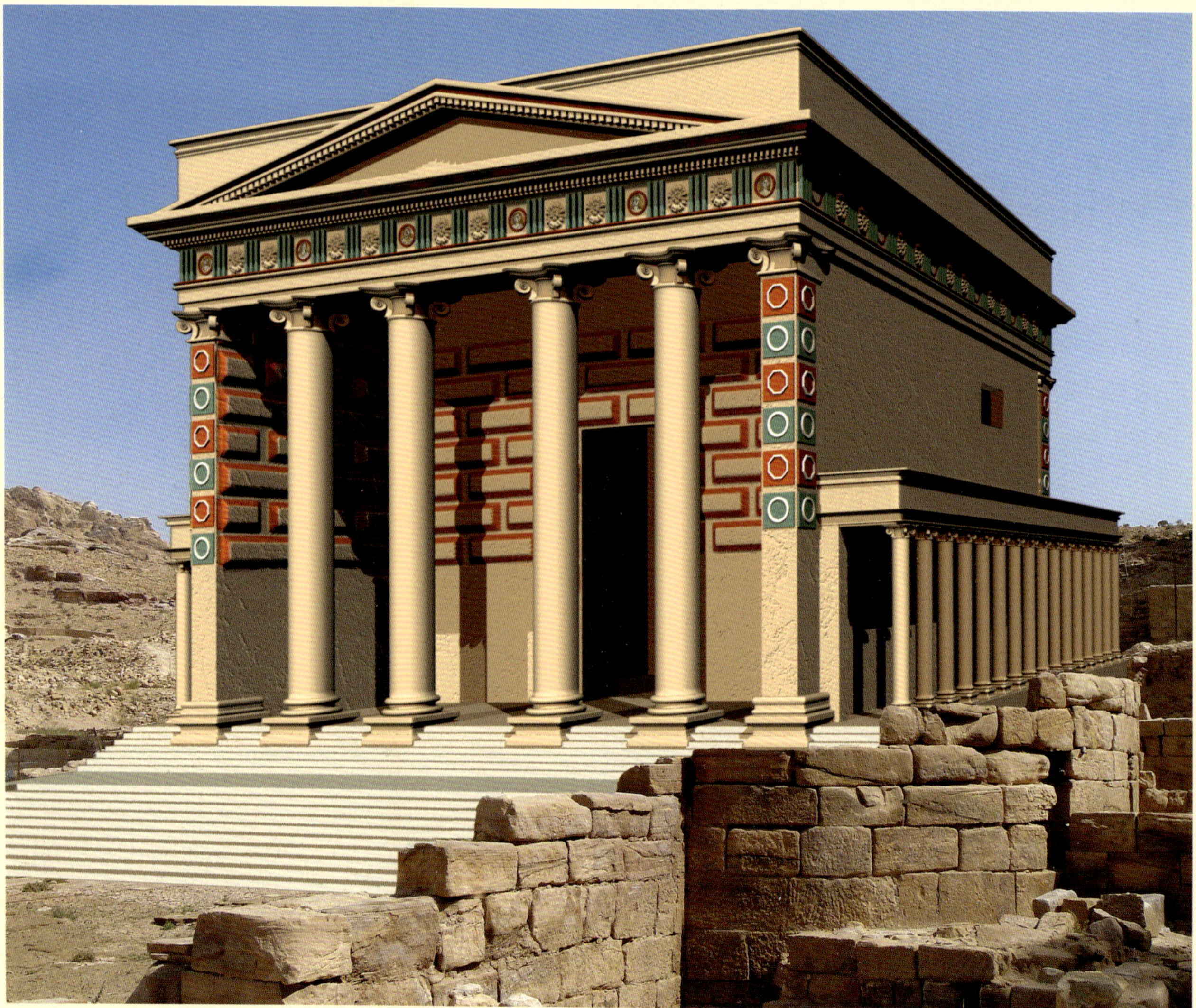

F. Bourbon - I. Cirillo

mantains its relieving arch. It is easy to imagine all the internal walls of the temple plastered and painted. Three adjoining rooms overlook the cell. In the central one, the *adyton*, the sacred image of the deity was housed. This chamber, which had pilasters around its walls, was about a metre and a half higher than the floor of the cella and was accessible by climbing two ladders at the sides. The other two rooms, where symposiums in honour of the gods may have been held, were laid out on two floors, and the mezzanines were held up by pairs of columns. The upper floors could be reached by climbing two staircases, built within the thickness of the perimeter walls. It is also likely that these staircases, or at least one of them, led to a flat roof, or in any case a terrace, where religious ceremonies may have been held, as described by Strabo, and like the ones that took place in Egyptian temples (for example in Dendera).

Today it is said that the temple, by virtue of its dominant position and considerable size, was consecrated to the god Dushara; however, so far, no archaeological finds have confirmed this supposition. The discovery of parts of two inscriptions written in Greek, but dating back to the Roman period, would suggest a different explanation. In fact, one of the fragments mentions the goddess Aphrodite (a deity assimilated with Al Uzza), while the other mentions Zeus Hypsistos, epithet with which the god Ba'al-shamin was identified. It is therefore possible that the temple was dedicated to more than one deity, perhaps even a trinity. The name of the third divinity, however, is unknown. On the subject of names, the complete one by which the monument is known is Qasr el Bint Faroun (which means "Palace of the Pharaoh's Daughter"), and it refers to yet another colourful Bedouin legend with no historical basis whatsoever.

Opposite the Qasr el Bint, the *temenos* is partly occupied by the remains of a large rectangular altar, which is about 13 metres long, just under three metres high in its current state, and positioned along an east-west axis. It is accessible via a staircase. Sacrifices were carried out here, in honour of the most important deities in the Nabataean pantheon.

In the north-west corner of the *temenos*, behind the great altar, the remains of a monumental building from the Roman era have been uncovered, with an exedra flanked by columns and niches. Fragments of inscriptions referring to Marcus Aurelius and Lucius Verus, joint emperors between 161 and 169, and the discovery of two busts of them nearby, suggest that the building was dedicated to them. The exedra and the Qasr el Bint were badly damaged by the earthquake of 363. During the occupation by the Crusaders, some of the temple's ashlars were probably used to build the castle on top of the Jebel al Habis.

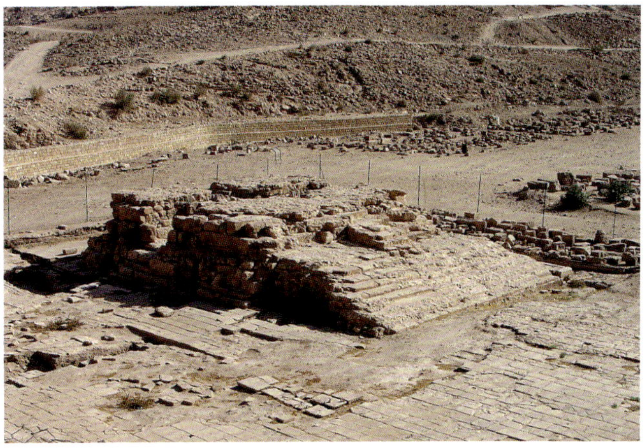

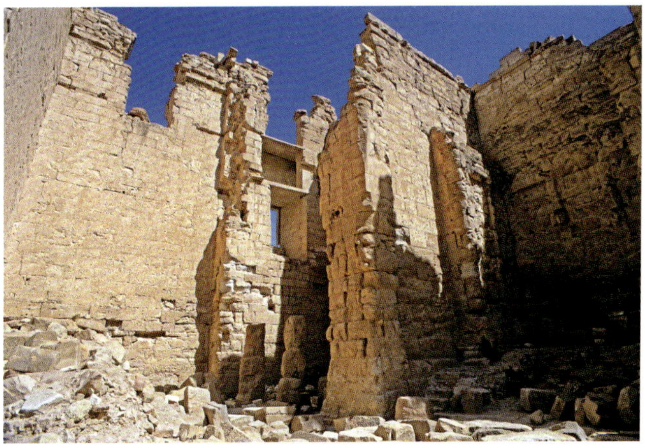

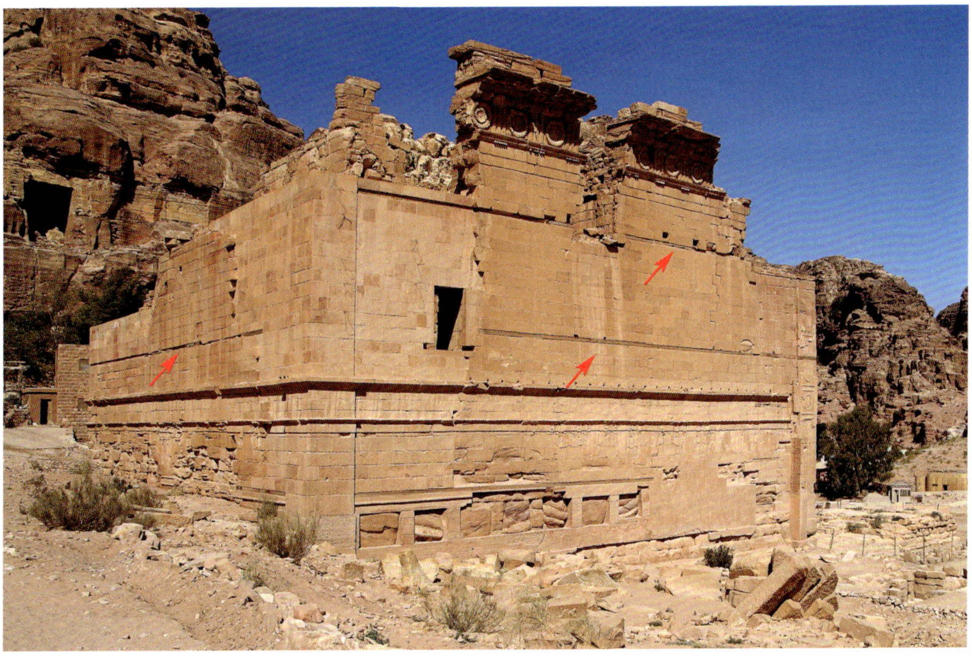

Top - *The large altar that stands in front of the Qasr el Bint; originally it was covered with marble slabs.*

Centre - *A view of the interior of the temple, with the central* adyton *and the eastern room.*

Bottom - *The south-eastern corner of the Qasr el Bint was rebuilt by the Jordan Antiquities Department. The point where the modern and the original masonry meet is clearly visible, as the latter one is slightly overhanging. The arrows indicate the layers of wood (maybe Lebanon cedar) inserted into the walls.*

THE BYZANTINE RELIGIOUS BUILDINGS

Together with some restaurants, cafés and toilets, in an area near the Qasr el Bint known as Nazzal's Camp, stands the old Museum. It was built in the nineties to house artefacts found during the archaeological digs carried out in Petra. Up until 2016, fragments of sculpture, Nabataean and Roman coins, jewellery, everyday objects, carefully restored mosaic floors, and a wide range of very delicate Nabataean ceramics could be admired here. There was also an extraordinary capital with elephant protomes, the best preserved of those discovered among the ruins of the "Great Temple". These items were then moved to the exhibition space inside the Visitors Centre, at the entrance to the site. Since 2019, they are on display in the very modern Archaeological Museum, not far away.

Finally, it remains to explain what lies under the eye catching white tensile structure on the hill overlooking the northern bank of the wadi Musa: it is a **Byzantine Church** dating back to the last decades of the 5th century, which was uncovered in the early nineties. Since Petra was a bishop's seat in that era, it was probably a cathedral. Oriented from east to west and 26 meters long, it had a basilica plan. The facade was preceded by an atrium and the aisles, held up by two rows of columns, had three apses at the end. The floors were sumptuously decorated with mosaics. Although the floor of the central

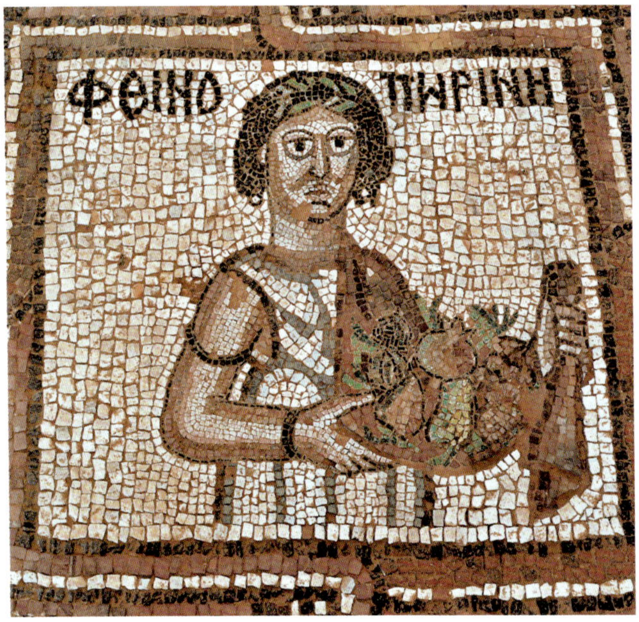

nave is not well preserved, the side naves are in much better condition, covered with an elaborate mosaic carpet. The mosaics are made up of lines of geometrical frames containing depictions of people, animals and objects connected with both the Christian liturgy and the classical tradition, endowed with new meanings. In particular, the personifications of the four seasons and Oceanus demonstrate this syncretism. The building was mainly constructed with re-used materials, probably taken from the ruins of the pagan temples destroyed in the two violent earthquakes of 363 and 419. In fact, one of the Corinthian capitals recovered during the excavations appears to come from the Winged Lions Temple.

In 1993, 140 scrolls were discovered in a room adjacent to the church. Most of them are legal documents relating to three generations of an influential local family (contracts, land register deeds, receipts, etc.) Although damaged in the fire that destroyed the church (possibly in 551 after one of the many earthquakes),

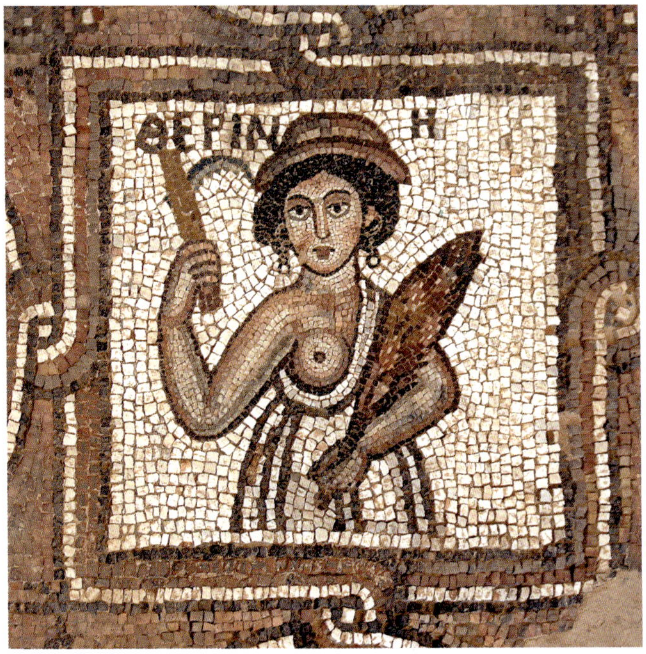

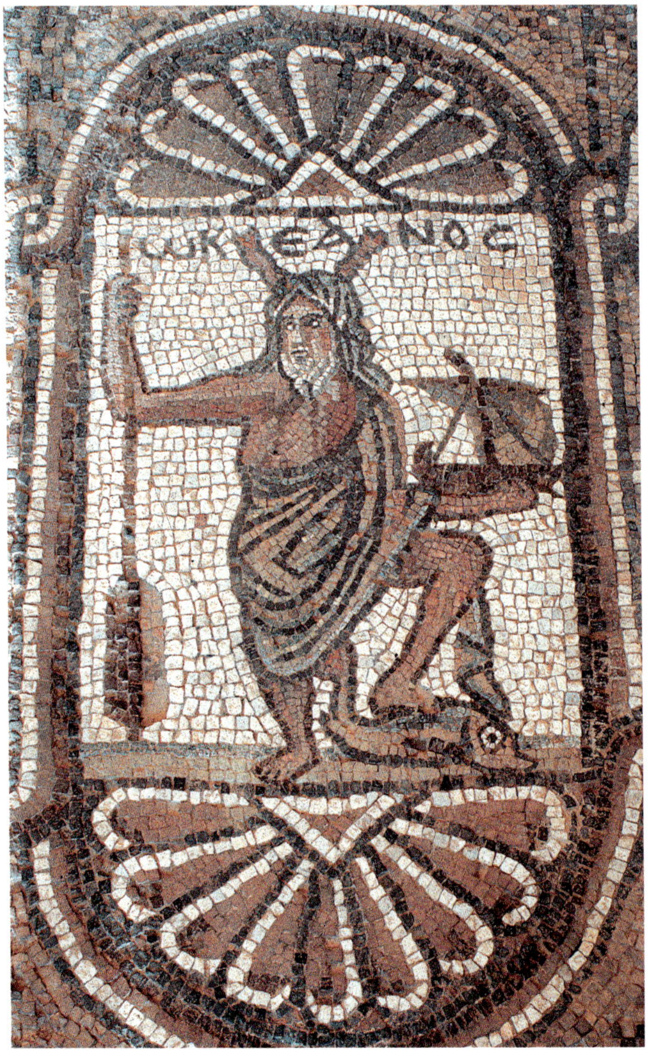

they are still legible and are now being studied as they shed light on the society of Petra in the Byzantine era.
To the north of the church, next to the city wall and on top of the ridge that dominates both the valley of the Wadi Musa and that of the Wadi Turkmaniyya, recent archaeological digs have uncovered the foundations of a Nabataean building, converted into a church in the second half of the 4th century (today known as the **Ridge Church**). It had three naves and is thought to be one of the oldest Christian churches in Jordan. The building was abandoned at the beginning of the 7th century, but was later partially reused as living quarters by the people of Petra. At the time, the population was in sharp decline as a result of the devastation caused by earthquakes.
In the area between the Ridge Church and the Byzantine Church, which was a residential quarter in the Nabataean and Roman eras, another structure has been discovered, which was also converted into a church, possibly at the beginning of the 6th century. This monument has been named the **Blue Chapel** because of its unusual bluish coloured granite columns, which come from an older Nabataean building. They have been reconstructed with anastylosis, and their well preserved and elegant looking "horned" capitals have been put back in place. These were probably taken from older pagan buildings, as well. It is believed that this little church-like building was adjacent to the residence of the bishop of Petra. This theory is supported by the fact that the base of the bishop's seat (*cathedra*) has been identified in the apse.
The excavations have also uncovered a beautiful marble pulpit and the balustrade of the presbytery, sculpted from the same material.

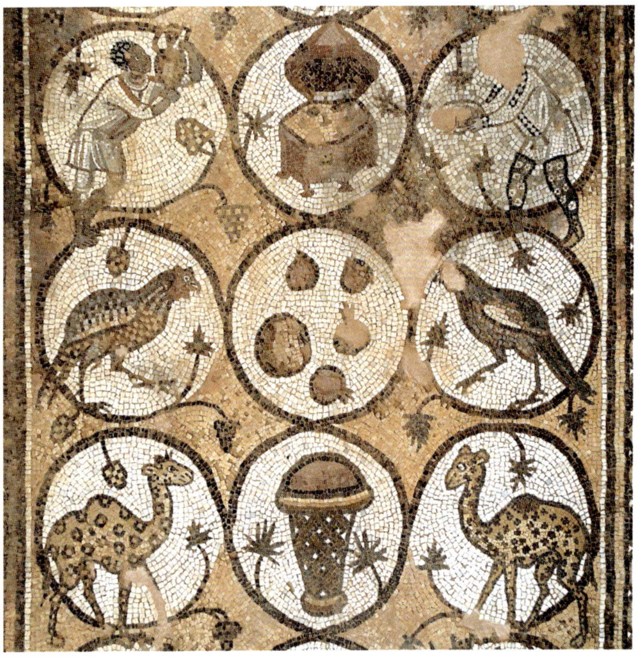

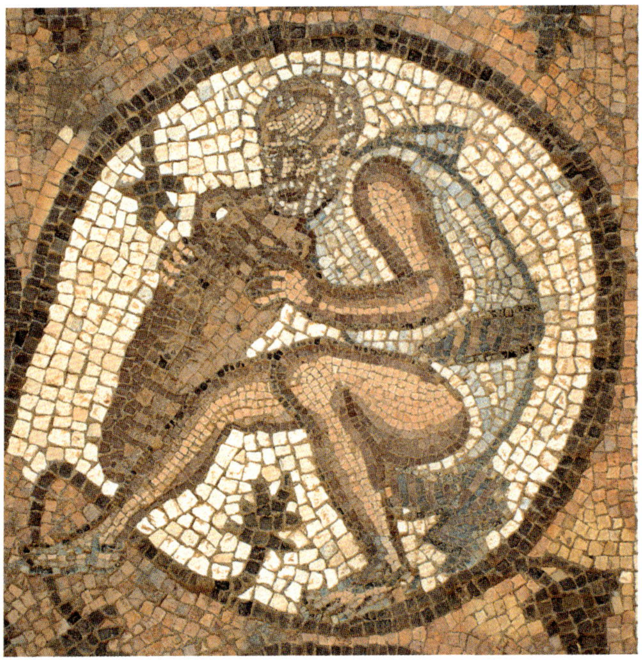

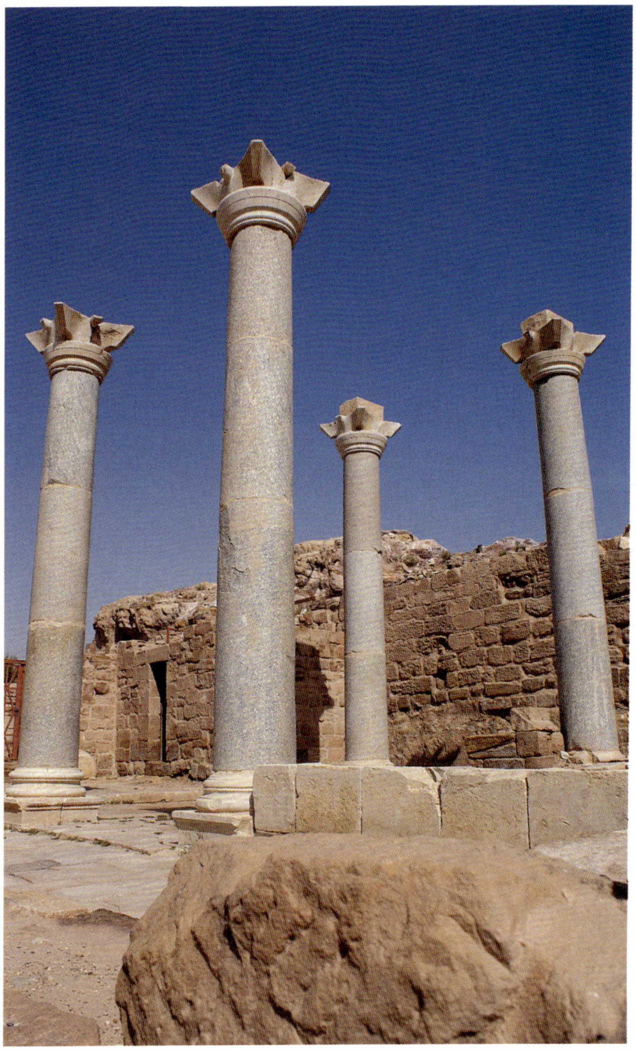

Opposite page - *The Byzantine Church is best known for the beautiful mosaics that decorate its two side aisles and which combine Christian iconographic themes with others from the Graeco-Roman tradition.*
Clockwise from the top, here are the personification of Summer, Oceanus and the personification of Autumn.

Left and top right - *Another two details of the mosaics that embellish the Byzantine Church and represent the flora and fauna of the world, as well as human activities.*

Bottom right - *The four elegant columns that gave the Blue Chapel its name probably were taken from an older Nabataean temple.*

THE JEBEL AL HABIS

The rocky hill that dominates the old city of Petra and towers over the Qasr el Bint is called Jebel al Habis. The perimeter of its base measures just over a kilometre and a half. According to some, it was the "citadel" of Petra, a place that could easily be reached and defended in times of need. Others believe it was the "acropolis", or yet another sacred site. Curiously enough, its modern name in Arabic means "the Prison". What is certain is that a large part of the city once stretched out beneath it, and there were several houses cut into the lower slopes of the rock, some of which still have traces of wall plaster and paint. Doubts remain about the function of some other giant rooms with no facades, which are like gaping jaws.

The suggested itinerary is not particularly demanding and can be completed in a couple of hours, or a little longer; only the climb to the top of the Gebel al Habis requires moderate physical effort. The trail starts and finishes in the same place, so you can choose which direction to take, based on the position of the sun, in order to stay in the shade as much as possible during the walk. However, the suggested route is the most practical in the end. From the area known as Nazzal's Camp, where the old Museum and the restaurants are, a stairway rises up steeply towards the towering face of the rock and turns to the left. As you go up, you can see some cave dwellings with modern doors. They were probably Nabataean houses, which later became Bedouin homes, and are today used as storage space and service rooms. A bit further on there is a strange room with some enormous windows (a feature that is almost unique in Petra's rock cut architecture). It is made up of three adjoining rooms and has a terrace in front of it, cut into the side of the mountain. Its function is not known, but it was probably a temple, or a place to rest and prepare for the processions that led up to the "high place of sacrifice" or to the top of the al Habis. At one time, it housed the first Museum in Petra, but all the artefacts have been moved to the new building close to the Visitors Centre. The astounding array of colours on the walls makes it worth a visit, but it cannot normally be accessed, as it has not yet been as-

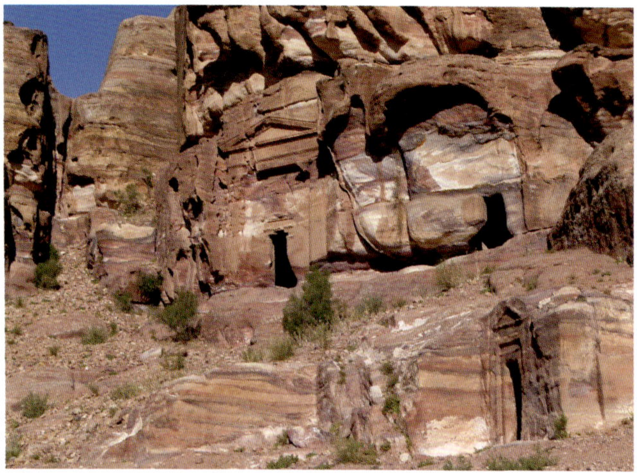

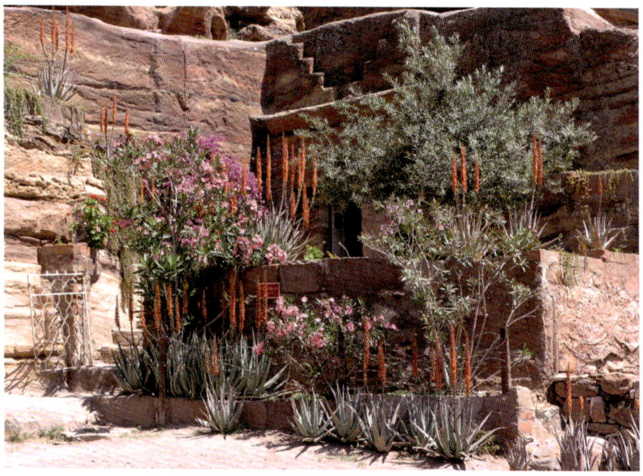

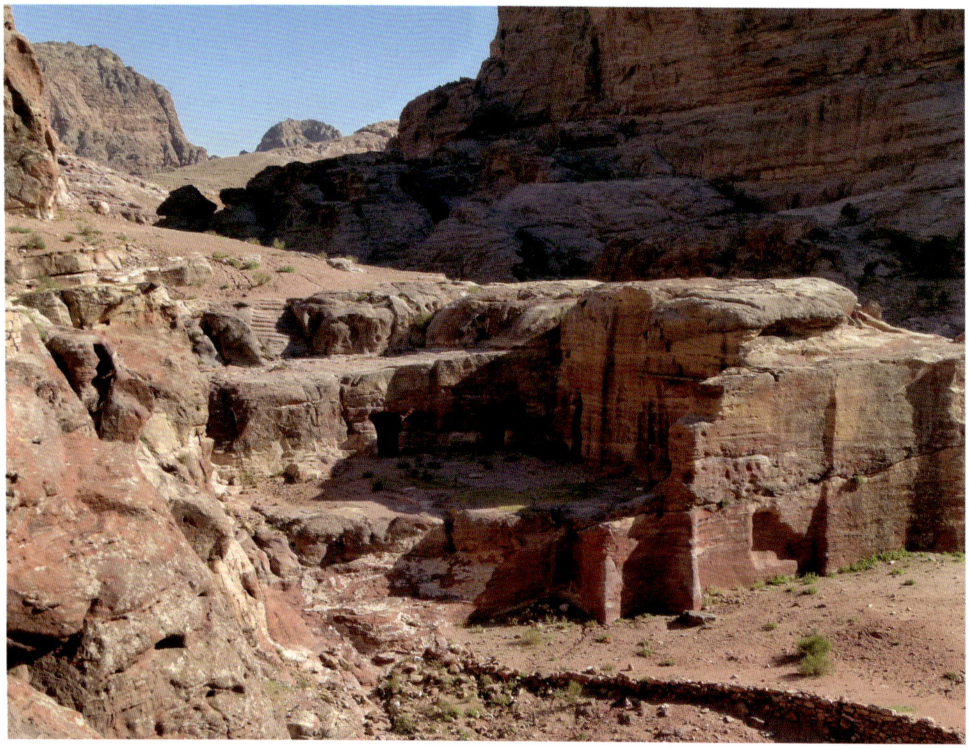

Above left - *The two pediment facades that adorn the north-western spur of the Jebel al Habis.*

Above right - *Mofleh Bdoul's rupestrian house has a lush, poetic flower garden in front of it.*

Below - *The curious complex of hypogea known as the Convent; on the western side there is a cavetto tomb.*

Opposite page - *Although modest in size, the high place (or open-air triclinium) of Jebel the Habis attracts attention by virtue of its spectacular location, right on the edge of the cliff overlooking Wadi Thughra.*

signed a new function. From this point, which already has a good view, the spectacular processional path, carved deep into the side of the mountain, turns sharply to the west and the Wadi Siyyagh can then be seen vertically below, with its innumerable rupestrian houses and oleander groves. You soon come to a sort of table-shelf formed from horizontal layers of sandstone, bordered further to the east by the precipice of the Wadi Thugra. Here, the rocks take on a glittering array of colours and all around you can see staircases cut into the rock, hypogea, and little aqueducts that once supplied a densely populated quarter of the city. On the jagged spur of the Jebel al Habris, there is an elegant well-preserved pediment facade. It is a well preserved triclinium, to the right of which there is another very eroded room. A little further down there is another smaller pediment facade carved into the rock. At the foot of the triclinium, along the dirt track that heads south, there is a tomb of the cavetto type, with two small windows in its facade and a luxuriant garden in front of it. This is the home of Mofleh Bdoul, a Bedouin with an innate sense of hospitality, who will be pleased to offer

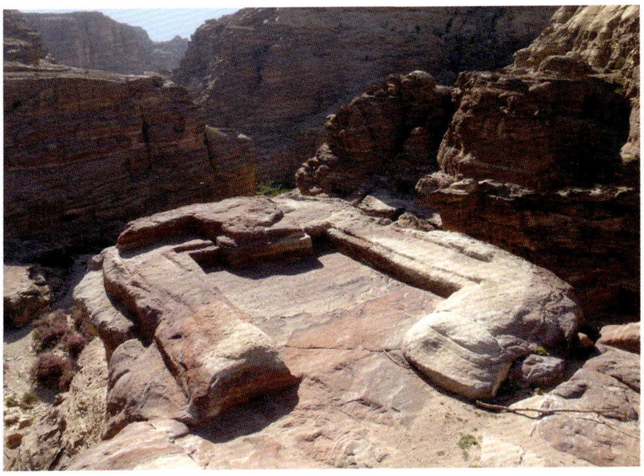

you a cup of tea and have a chat in one of the many languages he has learned. He is a sort of living legend, one of the few who refused to abandon his ancestral traditions and move to the village of Umm Sahyoun. You can always learn something interesting by listening to him.

If you go down some stairs, a bit further down, in front of his house, you will reach a suggestive rupestrian complex known as the **Convent**. It consists of a square courtyard, carved about six metres into the bed of sandstone, and is surrounded on three sides by the entrances to several caves. It is popular belief that the priests in charge of the cults in the nearby "high place of sacrifices" resided here, but in reality they are tombs and other service rooms dug inside a disused stone quarry. On the spur of rock situated a few metres west of the Convent, jutting out over Wadi Thughra (which joins with Wadi Siyyagh at this point), is the "**high place of sacrifice**" mentioned above. It is fairly similar to the one found on the Jebel al Madhbah, but smaller in size (about 5 metres by just over 3 and a half). Today it is opinion that it was in fact an open-air triclinium, used for celebrations in honour of the deceased buried in the nerby little necropolis.

PETRA'S INHABITANTS TODAY

Up until a few decades ago, Petra was not a "dead city". Bedouins of the Bdoul tribe lived in hundreds of tombs and other hypogea carved into the stone, which they simply called al mughar, *"the caves". However, in 1985, as part of a sponsored plan by UNESCO, the government pushed residents to settle in the village of Wadi Musa and in the purposely built settlement of Umm Sahyoun (which counts around 3000 residents today), which was supplied with all essential services like running water and electricity in addition to schools and other facilities. Over 250 families moved into new residences but not everyone accepted the change willingly, including Mofleh Bdoul. He still lives in a tomb today, but it has been completely transformed with a garden, electricity supplied by a generator and water, thanks to a large cistern. He explains his decision in a few words, "My family has always lived here and there's nowhere else in the world I would want to live".*

Compared to the past, the living conditions of the Bdoul tribe have definitely improved, also thanks to proceeds from tourism-related activities. Indeed, practically all the souvenir vendors, guides and animal handlers belong to that same tribe. The young people also have access to education, and many of them end up going to Jordanian universities. It can happen to meet a young shepherd who is following the lessons online on his laptop, while the goats graze nearby.

However, the increasing rise in population and the limited size of Umm Sahyoun, not suited to expansion due to the lie of the land, are creating difficulties, so much so that, although the figure is not official, about fifty families have returned to live in the ancient tombs, although entirely in the suburbs of the Nabataean capital.

Another problem is that Bdoul street vendors refuse to stay in specific areas, as suggested by the government, and each one prefers to choose their own place, sometimes causing damage to the ancient ruins. It is therefore clear that one of the next objectives at a cultural and governmental level will focus on resolving these sensitive issues.

Mofleh welcomes the author with his usual hospitality.

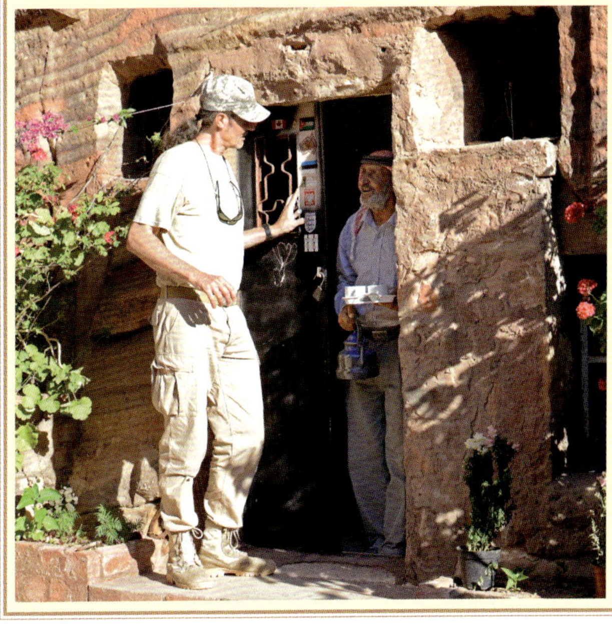

Returning to the track that skirts round the extraordinary ridged sides of the Jebel al Habis, the enormous face of the Jebel Umm al Biyara towers above with a large necropolis at the foot of it. When you reach the southern spur of the rock, you notice a series of steps, which become increasingly steep. The current staircase was built on the remains of a similar ancient structure, erected by the Nabataeans and then used again during the brief occupation of Petra by the Crusaders. First, you scramble up towards some rock cut houses situated in a spectacular aerial position, and then continue on to the top. About half way up there is a walkway made of some boards put in place to cross a gap. There may once have been a drawbridge here, put there by the Crusaders to defend the access route to the rock.

The double peak of the Jebel al Habis appears as a set of ruined buildings which are difficult to interpret. It is a confusing combination of walls, rubble, staircases, cuttings, cisterns and the remains of Nabataean dams. There are the ruins of a **Crusader fort** here, which was erected on the foundations of a Nabataean fortification (or possibly a sanctuary) and the remains of a settlement dating back to the Iron Age. The fort must have been an outpost of the Li Vaux Moise Castle (Al Wu'eira), built by order of Baldwin I of Jerusalem in 1116 and just a few kilometres away, to the east. It appears that the knights' lodgings and the other service rooms were built on the southernmost peak of the rock, while the keep, which is still surrounded by a thick wall, was on the slightly lower one to the north. The two sections of the fortress were connected by an arch, which, miraculously, is still standing. From the remains of the keep the view can range over the northernmost part of the Gebel al Habis, which the locals call Jebel Makkhool (in Petra, the same place can have different names and there is an endless number of toponyms). The summit of the rocky spur, squared by numerous quarries, is reached by a bold carved staircase that, inexplicably, leads nowhere. While taking in this majestic view, we can only imagine what the Crusader knights must have felt, looking out over such a mysterious metaphysical landscape, after arriving from distant lands. Strangers in a strange land, encamped in the hearth of a dead city...

On the way back, at the foot of the staircase you arrived from, turn left, going down the eastern slope of the Gebel al Habis, littered with many boulders that have fallen there during the many earthquakes. You pass in front of a hypogeum that is intermittently inhabited by a family of goat herders, and soon arrive at one of the most mysterious spaces in Petra, the so-

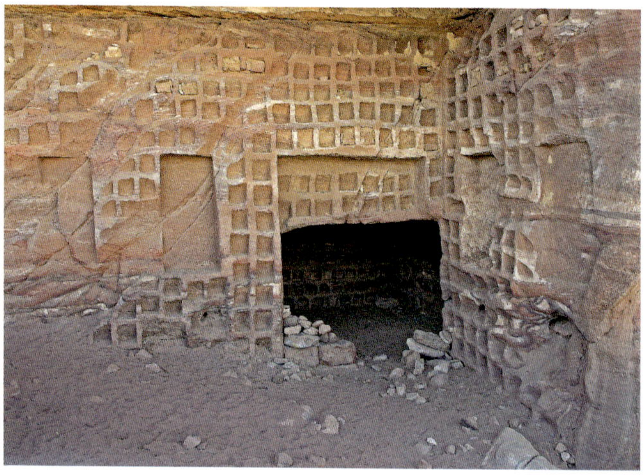

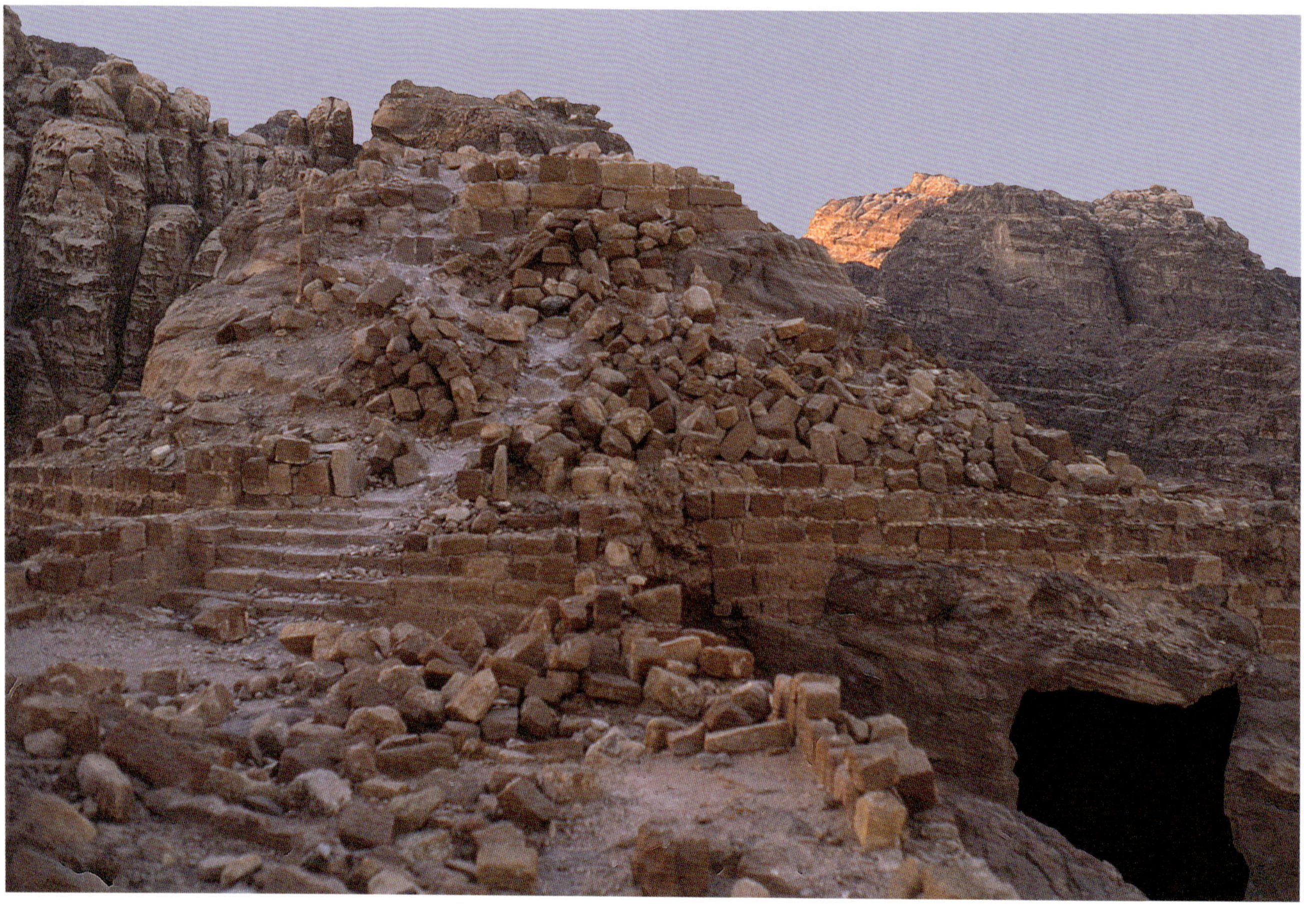

called **Columbarium**, the function of which is still unknown. Both the external walls of this space, and the ones inside, are scattered with a myriad of square niches, arranged in regular lines. This orderly framework is interrupted by some larger rectangular niches. The Latin term *columbarium* refers to a type of sepulchre with cavities carved in the walls, into which urns of ashes were placed. In this case, however, the niches are too small and shallow to have been used for this purpose. It may have been a rock cut sanctuary, in which images of deities were placed in the larger niches, while in the smaller ones the faithful might have left offerings, votive lanterns or little terracotta statuettes. This unusual monument may have been like today's sanctuaries in which a large quantity of ex voto offerings are piled up, but this is just a theory.
A little further on is the impressive facade of the **Unfinished Tomb**, which is noticeably set back in relation to the natural profile of the mountain. The only parts that were finished are the architrave and the four Nabataean capitals below it. The outer ones would have crowned the side pillars, and the two in the middle would have stood on top of two tall columns. Had it been finished, the facade would have been like an enormous portico *in antis*, similar to the ones that can be seen in the Little Petra (page 170), or in the Garden Triclinium (page 145), and would have been the biggest of its kind anywhere in Petra. The reason why the work was interrupted is unknown, but it was probably not a tomb, but rather a grandiose temple.
Following the path that now runs parallel to the fence in front of the Unfinished Tomb, you finally arrive back at the starting point, next to the Qasr El Bint.

Opposite page, top - *A peculiarity of the Columbarium is that the niches are not cubic and the rear walls incline outwards, from bottom to top. This makes them completely unsuitable for containing urns.*

Opposite page, bottom - *The Crusader fort was built on the remains of pre-existing Nabataean structures (perhaps a temple) and using recycled material. The ruins are not very impressive, but in this precarious position the seismic waves of the earthquakes occurred over the centuries must have reached the greatest destructive effects. In fact, the slopes of the hill are cluttered with ashlars and other stone blocks fallen from the summit.*

Below - *The front of the Unfinished Tomb.*

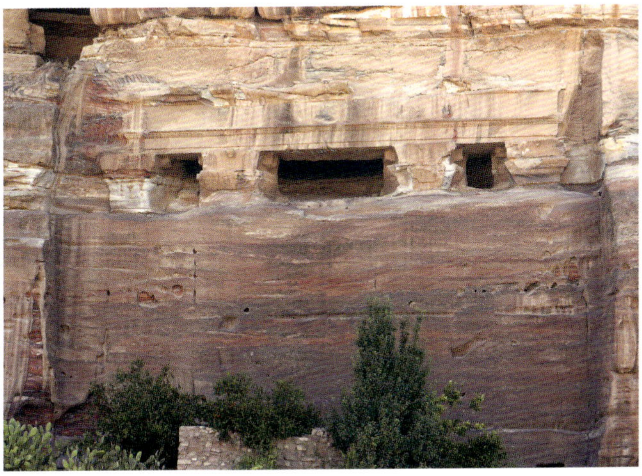

AN ALTERNATIVE HIKE

To reach the top of the Jebel al Habis, there is a little known, but very interesting route, which is only suitable for those who are prepared for a short, yet intense hike. At the back of Mofleh Bdoul's remarkable dwelling, an evident crack opens in the side of the rocky hill, immediately to the left of the large pediment facade. Here a staircase made in modern times of large stones and salvaged material, goes up, straight and steep, and then makes a few hairpin bends at a point where the marbling of the sandstone offers an extraordinary and beautiful sight. Suddenly you come out to a flat overhang, strewn with rubble; to the right towers the striking, massive wall of a large, well preserved water cistern (photo). Keeping to the right, you soon reach the last part of the already described path that goes up to the Crusader fort.

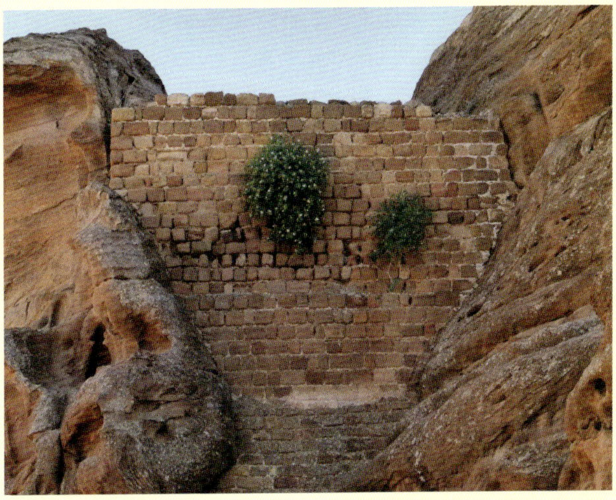

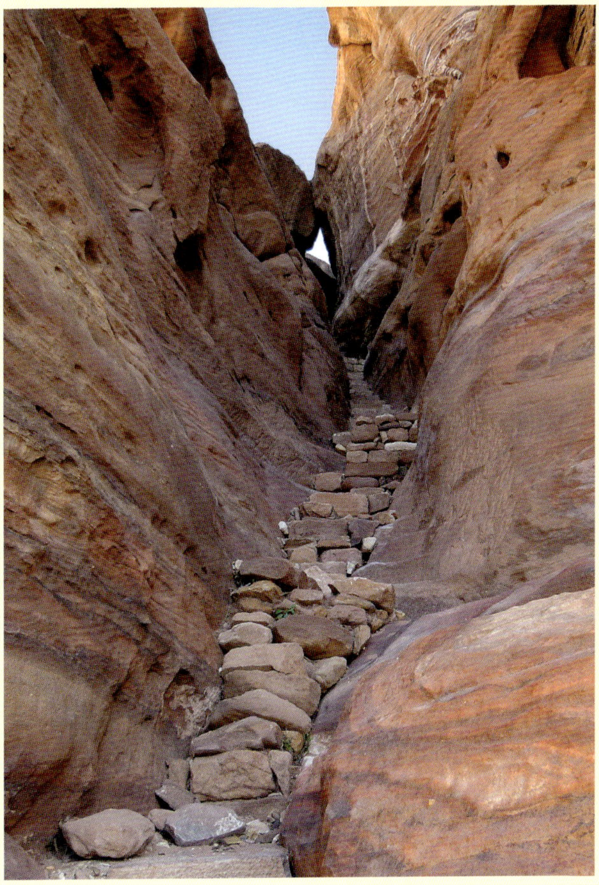

THE WADI AND THE JEBEL ED DEIR

Although the climb up to the Deir (or Monastery) is certainly long, steep and quite tiring, it should not be missed, as it leads to one of the most spectacular monuments in Petra and indeed the whole of the ancient world. It is recommended to start the walk in the early afternoon, because large parts of the valley are in the shade at that time, and also because the facade of the Deir faces west, and and therefore appears in full light during the second half of the day.
As always, it is a good idea to take at least a litre of water, although there are many places you can drink and get refreshments when you arrive (perhaps too many), set up by the Bedouins.
The path is not difficult but it is a good idea to wear shoes suitable for walking. The less athletic can make the climb on the back of a donkey. On foot, it takes about forty minutes. The whole expedition takes at least three hours, or even more if you decide to go on to the spectacular viewpoints situated on the edge of the ed Deir plateau, with an exciting view of the Wadi Arabah.

Monica Falcone

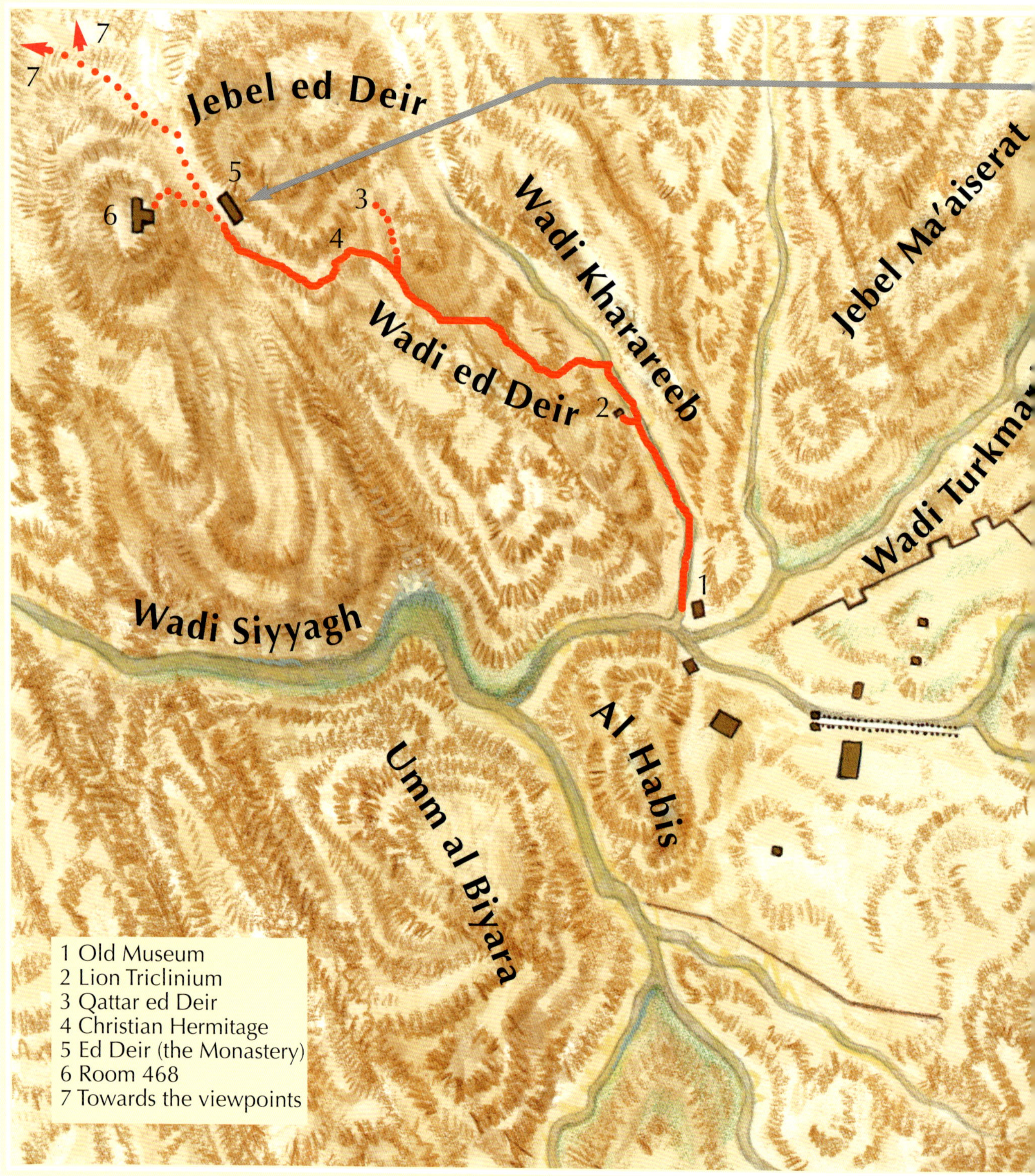

Top right - *The Lion Triclinium is one of the most elegant examples of a pediment facade in Petra.*

Centre right - *Without doubt the most imposing monument in Petra, the Deir stands in an isolated position on top of a wide mountain plateau. The façade of the immense rupestrian building seems to spring from the living rock as if to proudly proclaim the victory of human ingenuity over brute matter.*

Bottom right -*From the steep extreme western edge of the ed Deir plateau, you can enjoy a breathtaking view of the underlying Wadi Siyyagh and the distant Wadi Arabah. An open-air triclinium is carved on the rocky spur in the foreground. The whole area is dotted with caves, votive niches and shrines.*

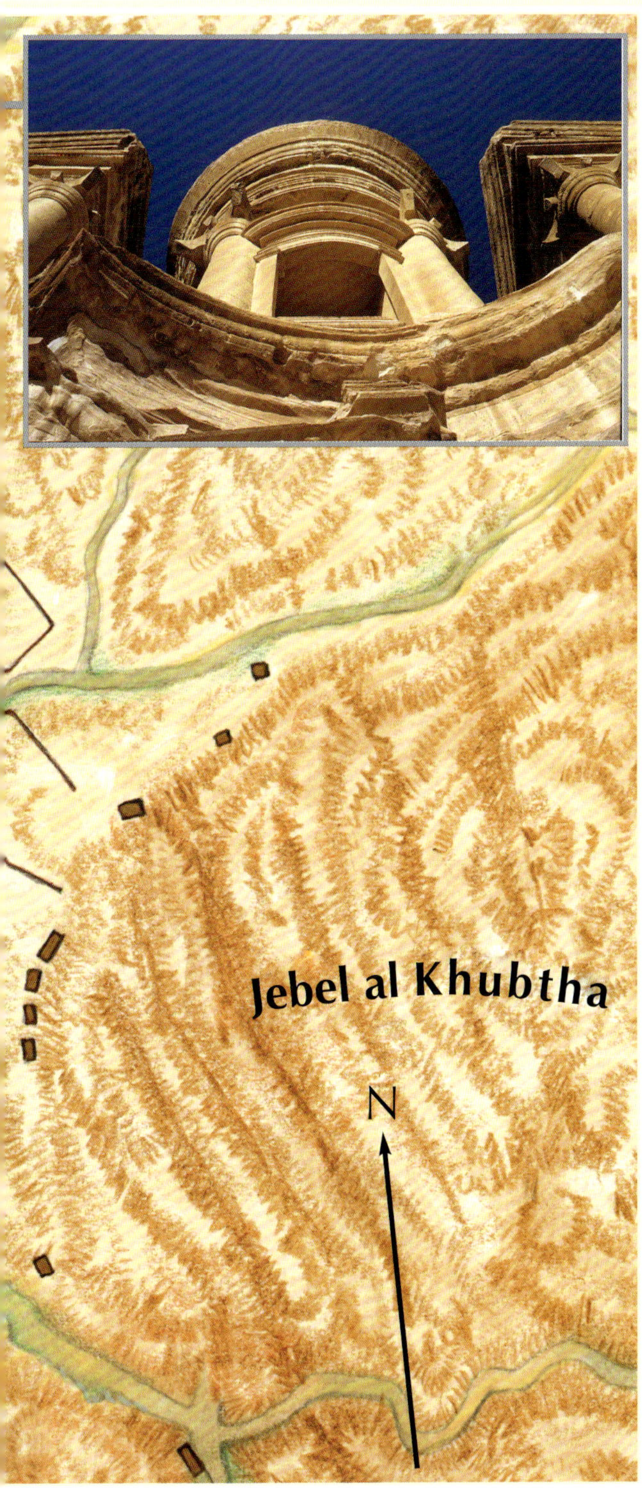

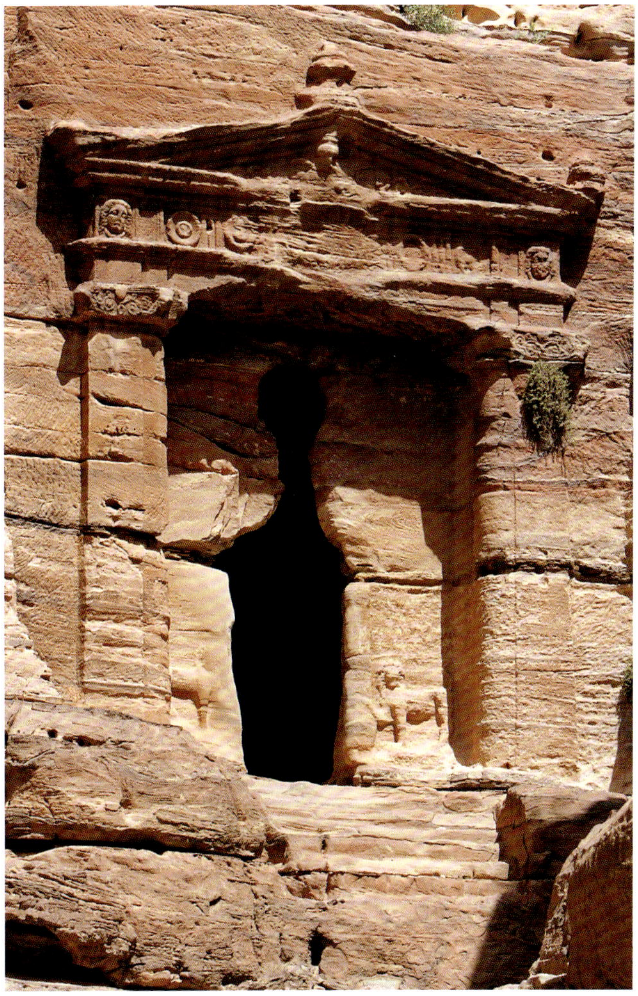

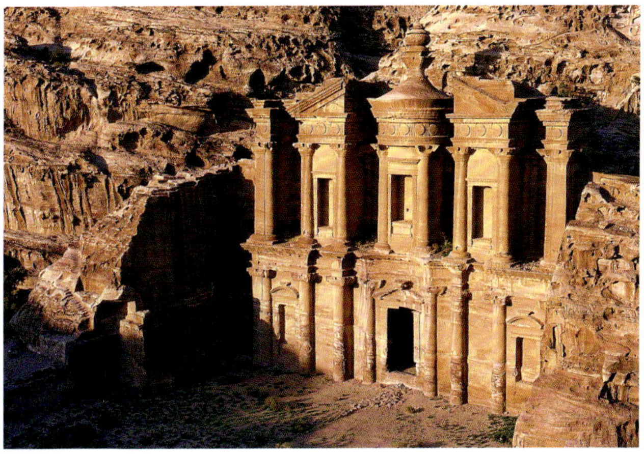

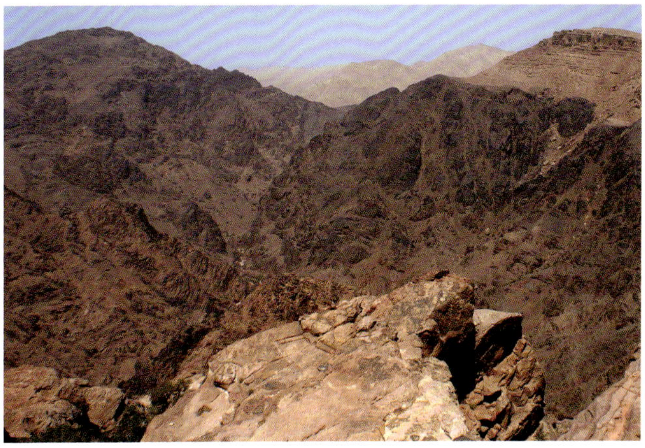

THE PROCESSIONAL ROUTE

The path starts near the old Museum, which has a restaurant next door to it, and it is clearly signposted. First, it heads in a northwesterly direction along the dry bed of the Wadi Kharareeb, which is dotted with a large number of rock cut tombs in different styles on both sides. Before long, the ancient Nabataean route turns left along the Wadi ed Deir and starts to go up. Large parts of it are cut into the living rock, and it alternates between gentle upward slopes and endless winding flights of stairs, with a total of 800 steps. Considering the remarkable excavation work necessary in several different places, the carving of the large staircases (now very eroded) and the need to build at least one little bridge to cross the wadi, which has now been substituted by a modern reinforced concrete structure, it is clear that this route must have been very important for the inhabitants of Petra. It was probably a sacred path (like the ones that go up to the top of the Jebel Attuf, the Jebel al Khubtha and the Umm al Biyara), along which the processions that periodically led to one of the most sacred sites in Petra would have made their way. In fact, as we shall see, in addition to the magnificent Deir there are a whole series of other monumental buildings on the saddle of the Jebel ed Deir, which are difficult to interpret today but must have been a very important complex of shrines.
You soon come to a fork in the track (partly hidden from view by the oleanders), where a sign indicates the presence of a rather interesting monument.
The **Lion Triclinium** (No. 452) can be reached by going along a short but rather difficult little gorge. This rock cut monument, sometimes mistakenly described as a

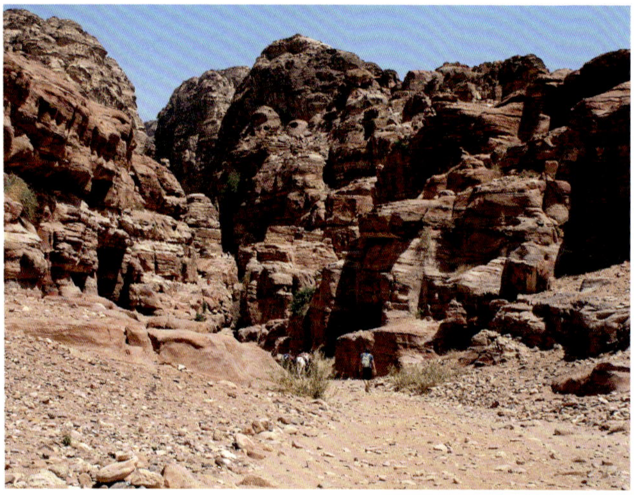

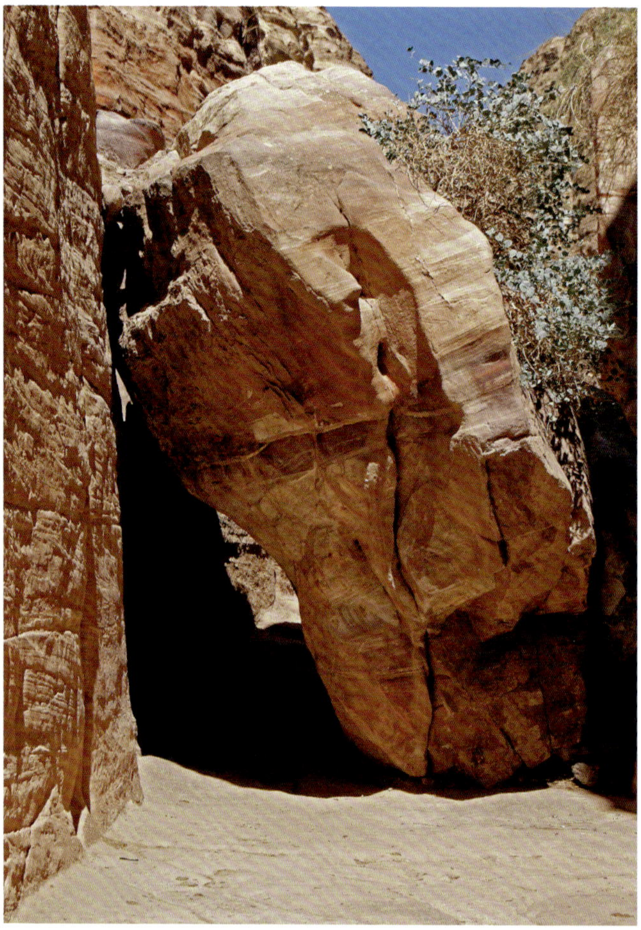

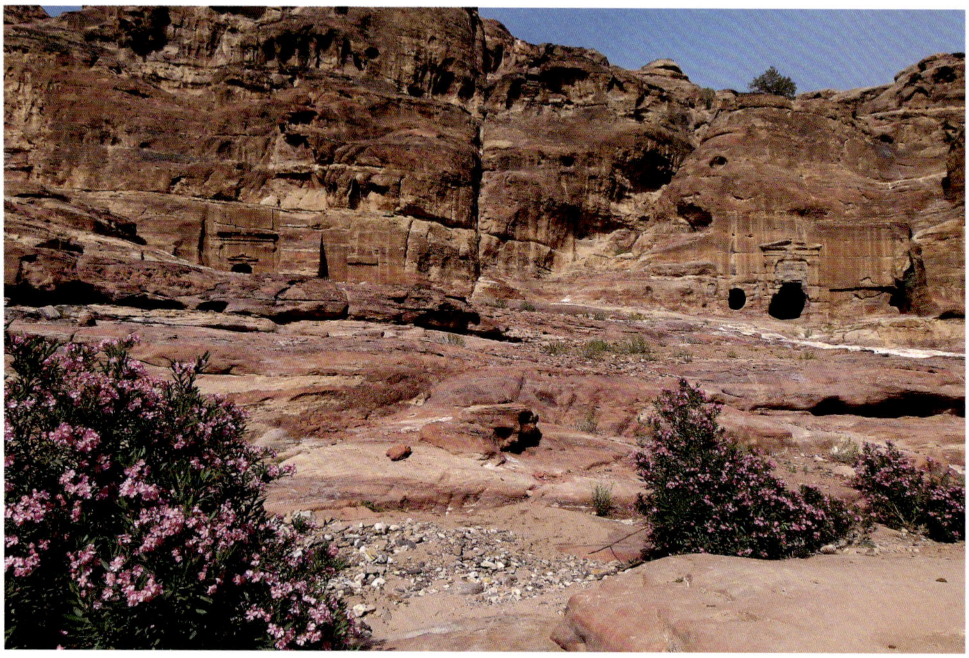

Top left – *At the beginning, the processional route that goes up to the Deir has been reduced to little more than a path, due to periodical floods, but in ancient times it would have been paved with stone.*

Top right - *Where the road steepens, you come across an enormous crack. It was here that an ancient earthquake caused a large boulder to detach, which partly obstructed the path but also created an evocative "arch".*

Bottom - *On the eastern side of the wadi there are some tombs and an elegant biclinium (on the right in the photo).*

tomb, deserves to be visited because it is one of the few *triclinia* in Petra that have survived intact. However, it should be pointed out that in reality the term biclinium would be more appropriate, because there are only two benches and not three. The monument was carved next to a gully in the headwall of the narrow gorge, the bottom of which has been deeply eroded by water. It is therefore likely that there was originally a little bridge in front of it, and that the gorge was regulated by by masonry embankments. The facade is rather beautiful. It is of the pediment type, framed by two pilasters with quarter columns and capitals that are unusually decorated with charming racemes. The trabeation has a Doric frieze in which triglyphs alternate with pateras in relief, with a woman's head at each end. They are commonly said to be Medusa heads, but there is not any factual evidence. Fortunately, these escaped the fury of the iconoclasts and are still clearly visible: this is both unusual and unexplainable, as the two masks would have been easy to reach.

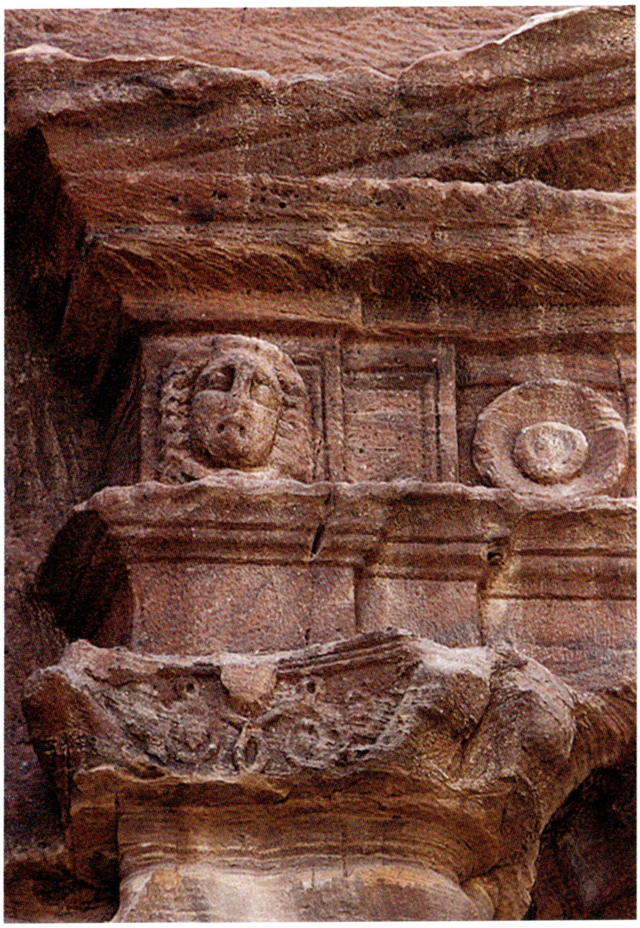

The pediment has a tympanum decorated with tendrils, which are very eroded and which frame an urn, and the acroterion on top of it is also in the shape of an urn. There was also acroterions at each end, but the one on the left has been destroyed. A staircase, now in rather bad condition, is cut into the sandstone in front of the doorway, on each side of which are reliefs depicting the lions (animals sacred to the goddess Al Uzza) that gave the monument its name. The two heraldic animals, which are unmistakably influenced by Syrian art, have been badly eroded by the elements. However, it is clear that they were not obliterated by the iconoclasts either.

The doorway was surmounted by an oculus, but earthquakes and erosion have transformed it into a strange "keyhole" shaped opening.

Based on its proportions and decorative apparatus, the monument most probably dates back to the second half of the first century AD, if not later.

A huge baetylus dedicated to Dushara is carved into the rock face to the left of the door. A short distance away there are two tombs side by side, and the biclinium is certainly connected with these. Both the facades have deep grooves in them, where originally mouldings made of harder stone were wedged, and then plastered.

Historical documents have revealed that in 1924 there were still human bones inside the two tombs. However, it is impossible to say whether these were remains from the Nabataean era, or if they were more recent.

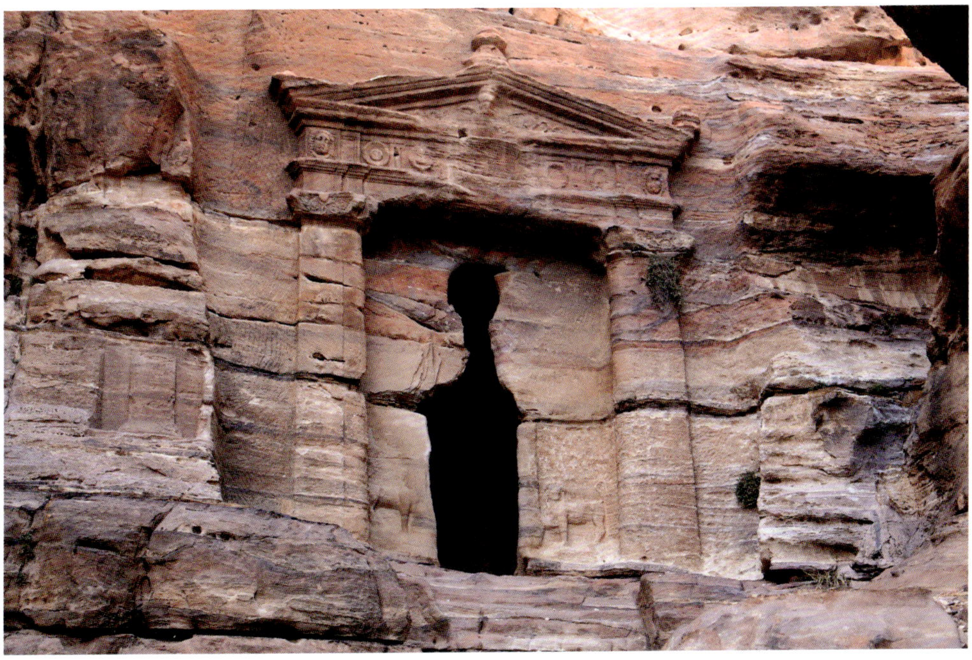

Above - *The mask located above the pilaster on the left is in good condition and is generally considered to be a representation of Medusa.*

Below - *The elegant proportions, the well-preserved decorative design and the scenic location at the bottom of the small gorge make the Lion Triclinium a monument worth visiting.*
In the photo the sizeable baetylus carved on the left of the facade is clearly visible.
As was customary, a gutter was carved high above the facade of this rock cut monument, to protect it from rainfall.

Back on the main path, you proceed along the Nabataean staircases in the Wadi ed Deir, in an increasingly exciting setting. Where the path leads onto an impressive ravine, forming an aerial belvedere of white sandstone which offers a breathtaking view of the Wadi Siyyagh from above, and of the spectacular mountain tops all around, it is worth paying attention to the rocky buttress on the right. In it opens, a few metres above ground, the front of an ancient stone quarry; here, in an unspecified period, two large rooms were excavated. One of them has the downstream side, facing the void, still buffered by some fairly irregular masonry, in which open a sort of window slit, a partially filled door and what seems to be the drain of a latrine, of the type found in mediaeval castles. Although their original function is unknown, it is certain that these rooms were converted into a **Christian hermitage** during the Byzantine era. Some crosses and other Christian symbols engraved on the walls are evidence of this. The hermitage is not easily accessible, and it is necessary to climb some unstable terrain to reach it. For this reason, you are strongly advised not to try (also, during his visits there the author has often come across scorpions, for some unknown reason).

Right in front of the hermitage, carved into a smooth, very light coloured pinnacle of sandstone, an astounding flight of stairs catches the eye, zigzagging upwards, apparently towards nothing. In reality it leads to a nearby open-air triclinium, which has been very worn away by the elements. Today, it is almost impossible to reach the staircase.

Back on the processional path, a little further on from the hermitage, only the most observant eye will notice the three crosses carved into the rock several metres above the ground, which resemble a Golgotha. These date back to the Crusader period.

Above - *The so-called "Christian Hermitage" is an enigmatic monument. It is certainly a fairly recent construction, as demonstrated by the infill wall built with what appears to be used materials, perhaps extracted from the colonnaded court of the nearby Deir.*

Below - *The spectacular stairway carved into the rock in front of the hermitage.*

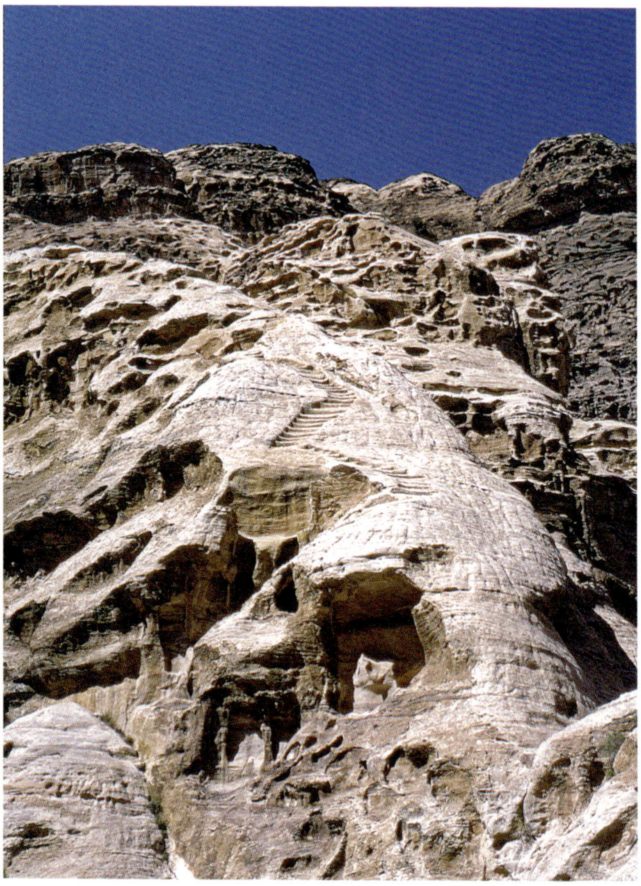

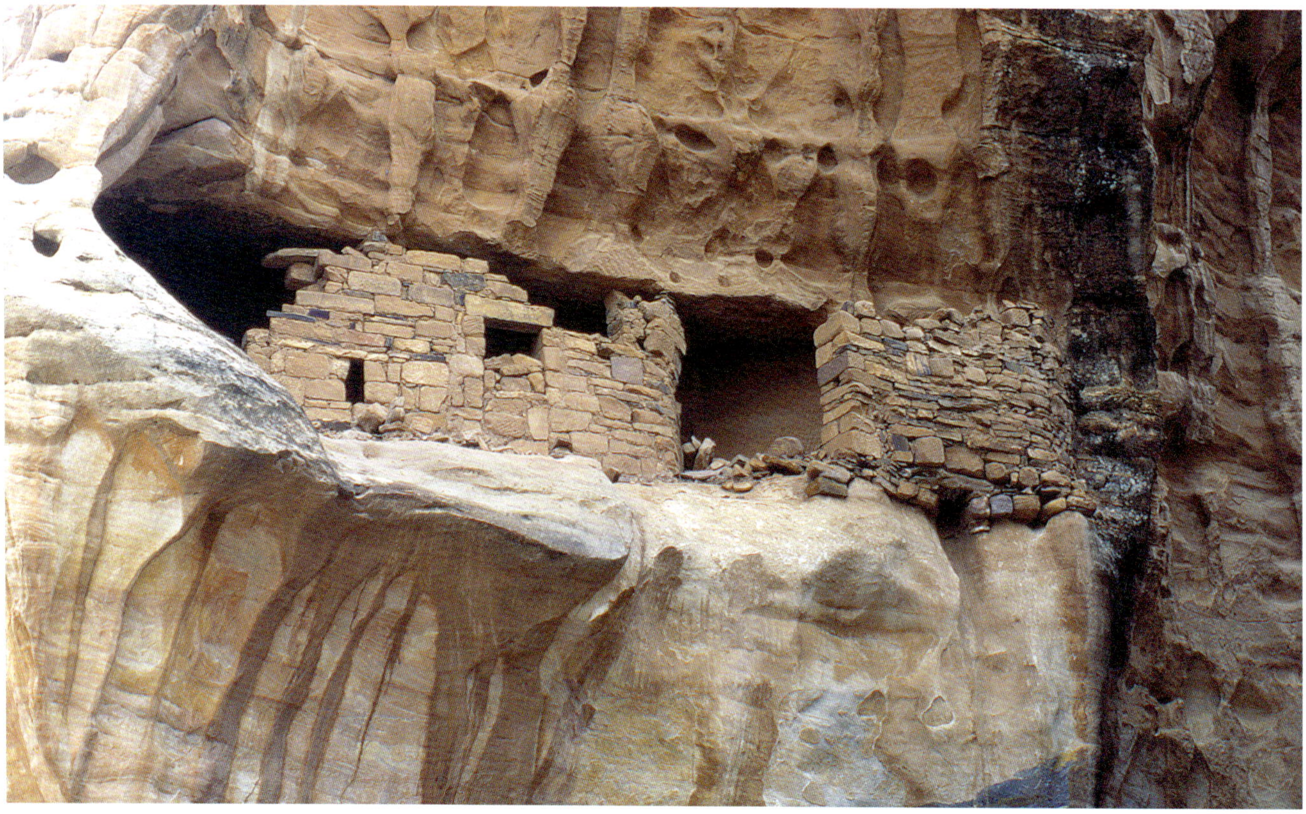

A PERENNIAL SPRING: THE QATTAR ED DEIR

About three quarters of the way along the processional route, where it is deeply dug into the sandstone and makes a hairpin turn to quickly rise in height, you will notice a deep and narrow, very steep gorge on your right. Here a barely noticeable path (in order to locate it, it is advisable to ask for directions from one of the many street vendors of souvenirs found here), leads in just a few minutes to a place with an arcane charm.
This is the Qattar and Deir, or a sort of deep natural recess of the looming rock wall, where rivulets of water perpetually ooze from the living rock (qattar means "the dripplace where it drips"). Here the Nabataeans carved a series of interconnected basins into the rock, fed by a web of drainage channels that collected the precious liquid from all around. This place was obviously sacred as evidenced by a triclinium, several niches with baetyli and a votive inscription devoted to king Rabbel II. On one of the baetyli, dedicated to Dushara, an eye-catching two-barred cross (or the Patriarchal cross) was carved. Clearly, whoever sculpted this symbol was well aware of the sacred significance of the baetyli and therefore wanted to "exorcise", for want of a better word, its pagan substance. It should be remembered that Petra had been extensively Christianised and had already become an episcopal seat at the start of the 4th century. Indeed, among the numerous bishops of Petra whose names are remembered are: Asterios, Germanus, Jason (who converted the Urn Tomb into a church) and Atenogene the Stylite, probably one of the last, lived in the 4th century. It is also interesting to mention the Spanish historian Carmen Blánquez Pérez's theory. She believes that Petra, now completely Christianised, was a sort of "ecclesiastical exile" for high priests suspected of heresy and therefore as undesirable to the emperor as they were to the patriarch of Byzantium. The marginal position of the city compared with the real heart of the Byzantine empire made it an excellent place for this type of confinement.

In the haunting silence, today's visitor can clearly feel the sacred atmosphere that still permeates the place, the only part of Petra where cisterns are still fed by springs throughout the entire year. It is easy to imagine how for centuries, the faithful heading towards the Deir would have stopped here (even after it had been transformed into a Christian place of worship), grateful to quench their thirst and enjoy the refreshing cool offered by the shady gorge. For safety reasons it is not advisable to visit the bare room carved into the opposite wall of the gorge.

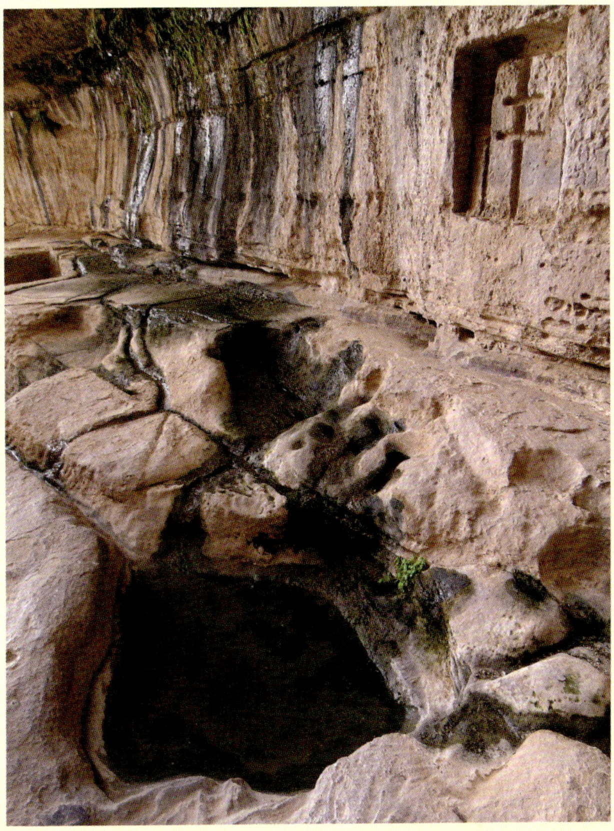

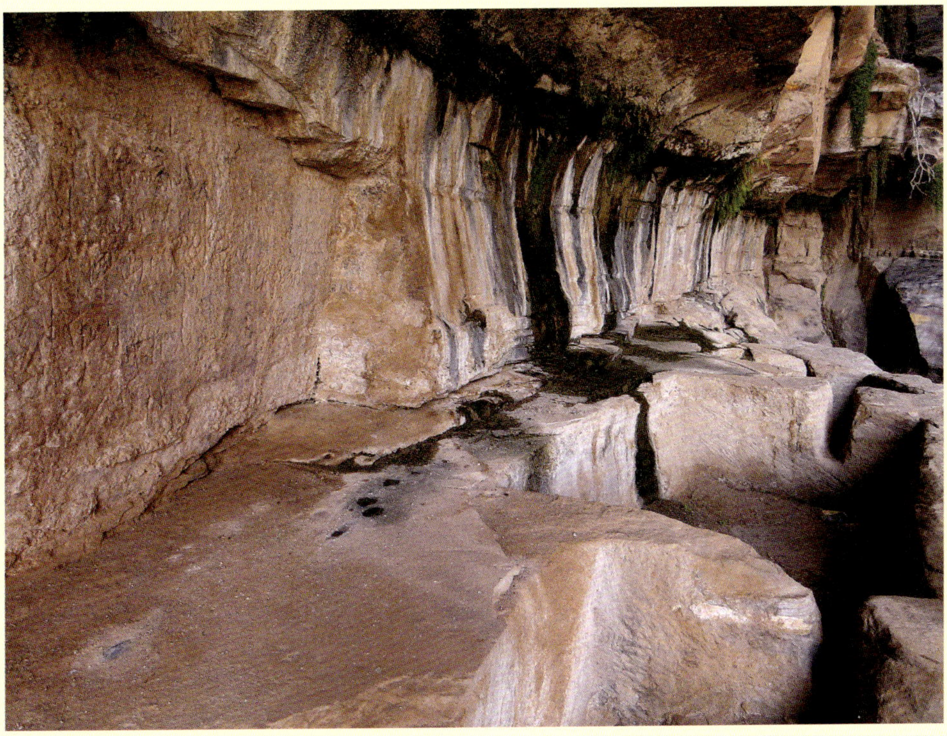

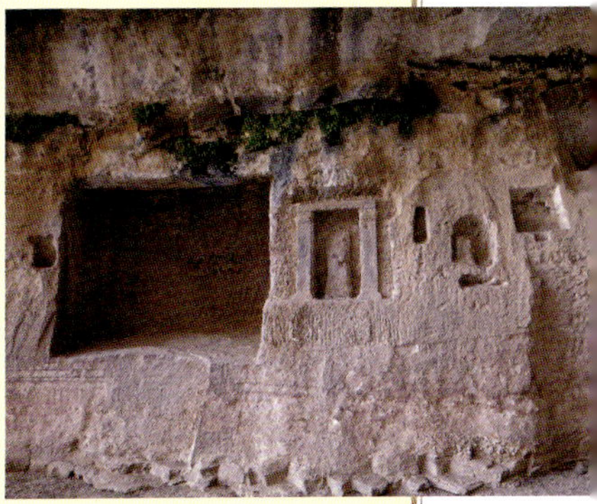

A few glimpses of the Qattar ed Deir: although the photographs were taken in the height of summer, you can see trickles of water coming from the rock face. Unfortunately, the flow of the spring is currently decreasing, but this said, the various basins fill to the brim again in springtime.

THE DEIR (or MONASTERY)

A short stretch of path quite exposed but now secured by a wall, which has taken away some of the charm of the place, and a few more flights of steps between high rock walls, finally lead to the vast plateau that opens up at the foot of the Jebel ed Deir. The facade of the Deir (or Monastery, No. 462) has been carved out in the slopes of this mountain. The presence of the monument is heralded by the sight of the colossal urn that crowns the *tholo*s, which appears unexpectedly from behind the rock.
However, this rock cut building is set back several metres from the side of the mountain, in such a way that it comes into view suddenly, leaving the visitor astounded by the size and purity of the architecture. This authentic masterpiece boasts extraordinary dimensions, just under 47 m in width by 48 m in height, but the most extraordinary thing about it is the perfection of its lines, which can be admired in all their glory thanks to its almost perfect state of preservation. The contrast between the insanely eroded rocks surrounding the building and its austere majesty accentuate the sense of wonder and respect. Seen from the side, the building seems to have miraculously freed itself from the mass of rock, transforming the incoherent shapes of the sandstone into a supreme geometrical arrangement.
Although it is situated in a less scenic position than the Khazneh, the Deir appears much more imposing and the restrained decoration increases its austere majesty. The facade has two floors with semi-columns crowned with the usual Nabataean capitals. In the lateral intercolumniations there are two niches crowned with curved tympanums. The portal, which is also framed between two semi-columns, is about 8 metres tall and surmounted by a triangular tympanum. Originally, there was a staircase in front of it, but it was destroyed at a later date, making it difficult to access the interior. Two small square holes, which originally held the bolts of the wooden doors, can be seen in the threshold of the doorway. A high broken pediment holds up the second floor, which is carved in very high relief, and made up of two avant-corps (or *antae*) with square pillars and two half pediments that frame the central *tholos*, which is covered by a conical roof, crowned with an enormous capital, upon which a great urn stands. The whole thing is about 9 metres tall on its own.
Like the two below, the three large rectangular niches in the *tholos* and in the shalf pediments may originally have contained statues, but there is no concrete evidence to support this theory. However, it should be said that according to some scholars, the enigmatic hole inside the niche in the *tholos* may have contained a sort of anchorage for a statue.
The architectural elements on the second floor are connected by a very elegant continuous Doric frieze, in which metopes, consisting of slightly raised discs, alternate with the usual triglyphs. It should be pointed out that the very successful contrast between the concave line of the trabeation above the doorway and the convex line of the *tholos* is evidence of the influence of Hellenistic architecture, and at the same time a surprising forerunner of Baroque architecture. In general, the recurring alternation between straight and curved lines, the chiaroscuro effect between full and empty, the use of typically Nabataean elements like "horned"

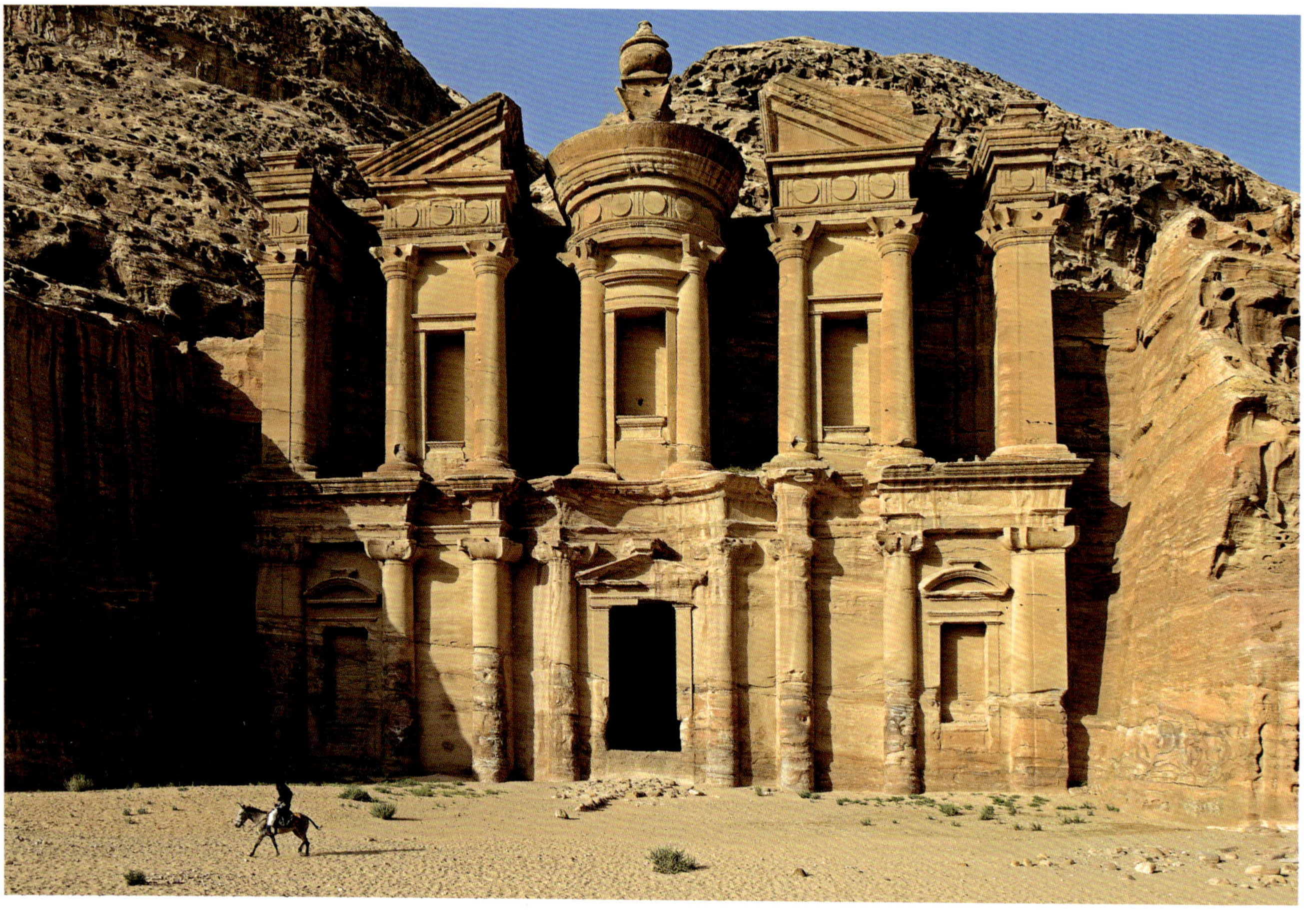

capitals and circular metopes, not only represent the perfect fusion of miscellaneous stylistic elements, mainly from the Hellenized world, but also the distinctive originality of Nabataean architecture.
The upper part of the monument could once be reached by climbing a flight of stairs cut into the left hand rock buttress, along which a couple of basins for collecting rainwater can be seen. Once again, it is clear that a system of channels was constructed to drain away the rain and prevent it from dripping down the facade of the monument. On the upper surface of the right hand avant-corps (as already pointed out by Judith McKenzie), some strange geometrical graffiti can be seen, which may have been part of an architectural plan drawn up by one of the builders. At the moment,

Opposite page - *The superb facade of the Deir, deeply embedded into the rock mass, is preceded by a large courtyard which was created by removing the living rock on a front of about 60 meters*

Left - *The arched niche in the chamber: you can see the two stairs that went up to the* motab *(or altar).*

Right - *The impressive dimensions of the Deir are clearly evident in this image.*

Plan of the Deir

A Large courtyard
B Remains of the southern colonnade
C Remains of the northern colonnade
D Large chamber
E Biclinium benches
F Arched niche

The facade of the Deir is oriented west-south-west. For this reason, it is fully illuminated by the sun in the afternoon and at sunset.

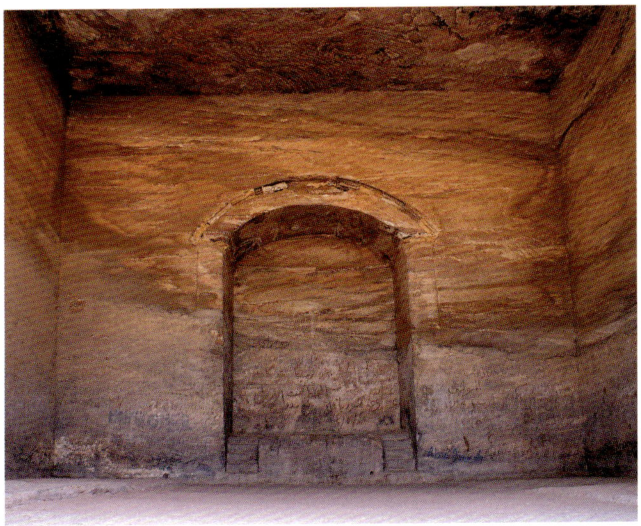

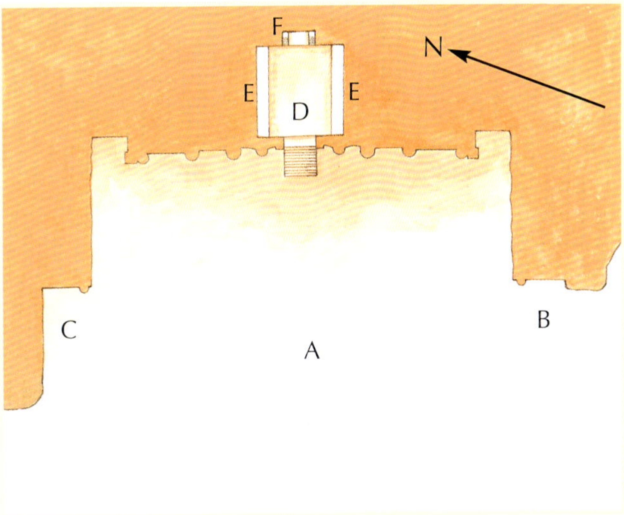

for obvious reasons of safety, the upper section of the Deir, and also the *tholos*, are off limits.
The interior is made up of one 11 m by 12 m chamber, which is about 9 m high and has no decoration apart from a large arched niche carved into the back wall, whose lowered arch has curvilinear cornices, which were inserted and then plastered.
At one time, it was believed that the Deir was the tomb of King Rabbel II (70-106 AD) and the last great monument built in Petra. However, there is a lot of evidence to suggest that in reality it had a very different function. First of all, since the internal chamber shows no sign of any loculi, it seems clear that it was not a sepulchre. The presence of two long benches along the side walls would suggest that it was in reality a biclinium (the floor of which is about 30 cm below the existing layer of detritus). However, it should be said that the base carved inside the arched niche, and framed between two symmetrical staircases, looks as if it once hosted a *motab* (or altar), then obliterated, which probably had a baetylus on top of it, or in any case a sacred image of some kind. The only remnant of the *motab* is a sort of shadow on the wall; just above this, some Christian crosses etched into the wall were once visible. Unfortunately, over the years the shameful habit that uncivilized visitors (or rather vandals) have of spoiling the walls with pointless graffiti has almost completely cancelled out this important evidence of the conversion of Petra to Christianity.

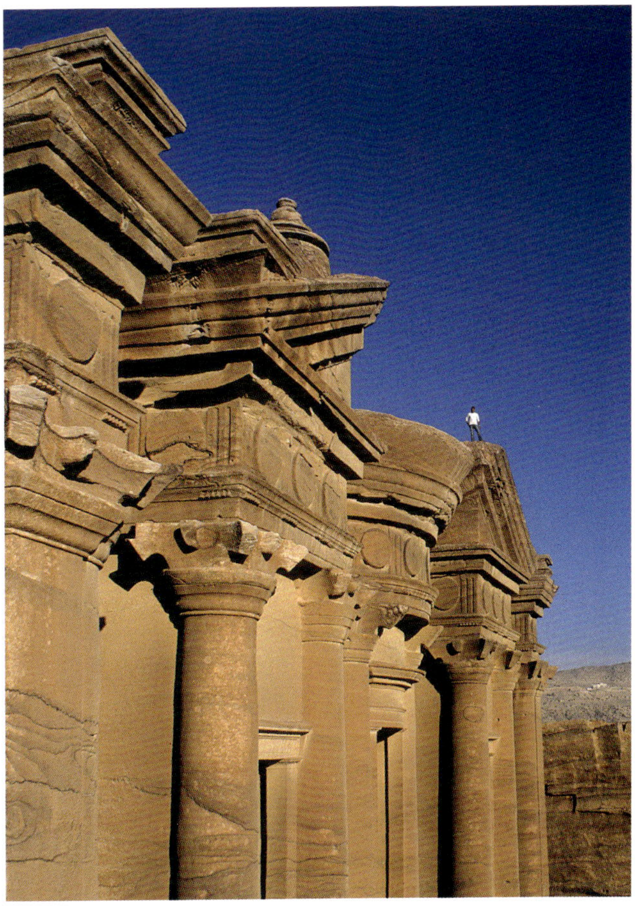

THE DEIR: A RECONSTRUCTIVE SUGGESTION

Today the approach to the Deir is perhaps the most exciting that Petra has in store for its visitors, because its view is cut off by a prominent buttress of rock until the very last second. In antiquity, however, the situation was different and in a certain sense more scenic as the pilgrim who had just reached the mountain pass of the Jebel ed Deir on foot, would have found himself in front of a high masonry wall, in which there must have been an imposing doorway. This led to a shaded portico enclosing an enormous flat space on three sides, entirely cut from the living rock, in front of the gigantic facade: a scene that took your breath away.

In this temenos *the celebrants of the sacred rites in honor of Oboda and perhaps of the god Dushara were to gather in hundreds and therefore it must be assumed that the portico was sumptuously ornate with wall paintings, stuccoes and perhaps even bas-reliefs.*

A survey carried out by the author in the spring of 1998 revealed that the columns of the portico were originally plastered in order to imitate a round of little pronounced flutings and painted white. That May, a violent storm had partially washed away some of the sand in the southern sector of the esplanade, bringing to light, amongst other things, a large lithic fragment that seemed to be the summit of an architectural tympanum, complete with a piece of the cornice. This fortunate observation led the author to imagine a great external wall, punctuated by pilasters aligned with the columns of the portico and framing several blind niches, surmounted by tympanums in the classical style.

Obviously, until systematic excavations are carried out, it remains a matter of conjecture, but it is certain that the great portico must have had proportions similar to those in the hypothetical reconstruction below.

Facing the main entrance on the southern side of the great colonnade was a similar doorway, testified by the short but wide cut in the sandstone still clearly visible on the northern side of the esplanade. Evidently, the processional path continued beyond the Deir, after passing a large rupestrian altar preceded by a few steps. Worth mentioning is that in order to build the great portico, it was first necessary to block the ravine, which from here begins to slope gradually southwards, with a massive masonry structure. A paved embankment was therefore created upstream from the great wall, which widened the area of the esplanade cut into the living rock, westwards.

Nabataean engineers also had to design a system for the disposal of rain water, which would otherwise have followed its natural course, eroding the court and the walls of the portico. As all of Petra's great monuments had their own hydraulic system and connected cisterns, it is easy to imagine that the Deir was no exception. Given the topographic layout of the area, it is even plausible that a large cistern is actually concealed under the esplanade

Moving a few metres away from the Deir, leaving behind the snack bar set within an ancient hypogeum, at a greater height compared to the temple and half buried in sand, there is a large circle cut into the sandstone bed (which until a few years ago was only just visible from above). This was a real enigma until the late spring of 2014 when an excavation probe, conducted by Brigham Young University in collaboration with Jordanian archaeologists, revealed it was a huge basin for collecting rainwater.

This amazing open-air reservoir, or "pool", stands out in

F. Bourbon M. Falcone

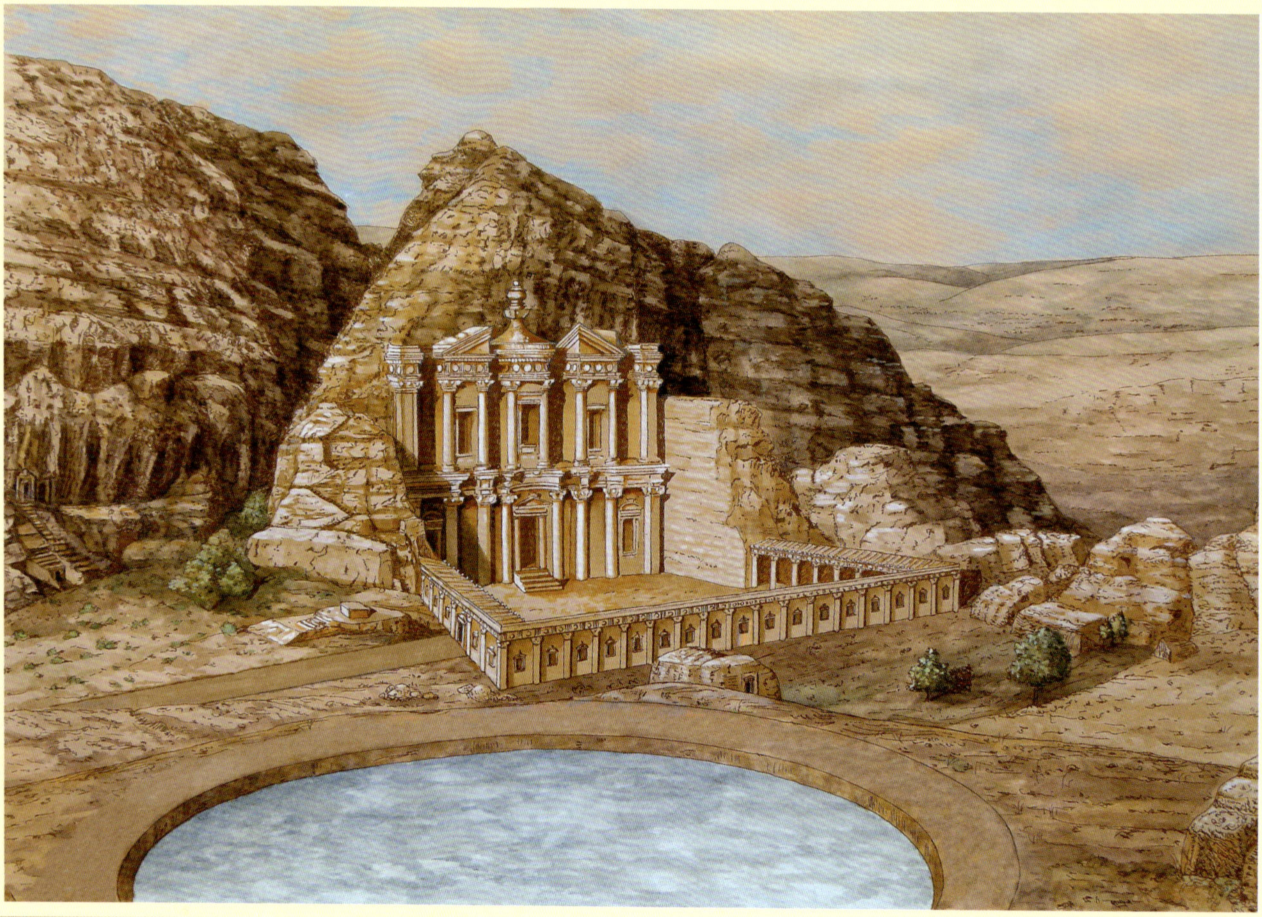

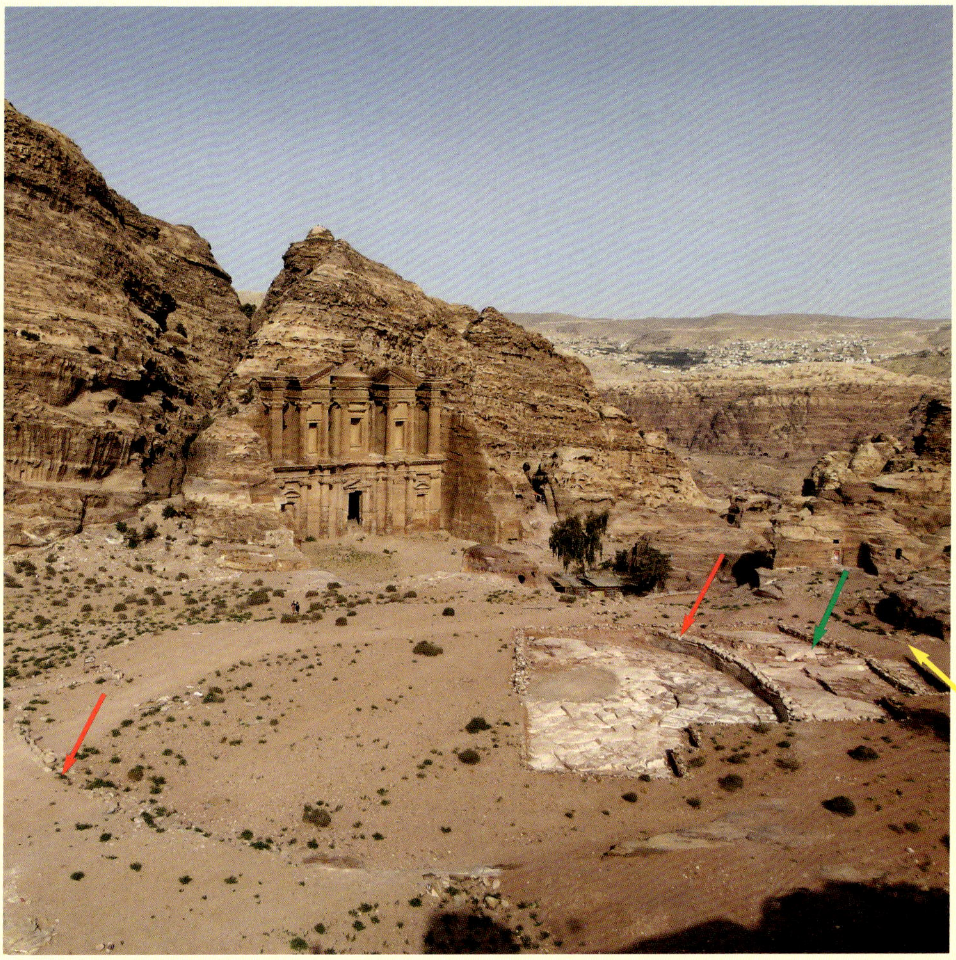

Above – *In this photo the outline of the "great circle" is clearly seen. The red arrow points to the internal perimeter of the reservoir, the green to a second, concentric, peri-meter wall. The yellow arrow points to the foundations of a mysterious structure, which may have been related to the religious functions connected with the Maiuma festival. The entire surrounding area is also dotted with hypogea, staircases and rock-cut aqueducts. Ancient historical sources mention that the festival of Maiuma was widespread in this region and linked to fertility rites. In many of the places where it was celebrated, it was believed that a woman who threw herself into the consecrated pool would soon become pregnant.*

Below – *An excavation probe carried out in 2014 explained the hydraulic function of the "great circle".*

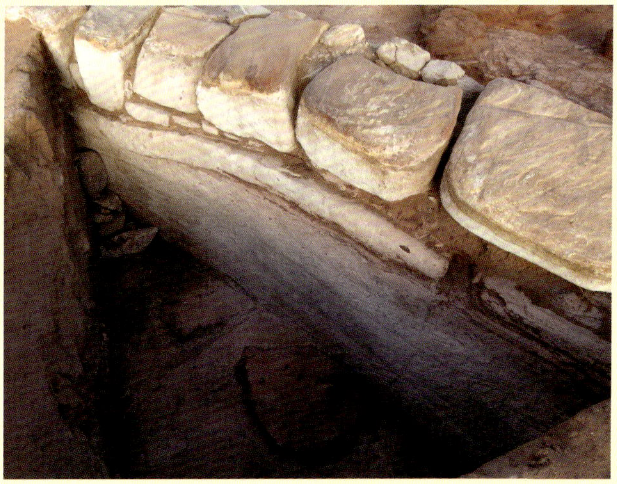

the reconstruction. Almost entirely obtained from the living rock, with a diameter a little less than 60 metres and with a depth of nearly one and a half metres, it was bordered by a circle of stone blocks carefully connected with mortar. A few metres from the internal perimeter of the "great circle" was a second circular wall, concentric to the first. Other curved walls can be made out further away from the pool. It appears that the entire area was levelled and terraced with a slight slope towards the basin. It is certain that the ring-shaped space around the pool could have held a large gathering.

*What the "pool" was used for is unknown, but it is unlikely that it only had a recreational function, or that it was only used to hold drinking water. In such a dry climate, evaporation would have been high and the sand, carried by the wind, would have very quickly polluted the water, encouraging, amongst other things, the spread of algae (as can be seen happening near Qattar ed Deir). According to the archaeologist Cynthia Finlayson, the function of the great circle was to collect rainwater and protect the Deir from erosion and possible flood waves. This theory seems quite likely. However, an analysis of the surrounding area reveals numerous little channels carved into the sandstone, as well as several smaller secondary basins. It can therefore be assumed that the great pool could have been filled and emptied on command by an intricate system of channels. Since everything suggests that the entire area of the Deir had been built up with monuments from the beginning of the 1st century AD, and perhaps also during the following period of Roman occupation, it is possible that the pool was used to celebrate the Maiuma, a pagan festival mentioned, amongst others, by the Byzantine historian John the Lydian (*De Mensibus *4.76-80). The Maiuma, probably of Syriac origin but widespread in various regions of the empire, took place in May and consisted of a sort of large and festive collective bath, in which participants pushed each other into the water. In some cases, priestesses of Aphrodite were thrown into the water followed by the crowd. Clearly this practice celebrated the generative power of water and suggested the divine birth of Venus-Aphrodite. Considered to be extremely licentious, the Maiuma festival was bitterly opposed by Christianity and in the end prohibited. It is possible that after the festival the pool was emptied and used as collecting basin, for the purpose of protecting the Deir.*

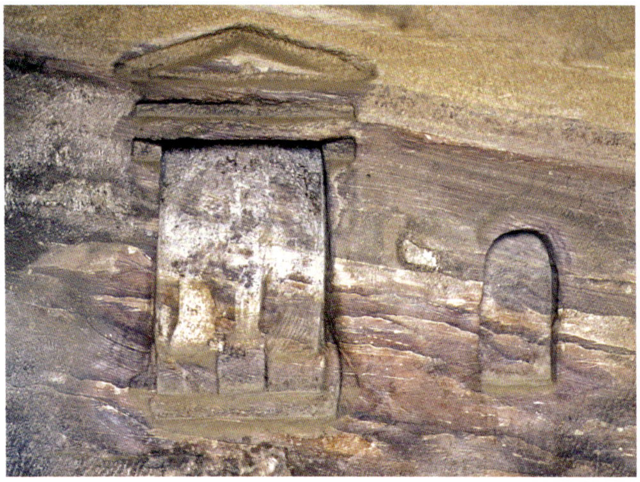

It was this event that gave it the name Deir, which means "monastery" in Arabic. In fact, when they saw those crosses, the Bedouins were convinced that the great hall was once used as a church or retreat for Christian monks. In addition to the evidence above, the presence of an inscription that mentions the "symposium of Obodas, the god" along the processional path, suggests that the Deir was in reality a *heroon*, or rather a temple-cenotaph to commemorate a deified monarch. This must have been King Obodas I (96-87 BC), saviour of the Nabataean kingdom, who died heroically in battle fighting against the Seleucid leader Antiochus XII, and was buried in Advat, a Nabataean city in the Negev Desert. The great chamber would once have hosted banquets, symposiums and ceremonies in his honour. The facade of the temple faces west, towards the place where the ancient caravan centre lies (see page 35).

The wide open space in front of the rock cut building, which was once surrounded on three sides by a colonnade, may also be connected with the cult of Obodas I, and perhaps also with the god Dushara. The semi columns carved into the rock, which can be made out on the front of the two rocky buttresses on either side of the Deir are evidence of the existence of the colonnade, as are the stone drums that were once part of the columns, buried in the sand.

Dating the Deir, like the Khazneh and most of the other monuments in Petra, is an arduous task, and even the author has expressed contradictory opinions over time (which is not surprising, given the lack of evidence available). In short, we can now say that the Deir is considered a product of late Nabataean architecture, and therefore dates back to a period between the second half of the 1st century AD and the first quarter of the subsequent century. Considering the minimalist look of the temple (which has no figurative Hellenistic decorative elements, like leafy spirals and racemes), and the frequent use of particularly Nabataean elements like "horned" capitals, this colossal monument could date back to the reign of the last Nabataean monarch, Rabbel II (70 - 106 AD), who was intent on taking his people back to their ancient glory by rejecting foreign influences as much as possible. Because of its balanced architectural composition, the extraordinary expertise needed to create it and the huge technical difficulties, so brilliantly overcome, the Deir should be considered one of humanity's greatest artistic achievements.

The entire plateau where the Monastery stands once had a very different appearance, with monuments spread out around it, which have unfortunately been destroyed. The foothills of the Jebel ed Deir have a large number of caves in them, as well as votive niches, shrines, staircases, at least two open-air triclinia, and other works that are hard to interpret. The most northerly part of the mountain face was partially excavated to create a huge rectangular open space. In the carefully worked rock face, a sort of basin and three niches can be seen. Immediately to the left of the Deir, a narrow wadi was blocked by a dam (recently restored), and next to that we can see a rock cut aqueduct, and even an enormous unusually shaped cistern, the opening of which is still partially blocked by some stone slabs. The hydraulic expertise of the Nabataeans is demonstrated by the fact that the basin is still full of water today, and used by local shepherds to water their flocks.

At the mouth of the second gorge to the left of the Deir, next to the door of a hypogeum (No. 466), you can still see a very eroded bas-relief depicting two Nabataean merchants, each leading a dromedary by the reins. Between them there is a shrine. The bas-relief is similar to the one in the Siq, although it is smaller in size.

The saddle between the Jebel ed Deir and the reliefs in front of it is covered with an unbelievable amount of rubble: ashlars, remains of trabeations, and even some fragments of fluted columns. In a couple of places, a trained eye can identify two large piles of rubble. Although these cannot now be read, under one of them

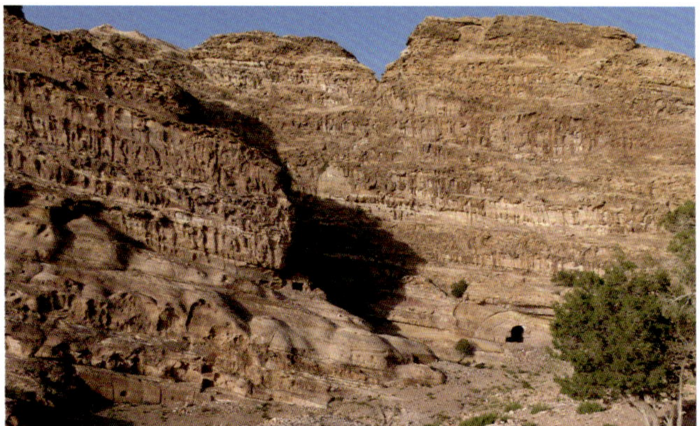

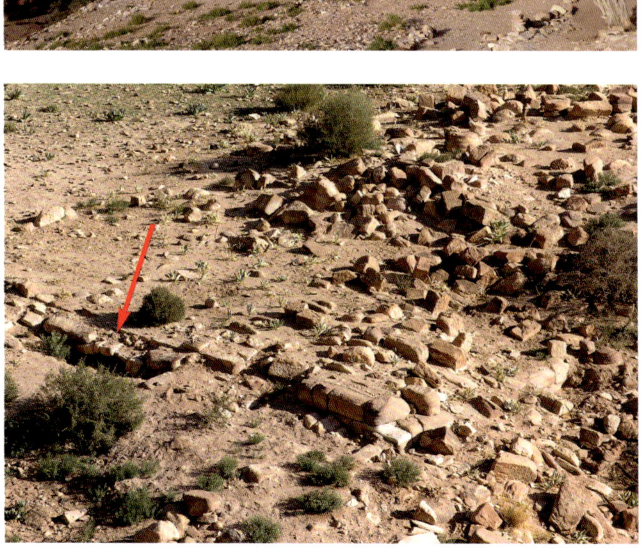

(situated almost in front of the big cave room with the distinctive arched opening) is a large vaulted cistern with a similar structure to the one illustrated on page 34.
In the area between the Deir and the spur of rock that rises up almost opposite is the so-called "great circle", a basin with a diameter of 60 metres, the possible function of which has been explained on the previous pages.
Considering the absence of tombs, we can say with certainty that in Nabataean and Roman times the entire area constituted a sanctuary complex of enormous importance and was densely built up. This theory is also confirmed by the so-called Room 468, which has already been discussed, and the open air triclinia (or "high places of sacrifice") carved in the extreme western edge of the plateau, in spectacular positions looking down on the Wadi Siyyagh below. From these privileged viewpoints - near which today there are some picturesque, but questionable kiosks for the use and consumption of tourists - you can enjoy a spectacular view over the Wadi Arabah, the immense valley of about 170 kilometres in length that lies between the Gulf of Aqaba and the Dead Sea, the deepest depression on the surface of the earth. The return to Petra retraces the same route.

Opposite page, left - *To the left of the Deir there is a cave (No. 465) in which this beautiful aedicule is carved.*

Opposite page, top right - *A view of the plateau at the foot of the Jebel ed Deir; the area is rich in hypogeums, votive niches and ruins of collapsed structures.*

Opposite page, bottom right *The arrow indicates the position of the cistern located under an enigmatic pile of rubble, visible at the foot of the Jebel ed Deir.*

Below left - *This bas-relief, although very eroded, shows two Nabataean merchants with their dromedaries.*

Below right - *The large cistern excavated at the foot of the rocky buttress to the left of the Deir.*

A SHORT BUT INTERESTING DIVERSION

This short but slightly strenuous walk is advised for the more curious visitors, archaeology enthusiasts and photography lovers, who will be able appreciate some uncommon views.
Right in front of the Deir a snack bar is partially set within a spacious hypogeum. This could have been a triclinium and it is fascinating to think that is has more or less returned to its ancient use. Climbing the few steps to the right, you turn left, walk around a second rocky outcrop and head towards the mountain peak opposite. You will immediately see two large caves side by side, topped with a third hypogeum (difficult to say what it was used for, certainly not as a tomb). To the right a steep rock-cut staircase climbs up, going higher and higher with a series of flights of steps. You will see other staircases in the same area, now partially impassable and small channels carved into the rock. Finally, you will arrive at the top of the mountain. From here you can enjoy a very unusual view of the Deir and the entire valley where Petra lies. The sacred area (or "high place") reachable by the staircase is not easy to locate and has been almost completely worn away by weather erosion.

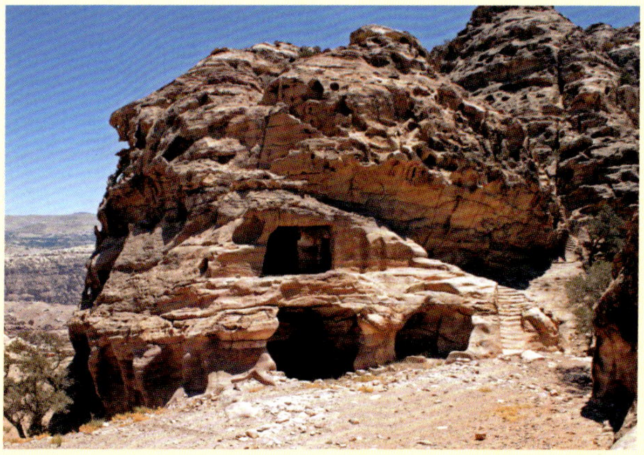

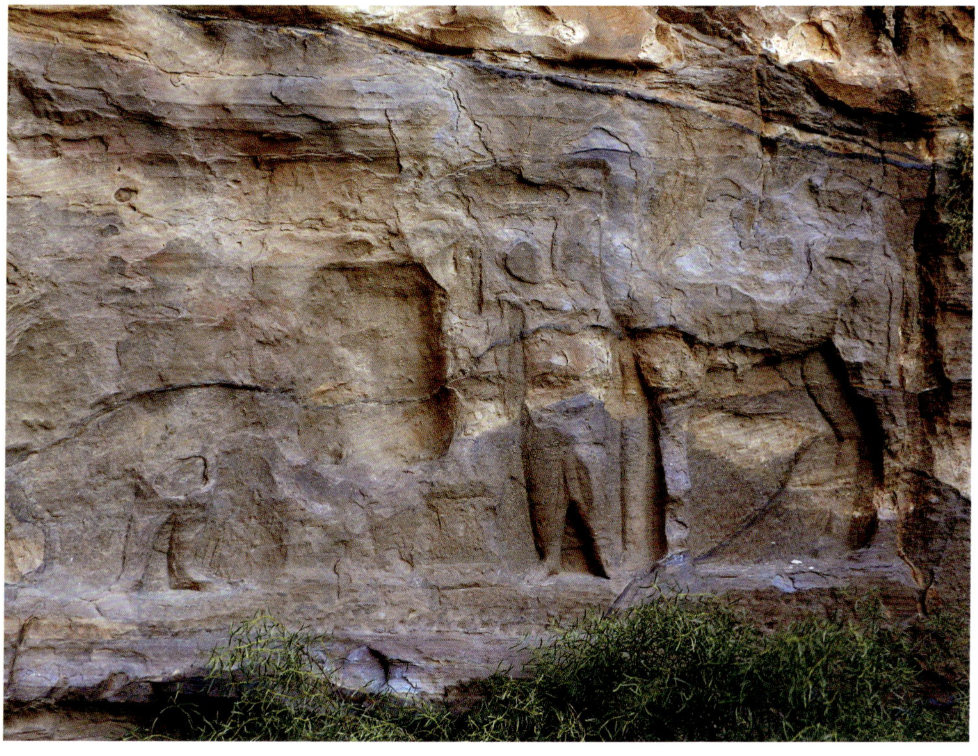

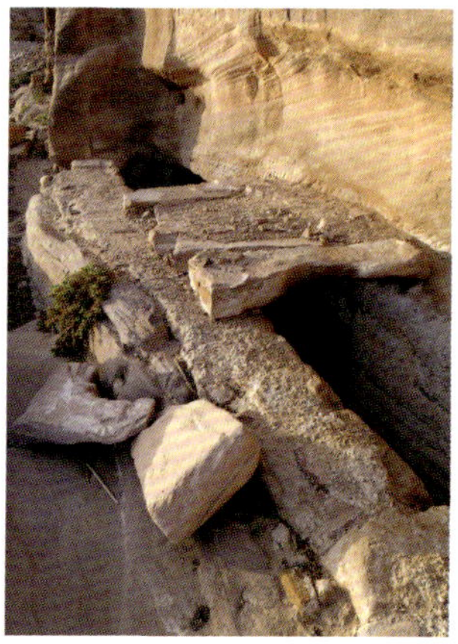

THE ROOM 468

In the rocky hummock that rises up almost opposite the Deir, to the south-west, there is a large cubic room with no facade, which is today known as Room 468 in the Brünnow classification. This huge cave was the cella of a temple of enormous proportions (undoubtedly one of the most imposing in all of Petra), with a massive masonry substructure that probably had a vast pronaos made up of 14 or 16 columns at the front, the bases of which can still be seen in situ. A monumental staircase on the right, now almost completely ruined, led up to this building, which was razed to the ground by one of

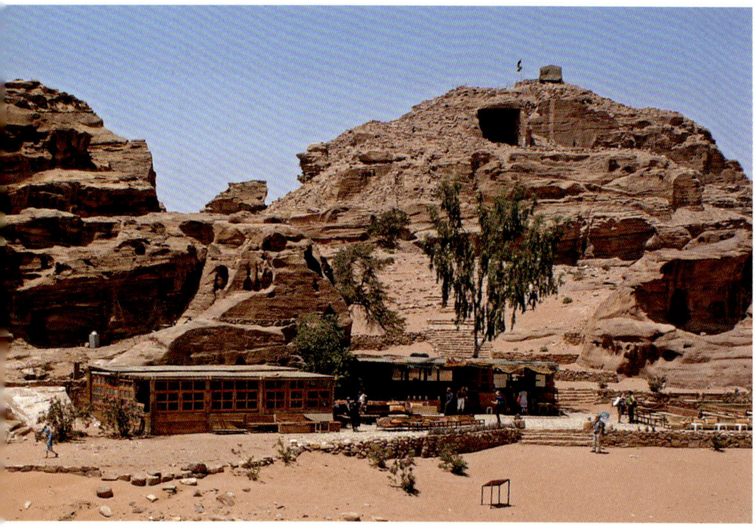

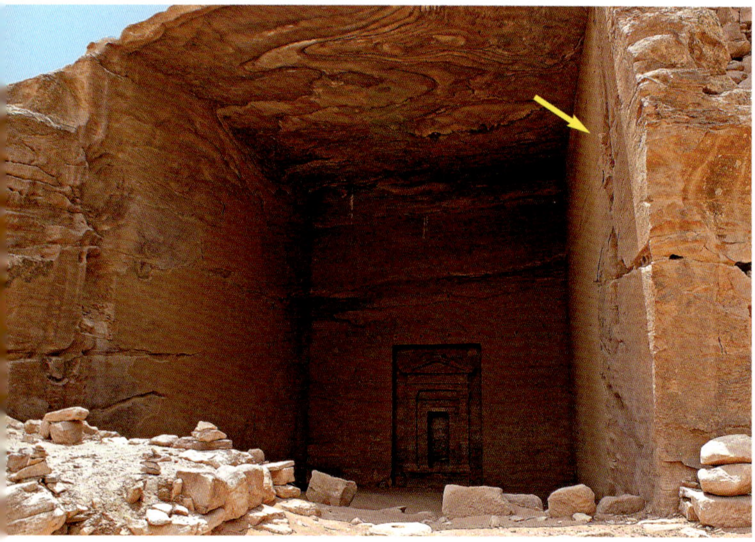

the terrible earthquakes that struck the region in the past. At the foot of the flight of stairs there is a large rock cut cistern.

Carved into the rear wall of the room, which is 8.5 m by 12 m, is the most elaborate and best preserved aedicula in Petra. It consists of a niche, where an image of the deity was placed between pilasters surmounted by a Doric trabeation, which is the same as the one in the Deir, framed with two further pilasters with Nabataean capitals. These support a trabeation with a smooth frieze on it, decorated with a bust at each end. Although the faces have been destroyed, it is possible to make out two figures, probably female, each holding a torch (or a cornucopia). The whole thing is crowned by a pediment with three acroterions, and exquisitely crafted in a resplendent Hellenistic style. The unusual decoration of the outermost pilasters, made up of six overlapping rectangles in bas-relief, resembles that of Tomb 66 (page 76) and it is a distinctive feature of the architecture of Petra during the 1st century AD. The presence of this shrine demonstrates beyond doubt that Room 468 was a temple, but the deity to which it was dedicated is not known (perhaps Al Uzza).

The square holes in the walls must have been to support the sacred furnishings, probably in wood. Bearing in mind their position, the shrine may have been framed within a larger and more sumptuous altar, which we can imagine richly decorated and leaning against the wall. On the right hand wall, at a height of about 5 metres, an elaborate semi-capital with floral decoration can be seen, still wedged into the sandstone and held in place by mortar.

Top left - *The temple cella, known as Room 468, is clearly visible from the court facing the Deir.*

Bottom left - *A view of the monument's cella, with the aedicule carved into the back wall. The arrow shows the position of the elaborate semi-capital still embedded in the right wall. It would have supported an arch, part of a sort of iconostasis (a dividing partition).*

Bottom right - *This splendid shrine is miraculously well preserved, even though it has been defaced by tourist graffiti. Unfortunately, in recent years this damaging habit has experienced a remarkable resurgence.*

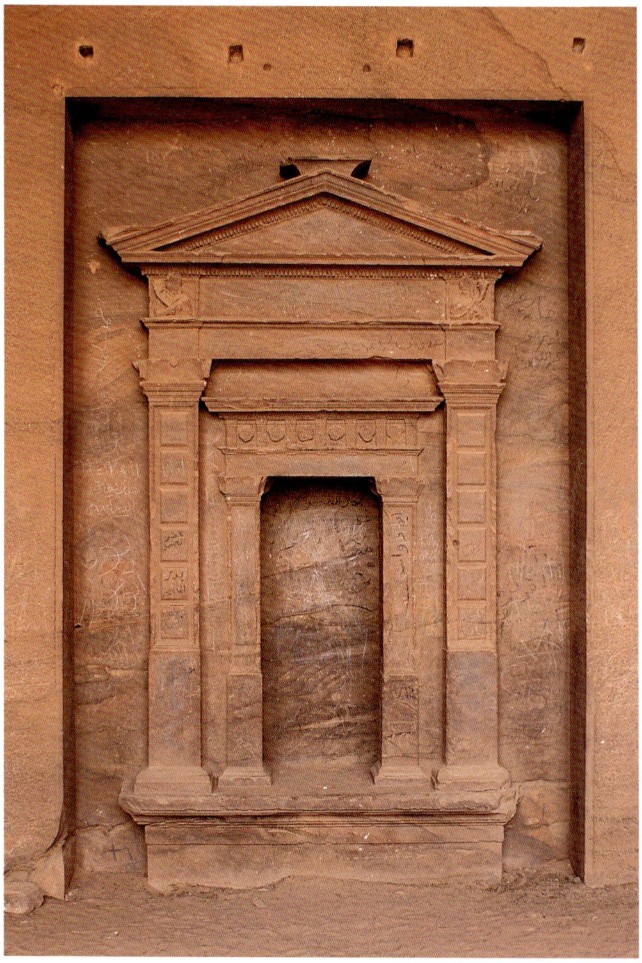

THE ROOM 468: A RECONSTRUCTIVE SUGGESTION

The Room or Monument 468 is one of the structures most affected by the terrible earthquakes that hit Petra, and it suffered very serious damage. However, thanks to its wonderful aedicule, it caught the attention of several distinguished visitors in the 19th century, including the French Lèon de Laborde, who included it in a map of the area (showing the massive scale of the pronaos), and the Scottish landscape artist David Roberts, who included part of the pronaos and some of the related column bases in a magnificent lithograph portraying the Deir (p. 17).
Going up here, you can easily see that the broad terrace, facing the cella of the temple, was partly obtained by excavating the natural profile of the rock hummock and partly by erecting a massive masonry wall. This substructure supported a huge pronaos with at least 14 columns, whose bases are still in situ but are partially buried. The whole appearance of the hill above was very different compared to how it appears today.
Up until a few years ago, you could see the remains of masonry buildings, including the foundations of two small circular structures, one of which had a ring of semi-columns on the inside (it could even be small baths for ritual use). There were even fragments of a floor with a black and white mosaic, and, on the edge of the precipice, an unusual floor made of hexagonal tiles and largely covered with detritus (shown by the arrows in the photo, taken during the late spring of 2006). This demonstrates without a doubt that the pronaos of the temple below rose to a considerable height and, joining the mountain, must have made a sort of enormous terrace. It is impossible to say what stood on this terrace and nearby, but it is clear that Room 468, and the structures below it, must have been part of a monumental complex of great importance, considering its elevated position, looking out over the Jebel ed Deir to the east, and the immense valley of Wadi Arabah on the opposite side. In fact, it is known that the Nabataeans usually erected important sanctuaries on mountain tops.
Unfortunately, the recent and deplorable construction of a kiosk for tourists has severely damaged the ancient remains, just as the opening of the path that leads up here has caused serious damage to structures that should have been carefully investigated. These reckless actions have compromised much-needed, future archaeological investigations of an architectural complex whose understanding is fundamental for a broader and complete analysis of this sacred area at the foot of the Jebel ed Deir.

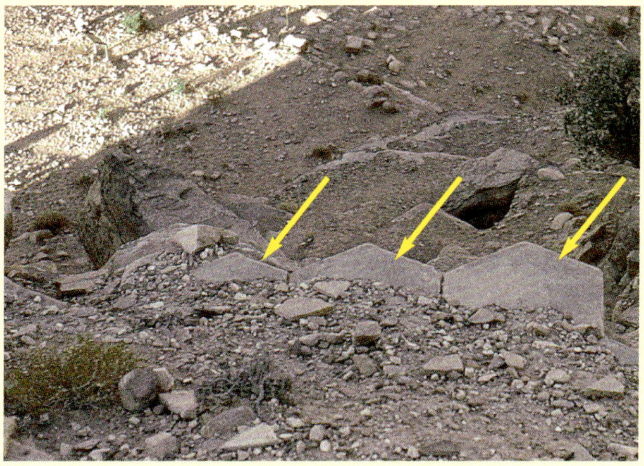

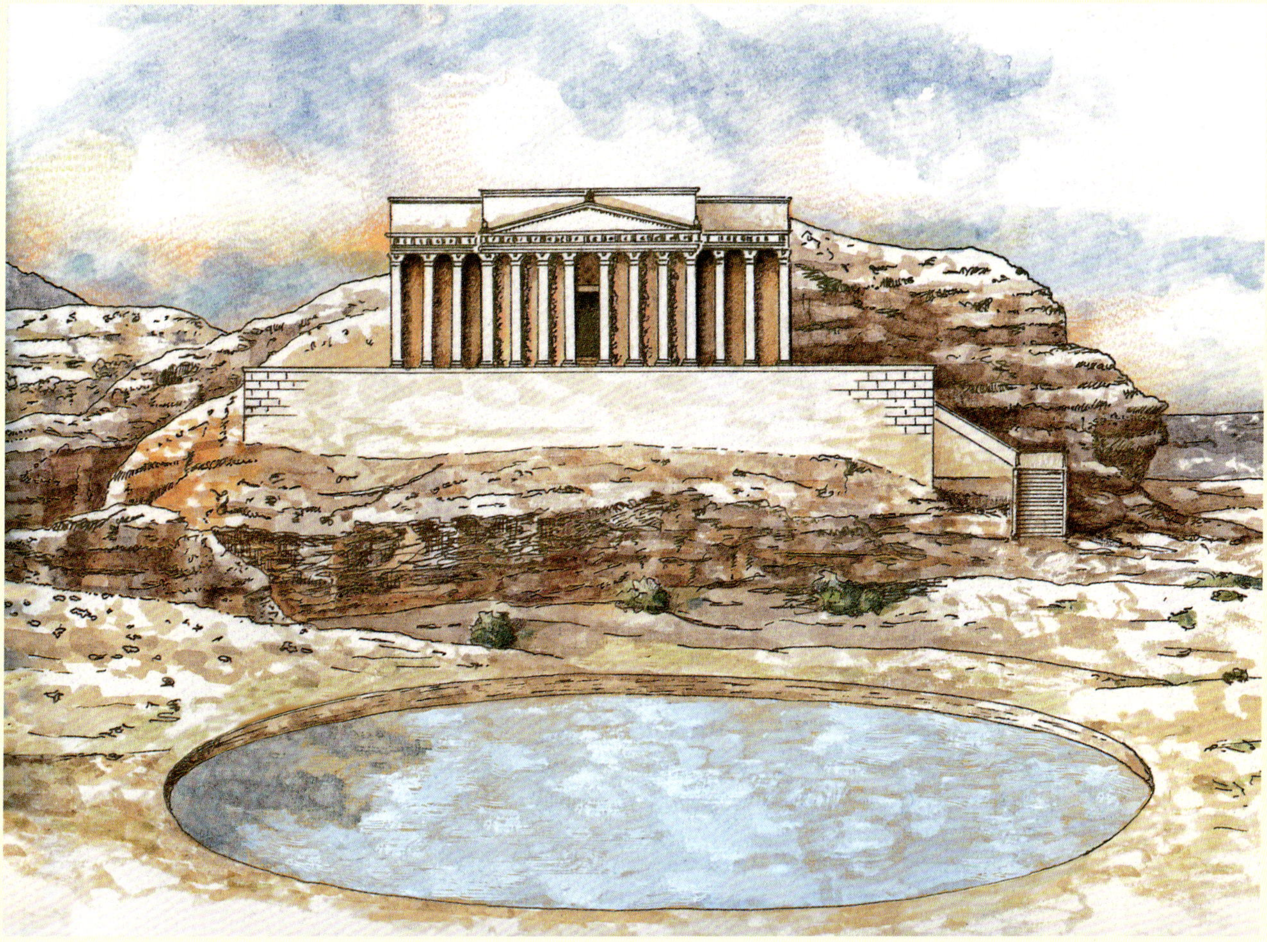

F. Bourbon M. Falcone

THE JEBEL AL MADHBAH

The climb up the Jebel al Madhbah, and the "High Place of Sacrifice" carved into the mountain top, is also more tiring than the one that leads up to the Deir, but it is worth taking into consideration, both for the beauty of the monuments and the spectacular views that can be seen along the way. The route (which lasts at least 3 hours) can be undertaken in both directions. The processional path that climbs up from the external Siq, a little further on from Tomb 70 (page 78), and before the Theatre, is easy to follow, but it soon becomes an interminable succession of staircases cut into the living rock, which are impressive but rather steep. The narrow valley they climb up is already exposed to the sun from the second half of the morning and this makes the walk even more tiring, especially if there is no wind. The ascent from the Wadi Farasa side, on the other hand, is more gradual, and although the path is in the sun for the whole of the afternoon, it is less tiring thanks to frequent gusts of wind. If you start the walk after the hottest part of the day, you can enjoy the shade of the rock chambers along the way, and arrive at the summit of Jebel al Madhbah when the light is perfect for admiring the magnificent view over the whole of Petra, the surrounding mountains, and the Tomb of Aaron in the distance.
Finally, you descend in the cool shade, and once you reach the external Siq, it is not too far to the entrance gate of the archaeological area.

Monica Falcone

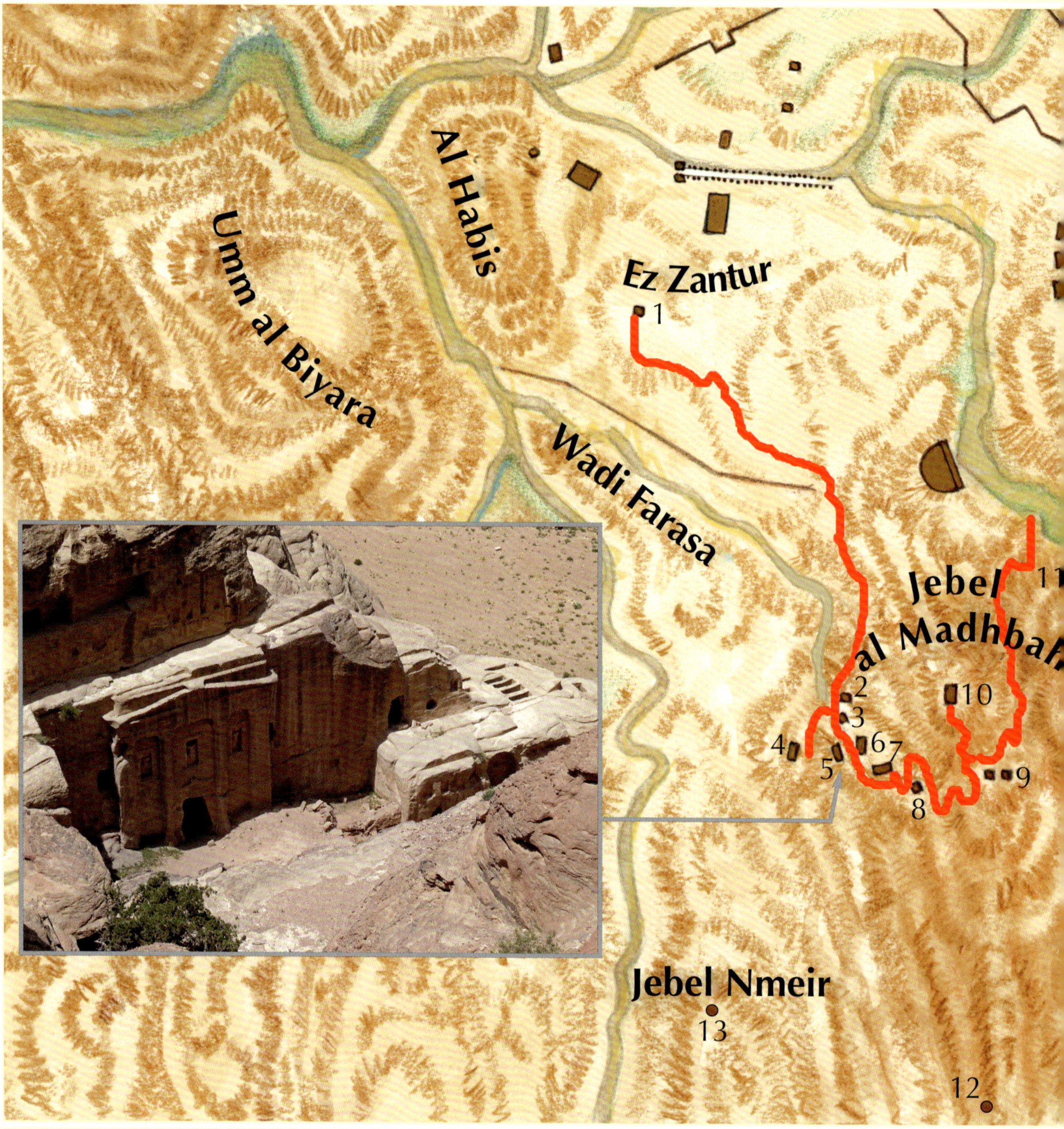

Top left - *The Broken Pediment Tomb, with its austere composure, stands on a terrace preceded by a flight of stairs. The facade, a magnificent example of the "classical Nabataean style", is visible from a considerable distance and marks the entrance to the Wadi Farasa East.*

Centre left - *The Roman Soldier Tomb is the main monument in the Wadi Farasa. Although it is classically inspired, it still retains typical Nabataean elements, such as capitals and pilasters with quarter columns on them.*

Bottom left - *On the Jebel al Madhbah summit, 1035 meters above sea level, the most famous "High Place of Sacrifice" in Petra can be found. Entirely carved out of stone, it consists of a large esplanade and two adjoining altars, in one of which a round basin opens up to collect the blood of the victims immolated to the gods. Not surprisingly, the name of the massif means "Mountain of the Altar".*

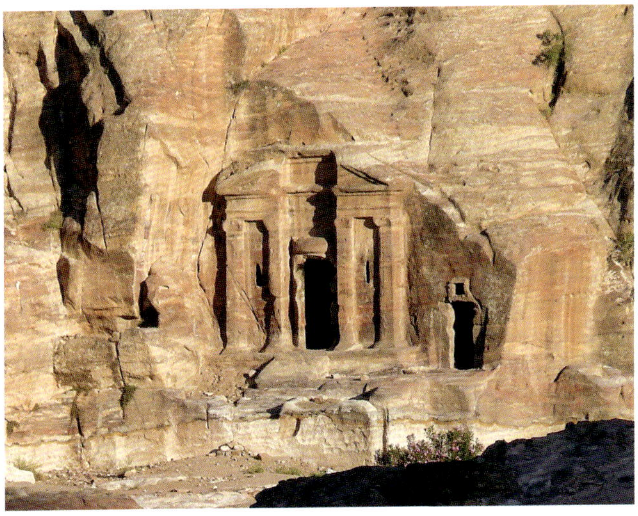

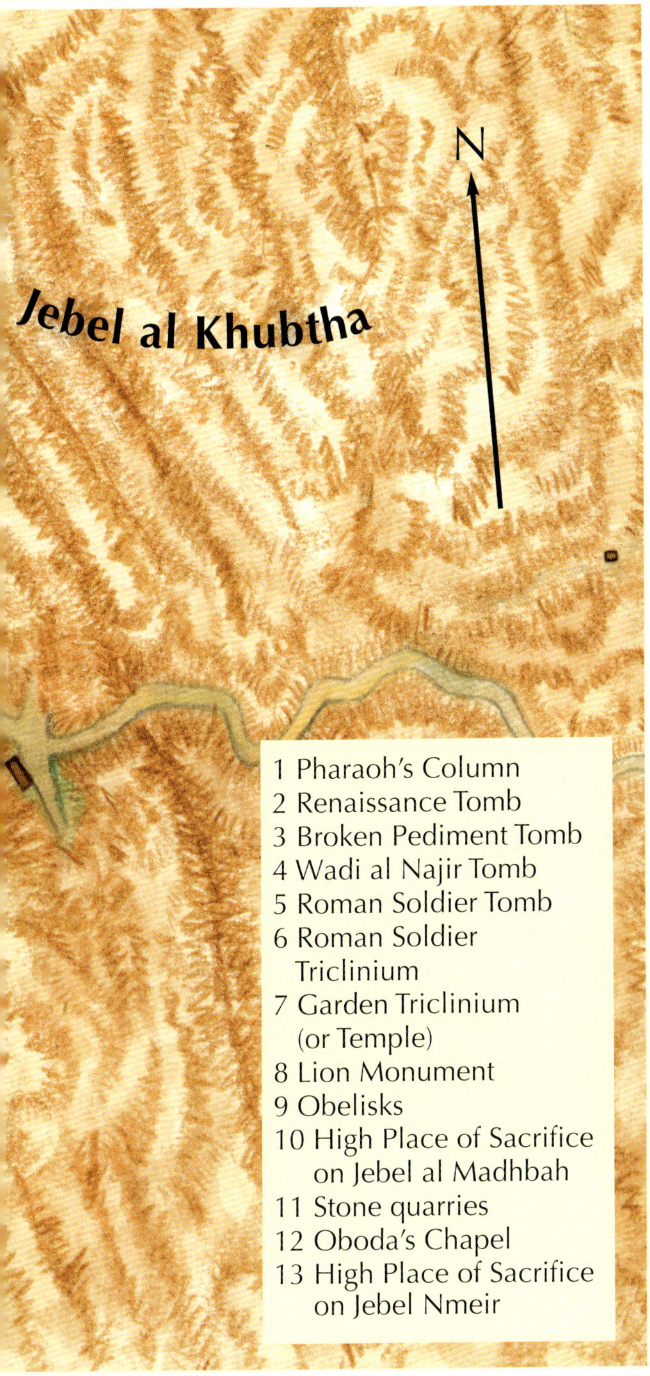

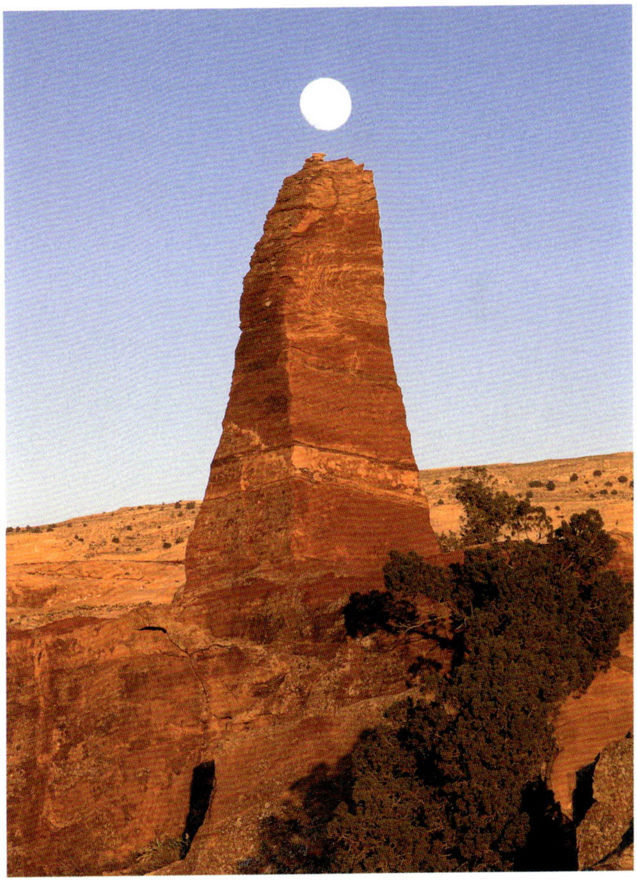

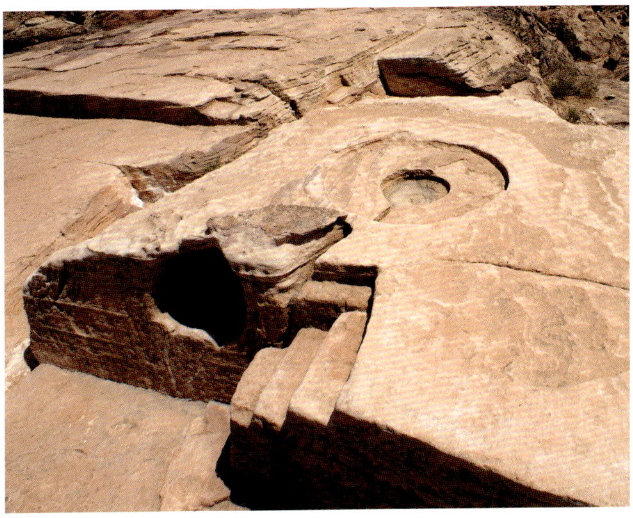

THE WADI FARASA

If you want to follow the suggested itinerary on the previous page, it begins behind the Great Temple. From there, you need to follow a dirt road towards the isolated "Pharao's Column" (page 108) and after a few metres you will see a crossroads where you will need to turn left. The path is still plainly visible and goes past the large Nabataean rubbish dump and under the excavations of the Ez-Zanthur IV house. The conical shape of the rubbish dump stands out on the tormented surrounding terrain for its regular and smooth surface. The path heads southeast and goes along the Wadi Farasa, a valley that has intense, brick red coloured sandstone. On the left, the rocky walls of the wadi can be seen, dotted with rock facades arranged on many different levels. They are quite similar to the ones in the Outer Siq, and in particular one of them, which has been eroded by the wind but is still rather photogenic looking, resembles a mask with its mouth wide open. In fact, the whole of this low rugged slope of the Jebel al Madhbah is full of tombs, votive niches, cisterns and aqueducts, not to mention a couple of open-air triclinia. Nevertheless, it is still not very popular with visitors, so those wishing to explore the place need to know that there is a path that runs along the side of the mountain, which leads to the Outer Siq outlet, right in front of the Royal Tombs and downstream of the theatre. In this area, you will find the open-air triclinium illustrated on page 36, and nearby, a cavity with an altar carved inside it, and a strange serpentine figure in high relief above, probably an effigy of a divinity from the underworld.

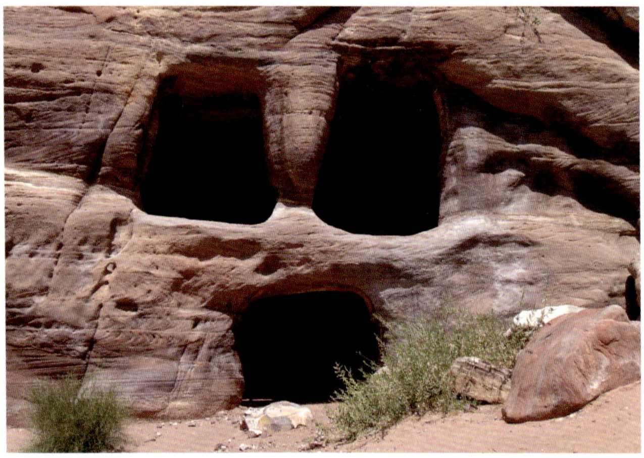

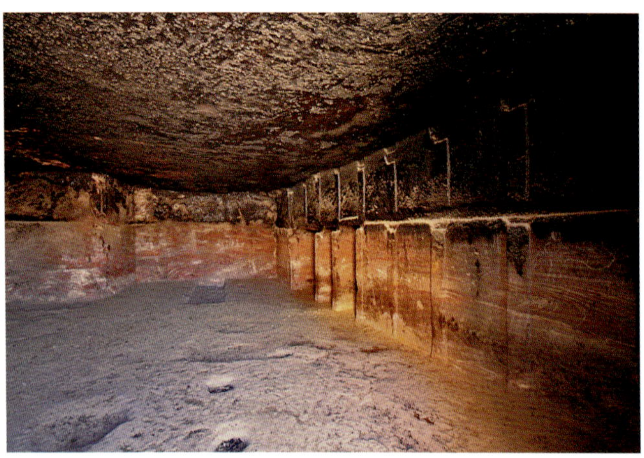

Judging from the tombs that are carved in the upper part of Wadi Farasa, where those of the Assyrian or cavetto type are becoming more and more rare, to be supplanted by Hellenistic and Roman influenced monuments, it is likely that this whole area was monumentalized rather late, probably from the middle of the 1st century AD up until the period of Roman domination. Even from a great distance, it is possible to see the peculiar facade of the **Broken Pediment Tomb** (No. 228), surely one of the more stylistically balanced structures in Petra. In this monument the perfect balance between Greco-Roman architecture and the Nabataean taste for the multiplication of lines seems to have been achieved. The tomb is carved into an elevated position on a north-facing rocky buttress, opposite a large courtyard that is carved out of sandstone. It appears to be unique due to the contrast of the formal Hellenistic design and the Nabataean taste for bundling decorative

Top - *Erosion has modelled this hypogeum in the Wadi Farasa in a bizarre way; it is likely that it was a dwelling or a triclinium room.*

Centre - *The interior of the Broken Pediment tomb is of some interest due to the decorative design on the walls, articulated by a double theory of pilasters with inserted capitals, which unfortunately are missing.*

Bottom - *The facade of the Broken Pediment Tomb is quite unique in Petra's architectural panorama.*

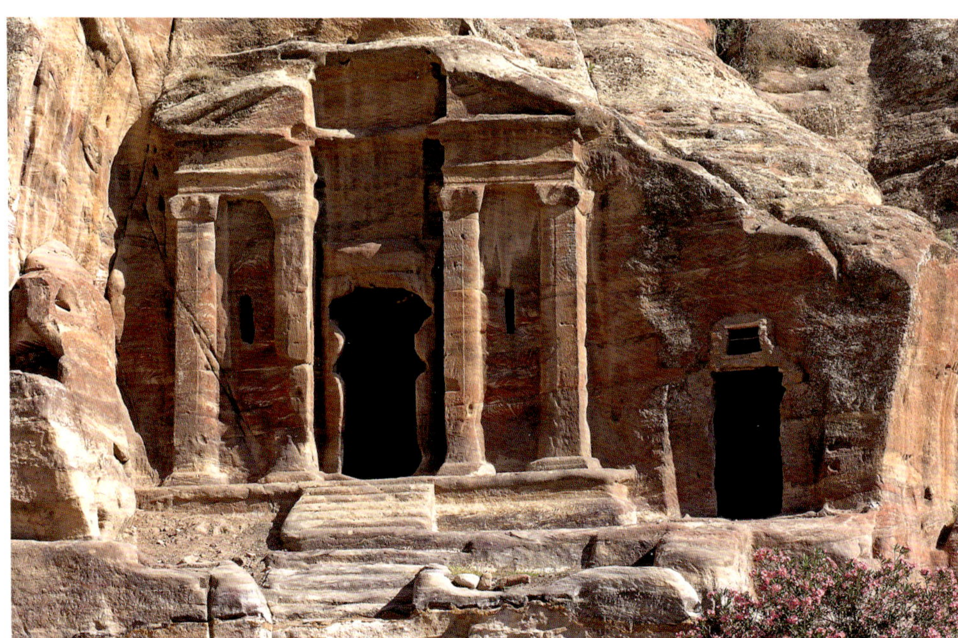

elements together. The facade is punctuated by four prominent pilasters with "horned" capitals with a simple entablature that supports a broken pediment. The doorway, reached by a broad flight of steps, was probably damaged by an earthquake and this is the reason for its strange appearance. The two slit windows constitute a late intervention. The interior is of some interest, as the wall on the right is marked by a series of low pilasters arranged into two orders with built-in capitals that have since gone missing. The architrave that divided the two orders of pilasters was also built-in. In the lower order, four burial niches were originally excavated (today there appear to be three, as two were joined together in an earlier intervention) and there is a pit grave in the floor, towards the back wall. The left side of the tomb, which would have had several niches separated by slender pilasters, was drastically modified in antiquity when the walls that separated the niches were demolished (perhaps following the transformation of the tomb into a Bedouin home). Ultimately, it seems that for some reason the interior of this tomb was never completed. Judith McKenzie dates the monument to an era between 40 and 70 AD. The small room, on the right of the tomb, must have been a triclinium. On the terrace, in front of the tomb, two large cisterns have been excavated: one square, the other octagonal. A dizzying staircase, with several ramps, is carved into the stone above the facade (protected by a gutter channel, as is usually the case), but it is impossible to say where it would have led. Perhaps it would have gone up to the aqueduct that was dug out of the steep Jebel al Madhbah slope, taking water from the Ain Braq perennial spring to the south-western quarters of the city, now the Wadi Farasa East valley as it is conventionally called by archaeologists.

Just beyond the Broken Pediment Tomb, you come across the elegant **Renaissance Tomb** (No. 229), which was given this name due to its magnificent proportions, which recall the Italian architecture of the sixteenth century. The facade – facing west – is framed between two pilasters with a quarter column, which support an entablature with a smooth frieze and a rather low tympanum, surmounted by three acroterions. The doorway is inserted into a second frame made up of the usual pilasters with half Nabataean capitals, upon which, instead of a normal entablature, there is an open gable arched pediment, with three small urns on the extrados.

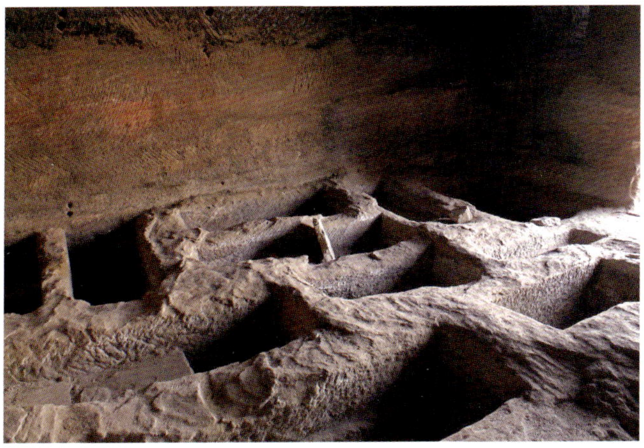

Left - *The pit graves discovered inside the Renaissance Tomb had already been looted in antiquity.*

Right - *Even the elegant facade of the Renaissance Tombhas two slit windows. This detail is visible in several other sepulchres and is the result of relatively recent interventions, carried out when many of the tombs were used as dwellings. This practice continued until the third quarter of the twentieth century and explains the appearance of many of the hypogea, blackened for centuries by the smoke of the fires used by the beduins to cook and keep warm.*

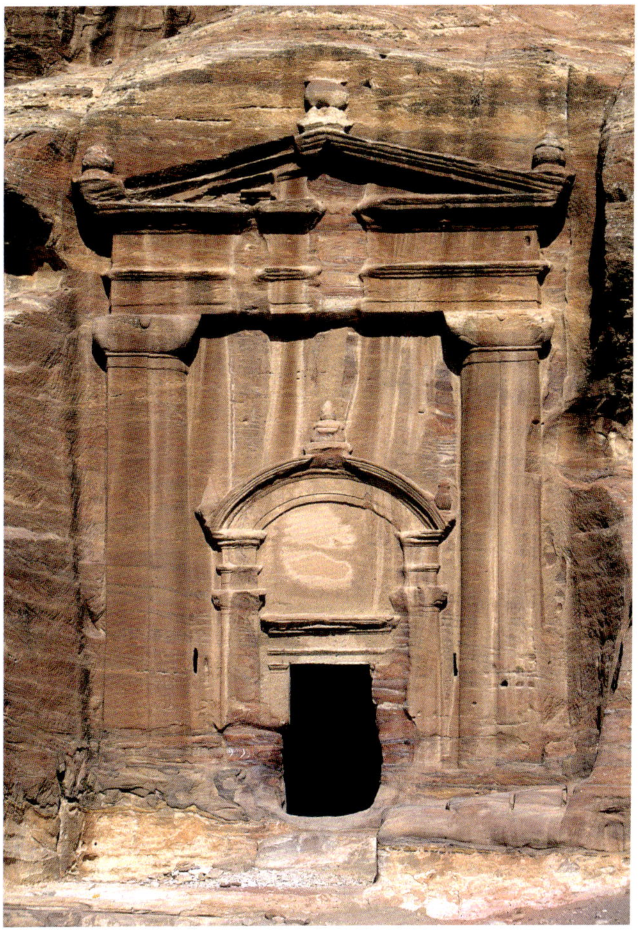

An excavation campaign, conducted in 2003 inside the tomb, led to an exceptional and unexpected discovery: as many as 14 burial pits were found beneath a layer of debris. They were so well-preserved that it was even possible to recover the remains of the bones of the deceased. In addition, the discovery confirmed that burials were regularly provided with grave goods. The analysis of similar fragments confirms that these goods consisted of ampoules (ointments) and ceramic plates, terracotta or bronze statuettes, oil lamps, bronze bells, jewellery and even coins. A study of the pottery from the Renaissance Tomb has allowed us to date the burials back to the last quarter of the first century AD. This dramatically contradicted the previous attribution, which dated them to the first half of the second century AD (as proposed by Judith Mckenzie) based on their formal similarity with the Sextius Florentinus Tomb. It is therefore likely that the latter was modelled on the Renaissance Tomb, fifty years later.

In the rock wall on both sides of the Renaissance Tomb you can see the deep grooves of yet another aqueduct.

THE WADI AL NAJIR (WADI FARASA WEST)

The short itinerary suggested here allows you to go to a very interesting group of monuments, which are not often visited. The area, usually deserted, is particularly evocative and offers glimpses of arcane beauty. In addition, the tour can act as a type of introduction to the monuments that will be visited later, in terms of similar styles and architectural features.
From the Renaissance Tomb you need to leave the path that goes into what is often referred to as Wadi Farasa East. Instead, turn to your right and head south-west towards the clear entrance to a secondary valley, conventionally called Wadi Farasa West, but known to the locals as "Wadi al Najir". Approaching the entrance to the wadi you will see that the ground is cluttered with ruins; a huge retaining wall made for strengthening the upper part of the valley must have stood here. On the right side of the wadi, the unusual facade of Tomb 258 (or the al Najir Tomb) immediately appears, bringing to mind the front of a classic tetrastyle temple. The facade is characterised by four, tall half-columns (the outer ones are actually half-pilasters with leaning quarter columns), crowned with Nabataean capitals. The trabeation is smooth and arranged with a simple cornice. A pediment, crowned with three not very pronounced acroterions rests on the upper architrave. The architrave is set in an attic ending in a slim cornice. The doorway opens in the central intercolumniation, set between two half pilasters with Nabataean capitals that support an architrave and a Doric frieze with five triglyphs and four metopes formed by slightly raised discs. It is completed by a smooth tympanum with three acroterions. This entrance is very similar to the one on the Urn Tomb. The inside, lit by two large open windows on the sides of the facade, probably the result of later works, is devoid of decorations. Only six burial niches open up in the upper part of the back wall. In its entirety, the tomb seems like a smaller and simplified version of the Roman Soldier Tomb. Considering the similar stylistic-architectural features, it is likely the two monuments were more or less contemporary, datable to the third quarter of the 1st century AD.
On the left side of the tomb there is an ancillary room, then a spacious triclinium (No. 256), lit by a large window above the door. Apart from the excellent conservation of the three benches lined to the walls, this room is special because of the five loculi carved into the upper part of the walls. This is not a unique inconsistency in Petra's varied architectural panorama, but it still remains unexplained. In fact, why a number of triclinium were also used as sepulchres is not clear.
On the outside of the hypogeum, to the left of the door, is a rectangular basin carved into the solid sandstone, perhaps used for ritual ablutions, while to the right a long bench can be seen, with short pilasters along it. A few metres in front of this, although the ground is cluttered with detritus, you can glimpse another bench carved into the stone, connected at right angles to the first one by a third, facing uphill. A few clues (including a pilaster with a trapezoidal capital carved into the rocky wall) suggests that there was a court or cultual space here. This sort of open-air triclinium was perhaps shaded by a large canopy, held in position by a sys-

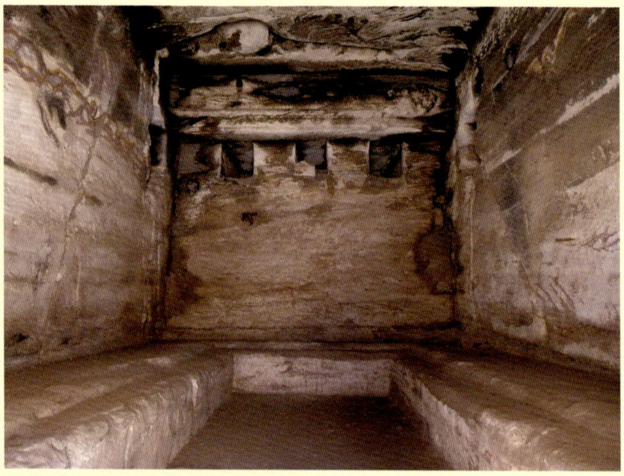

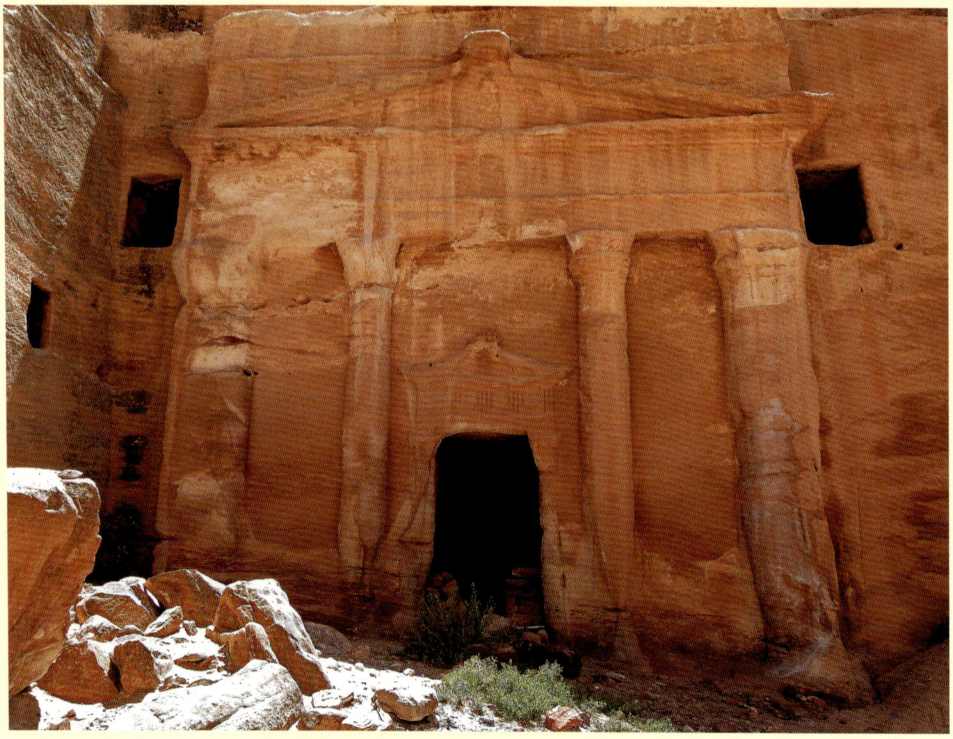

Left - *Reachable in about ten minutes from the path that climbs along the wadi Farasa, the Tomb of the wadi al Njir is of considerable interest because it appears to be a slightly reduced and simplified variant of the Tomb of the Roman Soldier.*

Right - *Inside the triclinium located next to the tomb, five loculi are clearly visible in the upper part of the walls. Their presence is contradictory, although in Petra there are similar cases in some other triclinia. It is possible that in late times some of these banquet rooms, having lost their original function, were used as burial sites.*

tem of ropes secured to the rock by two conspicuous through holes carved into it.

The narrow gorge situated to the left of the triclinium is still blocked by a rather well-preserved storage dam. Upstream from this there are the remains of a second dam, which held back the force of theflash floods. The water collected in the basin downstream was then sent to a covered cistern that now lies in ruins, built on the left of the large wall.

Next to it, carved into the vertical walls of the rock buttress, the elegant facade of a pediment tomb (No. 253) stands out, whose lower section is unfortunately rather damaged. The Doric frieze, with the common design of triglyphs and round metopes, is unusual because there are a seven of these round metopes. This links the facade to the Lion Triclinium and suggests a similar date, namely the second half of the 1st century AD, if not later. The inside is pretty interesting: a low bench, not very noticeable, runs along the sides of the walls of the room, forming a decidedly unusual feature, while the walls are characterised by simple pilasters crowned with trapezoidal capitals (some were inserted), which support a smooth trabeation without cornices. Spaces between one pilaster and another were carved to make room for loculi only in the back and left walls. Strangely enough, it was only in the floors of the three rear loculi that pit graves were dug.

On the eastern side of the wadi, just in front of the triclinium, there are two hypogea which are very damaged from erosion and whose function is unknown.

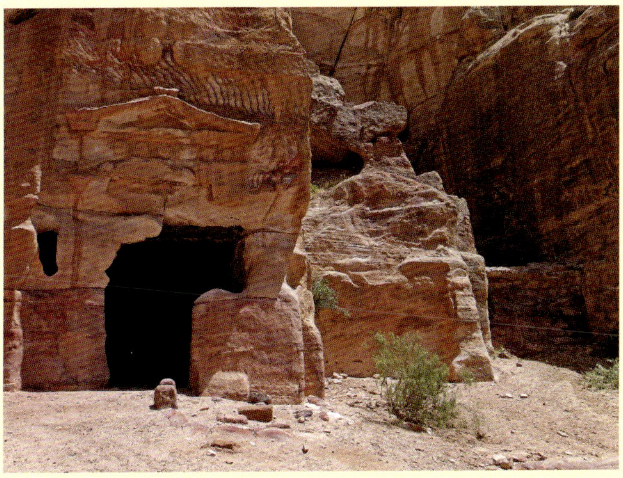

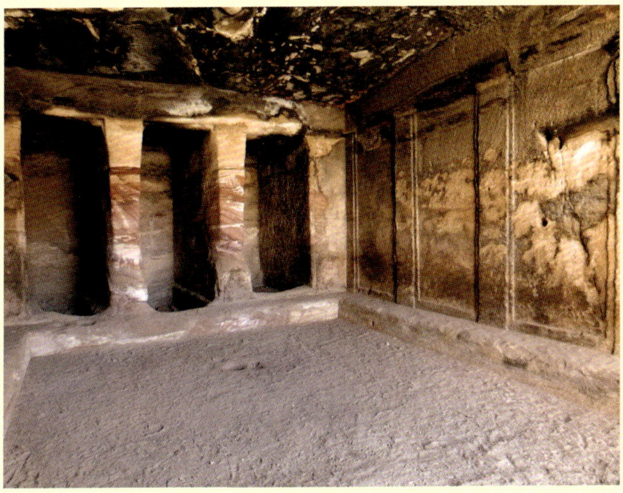

Above – Unfortunately, the facade of the pediment tomb 253 has been badly damaged by the elements The opening in a later period of two large windows at the sides of the door, has also contributed to this.

Below– The inside of Tomb 253 is unusual because of the articulation of the walls, the presence of a low bench running on three sides, and the ceiling, which seems to be formed of two slightly inclined slopes.

THE AREA OF JEBEL NMEIR

West of the Wadi al Najir, where the rough slopes of the Jebel Nmeir (or Numayr) extend, is the least visited area in all of Petra. There is a huge necropolis, which includes also some block tombs, at the foot of the mountain. This area, accessible by following the ancient paths on the right of the entrance to Wadi al Najir, hosts numerous cisterns, two stibadia, the bas-relief of a man in armour, the remains of dams and substructures that must have formed terraces for farming in antiquity.

As it is in a difficult position to reach, it takes a lot of effort to go up the Wadi Nmeir track, which quickly transforms into quite a rugged gorge (this is why you need to be guided by a local), and reach a sanctuary known as the "Chapel of Obodas", still in a study phase (2019). The large complex, situated in a very evocative landscape setting, can be reached by following a narrow passage carved into the living rock. The cult area is formed of a number of rooms (several carved into the stone and others built in masonry, which have been reduced to rubble), including triclinia, a stibadium, service hypogea and a cistern. In the main chamber, which looks like a triclinium, a deep niche is carved, which must have had a statue in it. In fact, a dedicatory epigraph says, "This is the statue of the god Obodas (Ubdat), made by the sons of Hnynw...". The archaeological excavations carried out by Laurent Tholbec have brought to light three main construction phases, the oldest dating back to the 2nd century BC. This makes the Chapel of Obodas one of the oldest monuments in Petra.

Throughout Petra, you can see about thirty similar structures, called "chapels", whose exact use is still not fully understood. It is thought, however, that these cultual places were periodically visited by specific confraternities (thiasoi), perhaps organised on the basis of tribal subdivisions.

Shining light on the subject are the investigations carried out by the scholar Laïla Nehmé, who discovered that the vast majority of Petra's epigraphs are carved close to the triclinia and hypogaea containing baetyli (others mostly accompany nefesh). These epigraphs form real groups, concentrated in specific zones around the urban centre. Within each group, the cult of a single divinity is evident: Dushara in the area of al Madrasa, Zeus Hagios on the Umm al Biyara, Al Kutba in the Wadi Siyyagh, Obodas on the Jebel Nmeir, etcetera. Data from studying the Chapel of Obodas suggests that already in the early phases of population, specific mountain areas situated around the urban centre had been consecrated for worshipping a particular divinity. In addition, such religious distinctions may also attest to an ancestral subdivision of the population in clans. Likely, at the dawn of the permanent occupation of Petra, several Nabataean clans established consecrated areas to their own tribal divinity in precise meeting places. Such customs continued over time with various confraternities that periodically met up in the original localities to bear witness to their faith.

It is interesting to note that up until now, 980 Nabataean inscriptions have been located in Petra and a 133 of them are concentrated in the Jabal Nmeir area.

A little further on, where the Wadi Farasa narrows and becomes steeper, you reach the **Roman Soldier Tomb** (No. 239), opposite a large triclinium and an esplanade that is partly carved into the rock. The facade, hewn out of the west facing wall, is the most famous and accomplished example of the "Roman style" (along with the Wadi al Najir Tomb) and very reminiscent of the front of a tetrastyle temple. There are two pilasters with quarter columns and the portal opens between two half-columns. The capitals appear to be Nabataean although they are very eroded and the entablature, without a frieze, supports a low pediment, framed within a rectangular attic and, perhaps, originally adorned by three acroterions. The portal is crowned by a beautiful Doric frieze, which supports a pediment. The peculiarity of the tomb lies in the three niches that are carved in the intercolumniations and framed by pilasters and a smooth entablature. Inside, as many high relief human figures are clearly visible, each consisting of six overlapping slabs. The central male figure, today without legs and headless, wears a Roman style cuirass, while the two placed on the sides, unfortunately also very worn, seem to be male individuals dressed in short military-style tunics. The few traces of stucco that have survived lead us to believe that these figures were plastered and polychrome. Until recently, it was thought that the man in the centre was a high-ranking Roman soldier (perhaps an imperial legate) and that the other two were his children. Due to the type of clothing and the general appearance of the sepulchre it was believed that it was excavated around the first decades of the second century AD, i.e. after the annexation of Petra to the empire. However, today, it is known that the tomb, and most of the structures connected to it, date back to the third quarter of the first century AD. It is therefore evident that the portrayed figure must have been Nabataean and of conspicuous lineage, certainly a high-ranking military man, perhaps belonging to the royal dynasty, considering the grandeur of the burial complex.

The interior of the tomb consists of two square-shaped burial chambers; a loculus and four arcosolium niches were carved into the walls of the first one.

A long excavation campaign began in 2001 involved the vast courtyard (21 m x 33 m) in front of the tomb, demonstrating that the area - obtained by flattening the bottom of the wadi and channeling the watercourse

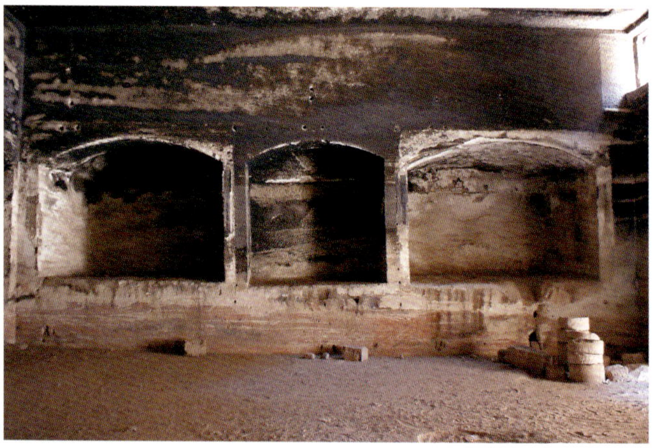

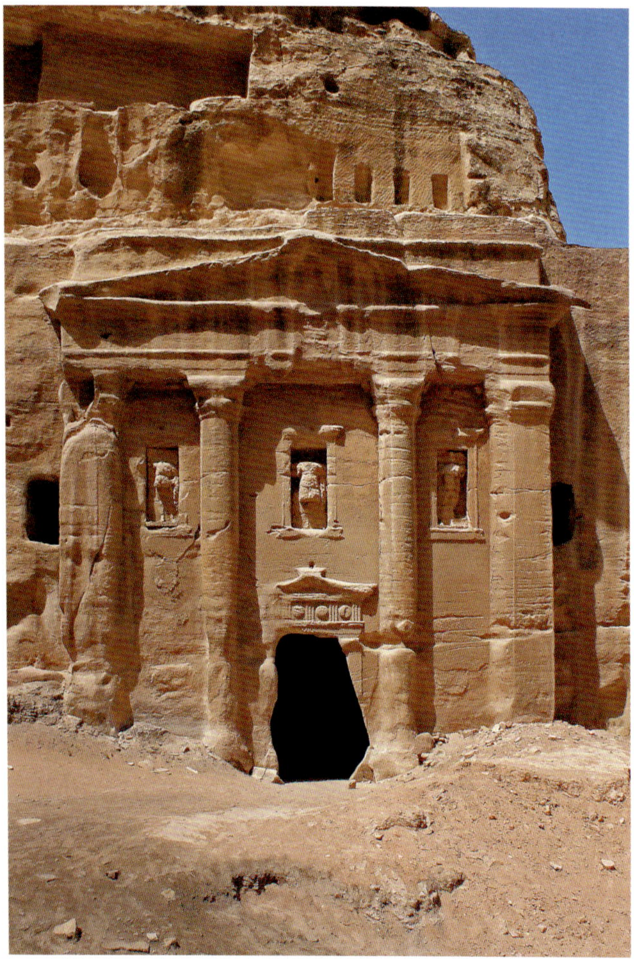

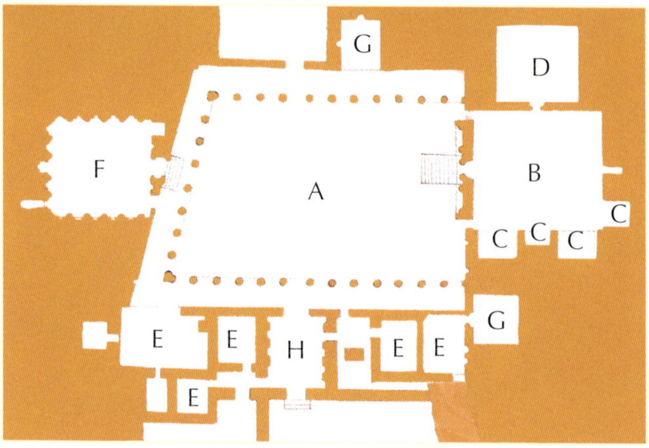

Left - *Above the facade of the Roman Soldier Tomb there is a deep rectangular cavity with an unknown function. Comparing it with the similar rooms opening in the back wall of the theater, it can be imagined that it was an older hypogeum, sliced through to allow the carving of the new tomb complex.*

Right - *A view of the main burial chamber, with the arcosolium carved into the northern wall.*

Plan of the Roman Soldier Tomb

A Colonnaded courtyard
B Main burial chamber
C Arcosolium niches
D Secondary burial chamber
E Ancillary rooms
F Large triclinium
G Secondary triclinia

that is formed during periods of heavy rainfalls - was surrounded on three sides by a portico supported by 4 metre high columns. The downstream wing, supported by a retaining wall, included several other ancillary rooms arranged onto two floors. A dense network of channels hewn into the rock, terracotta pipes and a cistern show that the complex had plenty of water. Since the Ain Braq aqueduct runs much higher and there were no connections, it is clear that the supply was guaranteed by a system of dams, cisterns and settling basins located upstream and fed by rain.
Ceramic fragments and coins from the excavations have shown that the Roman Soldier Tomb complex was enlarged after the Trajan annexation and remained in use for a long time; its destruction was probably caused by the deadly earthquake of 363.

The room that is located in front of the tomb was a large triclinium (No. 235). It is unique in its kind in Petra due to its elaborate decoration. The multicolored walls, in fact, are divided into sections by a number of fluted half-columns, crowned by capitals with an unusual shape, which support a trabeation with a continuous cornice; rectangular niches open in the upper register of the intercolumations, once surmounted by stone mouldings embedded in deep grooves (only a few have remained in situ). It is possible that these niches also housed high-reliefs, similar to those of the tomb. The bench that runs along three sides of the chamber attests to its original function of room for ritual banquets.
The excavations of the Roman Soldier Tomb once again demonstrate how the tombs, the related triclinia and the porticoed courtyards formed an indissoluble

Above - *The Roman Soldier tomb is unusual because of the three high-reliefs that decorate the facade. The overall appearance of the sepulcher closely resemble the Urn Tomb; precisely because of these similarities, several scholars believe that the latter was a model for the tomb carved in theWadi Farasa East.*
Although it is impossible to say whose tomb it was, it is certain that it was destined for a high-ranking individual and his family.
It could even be a royal tomb, but in the absence of specific data this remains a hypothesis.

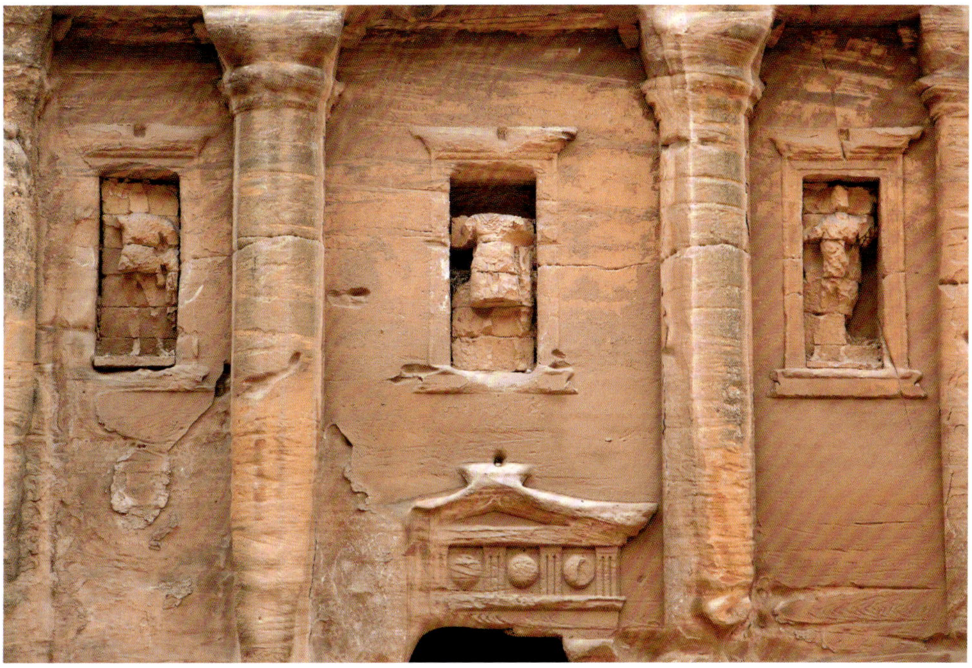

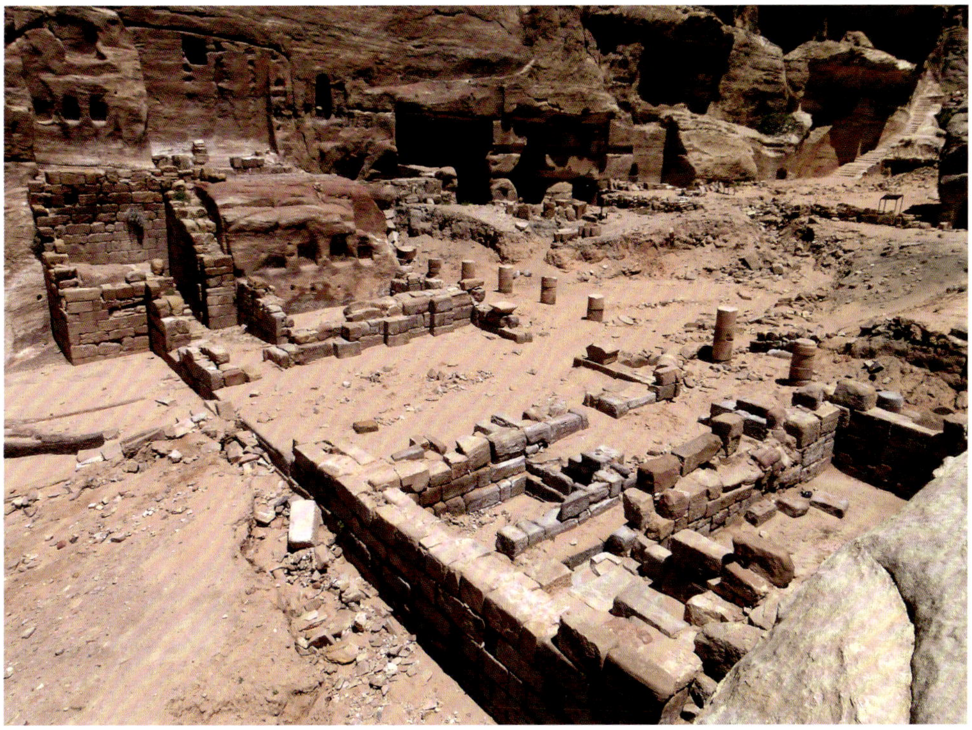

Below - *The excavations carried out in front of the tomb have brought to light not only the remains of the large portico, but also a cistern covered by four arches, a complex network of canalizations, earthenware pipes and even a small bath.*

Next pages - *The splendid triclinium located in front of the tomb. The delicate flutings still visible on the pilasters lead us to believe that the walls of the room were neither plastered nor painted. The entablature and the ceiling were certainly so, as can be seen from some still recognizable traces. The capitals are called pseudo-ionic. The deep hole in the left niche of the back wall dates from post Nabataean times and could have been a tomb.*

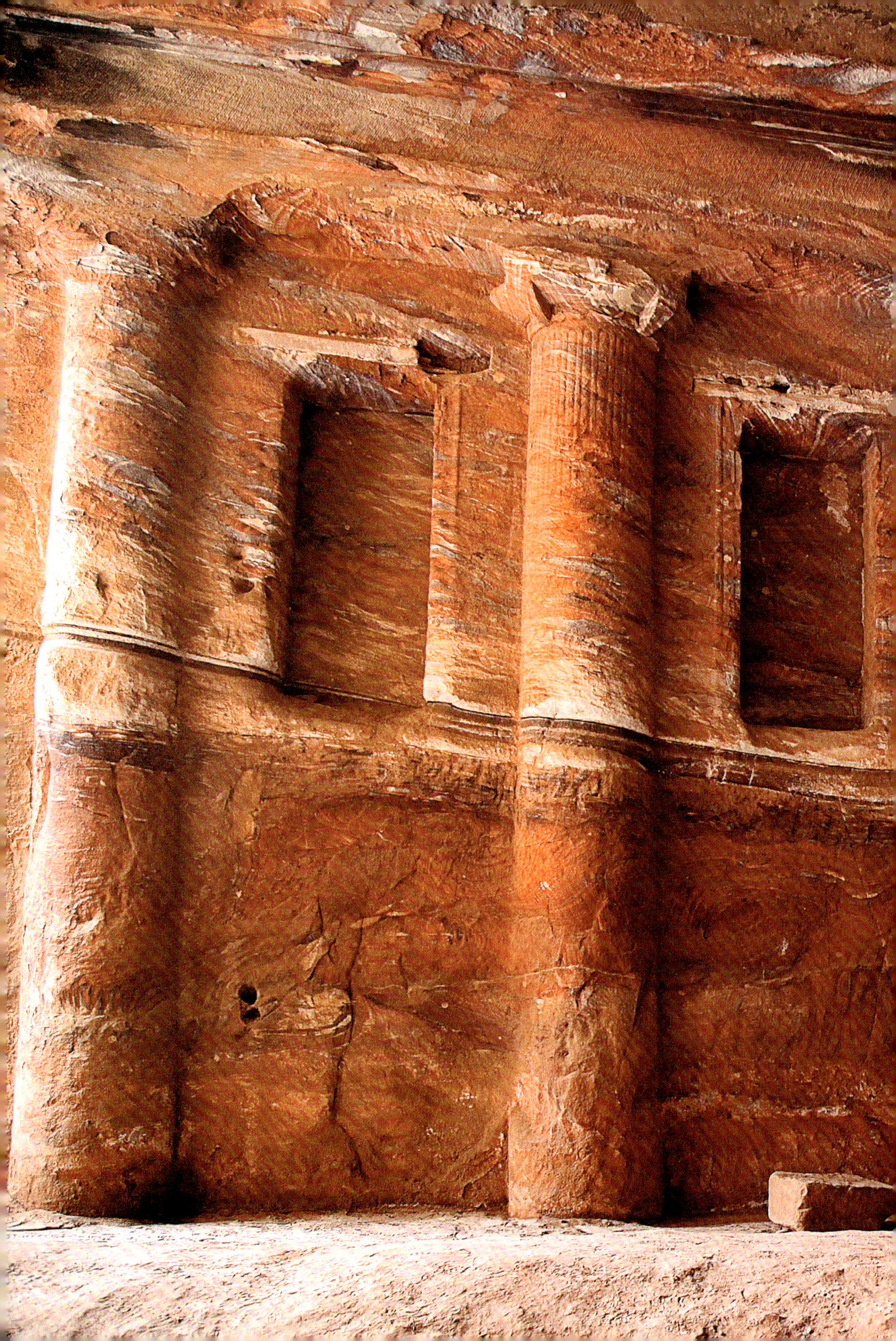

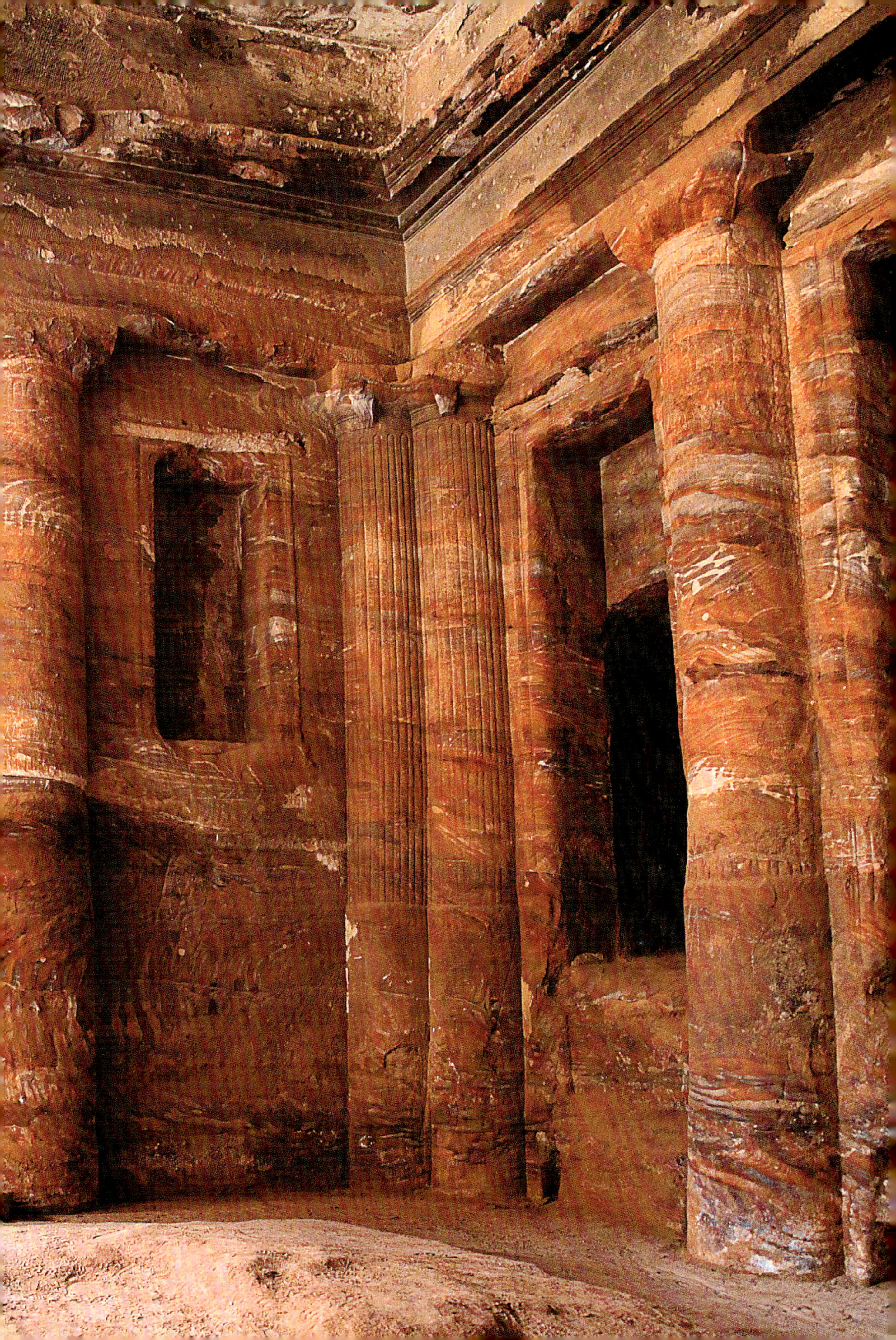

THE ROMAN SOLDIER TOMB: A RECONSTRUCTIVE SUGGESTION

In 1921, Bachmann had already come to the conclusion that there was a large, porticoed courtyard in front of the Roman Soldier Tomb and proposed a hypothetical reconstruction of it. Essentially, the archaeological investigations carried out from the beginnig of 2001 have largely confirmed this hypothesis, but also added some important data. The wing facing north, which reached from one side of the wadi to the other and sealed it off, was formed of a series of different sized rooms, several of which had ceilings supported by parallel arches. At the east and west extremities, these rooms were on two floors, partly added onto the side of mountain and partly carved into the rock. Clearly, the path heading towards the top of Jebel al Madhbah must have crossed the courtyard from north to south, passing through two doorways. In the north wing, a large room (10 x 9 metres), also covered with a system of arches, gave access to the complex, while a second door allowed entry into another room on the ground floor. The wooden thresholds of the doors were perhaps decorated with bronze studs some of which have been recovered by archaeologists of the IWFP (International Wadi Farasa Project). It is not known if there were windows facing outwards in the north wing, but it is quite probable that there were.

The portico on the north, east and south sides of the great courtyard was about three metres wide. From the few remains recovered to date, it is thought that the capitals were in the Doric style. The columns were not fluted, but were probably covered with a thick layer of plaster. The paving was made of rectangular stone slabs, similar to the paving in the various rooms. On the bottom of the cistern, carved underground outside the north wing, many items of pottery made for everyday use have been found, including a large number of plates. This suggests that the complex had at least one kitchen where meals for ritual banquets were prepared. The presence of some heated rooms, part of a small bath complex, also throws new light on Nabataean funeral customs. In fact, while it has been well noted that the tombs were accompanied by triclinia, cisterns and other rooms necessary for putting on banquets and symposiums in honour of the deceased, it is clear that the ceremonies must have been considerably more complex, lasting for days perhaps, thus necessitating rooms for ablutions and maybe even sojourning.

Finally we come to the question of the date of the monument. If it is true that the pottery fragments and other relics discovered among the ruins date to the middle of the last quarter of the 1st century AD, what raises a question is the remarkable resemblance of the armour, worn by the male figure portrayed in the central intercolumniation, with Roman cuirasses. In particular, observing the high-relief in detail and comparing it with statues of the imperial age, you see that the distinctive configuration of the ligature of the shoulder straps and the pterygium (namely the strips of leather used for protecting the bottom of the stomach and the thighs), are very similar to those of the Roman muscle cuirass (lorica musculata)*, used by high ranking soldiers between the late 1st century AD and the first decades of the following century. In the light of this evidence, a likely explanation is that, in the 1st century AD, the Nabataean officers had already adopted the habit of wearing this type of protection from the Roman army, which at the same time showed their status. In fact, some rare coins minted under King Aretas IV show that such armours were also common among the Nabataeans.*

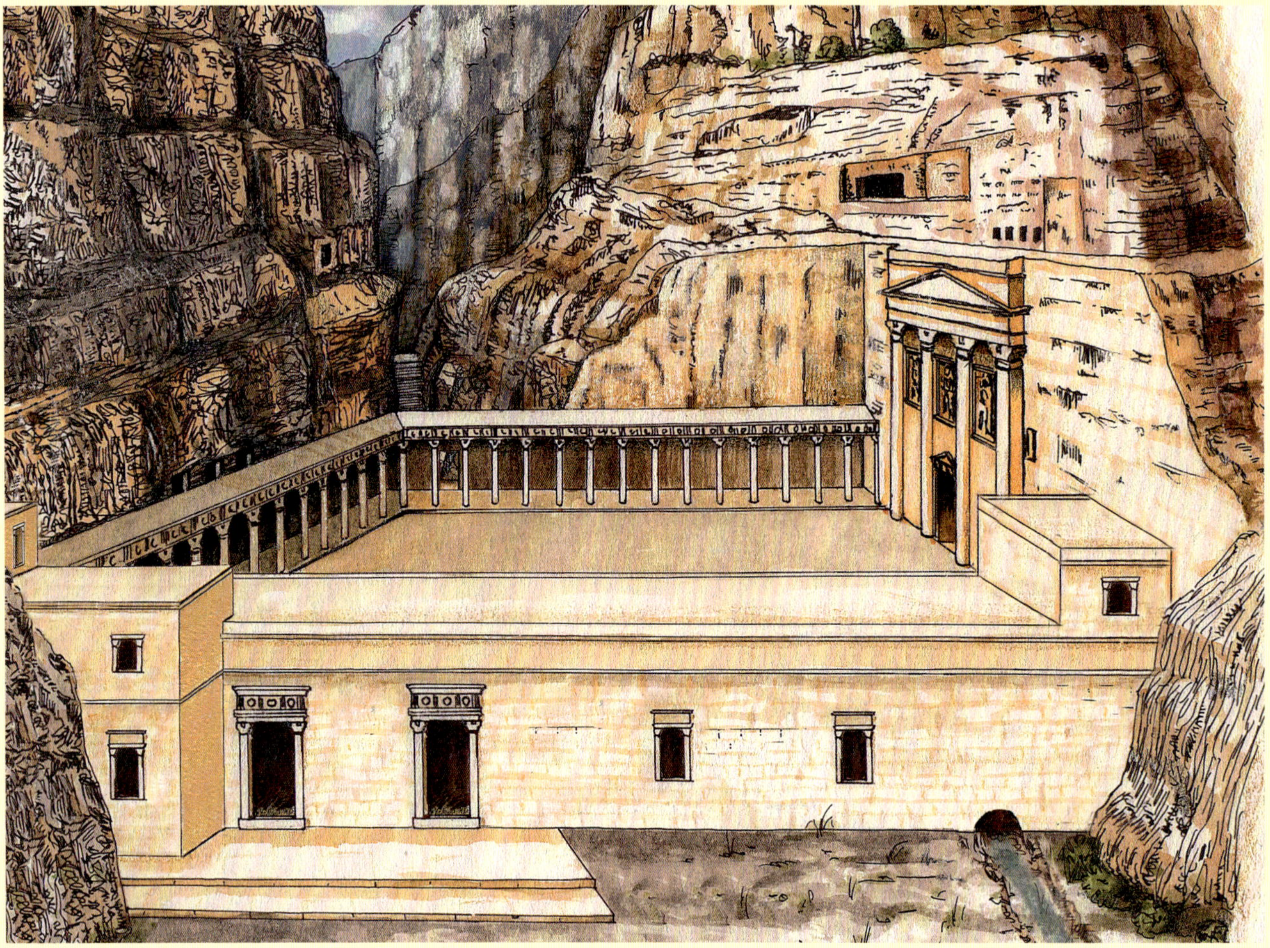

F.Bourbon M. Falcone

whole in Nabataean monumental funerary architecture.
Before leaving the Roman Soldier Tomb behind, it could be interesting to climb the rocky spur, with its rounded shapes, to the right of the facade. There is a stairway leading to the top, where there is a small necropolis with fifteen pit graves. In 2005 they were identified and investigated, revealing that they had already been looted in antiquity, but nevertheless they are interesting because they allow us to understand what these particular burials were like. Several of them retain parts of the closure slabs, while one is simply outlined in the sandstone bank. The stone cutting tool marks are still clearly visible in the rock.
Continuing along the Wadi Farasa (accessible via a steep staircase) you will soon reach a beautiful rupestrian structure, known as the **Garden Triclinium** (No. 244), excavated into a rock buttress in a spectacular position. The front looks like a simple but suggestive portico with two columns *in antis*, surmounted by the usual Nabataean capitals and an entablature with a smooth frieze. The interior consists of a slightly trapezoidal room, which leads to a second, smaller, square-shaped room. Both rooms are completely bare. At the top of the facade, to the left of the pilaster, it is interesting to note a remnant of stucco imitating the ashlars of a isodome wall structure. Yet another clue supporting the theory that the monuments in Petra were partially plastered and painted.
In the first room, until around 1910, the presence of a stele engraved with a rudimentary cross was attested, but it then went missing: it could have been a burial testimony dating back to the Crusader occupation in Petra. The discovery (in 2001) of five other similar tomb stones suggest that this section of Wadi Farasa East was used as a cemetery in medieval times.
In the small courtyard, in front of the facade, there is a cistern dug into the rocky ground and originally covered with the usual system of parallel arches, whose imposts are still clearly visible. This cistern is connected to a smaller one, from which the drinking water was drawn. Nineteenth century travellers gave the monument its name due to its two basins. When the roof collapsed the cisterns were filled with debris and soil, which retained humidity for a long after rainfall, thus helping an authentic grove of oleanders to grow (although in recent times it has been sacrificed for archaeological purposes).
The walls that have been brought to light in the courtyard belong to the Ayyubid-Mamluk period (XI-XIII century) and attest to a reuse of the monument.
The question remains as to what the function of the hypogeum was. It has long been thought, since there are no traces of any loculi in it, that it was a small temple, perhaps there to "protect" the huge nearby reservoir, with its mighty southern retaining wall looming to the right. However, the religious function of the complex has been contradicted due to some elements that now suggest it could have been used for a different purpose.

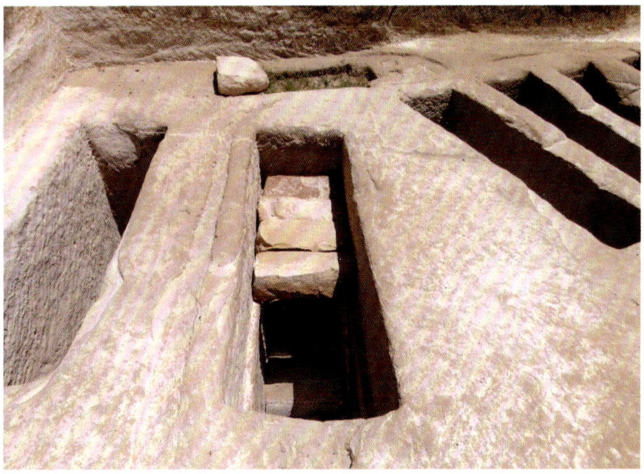

Above - *A glimpse of the small necropolis located north-west of the Roman Soldier Tomb.*
The loculus, excavated a couple of meters deep and vaguely anthropomorphic in shape, was covered with a series of slabs resting on a setback and cemented with mortar. About a metre higher up, a similar cover was prepared. This often allowed two or three bodies to be placed in the same tomb. The upper part was finally sealed with a layer of stone and mortar.
Several skeletons and even a pair of gold earrings were found inside these pit graves.

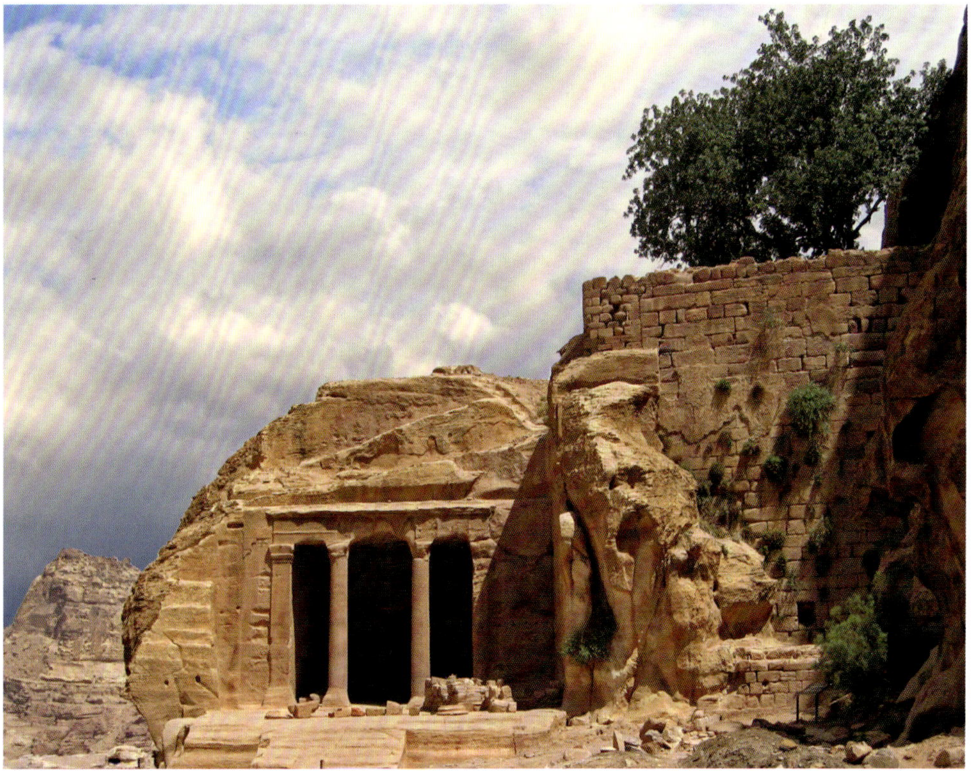

Below - *The so-called Garden Triclinium and the nearby reservoir.*

In particular, the two deep grooves that can be seen, one above the facade and the other in the wall perpendicular to it, suggest that the two columns could have been preceded by a peristyle, with a second floor consisting of several rooms above it. It could therefore be a luxurious home, of a type widespread in Roman times in the eastern provinces of the empire and characterized by a marked alignment of the internal rooms. Among other things, the south-north orientation favored less solar radiation in summer and greater in winter.
Of this housing complex (dating back to the turn of the first century AD) was also part an enigmatic room partially carved into the rock just behind the large reservoir, whose wall made of isodomic ashlars still retains conspicuous traces of the original plaster. In fact, the Nabataeans used to waterproof both sides of the retaining walls with a thick layer of hydraulic mortar, often mixed with finely crushed bricks and ceramic shards. The cistern was 18 metres long, 6 metres wide and the same depth. It was equipped with an internal staircase for maintenance purposes and it would have supplied the whole area of this part of Petra. These days, the large room located north of the cistern is difficult to access, but it is still clearly visible from above and is a bit of an enigma. Indeed, without the facade, it looks like a room with twelve empty niches in the walls. The roof, as shown by the deep grooves in the sandstone, consisted of a stone built barrel vault: an authentic unicum in the architecture of Petra. This mysterious chamber could have been a triclinium, but only an adequate future investigation would be able to confirm this hypothesis. Moreover, a hypogeum with a barrel vault has only been found in Umm Qussa, near Little Petra.

From the Garden Triclinium the road begins to climb up the west face of the Jebel al Madhbah, turning into very steep stairways. Along the first ramps there is yet another hydraulic system, including a square-shaped cistern, which is now full of sand. Continuing along the steep path, at a certain point, you will be able to enjoy a very panoramic view of the Roman Soldier Tomb and the Garden Triclinium, with the large cistern and the niche room. Along the path you soon come across the **Lion Monument**, which was actually a monumental fountain. The large animal, which is dug out of the rocky wall, appears to be headless. The missing head would certainly have had its jaws wide open and from them gushed the water coming from an overlying cistern, served by a

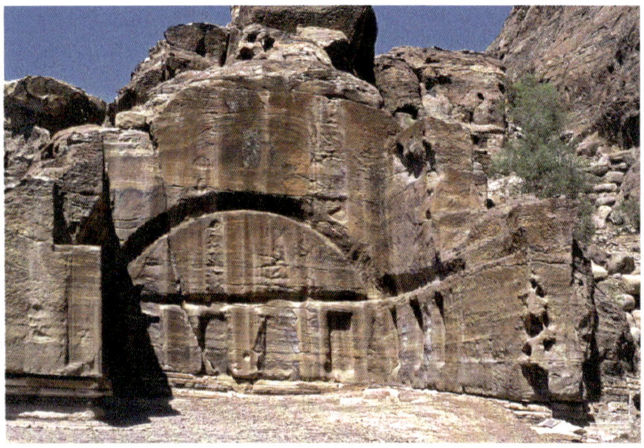

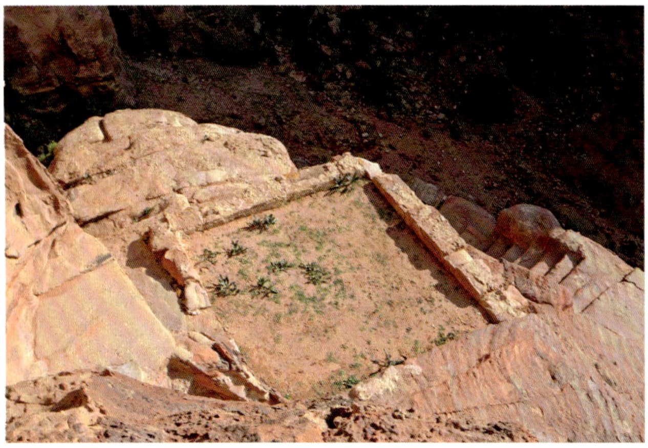

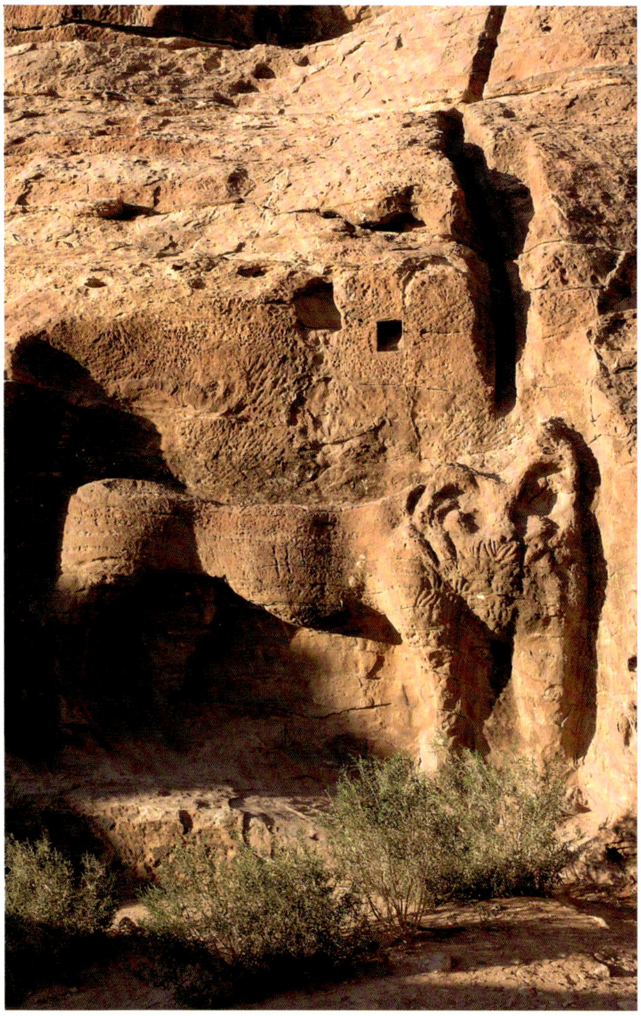

Top left - *The large hall with niches, located north of the large cistern in the Garden Triclinium. This room can be reached by climbing up a very steep staircase to the right of the cistern, but this can be quite dangerous.*

Bottom left - *This large square cistern was part of the hydraulic system that supplied the upper part of the Wadi Farasa East.*

Right - *The Lion Monument was actually a fountain, with a basin in front of it. The lion was one of the animal symbols of the goddess Al Uzza, and it was certainly not placed along a processional path by chance.*
Years ago, the author of an "archaeology-mystery" book claimed that the blood of the victims who were sacrificed on the Jebel al Madhbah high place would have streamed out of the lion's jaws, but this is a fantasy without any foundation.

stair. It is still possible today to see a groove in the rock where the water pipe would have been.
A little further on, somewhat off the trail, there is a large rectangular baetylus, carved into a rock spur that juts out over the abyss. It is inserted inside a double frame and above it there is a circular medallion with a sadly worn bust sculpted into it, probably depicting the god Dushara (assimilated to Dionysus). It is interesting because it is one of the rare figurative representations of a Nabataean divinity, which was immune to the furious iconoclasts, but not to natural erosion. The more curious will notice, among other things, that the divinity wears two *armillae* (i.e. armbands) on his forearms.
A little further on, the processional path continues deeply embedded in an artificial fissure and it is clear that a portal must have been located here, to block access to the "high place of sacrifice". Similar measures are common to several petree rocky roads. Indeed other rock-cut roads in Petra share similar precautionary measures.
The route - very aerial at times - proceeds decidedly on towards the top of Jebel al Madhbah. Almost halfway up, the most attentive ones will notice several votive inscriptions carved in the sinuous Nabataean alphabet on the rocky walls. At a certain point it is possible to gaze down over the Roman Soldier Tomb and the similar tomb in the Wadi al Najir. On the right, a little further along, the tops of two large tower tombs can be seen jutting out. Where the sandstone bank is particularly white, there is a curious semi-circular structure: it is a stibadium, that is, as already mentioned, a rather late type of open-air triclinium. In the distance, the slopes of the Jebel Nmeir extend out as far as the Oboda Chapel and the so-called Southern Necropolis slightly further away. Towards the end of the path, by the side of the road, a deep channel can be seen; this is a section of the Ain Braq aqueduct.
Suddenly you come to a mountain saddle, where there are two stunning rock-cut **obelisks** (No. 89, 90) towering above. In fact, the top of Jebel al Madhbah (1035 metres) is divided into two: the part facing north is occupied by a "high place of sacrifice" (or al Madhbah, namely "the Altar"), while the part facing south is famous for the two obelisks, which are about 7 metres high. Thirty meters away from each other and made out of the rock mass, the monoliths stand isolated on an esplanade that was obtained by digging the top of the mountain. It is commonly thought that they represented the gods Dushara and Al Uzza, but in addition to this, they probably had some kind of an astronomical function, as they are both perfectly aligned along the east-western axis. Since on the Jebel al Madhbah there is a curious votive shrine (No. 199), framed between two pilasters crowned by crescents, it is plausible that the whole area was connected to a lunar cult.
They could also be huge *nefesh* left by the quarrymen in honor of their colleagues died in accidents.

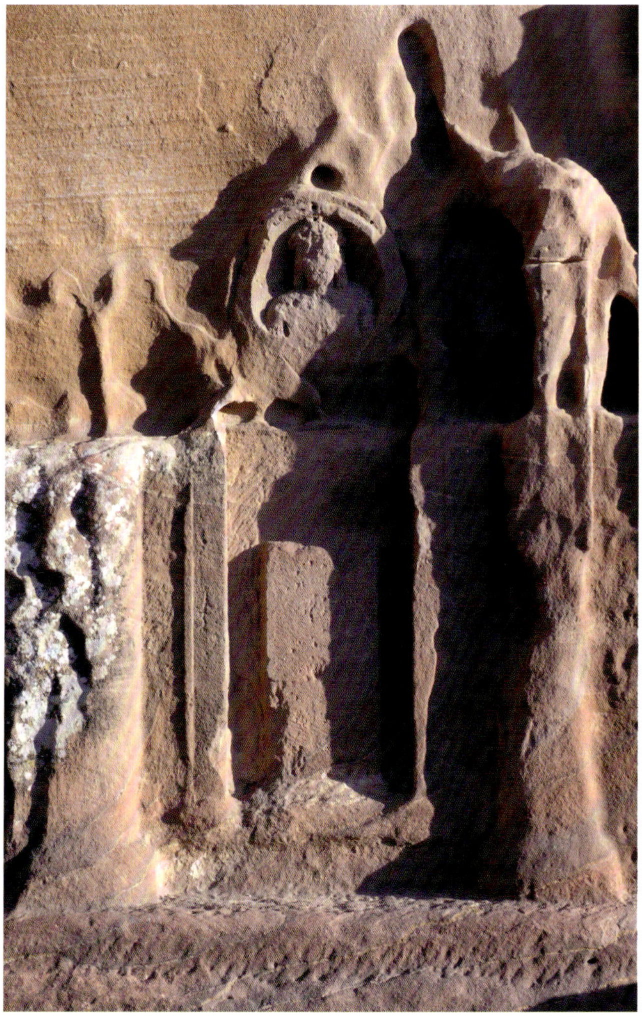

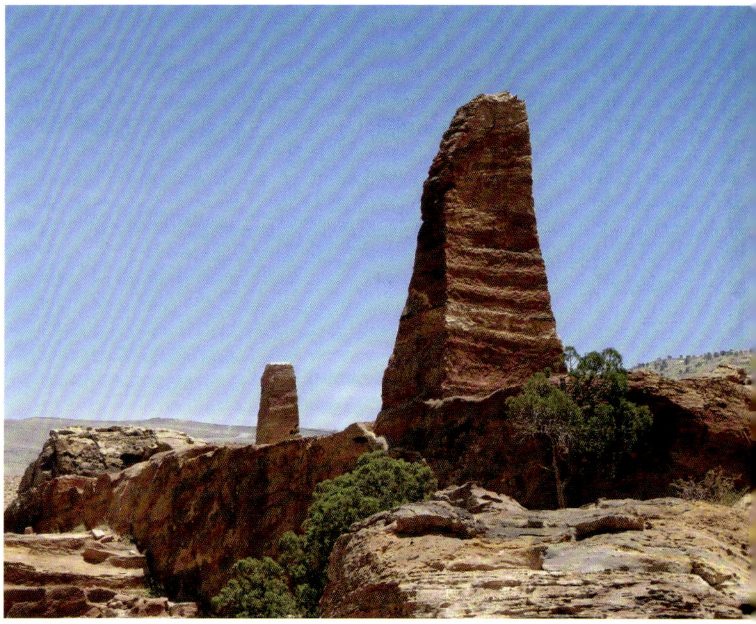

Left - *The votive aedicule carved along the processional path is unique, as it combines the aniconic tradition (represented by the lower baetylus) with the figurative one, consisting of the bust inside the medallion. Some stylistic elements lead us to believe that this is a representation of Dushara. Others say it is the deified king Obodas.*

Right - *It has been calculated that to obtain the colossal obelisks from the living rock of the Jebel al Madhbah, the Nabataeans must have had to remove no less than 3,200 cubic metres of sandstone. However, according to some, this calculation is an underestimation. The local name by which they are known - Zibb Attuf, or "propitiatory phalluses" – has also led to the suggestion that the two monoliths were symbols of fertility, but this theory does not appear very solid.*

THE HIGH PLACE OF SACRIFICE

A rather solitary ruined tower, which was once part of a more complex structure that was erected on the edge of a Nabataean quarry, guards the entrance to the "high place of sacrifice" (No. 86). Brunnow simply called it a "citadel" but a more widespread opinion wanted this to be a fortification dating back to the Crusader period; according to others it was a building dating back to the Byzantine era. Currently, following an analysis of the materials used, and due to how the stone ashlars were processed, it has been concluded that the remains belong to the monumental propylaea (representative gate) of the sacred area on the Jebel al Madhbah, erected during the Nabataean era. Such a large scale construction would undoubtedly attest that this was one of the major places of worship in the whole of Petra to which periodically - perhaps in observance of a calendar linked to the cycle of seasons - the processions of the faithful went up along the sacred road coming from the city. The steep path passes right through the ruins until you get to the top of the mountain. Here, there is the best preserved open air sanctuary in Petra, preceded by a large cistern dug out of the sandstone. At first glance the sanctuary

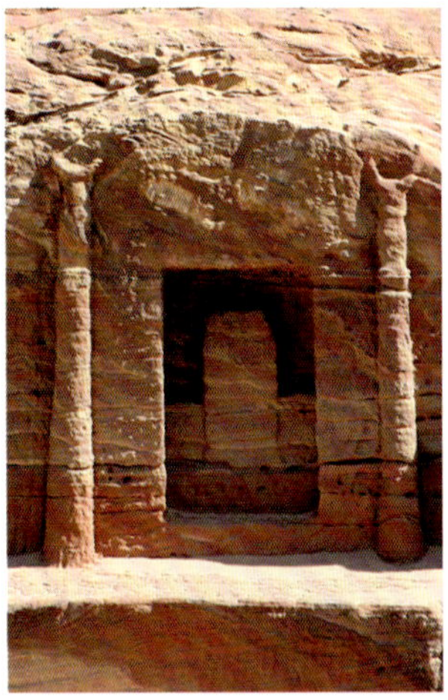

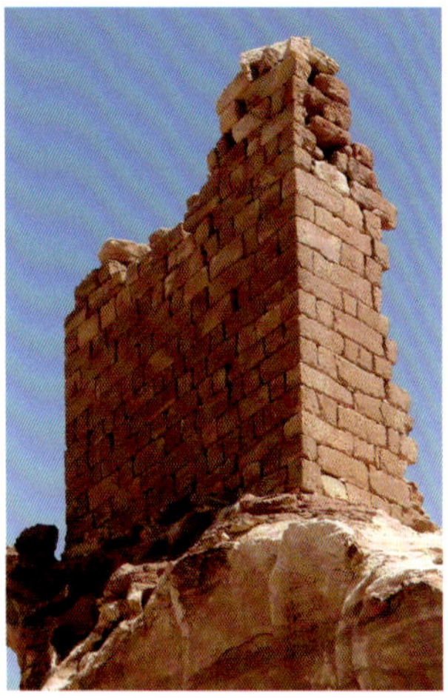

does not look very spectacular, but it is necessary to consider that to obtain this rectangular "courtyard", oriented from north to south, roughly 15 metres long and 6 and a half metres wide, the Nabataeans must have had to flatten the top of the mountain perfectly. The area is surrounded by a low step which probably acted as a triclinium bench for those who participated in the rites and it has a fifteen centimetre high rectangular platform (a sacred table) in the middle, upon which offerings, certainly not bloody ones, would have been placed for the gods (ears of wheat, food and drink). On the western side of the courtyard, in front of the sacred table, a monolithic altar (*motab*) was excavated. It is just under a metre high and is preceded by three steps; everything is oriented along the east-west axis. As there is a rectangular hole on the surface of the altar, it can be presumed that a baetylus, which was a symbol of divinity, was fitted into it. Such a baetylus would have had the appearance of a well-polished block of stone. This ancestral use originates from the Arabian Peninsula; its reminiscence is attested to by the veneration that is still attributed to the Black Stone today, which can be found nestled along the eastern edge of the Ka'ba, in Mecca.

To the left of the altar there is a podium, in which a rectangular cistern and a large circular basin are carved. There are four steps leading up to the latter one, that is equipped with a channel for the outflow of liquids. It is thought to have been a lustral basin, in which the blood of the victims (lambs, goats) immolated to the gods was collected and sprinkled onto the baetylus. The small rectangular basin was probably used for purification ceremonies, in order for the priests to wash their hands and wash sacrificial equipment.

Over the years, some have periodically claimed that this must be Mount Sinai from the biblical tradition, due to its position and the sacred apparatus found on Jebel al Madhbah. However, this theory, which was proposed by Ditlef Nielsen in 1927, does not enjoy much credit. In fact, the references to the biblical patriarch still evident in the local toponyms (Wadi Musa: the valley of Moses;

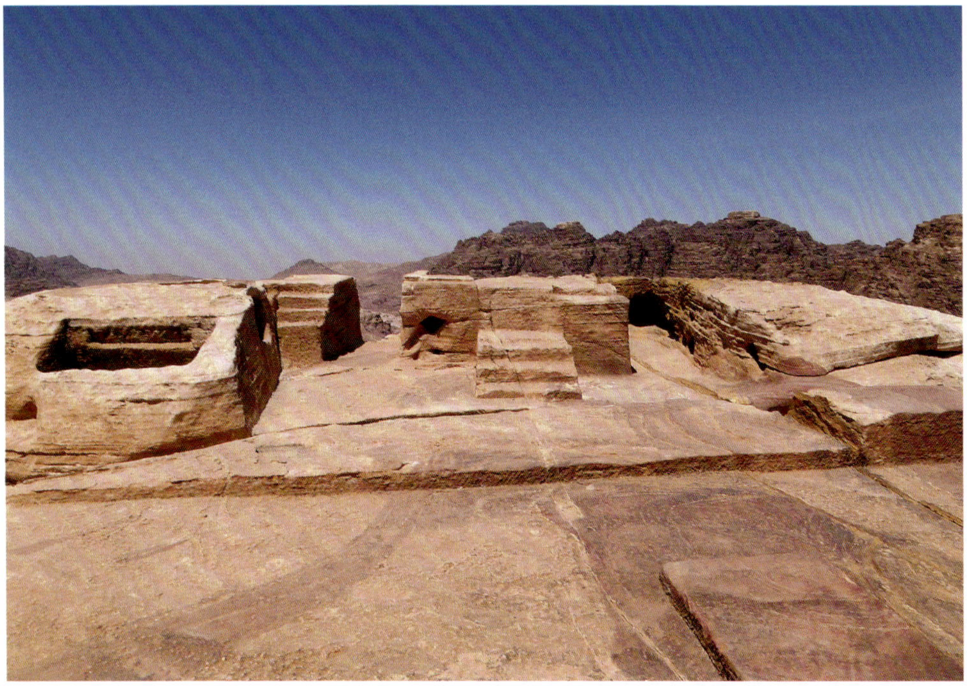

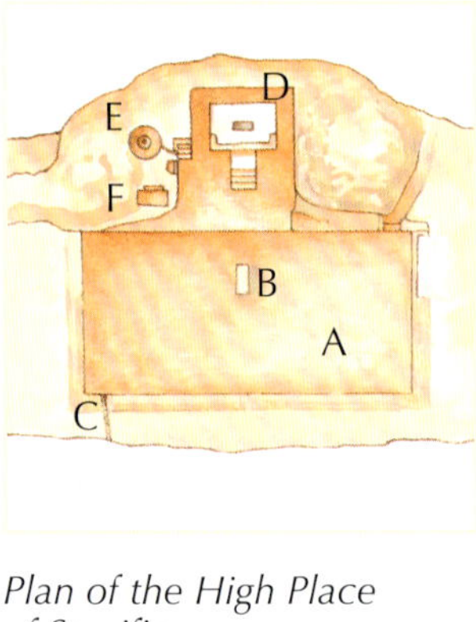

Plan of the High Place of Sacrifice

A Esplanade
B Sacred table *(mensa sacra)*
C Rainwater drainage channel
D Altar *(motab)*
E Lustral Basin
F Cistern

Ain Musa: the Source of Moses) belong more to the legend - or to the faith - than to history.
Venturing on, a little further away from the High Place of Sacrifice, towards the northern edge of the Jebel al Madhbah, you can enjoy a spectacular view of the Petra valley and the Royal Tombs. The aforementioned votive niche with two crescents is located in this area, facing west. It is carved out of a rocky prominence along the slopes of the mountain. A hundred metres lower, there is also an open-air triclinium (photo on page 36).
To go down to the valley you have to retrace your steps until you get to the foot of the tower and you can see the obelisks (there is also a refreshment point nearby): from here the path descends very steeply eastwards towards the narrow valley of Wadi al Mahfur. On both sides, the vertical walls of ancient Nabataean quarries tower over the land; the construction materials for the propylaea were extracted from here. On the wall of the one on the left (that is, facing north) there are several curious V-shaped signs, which can be interpreted as a crescent moon or a comet (or markers left by the stonemasons). The trail soon transforms into a series of stairways, which at times are rather eroded, leading up to the Outer Siq and finishing near Tomb 70.

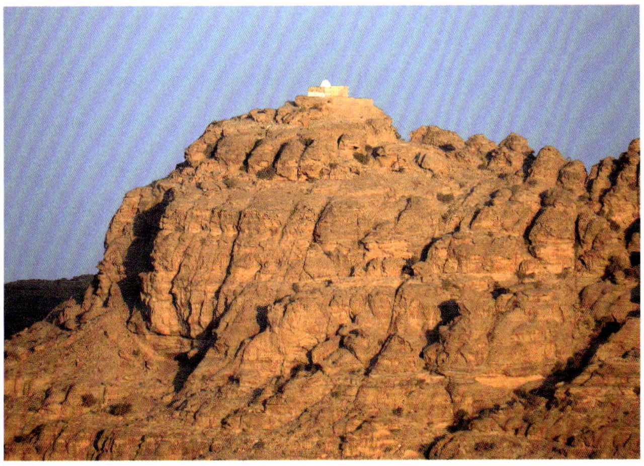

Opposite page, top left - *The curious votive niche decorated with two crescents, located on the western side of the Jebel al Madhbah. Another crescent is visible in the sanctuary known as Sidd el Majin (page 153).*

Opposite page, top right - *The remains of the mighty tower that watches over the access to the High Place of Sacrifice.*

Opposite page, bottom - *The High Place of the Sacrifice was not conceived to accommodate large crowds of worshippers; this is a common characteristic in all the other open-air sacred places in Petra. It is believed that the sacrificial victims were mostly young goats.*

Above - *As noted on the opposite page, the high place altar is oriented towards the top of Jebel Haroun; perhaps the mountain was sacred for a Nabataean deity.*
It is located about 11 kilometres southeast of Petra and it can be identified with the biblical Mount Hor. Tradition has it that on its peak, Aaron, the brother of Moses, died and was buried according to divine dictates. Today, on the summit, there is a small, blinding white mosque, built in the XIV century on an existing structure. A little further down there are the remains of a Byzantine monastery. The tomb, sacred to the three monotheistic faiths, is still a pilgrimage destination; a 5 to 6 hour walk from Petra to its summit.

THE STONE QUARRIES

As you near the end of the processional path, it is worth turning your attention to the vertical wall that rises up to your right. This is the front of a quarry, along which a steep staircase climbs, formed by rows of square, parallel holes (photo above). It gives you the shivers just thinking how Nabataean quarrymen nonchalantly used these vertical staircases, although some Bdoul teenagers still use them today... Similar quarries are found pretty much everywhere. The material used to construct buildings, temples, dams and substructures came from here. The stone still shows signs left by the simple tools of quarrymen: pickaxes, hammers, scalpels, chisels, gouges and awls. Blocks were gradually extracted from top to bottom, in line with what is known as "step cultivation" and moved by sledhes on inclined planes made of crushed stone and sand. The final result was a vertical wall like those visible in the two photos. This ancient methodology remained popular for millennia, even in places far away from each other - a testament to the fact that man finds similar solutions to the same old problems regardless of time and space. This is displayed in the photo below, which portrays an old volcanic tuff quarry on the island of Santa Maria, in the Azores.

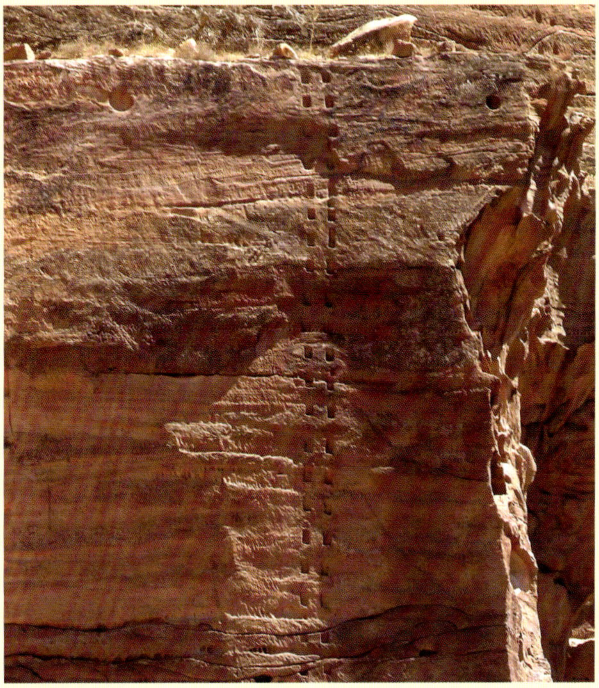

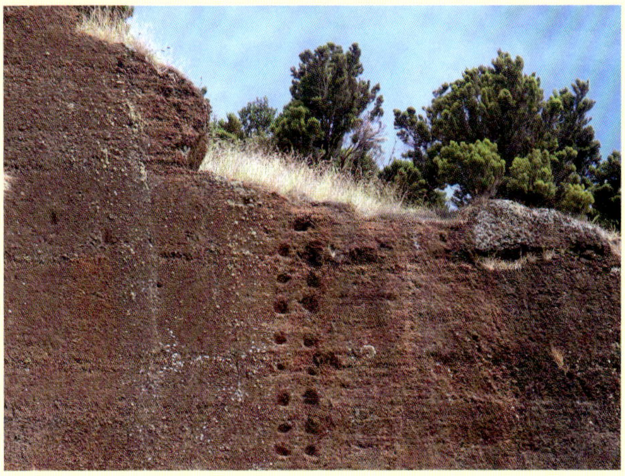

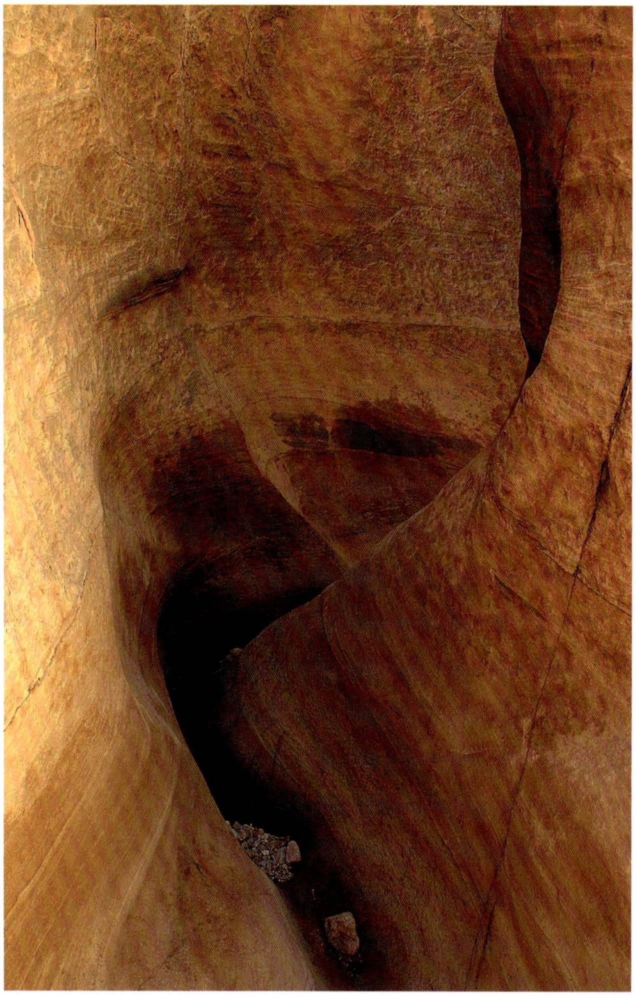

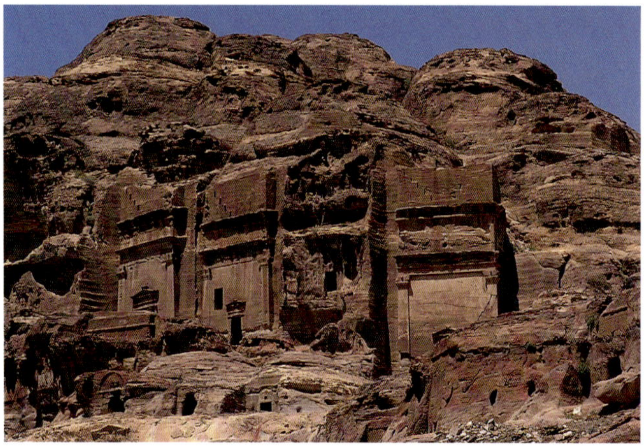

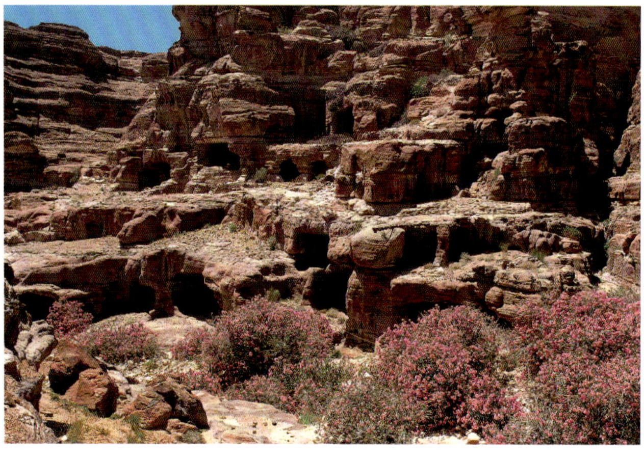

Top left - *The Wadi Muthlim trail - or Little Siq - is exciting all the way, especially along the last stretch, where the gorge transforms into a very narrow gulley, and it is only possible to pass through one at a time. The rocks have been shaped over thousands of years by seasonal water-course erosion.*

Centre left - *The slopes of Jebel Ma'aiserat are home to a vast necropolis, which extends between the Wadi Turkmaniyya and the Wadi Kharareeb. On the latter there are some large tombs (No. 523 and 522), near to which there is a bas-relief of a man on horseback.*

Bottom left - *The pebbly shore of Wadi Siyyagh is dotted with lovely oleander groves. Here there is also a sanctuary dedicated to Isis.*

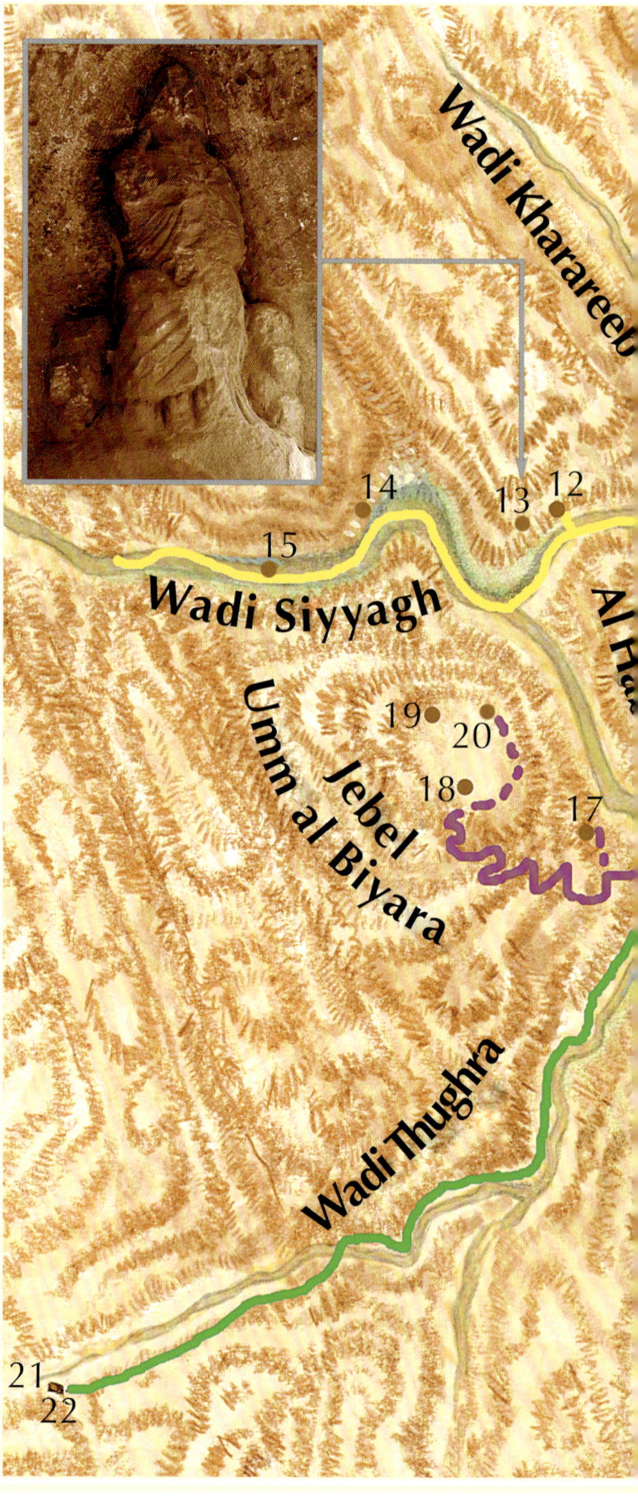

OTHER AREAS

The areas illustrated on the following pages are recommended for all of those who wish to deepen their knowledge of Petra, which will of course involve more effort and some long walks. As there is hardly anyone in these parts, taking a good supply of food and water is recommended. Furthermore, given the impervious nature of the routes, appropriate footwear and clothing should be worn.
Anyone wishing to tackle the descent to the Little Siq - or Wadi Muthlim – should carefully consider the weather conditions: the itinerary must not be attempted during the rainy period, or if storms are expected in the area. The sudden floods literally live up to their name, and hit the valley with extraordinary violence, as happened in November 2018.
The climb to the top of Um al Byiara is not recommended for those suffering from vertigo.
On the other hand, these excursions allow you to discover some very characteristic monuments, all in the context of extraordinarily pleasant landscapes.

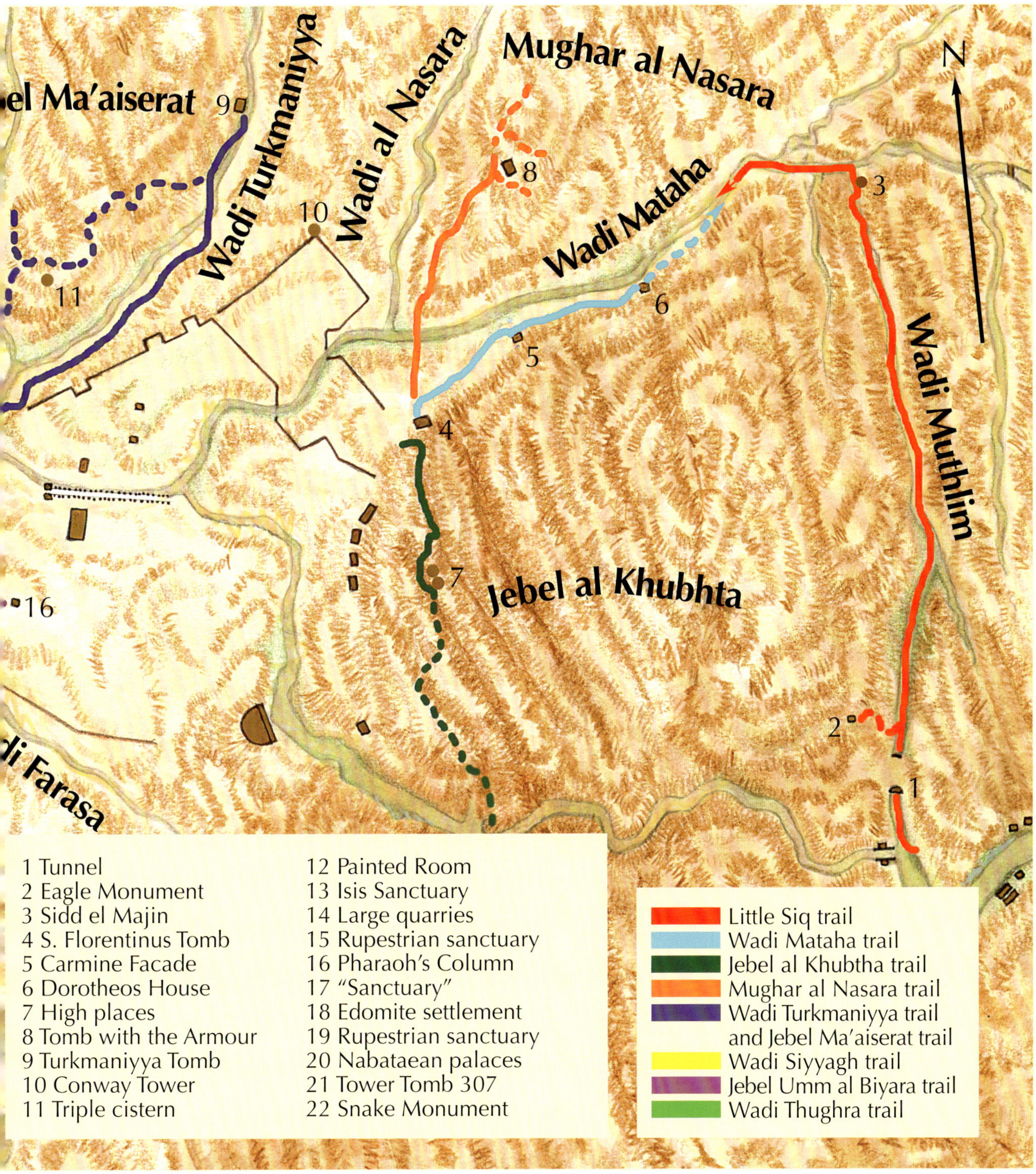

Monica Falcone

THE LITTLE SIQ

This itinerary involves a long march along the shore of a seasonal stream, where floods are continuously changing the conditions of the route. It is only suitable for expert walkers who are used to taking on steep slopes using mountaineering techniques, because at a certain point it is necessary to descend a cliff of about 6 meters, where a waterfall periodically forms. The area is deserted and so in the event of an accident it would be almost impossible to call for help. Additionally, in hot weather, an abundant supply of water is required.
Apart from these considerations, the natural environment is spectacular, with sandstone outcrops that display incredible polychrome marbling. Moreover, it is quite common to come across an *Agama sinaita* with its bright blue livery. Ultimately, thanks also to the arcane silence that pervades the ravine and the tightness of some spectacular passages (where the opposite walls of the canyon are about a metre away), this is certainly one of the most exciting routes in the Petra area, however difficult it may be.
Little Siq, or Wadi Muthlim, collects its water from Wadi Musa through a deep ditch and a tunnel dug by the Nabataeans to the right of the mouth of the Siq to divert the river's disastrous sudden floods. So firstly, you need to go into the ditch - which may have had an arch spanning it, erected to commemorate the extraordinary hydraulic work - then go through the tunnel. Just beyond the tunnel (not to be entered into in the event of impending thunderstorms), you will see a rather steep and poorly traced ramp on the left-hand side, which allows you to climb up to the rocky plateau above, but with a certain degree of difficulty especially when, in the hottest hours of the day, it literally turns into an oven. Turning your back on the wadi, you immediately notice - just to the right - a rocky wall with several niches and baetyli carved into it. The most conspicuous of them is the so-called **Eagle Monument** (No. 51), a votive shrine that may date back to the Roman domination due to the bird of prey in between two slender pilasters that support a sort of broken pediment; its wings are spread out in a similar way to the legionary insignia. However, it is worth remembering that the eagle was also one of the symbols of the god Ba'al-shamin.
From here it is advisable to retrace your steps. The more adventurous can instead venture into the wadi, whose left side is dominated by a very light sandstone rounded hill, with a long dizzying staircase carved along its

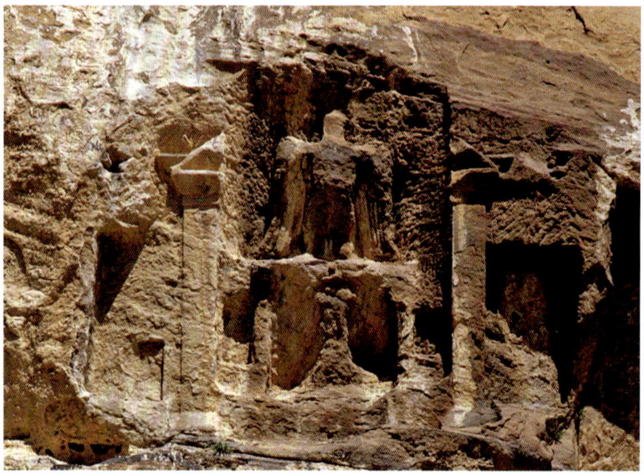

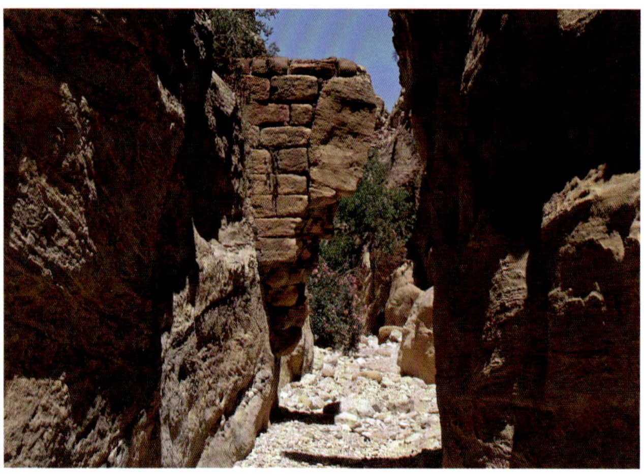

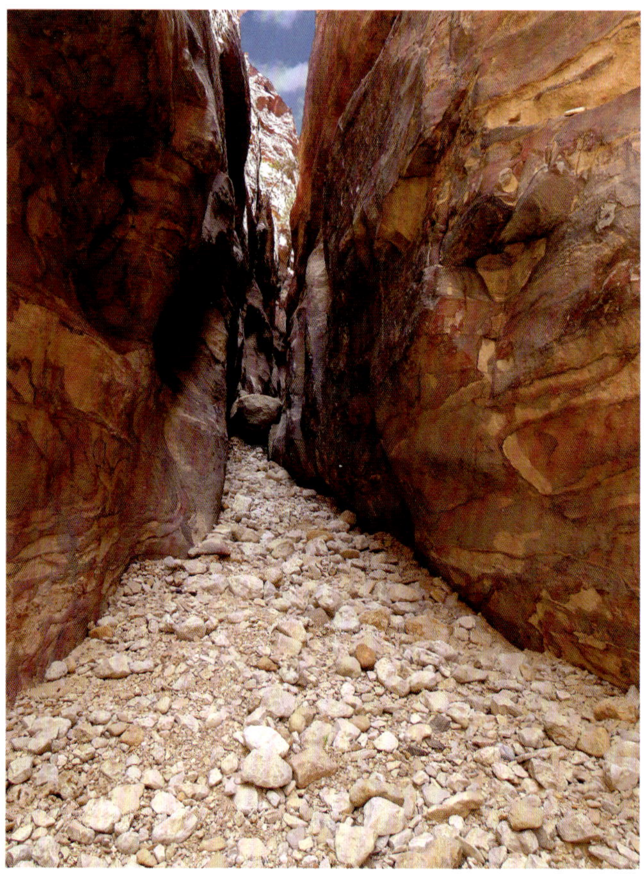

Top left - *The Eagle Niche, maybe a Roman monument.*

Bottom left - *The remains of a Nabataean dam are visible along the Little Siq, or Wadi Muthlim. As can be seen, the construction technique was very robust. The masonry was secured to the rock face with a skilful system of mortise and tenon joints*

Right - *One of the impressive and colourful bottlenecks in the Wadi Muthlim.*

Opposite page, top left - *The votive niche inside which is carved the Isiac crescent.*

Opposite page, bottom left - *Another view of the Little Siq, along one of its narrower passages. Here the walls are just over a meter apart.*

Opposite page, right - *The large aedicula carved into a side of the Sidd el Majin, a suggestive rock sanctuary perhaps connected to the cult of the waters or of Isis.*

slopes; very eroded, it leads to an isolated "high place of sacrifices", or open-air triclinium. However, getting to it is virtually impossible, and also dangerous due to the considerable steepness and exposure of the ramps.
The pebble and gravel bed, dotted with oleanders, becomes narrower and more recessed as it passes through rough, sandstone walls. On several occasions it almost appears to slip into a kind of cul-de-sac, but this is just an illusion caused by the way the gorge makes sudden curves and right angled turns. After the crag, that has already been mentioned, the canyon becomes a fissure with sides that have been smoothed by thousands of years of erosion, causing the most fantastic shapes and colours to form. In some places the gorge is so narrow it barely allows even one person to pass through and the bizarre rock shapes require cautious movements. Without a doubt this is one of the most photogenic places in Petra. However, in case it has rained recently, it is not unusual

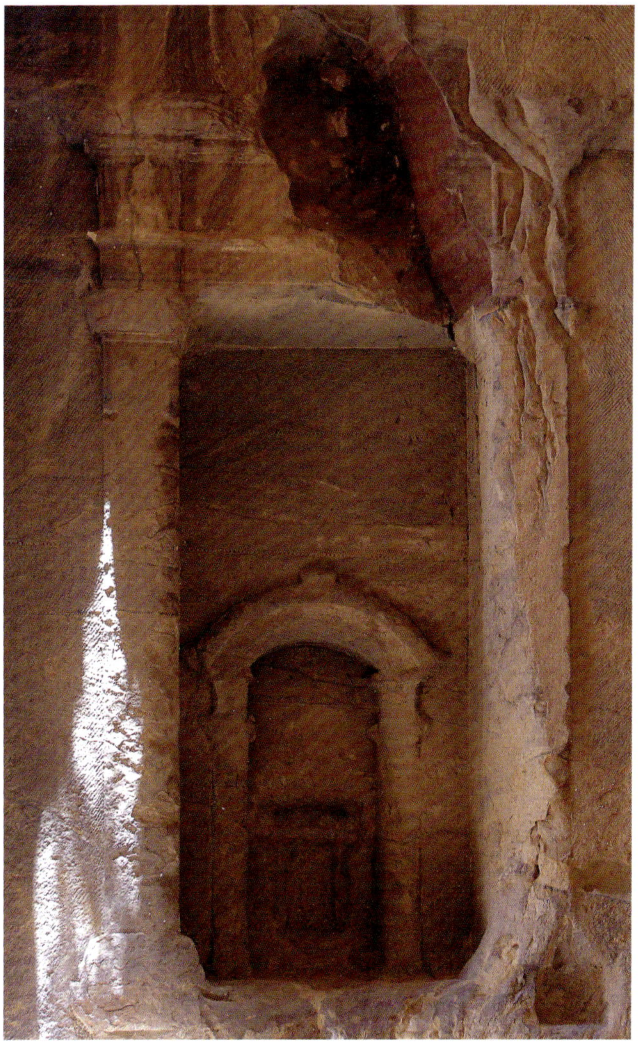

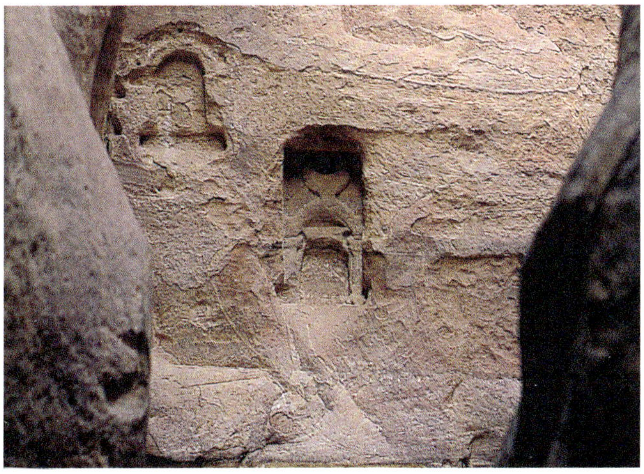

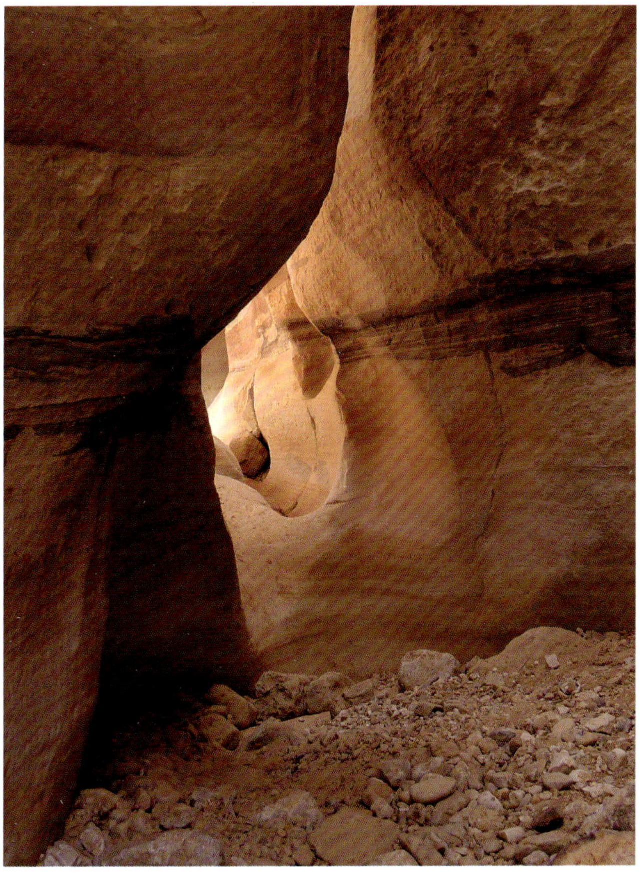

to have to wade through shallow pools of water. The sudden appearance of numerous votive niches, carved along the canyon's vertical walls, indicates that this little adventure is coming to an end. One of the niches has a crescent moon inside, a symbol of the goddess Al Uzza-Isis. A few meters further there is one of the best kept secrets of Petra, namely an evocative rock sanctuary, called **Sidd el Majin** and carved into the walls of a huge pothole. On its eastern side there is an astonishing 5-metre high aedicule with very elegant proportions. It consists of a small niche (where the image of the divinity was placed, probably a baetylus), framed between two half-columns and connected by a curvilinear pediment, which in turn are set between two high pilasters crowned with capitals and an architrave adorned with two busts. The effect is stunning and calls for quiet contemplation. The extraordinary similarity of the bust on the left (the other is very damaged) to the ones that adorn the aedicule inside the Room 468 (p.132) allow us to date the monument to the middle of the first century AD. Also in this case it is a female figure holding a torch (or a cornucopia) and it is therefore very probable that the same divinity was worshiped in both sanctuaries, perhaps the goddess Isis.
Leaving behind the welcoming shade of the sanctuary - where local shepherds often cool off - we reach the point where the Wadi Muthlim converges into the Wadi Mataha, following which we will finally arrive to the Palace Tomb.

THE WADI MATAHA

Although the proposed route is not particularly difficult, it should be tackled during the coolest part of the day, and a good supply of drinking water should be taken; it is worth remembering that the sun heats up the valley from mid morning to sunset.
From the Sextius Florentinus Tomb (page 98), continue along the rather visible path which goes into the valley of the Wadi Mataha and runs alongside the overhanging slopes of the Jebel al Khubtha. A few dozen metres from the ground, along the mountain wall, you can clearly see the deep groove where one of the main aqueducts of Petra, the so-called Khubtha North (page 25) ran, carrying water to the large basins dug out next to the Palace Tomb.
It is interesting to note, that in several points, the horizontal pipeline is intersected by natural vertical fissures, which every now and again contain temporary waterfalls created by storms. In recent times it has been demonstrated, contrary to popular belief, that the main aqueducts were carefully sealed and did not receive any additional rainwater. This has been confirmed due to a technical feature that is preserved along the route of the aqueduct: a small, masonry-built viaduct, allowing the pipeline to cross a gully, while still permitting rainwater to flow beneath it. These temporary waterfalls, where necessary, were intercepted by channels and small artificial basins downstream, supplying the cisterns that were dug out near the numerous cave dwellings throughout the urban area. In fact, the entire

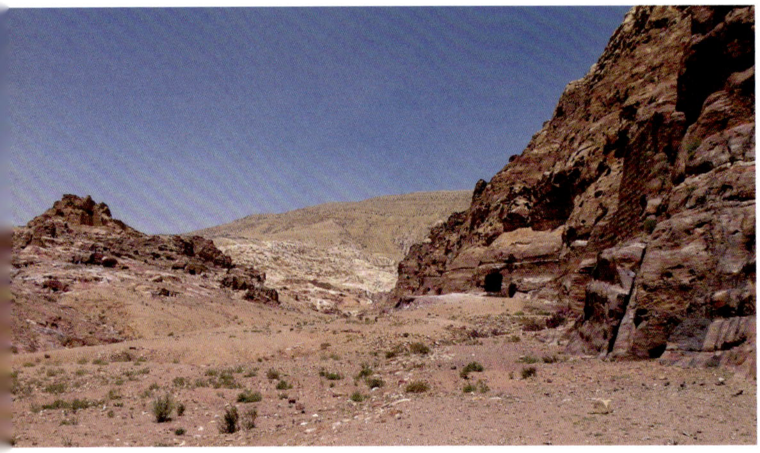

side of the mountain is dotted with large numbers of hypogea, votive niches, tricliniums, cisterns and stairs made of foothokds especially carved for the maintenance of the aqueduct. The absence of tombs in the area demonstrates that this must have been a residential suburb of the city. Following the drastic fall in population in Petra after the earthquake of 363 in the Byzantine era, the area became depopulated and remained outside the city walls.
After walking for a few minutes you will see the dramatic wide open mouths of the two hypogea on your right. The largest one is a triclinium, while the one next door was possibly a service room. To the right of the triclinium there is a deep gutter carved into the rock, which would have fed an underground cistern. It is not easy to see from this position, but just above the two hypogea, at a height of a few dozen metres, there is an incredibly complex system of artificial terraces, all arranged at different levels, as well as stairs, channels, reservoirs and small dams which were used to collect rainwater and convey it to the terraces. There are still several trees and even a "hanging" grove that thrive in them. It has not been officially studied but this complex demonstrates, once again, the extraordinary engineering expertise of the Nabataeans, although it is not possible to say with any certainty what the real function was. As it is difficult to envisage how these "terraces" were just simply basins, buried over time, it is possible to imagine that this area was somehow intended for agricultural purposes.
Once you have passed other smaller hypogea and cisterns tanks now largely filled with soil, you soon come

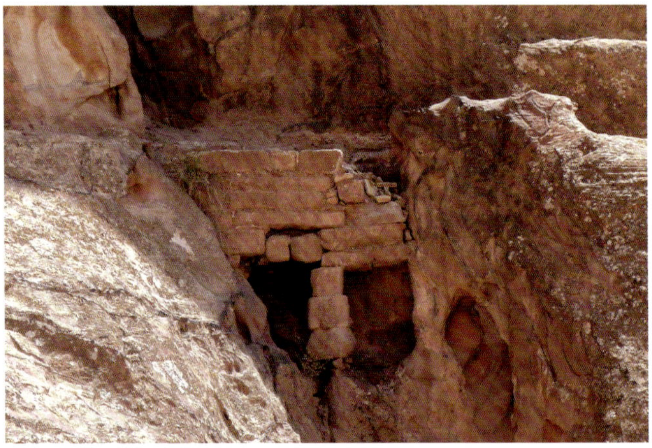

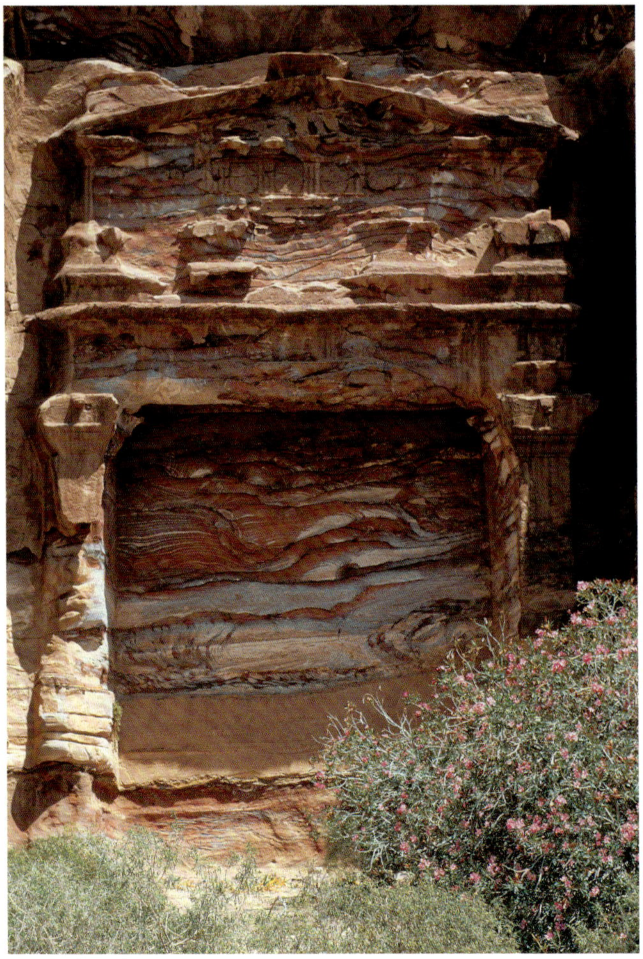

across the so-called **Carmine Facade** (No. 731), with the spectacular polychrome to which it owes its name. It is dug deep into the rocky wall and faces what appears to be a vast courtyard, separated from the valley by a partly ruined wall covered in a thriving oleander grove. The structure is of the pediment type; the two lateral pillars are completed by "horn» capitals, which support an architrave and a double cornice, surmounted by four very short pilasters. These in turn support a beautiful Doric frieze in Nabataean style, that is, with flat round metopes . The tympanum is crowned by a small acroterion. What makes the monument so unusual is the fact that it lacks a door, and therefore an internal room. According to some, this monument could be an unfinished triclinium, but it is likely (given the degree of finishing of the various architectural details) that its purpose was quite different: perhaps an enormous votive shrine.
The frieze with metopes and triglyphs is very reminiscent of the Deir and this, together with other technical details, leads us to date the monument to at least the second half of the first century AD, if not later.
Near the Carmine facade there is a large cistern, which has had the sand emptied out of it, and now serves as a watering hole for goats.
Continuing along, we finally get to the **Dorotheos House**, that is, a group of hypogean rooms arranged on several levels with a steep stairway leading to them. It would have been home to a wealthy family and would have been equipped with every comfort, including some large tanks that are still in use; however,

Opposite page, left - *On the right of the Wadi Mataha towers the wall of the Jebel al Khubtha, while on the left extends the Mughar al Nasara.*

Opposite page, top right - *This viaduct is still visible along the path of the aqueduct excavated on the northern slope of the Jebel Al Khubtha.*

Opposite page, bottom right - *The Carmine Facade, without a hypogeum, is a real enigma for archaeologists. Since this was a residential area and there are no tombs, it is possible that the monument was designed as a triclinium room, which was left unfinished.*

Above - *A glimpse of the upper part of the so-called Dorotheos House.*

Below - *The Dorotheos House is one of the best preserved dwellings in Petra. The acqueduct groove stands above it.*

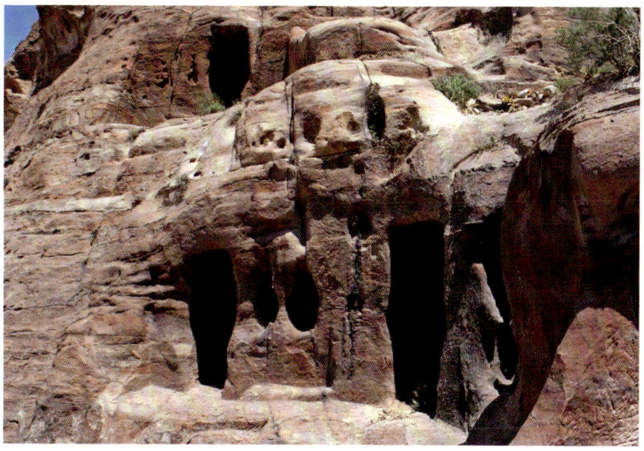

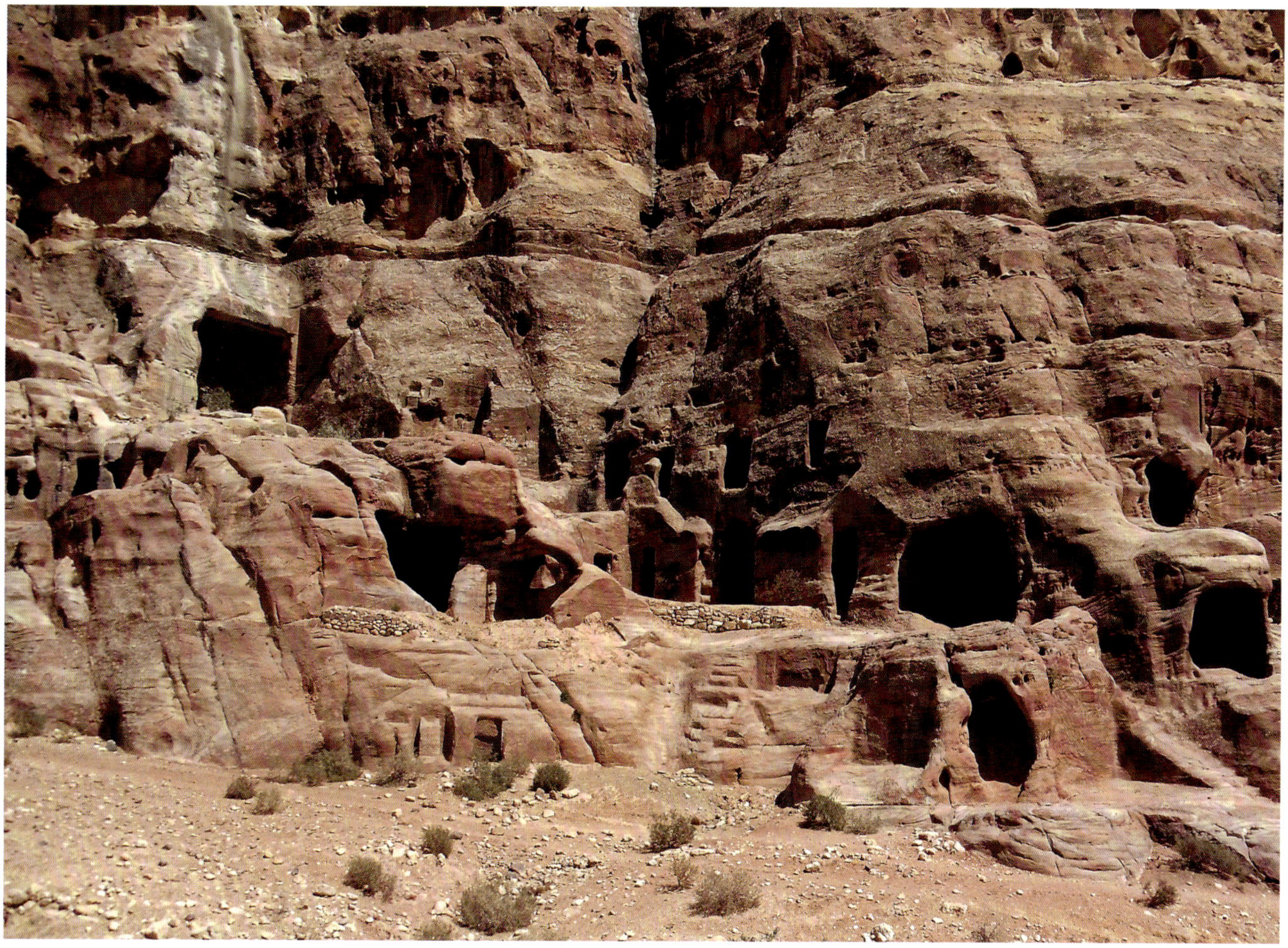

it is difficult to guess what the real functions of the various rooms were. The name attributed to it derives from two identical Greek inscriptions that are engraved on the benches of the largest room, which was a triclinium. This spacious chamber is accessible through three doorways, surmounted by as many windows. The wonderful coolness in this room demonstrates how wise it was to live in a hypogeum. The complex, which has a dozen rooms, even includes a private cult area, complete with a monolithic altar. Some rooms are lit up by the sunlight seeping through windows carved into the stone, others have a door preceded by a sort of terrace. It is not known whether the facades originally had architectural decorations or if they were plastered.
To the left of the large triclinium, a very steep flight of stairs leads up to the rock aqueduct, probably for maintenance purposes. The interesting fact is that the groove looks like a deep L-shaped incision in the side of the mountain, but from here on it is completely devoid of a side wall facing downstream. So much so, that at first glance, it is like being in front of an incongruous, aerial walkway. Evidently, at least in this section, the water did not flow into a channel (as in the case of the southern Siq aqueduct); instead, it went through a terracotta piping, the elements of which have disappeared, however.
From the Dorotheos House, the more curious can go even further on, continuing along the slopes of the Jebel al Khubtha, where several other ancient cave dwellings can be seen (some of which are still in use). On the right of the modern masonry embankment, which checks the occasional and violent flood waves, there is a narrow ravine: this is the downstream outlet of the Wadi Muthlim, or the Little Siq, as already described. Continuing along, just a few metres more, into the silent canyon (never if a storm is forecast), you will very easily reach the rather evocative sanctuary of Sidd el Majin, but the ascent up the ravine to the tunnel is rather demanding from a physical standpoint, and so it is not recommended. It is better to retrace your steps, or look for the best way to cross the stony bed of the Wadi Mataha and go up the northern side, entering into what was once a suburb of Petra, but is today known as Mughar al Nasara.

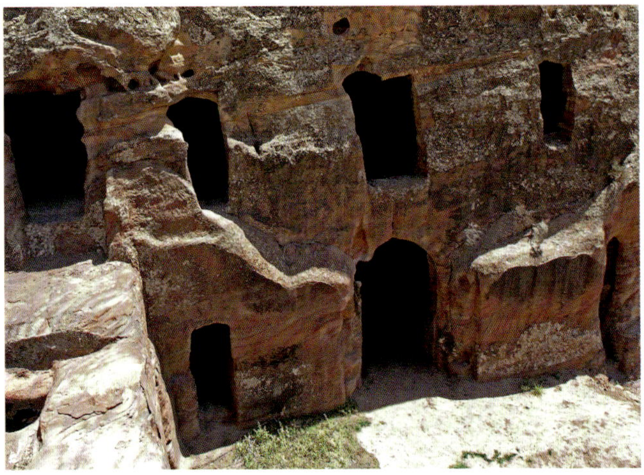

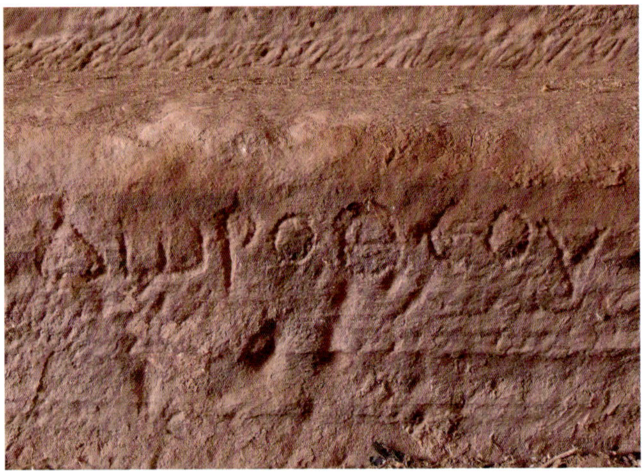

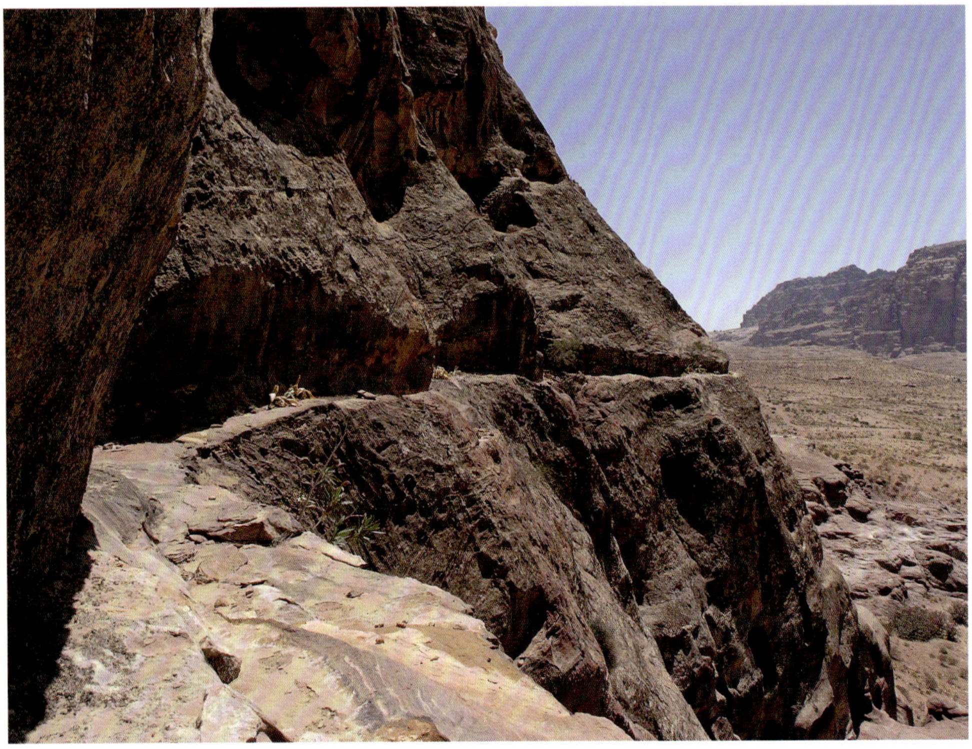

Top - *The large triclinium is the most impressive room in the Dorotheos House.*

Centre - *One of the graffiti that gave the complex its name: it reads Δωροθεου, "of Dorotheos". It is unknown what or whom it refers to.*

Bottom - *A spectacular view of the aqueduct, almost on the vertical of the large triclinium. Strangely, from this point on the deep groove does not have a sidewall, which is instead present in the upstream section. Perhaps this indicates two temporal phases in the construction of the aqueduct, which initially arrived here and only later was continued. From this point on, the water had to flow into a pipeline.*

THE JEBEL AL KHUBTHA

To the left of the Palace Tomb, a well-marked path runs alongside the slopes of the mountain, and soon turns into steep staircases that are partly carved and partly built with ashlars. The spectacular processional road that that winds its way up to the top of the Gebel al Khubtha, with a theory of long hairpin turns carved in the living rock, starts from a formidable cut where still today two wooden jambs and a beam mark the position of an ancient portal, evidently guarding the path. From here on, the gaze is captured by extraordinary views of the gorge and the underlying valey. At a certain point the rear part of the surviving wall structure at the top of the PalaceTomb can be easily observed; though further on, the huge auditorium of the theatre monopolizes attention. The inclining planes are followed by endless sequences of steps that are either very worn or have been redone in recent times. In fact, the real interest in this arduous climb lies in the path itself and in the formidable panorama that can be enjoyed during the journey. The real achievement is seeing two contiguous high places of sacrifice, carved out of two rocky outcrops, though much more modest than the one on Jebel al Madhbah. One of the two esplanades - or open air triclinia - has a curious shape, as the shorter side is made up of a small stibadium (No.769); there would have been a building or even a temple nearby. The other one is rectangular, with two large basins dug alongside it.
Here, it is also evident how the high places of sacrifice were positioned in such a way as to ensure that there was a perfect view over the city and other high places, and therefore they would have formed a sort of circle - or crown – maybe having a mystical-religious or even apotropaic function.
Nearby, there are also a dam, a cistern that still retains an arch from the original roof, a large underground area and the ruins of some difficult to interpret structures, one of which was probably a watchtower or an observatory.
In the western sector of the massif (also known as Jebel Umm al 'Amr) a recent archaeological investigation has identified the remains of a small thermal plant, partly rock-cut and partly built in elevation, with two large cisterns, originally fed by a complex channel system and two sturdy, rock-cut aqueducts. The surprising complex, including a canonic frigidarium, tepidarium and calidarium, appear to belong to the period after the Trajan conquest of Petra (106 AD). Since the baths do not seem to be connected to any ritual function, and as there are the remains of other buildings, some of which have been identified as dwellings in the surrounding area, it is certainly possible that a residential district could have developed on top of Jebel al Khubtha in Roman times. This appears to be the case due to some findings of ceramic fragments dating back to the second and fourth centuries AD, confirming that Jebel al Khubtha may not just have had a religious-sanctuary role but it could also have had a civil one too.
A well-marked panoramic path leads to a belvedere - where there is an unmissable Bedouin tent - and from which you can enjoy an unusual view of the Khazneh below. Another trail goes down to the Urn Tomb, but it is very impervious and too dangerous. On the way back it is essential to take the well-known path.

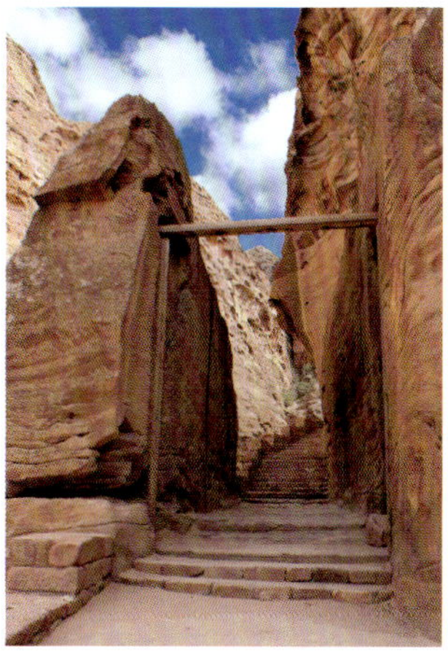

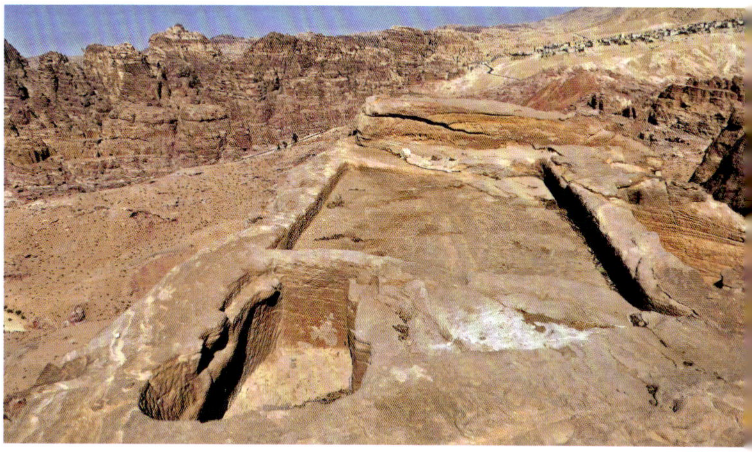

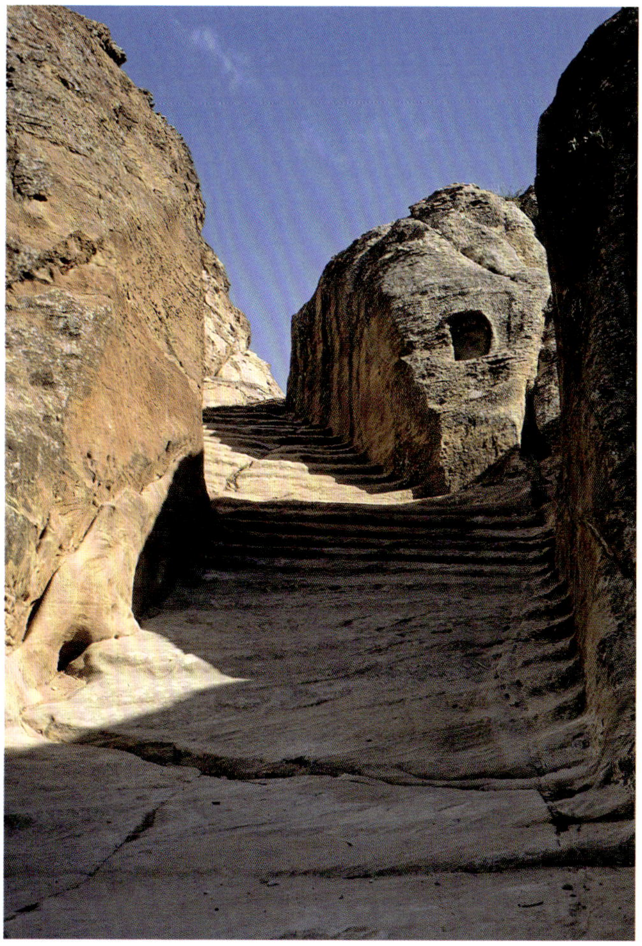

Top left - *The point where the processional road was closed by a portal.*

Bottom left - *It is the route itself that makes the climb to the top of the Jebel al Khubtha so fascinating.*

Right - *One of the two high places of sacrifice excavated on the summit of the Jebel al Khubtha. Close to the nearby stibadium stood a large sacred building or a pavilion of unknown use.*

THE MUGHAR AL NASARA

As this itinerary goes across rather difficult terrain, it should be tackled in the coolest part of the day. From the Sextius Florentinus Tomb (page 98), which should be kept behind as a reference, it is necessary to head north-east, upstream across the bed of Wadi Mataha, and then, just as you meet Wadi an Nasara (easily recognizable by the intense reddish hue of sand and rocks), you need to bend to the right and follow a rather distinct track. Diverging slightly to the left, the more curious can observe the remains of a massive wall structure, made of huge, well-connected blocks. This is what is left of a mighty dam that was put into place to block the Wadi al Nasara water course: it was part of an elaborate weir system designed to protect the city centre from sudden floods during the spring and winter months.
Keeping Wadi an Nasara on the left, go up to the rocky outcrop pierced by ancient quarries and numerous tombs. This is Mughar al Nasara, a sector of Petra which is outside the city walls and owes its current name – Caves of the Christians – to the numerous crosses found in the monuments in that specific area, which are signs of ancient Nabataean tomb reuse. Indeed, the term Nasara means "Nazarene", the name by which the Arabs once called Christians. Bear in mind that there are numerous treacherous pit graves in the multi-coloured sandstone banks. In the surrounding area there are several other less well-preserved tombs (a real catalogue of the Nabataean architectural types) and related courtyards carved into the rock. However, the monument that deserves the greatest attention is the so-called **Tomb with the Armour** (No. 649), with a double cornice (Hegra) facade and an attic marked by four short pilasters with Nabataean capitals. In the spaces between, there are two large sculpted masks in relief and in the centre there is an trophy of arms with an armour in the middle, which evidently gives the monument its name. This decoration is the only one of its kind found in Petra. Considering the subject matter of the bas-relief, the sepulchre could have been prepared for a high-ranking military man and his family (inside there are at least 8 niches) but this is only a guess.
The facade is preceded by a large courtyard carved out of stone, which was probably surrounded by a colonnaded portico.
The road deeply carved into the rock (and very eroded by the washout) that passes right in front of the Tomb of the Armour, is rather enigmatic; excluding the possibility that it could have been a sacred route, it remains to be thought that it was a Nabataean caravan track directed north-east towards the Namla pass, about fifteen kilometers away from Petra. From here the road then descended towards the Wadi Arabah, passing some springs along the way, and probably continued towards the Negev and the Moyet Awad caravan station; this route also connected Petra to the important copper mines in Faynan.
It should be remembered, that in ancient times, there were several other caravan routes that went from Petra to the Wadi Arabah depression, continuing on to commercial stations in the north, south and west, and to the port cities of Gaza and Aqaba. These roads were traveled

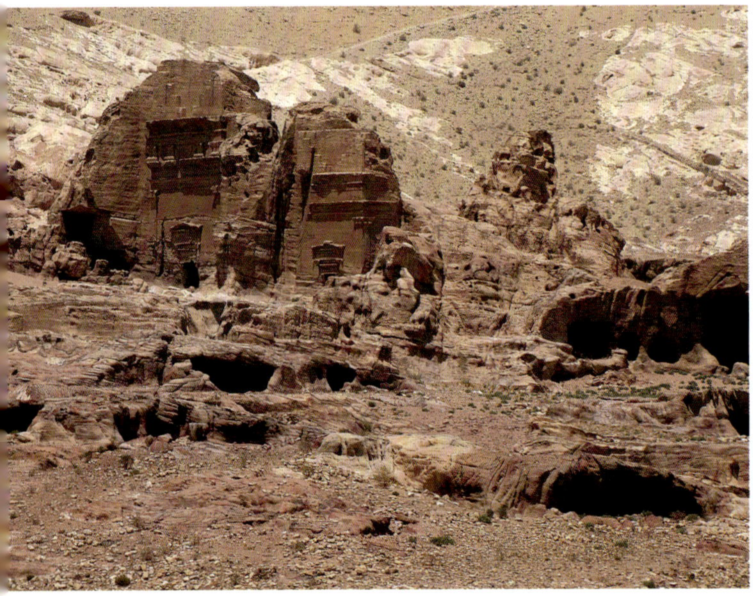

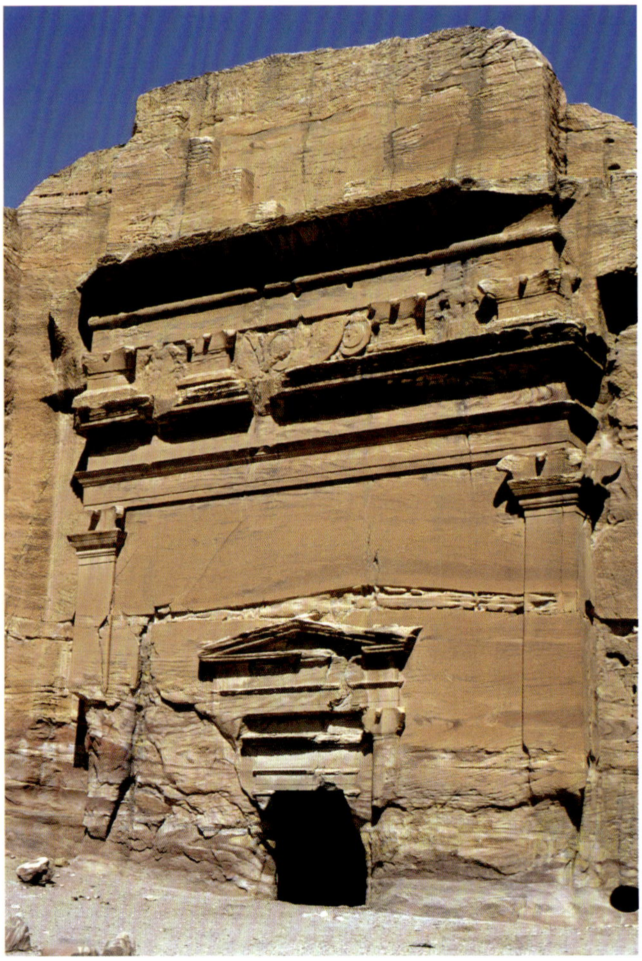

Left - *The characteristic reddish rocky ridge where the Mughar al Nasara tombs are carved is recognizable from afar. As you get closer, you can see that the whole area is littered with rubble (ashlars, even fragments of columns) and that remains of walls emerge here and there In ancient times this was a densely populated residential district of Petra.*

Right - *Because of its weapons and armour frieze, the Tomb with the Armour is one of a kind, not only in Petra, but in all Nabataean funerary architecture. Not even Hegra can boast a similar decoration.*

according to the season, the convenience of the Nabataean caravans and the type of pack animals used (donkeys or dromedaries). One of these routes, it seems rather used, went up along the Wadi Ma'aiserat, passed through al Barid (namely Little Petra) and then forked, reaching the Wadi Arabah crossing different mountain passes (Namla, Slaysil and Aqib). It is believed that al Barid was in fact a "terminal" for the large caravans that were bound for Petra, which did not go down to the city, but unloaded and loaded their wares right here. This point is rather important as it allows us to understand how Petra's "urban landscape" would have looked. It is unthinkable that caravans made up of hundreds of dromedaries could have made their way to the city centre and used it as a stopping point. It is easy to imagine how bad the traffic would have been and how public hygiene

Petra. The road continues north, winding through a series of cuttings into the rock, until it disappears at the foot of Umm Sayhoun, the modern Bedouin village.

To the right of the Tomb with the Armour there are some other sepulchres: one of them (No. 652), of the double cornice type, adorned with an elegant tympanum portal framed between two pilasters, has the right side of the facade collapsed to the groud. The comparison with a photograph published by Brünnow in his *Die Provincia Arabia* (1904-1909) attests that the collapse occurred in the early twentieth century.This reminds us that infiltrations and rock subsidence constantly threaten the monuments in Petra.

Visiting the surrounding area can take a few hours so remember that the journey back to the entrance gate is quite a way from here.

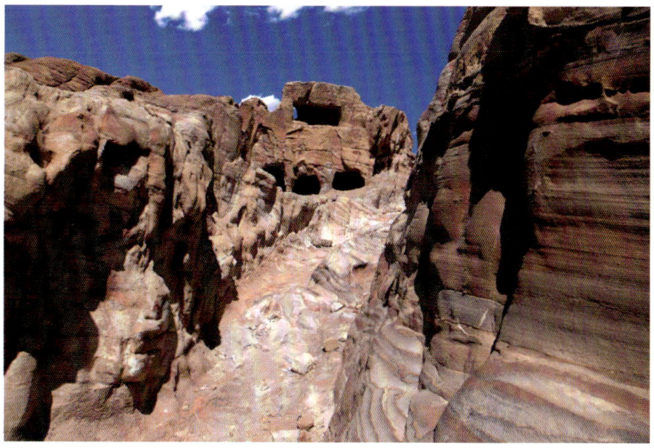

Top - *A stretch of the road, deeply carved into the rock, that runs right in front of the Tomb with the Armour.*

Centre - *A detail of the elaborate frieze on the Tomb with the Armour. Although it is very eroded, it is still possible to distinguish (from left to right): a large mask with a thick beard, an oval shield with a double-edged axe, a round shield adorned with a Medusa head in the umbo, an armour (breastplate) with pteryges, an oval shield with another head of Medusa (?), an axe and a round shield decorated with a lion protome, a mask similar to the first one. It is interesting to note that the breastplate is very similar to the one in the Roman Soldier Tomb.*

Bottom - *The half-collapsed tomb that stands on the right hand side of the Tomb with the Armour.*

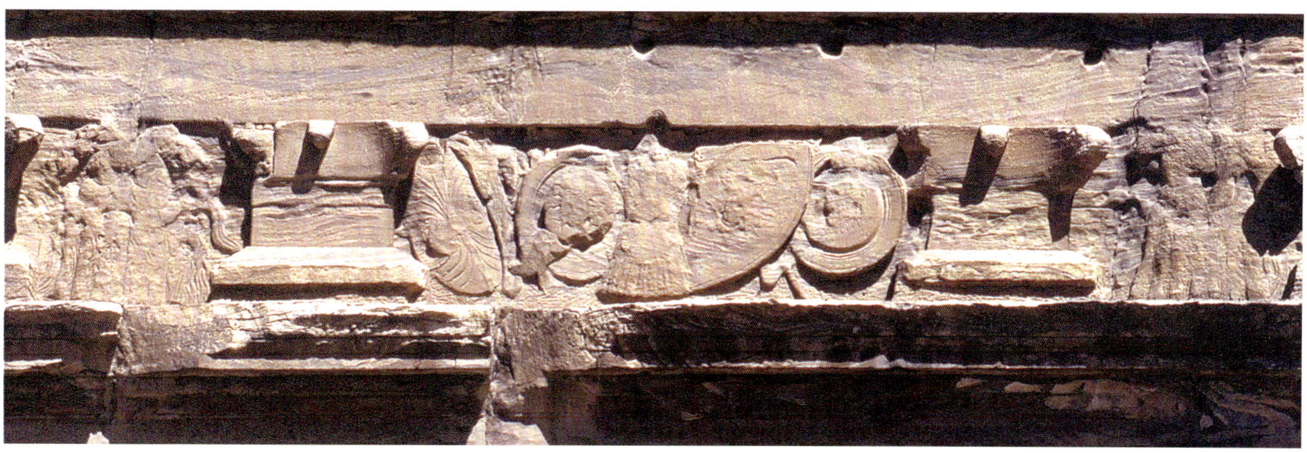

would have suffered as a consequence of such a cumbersome presence. It is therefore probable that the "ships of the desert" would have had special parking areas for loading and unloading their goods, which would have been located all around the metropolis, along the major roads. From and to these satellite stations, the merchandise would have been taken and moved around manually or by donkeys or mules.

Following the road a little way upstream, away from the Tomb with the Armour, you will see an altar that is preceded by some steps on the right, and an open-air (unfortunately rather eroded) triclinium a little further along. Here, the sandstone has an almost blinding whiteness, in stark contrast to the reddish rocks all around. Undoubtedly this is one of the most colorful and exciting scenarios among those offered by the "multicoloured"

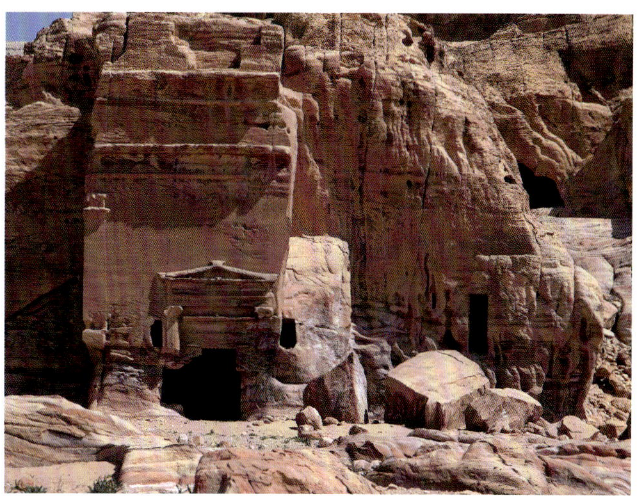

THE WADI TURKMANIYYA AND JEBEL MA'AISERAT

This itinerary starts in front of Qasr el Bint, following the modern, travel-friendly road that goes through Wadi Turkmaniyya (also called Wadi Abu Olleqa): consequently it is practicable without any difficulty.
What immediately catches the eye is the large amount of oleander plants, which suggest that there is a relative abundance of water in this area. In fact, here there were large crops already at the time of the Nabataeans, watered by the usual system of channels but also by the wadi itself, whose bed was once barred by a dam. These days, the agricultural vocation has been restored in the area, so much so that the locals doggedly manage to irrigate several orchards as well as olive groves. For the most part, they still use the ancient hydraulic systems and the Ain Abu Olleqa spring, which flows right into the lower part of the wadi (it is in a pipe today and no longer visible).
On the right, in an elevated and rather evocative position, there is an eye-catching tomb, with a facade that was excavated out of a tower of square-shaped rock, the last testimony of a Nabataean stone quarry. Other quarries are visible throughout the entire valley, and an empirical probability calculation of just how much material was extracted in the area suggests that many more buildings were built in the Petra basin than can be imagined today.
All of a sudden, after taking a slight bend to the left, you will come across the unmistakable facade of the **Turkmaniyya Tomb** (No. 633). It is easily recognizable because the lower half is completely missing (perhaps eroded over the centuries by the disastrous floods of the wadi, or perhaps intentionally demolished when the tomb was used for other uses). It is a double-framed tomb (Hegra type), with the front closed between two half pilasters with a quarter column attached, and punctuated by two half columns framing the entrance. The lower attic floor is punctuated by four short pilasters, which are in line with the underlying half columns, and crowned with typical Nabataean capitals; on the upper attic floor there are two tall half merlons. Unusually, the interior consists of two large intercommunicating rooms.
The reason why the tomb is so important lies in the carved inscription in the central intercolumniation under the rectangular niche, whose function remains unknown. Although the owner's name is not mentioned, all the elements of the sepulchre are meticulously enumerated, including the vestibule and the funeral chamber with relative niches, the porticoed courtyard in front of the tomb, the triclinium room, the cisterns and the retaining walls. All these properties are placed under the tutelage of the god Dushara, and finally it reminds us that no one else can be buried in the tomb except those who have the right (i.e. the sons and relatives of the deceased). This confirms that the Nabataean tombs were dedicated and "bound" to a god (for the most part Dushara), who acted as a protector against thieves.
This epigraph, the longest existing in Petra, is of fundamental importance for the study of the ancient language but also for understanding that the Nabatean burials, in addition to the actual tombs, included numerous accessory structures, most of which were destroyed by earthquakes and floods. Furthermore, as the inscription was

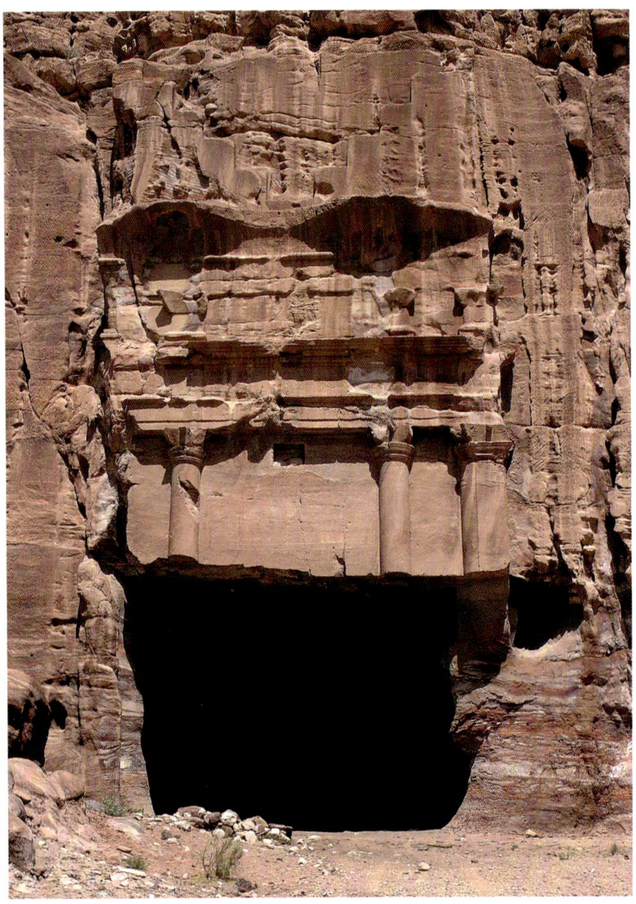

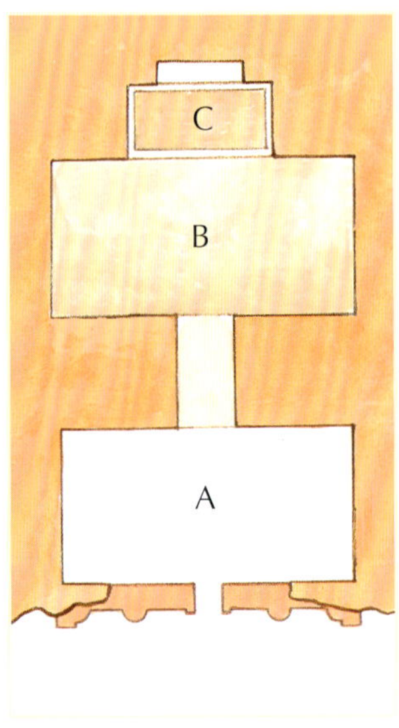

Plan of the Turkmaniyya Tomb

A Vestibule
B Burial chamber
C Recess

A spacious room with two niches inside is located above the corridor that connects the two chambers

Left - *The palaeographical analysis of the long inscription carved on the facade of the Turkmaniyya Tomb has allowed us to date the tomb to the second half of the 1st century AD.*
The present name of the monument literally means the Tomb of the Turkman, but it is not known who this legendary character was.

Opposite page, left - *The Conway Tower owes its name to Agnes Conway, an English archaeologist who worked in Petra in the 1920s.*

Opposite page, top right - *The little open-air triclinium carved along the slopes of Jebel Ma'aiserat is in a good state of conservation.*

Opposite page, bottom right - *The Jebel Ma'aiserat is dotted with hypogea; the function of some of them remains a mystery.*

carved on the same level as the facade – and not on a relief panel – it is clear that the front of the tomb was never covered with plaster; thus challenging the hypothesis expressed by some, that Petra's tombs were entirely plastered and painted. Instead, it is highly probable that only a few details – crowsteps and cornices – were treated in such a way. Given that many of the rupestrian tombs in Hegra are accompanied by an inscription, it is probable that similar epigraphs to the Turkmaniyya Tomb were common on all sepulchres in Petra, but written on a perishable support such as a stucco panel.
From the Turkmaniyya Tomb the road continues to go gradually upwards towards one of the secondary entrances to the archaeological area, and consequently it is advisable to backtrack towards the museum. Gazing towards the ancient town of Petra, you can see the remains of a powerful circular wall on a nearby rocky promontory: the so-called **Conway Tower**, a bastion erected at the northernmost point of the city wall. As it surrounds a rocky outcrop, it is thought that this may have been a sacred place, accessed by a processional road, and not a defensive system, but this hypothesis still has to be confirmed. Nearby there are the remains of a circular structure, once surrounded by eight columns; some maintain it is a temple, others believe it is a civil monument.
From the Turkmaniyya Tomb, the overtly curious can go back along the road for about 200 metres, trail off and then go very carefully up along the northern side of the valley, following one of the many goat trails. With a little luck you will come across a large, very well preserved open-air triclinium, next to which there is a small altar and what appear to be two underground cisterns.
Directly opposite, about 150 metres south-west, there is an interesting "high place of sacrifice" which is quite dangerous to get to. It is carved on top of an impressive pinnacle of rock with a cavetto tomb by its side. Once you reach the nearby ridge, you can enjoy a fascinating, multi-coloured spectacle offered by the sandstone banks of the Jebel Ma'aiserat, marked with deep crevices and perforated with a myriad of tombs in various styles. Although the area was once full of monuments, these days it is still poorly studied and not so popular with visitors. The spectacular triple cistern illustrated on page 27 can also be found here. The entire area is dotted with small and large Nabataean quarries and the terrain is rather impervious; it is therefore advisable to head towards the bottom of the wadi and the road. However, if they wish, expert walkers can go round the mountain halfway up the side of it, and head west where they will reach the deep depression of Wadi Ma'aiserat. All around there are some rather enigmatic structures, stairways, aqueducts and deep excavations. Then, very carefully, you can go down to the wadi river bed and go up the opposite side. In this vast area between Wadi Ma'aiserat and Wadi Kharareeb there is a profusion of tombs, votive niches and strange hypogea, the purpose of which is unknown. Amongst all of these, a curious complex can be found, surrounded by a courtyard, and deeply carved into the sandstone (probably a sacred area). Situated above there is a huge Hegra type tomb (No. 559), preceded by an outdoor triclinium. Many other sepulchres are lined up along the steep slopes overlooking the wadi Kharareeb, some of the arch type. To the left of the two northern tombs located at a higher altitude (No. 523 and No. 522), there is a bas-relief depicting a man on horseback (No. 520), although unfortunately it is almost unrecognizable due to erosion. In any event, given the vastness and roughness of the whole area at the foot of the Jebel Ma'aiserat, anyone wishing to explore the place in-depth should really rely on a local guide.

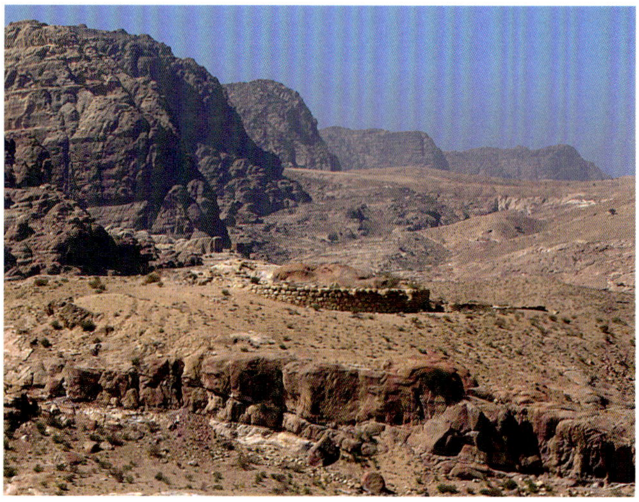

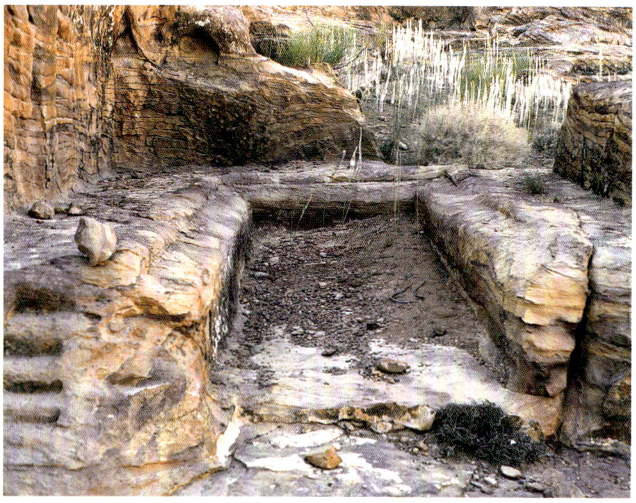

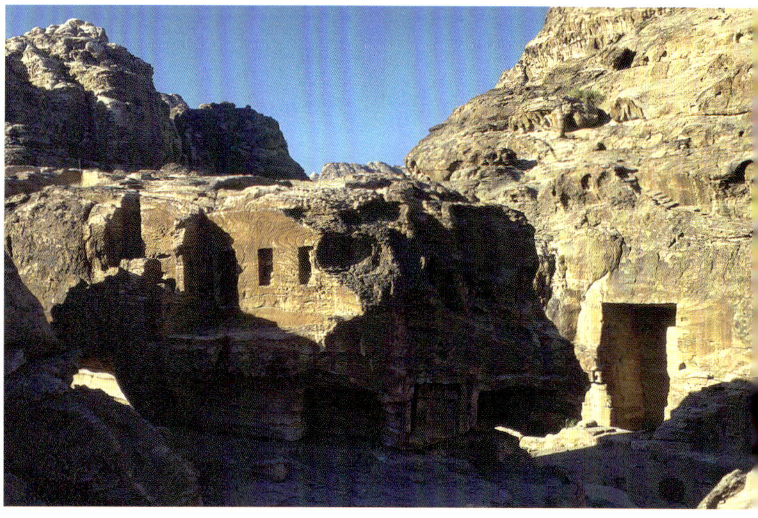

THE WADI SIYYAGH

This itinerary - which evolves over a rather difficult terrain – also begins near the old museum and the concrete bridge that crosses the Wadi Musa river bed. First of all, it is essential to go down to the river bed (which is also a partially adapted track for off-road vehicles) and then head towards the mouth of the gorge between the Jebel al Habis and the steep slopes of Jebel ed Deir; here the valley changes its name to Wadi Siyyagh. This gorge is the only way out towards the Wadi Arabah depression of all the rainwater that flows into the Petra valley. After about a hundred metres on the right, you will see the beginning of a short, steep path, which has patches of aloe and oleander bushes dotted around it. This trail soon turns into a short and rather exposed staircase, which leads to the threshold of the so-called **Painted Room**, part of a rupestrian house where there is a very rare example of Nabataean wall paintings preserved inside. Although the room – only officially discovered in 1979 – is closed by an iron railing door (the keys are kept in the museum, but it is difficult to get hold of them), you can easily observe the walls, which are plastered and painted in bright colours, with false doors, panels and frames in red, yellow, orange and blue. There is a striking similarity between these panels and those found in the Great Temple, which strongly suggests that the same workers would have produced them. The ceiling has an incredible radial painted motif with a stucco centrepiece at its fulcrum, very similar to the ones found in European homes up until the middle of the last century. A similar, but better preserved stucco centerpiece can also be observed on the ceiling of an adjoining room with the wall facing downstream missing.

From this privileged observation point, it is noticeable how the rocky walls on both sides of the wadi are dotted with dozens of rupestrian rooms, and connected by dizzying flights of stairs and walkways jutting into the void. This was a residential suburb of Petra and, evidently, the Nabataeans did not suffer from vertigo. All around you can see the grooves of the many aqueducts that collected rainwater, as well as the dark cavities of the cisterns. It is also clear that many Nabataean cave houses had masonry walls that faced down the valley (in which one or more of the windows would have opened), though this structural element has only been preserved in a few cases. Back to the wadi river bed, the most resilient and curious walkers will be able to go further along into a surreal world of colourful rocks and blooming oleanders. In recent years, this area returned to being cultivated, mainly because of the spring, which was not forced into an aqueduct during the Nabataean period because it was at a lower height than the urban area. Today, as in the past, the descendants of the Nabataeans cultivate fruit trees and vegetables.

In the ravine (called Sadd al Murayrrya) that opens along the right bank of the wadi immediately after the

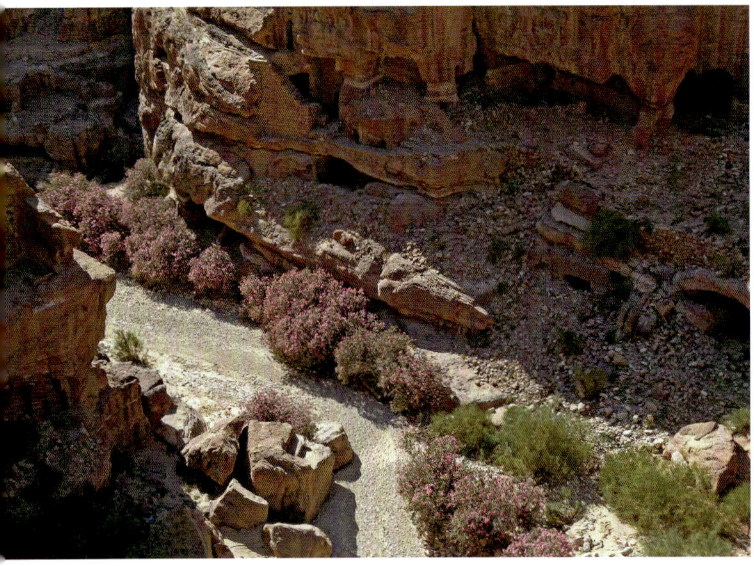

Above - *The gorge of the Wadi Siyyagh, whose walls are perforated by dozens of rupestrian houses, is all sprinkled with oleanders and aloe plants.*
Access to the Painted Room, preceded by a modern staircase, is visible at the top left in the photo.
In this area there is also a rupestrian sanctuary dedicated to the cult of Isis.

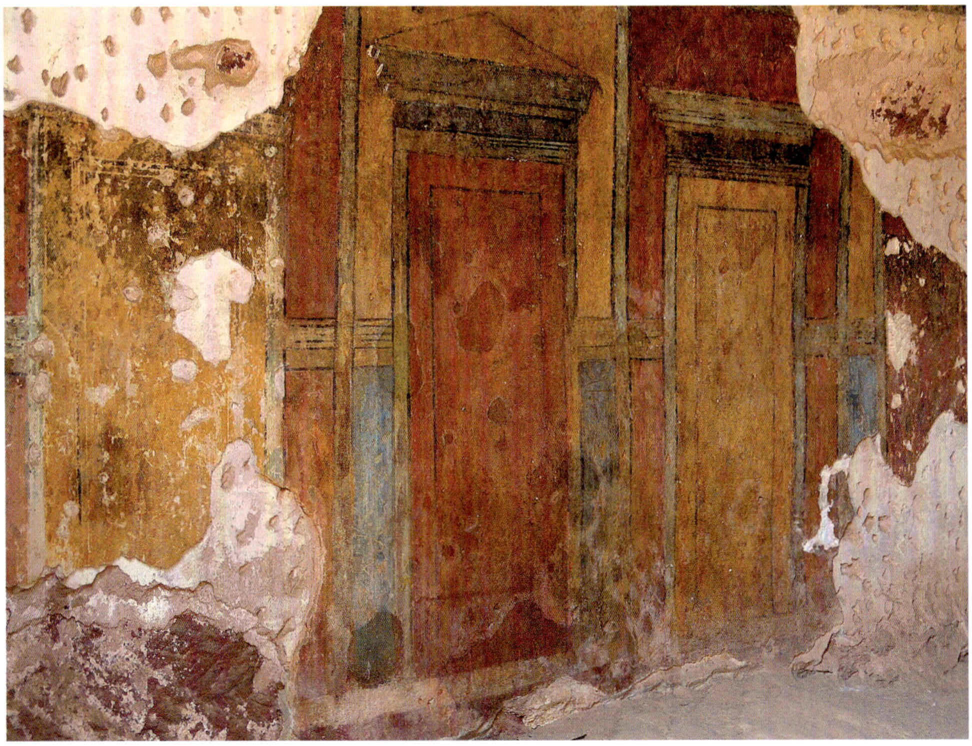

Below - *A detail of the wall paintings with an architectural subject, two false doors, which decorate the Painted Room. Fortunately, the paintings have been preserved until today because during the Ayubid-Mamluk period of occupation (XI-XIII century), the walls were plastered in white.*

Painted Room, a rocky prominence about 5 meters wide is perforated by some votive niches and a basin for ritual ablutions. The human figure carved in one of the niches was devastated by the iconoclasts, but it is still recognizable as Isis, the mother of Horus, seated on the throne (photo on page 150); an inscription (dated to the last quarter of the first century BC) expressly mentions the goddess.
A little further on, the walls of Wadi Siyyagh appear to have been altered the clean cuts of numerous Nabataean quarries, from which the ashlars necessary for the construction of the city's monuments were extracted. There is one quarry in particular which stands out due to its boldness, presenting itself as an immense surreal cubic gash in the mountainside. Another, on the left-hand side, was excavated high above the wadi shore. Evidently the sandstone at that point had particularly attractive characteristics for construction purposes, thus justifying a considerable physical and technical commitment. A large *nefesh* stands out on the curvilinear front of the quarry.
Where the gorge narrows, the sudden thickening of the vegetation reveals the presence of a perennial spring, partly intubated for irrigation purposes. The place was particularly sacred to the ancient gods and this is attested by the numerous inscriptions and baetyli that decorate the rocky walls. At another point there is a carved baetylus with a very stylized pair of eyes and a nose: the fragmentary inscription that accompanies it appears to quote the goddess Atargatis. Further on, after passing through a thick grove of oleanders, on the right side of the canyon stands the concavity of a huge Nabataean quarry. In the rock, at its foot, a "horned" altar is carved, framed between two "trees of life" surprisingly painted with a reddish pigment. Under the graffiti there are three circles; one of them is divided by 8 rays and another one is polylobed. They could be representations of celestial bodies (maybe the Moon and Venus) relating to particular deities. It is possible to link an astronomical character to it all due to the unmistakeable swastika on the right, an ancestral solar symbol found almost everywhere in the ancient world. These paintings, which have not yet been adequately studied, are the only ones found in the Petra area, and are a bit of an enigma. Next to the graffiti there is a through-hole, similar to ones that can be seen next to many votive aedicules and baetyli. It is believed that the offerings were made to the gods here (i.e. terracotta figurines), tied to little cords.
On the quarry front alongside stands out another graffiti, depicting an altar between two palm trees. In fact, the peculiar shape of an altar with high angular prominences (or "horns") is often found carved in the quarries and believed to have been a sign of devotion to the god Dushara. This fact could be related to the role of this deity as "lord of the mountains" or, perhaps, patron of the quarrymen.
Further along, beyond the spring water, there are a series of small natural pools and even a little waterfall, but going too far can be rather rash, and a local guide is strongly recommended when visiting the area.
On the right, there is a partially visible path that rises up through a magnificent natural setting towards the Deir, but again, an expert guide is necessary.

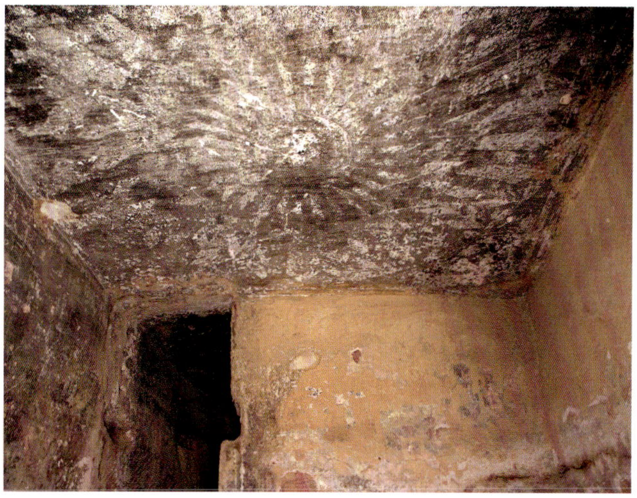

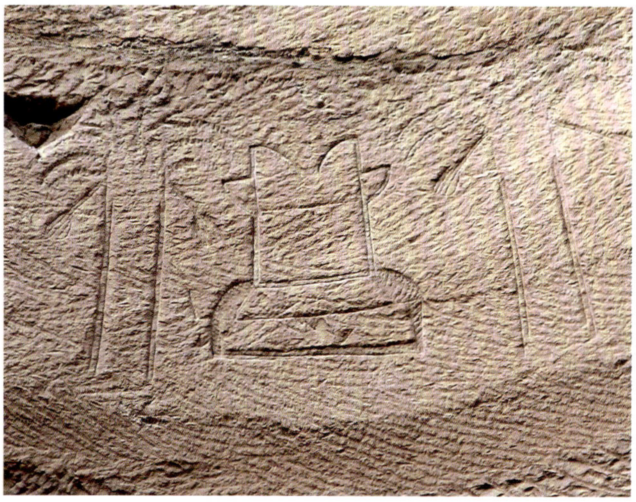

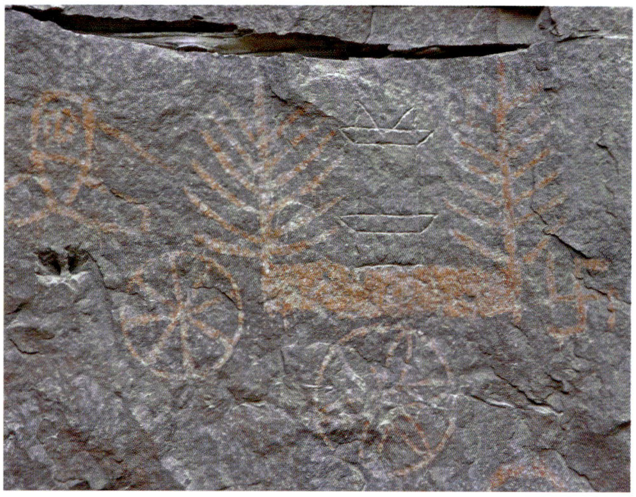

Top - *The Painted Room has a ceiling decorated with a lively black and white pattern that radiates out from the plaster centrepiece.*

Centre - *In this graffiti, clearly visible on a quarry front in the Wadi Siyyagh, the usual altar dedicated to Dushara is between two stylized palms.*

Bottom- *The unique paintings placed around the stylized altar consecrated to Dushara. The swastika, the circles and the strange symbol on the left are difficult to interpret. Brünnow catalogued them without giving an explanation for them. However, it is possible that the composition had an astronomical character.*

THE JEBEL UMM AL BIYARA

This excursion, although certainly the most tiring, is really the one that allows you to admire the most incredible panorama overlooking the entire basin where Petra stood. It is essential to be equipped with suitable footwear and an abundant supply of water, remembering that there is no refreshment point here.
Leaving the Pharaoh's Column behind you, take the dirt road that turns right and immediately begins to descend towards the bed of the Wadi Thughra, which is the valley that is wedged between the Jebel al Habis and the towering Jebel Umm al Biyara, with a fascinating rock necropolis at its foot. After crossing the wadi on the modern reinforced concrete bridge, you can head towards the showy **Tomb 361**, whose gigantic double cornice facade (Hegra type) is deeply set back into the natural mountain profile. It is articulated by four pilasters with Nabataean capitals, but unfortunately it is much more eroded than it seems from afar. If you want, you can spend some time wandering around the area which is full of hypogea, among which three curiously shaped tower tombs stand out (Nos. 379, 380, 381), leaning against each other, and two arch tombs (Nos. 365 , 366) side by side. The place is incredibly impressive, but be careful where you put your feet.
To the left of the enormous Tomb 361 there is the beginning of a path, or what seems be a path, but it soon turns into a stunning series of stairs, hairpin bends and rock cuttings that in about an hour take you to the top of Umm al Biyara (1178 m.). Where the path, carved into the rock and dotted with votive shrines, creeps into the narrow ravine, you will notice - dug in the opposite wall of the gorge - a bold aqueduct served by a walkway. The channel produces a deep horizontal line that runs a few metres above the large double cornice tombs (needless to say, trying to follow its path could have fatal consequences). Suddenly, the path takes on the appearance of an extraordinary sloping plane carved out of the living rock (known as *couloir*), which suddenly forks into two huge opposing ramps, one rising to the left, the other to the right.
To get to the top, you need to go up the ramp on the left-hand side; although, a similar excavation demonstrates how two important destinations were planned, not just one. In fact, if you go up the right ramp, and circumvented a gigantic landslide caused by an earthquake in remote times, you will soon reach a rather enigmatic place consisting of a vast, natural, wide-open cavity located in the side of the mountain. The cavity opens at about a third of the massif's height and can be seen from afar. Several hypogean rooms have been excavated along the walls of this spectacular balcony. The two facing south were sculpted at a considerable height and are truly surprising, not only for their appearance, but also because it is unclear how accessing them could ever have been possible. However, some remains of masonry and the considerable amount of stone material scattered around and largely collapsed in the valley, at

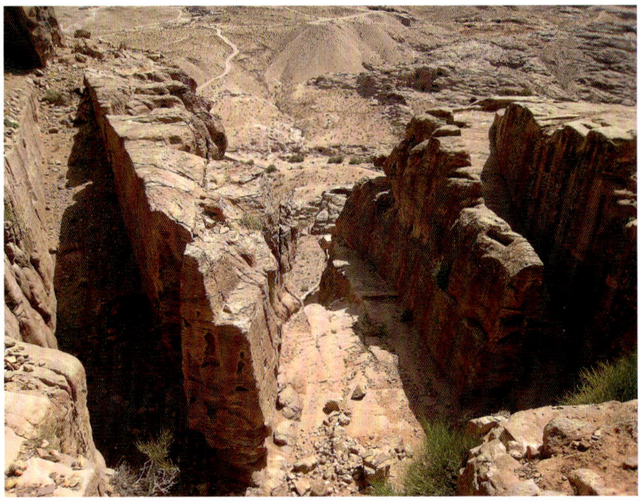

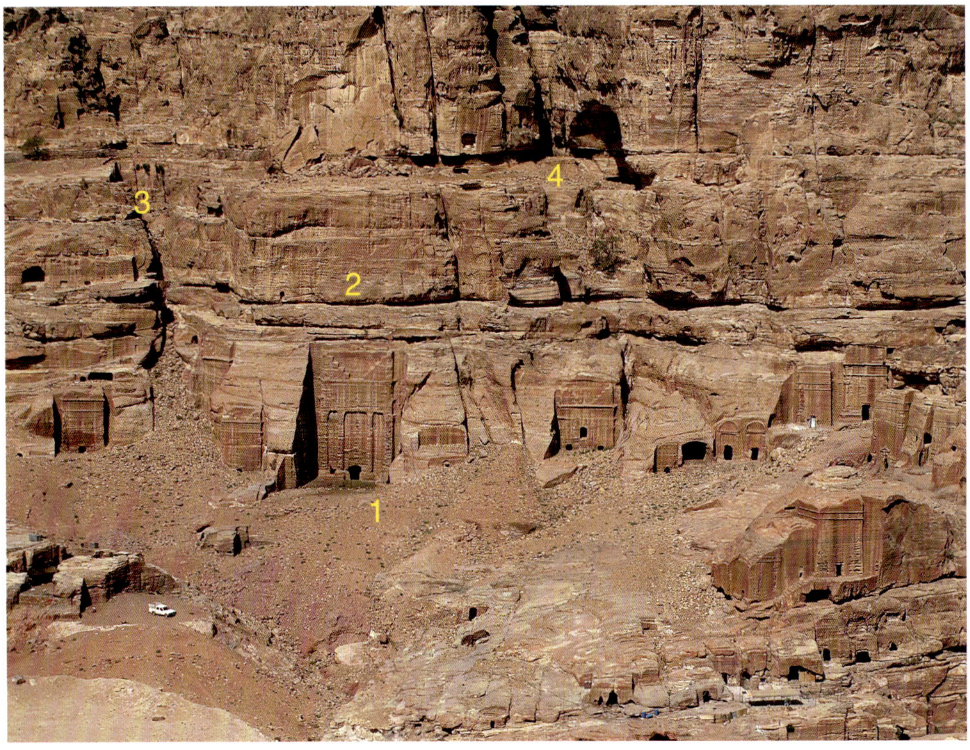

Above - *The spectacular couloir, with the two divergent ramps.*

Below - *In the picture, the following are marked: 1) the imposing Tomb 361, of the double cornice type; 2) the aqueduct; 3) the large couloir; 4) the so-called "sanctuary".*

Opposite page, top - *The northern side of the "sanctuary", with the entrances to the hypogean rooms, unfortunately devastated by earthquakes. On the left is the large hanging recess, in which a motab seems to be carved.*

Opposite page, bottom - *The opposite side, with a mysterious inaccessible room and the outlet of the narrow gully.*

the foot of the tombs below, suggest that there were substantial structures built here, and possibly even flights of stairs. The recess facing south seems to contain a large *motab*; above it there may have been a baetylus or a sacred image, visible from a great distance. The narrow cleft that cuts the mountain vertically was once blocked by a dam, and as a result, even today, a pool of water forms in the springtime. To its right there are other hypogean rooms (probably 7), though most of the ceilings have collapsed, making access very dangerous and volumetric analysis virtually impossible. Above these rooms there is another deep recess, but it is also impossible to get to. Given the grandeur of the access road, it is clear that this place, defined as a "sanctuary" by Dalman as early as 1908, would certainly have played a role of primary importance for the inhabitants of Petra. The vaguely uterine aspect of the large natural cavity, the presence of water and the deep vertical slit, all suggest that this really could have been an important place of worship, perhaps of a female deity.
The rock-cut road that from the colossal couloir climbs

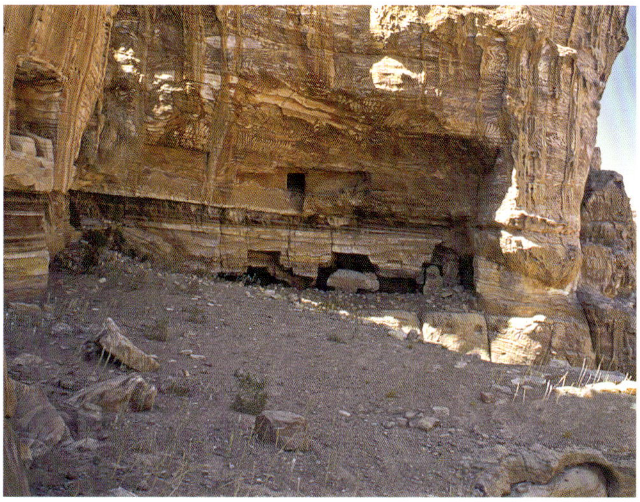

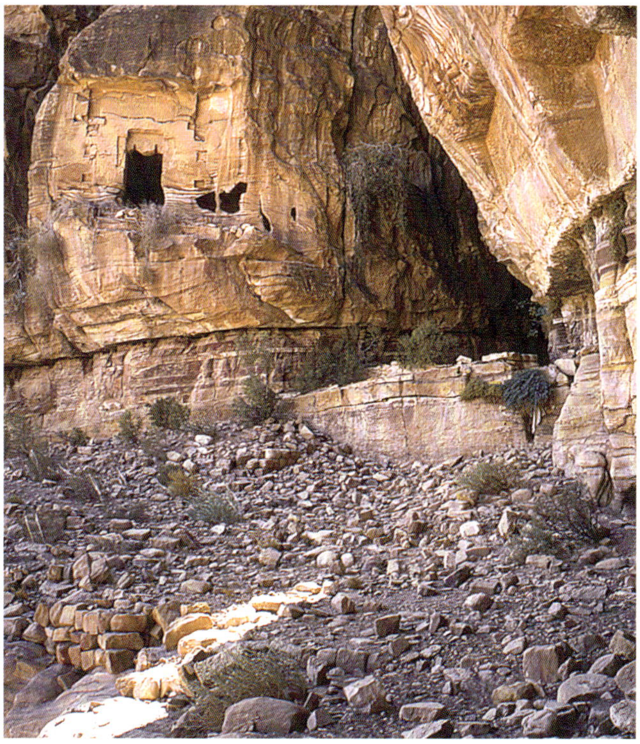

A ROYAL TOMB?

The colossal Tomb 361, situated at the feet of the Umm al Biyara, raises the question, "who could have afforded such a large sepulchre?" If it is an established fact that the greater the social status of the deceased the greater the splendour of a tomb, then it is reasonable to suppose that this could have been a royal sepulchre. In fact, it is clear that the monument required a huge amount of excavation work and that it was fronted by a large courtyard – probably colonnaded, in part cut into the sandstone and in part built in masonry – equal to the most important sepulchres in Petra. If we consider that the existence of at least eleven Nabataean kings has been ascertained, assuming that Obodas II was buried in Advat and the Deir is his cenotaph, it is evident that the number of presumed royal sepulchres (made up of the Khazneh, the Urn Tomb and the Corinthian Tomb, and excluding the so-called Palace Tomb for the reasons already mentioned) is actually relatively small. If the architectural revolution represented by the Classical Nabataean Style was launched by Aretas IV, it is also very likely that his royal predecessors had themselves buried in Assyrian style tombs or tombs with double cornices, only distinguishable from others by their unusual size. Taking into account the entire panorama of Petra, the tombs that stand out for their unusual dimensions and pre-eminent position are, above all, Tomb 808 in the Outer Siq, the Tower Tomb 303 next to the Snake Monument, the neighbouring Tower Tomb 307 and indeed, the one on the slopes of the Umm al Biyara. The location of these tombs, amongst other things, would seem to highlight their importance. In fact, it was customary in antiquity to put the great sepulchres along the main access roads of cities. Before the monumentalization of the Siq, between the middle of the 1st century BC and the beginning of the following century, the road that headed south along the Wadi Thughra, in the direction of Aila (Aqaba), was the main access road to Petra for a long time. Therefore, it is logical enough to think that the kings of Petra wanted their sepulchres here, at least in the most remote times.

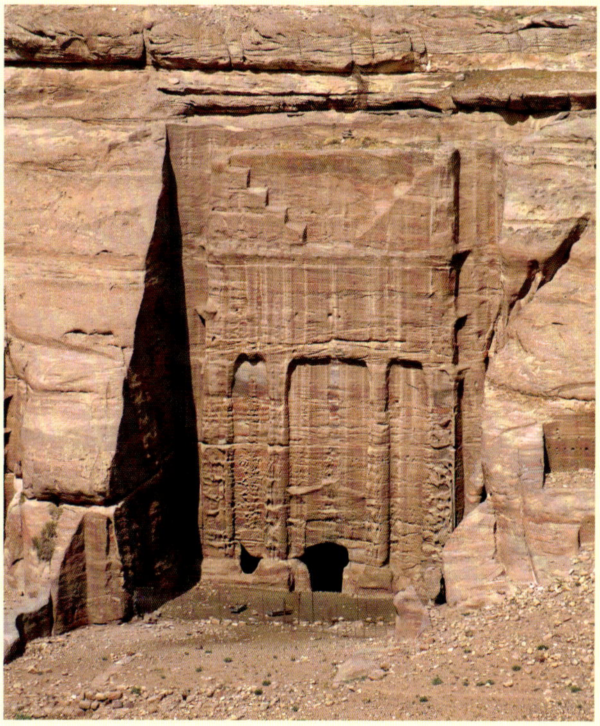

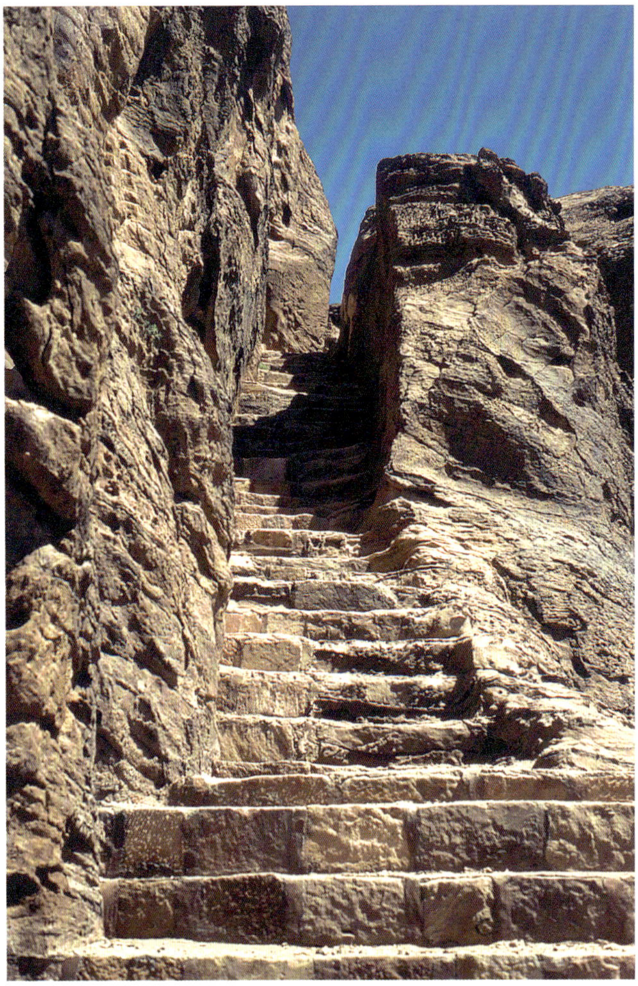

Top left - *One of the vertiginous flights of stairs that lead to the almost flat top of the Umm al Biyara.*

Bottom left - *The remains of the Edomite settlement, with drystone walls.*

Right - *A rock carving depicting four oryxes; according to some they date back to the Edomite era, for others they are much older, dating back to the Bronze (or Chalcolithic) Age.*

Opposite page, top - *Fragment of a sculptural frieze, related to one of the monumental structures (today known as T26).*

Opposite page, centre - *The curious spur of rock and debrids that stands almost in the centre of the plateau.*

Opposite page, bottom - *At the north western end of the plateau is a small, well-hidden rock sanctuary that houses several carved baetyli.*

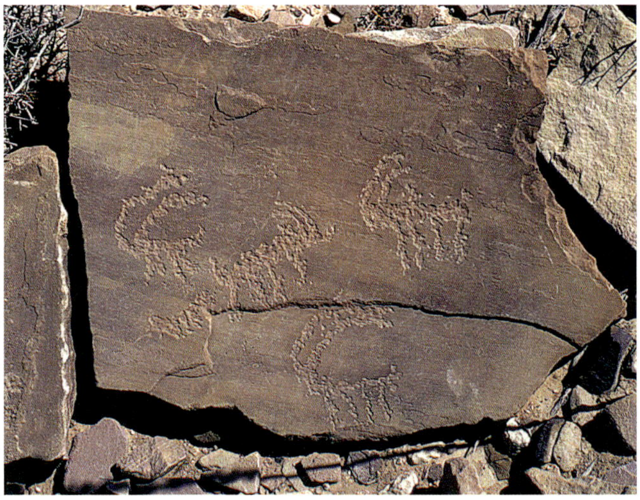

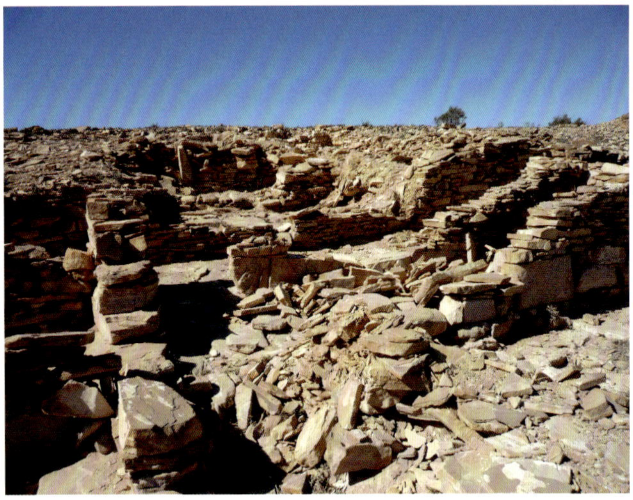

to the left, continues towards the top of the massif with a steep sequence of hairpin bends and flights of stairs often very aerial and exposed, but made rather safe by a series of restoration interventions.

At the top of the mountain are the remains of an Edomite settlement from the Iron Age, inhabited between the seventh and sixth centuries BC. About a third of the inhabited area was excavated and studied by the archaeologist Crystal Bennett from 1960 to 1965. Here, among other things, a terracotta seal was found with the name of Qosr-Gabr, "King of Edom" (670 BC ca.). Other evidence of early settlement of the site is provided by some rock carvings: one represents a desert partridge and others depict long-horned oryxes. It is not known what event caused the end of the Edomite settlement phase, but it is certain that the earliest evidence of a stable settlement in Umm al Biyara by the Nabataeans only dates back to the first century BC.

In 2010, meticulous excavation campaigns by the International Umm al Biyara Project began on the vast plateau that forms the top of the massif. These have made it possible to identify the foundations of about twenty Nabataean buildings, dating back to a period between the 1st century BC and the end of the 1st century AD. On the western edge there was a watchtower of fundamental importance for the defence of the city; this was in fact optically connected to similar structures scattered all over the region to control the access routes.

At the northwestern end of the plateau, a small rupestrian sanctuary was built under a rock overhang; here a series of niches is carved, one of which contains an altar where a tiny baetylus is inserted. An inscription in Greek tells us that the place was dedicated to "Zeus (i.e. Dushara) the redeemer".

On the edge of the precipice facing northeast, where you can enjoy the most spectacular view of Petra, there were some sumptuous palaces, equipped with Roman-style toilets (*latrinae*) and even thermal baths. Fragments of pottery, water pipes, and precious wall and floor coverings (in various types of marble) have been found there, as well as a few blocks with bas-reliefs similar to the Khazneh decorations. The water supply for the various structures was guaranteed by at least seven of the

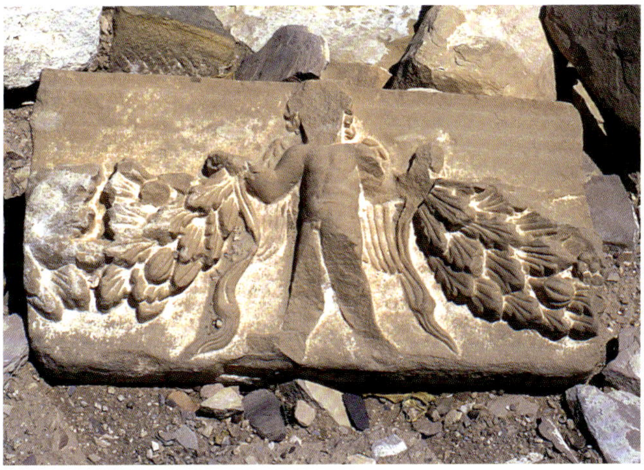

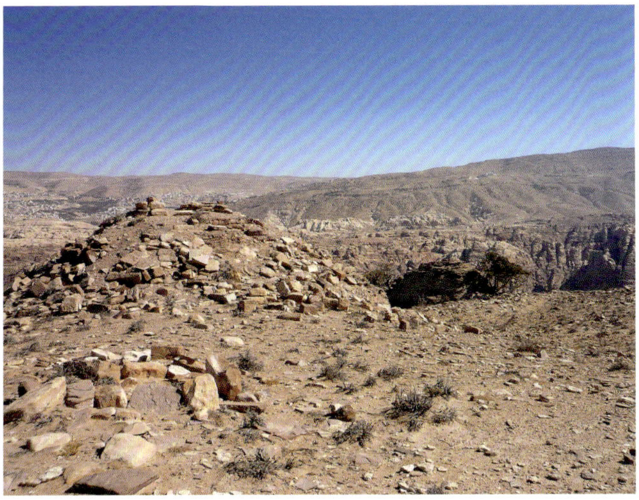

eight large bell-shaped underground cisterns located on the plateau and connected by channels carved into the rock. These are what gave the mountain its Arabic name: "Mother of the cisterns".

The most recent investigations lead us to believe that much of the top of the mountain was covered in buildings from the Nabataean era, and that quite possibly a royal palace could have existed too. If so, it could have been equipped with every comfort according to the fashion imported from Rome and perhaps influenced by the palace of King Herod, built on the fortress of Masada (in present-day Israel). Erected on the turn of the first century AD, it overlooked the abyss and was clearly visible from the city below. The remains of Roman and Byzantine ceramics suggest that all the structures were probably in use until the disastrous earthquake in 363. Considering the pre-eminent geographical position of Umm al Biyara, which dominates the whole of Petra, it is very likely that an important sanctuary could also have stood here, maybe built around the curious spur of rock that rises almost in the center of the plateau. Among other things, it is very intriguing to note that from here, all the main "high places" that surround Petra are perfectly visible. As already mentioned, it seems that they were arranged so as to be visually connected to each other. Although it is just a supposition, it is nice to imagine how various processions would have gone up from the town to the sacred places on top of the mountains on particular days of the year, to simultaneously celebrate sacred rituals. If these ceremonies carried on throughout the night, the lights of the torches or bonfires would almost certainly have created an image of great emotional impact...

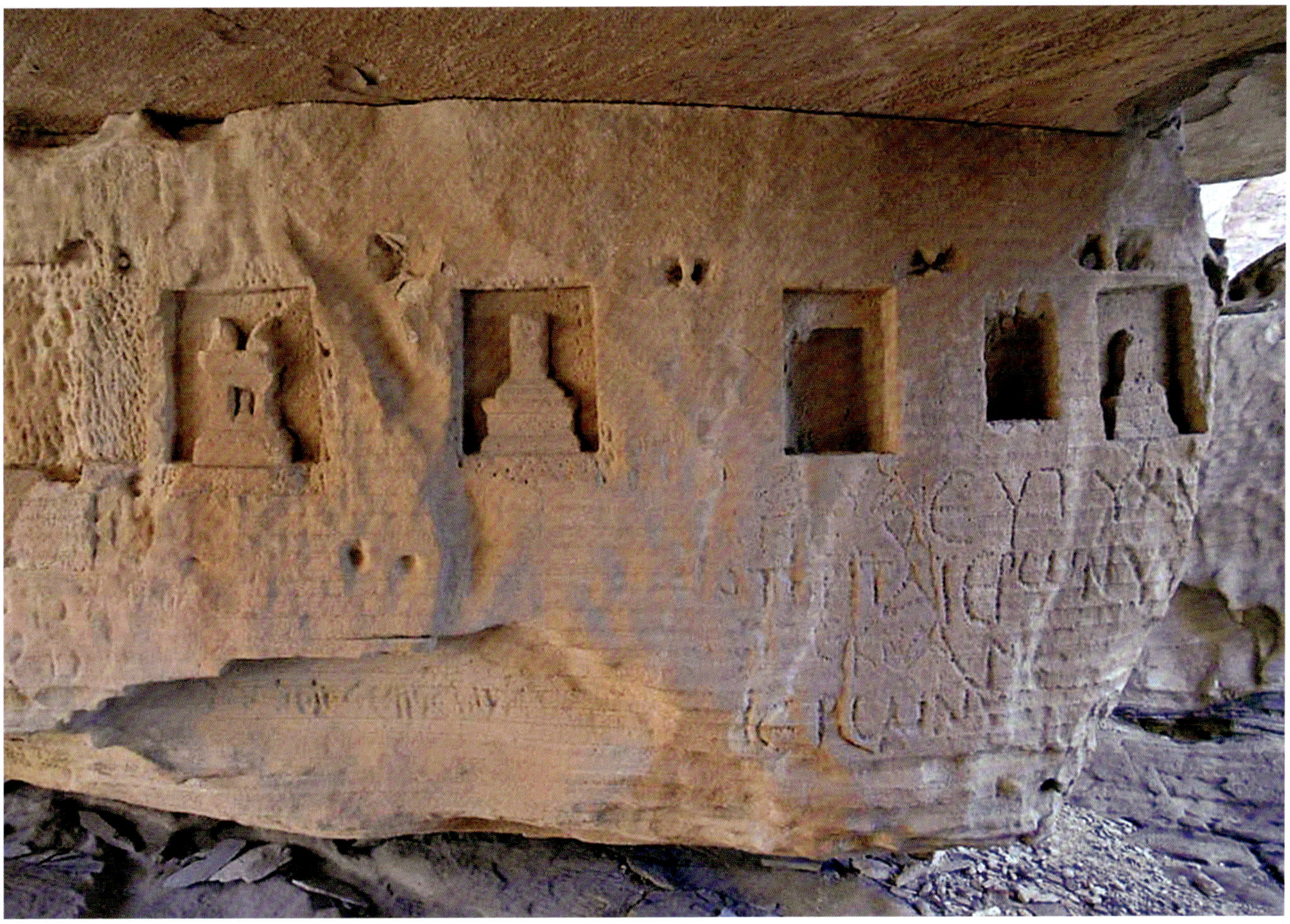

THE WADI THUGHRA (RAS SULAYMAN)

To explore the upper part of Wadi Thughra (an area also known as Ras Sulayman) it is necessary to start from the Pharaoh's Column, descend the dirt road already described (page 164) and follow its path south-westwards. Red and ochre colours dominate along both sides, in a scene of glittering beauty. After about a kilometer and a half and having gained altitude, the road comes in sight of a bench of light sandstone and the attention is immediately drawn to a large tower tomb carved on a high podium (No. 307), in which it opens a room. This monument is unique in its kind. Some olive trees grow in the courtyard that opens in front of it, giving the whole a bucolic and vaguely surreal aspect. The surrounding area is dotted with other hypogea and several quarry fronts, but the most striking monument is a second, huge tower tomb (No. 303), located just in front of the first. It stands on a rocky prominence in which two hypogea open wide, and there is a small room excavated in its body. The monument has a lower round of Assyrian crowsteps varved in bas-relief; the top still retains a large part of the cornice and some of the crowsteps, made up of lithic blocks and put in place separately.
To the left of the tower tomb, believed to date back to the last years of the second century BC, or the first years of the first century BC, one of the most enigmatic monuments in Petra can be found: the **Serpent Monument** (No. 302). Carved on top of a rocky outcrop, it looks like a squat djinn block on which are twisted the coils of a huge reptile, which erosion has deprived of the head. Since there are no tombs in its immediate vicinity, it is likely that this was a depiction of a divinity (Dushara) or perhaps an apotropaic symbol. Incidentally, snakes were often associated with the world of the dead, so a monument of this kind could have been a marker to protect the surrounding cemetery area, which is known as the Southern Necropolis today.
In this area are still visible some sections carved into the rock of one of the roads leading from Petra to the great depression of the wadi Arabah, where, among other things, there was the important Roman fortress of Gharandal; from here the road then continued towards Aila, today's Aqaba. About 4 meters wide, the track still visible was created after the Trajan conquest; it is basically a Roman modernization of a much older Nabataean caravan track. This artery (probably from the Diocletian era) was defended by forts and watchtowers along its course.
In the nineteenth century, the first visitors to Petra entered the city using this route.

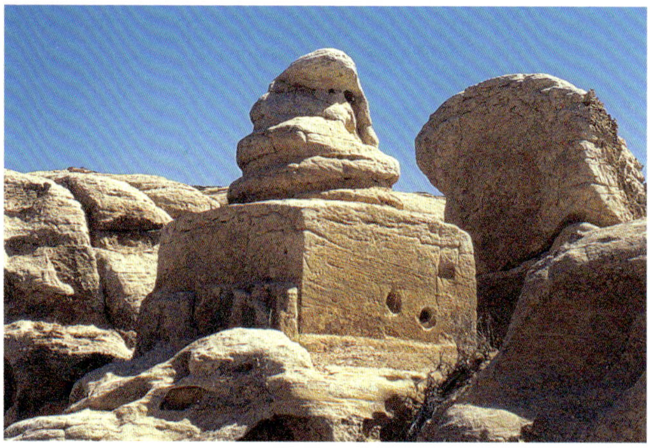

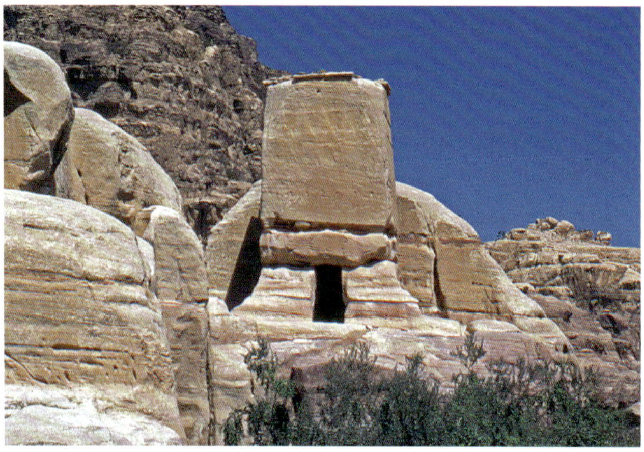

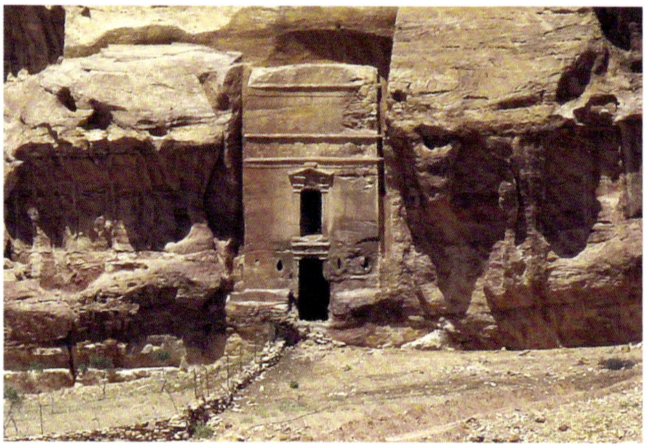

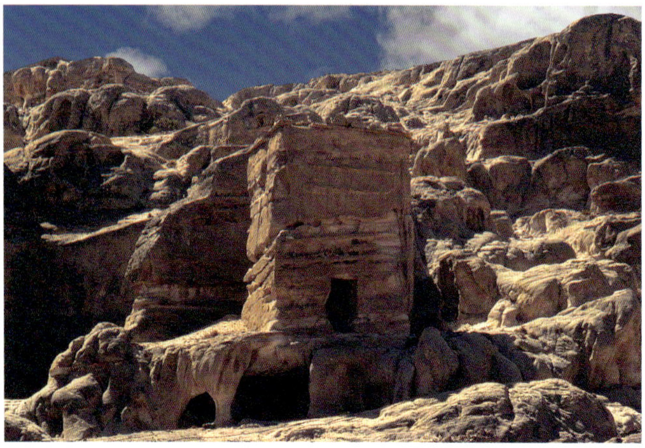

Top left - *The tower Tomb 307 is the only one with two floors; perhaps the lower room, whose view is precluded by trees, was used as a triclinium.*

Bottom left - *The imposing tower tomb 303; it is possible that a pit grave is still hidden at the top.*

Top right - *The bizarre Serpent Monument; in antiquity its appearance must have been surprising for those who came to Petra from Aila (Aqaba). Perhaps it had an apotropaic function*

Bottom right - *The Ras Sulayman area is hardly ever visited, although there are some monuments of great interest. Tomb 313 stands on the slopes of the mountain called Umm Hrerib. It is the only one of the Assyrian type with two chambers, one on top of the other.*

AL BARID: LITTLE PETRA

About 9 kilometres north of Wadi Musa there is another archaeological area, much smaller in size than Petra but still of some interest; it is called al Barid, better known as "Little Petra". Although it is possible to walk (about a two hour walk along the asphalt road from Wadi Musa, or from Petra, going up the Wadi Turkmaniyya, which takes at least two and a half hours), it is better to take a taxi there and back (the journey takes about fifteen minutes and it is not costly). If you opt for this solution, you can even ask the driver to stop for a few minutes along the way, so you can briefly visit the ruins of the Al Wu'eira crusader castle, which is perched on the edge of a ravine in a formidable position (page 15). To enter the ruins you need to cross a modern footbridge, which has literally been thrown over an abyss, replacing the original drawbridge. The fortification, built under the reign of King Baldwin I of Jerusalem in 1116, was known to the Crusaders as Li Vaux Moise, and was part of a defensive system set up to control trade along the road from Damascus to Cairo. It was besieged by Muslim forces several times, with little success, but finally taken in 1189 after Saladin had defeated the Christian armies in the Holy Land in the battle of Hattin. It was the last Crusader outpost to surrender, and since the defenders offered strenuous resistance, Saladin was said to have spared their lives and set them free. The castle was then occupied by an Ayubbid garrison until the early 13th century, after which it was finally abandoned and fell into disrepair. Al Barid is preceded by a vast open space, which is used for parking, and there are some kiosks overlooking it, where you can buy some souvenirs, or better still, quench your thirst with some excellent local tea. Looking around, it almost seems impossible that this was once a populous satellite village of Petra, where goods were stored and large caravans would arrive and depart. There were also numerous houses and spacious warehouses built in masonry, as well as several underground cisterns that were fed by aqueducts. The only way to fully recognize the foundations of the various structures, and appreciate the full extent of the town, is to see it from the sky, and in the right light. It can even be perceived that in the large wadi facing north (Wadi al Imti) there must have been a gigantic basin to collect rainwater, and an aqueduct would have begun there. There are also some tombs, a triclinium and two basins (interpreted as grape presses) here. It is easy to imagine that the flat areas on the edge of the town would have hosted crops, vineyards and orchards. When the time comes for an adequate archaeological investigation, "Little Petra" will certainly reveal countless surprises.

For the moment it is worthwhile being accompanied by a few locals to visit the nearby cistern called Bir el Arays, a real miracle of Nabataean hydraulic engineering (it looks a bit like a hut leaning against the mountain, with a few steps up to the door). It is still fully functional and accessible via a masonry staircase that descends down into the depths of its three concamerations, where it could contain about 12 million litres! Its name means "cistern of the brides" which is linked to an ancient Bedouin tradition.

The visit to Al Barid starts from the small but very elegant **Facade 846** (pediment type), preceded by a short flight of stairs. The doorway, which is framed by two pilasters with Nabataean capitals, is surmounted by a beautiful Nabataean Doric frieze and a curvilinear pediment. Despite its appearance, it does not appear to be a tomb, as al Barid was a place of transit and trade, or rather a caravanserai where large caravans were stationed and where water was given to their dromedaries.

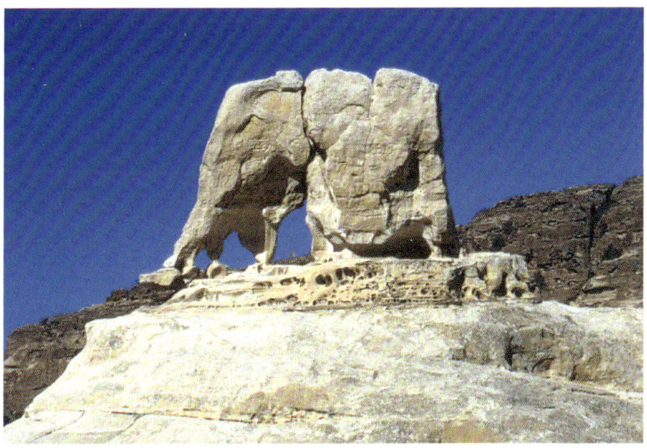

Left - *Along the road from Wadi Musa to al Barid stands a curious natural formation can, known as the "elephant rock". It was shaped by the erosive action of the wind.*

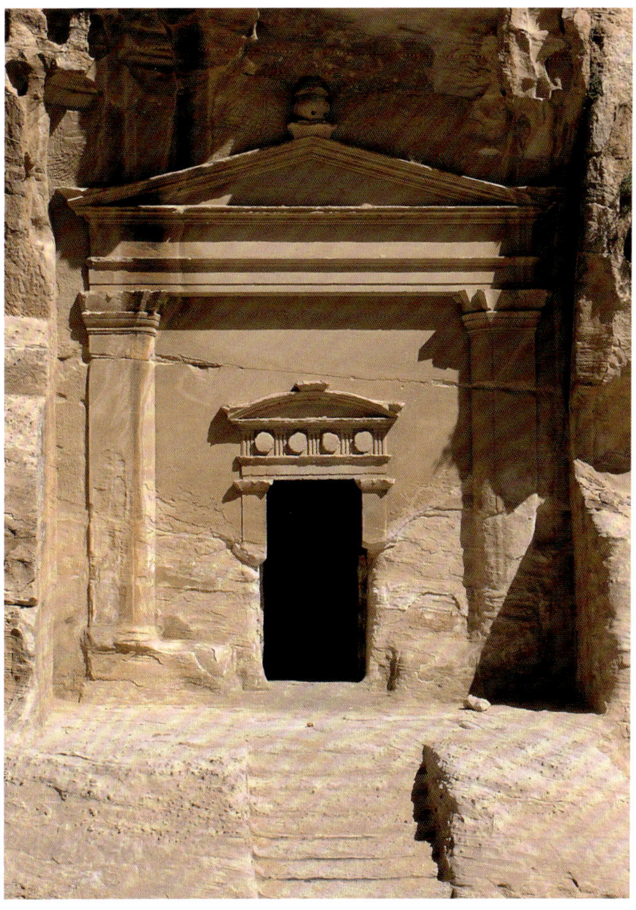

Right - *The room inside the monument called Facade 846 is really small. However, the traces left by the doors on the threshold indicate that it was used frequently.*

Here the merchants who shuttled between Arabia and the Mediterranean coasts stopped, here the goods destined for the markets of the nearby Nabataean capital were stored. Bearing this in mind, some authors think that the beautiful rock structure may have been a sort of guard post, or even a "customs duty office" where tax officials would have been stationed, but it is difficult to say if this hypothesis has any substance. According to others, more simply, it might have been a temple, dating back to the middle of the 1st century AD, like most of the other monuments in Little Petra.
A little further on, the surrounding rock walls - which form a sort of natural amphitheatre - almost touch each other, forming a very narrow and suggestive crack, about ten metres long. In ancient times it was protected by a door, but this has since been replaced by an iron gate. This sort of miniature Siq (not by chance called Siq al Barid) then forms a kind of natural plaza dominated by the beautiful facade of the so-called **Distyle Temple**, carved in an elevated position. Its appearance, with the two columns *in antis*, crowned by Nabatean capitals and a sober, unadorned frieze, suggests that it was in fact a temple, perhaps dedicated to the main Nabatean deities, Dushara and Al Uzza. This hypothesis seems realistic, particularly because there are no traces of burial niches inside it, and furthermore it seems logical that it was a sacred building that would have welcomed the caravans to the safety of the caravanserai. The room must have had a high staircase in front of it, built in masonry, to allow access to the small platform in front of the facade, but this has been destroyed. The two rooms carved into the rock (now broken through) that opened on the sides were probably service areas linked to the sacred offices.
There are other hypogea close by - mainly triclinia, but also huge cisterns - while a dizzying staircase winds its way up into a natural crack near the rock cut temple. Staircases in mid-air like this one, that can be seen almost everywhere, led up to numerous channels that collected the rainwater, and also to the ever present "high places of sacrifice", which were placed all around the settlement, as they were in Petra.
If you are lucky enough to have al Barid all to yourself, the silence of the place, the pouring of light that rains

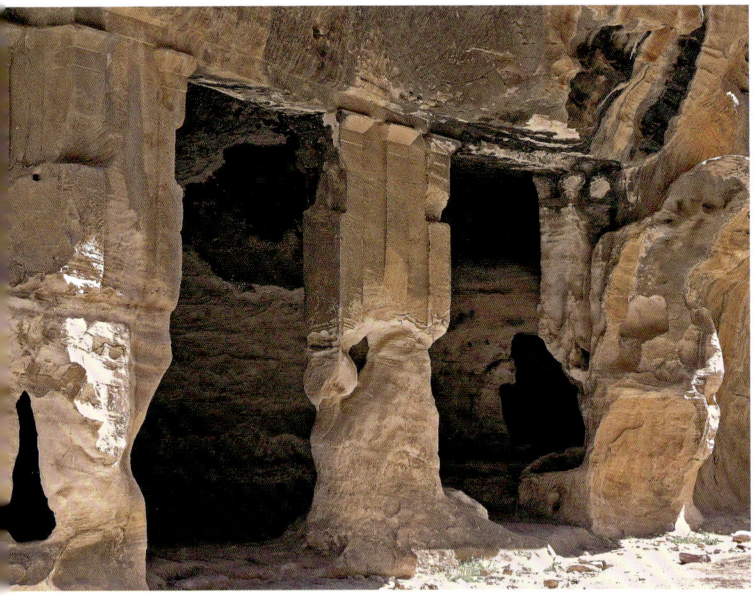

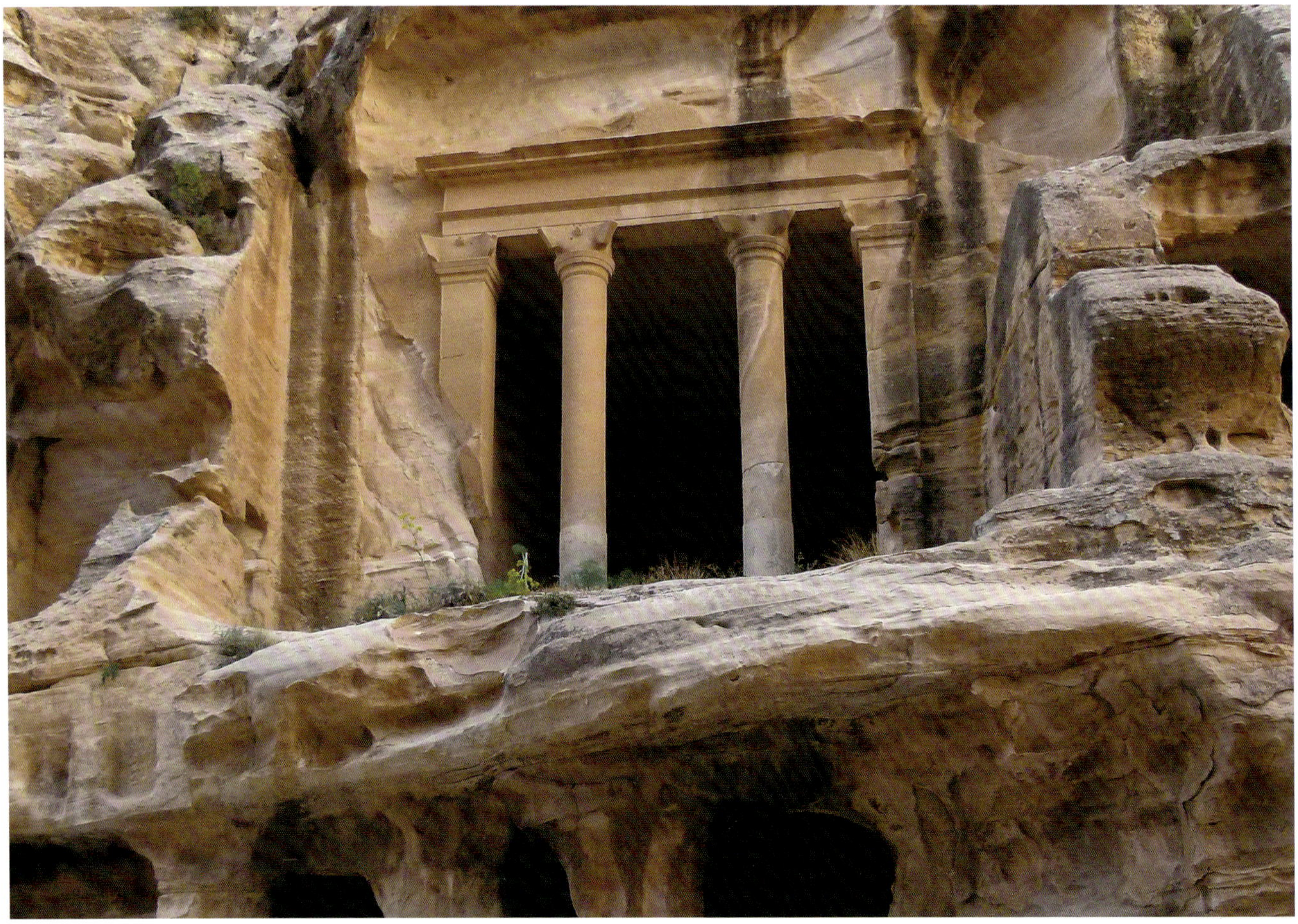

from above and falls on the insanely eroded rocks, the multi-coloured shades of the sandstone, the chance encounters with blue lizards, all help to make it an experience you will never forget. Indeed, it is easy to imagine the ancient merchants livening up this cool and sheltered place, haggling over spices or chatting about the latest news. These sensations can also be felt in the second wider area of the gorge, where a staircase and a short walkway lead into the famous **Painted House** (No. 849), which is actually a biclinium with walls that still retain part of the plaster painted with imitation ashlar. The vault of the arched recess in the back wall holds precious and very rare traces of a rich pictorial decoration, with racemes, flowers, vine shoots, birds of various species and cupids. One of these has been identified as a young Pan, playing a flute, while a second, perhaps Eros, is armed with a bow and arrow; a third is possibly holding an ear of corn. It is

Opposite page, top - *These spacious rooms were triclinia. We can imagine that the Nabataean merchants gathered here to enjoy the refreshment offered by the shadow, to feast and negotiate the price of the goods.*

Opposite page, bottom - *The first natural court of the canyon is overlooked by a hypogeum with two* in antis *columns, probably a temple.*

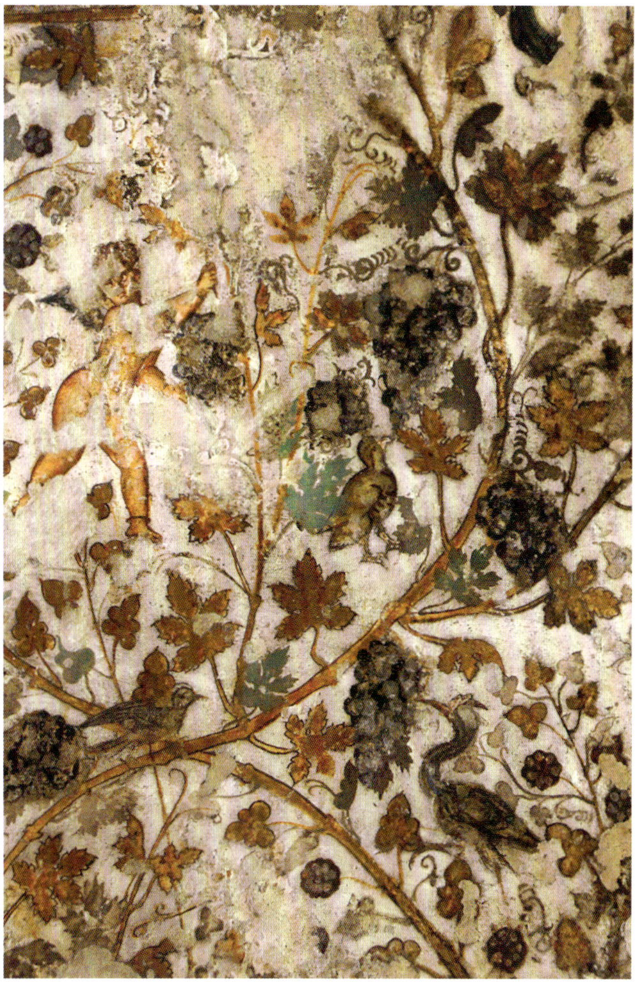

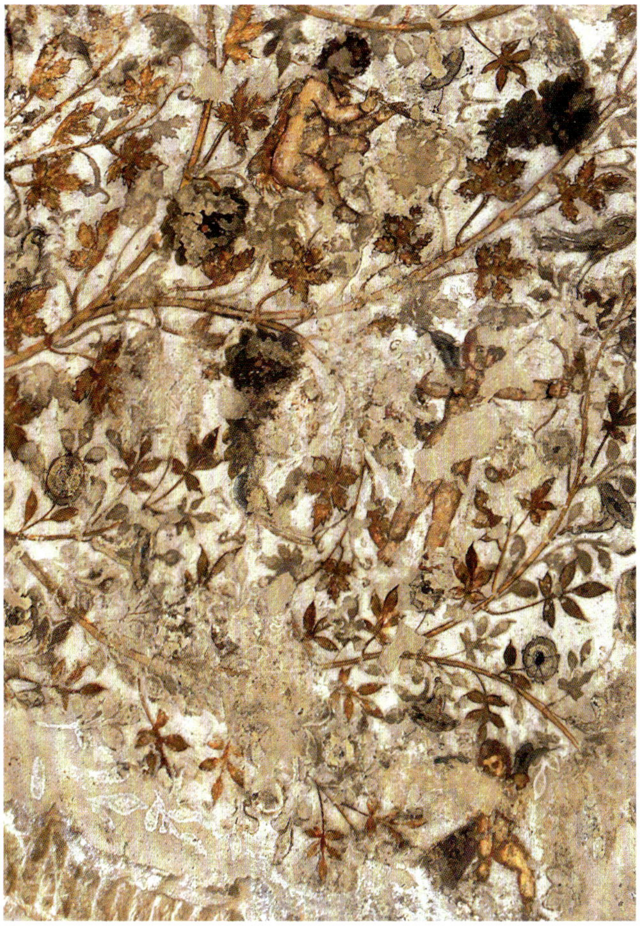

This page - *Two details of the frescoes that adorn the Painted House; the vine leaves retain traces of gilding. Near the biclinium, there are what appear to be actual rock cut houses, and several triclinia. Judging from what can be seen in Little Petra, we can assume that in addition to funerary and cultual uses, the triclinia would have served as a place to get together and have a meal.*

the only example of Nabataean wall painting in the figurative style that has survived to this day. It is clearly influenced by Hellenistic and Roman art and can be dated to the years between 40 BC and 25 AD. Restored in 2010, it allows us to imagine how colourful and sumptuous many other similar rooms would have been, when their colours were bright and life was buzzing all around. According to a recent theory, the so-called Painted House, together with the neighboring rooms, was actually part of a sanctuary dedicated to the cult of Isis. This is not surprising because it is ascertained that the goddess was highly revered in Petra.
Explorers in a hurry can return to the starting point, while those who have more time can go to the end of the gorge, where a dramatic staircase carved into a narrow crack leads out of Al Barid (nearby there is also a "high place of sacrifice"). Although, it is wise not to go too far, as the geography of the place is rather rough.
From al Barid there is a long track going through a charming landscape that leads to the Deir, but this is a demanding excursion and should not be attempted without a local guide under any circumstances.
About a kilometre southeast of Little Petra, in an alluvial plain, the remains of a prehistoric village called al Beidha (the White) have been found, dating back to about 6800 BC. Here, the foundations of numerous houses have been brought to light, the oldest of which have a circular plan; near these some hand-operated grindstones can be seen, left in situ.

In these last pages I would like to look at several questions that have long fascinated me and for which I can only provide theories, but I hope that one day investigations carried out using the right methods will lead to them being answered.

PETRA'S SEWAGE SYSTEM

For years, I have studied the complex water supply system put in place by the Nabataeans with admiration, but I have often wondered what Petra's sewage system would have been like, as it is a subject that has hardly been mentioned. Yet the question seems fundamental and completely legitimate to me. Obviously, a population of between twenty and thirty thousand people produces an enormous amount of sewage on a daily basis. Statistical data to hand: 4.6 to 6.9 tons of faeces, 34,000 to 51,000 litres of urine. Clearly, its drainage was a priority to ensure acceptable living standards. However, the problem could not be solved by simply digging holes in the ground. Among other things, the spread of pestilence and pandemics has always been connected to poor hygienic conditions, which is how people usually lived in the past. In Greek and Hellenistic cities, sewage was usually dumped in channels in the centre of the roads or in side ditches, but either way, everything ran out into the open air, or in rare cases into underground pipes. Although a primitive sewage system already existed in Babylonia, it was the Romans that devised proper sewage systems, perhaps taking the idea from the Etruscans. The most well known example is the Cloaca Maxima built in Rome in the 6th century BC. The disposal of sewage also had to be efficiently dealt with in Petra, but up to now there has been very little evidence during archaeological excavations in various areas. On a purely speculative level, I believe that water coming from aqueducts fed by perennial sources, and by those served by the large reservoirs supplied by rain water, were at least in part used for disposing of organic waste, collected in "chamber pots" (which the Greeks called amis*); almost certainly, the water that gushed out of the city's nymphaea must have then fed some sort of sewage channels. In fact, I imagine that at least the main streets, going in the direction of the Colonnaded Street, had covered channels under the paving, which must have poured out into a large sewer, built along the course of the Wadi Musa and then the Wadi Siyyagh. The sewage was probably discharged well beyond the source that flows into this ravine, the first section of which was densely populated. For sure a large part of the sewage system was irreparably destroyed by earthquakes and then by successive rampaging floods over the centuries, but I am convinced that, in the future, the work of archaeologists will also be able to clarify this vital aspect of the life of Petra's citizens.*

THE VAULTED ROOMS IN FRONT OF THE URN TOMB

One of the unresolved questions about Petra's monumental architecture regards the function of the imposing vaulted rooms in front of the Urn Tomb. Looking at these massive masonry structures, I have always been impressed by their thickness, but most of all by the unusual roofs of the chambers, arranged on two floors. Entirely formed of parallel arches, interconnected by flat slabs, they are very similar to those of the large Nabataean cisterns (photo on page 26). Since all the monumental tombs of Petra were fitted with cisterns, I believe that, at least in part, this is exactly what we are dealing with here. Most likely, the great internal strain was counterbalanced by the blind wall facing the valley, fortified by sturdy pilasters (five of which are still partly conserved towards the north). This tank was perhaps fed by the Siq's aqueduct and could have been connected to the nymphaeum positioned along the Colonnade. The noticeable difference in height between the two monuments would have ensured the necessary pressure for the water that gushed out of the monumental fountain.

THE HOLES IN THE HYPOGEA

Drilled into the internal walls of the majority of the triclinia (but also in other hypogea) are groups of three holes that are always arranged in the same pattern, that is, in the shape of a triangle. These holes are invariably situated at a certain height from the ground, and in general equidistant and aligned with each other. Several scholars including Laïla Nehmé, believe that metallic brackets were inserted into them and used to support some sort of decoration. However, I think that they have a different explanation, linked to a simple question: how did the Nabataeans light the insides of their rooms? My guess is that oil lamps were suspended from the brackets by chains.

F. Bourbon M. Falcone

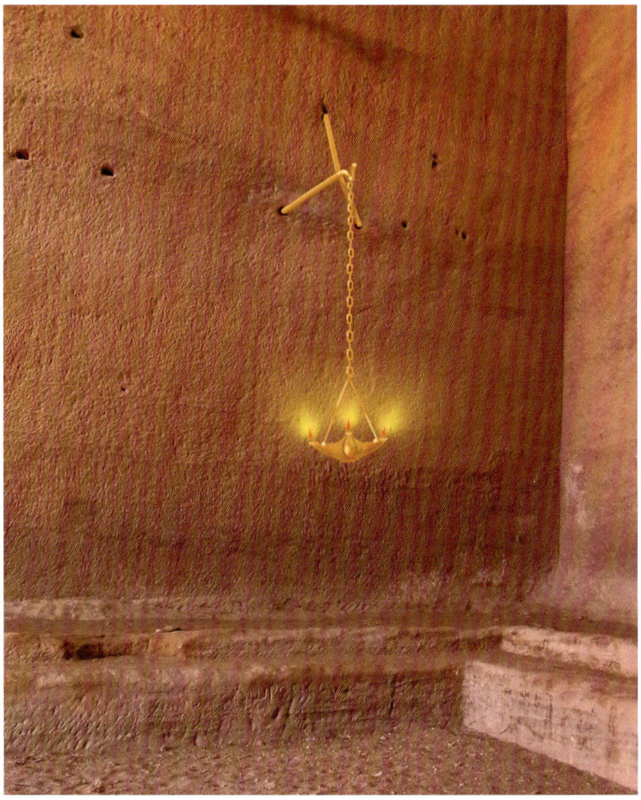

A FINAL THOUGHT ON THE KHAZNEH

As already mentioned, many scholars have tried to identify the architectural influence behind the origin of the Treasury. In 1862 the architect Jakob Ignaz Hittorff highlighted the surprising similarity between Petra's monument and a fresco belonging to the Second Style visible in the House of the Labyrinth in Pompeii, where a tholos *with a bell roof appears between two half pediments. It is an established fact that the Second Style spread in the Roman world during the second half of the 1st century BC. However, it is commonly believed that the amazing structures that animate these wall paintings*

are a work of fantasy, rather like theatre backdrops. In fact, real buildings that are from the same period as the Pompeian paintings and make use of the same technical solutions do not exist. Certain elements appeared only much later in monumental Roman architecture, namely in the 2nd century AD, in the times of Hadrian and Antoninus.
In the nineties, Judith McKenzie suggested that, in reality, the Second Pompeian Style had been strongly influenced by the Hellenistic architecture of Alexandria. The scholar showed that some architectural remains found in the Egyptian metropolis, and strikingly similar to details of the Khazneh (including the floral capitals), date back to the Ptolemaic period, in any case before 100 BC. McKenzie therefore reached the conclusion that monumental buildings, characterised by a style that today we would call "Baroque" had existed in Alexandria, and that these monuments inspired both the Second Pompeian Style and the Khazneh (and also later monuments like the Corinthian Tomb and the Deir). Therefore, the proposed date for the creation of the Treasury was the 1st century BC. However, archaeological excavations carried out in front of the monument have shown that the Khazneh was created in the following century, contradicting this theory.
Considering the macroscopic differences between the typical Nabataean rock cut architecture – Assyrian style tombs, Hegra type tombs, etc. – and the Khazneh, many writers have asserted that it was built by master stonecutters from Alexandria or at least from that area.
I would like to take this opportunity to express my own theory. First and foremost, if you carefully look at the Pompeiian fresco in the House of the Labyrinth, you will see that the tholos *is not alligned between the two broken pediments, but is set back from them and therefore is not part of one single building. Moreover, similar* tholoi, *framed in perspective between colonnades or broken pediments, appear in frescos in the Villa of the Mysteries in Pompeii and in the villa of P. Fannius Synistor in Boscoreale and now kept in the Metropolitan Museum of New York (adjacent photo). Moreover, in each of these representations, in addition to the fact that the* tholos *is set back from the buildings that frame it, all the structures rest on the ground, while in the case of the Treasury, these architectural elements form the second floor and are aligned on the same line. In addition, all the Pompeiian frescos appear to be characterised by an unreal architectural levity, with tall, thin columns that support delicate trabeations of absolutely unusual proportions. I believe the Roman wall paintings are a magnificent invention and do not represent real structures at all, but are to be considered examples of fanciful theatrical scenery.*
If the Treasury is then considered from a purely engineering point of view, it is obvious that in reality, a building constructed in masonry with similar proportions would not make sense. In fact, it probably would not be standing; the considerable weight of the tholos, *without an underlying system of transverse, supporting arches, would entirely rest on the trabeation of the portico, as well as on the doorway giving access to the interior, leading to an almost irresolvable problem of static equilibrium. In addition, it is difficult to imagine what the horizontal development of such a building could be; in other words, what kind of structure there could be behind such a facade. The same can be said for the Deir.*
Ultimately, I believe that the Pompeiian painting and the oldest, sepulchral painting attested in Alexandria are both magnificent works of fantasy and by any means imply the existence of real buildings. It is however very possible, indeed very probable, that the Roman decorators were influenced by a pictorial school that was already active in Alexandria in the 2nd century BC, and that this inspired the architect, or architects, of the Treasury, who perhaps had actually been called to Petra from Alexandria, with all his stylistic background. However, I believe that the paternity of the Khasné and all the other great monuments of the so-called Classical Style is to be attributed to architects and artisans from Petra. In fact, the local skilled workmen had gained unparalleled experience and maturity in the field of the construction of monumental rock cut structures; neither in Alexandria nor elsewhere were there builders so accustomed to working with stone on such a vast scale at that time. In Alexandria, as in the rest of the Mediterranean basin, masons were accustomed to constructing buildings, not carving them out of a rock mass. If we consider the purely technical problems the builders of the Khasnè (and of the Deir and the Corinthian Tomb) had to solve, we realize that these are of a sculptural nature, even on an enormous scale, and not an architectural one. Imagine, for example, what it means to rough out the large bell-shaped roof of a tholos *from a rock mass, or to give form to huge free-standing columns, proceeding from the top to the bottom. It is a job that involves acquired experience and the use of tools such as templates, compasses, squares, not wheelbarrows and trowels. I therefore believe that it is likely that architects or experts summoned to Petra from Alexandria were able to transform the two-dimensional pictorial fantasies of the Hellenistic school into three-dimensional realities; however,*

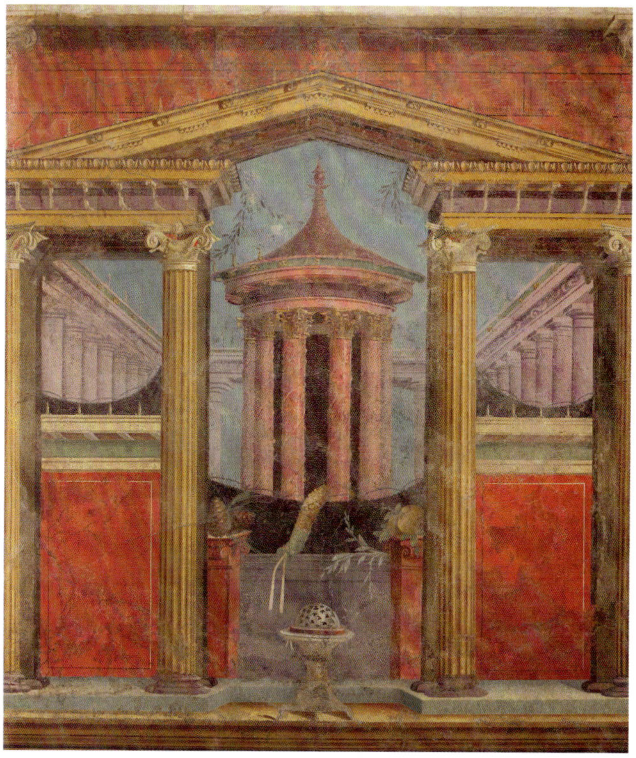

those who physically carried out the extraordinary work were skilled Nabataeans.
Lastly, a final consideration, ruled by sentiment rather than reason: what if the person who designed the superb facade of the Khazneh had not come from Alexandria at all, but was a Nabataean architect, who, returning from that amazing metropolis, had brought back the designs and ideas of the art flourishing there at the time? This would explain certain stylistic incongruities such as the lack of entasis in the columns, the lack of proportion of the acroterion eagles, the use of decorative elements no longer used in the contemporary Alexandrian lexicon like rosettes and facing griffons. In the end, I would like to think that this wonder of the world was conceived by a son of Petra and carried out by men like him – Nabataeans.

Acroterion: a classical architectural decoration, in the form of a palmette, vase, sphere or other, placed at the apex and the two ends of a pediment. It can also have a more complex shape (for example, a statue).

Aniconic: not allowing the use of images, in particular those depicting human beings.

Apotropaic: a term that refers to any object that has the function of staving off or eradicating malign influence.

Arcosolium: a niche with an arched ceiling, mostly in funerary temples or tombs, inside which a tomb was usually placed.

Attic: the raised part above the cornice of a building or the entablature of a temple.

Baetylus: a non-figurative representation of the Nabatean deities. It usually has the appearance of a simple parallelepiped. This word literally means "house of the deity". Baetyli are scattered throughout the Petra area: near tombs (where they confirmed the presence of God), along roads and processional paths (where they served as prayer stations) and in houses (where they served as family sanctuaries).

Biclinium (pl. biclinia): a banqueting chamber similar to the triclinium, but with just two benches, usually placed opposite one another along the long sides of a room.

Cavetto: a concave moulding with a regular curved profile, which juts forward and corresponds to a quarter of a circle, more or less.

Crescent: depiction of a falcated moon, usually a symbol of the goddess Isis-Al Uzza.

Entablature (or trabeation): a horizontal architectural element that rests on columns, composed of an architrave, a frieze and a frame.

Exedra: an architectural structure with a semi-circular plan.

Frieze: an elongated, painted or sculpted decorative architectural element. It is usually part of the entablature.

Intercolumniation: the space between two columns.

In antis: a term indicating a temple that has two or more columns on the facade, framed between two pillars (*antae*) that are located at the end of the side walls of the building.

Hellenism: the historical period between the death of Alexander the Great (323 BC) and the Roman conquest of Egypt (31 BC). In those three centuries, Greek art was influenced by Eastern art and assumed a marked propensity for realism, until it transcended into patheticism.

Metope: in the frieze of the Doric order, each of the spaces between one triglyph and another. It is usually adorned with sculptures in relief or simple disks.

Motab: the base on which a baetylus rests, with a simple platform shape, a trapezoidal base or a podium with steps.

Naos: the inner recess or chamber inside a temple, in which is hosted the statue of the deity. In Roman temples it is called cella.

Nymphaeum: originally the sanctuary of the Nymphs; in Roman times it became a public fountain, adorned with water features and statues, formed by one or more basins framed in a monumental facade with one or more floors.

Patera: a low wide bowl-shaped cup, used in antiquity during sacred libations. Once stylized it becomes a decorative element in architecture, where it often takes the place of a metope.

Pediment: a triangular architectural element with two slopes, located at the top of buildings, doors, windows and niches.

Pilaster: a decorative architectural element without a supporting function, consisting of half a column or half a pillar, protruding from the edge of the wall and surmounted by half a capital.

Pronaos: the covered space between the colonnade on the facade and the interior of a temple or building.

Raceme: a decorative element consisting of foliage arranged in volutes.

Stibadium (pl. Stibadia): a rather late form of triclinium, in which the bed (or bench) takes on a horseshoe or semi-circular shape.

Substructure: a masonry structure that constitutes the support base of a construction above.

Temenos: an open-air area, delimited by a sacred enclosure, where religious ceremonies took place.

Tetrastyle: any temple that has four columns on the facade.

Tholos: a circular temple with a conical or bell-shaped roof.

Triclinium (pl. triclinia): a banqueting chamber with three benches or triclinium beds arranged in Π along the walls, on which the diners would have lain, leaning on their sides. Here, the religious brotherhoods (*thiasoi*) used to meet to pay homage to a god, a sovereign or a deceased person.

Triglyph: a decorative motif in a Doric frieze consisting of a tablet with two vertical grooves, which is applied in alternation with the metopes.

Tympanum: a triangular, vertical architectural element, found between the two slopes of the pediment and the architrave line. It can be smooth or decorated with reliefs or sculptural groups.

Vestibule: the portico that precedes the cella of a temple.

ESSENTIAL BIBLIOGRAPHY

Adam J. P., *La construction romaine. Materiaux et techniques*, 1988.

Akaseheh T., *Nabataean and Modern Watershed Management Around the Siq and Wadi Mousa in Petra*, 2003.

Bachmann W., Watzinger C., Wiegand T. (and Wulzinger K.), *Petra*, 1921.

Bedal L. A.,*The Petra Pool-complex: a Hellenistic Paradeisos in the Nabataean Capital*, 2003.

Belmonte J. A., González-García A. C., Polcaro A., *Light and Shadows over Petra: Astronomy and Landscape in Nabataean Lands*, 2012.

Ben David C., *The Paved Road from Petra to 'Arabah - Commercial Nabataean or Military Roman?*, in *The Late Roman Army in the Near East from Diocletian to the Arab Conquest*, edited by Lewin A. S. e Pellegrini P., 2007.

Ben David C., *The Ancient Routes to Petra*, in *The Mountain of Aaron, Vol. III*, edited by Kouki P. e Lavento M., 2013.

Bienkowski P. (edited by), *The Art of Jordan: Treasures from an Ancient Land*, 1991.

Browning I., *Petra*, 1989.

Brünnow R-E., Domaszewski A. V., *Die Provincia Arabia auf Grund zweier in den Jahren 1897 und 1898 unternommenen reisen und der Berichte früherer Reisender*, 1904-1909.

Dalman G., *Petra und seine Felsheiligtümer*, 1908.

Blánquez Pérez C., *Bar Sauma versus Dushara: the Christianisation of Petra and its Surroundings*, in De Francisco Heredero A., Hernández de la Fuente D., Torres Prieto S. (edited by), *New Perspectives on Late Antiquity in the Eastern Roman Empire*, 2014.

Farajat S., Nawafleh S., *Report on the al-Khazna Courtyard excavation at Petra (2003 season)*, in *Annual of Department of Antiquities of Jordan 49*, 2005.

Fassitelli E., *Tubi e valvole di Roma Antica*, 1972.

Guzzo M. G. A., Schneider E. E., *Petra*, 1997.

Healey J. F., *The Religion of the Nabataeans. A Conspectus*, 1999.

Hoyland G., *Arabia and the Arabs: from the Bronze Age to the Coming of Islam*, 2001.

Joukowsky M. S., *Petra Great Temple*, 1998.

Markoe G. (edited by), *Petra Rediscovered*, 2003.

McKenzie J. S., *The Architecture of Petra*, 1990.

Mouton M., *The Monolithic Djin Blocks at Petra: a Funerary Practice of Pre-Islamic Arabia*, in L. Weeks (edited by) *Death and burial in Arabia and Beyond*, 2010.

MacDonald B., Adams R., Bienkowski P. (edited by), *The Archaeology of Jordan*, 2001.

Mouton M., Schmid S. G. (edited by), *Men on the rocks. The Formation of Nabataean Petra*, 2012.

Negev A., *Nabataean Archaeology Today*, 1986.

Nehmé L., Pétra. *Atlas archéologique et épigraphique, De Bab as-Siq au Wadi al-Farasah*, 2012.

Ohlig C. (edited by), *Cura Aquarum in Jordanien*, 2008.

Oleson J. P., *Strategies for Water Supply in Arabia Petraea during the Nabataean through Early Islamic Periods: Local Adaptations of the Regional 'Technological Shelf'*, in *Water Management in Ancient Civilizations. Berlin Studies of the Ancient World, 53*, edited by J. Berking, 2018.

Ortloff C. R., *Water Management in Petra*, in *Encyclopaedia of the History of Science, Technology, and Medicine in Non-Western Cultures*, 2008.

Ortloff C. R., *The Water Supply and Distribution System of the Nabataean City of Petra*, in *Cambridge Archaeological Journal*, Volume 15, pp.93-109, 2005.

Ortloff C. R., *Water Engineering in the Ancient World. Archaeological and Climate Perspective in Societies of Ancient South America, the Middle East and South-East Asia*, 2009.

Ruben I. (edited by), *The Petra Siq: Nabataean Hydrology Uncovered*, 2003.

Shiyyab A., *Recent discoveries in city center of Petra, Jordan: a preliminary excavation report*, 2014.

Sidebotham S., Thomas R., Sidebotham M., Rivard J-L., *Petra decumanus maximus survey 2008*, 2017

Sobieraj B., *Peristyle in Nabatean architecture*, in *Acta Universitatis Lodziensis*, 2009.

Tholbeq L., Renel F. , *Sanctuaires, stibadia et bains à Pétra (Jordanie): Recherches récentes de la mission archéologique française*, (INHA) 2017.

Tholbeq L., Vergnaud B., *Pétra - Un stibadium associé à un édifice sacré ou pavillonnaire sur le sommet du Jabal Khubthah*, in *Mission archéologique française "De Pétra au Wadi Ramm: le sud jordanien nabatéen et arabe": Rapport des campagnes archéologiques 2014 - 2015*, 2015.

Tholbeq L., *Sanctuaires de Pétra: Chapelle d'Obodas et "Haut-lieu" du Jabal Khubthah*, in *Mission archéologique française "De Pétra au wadi Ramm: le sud jordanien nabatéen et arabe". Rapport des campagnes archéologiques 2012*, 2013.

Tholbeq L., Bechetoille S., Durand C., Thibaud F., Lauwers C., Paridaens N., *Mission archéologique française à Pétra. Rapport des campagnes archéologiques 2016-2017*, 2017.

Wadeson L., *Nabataean Tomb Complexes at Petra: New Insights in the Light of Recent Fieldwork*, 2011.

Zayadine F. (edited by), *Petra and the Caravan Cities*, 1990.

PHOTOGRAPHIC REFERENCES

All photographs are by F. Bourbon, with the exception of the following:

Glenn J. Corbis: page 10b.
Ionis Thompson: page 11c.
The Library of Congress, Washington DC: pages 16r, 17a, 17b, 18-19, 58tr.
Wilke Schram: page 26b.
Alejandro Britos: page 28b.
Department of Antiquities of Jordan: pages 31, 32, 33r.
Livio Bourbon: page 46.
Kendal K. Down: page 56a (public domain).
Joe Carnegie: page 97b.
Bernard Gagnon: page 102.
Fabio Idini: page 117r.
Metropolitan Museum, New York: page 173.

Special thanks go to the Jordanian archaeologist Sami Mohammed Al Nawafleh, to Suleiman Farajat, chief commissioner for the Petra Development and Tourism Region Authority, to the Italian archaeologist Andrea Polcaro and to my late friend Gianni Gè.

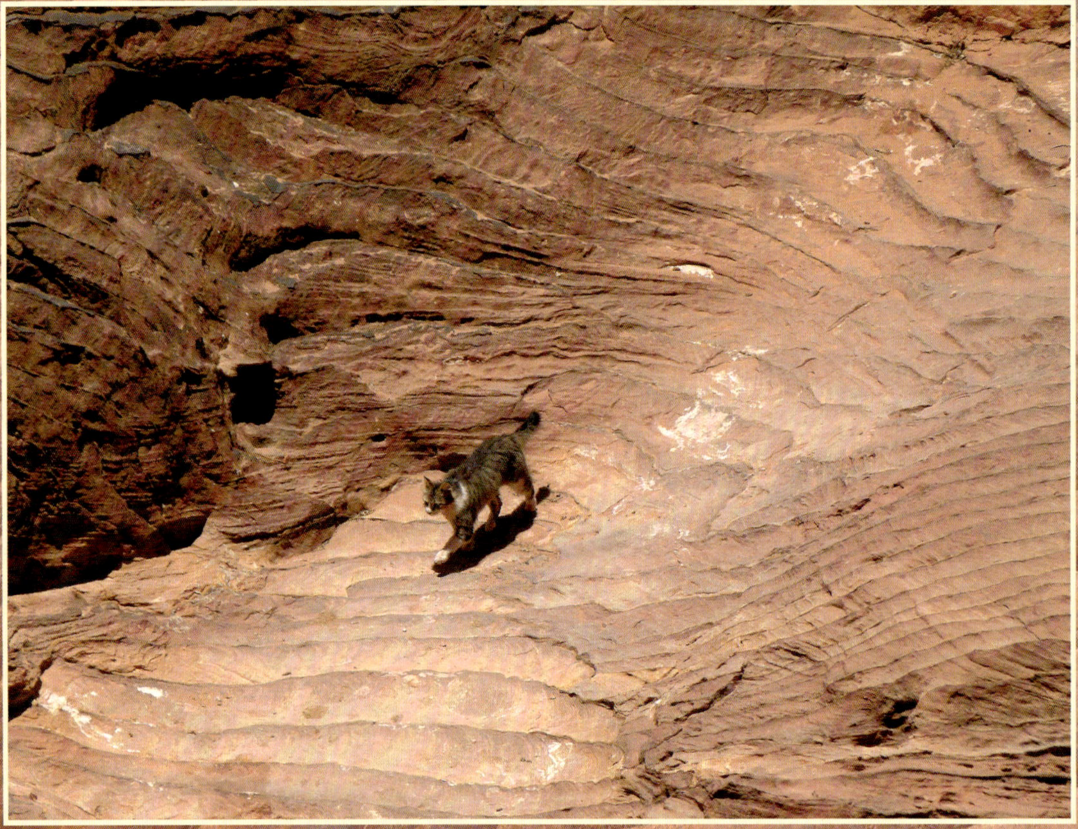

I dedicate this book, which is the result of a lot of passion and many years of work, to my parents Gianni and Vera, the Jordanian people and the people of Petra, who have always generously helped me in various ways during my many visits to the Rose City.
And, above all, to my wife Monica:
UBI TU GAIA, IBI EGO GAIUS.